THE RUSSIAN
AMERICAN
COLONIES

Ежели бъ ранее мыслило Правительство о сей части света, ежели бъ уважало ею как должно, ежели бъ безпрерывно следовало прозорливым видам Петра Великаго при малых тогдашних способах Берингову експедицию для чего нибуд начертавшаго, то утвердительно сказать можно, что Новая Калифорния никогда бъ небыла Гишпанскою принадлежностию. . . .

Николай П. Резанов

If [our] Government had given its attention to this part of the world earlier, if it had had proper respect for it, if it had persistently pursued the sagacious visions of Peter the Great, who with the small resources of his time dispatched Bering's mapping expedition, one may be certain that New California would never have become a Spanish possession. . . .

Nikolai P. Rezanov

THE ⋮RUSSIAN

TO SIBERIA AND

AMERICAN

RUSSIAN AMERICA

COLONIES

THREE CENTURIES OF
RUSSIAN EASTWARD EXPANSION

1798-1867

VOLUME THREE
A DOCUMENTARY RECORD

EDITED AND TRANSLATED BY
BASIL DMYTRYSHYN
E.A.P. CROWNHART-VAUGHAN
THOMAS VAUGHAN

OREGON
HISTORICAL SOCIETY
PRESS
1989

Endpapers: Map of New Arkhangel done prior to 1845, hand drawn and painted on heavy paper. Initially thought to have been drawn by a native, the predominance of ruled lines and the firmness with which the ships are drawn seem to point to someone working in a strong maritime tradition, possibly a New Englander or a very acculturated native. It can be found in the collections of the Sheldon Jackson Museum of Sitka, Alaska. It is printed here with permission of the Alaska State Museums.

The preparation of this volume was made possible in part by a grant from the Translations Program of the National Endowment for the Humanities, an independent federal agency.

This volume was designed and produced by
the Oregon Historical Society Press.

Library of Congress Cataloging-in-Publication Data
(Revised for vol. 3)

To Siberia and Russian America.

    (North Pacific studies series ; no. 9-11)
    Translated from Russian
    Includes bibliographies and indexes.
    Contents: v. 1. Russia's conquest of Siberia, 1558–1700—v. 2 Russian penetration of the North Pacific Ocean, 1700–1797—v. 3 The Russian American colonies, 1798–1867.
    1. Soviet Union—territorial expansion—Sources. 2. Siberia (R.S.R.S.R.)—Discovery and exploration Sources. 3. Northwest Coast of North America—Discovery and exploration—Russian—Sources. 4. Pacific Coast (North America)—Discovery and exploration—Russian—Sources. I. Dmytryshyn, Basil, 1925– . II. Crownhart-Vaughan, E.A.P. 1929– . III. Vaughan, T. 1924– . IV. Series: North Pacific Studies series ; no. 9, etc.
DK43.T6 1985   947   84-29079
ISBN 0-87595-147-3 (set : alk. paper)

The paper used in this publication meets the minimum requirements of American National Standard for Information Sciences—Permanence of Paper for Printed Library Materials, ANSI Z39.48-1984.

Printed in the United States of America.

DEDICATION

With the completion of this documentary trilogy we wish, with the very warmest memories, to pay homage to our parents and to express our gratitude for their profound sense of the past.

Hildegarde Wooll Crownhart
Jesse George Crownhart
Euphrosina Senchak Dmytryshyn
Frank Dmytryshyn
Kathryn Browne Vaughan
Daniel George Vaughan

NORTH PACIFIC STUDIES SERIES

Edited with introduction and notes by Kenneth N. Owens.
Translated by Alton S. Donnelly.
1985

No. 9   *Russia's Conquest of Siberia, 1558–1700: A Documentary Record.*
Edited and translated by Basil Dmytryshyn, E. A. P. Crownhart-
Vaughan and Thomas Vaughan.
*To Siberia and Russian America: Three Centuries of Russian Eastward
Expansion, 1558–1867.* Volume one.
1985

No. 10   *Russian Penetration of the North Pacific Ocean, 1700–1797: A Docu-
mentary Record.*
Edited and translated by Basil Dmytryshyn, E. A. P. Crownhart-
Vaughan and Thomas Vaughan.
*To Siberia and Russian America: Three Centuries of Russian Eastward
Expansion, 1558–1867.* Volume two.
1988

No. 11   *The Russian American Colonies, 1798–1867: A Documentary Record.*
Edited and translated by Basil Dmytryshyn, E. A. P. Crownhart-
Vaughan and Thomas Vaughan.
*To Siberia and Russian America: Three Centuries of Russian Eastward
Expansion, 1558–1867.* Volume three.
1989

CONTENTS

ministration of the Russian American Company regarding its expedition to the island of Kauai.

ILLUSTRATIONS

FOREWORD

In this volume, the many-tiered imperial Russian colonial design unfolds onto the tidal shelf of continental North America. In this once hazy and unfamiliar epoch, Russia for the first time quickly and confidently annexes extra-continental territory, following in the path of Rome, Portugal, Spain, France and Great Britain.

For the first time, Russian diplomats, explorers, scientists and fur hunters encounter forces on the North American continent. In this century of European tensions, Sweden, Austria, Poland, Ottoman Turkey and China are the contestants, who in countless ways provide competition and infinite geopolitical problems. These in no way diminish as Russian forces become entangled in the thrusting designs of imperial Spain, England, Bourbon France, revolution and Bonaparte's dynasty.

These powerful players from the far end of Europe complicate the chessboard, as do their merchants and missionaries. Added to the intricacies of this third volume are the expanding interests of a vast hegemony, the fur trading Hudson's Bay Company, the continuing reclusiveness of Japan and the audacious proposals of the "Bostonians" representing the young cocksure American states.

Famous and forgotten men and women of many races and persuasions push through the unknown channels and hazards of tide-ripped bays and labyrinthine forest corridors. Long-planned expeditions suddenly vanish, ships sink or splinter on reefs, hopes are dashed, and explanations are demanded by power brokers in distant palaces. Breathtaking ethnographic, botanical and ornithological collections are taken back to European capitols, but even these cannot convey the menacing climate and topography and the fierce encounters between natives and newcomers. Indigenous peoples from the Kuril Islands along a great arching path down to Bodega Bay in California, and across to Hawaii, resist incursions. To the natives, these white men, whatever their nationality or internecine competition, are invaders who bring endless catastrophe into every element of tribal life for the Ainus, Aleuts, Tlingits, Chinooks, Pomos and Hawaiians. Large native populations and entire settlements are wiped out by new diseases, alcohol and guns. Although the Russian Orthodox Church is a powerful force, it cannot stem the destruction.

Russians in Alaska undertake extensive commercial enterprises—ice production, coaling stations, whaling—and these are successful only to a degree. But attempts to solidify the California and Hawaii ventures do not prevail. The Crimean War with its worldwide ramifications intrudes mid-century. As in an epochal drama, the last scene comes into focus and plays out in the triumphant conclusion of the sale of Alaska to the United States, a less threatening associate than France or England.

With the sale, much archival material was passed on, a great deal of it available in American repositories. And as better access to Soviet archives is granted, we will expand the record of this remarkable Russian adventure and have a greater understanding of much beyond the residuals of family and topographical place names, lonely bell towers and ruined palisades in rocky inlets.

In 1968, this writer, one of the editors of this series, was working in East Central Siberia with newfound colleagues in Irkutsk. "Tell us," urged one at our first meeting, "do Americans know this part of our history? Do American school children learn that Russia once owned Alaska? Or is all of that forgotten?" "Oh yes," was the response, "we do remember. Such a story will never fade from memory." More than twenty years have passed since that evocative exchange, and with each year comes more information and understanding and an ever more powerful memory of an increasingly distant but now even more sharply drawn past.

Colleagues in many countries have provided most generous assistance to many aspects of our work. *USSR*: Moscow: Academy of Sciences, Iulian V. Bromley, Nikolai N. Bolkhovitinov, Svetlana G. Fedorova; Lenin Library, B.P. Kanevsky. Leningrad: Academy of Sciences, Rostislav V. Kinzhalov, Roza G. Liapunova, Avram D. Dridzo, Galina I. Dzeniskevich, Elena A. Okladnikova, the late Erna V. Siebert and Mikhail I. Belov; Central State Naval Museum, the late Evgenii G. Kushnarev; Saltykov-Shchedrin State Public Library; Geographical Society Library. Novosibirsk: Library of the Academy of Sciences. Irkutsk: Zhdanov State University library. Khabarovsk: Geographical Society, Far Eastern Sector. Vladivostok: Far Eastern Scientific Center.

France: Paris: Andre Roubertou, Service Hydrographique et Oceanographique de la Marine, Bibliotheque Nationale, Archives Nationales. Vincennes: le contre-amiral Chatelle and Pierre Waksman, Bibliotheque Historique de la Marine. Brest: le commandant J. Daguzan, Bibliotheque de la Marine. *Spain*: Madrid: Archivo Nacional. Seville: Archivo de Indias. Simancas: Archivo de Simancas. *Mexico*: Mexico City: Archivo nacional. *Great Britain*: London: Helen Wallis, OBE, British Library. Taunton: Lt. Commander A.C.F. David, Ministry of Defence. *Canada*: Toronto: James R. Gibson. *USA*: Washington, D.C.: Robert V. Allen, Library of Congress; Susan Mango, Raymond H. Harvey, Molly Raymond. Sitka: Right Reverend Gregory, Bishop of Sitka and Alaska. Portland: Col. M.J. Poniatowski-d'Ermengard and the late Ivan L. Best. Los Angeles: Raymond H. Fisher. Berkeley: The Bancroft Library. Sacramento: Glenn J. Farris. St. Paul: John D. Taylor. Honolulu: John Stephan and Patricia Polansky.

Support for research and publication has come from the National Endowment for the Humanities, the Northwest Area Foundation, the Westland Foundation and the S.S. Johnson Foundation, as well as from many private benefactors who, under the aegis of the Oregon Historical Society in 1968 established the Irkutsk Archival Research Group. This group, headed successively by John Youell, Samuel S. Johnson, Jane West Youell and James B. Thayer, was under the direction of OHS Executive Director Thomas Vaughan.

In 1988 the importance of this program was recognized at the Federal level, and with the support of Senators Mark O. Hatfield and Robert Packwood, Congressman Les AuCoin and Charles Z. Wick, director of the United States Information Agency, legislation was signed by President Ronald Reagan establishing the North Pacific Studies Center at the Oregon Historical Society, responsible to the Board and membership of that society. Noydena Leonard Brix serves as Board Chairman of the Center.

The extensive and ever-growing research collections of the Oregon Historical Society are the backbone of all three volumes in this series.

Design, editing and production of the series are the work of the Oregon Historical Society Press; Bruce Taylor Hamilton, OHS Assistant Director-Publications, and the Society Press staff: Susan Applegate, Colleen Compton, Adair M. Law, Virginia Linnman, Lori R. McEldowney, and George T. Resch. Indexing of the *To Siberia and Russian America* series is done by Jean Brownell.

To all who have worked with us in this effort of international cooperation, we extend our gratitude and our warmest thanks.

Basil Dmytryshyn
E.A.P. Crownhart-Vaughan
Thomas Vaughan

INTRODUCTION

The Russians laid the foundations of their colonial empire in the North Pacific and in North America between 1700 and the end of the century. They accomplished this through two bold approaches. The first was a series of carefully planned and executed government-sponsored expeditions. The First Kamchatka Expedition, 1725–1730, under Captain Vitus J. Bering, sought to ascertain whether a land bridge connected the continents of Asia and America. The Second Kamchatka Expedition, 1733–1741, under Bering and Captain Aleksei I. Chirikov, explored Aleutian and Alaskan waters and by right of first discovery laid Russia's claim to the entire region. Captains Petr K. Krenitsyn and Mikhail D. Levashev led a secret expedition, 1764–1769 to explore further and to verify discoveries made by Russian *promyshlenniks* [hunters]. And in the years 1785–1792 captains Joseph J. Billings and Gavriil A. Sarychev led a semi-secret expedition to describe and map new discoveries and to warn other maritime powers to respect Russia's North Pacific preserve.

Through these governmental expeditions Russia became the first European nation to discover the Northwest Coast of North America and the many islands in the North Pacific. They were also the first to encounter and describe the indigenous peoples and to survey the region's resources. Russians were the first to set foot on the Alaskan mainland and formally laid claim to the entire region. Their explorations and cartographic surveys enabled them to correct many misconceptions about the geography of the North Pacific as they laid in a coastal outline of North America.

Russians likewise established their presence in the North Pacific through many voyages undertaken without direct government sponsorship. While private entrepreneurs organized and financed these costly and dangerous voyages, government officials carefully monitored and controlled them. This was usual procedure, for Russian governments have never recognized private entrepreneurship, especially if its activity might cause international complications. Russian private entrepreneurs dispatched at least 110 such voyages between 1743 and 1800! Their two-fold purpose was to take as many furs as possible while bringing all lands and peoples encountered under Russian control. These two goals were accomplished with astounding success. In spite of hardships, reverses and disasters, by 1800 Russians had discovered and subdued nearly all the islands in the Aleutian archipelago, established several permanent settlements, and were poised to move on to the Alaskan mainland.

A most remarkable aspect of this Russian venture in an inhospitable part of the world, as yet unknown to other powers, was the speed with which the adventurers accomplished their aims. Here, as in the Russian drive across Siberia, an important factor was government support. The invaders also had weapon superiority; no substantial resistance on a sustained basis was possible. No significant European force was on hand to compete in the new arena. Further, the intense momentum of success fueled ambition and avarice among the Russian seafarers. They were determined and resourceful; they could be cruel, brutal and ruthless; and they continued to be courageous, intrepid and as always, audacious. In the way of things natural leaders emerged. Some made extraordinary contributions.

Emilian S. Basov, a sergeant in the Lower Kamchatka command, in 1743 led the Russian drive of private entrepreneurs across the North Pacific. Andrean Tolstykh in two decades, 1746–1765, discovered a number of the Aleutian Islands; the Andreanov group to this day bears his name. Potap K. Zaikov, voyaging 1772–1792, brought immense wealth to his sponsors from peltry. Gerasim A. Izmailov provided valuable information to Captain James Cook's third voyage in the North Pacific. Gerasim L. Pribylov discovered the islands that bear his name; from his voyage he brought back one of the richest cargoes on record—furs worth the immense sum of 258,018 rubles. Nikifor Trapeznikov promoted eighteen voyages between 1743–1764, made and lost an enormous fortune from the fur trade and died a pauper. Pavel L. Lebedev-Lastochkin organized a successful trading company, financed a number of voyages into the North Pacific and established three permanent settlements. Ivan L. Golikov's company promoted much successful activity in the region. But most memorable of all these merchant giants is Grigorii I. Shelikhov, whose energetic promotion of Russian colonial expansion made him Russia's equal to the world's great leaders and dreamers of any era.

At best the Russians published minimal amounts of geographic and scientific data gathered by their expeditions during the eighteenth century, but most secrets remained just that. Some information appeared in print in Western Europe through foreign participants in the government-sponsored expeditions or by indirect means such as diplomatic observation and espionage. These publications sparked immediate attention, soon adding to the impetus for Britain, Spain, France and America to organize and dispatch their own expeditions to the North Pacific.

The most important Spanish voyages of 1775–1792 explored the waters along Vancouver Island; the coast of Alaska north of Cape St. Elias, Chugach and Yakutat bays; Nootka Sound; and the islands of Kodiak, Shumagin, Umnak and Unalaska. The British sent both official and private expeditions. Government expeditions commanded by captains James Cook and Charles Clerke sailed to Nootka Sound, Kodiak, Unalaska, Unimak and other islands, Bering Strait, and to Petropavlovsk harbor in Kamchatka. Unofficial voyages were sponsored by the East India Company, whose sturdy vessels undertook numerous voyages, 1785–1792, to various points in Russia's North Pacific preserve to trade with the indigenous peoples. The French, under Jean François de Galaup, compte de La Pérouse, sailed 1785–1788; and the Americans under Captain Robert Gray between 1789–1792.

The aim of these non-Russian voyages was threefold: to gather information about this vast area which outside Russia was essentially *terra incognita*; to investigate Russian activity in the region and evaluate their claims; and to establish trade with the natives. These expeditions, troublesome to the Russians because they often supplied the natives with spirits and fire-arms, never contemplated force to unseat the Russians from the region. The Russians were wary of any intrusion, but they were in no position to resist, because they had too little man-power and feared armed conflict which they might not win. Further, Russia was then embroiled in many complex and costly involvements in Europe.

Although harassed and annoyed by European surveillance in the North Pacific, the Russians were not distracted from their aim of establishing a permanent Russian colony on the North American continent. Credit for this resolve belongs to two small groups of dedicated persons: the few ambitious merchants of eastern Siberia who conceived the idea, and the handful of high government officials of the region who encouraged and supported this venture. The first group included Lebedev-Lastochkin, Golikov, Shelikhov, Nikolai Mylnikov and Grigorii Panov. Government supporters were three Governors General of Siberia, Denis I. Chicherin, Ivan A. Pil and Ivan V. Iakobii; two of Catherine's personal secretaries, P. A. Soimonov and Count A. A. Bezborodko; and Prince A. R. Vorontsov, head of the College of Commerce.

Shelikhov was the most energetic promoter of Russian colonial expansion into the North Pacific. Born in 1747 into a petty merchant family in the town of Rylsk in Kursk *gubernia* [large administrative unit], Shelikhov eventually made his way to Irkutsk in 1772 with others seeking fortune and adventure. In Irkutsk, the administrative and commercial center of eastern Siberia, he joined forces with Lebedev-Lastochkin and Golikov. In 1775 he married Nataliia Alekseevna, a young, well-educated and ambitious noblewoman, widow of a wealthy Irkutsk merchant. Shelikhov used her social connections and her wealth, and over a period of eight years, 1775–1783, joined with several groups of merchant promoters in financing fur trade expeditions to the Kuril and Aleutian islands. In a long run of good fortune each venture brought him profit and subsequent social and political influence.

In the early 1780's, with financial backing from the influential Demidov family who had founded the iron industry in the Ural Mountains, Shelikhov and Golikov formed a company and built and outfitted three ships: *Tri Sviatitelia, Arkhistratig Mikhail,* and *Simeon Bogopriemets i Anna Prorochitsa.* In August, 1783, accompanied by his wife and four experienced seafarers (Gerasim Izmailov, Konstantin Samoilov, Potap Zaikov and Evstrat Delarov), Shelikhov set out from Okhotsk for Alaskan waters. Storms separated the ships and wrecked one. Shelikhov, aboard *Tri Sviatitelia,* spent the winter on Bering Island and then continued on to Unalaska and Kodiak Island, where he remained for two years. The Koniag natives of Kodiak attacked the Russians to prevent them from landing, but Shelikhov's men with their basic superiority in weaponry forced the natives not only to desist, but to surrender hostages and eventually to hunt sea otters for the Russians.

To ensure his safety Shelikhov built a fortified post at Three Saints Harbor on Kodiak, and set up additional outposts on Afognak, at Cook Inlet and at Cape St. Elias. He also pacified the natives through gifts and reasonable treatment, and even persuaded some to be baptized into the Russian Orthodox Church. While on Kodiak Shelikhov gathered important cultural and ethnological information about the Koniagas. The natives and Shelikhov's own promyshlenniks procured many furs, which made this voyage an extremely profitable venture.

This three-year voyage had a profound impact on Shelikhov; he now had first hand experience of the rigors and severity of the voyage, and he had learned much from his encounters with the natives. His experiences convinced him that in order to keep the North Pacific Ocean, its islands and adjacent territories as an exclusive Russian preserve, his countrymen must develop special rules to govern their activities in this vast and inhospitable but extraordinarily rich region. He believed the Russians must develop a network of permanent settlements on key islands and along the coast of Alaska. Such settlements of peasants, artisans, military units and administrative personnel would enable the Russians to exploit the region's resources efficiently and economically; they would make Russia's claim to the region a reality; and they would prevent foreign intrusions into the area. He maintained this program could only be implemented if the government would entrust it to a single company, giving that company substantial financial subsidies and extensive exclusive rights and privileges, including that of trade with other countries on the Pacific littoral. Such privileges should also carry the obligation to provide some education to the native peoples, and to proselytize among them.

When Shelikhov returned to Irkutsk in April, 1787, he incorporated these views in a written account of his experiences, and in a series of communications to highly placed government officials. Because his plans called for giving a single company a monopoly on hunting and trading, many Russian merchants in Siberia, already envious and distrustful of Shelikhov, naturally resisted the proposal. But a number of Russian officials, especially Governors-General of Siberia Pil and Iakobii, as well the head of the Commerce College, Vorontsov, welcomed it and arranged for Shelikhov and Golikov to present their plans to Empress Catherine II.

Catherine praised Shelikhov for his explorations and for the valuable information he had brought back, but rejected his request to form a company that would enjoy exclusive rights to hunting, trade and exploration in the entire North Pacific. She based her refusal on philosophical grounds, influenced in this matter by the writings of Montesquieu and Adam Smith. However she was also no doubt exercising caution to avoid potential international confrontations in a distant arena she could not defend. At this time the crisis in Poland, strained relations with the Ottoman Empire and with Sweden, as well as the growing political instability in France demanded her attention.

Catherine did acquiesce, nevertheless, to others of Shelikhov's requests. She approved his plan for establishing a permanent Russian settlement in Alaskan waters at Three Saints Harbor, and authorized officials in Siberia to send exiled peasant and artisan families there to be a symbol of permanent Russian presence in North America. She also authorized the Admiralty College to dispatch a naval flotilla to the region to monitor the increasing British, Spanish, French and American maritime activity in the area. Moreover, she ordered an expedition to be organized under Captain Grigorii I. Mulovskii, but the outbreak of war with the Ottoman Empire and Sweden forced her to cancel it on the eve of its departure. Finally, to reward their efforts on Russia's behalf, Catherine decorated Shelikhov and Golikov and elevated them to the status of nobility.

With imperial endorsement and the support of local officials, Shelikhov expanded his activities upon his return to Irkutsk; and he sought subordinates who would support his visions and bring them to reality. In 1790 and 1791 he chartered three new companies: the Predtechenskaia ["Inaugural"] Company to develop the fur seal resources of the Pribilov Islands; the Unalaska Company to build the fur trade on Unalaska; and the North American Company to profit from the great wealth of resources on the Alaskan mainland. Shelikhov was also the prime promoter in the attempt to establish commercial contacts with the Japanese. He offered his ship *Dobroe Predpriatie* to the government for that purpose. In 1794 he hoped to establish permanent Russian settlements in the Kuril archipelago on the islands of Urup, Uturup and Kunashiri. He also ardently promoted Russian acquisition of the Chinese-held Amur River basin, while at the same time expanding the sea otter fur trade with Chinese merchants at Kiakhta. In all of these ventures Shelikhov made certain that all participants, whether investors, ship captains or his own administrative assistants, supported his grand vision of a colonial empire.

During the early 1790's Shelikhov's bold plans were further advanced by three occurrences. Aleksandr A. Baranov agreed to serve as Shelikhov's principal administrator and promoter of the great plans for Alaska. In 1791 Shelikhov's account of his voyage to Kodiak was published in St. Petersburg and was widely discussed in influential Russian circles. And in 1794 his daughter Anna married Nikolai P.Rezanov, an ambitious and aggressive St. Petersburg courtier who also shared Shelikhov's vision.

Shelikhov's titanic enterprises were interrupted by his death on July 20, 1795, but his loyal and enthusiastic adherents pressed on with his great plans. For two years his widow Nataliia skillfully directed the company's affairs. In 1798 his various companies merged with one of his competitors, the Irkutsk-based Mylnikov Company, to form the United American Company. And on July 8, 1799, Emperor Paul I formally approved the merger and named the new company the Russian American Company. The Emperor granted the Company many rights and privileges, commanding that it guide the destinies of the Russian colonies in North America. The Company carried out this directive until March 31, 1867, when the

Russian government sold its North American colonial possessions to the United States of America.

THE PRIVILEGES AND THE ADMINISTRATIVE STRUCTURE OF THE RUSSIAN AMERICAN COMPANY

In scholarly literature and in the popular view the Russian
American Company has been perceived as a private enterprise patterned after the East India Company and other European trading companies. The proponents of this view cite as
evidence the fact that the Russian American Company issued
shares of stock, that some parts of its administration had a business structure, and that its operations were purely commercial.
This perception is mistaken. From its formation in 1799 to its
demise in 1868, the Russian American Company was never a
private enterprise as that term is applied, practiced and understood in the West. Rather, the Company was an important aux-
iliary of the Imperial Russian government. Social, economic
and political realities in the Russian Empire at the time dictated
this status. Russian authorities have never allowed an institution or organization of any nature or purpose to exist outside
government control.

That the Company was an important agency of the government is also clearly evident in the fact that the Emperor, the
source of all authority and power in Imperial Russia, was the
principal patron and shareholder of the Company. Members of
his family and a number of his ministers were also shareholders. In addition, most important administrators of the Russian
American Company from 1818 on were government employees, enjoyed ranks and title, and the years they spent in Company service entitled them to receive the same pensions and
awards they would have received had they been in regular government service. Finally, government authorities maintained
close scrutiny over the Company's revenues, expenditures and
activities, and made all major decisions affecting the Company
and its eventual dissolution.

An effective way of clarifying the question of whether the
Company was a private or a government entity is to examine
its privileges and administrative structure. Under the terms of
three Imperial charters, 1799, 1821 and 1841, the Company

enjoyed extensive monopoly privileges. It had the exclusive right to establish and profit from all of its current and future economic ventures in the Aleutian, Kuril and all other islands in the North Pacific and along the coast of North America above 55° northern latitude. This right also applied to resources above and below ground in all known territories, as well as in those the Company might discover in the future.

In addition, the government granted the Company the right to establish in those regions permanent Russian settlements and fortified outposts; to hire essential personnel, both Russian and non-Russian, to run its colonial possessions; to introduce agriculture and raise livestock in the region; to cut timber to build Company ships, without securing cutting permits from Russian naval authorities; and to dispatch ships out of Russian ports carrying cargo necessary for the colonies. Moreover the Company had the right to trade throughout the Russian Empire and to develop trade relations with China, Japan and all other countries and regions in the North Pacific. The Emperor enjoined all other Russian trading companies and all military, naval and civil officials from interfering with the Company's privileges and operations. Indeed, in case of necessity, the Company could receive protection from Russian military and naval forces. This protection was actually automatic, since all during the existence of the Russian American Company a small Russian military force with both naval and army personnel was stationed in Company headquarters at New Arkhangel on Sitka Island. Further, after 1818 all top administrative officials in charge of Company affairs in New Arkhangel were high-ranking naval officers who represented national as well as Company interests.

The government also granted the Company legal powers to punish its employees for damaging Company property or for dereliction of duty; and it had the right to grant awards and to recommend outstanding persons for promotion. The Company had the authority to purchase gunpowder, shot and weapons from government depots, to employ male natives between the ages of 18 and 50, and to insist that all natives in the Russian colonies in North America sell their furs only to the Company, at a set price. Finally, all Company structures were exempted from billeting.

In return for these extensive rights and privileges, the Russian American Company assumed a number of obligations. The Company pledged to preserve the unity and integrity of the territories the government had entrusted to its exclusive use, and vowed to avoid entanglements with foreign powers. It also promised to arrange its business operations in such a way that these would benefit the entire nation, and would never overstep the framework of its privileges. The Company agreed to keep the Emperor informed of its operations, either directly or through the Minister of Finance. It also agreed to spread the Russian Orthodox faith among the indigenous peoples and to build churches and pay all maintenance costs for them. This was a natural extension of responsibility, since in Imperial Russia church affairs were inseparable from state affairs, and the Emperor was the titular head of the church.

The Company further pledged to provide its employees proper living quarters, clothing, food and medical care; to give humane treatment and protection to all native inhabitants under its jurisdiction as lawful Russian subjects; to pay them reasonable wages for their work; and to offer them some educational opportunities. Finally, the Company agreed to keep a close record of marriages between Russians and natives, and pledged to allow the natives to fish and hunt on Company land so they could secure for themselves and their families basic necessities, and not become a national burden.

The three Charters which the Company received from the government put the enforcement and administration of the privileges and obligations in the hands of an elaborate administrative apparatus. Various departments of the government handled a number of matters. The Ministry of Foreign Affairs dealt with problems affecting the Company's relations with foreign powers; the Ministry of Finance supervised the Company finances; the Ministry of the Navy defended Company interests at sea, transported its cargo and mail, and after 1818 assigned naval staff officers to serve the Company in various capacities; the Ministry of Internal Affairs oversaw criminal matters and related issues; and the Holy Synod had jurisdiction over religious matters. In 1804 the government appointed a special Council of highly placed officials to supervise the political aspects of Company activity, and in 1813 made that body a Permanent Council.

The top agency of the Russian American Company was the Main Administration. Initially the Main Administration had its headquarters in Irkutsk, but in 1800 it moved its office to St. Petersburg. The move was beneficial to the government and to the Company, since it allowed government officials to exercise closer control over Company activities, and gave Company spokesmen better access to powerful officials. The principal spokesmen for the Main Administration, and hence for the Company, were four Directors, elected by majority vote of Company shareholders at a general meeting. Only shareholders with ten shares could vote for Directors, for which eligibility included ownership of 25 shares, practical business experience, and a sound, well-informed knowledge of all aspects of Company affairs. Each Director received an annual stipend of 2,000 rubles, a generous sum for the time. Once elected a Director could serve indefinitely, unless removed by majority vote at a general meeting, if investigation proved that his negligence had been detrimental to the Company.

Individually and collectively, the Directors were responsible for keeping Company accounts in order, preserving its capital assets and increasing its earnings. They were accountable for the Company's cash, notes, goods and all property, and also for the purchase and disposition of all equipment and supplies. They negotiated contracts with the Russian promyshlenniks and dispatched them to their destinations in the North Pacific. They hired agents and other personnel essential to the Company's service and were accountable for their conduct. They issued instructions for hunting and trade and carried out the objectives and intentions of the Company. Directors represented the Company in all legal and civil matters, oversaw correspondence and audits and prepared annual reports. They were also accountable for any loss the Company suffered as a result of their negligence or dereliction of duty. In short, the Directors were responsible for administering the entire business of the Russian American Company.

Many subordinates assisted the Directors in carrying out their responsibilities. In Company headquarters in St. Petersburg there were legal counselors, secretaries, specialists in various fields, copyists, appraisers and others. In the Company's ten branch offices in Moscow, Irkutsk, Kiakhta, Iakutsk, Okhotsk, Kazan, Tiumen, Tomsk, Gizhiga and Kamchatka, the Directors appointed local managers. In the Russian colonies in North America their representative was the Chief Administrator, who supervised an extensive staff.

The role of the Chief Administrator was critical, especially in colonial operations. Until 1818 the responsibilities of the Chief Administrator were loosely defined, formulated by various persons at different times. Some evolved from Shelikhov's initial instructions to Baranov concerning his duties and responsibilities. Others stemmed from later instructions from Company Directors to Baranov. Still others arose from Baranov's own interpretations of these instructions, in light of local situations and his own perception of his position and mission. The vast distance that separated Baranov from his superiors in St. Petersburg, and the slow process of communication bred lethargy. Finally, government officials' preoccupation with such pressing problems as stormy relations with Napoleonic France (1799–1814), war with Persia (1803–1813), war with the Ottoman Empire (1808–1812), the Congress of Vienna (1814–1815), and the growing revolutionary restlessness in Europe and in Russia after 1814, prevented them from giving focused and steady attention to conditions in Russia's American colonies.

Changes occurred in 1818 when on the advice of Russian naval authorities the Directors of the Russian American Company allowed Baranov to retire at last, and named as his replacement a career naval officer, Leontii A. Hagemeister. His appointment inaugurated a new era that lasted until the sale of Alaska in 1867. In contrast to Baranov, who although capable and practical was a self-made man with limited formal schooling, all of his successors were well educated, high-ranking officers of the Russian Imperial Navy. And unlike Baranov's nineteen-year often tyrannical tenure, appointments for the new Chief Administrators were at first for three, and later for five years. Finally, to prevent a possible re-emergence of the arbitrary and abusive behavior which had characterized Baranov's tenure, in 1821 the government clarified and formally codified the rights and responsibilities of the Chief Administrator.

Under the new rules the Emperor appointed the Chief Administrator from among senior Russian naval officers, upon recommendation of the Ministry of the Navy and the Directors of the Main Administration, to whom the Chief Administrator was responsible. In regard to military and naval personnel, the authority of the Chief Administrator corresponded to that of a Port Commandant. In his relations with foreign powers he acted as the governor of a gubernia of the Russian Empire. He enjoyed considerable judicial powers in matters which in Russia would be handled by judicial and police officials. He had the power to appoint and dismiss commanding officers of Company ships, accountants, secretaries, warehouse supervisors and all other Russian and native officials. He supervised the activity of the Company's branch offices in Okhotsk, Kodiak, Fort Ross and other administrative outposts, and distributed awards for exceptional services and reprimands and punishments for failures. He had the right to establish wages for native hunters and to reprove, demote and dismiss any Russian employees of the Company, decrease their wages or even deport them to Russia to face criminal charges if their conduct or actions harmed Company interests.

With these rights, the Chief Administrator had many obligations. He was accountable for the proper functioning of colonial defenses on land and sea. He was responsible for the strict observance on the part of all his subordinates of the Company's privileges and laws, not only of Imperial Russia, but those stemming from international treaties as well. He was required to submit an annual report to the Directors of the Main Administration on the state of the colonies, including a full review of overall conditions in the colonies, the state of education, results of hunting and fishing, goods imported and exported, an inventory of supplies on hand and a list of those needed, a report on current construction projects and a review of policy decisions affecting Company interests.

The Chief Administrator also had the obligation to see, at least in theory, that no one under his jurisdiction, either Russian or native, was abused, humiliated, exploited, deprived of his legitimate recompense and basic needs, or unjustly detained. To guard Company interests he had to make certain no one had unauthorized contact with foreign ships. He was required to set an example for employees of the Company in high standards of personal conduct. He had to be ever vigilant in the Company's interests, see that its property was well maintained and that its ships and crews were ready to sail. He had to make an annual inspection of enterprises, see that equipment functioned properly and that supplies were in order. Finally, the Chief Administrator was to exercise economy in all Company undertakings, organize a school system to teach natives useful trades, and make a fair distribution of provisions and other essentials to all persons under his jurisdiction. The Chief Administrator wielded enormous power and exercised viceregal responsibilities.

To enable the Chief Administrator to manage the Company's colonial possessions more efficiently, the Directors divided the vast area into administrative units: 1) *Sitka*, which included the Northwest Coast of America from Mount St. Elias south to 54° 40′ and all offshore islands in the area; 2) *Kodiak*, which embraced islands of Kodiak, Ukamok, Semidi and others in the area, the coast of the Alaska Peninsula to the meridian of the Shumagin Islands, and the coast of Bristol Bay and the basins of the Nushagak and Kuskokvim rivers; 3) *Mikhailovsk Redoubt*, which covered the Kuskokvim and Kvikpak River basins and the coast of Norton Sound to Bering Strait; 4) *Unalaska*, which embodied the Alaska Peninsula from the meridian of the Shumagin Islands, the Fox, Sanak and Pribilof islands; 5) *Atkhinsk*, which comprised the Andreanov, Rat, Near and Komandorskie islands; 6) *Kuril*, which consisted of the Kuril archipelago from Urup to the Kamchatka Peninsula; and 7) *Fort Ross*, a small outpost north of San Francisco, California, which the Russian American Company held from 1812 to 1841.

All of these administrative units were under the jurisdiction of the Chief Administrator of the Russian America Company, whose principal office was in New Arkhangel on Sitka [now Baranov] Island. The Chief Administrator appointed all officials of these units, delegated to them their duties and responsibilities and held them accountable for their conduct and performance. In a few instances these officials, with the consent of the Chief Administrator, entrusted their *prikashchiks* [assistants] with the administration of remote regions of their territories, such as the islands of Urup, Atka, Attu, Bering, Copper, Unalaska and Unga. Below these officials were the heads of various redoubts and *odinochkas* [one-man posts], who supervised Company trade with the natives and exercised control over the natives themselves. All officials were either Russian or *creole* [mixed Russian-native parentage].

At the lowest rung of the formal administrative structure was the network of *toions* [native leaders]. The Company adopted the practice of using these native leaders from Russia's colonial experience in northern Asia: the word "toion" is indeed from the Tungus language. Officials of the Company selected these native leaders to carry out several tasks: organize native hunting parties; distribute food to needy natives; keep peace and order in the native community; resolve conflicts, settle arguments, and see that every member of the native community was engaged in constructive activity. For their efforts the toions frequently received from the Company extra supplies of tobacco, alcoholic beverages, clothing, uniform, medals and special letters of thanks, which they displayed prominently in their homes. On special occasions the Chief Administrator would even receive certain toions in his office, to hear their concerns.

The final link in the Company's administrative structure was the Russian Orthodox Church. Its presence in the colonies was mandated by two fundamental considerations. The Church was an inseparable part of the Russian Imperial system, with the Emperor as its titular head. Further, several provisions in its Charters mandated that the Company give full economic assistance and support to the Church in fulfilling its mission, which was to care for the spiritual needs of Russian Orthodox employees of the Company and to attempt to convert colony natives to Orthodox Christianity.

Although Shelikhov first baptized Kodiak Island natives in 1784, real proselytizing began ten years later when a group of missionaries from Valaam Monastery near Lake Ladoga, north of St. Petersburg, headed by Arkhimandrit Ioasaf, arrived to establish the first mission in Alaska. Until 1840 the Russian missionaries were under the jurisdiction of the Irkutsk Consistory, and on many occasions they clashed with Company administrators, especially with Baranov, over their respective assignments. Conditions changed in 1840 with the establishment of the Diocese of Alaska and the appointment of Archpriest Ivan Veniaminov to the rank of Bishop of Kamchatka, the Kurils and the Aleutians, under the name of Bishop Innokentii. Veniaminov was not only a zealous missionary, but an able administrator and profound scholar. He devised an alphabet and a grammar for the Aleuts and translated a number of religious works into that language. He built the Cathedral of St. Michael in New Arkhangel and made that town the religious center for the Russian colonies in North America, and for much of eastern Siberia as well, since that entire region came under his jurisdiction as archbishop. In 1868, after the sale of Alaska, he was made Metropolitan of Moscow. This priest of phenomenal achievements is known today as "The Apostle of Alaska."

The success of the Church in fulfilling its missionary task is difficult to assess, because no serious attempt has as yet been made to analyze this question. Critics have argued that there were simply too few missionaries to accomplish the task and that the Russian employees of the Company themselves provided a very poor Christian example for the natives; they further argue that the missionaries exaggerated their successes, and that, as one critic suggested, in exchange for gifts of food, tobacco and liquor, a native would embrace even Islam or any other religion. Baranov was constantly at odds with the clergy, who were outspokenly critical of his treatment of the natives. Many of the clergy assigned to the colonies were undistinguished spiritually and intellectually, seldom left the security of the Russians forts, and made no effort to learn native languages. However there were a number of outstanding priests in addition to the great Veniaminov. The *ieromonk* Herman has recently been sanctified by the Russian Orthodox Church for his missionary labors. A creole priest, Iakov Nesvetsov, furthered Veniaminov's work of translating parts of the Bible into native tongues and traveled extensively, both along the coast and into the interior, to convert the natives. But perhaps the best evidence that the Church was successful in its work is the fact that even today there are some 90 active Russian Orthodox places of worship in Alaska, and the area has its own bishop, who presides over this vast eparchy.

In addition to this formal administrative structure, the Russian American Company occasionally sent inspectors to make independent reports. These men represented the interests and concerns of the Emperor, the Directors, the Ministry of the Navy and the Ministry of Finance. They went to the colonies to check on reported abuses by officials, make appropriate changes in administrative personnel, and recommend new policies or programs of colonial administration. The best known of these were Nikolai P. Rezanov, 1805–1806; Leontii A. Hagemeister, 1818–1819; and Pavel N. Golovin and Sergei A. Kostlivtsov, 1860–1861.

RUSSIAN AND NON-RUSSIAN SUBJECTS IN RUSSIA'S AMERICAN COLONIES

From 1799 to 1867 the jurisdiction of the Russian American Company extended over Sakhalin, the Kuril, Aleutian and other islands in the North Pacific, Alaska, and from 1812 to 1841 over an outpost in northern California. In addition to numerous Russians employed by the Company as officials, military personnel and laborers, many native peoples inhabited this vast area. Giliaks and Ainus lived on Sakhalin; Kurils on the Kuril Islands; various Aleut peoples on the Aleutians; Koniags on Kodiak; diverse Tlingit peoples between Vancouver Strait and Chugach Bay; Chugach along the bay itself; Inuits in northern Alaska; and Pomos in northern California.

Based on their economic ties to the Company, these peoples comprised the following basic groups: *Russians* in Company service; *creoles*, persons of mixed Russian and native parentage; and the *indigenous* population. The latter was divided into those who were classified as *dependent*, and included Kurils, Aleuts and Koniagas; *semi-independent*, the Kenais and Chugach; and *independent*, the Tlingits, Kolchans, Malegmiuts, Inuits, inhabitants of the Komandorskie Islands and Pomos. Available evidence indicates that despite policy directives the Company regularly exploited and mistreated these subjects. Observations of foreign visitors to the region corroborate this, as do reports of Russian government inspectors, petitions from natives to Russian authorities, and large scale desertions and violent rebellions. The situation was so unstable that throughout the existence of the Russian American Company most fortified Russian posts were on a 24-hour formal alert against native attacks, especially from the Tlingits. This paralysis combined with the constant shortage of Russian manpower confined the invaders to the coastal lowlands and prevented any extended exploration of the interior of Alaska and later of northern California.

Many factors contributed to this state of affairs, but perhaps the most important was historical precedent. Officials of the Russian American Company treated their colonial subjects in North America in the same manner as Russian government officials and private entrepreneurs had earlier treated the natives of Siberia. Russian rulers neither authorized nor officially sanctioned a policy of abuse and mistreatment; their basic interest, however, was to bring these people under Russian rule by any means possible. Distance, lack of communication and other priorities obviated punishment for excessive zeal in this endeavor. Furthermore, the situation in North America differed from that which had existed in northern Asia, where the Russians had had a monopoly on their hegemony. In North America administrators increasingly had to contend with British and American competitors who sometimes assisted the Russians in their struggle for survival, but just as often traded natives firearms for furs and encouraged resistance whenever the Russians protested these transactions.

Russian employees of the Company were better treated than others in the North American colonies. Depending on their responsibilities, Russian employees were top administrators of the Company, military or naval personnel in Company service, or promyshlenniks and other lower echelon workers. The top administrators, staff officers and commanding officers of vessels were the most powerful, and were designated as "distinguished persons." Below these were "semi-distinguished" persons: prikashchiks, hired navigators and persons in subordinate positions. The lowest and largest category included sailors, soldiers and common laborers. This stratification was in no way unique, but rather a standard feature throughout the Russian Empire.

Least fortunate of the Russian employees were the laborers. Under the terms of its Charter, the Company had the right to recruit these people throughout the empire, provided they were not serfs, were not under suspicion, and had valid passports. The Charter stipulated that the minimum term of contract was to be seven years. Since Russians who lived in Siberia enjoyed greater freedom of mobility than those in European Russia, the majority of the Company's Russian work force came from Siberia, and it was of course a mixed bag.

To attract these often gullible, desperate and reckless men, Company recruiters hinted at fortunes to be made and other enticements. Seldom did they reveal to recruits their obligations, the dangers and the brute hardships they would face. Many recruits, of course, signed on after they had consumed generous amounts of spirits supplied by recruiters. If they actually reached their destinations they found a harsh reality. They were already indebted to the Company, for in America they found they even had to pay for the drink they had consumed before agreeing to work abroad for the Company! The Company charged them for everything—food, lodging, clothing, footwear, equipment and all other necessities. Their wages were so low they could rarely free themselves from indebtedness to the Company, and without repayment, they could not leave. In essence they became Company slaves, and as they wore out, a serious burden.

The lot of these Russian laborers was miserable, especially in the early years. Company barracks were damp and pest-ridden. Low wages prevented the men from buying spare clothing, so they wore only what they had, day and night, wet or dry. The Company provided food from communal kitchens, but the diet was limited to what was available, which often was only fish soup, whale meat and blubber, sometimes putrefied and unfit to eat. Many of the men became seriously or fatally ill with scurvy and pneumonia. A good many also became infected with venereal diseases brought to the native population by earlier Russians as well as by their contemporaries. Medical aid, when available, was primitive. All assigned work was strenuous and hazardous, but the greatest danger was from attack or ambush by hostile natives. Company officials punished employees who criticized conditions, and treated rebels as traitors. Men often died young; others were ravaged by malnutrition and exposure, still others were permanently disabled. Most could never hope to return to Russia, because they could not repay their debts to the Company. In the 1850's their plight came to the attention of government officials, who decided to confer on these persons the title of "colonial citizen." Each was entitled to own a small plot of land to grow his own food, and the Company granted each an annual pension and the privilege of purchasing certain necessities at Company stores.

The status of the creoles was below that of the Russian laborers. As the number of creoles increased, government and Company officials reassigned them into a special category of colonial population known as the *meshchanstvo* [town dwellers], since most of them lived in the fortified outposts which the Russians called towns. Initially creoles were exempt from taxes. Creoles, like all other subjects under Company jurisdiction, were obligated to work for the Company, and if Company officials judged their performance satisfactory, they were entitled to the same awards and titles the Company granted their Russian counterparts. Creoles who were educated at Company expense were required to serve the Company for at least ten years. Creoles welcomed these advantages but were considered outcasts by other natives, as well as by the Russian work force. They were trapped between two worlds.

Certainly the most unfortunate subjects of the Russian American Company were the native peoples of the Aleutian archipelago whom the Russians had subjugated in the second half of the eighteenth century. Many of these tribes perished in the process of Russian conquest; those who survived became servants of the Company. The Russian government freed them from the payment of *iasak* [tribute], but required them to hunt sea animals and to perform other labor for the Company. This obligation fell primarily on men between 18 and 50 years old. Local toions had the responsibility for assigning the native men to the hunts, which were prolonged and often far distant from their families. Many perished en route, either through intertribal hostilities, as in 1802 when Tlingits killed hundreds of Aleuts who were hunting for the Company, or through maritime disaster, as in 1804 when twenty Aleut baidaras were swept away by storm, and scores of Aleuts lost their lives.

The Aleuts were superb sea hunters, especially of the sea otter. The Company could not have maintained its operations without them. In addition to this, the Company assigned Aleuts to cut timber, build dwellings for the Russians, build warehouses and other structures, fish, make bricks, and after 1850, cut ice for the Company to sell in San Francisco. The Company also employed elderly Aleuts, both men and women, and Aleut children, to garden, tend livestock, pick berries, prepare fish, sew garments, gather birds' eggs and perform other chores.

Unremitting obligations to the Company disrupted traditional Aleut family life and made their long-term survival problematical. Company work took most men away from the Aleut communities, often bringing famine to the rest. At times their only nourishment was whatever the tides cast up on shore. Many died from eating decayed or toxic shellfish or other rotted sea creatures. Understandably the Aleut population was drastically diminished during the Russian period.

Under the terms of the Charter, the Company theoretically compensated the Aleuts for their work, but compensation was very low. This amounted to 200 paper rubles per year in the 1830's, a sum inadequate to buy even necessities. Moreover, the Company generally paid the Aleuts not in rubles but in goods of very poor quality. Further, Company officials appraised Aleut furs at very low prices and put a high overhead on goods purchased from Company stores. If the Aleuts protested, Company officials accused them of insubordination and employed harsh methods to keep them in line. Under such circumstances Aleuts were unable to free themselves from their obligations to the Company.

Under the terms of its Charter, the Company provided housing for Aleut employees, but like the wages and food, housing was deplorable. These employees lived in communal structures more like livestock sheds than human dwellings. Crowded with 150 to 500 persons, these sheds were filthy and the stench unbearable because they were also used for cleaning fish and preparing furs and hides. Colonial officials naturally avoided mentioning such matters in their annual reports to St. Petersburg; rather, they presented favorable statistics and descriptions of progress.

Aleut girls and women suffered the additional abuse of concubinage to the Russian men, and their creole children faced an uncertain status and existence. Many Aleuts fell victim to smallpox, scurvy, dysentery, respiratory ailments and venereal disease. Thousands perished from lack of medical care. The previously hearty, energetic Aleuts became lethargic and indifferent and ceased to care for their own needs—they were then a liability to the Company rather than an asset. After 1820, in order to reverse some of these problems, the Company organized educational facilities for native children, as well as for the children of Company servitors. The curriculum for boys included catechism, Russian language, arithmetic, geometry, navigation, astronomy, geography, history and bookkeeping. Girls' studies emphasized handicrafts, sewing, cleaning and cooking. Facilities, budgets and enrollment were limited, and the quality of teaching not of the best, but a number of youngsters educated in these schools later served the Company as clerks and seamen. Some of the brightest pupils were even sent back to Russia for more professional training, especially in cartography and navigational science.

In the three decades, 1812–1841, that the Russians held Fort Ross and the Ross settlement, Russian American Company officials and Imperial Russian naval officers had contacts with the Kashaya Pomo Indians of northern California, on whose lands the Russians had erected their fort. The Russians hired the Pomos as laborers and agricultural workers, and a few marriages took place between Pomo women and Aleut hunters employed by the Russians in the San Francisco Bay area. In 1817 Russian naval officers persuaded the Pomos to sign a treaty which gave the Russians possession of the land they already occupied at Fort Ross—land the Spaniards considered their own.

Contemporary accounts by Russian administrators of Fort Ross and Russian navigators who visited the installation speak of the friendly relations between the Pomos and the Russians. This was perhaps the case initially, but not after the Russians, perennially short of manpower, forced the Pomos to work for them without meaningful compensation. However the permanent importance of Russian contact with these people was not economic, but ethnological. The Russians made invaluable

These seemingly sedentary, stoic poses mask the ferocity of the Kolosh [Tlingit] people. Strong tribal allegiances combined with the equally fierce climate and topography and made subjugation impossible. For the first time in Russian America the Russians had met their match in tenacity, cruelty, valor and grim determination. Until the very end, Russian administrators mounted armed guards around the clock. *La Corvette Senavine.* (OHS OrHi neg. 82407)

accounts of the Pomos' physical appearance, clothing, diet, dwellings, customs and crafts. Since neither British, American, Spanish or French explorers appear to have left such accounts, this Russian material is all the more valuable, including large artifactual holdings in Soviet museums.

In contrast to Company relations with its Russian, creole, Aleut and Pomo subjects, the Tlingits, whom Russians called Kolosh, were never subdued; rather, they were at all times a serious threat to Russian settlers. The powerful Kolosh inhabited the Northwest Coast from Yakutat Bay to the Stikine River, and offshore islands as well. They were subdivided into two clans, the Wolf and Crow, and were identified by the name of the settlement they occupied. The most prominent groups inhabited Yakutat, Sitka, Stikine, Lituya Bay, Kenai, Kaigan and the tundra. Such widespread divisions indicate that the Kolosh population was very large. The exact numbers are not known, for no one took an accurate census of these independent people. An 1860 Russian estimate placed the population at between 15,000 and 20,000. Contemporary Russian accounts describe the Kolosh as savage, brave, cunning, vengeful, able to endure pain and deprivation, and above all, intensely proud and independent. These are accurate observations, and for these reasons and because they were better organized and had stronger leaders than other tribes, the Kolosh never submitted to the Russians. They made every attempt to destroy them, as at Slavorossia and New Arkhangel.

They harrassed on a 24-hour basis and ambushed Company hunting, fishing and timber cutting parties, inflicting demoralizing losses. Their hostility, determination and strong resistance forced constant Russian vigilance and penned them close into their fortified settlements. In effect they denied the Russians access to the interior of Alaska to inventory and exploit the region's resources and potential.

The Kolosh women were a formidable challenge to the Russians, too, for they were highly skilled bargainers. They would supply the Russians with furs, fresh meat, fish, berries and other produce, which the Russians desperately needed, but only for high prices. If the Russians refused to pay the asking price, the Kolosh men would direct trade to American and British merchant traders in exchange for guns, powder and shot. As a basic security measure, Russian officers barred Kolosh from entering Russian settlements. Of necessity they had to allow Kolosh traders to camp near some of the Company forts, but loaded cannon were constantly trained on these encampments from the walls.

Records reveal the Kolosh and other tribes in Russia's American colonies had good cause to hate the Russians, for they tried to enslave them; exploited, degraded and abused them; tried to prevent them from profitable trade with American and British merchants; imposed restrictions on their mobility; and introduced smallpox, venereal disease and other illnesses that took an enormous toll on the natives. Company officials did, however, offer the Kolosh some opportunities for paid work and for education, introduced them to Russian and European food and drink, tobacco, customs and way of life, and converted some to Orthodox Christianity. Important to us, however, is the fact that Company and government officials recorded for posterity detailed descriptions of the Kolosh and collected artifacts that today enrich museum ethnological collections on four continents.

THE DIVERSE ACTIVITIES OF THE RUSSIAN AMERICAN COMPANY

Analysts of the Russian American Company usually maintain that the Company was a private enterprise and that hunting for furbearing animals was its principal activity, indeed its reason for existence. We believe this perception of Company activity is incorrect. The Company, as we have documented, was not a private venture, but a de facto agency of the Imperial Russian government. And while hunting was one of its ventures, it was not its prime purpose. In our view the purpose of the Company, from the point of view of the Imperial government, was to found permanent Russian settlements on islands in the North Pacific and along the Northwest Coast of North America, in order to make that vast area an exclusive Russian colonial preserve.

These settlements had a four-fold purpose. They were to serve as Russian national outposts in the North Pacific, warning off any other maritime powers from Russia's colonial possessions. They were to be advanced bases from which the Russians could move on to Spanish California, Hawaii, the Amur Basin, Sakhalin, China, the Philippines and other regions of the Pacific Rim, in pursuit of Shelikhov's grand vision, and indeed the stated provisions of the Company's Charter. These settlements were also to function as the administrative, commercial and cultural outposts from which the Russians could exploit the region's resources, exert rigid control over the indigenous population and bend them to the Russian way of life. Finally, these outposts were intended to reduce costly voyages between Russian home ports along the northeastern Asian coast, such as Okhotsk, Petropavlovsk and Nizhnekamchatsk and Russia's American colonies. These then were imperialistic and hegemonistic goals, similar to those devised and used in the Russian conquest of Siberia.

To implement these objectives between 1799 and 1821 the Russians founded fifteen permanent and numerous temporary or seasonal settlements. They located permanent outposts on the Komandorskie and Pribilov islands, and on Atka, Unalaska, Kodiak and Sitka (Baranov) islands; at Cook Inlet, Chugach Sound and the Kenai Peninsula; in northern California (1812–1841); and in Hawaii (1815–1817). In the 1850's government and Company servitors surveyed and annexed to Russia the Chinese-claimed territories of Sakhalin Island, the Amur Basin and the Maritime Province, where they immediately established a network of permanent outposts, focused on Vladivostok. The Russians also established temporary outposts on the Kuril and Aleutian islands, the Alaska Peninsula, Afognak Island and Norton Sound. They attempted to enter and colonize the Columbia River Basin, but failed in that endeavor. Regardless of whether they were permanent or temporary, all outposts were designed to serve Russian national interests, and accordingly developed communication links with one another and with the colonial capital of New Arkhangel.

Under the terms of the Charter the government required the Company to fortify all permanent and temporary outposts and permitted it to purchase cannon, gunpowder and shot from government ordnance depots. To assure that Russian colonial interests in the North Pacific and in North America were well protected, the government also stationed military and naval units in New Arkhangel. Likewise, between 1805 and 1865 the government dispatched men-of-war to the North Pacific to demonstrate its constant commitment to the security of its far-flung empire. Further, it authorized the Company to recruit Russian nationals and Russian clergy to supervise the daily activity of the indigenous population and to attract them to the Russian way of life. In short, based on previous experience in Siberia, the Russian government and Company officials attempted to utilize a system of permanent and temporary settlements as an essential means to hold the North Pacific region and the Northwest Coast of North America, and transform it into an exclusive Russian preserve.

However, from the time the Russians first established settlements in their newly acquired colonies they faced a host of serious problems. The most pressing were shelter and food. The Russians solved the problem of shelter in the same manner as they had in Siberia. They patterned their permanent settlements in the American colonies on their Siberian *ostrogs* [forts];

and their *odinochkas* [one-man outposts] closely resembled their Siberian *zimov'es* [winter huts]. The odinochkas were primitive, and offered little security, while the forts were larger and more comfortable, and certainly safer. Within its walls each fort included the office and living quarters of the Chief Administrator, a church, living quarters for Russian government and Company personnel, living quarters for non-Russian employees, a communal kitchen, warehouses and artisans' shops, a stockade and other structures. Sitka's headquarters boasted steambaths, plus a private one for the Chief Administrator.

It was more difficult to solve the food problem because of the northerly location, inhospitable climate and the vast distance that separated the colony from its home base. Almost the entire colony consisted of barren or semi-barren islands and a coastline which although picturesque, was rugged and hazardous. The entire region was above the 55th parallel; the temperature was extreme, arable land in short supply and the growing season brief. Moreover, no matter how one journeyed to the colonies, overland across Siberia and thence by sea, or by sea from St. Petersburg, the hazard-filled distance was an appalling 10,000 miles or more! Under ideal conditions, with the transport available at the time, a trip from St. Petersburg to New Arkhangel could not be completed in under seven months. These considerations forced the Company to develop diverse sources of provisioning not only for its own Russian servitors but also for many of its non-Russian employees and their dependents.

The waters of the North Pacific abounded in superb fish, which proved to be the most reliable and least expensive source of food. Fishing was one of the basic activities of the Company. Indigenous subjects of the Company did most of the fishing; they caught cod, halibut, pike, perch and bream throughout the year, and herring and salmon seasonally. They took herring from February to April, salted it and stored it in wooden barrels or tubs. Salmon ran from June to September. During this time the Company distributed fresh salmon to all service personnel without cost, and also salted and stored large quantities. They dried additional amounts of salted salmon; in this condition it was known as *iukola*, and was a staple for the Aleuts during sea otter hunts. Carelessness and unsanitary conditions in processing and storage facilities, and the insidious wet climate caused large amounts of fish to spoil. During the 1850's the Company annually prepared some 380,000 dried fish, 114,000 salted fish and provided 64,000 fresh fish.

In addition to preserving fish for its own people, the Company salted many barrels of fish to sell to foreign customers—in 1858 more than 1,000 barrels. This was an expensive venture, however, for each barrel of fish required five *puds* [one pud = 36.11 pounds] of salt; for this reason and because of frequent unfavorable market conditions, the Company suffered heavy losses in this undertaking.

The Company also engaged in whaling, at first assigning Aleuts and creoles to this hunt, and later, in the 1850's, forming a joint venture, the Russian-Finnish Whaling Company. Whales provided meat, blubber, whiskers and sinews, as well as the versatile oil for lamps, for consumption by the Aleuts, lubrication for baidarkas and mill machinery, and an essential ingredient for tanners and caulkers.

In addition to efforts to obtain food from the sea, the Company tried to wrest it from the land. Shelikhov envisaged the development of agriculture and livestock breeding in the colonies, and tested some seeds while on Kodiak. He later persuaded government officials to allow him to settle a few families of exiled Russian peasants on Kodiak, with their livestock. The Company charter specified the development of agriculture as a prerequisite to success for the colonial venture, but the Company never managed to accomplish this to a bountiful degree. Many factors prevented this: the unfavorable climate, paucity of arable land, colonial officials' lack of knowledge of farming and animal husbandry, and the fact that the threat of Kolosh attacks confined the Russians to the foggy coastal reaches. The Company did bring cattle, swine and poultry to Alaska, but never provided shelter or feed. Left to roam and forage for themselves, much of the livestock starved; those that survived by living on fish and sea growth proved to be almost inedible because their meat had such a strong taste.

Conditions improved somewhat after 1812 when the Company established Fort Ross, some 100 miles north of San Francisco on the coast of California. The Russians immediately planted gardens and orchards around the new settlement, and in 1818 began to grow barley, wheat and other grains on three farm sites, the Khlebnikov, Kostromitinov and Chernykh ranches. The total amount of land under cultivation, however, was less than 200 acres. This venture produced several good harvests which made Company officials optimistic that Fort Ross might eventually be able to provide enough food to satisfy the needs not only of the Russian colonies in Alaska, but also of Kamchatka and the Okhotsk seaboard.

These hopes proved in vain because labor shortages forced the Company to use unskilled natives to work the land; heavy fog which prevails during the summer growing season caused blast; and Company officials themselves lacked basic agricultural knowledge and experience. By the late 1830's prospects for improved production yields were extremely poor. Fortunately in 1839 the Company concluded an agreement with Hudson's Bay Company which in part provided that the English company would annually provision the Russian American Company with wheat, flour, peas, groats, corned beef, butter and ham, all delivered to New Arkhangel from the Columbia and Nisqually river valleys. This arrangement enabled the Company to sell Fort Ross in 1841 to John Augustus Sutter for 30,000 Spanish piasters. In the effort to secure adequate supplies of food, the Company sought assistance from other sources as well. They bartered furs for provisions from American and British ship captains who occasionally came to the region, but this was unreliable, since it was uncertain when such ships might put in to the Russian colonial ports. Spanish California, which after 1825 became Mexican California, was another source. Rezanov had utilized this in 1806, but after 1807, as is discussed later, a number of problems interfered.

The Company also tried to establish provisionment from other sources. In 1812 Russian diplomats in New York and Washington helped the Company negotiate an agreement with John Jacob Astor's American Fur Company to barter supplies for furs. Between 1815 and 1817 the Company established a foothold and a plantation in Hawaii, but fearing complications with Britain, abandoned the venture at the behest of government officials in St. Petersburg. Throughout this period the Company obtained fresh meat and wild produce from the Kolosh, in exchange for manufactured goods, an arrangement fraught with uncertainty because of tribal malevolence. Large amounts of grain and meat were also shipped to the colonies from Siberia, but the cost was prohibitive and the quality often poor. Finally, the Company obtained a substantial amount of its foodstuffs and other necessities from Russia and Europe aboard Russian naval vessels and Company ships which sailed every year to and from the colonies. In addition to time, distance and cost, rot was a problem here. In short, the basic problem was that every source of provisionment was unreliable and costly, a situation never resolved, and a principal reason for the demise of the Russian American Company.

The fur trade was a prime source of income for the Company. The Aleuts, Koniags, Ainus and Chugach were the most skillful hunters; sea otters, sea lions and seals the most prized targets, although other furbearing animals hunted included bears, river otters, beavers, wolverines, lynxes, reindeer, foxes, muskrats, minks and wolves. Sea otters ranged the coastal waters from the Kurils to California. Because their pelts were warm, durable and luxurious, they were much in demand. The Russians forced the Aleuts to hunt and take excessive numbers of these animals. Hunting was an elaborate process of careful planning and execution. The annual undertaking began in December, when local toions formally decided how many Aleuts and how many baidarkas would set out from their settlements on the coming expedition. The community decided on the time and location of the hunts, and on the assignment of the preliminary tasks.

Generally the Company provided the lumber, *lavtaks* [cured pelts used to cover the baidarka frames] and other necessary materials for making the light, slender crafts. If the Aleuts provided their own materials, the Company compensated them. The Company also supplied each hunting party with provisions of food, spirits, tea, tobacco, iukola, blubber, arrows, guns, powder and shot. Hunting parties set out early in April and returned in the first part of July. The Company paid a set price per pelt. The Company took no steps for conservation, until threatened with the extinction of the animals, and of profit.

Second to sea otters, northern fur seals were the prime targets of Company hunts. The Komandorskie and Pribilof islands were the traditional breeding grounds. Official reports reveal that from 1786 to 1832, 3,178,562 fur seals were killed on the two islands of St. Paul and St. George! This slaughter of course drastically depleted the animals. An average of 185 animals were slaughtered each day, and carcasses simply left to rot. The stench of decomposition was so great that often seals would avoid the islands. Further, the wet climate hindered proper drying of the pelts, and over a period of time the loss of pelts amounted to hundreds of thousands. Finally, the excessive kill created a glut in the fur market and a decline in price. In the mid-1830's the Company introduced initial conservation measures; by the end of the 1850's they took fewer than 20,000 fur seals each year.

In addition to sea otters and fur seals, the Company also took a great number of harbor seals and sea lions, not for the furs but for the hides to be used for baidarkas, the gut for *kamleikas* [outergarments], flippers for soles of footwear, and the meat, fresh, dried or salted, for food. From late September to mid-December the Company sent Aleuts out to hunt the furbearing land animals, and it also obtained pelts from dependent and independent natives. Official reports reveal that the value of all the furs taken in the colonies between January 1, 1849 and July 1, 1860, was 1,776,878 paper rubles.

The Company marketed its furs in Russia, Western Europe, the United States and China, the latter providing the most lucrative market. Furs entered China through two outlets: Canton, with the help of British or American intermediaries, since until the mid-19th century the Chinese would not allow Russian ships to enter Chinese ports; and Kiakhta, an outpost south of Lake Baikal where from the early 18th century the Russians and Chinese had maintained commercial and diplomatic contacts. The Kiakhta route was arduous and expensive because to reach that outlet from New Arkhangel involved using the Okhotsk-Iakutsk-Irkutsk route. At Kiakhta Company agents exchanged furs for Chinese tea, fabrics, porcelain and other items of Chinese manufacture. The Russian government profited again from these transactions through the imposition of import duties.

The location of the Russian colonies in North America, the vast distances that separated various administrative units from one another and the colonies from the Motherland, and Company activities of hunting, fishing, trading and maritime exploration, all required that the Company have ships available. The Company's fleet included two categories. The first consisted of ships capable of circumnavigating to bring goods from the Baltic port of Kronstadt, the St. Petersburg entrepôt, and after 1840 from other European ports, to the colonial outposts and transporting colonial cargoes back to Europe. Many of these ships were Imperial Russian naval vessels manned by naval personnel but financed in part by the Company. Others were commercial vessels manned primarily by Finnish crews. The Company bought most of these bottoms from Germany, England and America. The second category consisted of smaller vessels for use in colonial waters. The Company purchased a few of these from visiting American and British captains, but also built a number in colonial shipyards at Three Saints Harbor, Yakutat, New Arkhangel and Fort Ross. Colonial shipwrights generally used larch for sheathing, spruce for decks and yellow cedar for ribs, but Fort Ross builders used oak. Most of these shipyards could make repairs, including timbering and tarring. Ships built in colonial shipyards generally gave brief service because they were built of unseasoned lumber. The Company used disabled vessels as hulks to store provisions and supplies. Compared to world girdling vessels, those that plied colonial waters were poorly maintained. Their crews consisted mostly of creoles and Aleuts.

Official reports indicate that between 1798 and 1833 the Company built 41 vessels in its colonial shipyards; but because of shipwreck and decay, by 1842 the Company had only fifteen seaworthy ships; five others were used for port duty. By 1860 the figure stood at twelve seaworthy vessels: four frigates, four steamers, two brigs and two barks.

Throughout its existence the Company engaged in lumbering. A special crew of woodsmen, and later soldiers, cut lumber all year long for dwellings, other structures, ostrogs, fences, vessels, barrels, furniture, implements and firewood. Rot, fires and the expansion of Company operations increased the demand for lumber. To meet this demand the Company installed waterpowered, and later steam-driven mills. The main lumbering centers were on Baranov and Kodiak islands and at Fort Ross.

Other Company ventures included a flour mill built at New Arkhangel which by 1846 could grind more than 650 tons of grain per year, if available. The Company owned a brickyard to produce bricks for ovens and chimneys. Company servitors tried to develop and utilize coal deposits on the Kenai Peninsula and on Unga Island in the late 1840's, but the high cost of production led the Company to discontinue this operation. As previously mentioned, the Company had a joint venture with Finnish subjects for whaling. And finally, in the early 1850's the Company began to cut and ship ice. The principal market was California, due to the sudden increase of population caused by the gold rush. Centers for the ice trade were New Arkhangel and Lesnoi Island off Kodiak. The Company marketed ice through the California-based American-Russian Commercial Company. The annual production reached over 3,000 tons of ice, but the high cost of cutting, storing and shipping forced the Company to abandon this venture as unprofitable.

The Company was also active in promoting education, both secular and religious, among the colonial children. By the terms of its charter the Company had to build and maintain elementary schools for the native children and help the Russian Orthodox clergy spread Christianity. By 1840 the Company had established four schools for boys and another four for girls; these were in the departments of Sitka, Kodiak, Unalaska and Atka. Both sexes learned the catechism, to read and write, and practical skills to enable them to lead useful lives. Boys might become scribes, navigators, mechanics, tailors, painters, cooks or artisans. Girls learned basic homemaking skills. Both sexes were fed and clothed by the Company.

A theological seminary opened in 1845, and trained a number of native and creole clergy. In 1860 the All-Colonial School opened in New Arkhangel to provide education to children of Company servitors, both Russian and creole. This school offered a more advanced education than the earlier facilities, including both Russian and English language instruction, geography, history, advanced mathematics, navigation and astronomy. Both the facilities and the teaching staff of this school were superior to the others. Training lasted five years, and students who received financial assistance from the Company had to enter Company service for fifteen years after graduation. Many boys educated in this school became fine navigators and even articulate defenders of the Company. A few attained career positions in Petersburg. The educational program was so successful that even critics admit the Company deserves a great deal of credit.

Two additional developments in education were significant. The first, as earlier described, was the devising by religious personnel of an alphabet for the Aleut and Kolosh peoples. The second was the decision to send scientists from scholarly institutions in Russia to the colonies to describe all aspects of natural history and collect specimens. Their efforts were thorough and the results rewarding, as evident in the superb and rich collections of the Museum of Anthropology and Ethnography in Leningrad and Helsinki's National Museum.

RELATIONS OF THE RUSSIAN AMERICAN COMPANY WITH FOREIGN POWERS

During its existence from 1799 to 1867, the Russian American Company conducted its relations and maintained contacts with foreign powers on two distinct levels: representing the Russian government, and on its own behalf. This dichotomous approach stemmed from the nature of the Company. As noted earlier the Company was an agency of the Russian government, protected by the Emperor, and controlled by his appointed officials. At the same time it was an entity which for practical purposes was presented to the public as a private, shareholding enterprise. This arrangement offered Russian officials considerable maneuverability. It enabled them to advance boldly when there was little risk of confrontation, or to retreat tactically in the face of danger. Because of this dual nature of the Company, the Russians were able to avoid embarrassment or conflict with strong adversaries, yet with minimum effort they could protect and expand Russian Imperial interests in the Pacific Basin.

Relations with China offer an excellent example of how this policy operated. Officially, Russia's relations with China were based on the provisions of the Treaty of Nerchinsk (1689) and the two treaties of Kiakhta (1727 and 1768). These provided for the delineation of a common frontier between the two powers. The two nations agreed that the Amur Basin belonged to China, pledged they would settle their differences through peaceful means, and vowed they would not allow neighboring Mongol peoples to disrupt their friendship. The treaties laid down general rules for handling fugitives and criminals and granted the Russians the right to maintain a religious and diplomatic mission in Peking. The two signatories promised to maintain commercial relations and designated Kiakhta, a border outpost south of Lake Baikal, as the only point through which Russian diplomats and merchants could enter China.

Neither side adhered fully to these terms, but the provisions concerning commercial relations were very successful. Until 1762 the Russian government had a monopoly on all Russian trade with China; it obtained furs from Russian promyshlenniks and subject Siberian natives, and annually exchanged this peltry for Chinese tea, textiles and other goods. In 1762 the government relinquished this monopoly and allowed private entrepreneurs to carry on the fur trade with China, in exchange for paying heavy custom duties. Russia adopted this change not for philosophical but for practical reasons: it brought in substantial revenues, eliminated diplomatic problems and yet provided continued access to information on all commerce and intelligence gathered by merchants and missionaries. Moreover, this transfer enabled Russia to turn her full attention to the profound changes, challenges and problems engendered by the Scientific, French and Industrial revolutions, as well as to the affairs of Poland, the Ottoman Empire and Europe.

These European issues were geographically closer and politically more pressing. Furthermore, Russian leaders perceived China as a powerful giant and wished at all costs to avoid two confrontations, one in Europe and one in Asia. They were careful neither to provoke nor to react to frequent Chinese aggravations, such as her refusal to allow the first two

Russian circumnavigatory vessels, *Neva* and *Nadezhda* to put in at Canton to sell goods carried from Russia's American colonies. Since the Chinese stipulated the Russians could trade only in Kiakhta, Russian colonial officials had to use American and British vessels as carriers. Kiakhta was far distant from the colonies, and far inland as well. The overland route was arduous and dangerous; the Company made little profit from its effort and investment, especially when entry was refused or delayed by fractious Chinese officials.

Conditions changed dramatically during the Opium War of 1839–1842, when the British exposed China's weakness and imposed humiliating terms on her. Russia immediately took advantage of this, permitting the Russian American Company and other Russian merchants to trade at Kiakhta, but between 1842 and 1860 also endeavoring to improve her own position with China. In the early 1850's Russian naval officers and Company officials surveyed the entire coastal region south of Okhotsk, a region which the Treaty of Nerchinsk had affirmed as belonging to China. Russia now established a series of fortified outposts in that strategic area. In 1853 Emperor Nicholas I directed the Company to occupy the northern half of Sakhalin Island, then claimed by the Chinese; and in 1855 Japan occupied the southern part. At the same time Russians secured equal access with the British and French to Chinese ports, and forced the Chinese to sign three bilateral agreements: Aigun, 1858; Tientsin, 1858; and Peking, 1860. These agreements negated most of the terms of the Treaty of Nerchinsk. The Russians induced the Chinese to acknowledge Russia's occupation and annexation of the entire Amur Basin and the Maritime Region. In 1860 Russia founded Vladivostok to guard her imperial interests in the North Pacific.

Russia's policy toward Japan was similar to that toward China—except that it was not successful. Throughout the entire eighteenth century the Russians used various means to try to establish relations with Japan. One method was to return survivors from Japanese vessels wrecked off the coast of Kamchatka. In another attempt, the Second Kamchatka Expedition of 1739–1742 sought to map the Japanese coastline. In yet a further endeavor, using promyshlenniks, cossacks and merchants, Russia tried to reach Japan via the Kuril Islands. Finally, with the approbation of Empress Catherine II, in 1791 the government organized a small expedition headed by scientist Adam Laksman. After several months of negotiations Laksman secured limited permission for a Russian merchant vessel to visit Nagasaki once a year; however, rapidly unfolding events in Europe following the outbreak of the French Revolution prevented the Russians from taking advantage of this long-sought opportunity.

Early in the nineteenth century the Russians renewed their efforts. They assigned the mission to Rezanov, who was a confidant of Emperor Alexander I, as well as Shelikhov's son-in-law and a major shareholder of the Russian American Company. Rezanov hoped to secure permission from the Japanese government for Russian vessels to put in at a northern Japanese port on a regular basis; obtain a lease on land where the Russians could build a warehouse; negotiate long-term price and trade agreements for Russian goods to be exchanged for Japanese products; agree on rules governing procurement of supplies for visiting vessels; and build a foundation for establishing diplomatic relations between the two countries. Rezanov also carried a letter from the Emperor, gifts, and several survivors from Japanese vessels wrecked in Russian waters.

Although the Japanese were surprised by the Russian visit, they received the uninvited guests courteously, provided them with provisions without charge, and even accommodated Rezanov and his immediate staff in a large mansion outside Nagasaki. However, the inability to communicate, ignorance of each other's language, culture and manners, and Russian failure to observe Japanese diplomatic protocol during official meetings all caused misunderstandings and problems. Rezanov vented a public outburst of indignation over procrastination, isolation and the indifferent Japanese response to Alexander's letter, and their refusal to accept gifts from the Russians. When Rezanov in turn refused to accept gifts from the Japanese, they ordered him and his men to leave the country. Rezanov departed April 29, 1805, his mission a failure.

On a subsequent voyage from Kamchatka to New Arkhangel, Rezanov met two young Russian naval officers in Company service, lieutenants N. A. Khvostov and G. I. Davydov. With them he concocted a plan to raid Japan in retaliation for the alleged Japanese insult to Russia's honor. Rezanov sent word of his plan to Alexander I. The raiders were to attack and destroy Japanese settlements, take prisoners and resettle them on a small island near New Arkhangel where they would work for the Company. Rezanov later altered the plan so he would not personally take part in the raid. He set out for St. Petersburg, but on the way fell ill and died in Krasnoiarsk. Khvostov and Davydov planned and carried out the raid, twice attacking Japanese settlements, in October 1806 on southern Sakhalin, and the following June, on Etorofu Island. Although outnumbered, the Russians inflicted heavy damage, plundered, and returned to Okhotsk. They were arrested for this unauthorized action, but were soon released and eventually became heroes in their homeland.

Shocked by these raids, the Japanese dubbed the Russians *aka-oni*, Red Devils, and immediately began to strengthen their defenses and gather intelligence about this dangerous adversary. In 1811 they took revenge when, through a ruse, they captured Vasilii M. Golovnin, captain of the sloop *Diana*, and seven of his crew, on Kunashiri Island. They held the men prisoner for more than two years, releasing them only after the Russian officials convinced the Japanese that the raids had not been authorized.

Subsequently the Russians attempted several times to establish commercial and diplomatic relations with Japan. These efforts were futile, for the Japanese government continued to adhere to its longheld policy of isolation. Russian ships, however, continued to sail into Japanese waters to study currents and map the shoreline. But it was only in 1855 that the two countries finally established formal relations, after the American flotilla under Commodore Matthew C. Perry "opened Japan." The first sign of cooperation was an agreement calling for the division of Sakhalin Island, giving control of the northern area to Russia, and of the southern to Japan.

Russian relations with Spanish authorities, and after 1821 with Mexican authorities in California, alternated between suspicion and limited cooperation. This was inevitable, for ever since they had launched their trans-Pacific colonial venture, ambitious Russians, and Shelikhov especially, had aspired to establish a Russian base in California. That intent, however, ran counter to Spanish interests which contended that not only

California, but indeed the entire west coast of North America, belonged to Spain by right of first discovery. In the latter part of the eighteenth century the Spaniards dispatched several voyages to the North Pacific to check the Russian move south. They extended their network of missions and presidios up the California coast, while continuing their policy of total nonco-operation with competing European powers. Again they re-fused to condone any contact with them. But there were human factors.

The first Russo-Spanish encounter in California occurred in April 1806, when Rezanov, rested after his disastrous mis-sion to Japan, sailed south in an attempt to procure food for the starving personnel of the Russian American Company in New Arkhangel. Rezanov hoped to cross the hazardous bar at the mouth of the Columbia River, but storms frustrated his plan. He sailed south, and surprised local Spanish authorities by his appearance in San Francisco Bay to barter furs for pro-visions. In contrast to his mission to Japan, this voyage was a resounding success. Employing immense Slavic charm, and with generous help from local missionaries, Rezanov enlisted the aid of several influential administrators to purchase substan-tial quantities of grain and other foodstuffs. A widower since the death of his wife, Shelikhov's daughter, Rezanov climaxed his transaction with his betrothal to Doña Concepcion, the beautiful young daughter of Don Luis de Arguello, son of the commandant of the Presidio of San Francisco. Rezanov died before the marriage could take place, but the provisions he took back to New Arkhangel saved the lives of many Company em-ployees, and the legend of unrequited love exists today.

The next Russo-Spanish encounter occurred in 1808 when Baranov in New Arkhangel dispatched two Company vessels: the schooner *Nikolai* to survey the mouth and lower reaches of the Columbia River and select potential sites for a Russian set-tlement; and the brig *Kadiak*, to carry out the same assignment along the coast of northern California. *Nikolai* never completed her mission. She was wrecked on the Olympic Peninsula, and her crew members either perished or became prisoners of local natives. [See *The Wreck of the Sv. Nikolai*, OHS: 1985]. *Kadiak* fulfilled her assignment and selected Little Bodega Bay as the site for a new Russian settlement. With the usual two-year hia-tus, Company directors requested permission of Emperor Alexander I to build a fort there. The Emperor not only approved the request, he also took the fort under his protection. With that assurance, the Company in 1812 renamed the bay Rumiantsev Bay (in honor of Russian Foreign Minister N. P. Rumiantsev), and founded Fort Ross on a tableland overlooking a cove eighteen miles north of the bay.

Spanish officials were of course vexed by the sudden appearance of a Russian fort in their territory, but were in no position to eject the intruders. They pursued a policy of non-cooperation and harassment and founded new missions north of San Francisco to contain further Russian advance. The Russians, now ensconced at Fort Ross, sought to legitimize their presence. They exerted diplomatic pressure in Madrid to approve their action and when that failed, Russian naval officers on the scene in 1817 signed an agreement with Pomo Indian chieftains which gave the Russians the right not only to the immediate vicinity of Fort Ross, but also to the entire coastal region from Fort Ross to the mouth of the Columbia River. Because that unrealistic understanding posed possible conflict with Spain, England *and* the United States, Russian government officials gave no formal approval.

The successful overthrow of Spanish colonial rule by the Mexican Revolution in the early 1820's caused some bewilderment to Russian policy makers. However, Company officials hoped the change would benefit the Company. But the new Emperor Nicholas I, rejected and despised all revolutions and prohibited any contact between Company officials and revolutionary regimes, even though Mexican officials revoked all former Spanish prohibitions against foreign trade and opened their ports to all foreign vessels. Such ships, especially American, came in such numbers that the Russians could not compete. Russian American Company Chief Administrator Baron Ferdinand von Wrangel believed the Yankees posed a major threat both to Mexican and Russian interests, but no other officials took formal notice of his warning. In the 1840's it was too late to take any deterrent action, since California was by then bound on its own course, eventually to end up as the 31st of the fast growing United States.

Russian relations with the British also alternated between suspicion and limited cooperation. Suspicion stemmed from national and colonial competitions between the two empires around the world, as well as from frequent British intrusions, both official and private, into Russia's Baltic and North Pacific waters. Practical considerations of commerce and statecraft, however, mandated cooperation. Company officials strongly resisted British vessels putting into the Russian colonies, because it was known that British traded the natives firearms for furs. Since the Russian American Company did not have its own seagoing vessels and could not deliver its goods to Chinese ports, it was obliged to use British bottoms. Moreover, on a number of occasions British vessels appeared on the scene at crucial times, either to save the Russians from slaughter at the hands of hostile natives, or from starvation or economic disarray. Finally, a few British captains favorably sold their vessels and cargo to the Company lock, stock and barrel at times when it was absolutely imperative that such a transaction be consummated.

Russo-British relations reached a low point in September, 1821, when at the request of the Company but without prior notice Alexander I signed a decree extending Russian jurisdiction 100 miles offshore and denying foreign ships the right to enter those waters. All this took time to publicize, but as the major naval and colonial power, Britain rejected Russia's extension of territorial waters. Since Russia had no means of enforcing this decree, the two powers resolved their differences in the Convention of February 28, 1825. Shortly thereafter the Company concluded an agreement with the British Hudson's Bay Company, another vast holding enterprise, which assured the Russians access to needed goods at reasonable prices. This arrangement soon downgraded the importance of distant Fort Ross as the principal supply base for Alaska, and paved the way for its eventual sale.

Russo-British conflict flared up again during the Crimean War, 1853–1855. Most of the action took place in the Crimea, the Baltic and the White and Black seas, but a joint British and French flotilla invaded the Russian naval base at Petropavlovsk in Kamchatka in two successive years, and attacked Russian naval and Company vessels in an engagement between the mouth of the Amur River and Sakhalin. These were costly and embarrassing sideshows. At the same time, the Crimean War gave the Russians justification for occupying the entire Amur Basin, the Maritime Territory and the northern part of Sakhalin, to prevent the Anglo-French flotilla from capturing those areas. During the war the Company worked closely with government agencies, placing some of its ships at government disposal and receiving government authorization to occupy northern Sakhalin.

Finally, we address Russian estimates of the newly formed United States. Official relations were amicable, because in that era the interests of the two countries were not in conflict. They differed radically in ideology, of course, but vast distances separated them. Imperial Russia was an old autocratic monarchy, with essentially Euro-centered interests; the United States was a new nation with a republican form of government, whose interest centered primarily in the western hemisphere. Moreover, for many years leaders in each country were generally uninformed of problems and intentions of the other country. Because of this, the two conducted official business in relative harmony and through many able representatives.

This official concord between St. Petersburg and Washington influenced relations between the Company and numerous American entrepreneurs who had interests in the greater Pacific Northwest. In 1806 Baranov contracted with an American shipwright named Lincoln to build Company vessels in New Arkhangel. He also purchased several ships and their cargoes from American captains and engaged Americans to carry and sell Company furs in Chinese ports forbidden to the Russians. American and Company ships participated in a joint venture to hunt sea otters off the coast of northern California, along the sea islands and in San Francisco Bay. In 1811 the Russian American Company and the American Fur Company of John Jacob Astor signed a five-year cooperative agreement. Subsequently the Company sold many furs to American dealers and purchased from American sources many of its basic needs, including some of its best seagoing vessels.

In 1841 the Company sold Fort Ross to John Sutter, born in Switzerland but a naturalized American citizen. Following the admission of California to the Union in 1850 the Company opened a branch office in San Francisco near the now fashionable Russian Hill. Later the Company negotiated an agreement with Beverley C. Sanders, of the San Francisco-based American Russian Trading Company, for annual delivery of ice from Kodiak to San Francisco. There was a Russian consulate in San Francisco, and for many years the Bay served as a main resupply center for Company and Russian naval vessels. This is only a partial list of mutually beneficial cooperative ventures between the Russian American Company and diverse American entrepreneurs.

It should be noted, however, that concomitant with the many cooperative ventures there was also competition and on occasion discord between the Company and certain American entrepreneurs. During Rezanov's 1806 voyage he tried to enter the Columbia River, since he had learned of the intent of the Lewis and Clark Expedition. Further, Company officials were understandably outraged when Americans traded guns for furs with Alaskan natives. The Russians objected on two grounds. They regarded such transactions as flagrant violations of the Company's rights and privileges, since the Charter designated the Company as the sole agency empowered to purchase furs from the natives. They rightly believed this exchange endangered the lives of Company employees, since the guns obtained by the natives in trade were often used against Russians. For years Company and government officials pleaded with American and British skippers to cease this practice. The Americans ignored these protests, as well as those against the indiscriminate slaughter by Americans of whales in Russian waters—an undertaking that brought great fortunes to many "Bostonians," as the Russians referred to the New England underwriters.

Since protests had no effect on the Americans and British, Alexander I signed a stern decree in September, 1821, at the urging of the Company's Board of Directors. Under its terms all foreign vessels were prohibited from carrying on unauthorized trade in the Russian colonies in North America, and also from sailing within 100 Italian miles [1 Roman mile = 5000 feet] of the colonies. Any vessel violating this prohibition was subject to a heavy fine and confiscation, although certain provisions were made for emergencies. The Americans and British refused to abide by the terms of this decree, and the Russians had no effective means of enforcement. Thus in April, 1824, the governments of the United States and of Imperial Russia signed a convention that greatly modified the terms of the 1821 decree. The British signed a similar convention in February, 1825.

The final chapter of Russo-American relations in the Pacific Northwest is one of harmony and concerns the sale of Alaska. Events leading to the sale are extremely complex and in spite of the existence of many fine works on the subject scholars have failed thus far to provide definitive analysis. It is apparent, however, that the Russians sold their remaining colonies in North America to the United States for significant reasons. They could not defend the colonies either from foreign attacks or from any large-scale influx of persons in search of gold (which the Russians were aware of), other natural resources, or land itself. They could not adequately provision their colonies, and they lacked the necessary Russian personnel to administer them. The Russians were preoccupied with reforms following upon the emancipation of serfs. Their attention focused on consolidating recent gains in the Far East and Central Asia. They hoped to establish close strategic relations with the United States to thwart further British expansion in the area. There was a small but influential group of persons in Russia, headed by the Emperor's brother Constantine, who wanted to rid Russia of this financial and political liability. And, finally, there were a few powerful visionaries in the United States, headed by Secretary of State William H. Seward, who saw the great value to the United States of annexing the Russian colonies. After several years of adroit maneuvers on the part of both nations, they agreed upon a sale price of $7,200,000 and consummated the transaction on March 31, 1867.

SOURCES AND PRINCIPAL SCHOLARS OF RUSSIAN AMERICA

In contrast to the bare-boned and elusive first hand accounts of Russia's earlier ventures into Siberia and the North Pacific, there is a rich record of the building of her colonial empire in North America. The principals in this undertaking—administrators, ships' captains, persons on special assignments—were better educated and informed, and were often perceptive observers and reporters.

Source material on Russia's American colonies falls into four general categories: government decrees, instructions, rules and regulations; records of the Russian American Company; accounts by officials sent by the government, the church, the Company and educational and cultural institutions who spent considerable time in the colonies carrying out assignments; and memoirs of both Russian and foreign visitors to the region. Much of this material has never been published, and as usual much has been lost through carelessness, fire, inadequate conservation practices and other archival disasters. Further, unpublished manuscript materials in Soviet archives are usually extremely difficult of access, especially for non-Soviet scholars.

Government decrees, rules and regulations are significant because they include all the major official policy pronouncements issued either by the Emperor himself or in his name by authorized officials of various ministries, councils or departments. Most of this material, except for that dealing with very sensitive matters, has been published in *Polnoe Sobranie Zakonov Rossiiskoi Imperii* [Complete Collection of Laws of the Russian Empire], First and Second Series. No attempt has as yet been made to assemble and publish the germane material in a single volume. Students of Russian America would welcome such a publication.

The records of the Russian American Company, both published and unpublished, are a major source of the history of Russia's American colonies. Unfortunately there are many interruptions in these records because most of the archives of the Company's Main Administration office in St. Petersburg were lost in the 1870's when the Company was in the process of dissolution. Also lost are Baranov's papers which he was carrying with him at the time of his death while on his way back to Russia. The papers of Baranov's assistant, I. A. Kuskov, who was the first administrator of Fort Ross, are also missing. Other Company records are housed in a number of archives in the Soviet Union and the United States.

The major Soviet repositories are the Archive of the State Geographical Society; the State Archive of the Period of Feudalism and Serfdom; the Archive of Russian Foreign Policy; the Manuscript Division of the Lenin State Library; the Archive of the Academy of Sciences; the Archive of the Institute of History of the Academy of Sciences; the Central State Archive of Ancient Acts; the Central State Historical Archive; the Central State Archive of the Navy; the Historical Naval Archive; the Archive of the State Council; the Archive of the Ministry of Finance; the Archive of the Department of Manufacture and Domestic Commerce; the Archive of the Ministry of Foreign Affairs; the Archive of the State Senate; the Archive of the Chancery of the Holy Synod; the Archive of the Ministry of Public Instruction; and the Archive of His Majesty's Own Chancery. This partial list is yet another proof of the fact that many agencies of the Imperial Russian government were involved in the colonial venture in North America. It will require years of work by dedicated and competent scholars before this material is carefully identified, assessed and published. The challenge lies primarily with Soviet scholars since they have first access to the materials. There are many scholars outside the Soviet Union, as well, who would eagerly assist this important undertaking.

A number of documents from these archives have been published in special collections. The first appeared in 1863, as an appendix to P. A. Tikhmenev's monumental work on the history of the Russian American Company. Nearly a century later A. I. Bilinov edited and published a collection entitled *K istorii Rossiisko-Amerikanskoi kompanii. Sbornik dokumentalnykh materialov* [History of the Russian American Company. A Collection of Documentary Materials.] Other documents, especially those touching on Russian foreign policy, have been published in the multi-volume series *Vneshniaia politika Rossii XIX i nachala XX veka. Dokumenty Rossiiskogo Ministerstva Inostrannykh Del* [Foreign Policy of Russia in the 19th and Early 20th Century. Documents of the Russian Ministry of Foreign Affairs]. In 1980 a joint Soviet-American scholarly and governmental effort produced a volume, *Rossiia i SShA: Stanovlenie otnoshenii, 1765–1815* [Russia and the United States: The Beginning of Relations, 1765–1815]. This volume, simultaneously published in Russian in the Soviet Union and in English in the United States, includes a number of documents pertaining to Russia's American colonies.

In addition to Soviet repositories, United States archives and libraries have substantial holdings. The largest collection is in the National Archives in Washington, D.C.; this consists of communications between the Main Administration of the Russian American Company in St. Petersburg and the Chief Administrators in New Arkhangel, and includes materials for the year 1802, followed by a gap, and the years 1817–1866; outgoing communications of the Chief Administrator in New Arkhangel; logs of Company vessels, 1850–1867; and journals of Russian exploring expeditions into Alaska's interior, 1842–1846, 1860, and 1864. This material came into American possession under Article Two of the Convention which formalized the sale of Alaska on March 30, 1867. Initially the Department of State had custody, but at present the 66,000 pages of materials are in the National Archives, which in the early 1940's transferred the material onto 92 rolls of microfilm, and made it available to all research libraries everywhere.

A distinguished scholar in the field, Raymond H. Fisher, has prepared a partial calendar of these records. He has found that the records do not include the following: trade books listing the variety and amount of furs the Company acquired from its employees and from natives; account books recording purchases and indebtedness of Company employees; price lists for goods sold by the Company to its employees; correspondence between the Chief Administrator and district managers under his jurisdiction; reports by medical officers; enclosures sent out with cover letters; maps; log books of Company ships prior to 1851; and many journals of explorers. Documents relating to the activity of the Russian Orthodox Church are not included, since American authorities treated the Church as a nongovernmental institution. But in spite of these omissions, the material in the National Archives comprises the largest single collection of sources on Russian America.

The second major American repository is the Manuscript Division of the Library of Congress, also in Washington, D.C., which holds several hundred boxes of material on the Russian Orthodox Church in Alaska. This material, which the Library gathered from various parishes between 1928 and 1942 includes records of births, deaths, marriages, diseases, illegitimate births, counselling of parishioners, and diaries and travel journals of the missionary priests. A few of these documents are available on microfilm and some have been translated and published. However, because of past neglect and the poor quality of paper, many are in extremely fragile and almost illegible condition.

The Manuscript Division also holds a number of materials which it acquired in 1907 by purchasing a library of more than 80,000 volumes from Genadii V. Iudin, a wealthy Russian entrepreneur in Siberia. The Iudin Collection contains material on the activities of Shelikhov, Rezanov and Petr Korsakovskii, the first Russian explorer of Alaska's interior. When Iudin sold his collection to the Library of Congress, however, he did not include many important documents he kept in Novosibirsk; some of these were published in 1957 in the USSR.

Other American repositories are the Bancroft Library at the University of California, Berkeley, which holds the works and papers of Hubert H. Bancroft, a great bibliophile and historian of the American West; Stanford University Library, which has the papers of Frank A. Golder, who pioneered American study of Russia's expansion to the Pacific; the University of Washington Library, which has many translated transcript copies of documents; the University of Alaska Library which recently purchased many reels of microfilmed documents from Leonid A. Shur, an emigré Soviet scholar; and the Oregon Historical Society, which has amassed a significant research collection in the field.

Other important sources are the published accounts by persons who were sent to the colonies on long-term assignments by the government, the Company, church or educational institutions. These persons were well-informed of conditions in the colonies because they spent relatively long periods of time there and became familiar with the region's problems and potentials. The most informative of these are by Baranov; Kyrill T. Khlebnikov, assistant to Chief Administrators between 1815 and 1832; Ivan Veniaminov, later Archbishop Innokentii, Russian Orthodox missionary from 1825–1839; Baron Ferdinand von Wrangel, Chief Administrator 1830–1835; Lavrentii A. Zagoskin, explorer of Alaska's interior 1842–1844; and Ilia G. Voznesenskii, a scientist who spent ten years, 1839–1849, collecting materials from the colonies for the Academy of Sciences. Their accounts, which are detailed in the Bibliography, offer valuable information for scholars; some have recently been translated into English and published. However until Soviet scholars publish the rest of these accounts, the authors will not have the recognition due them.

The category of published memoirs by Russian and other visitors to the colonies is voluminous and consequential. It consists of impressions by naval officers, scientists, government officials and businessmen who for various reasons made brief visits to the colonies. Their accounts are informative, but often episodic since the authors were in the region for such brief periods of time. They did not have an opportunity to become truly knowledgeable about the complex problems, so these accounts should be cautiously used. The volume of this material is extensive as will be seen in the Bibliography. Among the most interesting accounts are those of Nikolai P. Rezanov, Vasilii N. Berkh, Nikolai A. Khvostov, Gavriil I. Davydov, Iurii F. Lisianskii, Georg von Langsdorff, Adam J. Krusenstern, Otto von Kotzebue, Fedor P. Lütke, Vasilii M. Golovnin, Andrei P. Lazarev and Pavel N. Golovin.

On the basis of all these increasingly available source materials, Russian, Soviet, American, English, French, Canadian, German, Spanish and Japanese scholars have produced numerous monographic and periodical studies on various aspects of Russia's colonial venture into North America. The quantity of these studies in the last twenty years is impressive, but the quality is uneven. While many are fine works, others are inadequate because of failure to consult original sources, ideological prejudice, careless research and unfamiliarity with the Russian language. In light of the increased availability of sources, scholars must take a fresh look at topics which have received inadequate attention and treatment in the past.

Scholars of Russian America acknowledge that Petr A. Tikhmenev was the first great student of the region and of the Russian American Company in particular. Tikhmenev was not an academically trained scholar. He spent his early years in the Imperial Russian Navy and in the early 1850's sailed to New Arkhangel. In 1857 he left the navy for service with the Russian American Company and undertook to write its history.

Company officials placed the records at his disposal, and Tikhmenev completed the two-volume study in five years. The first volume, *Istoricheskoe obozrenie obrazovaniia Rossiisko-Amerikanskoi kompanii i deistvii eia do nastoiashchego vremeni* [Historical Review of the Founding of the Russian-American Company and Its Activities to the Present Time], appeared in 1861; Volume II, was published in 1863.

Tikhmenev's work received immediate acclaim. The key to its success was his judicious treatment, based on documentary evidence, of the Company's economic activities, the diverse problems the Company faced, and its achievements from its inception to 1860. Tikhmenev did not attempt to treat political problems, provided little background information on various Company officials or on the daily routines of lower ranking employees, and paid little attention to foreign policy matters. But in spite of these omissions, Tikhmenev's work remains a monumental pioneering work which must be consulted by every scholar interested in Russia's American colonies.

The second great chronicler of the history of Russian America was Hubert H. Bancroft. Like Tikhmenev, Bancroft was not an academically trained scholar. He was at first a successful San Francisco bookstore owner and a collector of historical sources. He later became a publisher and with his associates, a major historian of the American West. Bancroft treated Russian America in two volumes of his *Works: History of Alaska* (Vol. 33) and *History of California* (Vol. 34). Both volumes offer treatment rich in detail, but since Bancroft did not read Russian, he was unable to use Russian sources and based his accounts on earlier published works of Russian scholars such as G. F. Müller, P. S. Pallas, V. N. Berkh, A. P. Sokolov and Tikhmenev. Unfortunately Bancroft also relied on a Russian-born assistant to make translations for him; Ivan Petrov not only translated but indeed invented documents. Although Petrov's fraud was eventually exposed, for years scholars accepted the work as authentic.

A third major scholar was Frank A. Golder. Born in Odessa in 1877, Golder came to the United States in 1881 and received his education at Bucknell and Harvard, as well as in Paris and Berlin. From 1899 to 1902 he served as United States Commissioner in Alaska, an experience which led to his interest in the history of the region. Golder taught at the universities of Missouri, Boston, Chicago, Washington and Stanford. During World War I, with the assistance of young Russian and American scholars, he gathered data for the Carnegie Institution from many Russian archives on Russian source materials pertaining to American history. From 1917 to 1919 he served as a member of the Colonel House Inquiry Commission, and from 1920 to 1923 as a special investigator for the American Relief Administration in revolution-torn Russia.

Golder's reputation rests on his publications and his archive. His major works are *Russian Expansion to the Pacific, 1641–1850* (1914 and 1968); *Guide to the Materials for American History in Russian Archives* (1917); *Bering's Voyages*, 2 vols. (1922–1925); and *Documents on Russian History, 1914–1917* (1927). Golder's archive on Russian history is a second achievement, and is housed at the Stanford University Library. It contains many holograph copies of documents presently held in archives in Moscow and Leningrad. Golder was skeptical of certain Russian accomplishments, which has led some Soviet scholars to consider him biased. In recent years his scholarship has also been criticized outside the Soviet Union, but in spite of these criticisms, serious students of Russian America will continue to consult Golder's work.

The fourth promoter of interest in the activities of the Russian American Company was Semen B. Okun. Like Golder, Okun was a professional scholar. He had his academic training at the University of Leningrad, specializing in tsarist colonial policy in the Russian Far East, and in socio-economic problems of Russia in the 18th and 19th centuries. His scholarly career included research in Soviet archives and lecturing in Soviet universities. Okun produced two major works concerned with Russian colonial expansion: *Ocherki po istorii kolonialnoi politiki tsarizma v Kamchatskom krae* [Historical Outlines on the Tsarist Colonial Policy in the Kamchatka Territory] and *Rossiisko-Amerikanskaia Kompaniia* [The Russian-American Company]. The latter work was translated into English in 1951, and is considered a classic among scholars.

Okun's work, like Tikhmenev's, is especially important because it is based on documents in Soviet archives. However, in contrast to Tikhmenev, who dealt primarily with the business aspects of the Russian American Company's activities, Okun emphasized its geopolitical implications, that is, the effort by Imperial Russia to use the Company as a screen to camouflage its colonial ambitions in the North Pacific and along the Northwest Coast of North America. Okun's emphasis coincided with the prevailing official Soviet criticism of tsarist imperialism, and as was usual also at that time, his writings show little awareness of works on Russian America by non-Russian scholars. It is not known whether this omission was officially mandated, but it does impair the scholarship of the work.

In addition to these important pioneers in the field, other influential scholars have emerged in more recent years. Stuart Ramsay Tompkins, born in Canada in 1886 and educated at the universities of Toronto, Alberta and Chicago, was one of Golder's assistants in collecting materials from Russian archives. From 1931 until his retirement he taught at the University of Oklahoma, authoring several general works on Russian history and a number of works on Russian America, including: *Alaska: Promyshlennik and Sourdough* (1945); "Drawing of the Alaska Boundary" (1945); "After Bering: Mapping of the North Pacific," (1955); and with Max L. Moorehead, "Russia's Approach to America: From Russian Sources (Part I) and From Spanish Sources (Part II)" (1949). Tompkin's articles appeared in the *British Columbia Historical Quarterly*; a principal merit is that they are based on documentary evidence.

A highly productive scholar in the field is Nikolai N. Bolkhovitinov. Born in Moscow in 1930 and educated at the Moscow State Institute of International Relations, Bolkhovitinov has been a senior member of the Institute of General History of the Academy of Sciences of the USSR since 1968 and in 1987 was named a Corresponding Member of the Academy. He has lectured at a number of Soviet and American universities, served on numerous editorial boards, presented papers at scholarly meetings in the USSR and abroad, and has published several excellent monographs and more than 100 articles and lengthy book reviews. His principal works are: *Proiskhozhdenie i kharakter doktriny Monro, 1823* [The Genesis and Nature of the Monroe Doctrine of 1823] (1957); *Stanovlenie Russko-Amerikanskikh otnoshenii, 1775–1815* [The Beginning of Russian-American Relations, 1775–1815] (1965); *Russko-Amerikanskie otnosheniia, 1815–1832* [Russian-American Relations, 1815–1832] (1975); *Rossiia i voina SShA za nezavisimost, 1775–1783* [Russia and the United States War for Independence, 1775–1783] (1976); *Rossiia i SShA: Razvitie snoshenii, 1815–1865* [Russia and the United States: The Development of Relations, 1815–1865] (1980); *Russko-amerikanskie otnosheniia i prodazha Aliaski, 1834–1867* [Russian-American Relations and the Sale of Alaska, 1834–1867] (1989). Several of Bolkhovitinov's books and articles have been translated into English and published in the United States. The respect his works enjoy rests on his scrupulous reliance on primary sources, both Russian and foreign, and his thorough familiarity with secondary literature.

Another fine scholar of Russian America is James R. Gibson. Born in Canada in 1935 and educated at the universities of British Columbia, Oregon and Wisconsin, Gibson's speciality is historical geography. He has lectured at many universities around the world and has presented papers at numerous scholarly conferences. His pertinent works include: *Feeding the Russian Fur Trade: Provisionment of the Okhotsk Seaboard and the Kamchatka Peninsula, 1639–1856* (1969); *Imperial Russia in Frontier America: The Changing Geography of Supply of Russian America, 1784–1867* (1976); *Russian Maps and Atlases as Historical Sources* (1971); *Studies in the History of Russian Cartography* (1975); and *Farming the Frontier: The Agricultural Opening of the Oregon Country, 1786–1846* (1985). In addition, Gibson has authored more than 100 articles, book reviews and papers for scholarly conferences. His works are highly regarded by his peers, because they are based on new evidence he has found in Soviet, Canadian, American, Mexican and other archives and repositories.

Another Soviet scholar who has devoted considerable attention to Russian America is Svetlana G. Fedorova. Born in Moscow in 1929, she received her academic training at Moscow State University, the State Historical Museum of the City of Moscow and the Institute of Ethnography of the Academy of Sciences of the USSR. Her first major publication was *Russkoe naselenie Aliaski i Kalifornii, konets XVIII veka-1867* [The Russian Population of Alaska and California, Late 18th century—1867] (1969). This soundly based scholarly work was well received and was translated into English in 1973. Her other publications include: *Russkaia Amerika v neopublikovanykh zapiskakh K. T.*

Khlebnikova [Russian America in the Unpublished Notes of K. T. Khlebnikov (1979), edited with R. G. Liapunova; and *Russkaia Amerika v "Zapiskakh" Kirila Khlebnikova: Novo Arkhangelsk* [Russian America in the Notes of Kiril Khlebnikov: New Arkhangel] (1985); articles on Company officials in the Russian colonies; and "Istoricheskie istochniki po russkoi Amerike v perevodakh zarubezhnykh uchenykh" [Historical Sources on Russian America in Translations by Foreign Scholars] (1987.)

And finally, two scholarly publishers have made available in English much source material pertaining to Russia's colonies in North America: Richard Pierce's Limestone Press has published a number of translated sources; and the Oregon Historical Society Press has published its series North Pacific Studies since 1972 as part of its program of collection, translation and publication of sources pertaining to the history of the North Pacific Rim. The present volume is Number Eleven in that series of which twenty-two are presently in planning and production.

EDITORIAL
PRINCIPLES

O ur goal in this volume, as in the previous two of this trilogy, is to retain the original flavor of these astonishingly rich and colorful documents, while presenting a faithful and accurate translation in clear, modern English.

We have selected documents which give insights into the remarkably diverse situations, activities, problems and individuals woven into the existence of Russia's American colonies. In some cases we have excerpted from documents too long and repetitive. A few documents, as noted, have at some time been translated in whole or part into English; but we have again elected to use our own translations for consistency, style and other reasons.

In transliterating Russian words into English we use the Library of Congress system, slightly simplified to omit ligatures and soft signs. We anglicize plurals of words which have no exact English equivalent: *promyshlenniks*. Given names of Russian rulers are anglicized: Paul, Alexander.

When a geographical name is not readily identifiable in it Russian form, we use contemporary English nomenclature: *Kauai*, not *Atuvai*. We use *California* and *Hawaii*, rather than *New Albion* and *Sandwich Islands*. Russians often referred to the Pacific Northwest as "northeast America," i.e., northeast of Russia's Pacific coast.

Russians refer to ships as "he;" we follow the English language practice of using the feminine pronoun. The word "Company" is capitalized when it refers specifically to the Russian American Company; otherwise it appears in lower case letters. Titles of Company personnel are explained in the Glossary.

In reproducing lists and tables, we standardize the use of Roman and Arabic numerals to designate main and subordinate points. Russian dates are given in the Julian or Old style, which in the nineteenth century was twelve days behind the Gregorian or New Style calendar used in Europe and America.

Editorial notations in the text are enclosed within brackets [ ]; asides by the author of the document are given in parentheses, as they appear in the original text.

Whenever possible we give the present archival location of each document so interested scholars may use the original in their own research. However, because of the massive reorganization of the entire Soviet archival system in recent years, and the paucity, not to say lack, of published Soviet finding guides to these often relocated archives, this is not always possible.

Archival initials used in this text:
  AVPR: Arkhiv vneshnei politiki Rossii [Archive of Russian Foreign Policy]
  TsGADA: Tsentralnyi gosudarstvennyi arkhiv drevnikh aktov [Central State Archive of Russian Foreign Policy]
  TsGAOR: Tsentralnyi gosudarstvennyi arkhiv oktiabrskoi revoliutsii [Central State Archive of the October Revolution]
  TsGIA: Tsentralnyi gosudarstvennyi istoricheskii arkhiv [Central State Historical Archive of the USSR]
  TsGAVMF: Tsentralnyi gosudarstvennyi arkhiv voenno-morskogo flota SSSR [Central State Archive of the Navy of the USSR]
  TsGIA ESSR: Tsentralnyi gosudarstvennyi istoricheskii arkhiv ESSR [Central State Historical Archive of the Estonian SSR]

Archival abbreviations used in this volume are:

d.: *delo*, item or unit

f.: *fond*, basic unit group of archival records

l.: *list* (plural *ll*), folio, leaf

ob.: *oborotnaia storona*, verso

sb.: *sbornik*, a collection of materials bound or fastened together.

GLOSSARY

Alcalde. A Spanish term for an administrative and judicial officer in villages, towns or districts in Spain and regions under Spanish influence.

Arroba. A Spanish measure of weight equal to 11.5 kilograms.

Arpent. A French measure of land equal to 1.5 acres.

Artel. A cooperative work party of Russian men, organized for the purpose of hunting, fishing, harvesting or other work.

Baidara. A large open boat with a wooden or bone framework covered with cured sea mammal hides [see *lavtak*] fastened with thongs. Used by Aleutian Island natives for hunting at sea. A baidara could carry up to 40 persons. It was also adapted for use by the Russians, sometimes with a mast, sail and rudder. The Inuit *umiak.*

Baidarka. A long narrow boat with a wooden frame covered with lavtaks. Smaller than a baidara, and completely enclosed by the hide covering, with one to three openings or hatches for a paddler, hunter or passenger. The hatch could be enclosed by a drawstring, pulling the hide covering around the torso of the person. Natives used the baidarka for hunting; the Russian American Company often used the three-hatch baidarka to transport passengers or to make coastal explorations. The Inuit *kayak.*

Baidarshchik. The several meanings include: skillful steersman; owner or builder of a baidara; overseer of the construction or crew of a baidara; head of an artel; head of a small Russian American Company trading post; elder in a small Russian American settlement.

Barabara, barabor. From the Kamchadal word *bazhabazh*, a temporary summer hut. Russian settlers in Alaska used this term to refer to native dwellings, especially the underground Aleut dwelling with the entrance through the roof.

Bobr. The adult male sea otter. See *morskoi bobr.*

Cable length. A maritime unit of length based on the length of a ship's cable. Variously reckoned from 100 to 120 fathoms. In this volume, 185.2 meters.

Chag. The Sitka spruce (*Picea sitchensis*).

Chavych. The King or Chinook salmon (*Oncorhynchus tshawytscha*).

Chernozem. A Russian word meaning "black earth." In agronomy, a term for a very fertile dark soil with a deep rich humus content.

Cossack. A word of Tatar origin (Kazak), which originally denoted a free frontiersman. In the period of Russian expansion to the North Pacific, the term referred to a member of a garrison in a fortified ostrog who performed military service under the jurisdiction of Siberian officials. Cossacks also served as government agents aboard ships that explored the Aleutian Islands and Alaska, and were often hired as promyshlenniks to hunt for the Russian American Company.

Cossack sotnik. A Russian term for a commander of 100 cossacks.

Creole. In the Russian American colonies, a person of mixed Russian and native parentage. After 1841 creoles had special legal status as members of the *meshchanstvo* class.

Fanega. A Spanish measure of grain and other dry produce, equal to 1.5 bushels. Also, a Spanish unit of land measurement: in Spain, 1.59 acres; in Mexico, 8.81 acres.

Feldsher. A term of German origin referring to a surgeon's or doctor's assistant. In the Russian American colonies, often the only medical personnel.

Golets. A loach; a small freshwater fish of the family *Cobitidae*, resembling a catfish.

Gorbusha. The humpback salmon (*Centropristes striatus*).

Gramota. A word of Greek origin which in Russia referred to a letter, deed, will, charter or any other official or private written document.

Gubernia. A Russian term for a province; an administrative division of land, comprised of *uezds*.

Iasak. A Mongol-Tatar term meaning tribute paid by the conquered to the conqueror. During the period covered by the present three-volume study, iasak refers to tribute paid primarily in furs. The practice was widespread in Siberia and introduced briefly in the Aleutian Islands; it was officially terminated by tsarist ukaz in 1768. Unofficially, however, it continued throughout the eighteenth and early nineteenth centuries in Russia's American colonies.

Ierodiakon. A priest-deacon in the Russian Orthodox Church.

Ieromonk, hieromonk. In the Russian Orthodox Church, a monk who has been ordained as a priest.

Igrushka. Literally, a toy or plaything. In Russian America, a term applied to native festivities such as those celebrating the hunting season and the prowess of tribal hunters.

Iukola. Dried meat or fish, especially salmon, used widely in Siberia and Alaska for winter provisions. The head and backbone of salmon iukola were often given to dogs, and the rest was eaten by natives and sometimes by Russians as well.

Kaiur. A Kamchadal word for a post or dogsled driver. In Alaska and the Aleutian Islands, a native worker for the Russian American Company, taken from among native *kalgas* [slaves].

Kalga. An Aleut, Inuit or Tlingit native, captured by a rival tribe, usually during battle, and subsequently enslaved.

Kalina. The white hazel.

Kamlei, kamleika. The upper garment worn by natives of northeast Asia, the Aleutian Islands and coastal Alaska. A hooded, waterproof garment made of sea lion throat membrane, seal gut or reindeer hide. Worn alone in summer, or over a fur or feather garment in cold weather.

Kazhim. In the Aleutian Islands and coastal Alaska, a communal structure serving as barracks for men. Often a partially excavated structure similar to, but larger than a native family dwelling.

Kizhuch. The silver salmon (*Oncorhynchus kisutch*).

Koch. A small, flat-bottomed sailing vessel for river and coastal use. It generally had a small deck and could carry ten persons, their equipment and provisions.

Kolosh. The name used by Russians in Alaska and the Aleutian Islands to refer to Tlingit natives.

Koshka. Literally, "little cat." The shallows in a river; the first part of a river course to emerge from low water or a receding tide, so called because the shape resembles the back of a sleeping kitten.

Koshlok.   A half-grown sea otter.

Krasnaia ryba.   The blueback or sockeye salmon (*Oncorhynchus nerka*).

Kyshka.   The title given by Kenaits natives in Russian America to a tribal elder.

Lavtak.   The cured hide of a seal, walrus or sea lion, used to cover baidaras and baidarkas. A lavtak could also be used as an emergency writing surface.

Lodka.   A river boat about 200 feet long, built of pine or fir planks. A lodka could transport up to 1,260 tons of cargo and 70 persons.

Lykyn.   A Kenaits name for a tribal shaman.

Matka.   An adult female sea otter.

Medvedka.   A young sea otter, a suckling not yet having full fur.

Meshchanin.   A townsman, member of the meshchanstvo or lower middle class in Russia.

Meshchanstvo.   The lower middle class or petty bourgeoisie in Russia. In Russian America after 1841 creoles were legally identified as members of the meshchanstvo.

Michman.   In the Imperial Russian Navy, a midshipman; in the Soviet Navy, a warrant officer.

Morskoi bobr.   Literally, "sea beaver." The Russian term for the sea otter (*Enhydra lutris*).

Nalivka.   A liquer made from fruit such as cherries, currants, raspberries or strawberries.

Nariadchik.   An aide or assistant, especially for maintaining order; also, (obsolete) a scout or spy.

Ober-Prokuror.   A word of German origin introduced during the reign of Peter the Great into Russian administrative vocabulary. Two persons held this rank: the presiding officer of the Senate, which in Russia was a judicial branch of the administration; and the overseer of the Holy Synod, who served as the lay overseer of religious affairs.

Oblast.   A Russian term for a province, region or administrative district.

Odinochka.   A small fortified outpost manned by one person; a remote trading post. Analagous to the zimov'e in Siberia.

Ostrog. A Russian term with several meanings: fort, fortification, blockhouse, settlement, town.

Ostrozhek. A small ostrog or blockhouse.

Palma. A broad knife with a single edge, used for hunting, cleaning and dressing hides, hacking through underbrush, and as a weapon in hand-to-hand combat.

Partovshchik. A member of a Russian hunting party.

Piaster. A Spanish coin also known as a "piece of eight;" in the nineteenth century, approximately equal in value to one U.S. dollar.

Pika. Boiled tar used in shipbuilding.

Pikul, picul. A Chinese measure of weight equal to 133-1/3 pounds; in the present volumes, a measure for sandalwood.

Pomeshchik. In Russia this term designated an owner of a *pomest'e,* a landed estate for which the owner was obligated to perform certain services to the state. From the eighteenth century on, the term is associated with the status of hereditary nobleman.

Pomoshchnik. An assistant, a helper.

Pravitel. An administrator, the head of a household, an elder, a supervisor.

Prikashchik. A low-ranking official or agent of an administrative department of the Russian government designated as a prikaz; a town or village administrator; a steward, manager of an estate; a merchant's agent. In Alaska the term also referred to a special agent employed by the Russian American Company, or a ship's supercargo.

Promyshlennik. In Siberia and Russian America, a hunter of furbearing animals, fish or birds. In Russian America the term was used to identify Russians hired as fur trade workers by the Russian American Company. During the period of Russian expansion into the North Pacific, it also referred to an individual Russian hunter, trader or trapper who worked for himself, in a group, or for a wealthy merchant; also, a government official on an assignment such as exploration, conquest and pacification of natives.

Promyslovie zvery. Furbearing animals which the Russian American Company employees had the exclusive right to hunt.

Pud. A Russian unit of weight equal to 36 pounds or 16.38 kilograms.

Quintal.   A Spanish measure of weight equal to 46 kilograms.

Ravenduk.   Russian sheeting, a coarse heavy linen used for light sails, tents, heavy sacks and work clothing.

Rhumb.   One of the 32 points of the compass.

Rozhnitsa.   From the Russian word *rozh*, rye. A Russian word for a wild cereal gathered by the Pomo Indians near Fort Ross, so called because it resembled rye.

Réamur thermometer.   A thermometer used in the eighteenth and nineteenth centuries, on which 0° represented the freezing temperature of water, and 80° its boiling point.

Ruble.   A Russian coin or note. In the early nineteenth century one ruble was approximately equal to $.50. In Russian America, "paper ruble" referred to scrip issued by the Russian American Company; its value was about 20 percent that of a silver ruble.

Sarana.   The martagon or Kamchatka lily (*Fritillaria kamchatcensis*), the root of which was widely used by natives of Siberia and Russian America for food.

Sazhen.   A Russian unit of linear measure equal to seven feet or 2.134 meters.

Soiuznyi.   An ally.

Starshina.   A Russian term for an elder. In Russian America, a responsible and trusted servitor of the Russian American Company appointed to oversee a native toion.

Toion.   A tribal leader appointed by the Russian American Company to carry out certain administrative responsibilities within his native settlement.

Toise.   A French unit of linear measurement equal to one fathom or 6.39 feet; *see* footnote to Document 74.

Toporka.   A marine bird (*Alca arctica*).

Uezd.   A Russian term for a district administrative unit which included not only a settlement but the surrounding rural area as well; a subdivision of a diocese or gubernia.

Ukaz.   A Russian term for a decree, edict or order issued by the Tsar or Emperor, or other important agencies of government.

Vaquero.   A Spanish word, variously transliterated by the Russians in Russian America as *baker, voker* or *vaker*. In Spanish California, a mounted herdsman, chosen from among the Christianized Indians, who could speak Spanish.

Such men protected herds of livestock and acted as a security force around a Spanish mission.

Vara.   A Spanish unit of linear measure equal to 33 inches.

Vedro.   A pail or bucket. A Russian unit of liquid measure equal to approximately 21 pints.

Verst.   A Russian unit of linear measure equal to 3,500 feet or 1.06 kilometers.

Zapusk.   In Russian America, a term applied to the temporary curtailment of hunting threatened species of furbearing animals, as a conservation measure.

Zhupan.   A word of extremely diverse meanings. The original Slavic word designated an official of an administrative unit, and also, especially in the Ukraine, the attire worn by that official, or by some other well-to-do person. In Siberia it referred to a heavy homespun caftan or a warm sheepskin coat. In Kamchatka, it was the opening cut into the side of an earthen iurt to permit the intake of fresh air and to allow the heat to escape. In certain Aleutian Islands, the word (also transliterated *schopan*) was used to refer to a "male wife" or transvestite, kept as a concubine and/or household worker. On Kodiak Island, the winter sleeping quarters for a native family.

Zimov'e.   A Russian term for a small winter outpost in a newly conquered region.

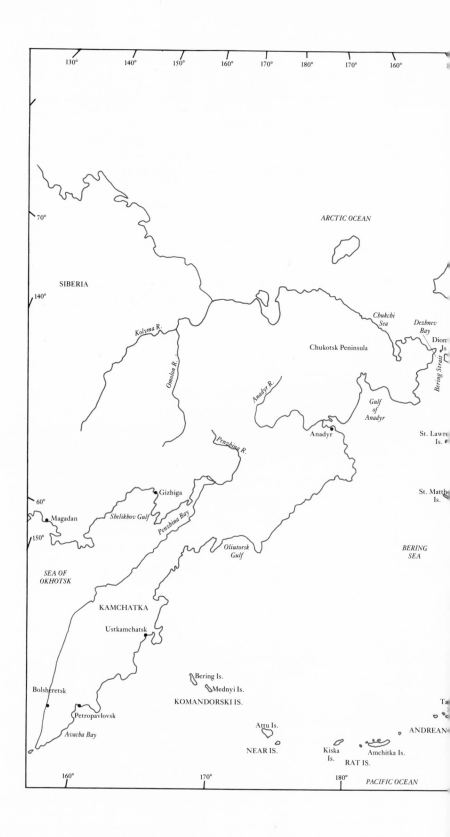

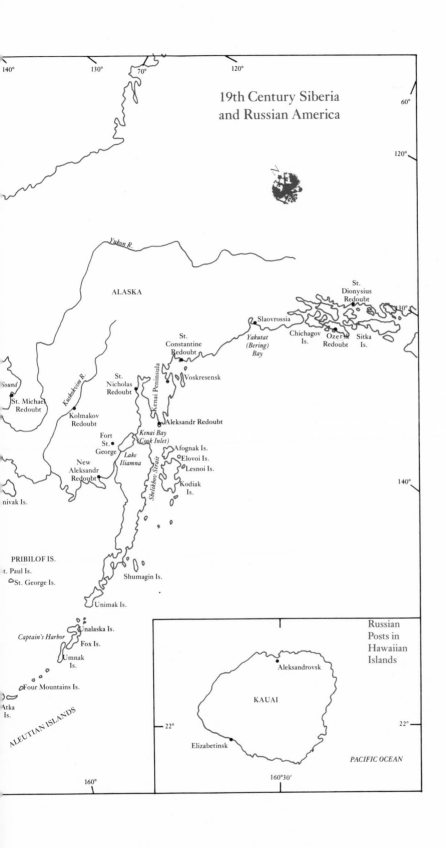

140°   130°   70°   120°

60°

19th Century Siberia
and Russian America

120°

Yukon R.

St.
Dionysius
Redoubt

ALASKA

130°

Slaovrossia

St.
Constantine
Redoubt

*Yakutat
(Bering)
Bay*

Chichagov
Is.

Ozersk
Redoubt

Sitka
Is.

Sound

Kuskokvim R.

St.
Nicholas
Redoubt

Voskresensk

St. Michael
Redoubt

Kolmakov
Redoubt

Aleksandr Redoubt

Fort
St.
George

*Kenai Bay
(Cook Inlet)*

Afognak Is.

140°

New
Aleksandr
Redoubt

*Lake
Iliamna*

Elovoi Is.

Lesnoi Is.

Kodiak
Is.

nivak Is.

PRIBILOF IS.

t. Paul Is.

St. George Is.

Shumagin Is.

Unimak Is.

Unalaska Is.

Captain's Harbor

Fox Is.

Umnak
Is.

Four Mountains Is.

Atka
Is.

ALEUTIAN ISLANDS

160°

Russian
Posts in
Hawaiian
Islands

Aleksandrovsk

22°

KAUAI

22°

Elizabetinsk

PACIFIC OCEAN

160°30′

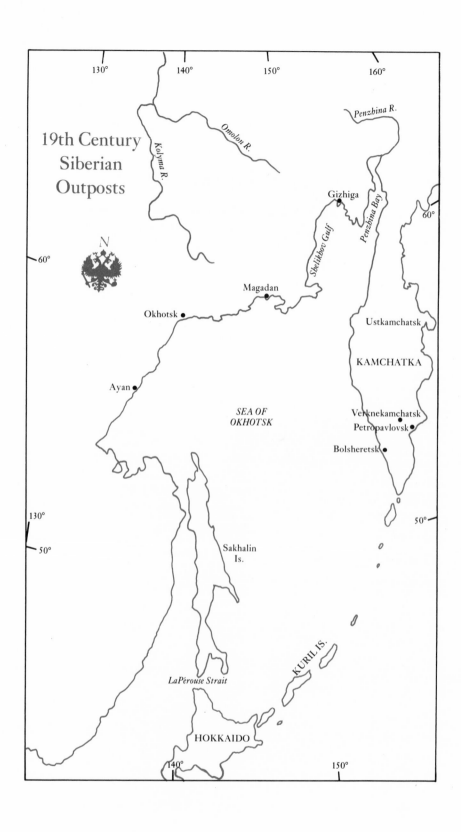

19th Century
Siberian
Outposts

140°   130°   120°

N

Yakutat Bay

Lynn Canal

Cross Sound

Sitka

19th Century
Colonial
Russian America

Sea Otter Bay

QUEEN CHARLOTTE IS.

50°   50°

Nootka   *Vancouver Island*

Strait of Juan de Fuca

Astoria   *Columbia R.*

Sitka
Approach

Lynn Canal

Litvya Bay

Akku

Cross Sound

Chichagov
Is.

Chatham Strait

KING GEORGE

Bay of Islands

Khutsnov

Cape
Edgecumbe

Norfolk Sound

Sitka

Baranov Is.

ARCHIPELAGO

Fort Ross

Bodega Bay

40°

San Francisco

South Point

THE RUSSIAN
AMERICAN
COLONIES

1

THE ACT OF INCORPORATION OF THE UNITED AMERICAN COMPANY

In the name of Almighty God, on August 3, 1798, we, the partners of the American and Irkutsk commercial companies, have considered how commerce benefits the state, the general public and private individuals. We further believe that still greater benefits can be achieved through the extension of trade into distant and still little-known seas and islands and into that part of America which is under Russian suzerainty.

We have also endeavored to expand and advance [the benefits of] the voyage made in the year 1781 by the distinguished citizens, [Grigorii I.] Shelikhov of the town of Rylsk and [Ivan L.] Golikov of the town of Kursk, to the northeast, to North America, the Aleutian and Kuril islands, and to other places and lands in the North Pacific which are under Imperial Russian sovereignty.

Therefore, on July 18 and 19, 1797, we reached a preliminary agreement to unite [our two companies], and this has been confirmed in a written document. As loyal and reverent subjects we have received from His Imperial Majesty, the Most Gracious Sovereign Emperor [Paul I], His Imperial permission to unite, with the sole Imperial stipulation that we organize and pattern our Company on the example of European companies, and following their experience, to formulate a trading company and its regulations which will truly benefit Russian merchantry.

Our Company, approving this preliminary union, implores God, the Almighty Creator and Benefactor, to grant us strength and wisdom to fulfill His Imperial Majesty's purpose. Trusting fully His Holy Guidance, we have drawn up the following agreement.

I.

The intent and purpose of creating our Company is as follows:

Pavolovsk (St. Paul) Harbor on Kodiak Island, from the
north. This 1798 drawing, attributed to James Shields, a
shipwright employed by Shelikhov, is the earliest known
view of the harbor. Although considerably out of scale, the
buildings on the inlet are identifiable, and the church is still
standing today. N. N. Bashkina, *The United States and Russia,
The Beginning of Relations*. (OHS neg. 37374)

1. To support the Christian Greek Catholic mission in
America which is working to teach the Holy Gospel and enable the illiterate people in America and on the islands [in the
North Pacific Ocean] to gain knowledge of the True God. The
Company, concerned for the well-being of the mission, will
strive to supply all its needs for the maintenance of the holy
churches. We are motivated in this concern by our love for
God, our duty as true Christians, concern for our fellow man,
diligence as loyal subjects to augment the interests of His Imperial Majesty, and finally, to increase the benefits which may
accrue to our Company.

2. To engage in all trade and commerce which is associated
with merchants and permitted by law throughout the Russian
Empire and abroad.

To send ships, at the expense of this Company, with goods and with *promyshlenniks* [hunters, traders], to America and to the northern, Kuril and Aleutian islands, and to all places where our Company presently engages in trade, and may do so in the future.

To search for new lands and islands in the North Pacific and in southern seas and to attempt to convert newly discovered peoples to Orthodox Christianity and bring them under the suzerainty of His Imperial Majesty.

To establish industries related to sea and land [furbearing] animals in all places in America and in the islands and in places the Company may occupy in the future.

To establish shipyards necessary for the Company, and in order to accomplish this, to seek an increase in the number of settlers in possessions already controlled by Russia, and to settle lands as yet unoccupied.

To develop in America and on the islands agriculture and livestock breeding, and to keep constantly in mind friendly treatment of American natives and islanders, establishing trade with them from Lituya Bay, and extending it north beyond Bering Strait.

To commence seafaring and trading with Japan, Canton and other places, provided this meets with the approval of His Imperial Majesty, our August Monarch.

All of these goals, under the patronage of the Imperial Autocrat, will be carried out wisely and assiduously, and insofar as possible, will be based on the rules of honor, justice, humanity and conscience, consonant with advantages to the state, the public and the Company.

II.

1. This Company is formed by uniting two companies, The Northeast American Northern and Kuril Company, or Shelikhov and Golikov Company; and the Commercial Company of Irkutsk, belonging to [Nikolai P.] Mylnikov and his associates.

2. Presently it belongs to the following merchant families:
   A. Nataliia Alekseevna Shelikhova, widow, and the heirs of the late distinguished citizen of Rylsk, Grigorii

Shelikhov, whom His Imperial Majesty raised to the status of nobility within the Russian Empire;

B. Ivan Larionov Golikov, distinguished citizen of Kursk, and his son, Nikolai;

C. Nikolai Prokopev Mylnikov, merchant of the First Irkutsk Guild, and his sons Dmitrii, Iakov and Mikhail;

D. Petr Dmitriev Michurin, merchant of the Second Irkutsk Guild, and his sons: Nikolai, Prokopii and Dmitrii; his brother, Nikolai, and nephews, the sons of his late brother, Ivan Dmitriev Michurin;

E. Semen Alekseev Startsov, merchant of the Second Irkutsk Guild, his son, Dmitrii, and nephew, Fedor Petrov Startsov;

F. Evstrat Ivanov Delarov, merchant of the Second Moscow Guild, and his son, Ivan;

G. Stepan Fedorov Dudorovskii, merchant of the Second Irkutsk Guild, and his son, Iosif;

H. Ivan Petrov Shelikhov, merchant of the Third Rylsk Guild;

I. Ivan Fedorov Dudorovskii, merchant of the Second Irkutsk Guild;

J. Emelian Grigorev Larionov, merchant of the Third Irkutsk Guild;

K. Andrei Petrov Litvintsov, merchant of the Third Irkutsk Guild, and his sons: Evdokii, Ivan and Andrei;

L. Lavrentii Ivanov Zubov, merchant of the Third Irkutsk Guild;

M. Fedor Fedorov Dudorovskii, merchant of the Second Irkutsk Guild;

N. Aleksei Fedorov Ostanin, merchant of the Third Irkutsk Guild;

O. Petr Fedorov Ivanov, merchant of the Third Irkutsk Guild, and his sons: Iakov, Pavel and Petr;

P. Vasilii Ivanov Shelikhov, merchant of the Third Rylsk Guild;

Q. Ivan Mikhailov Kiselev, merchant of the Third Irkutsk Guild;

R. Efim Nikitin Sykhikh, merchant of the Third Irkutsk Guild, and his son, Petr;

s. Prokopii Ivanov Davydov, merchant of the Third Irkutsk Guild, and his sons, Ivan and Stepan;

T. Petr Prokopii Mylnikov, merchant of the Third Irkutsk Guild.

3. Inasmuch as the merger of our companies has come about through unanimous agreement, and has as its purpose to increase and advance Russian trade in the north, northeast and in the North Pacific, through joint endeavor, it is hereby resolved that in accordance with our agreements and decisions, our two companies, united forever, shall be known as the United American Company.

III.

1. The general capital of the Company consists of stock capital and credit capital. At the beginning of 1797 the stock capital amounted to 800,000 rubles. However, in accordance with our agreement of June 18, 1798, 38 shares, amounting to 76,000 rubles, were withdrawn and given to Golikov (as stated below in Paragraph VI). Consequently, the present stock capital consists of 724,000 rubles. This capital has been paid in by the shareholders whose names appear in Paragraph II. This is divided into 724 shares. At the beginning of 1797 each share was worth 1,000 rubles. The number of shares each shareholder owns is detailed in the capital book. Credit capital resulted from the merger of the companies of Golikov and Madame Shelikhova, who received promissory notes from the former Commercial Company of Irkutsk. The exact sum, and the terms specifying when the notes become due, is stated in detail in the agreement between this Company and the above mentioned Golikov and Madame Shelikhova.

2. This general stock and credit capital of the Company comprises one indivisible sum, and includes earnings from 1797 and 1798, the amount to be determined in the general accounting; the entire sum consists of cash, notes, various enterprises and equipment in America, on the Northern, Aleutian and Kuril islands, in initial shares, ships, rigging, supplies, materials, credits, sea otter debts, and, finally, in trade enterprises in Kamchatka, Gizhiga, Okhotsk, Iakutsk, Irkutsk,

Kiakhta, Moscow and other places where our Company carries on trade and business. A detailed and full listing of the entire capital and property is provided in the inventory books of the office.

3. The stock capital of the Company is its real foundation. For that reason this capital is to remain forever untouched, with the Company, for as long as the Company exists. No present or future shareholder of the Company either may or can request to withdraw stock capital, even if he is in debt and unable to make restitution, either to the government or to a private lender. No part of the stock capital, either in funds or in goods, may be withdrawn to settle such a debt, even if the shareholder's [shares] are confiscated. This is based on the right of each shareholder to sell his shares [intact] and the stock capital of the Company to remain unencumbered.

4. If individual promyshlenniks wish to merge their operations and capital with our Company, they may do so on the following basis. Promyshlenniks who merge with the Company are to present their holdings to the Company's Main Office, where they will be appraised on the basis of valid contracts, records and other precise, accurate and authentic accounts and documents. The Company will establish the value of the holdings. The entire capital which the promyshlenniks give over will become joint capital and will be merged with the general capital of the Company. Shares representing equal value will be issued [to the promyshlenniks]. . . .

VII.

1. To conduct all the business of the Company we have established the Main Office in Irkutsk. This is hereby verified by this Act; it will remain permanently in Irkutsk.

2. The office in Irkutsk will be called the Main Irkutsk Office of the United American Company. Other offices which presently exist will be under the jurisdiction of this office: in Okhotsk and on the islands of Kodiak, Unalaska and the Kurils. The first will be known as the Urat Office of the United American Company; the second, the Kodiak Office of the United American Company; the third, the Unalaska Office of

the United American Company; the fourth, the Kuril Office of the United American Company.

3. If there is need later to establish other offices, such as for example in Iakutsk, Kiakhta and especially in Moscow, or in other places, this will be reviewed by the Main Office. However, such offices will only be established with the consent of the entire Company in a meeting of the shareholders. The administrators of these offices will be appointed by the directors, and their salaries will be determined on the basis of their experience and their duties.

4. Communication and correspondence between these offices will be informational in nature. Only the Main Irkutsk Office, as the principal agent, will send instructions to other offices.

VIII.

1. To administer the affairs of the Company, two directors will be elected (up to four, if necessary) from among the shareholders. These persons are to have practical business experience, be informed on all aspects of Company affairs, and be capable of assisting the Company in all matters through their counsel.

2. These directors will always be elected at a general meeting of the Company, from available shareholders, by majority vote. Both in the election of directors and in all other meetings of the Company, the number of votes will be determined by the number of shares; each share will have one vote.

3. Company directors bear full responsibility for administering and ordering all Company business. For this reason, once these directors have been elected and empowered by the Company, no shareholder may interfere or issue orders on behalf of the Company. That prerogative belongs exclusively to the directors. . . .

5. Because directors of the Company, by virtue of their position, are not able to devote full time to their own business affairs, the Company authorizes that each of them be paid 2,000 rubles per year, beginning January 1, 1798.

Directors of the Company who administer the Main Office and are responsible for all the business of the Company are to allocate the work among themselves on the basis of their expertise. They must work zealously and do everything possible to keep Company accounts in order, preserve capital and increase earnings.

They have the following obligations:

1. Be responsible and accountable for the integrity of the Company's cash, notes, goods and in general the entire property of the Company.

2. Purchase and have ready everything necessary for all the offices and other posts, especially the office in Okhotsk, and everywhere conduct business in such a manner that all of these places are supplied in a timely fashion with everything they need, and on the best possible terms for the Company.

3. Contract with promyshlenniks, outfit them and dispatch them to Okhotsk and from there to America and other places, islands and territories, in accordance with instructions from the Main Office.

4. Oversee all correspondence, audit and verify all accounts, and manage all written records pertaining to the office. They are further to carry out all objectives and intentions of the Company, as described in Section I, and devote all possible energy and zeal to this.

5. Discuss and take counsel on all Company matters; such meetings are to be held daily in the Main Office.

6. Represent the Company in all judicial and civil inquiries, in accordance with the authority granted to them. Prepare and submit records, reports, petitions and responses which are requested.

7. Hire *prikashchiks* [agents], authorized personnel and other servitors, using their best judgment, at Company expense, from among free persons, on contract, in accordance with law. The directors may hire other prikashchiks and commissioners in the Main Office, on contract, on the same basis as others from outside, from among shareholders. Compensation will depend on their duties.

8. The directors of the Company are responsible for the business affairs of all the Company's offices presently existing or to be established in the future. They are also responsible for all commissioners, prikashchiks and other legally authorized persons in the employ of the Company. They will issue instructions and direct such persons on matters of trade and hunting. They will audit their records and accounts and impose penalties for losses, waste and dereliction of duty.

9. The directors must personally prepare an annual report on the status of the entire Company. They must allow any and all shareholders or persons designated by shareholders to audit the accounts and operations of the Main Office; this may be done in June, July and August, which are months when Company business is lightest. Following such inspection, the directors may and should request and receive from the Company a written statement attesting to the fact that their obligations have been satisfactorily fulfilled.

10. The directors will be held responsible for any loss or harm to Company business resulting from their negligence or dereliction of duty.

11. Directors of the Company may hold their positions as long as they desire. They will not be replaced by the Company unless there are fundamental legal reasons, and then only with the consent of the entire Company. If this should happen, the director who is being replaced must hand over to his replacement all records in his possession. Any director who wishes to resign his position may do so, provided he gives due notice, but he is to remain in his position until the end of the year in which he gives notice of retirement.

If any director is found negligent by his associates, who then prove that his negligence has caused harm to Company business, this must be reported to the Company. Upon review of the situation at a general meeting of the shareholders, a new director will be chosen from among the shareholders.

See: *Polnoe sobranie zakonov rossiiskoi imperii s 1649 goda*, [hereafter *PSZ*] First Series, Vol. 25, No. 19,030, 704–718.

2

THE CHARTER OF THE RUSSIAN AMERICAN COMPANY, GRANTED BY
IMPERIAL DECREE OF EMPEROR PAUL I

The benefits and advantages accruing to Our Empire from hunting and trade conducted by Our loyal subjects in the North Pacific Ocean and in the parts of America in that region, have attracted Our Monarchial attention and esteem. For that reason We confer Our direct patronage upon the Company which is engaged in hunting and trading there and direct that it be called the Russian American Company under Our August patronage.

We further direct that in order to augment the enterprises of that Company, all officials heading Our land and naval forces are to provide support whenever the Company may request it to enable it to conduct its business.

In order to govern, facilitate and encourage the Company, We hereby graciously grant it a Charter and Privileges for a period of twenty years. These two decrees, which We have approved, as well as the Act of Incorporation executed on August 3, 1798, by the present shareholders, which We fully approve, are not changed by the regulations [below]. We hereby direct that these documents be transferred to Our Senate and that the Senate prepare an appropriate *gramota* [official document] in accordance with the content of these privileges, and submit this for Our signature. Additionally, the Senate will prepare appropriate instructions pertaining to this.

REGULATIONS FOR THE [RUSSIAN AMERICAN] COMPANY

1. This Company is established for the purpose of trading on the American mainland to the northeast [of Russia] and on the Aleutian and Kuril islands and in the North Pacific Ocean, which belong to Russia by right of first discovery. It is to be known as the Russian American Company under the patronage of His Imperial Majesty.

2. This is not a new company, but is formed by the union of two previously existing private companies, one belonging to [Ivan L.] Golikov and [Grigorii I.] Shelikhov, and the other to

[Nikolai P.] Mylnikov and his associates. Its stock capital consists of 724,000 rubles divided into 724 shares. One thousand more shares are being added to the previously issued 724 shares in order to allow others to participate. In addition to the present shareholders, this will permit any Russian subject who wishes to join in this Company.

3. Any Russian subject or foreigner who has become a permanent Russian subject may join in this Company, regardless of rank or station, in accordance with the regulations stipulated below, providing he is a property owner. If through collusion or forgery a foreigner should use the name of a Russian citizen to become a shareholder in this Company, and is exposed and convicted through an investigation by proper authorities, all capital invested by him shall belong to the Company, and the Russian subject who has permitted the fraudulent use of his name will be forced to pay half of that amount to the Company; if he is unable to pay, he will be punished according to law.

4. Since the time the companies of Golikov-Shelikhov and Mylnikov and associates were united, as set forth above, some ships have returned with valuable cargoes, favorable reports have been received about other ships, invested capital has increased and various enterprises are prospering. Consequently it is not possible to value the first-issued shares of stock at the price at which they were originally issued when the Company was first organized. For this reason the following procedures should be followed regarding the sale of the additional 1,000 shares.

Six months after the date of the adoption of these regulations and privileges granted to this Company by His Majesty, the united Company is to prepare a list of the names of shareholders who signed the Act of Incorporation of August 3, 1798, and also of all the others who did not sign, but who have some participation in the original capital of the Company.

If these persons consent to the new stock issue, a detailed inventory will be made of all joint property: ships, goods, establishments and the like. The entire sum will be divided by the present number of shares, 724, and thus the value of each share will be determined.

Then, no later than the stipulated time, a notice of this is to be published in newspapers in both capitals [St. Petersburg and Moscow]. Immediately thereafter, applications as well as capital will be accepted. Each share will be appraised within six months of the day of the announcement. If some person declares his wish to become a shareholder, but cannot raise the necessary funds in cash or goods to pay during this time period, if the Company agrees, he will lose the opportunity of becoming a shareholder of the Company until some later time.

5. This undertaking is new and many Russian subjects are unaware of the advantages to be gained by joining this Company. Therefore the additional 1,000 shares may not be sold at the first offering. In such a case the Company is to repeat the procedure explained in the preceding paragraph two years after the first announcement in the newspapers. In that case the value of the shares will be determined by the actual worth of the Company's affairs at that time. This procedure will be repeated until the additional 1,000 shares have been sold. No further shares are to be issued until the privileges granted this Company have expired.

6. Payment for the shares, at prices established by the inventory of the Company, are to be made in cash in Irkutsk. Payment may also be made in any other Russian city in goods, ships, establishments or other property, instead of cash, but only upon mutual agreement between the directors of the Company and those desiring to purchase the shares. If property is used instead of cash, it must be free from all liens, both government and private.

7. In addition to the persons who formed this united Company, there are other entrepreneurs in the same trade who have ships and establishments in these same places. If any of them, as Russian subjects, wishes to join the Company on the above terms, and agreement can be reached with the Company as to the value of Company shares and of the goods, ships and other property of the entrepreneur, then by mutual consent, within the prescribed time period, the Company may issue to such person, out of the 1,000 new shares, the number of shares equal to the value of his property which will be incorporated into the Company.

If a foreigner has an interest in such shares, the Company is to deal only in cash or hard goods, so that in the future it will be possible to redeem that participation.

However, if the Company cannot reach agreement with these or with other persons, neither Russian subjects nor foreigners are to be denied permission to continue their business and realize profits according to previously agreed terms. This [privilege] extends only until such time as their ships return.

8. The shares from the first incorporation of the Company and the additional shares will be issued on government paper of 30 kopecks value and will be printed according to the appended sample form. Shares are to be signed by all the directors. The accountant is to number each share and so enter it in the Company's books. Each share will be notarized, the Company's seal affixed, and the share will be given over to the Company.

9. The entire capital, which the shares represent, is to remain permanently in the Company. All shareholders will have equal rights as the founders of the Company in regard to present establishments and acquisitions. They will share in the profits of all Company operations now and in the future, and will also be liable for any losses which may be incurred.

10. Every shareholder is free to dispose of his shares at will by selling them to other persons, or in some other manner, providing the buyer signs his name and title so that the Company, in its general public accounting, can identify him. In addition, the buyer and seller shall within three months inform the Administration of the Company of this transaction, so the Company will know in good time who the partners are.

11. When making an annual accounting of the profits earned by the Company, these are to be divided by mutual agreement of the shareholders. Such division will be made not annually, but biennially, from the time of publication in the newspapers as per point number 5. The following procedures will be observed:

> A. One-tenth of the profits from each share will be reinvested to increase the Company's capital, and will be subject to the same regulations as the original capital.
>
> B. Profits will be calculated and divided after all current debt payments have been subtracted, so that all profit will be free of liens or uncertainty. The prohibition against requesting or withdrawing profits before credit capital is paid up, as set forth in the Act of In-

corporation of August 3, 1798, applies only to the owners of the existing 724 shares, not to purchasers of the additional 1,000 shares to be issued.

12. The head office of the Company in Irkutsk, which will order all Company business, will be known as the Main Administration of the Russian American Company under the patronage of His Imperial Majesty. That office will handle all matters affecting this Company, will issue all orders, and will report directly to His Imperial Majesty about the progress of the Company.

13. The [Main] Administration will have a seal bearing the Imperial crest surrounded by the inscription, "The Seal of the Russian American Company under the patronage of His Imperial Majesty."

14. Upon the agreement of the entire Company, this Administration will have authority to establish branch offices, depending on need, and will supervise and manage them.

15. These offices will receive from the Main Administration smaller seals with the same crest as that of the Main Administration, and with appropriate inscriptions.

16. Directors shall be elected from among the shareholders; the number of directors will not exceed four.

17. Election of directors is by means of ballots. Persons who own at least 25 shares of stock in the Company are eligible for directorships.

18. The right to vote for directors and to have a voice in general meetings is limited to persons owning at least ten shares of stock.

At shareholders' meetings voice votes will be counted not on the basis of the number of shares owned, but by the number of persons present and voting.

19. Directors elected to manage the affairs of the Company will take an oath to do their best, faithfully and scrupulously carrying out the wishes of the shareholders, all Imperial decrees and Company instructions.

20. The directors will issue instructions pertaining to business in accordance with rules determined by the Company. Directors will not undertake new projects without first discussing the matter in Irkutsk with Company members who are entitled to vote. Directors will carry out a unanimous decision

of voting shareholders. If the vote is not unanimous, a proposed measure will be decided by a majority vote.

21. The Company is to be guided by the Act of Incorporation of August 3, 1798, executed in Irkutsk, and is to carry out meticulously those articles which are not repealed by these regulations, and such terms as are mutually agreed upon by the partners. If in the future it is determined that this Act be amended, any such amendment is to be presented to His Imperial Majesty for approval before being put into effect.

See: *PSZ.* First Series, Vol. 25, No. 19,030, 699–703.

3

DECEMBER 27, 1799

AN IMPERIAL DECREE FROM EMPEROR PAUL I GRANTING SPECIAL
PRIVILEGES TO THE RUSSIAN AMERICAN COMPANY FOR A PERIOD
OF TWENTY YEARS

By the most auspicious grace of God, We, Paul the First, Emperor and Autocrat of All Russia, etc. etc. etc.

We Extend Our Most High Patronage to the Russian American Company.

The benefits and advantages which will accrue to Our Empire from the hunting and trade carried on by Our loyal subjects in the Pacific Ocean and in the land of America have attracted Our Monarchial attention and esteem. For that reason We extend Our immediate patronage to the Company which conducts hunting and trade there and direct that it be named the *Russian American Company*. We further direct that in order to augment the ventures of that Company, all military officers of Our country as well as Our naval forces are to provide support whenever the Company may request it to enable it to conduct its business.

In order to govern, facilitate and encourage the Company, We hereby establish its regulations. By virtue of Our Most Gracious Imperial charter, We hereby grant this Company the following privileges for a period of 20 years:

1. On the basis of the fact that long ago Russian seafarers were the first to discover the coast of America to the northeast [of us], beginning from 55° northern latitude, and the archipelago of islands extending from Kamchatka north to America, and south to Japan, and by Russia's right to possess these lands, We, the All Gracious, permit the company to profit from all hunting and other ventures presently established along the coast of America to the northeast, from the above mentioned 55° to Bering Strait and beyond and likewise on the Aleutian, Kuril and other islands located in the North Pacific Ocean.

2. The Company may undertake to make new discoveries, not only above 55° northern latitude, but to the south as well;

they may occupy lands they discover and claim them as Russian possessions, in accordance with the previously prescribed regulations, provided that these newly discovered territories have not previously been occupied by other nations or have come under their protection.

3. The Company may utilize, without any claims from others, everything above and below ground in places it has already discovered or may in the future discover.

4. We most graciously direct that in the future the Company may rely on its own judgment and, in accordance with need, build settlements and fortified places wherever necessary for the safety of its employees; and without any hindrance whatsoever it may also send promyshlenniks to that region as well as ships carrying goods.

5. In order to increase and strengthen its enterprises, the Company may sail to all nearby nations and enter into trade with all adjacent powers, providing it has their permission and Our Imperial consent.

6. For its voyages, hunting and other enterprises, the Company may hire people from all walks of life who are free and not under suspicion for some misdemeanor and who hold legal documents permitting them to be hired. Because the places these persons will be sent are so far distant, the *gubernia* [provincial] administration should issue passports valid for seven years to state settlers and free persons from other classes. The Company should not hire peasants and household serfs belonging to *pomeshchiks* [landowners] without permission from the pomeshchiks themselves. The Company must pay state taxes for all the persons they hire.

7. Although Our Imperial ukazes prohibit the cutting of timber without permission from the Admiralty College, nevertheless, considering the distance that separates the Admiralty from the Okhotsk *oblast* [administrative region] where this Company will need to repair ships, and sometimes to build new ships, the Company is to be permitted to [cut and] use lumber without any restrictions.

8. For use in hunting animals, firing sea signals and all unexpected emergencies that may arise on the American mainland and on the islands, the Company may use its own funds to purchase 40 to 50 *puds* [one pud = 36 pounds] of gunpowder

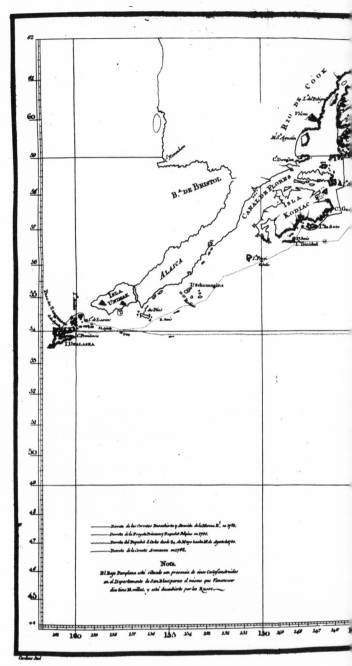

In 1799, Emperor Paul I granted a charter to the Russian American Company which bestowed the right "to search for new lands and islands in the North Pacific and the southern seas" to bring under the suzerainty of the Russian Emperor.

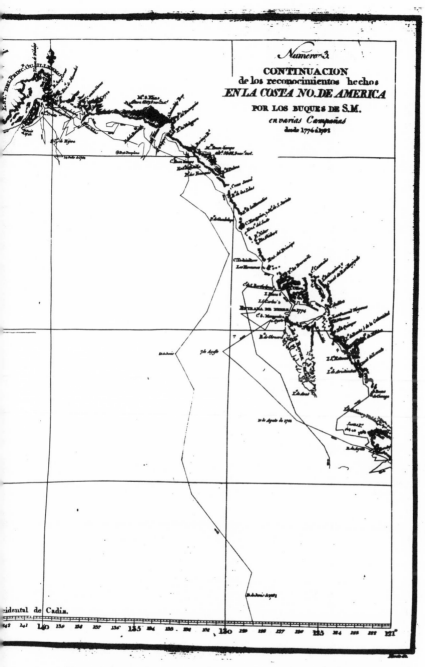

This late 18th century Spanish map indicates other European powers had already sent Cook, Vancouver, La Perouse and numerous Spanish explorers into the North Pacific. *Relacion del viaje.* . . . (OHS neg. OrHi 82105)

21

per year from the Government artillery depot in Irkutsk, and 200 puds of shot from the Nerchinsk factory.

9. If any shareholder of the Company becomes indebted to the Treasury or to private individuals, and has no means with which to repay the debt except for the shares he holds in the Company, in such a case, even though the capital he had invested in the Company is subject to confiscation, nevertheless, on the basis of the regulations of the Company, that capital is to remain untouched in the Company. The creditor cannot demand its release for payment of the debt; as first mortgagee he may only lay claim to the dividends when they are distributed. Upon termination of the Company's privileges, the debtor may claim what is due him in full.

10. Because We have most graciously granted the Company the exclusive rights, for a period of twenty years, to acquire everything necessary to hunt, trade, establish enterprises and discover new lands, throughout the entire region previously described, we hereby prohibit the enjoyment of these benefits and privileges not only to those who would like to voyage there on their own, but also to all previous promyshlenniks engaged in that trade who have ships and enterprises in those places, as well as to those persons who may have participated in the united company as shareholders but did not choose to join the Company. To these latter, in case of disagreements over joining this Company, as stipulated in the Company's regulations, We grant the right to continue their enterprises and enjoy the benefits under the same terms as previously, but only until their vessels return. After that, no one will have these privileges except said Company, under threat of confiscation of all their property.

11. Because the Main Administration of the Russian American Company is under Our Imperial protection, all offices [in the Empire] must note that the Main Administration is in charge of Company business. Should local courts desire information on Company matters, such requests must be directed to the Main Administration of the Company, not to any shareholders.

In concluding this, Our Imperial gramota placing the Russian American Company under Our Imperial protection, We instruct all Our military and civil officials and all government offices not to interfere with these privileges We have granted. Further, in case of need or any possible development which may bring loss or harm to the Company, such officials are to warn the Company, and if requested by the Company's Main Administration, to provide every assistance and defense. To add emphasis to this, Our gramota, We have signed it personally, and have ordered that it be sealed with Our Imperial Seal.

See: *PSZ*, First Series, Vol. 25, No. 19,030, 703–704; No. 19,233, 923–25.

4

A REPORT FROM THE MAIN ADMINISTRATION OF THE RUSSIAN
AMERICAN COMPANY IN IRKUTSK TO EMPEROR ALEXANDER I CON-
CERNING THE FUR TRADE IN THE NORTH PACIFIC OCEAN

To the Most Illustrious Reigning Great Sovereign, Emperor and Autocrat of All Russia [Alexander I], a most respectful report from the Main Administration of the Russian American Company.

The Main Administration of the Russian American Company is pleased to submit its most respectful report to Your Imperial Majesty, that on August 18, 1801, the Company vessel *Predpriiatie Sv. Aleksandry*, sailing from the Aleutian island of Unalaska to Okhotsk, managed to reach Petropavlovsk harbor [on Kamchatka] in spite of strong headwinds. That vessel was carrying a cargo of various furs conservatively valued at 228,380 rubles. The ship is expected to reach Okhotsk this summer.

That vessel also brought information from the Chief Administrator, the merchant [Aleksandr A.] Baranov on Kodiak Island, concerning prospects for the fur trade on the island of Unalaska, which he inspected on July 24, 1800. That information consists of the following.

1. The Company vessel *Orel*, which sailed from the settlement of Yakutat on the Bering Sea with a cargo of furs, was wrecked on the Chugach coast in the year 1799 with the loss of part of its cargo valued at 22,000 rubles, and the lives of five Company promyshlenniks.

2. The frigate *Feniks*, dispatched from Okhotsk to Kodiak in 1799 with a cargo, did not reach its assigned destination. According to Baranov's report, it appears that either it was wrecked or that it put in at an island which the Company plans to explore.

3. At the time he sent this information, Baranov noted that he was still holding furs valued at 494,634 rubles, but since he had only one large and two small vessels, he could not send this shipment this year.

The era of Russian American Company power is best re-
membered for the ruthless, autocratic and magnetic leadership of Chief Administrator Aleksandr Andreevich Baranov,
resident in his "castle" at New Arkhangel (Sitka). In this fine
painting, one sees the symbols of authority in his Order
of Saint Anne (second class) and the official seal and pen
clutched in a powerful fist whose strong fingers were equally
at home holding a tumbler of spirits. N. N. Bashkina, *The
United States and Russia, The Beginning of Relations*, (OHS neg.
OrHi 82934)

The Main Administration also respectfully reports to Your Imperial Majesty that Administrator Baranov has already devoted twelve years of his life to Imperial and Company interests. He has established control over a substantial part of the American coast and islands, and in the year 1800 he brought under the sceptre of Your Imperial Majesty the island of Sitka, located in 57° 15′ northern latitude, 241° eastern longitude. In that same year he built a wooden fort in honor of Arkhangel Mikhail on that island, as well as other structures for the promyshlenniks. In this manner he has strengthened his control. He is also considering a plan to annex to the Russian Empire the [Queen] Charlotte Islands and the Sound which the English have already abandoned.

Baranov further reports that while he was on Sitka there were European vessels there trading with the island natives. In the year 1799 there were three English and American ships from Boston, and two in the year 1800. Farther offshore from Sitka, there were three more. Baranov personally went aboard some of those ships, and he entertained the captains of others in his new fort. In conversation with these seafarers he learned about the local fur trade and of their trade with the Chinese in Canton.

Concerning these matters, the Main Administration will do everything possible to support Baranov with ships and personnel, and through other means, to bring benefit both to the Empire and to the Company. The [Main] Administration considers it an obligation to forward for Your Illustrious Imperial Majesty's review Baranov's report on these enterprises, established for the benefit of the fatherland.

Reference: Library of Congress, Manuscript Division. Yudin Collection, Box 1.
Undated, unnumbered.

5

SECRET INSTRUCTIONS FROM THE MAIN ADMINISTRATION OF THE
RUSSIAN AMERICAN COMPANY IN IRKUTSK TO CHIEF ADMINISTRA-
TOR ALEKSANDR A. BARANOV IN ALASKA

Strictly confidential. Instructions to Baranov, Chief Administrator in America.

The Main Administration has already sent you written instructions concerning certain matters, which several of your
subordinates should also be informed of, in order that they
may be properly effected. Now we are sending you instructions about matters for which you alone, as Chief Administrator, are responsible.

I.

Concerning the claim of the English to places which we
possess, you inquire how far your responsibility extends. The
Main Administration instructs you to try to establish the right
of Russia not only up as far as 55°, but farther, basing your
[claim] on the voyages [1725–31; 1735–41] of Captains [Vitus]
Bering and [Aleksei] Chirikov and others; you may also refer
to the voyages and fur hunting expeditions of private entrepreneurs which took place every year after that time. Try to use
these same arguments to extend our claims also into Nootka
Sound, so that the claims of the English court will be set [only
as far as] 50°, or halfway between 50° and 55°. This part of the
country is still unoccupied, and therefore up to the present
time Russia has the claim of first discovery there.

You should strive, as much and as quickly as possible, to
establish settlements near 55°, and a permanent fort, since you
now have enough people to do this. If possible, you should
settle that region with Russianized [native] Americans. But
however you do it, be certain that those persons whom you
settle there go voluntarily, which may be accomplished through
granting certain privileges to them. For maximum success in
those areas, it is recommended that you halt penetration to the
north and concentrate on the area where the English are trying
to establish themselves.

To this end, it is imperative that you submit to the Main Administration full annual reports, so the Main Administration can give you every needed assistance as quickly as possible. The Main Administration acknowledges your skill in managing to avoid contacts with the English and thus also avoid discussing with them delineation of frontiers. We hope that you will continue to do this in the future, using your best judgment and experience. But if the necessity for such an encounter arises, you are to remain firm regarding Russia's rights. Respond that you cannot assume responsibility on such a vital matter, and say that the British court should communicate only with the [Russian] Emperor regarding this situation.

From the appended travel accounts of [George] Vancouver and [Peter] Puget, and the map, you will see that they themselves indicated all the places occupied by the *artels* [work parties] of our promyshlenniks, which they refer to as Russian factories. Vancouver describes the relations between the Russians and the Americans [natives] with high praise [for the Russians], saying that they acquired control over the savages not by conquest, but by searching for a way to their hearts. The descriptions by these foreign seafarers does special honor to you, and it also emphasizes the wisdom of your kindly and judicious methods. These descriptions have brought your name to the special attention of our Sovereign Emperor. Your first report will bring you personal satisfaction and Imperial favor now and in the future.

We have noted in Volume Three of Vancouver's *Voyages* that some of your promyshlenniks gave English sailors maps of your voyages. The Main Administration feels it absolutely necessary to call to your attention the fact that when you select men you must not only take their loyalty into account, but also take every possible measure to prevent such an occurrence from happening again, for this is detrimental to the Fatherland.

II.

In regard to political developments in Europe, the Main Administration wishes to inform you that the French state has been proclaimed a Republic everywhere; the well-meaning government of First Consul [Napoleon] Bonaparte has ended bloodshed; a general peace has been concluded; and as evidence

28

of the good relations between the new Republic and us, the French General Geduville has been appointed as minister to our Court.

Enclosed are political journals from the past three years. From these and from *Vestnik Evropy* for this year, you will learn of all the changes that have occurred in the world. The Main Administration, for its part, feels it imperative to inform you that in October, 1800, a serious disagreement developed between England and our country. An embargo was placed against all English ships and goods in our ports, and against ours in London. Finally, in 1801 the situation deteriorated to the point of military action. In March the brave Admiral [Horatio] Nelson appeared in the Baltic Sea with a powerful flotilla, and although the Danes would not permit him to pass through the Sound, nevertheless Nelson fought them. He lost some of his ships, but managed to sail into our [Baltic] Sea. However, during the same period, His Imperial Majesty [Alexander I] ascended the throne and made fortuitous changes in all matters. Disagreements were ended and the friendship between the two countries was reestablished on the same basis as formerly.

All the same, the Main Administration instructs you to receive every foreign ship with great caution at all times, because distance prevents us from being able to keep you informed about rapidly changing political situations. To this same end the Main Administration instructs you, in accordance with the authority given you, to do everything possible to establish a depot in Petropavlovsk harbor where furs from all areas could be stored. This should not be too difficult to accomplish, because you will have experienced naval officers who will be able to complete these voyages [between Alaska and Kamchatka] in a shorter time and thus will be able to deliver furs more frequently. Next summer you will have an officer with each ship and you will also have doctors and a pharmacy.

III.

In regard to [James George] Shields*, although the Main Administration does not doubt his sincerity and already has

---

*Shields was an English shipbuilder in service to the Russian American Company. He had commanded the Company ship *Severo-Vostochnyi Orel* and proofs of his devotion, nonetheless by virtue of being English he may favor them and try to benefit them. Be as careful as possible in watching his actions, and keep the Main Administration informed about him. Try not to let him see that you suspect him of anything, and do not give him the slightest reason for any bitterness. On the contrary, reward him with kindness and with promises of honors from the Sovereign and medals and financial rewards from the Company, so as to bind him as much as possible to Russia, under the kindly rule of His Imperial Majesty, so this foreigner will be satisfied with his position and have no reason to seek fulfillment elsewhere. In this way he may become a most ardent and true Russian. You may employ him as a navigator for transporting goods, or to explore northern regions, but do not send him to regions belonging to England. You yourself know how to use him to best advantage now and in the future, and your common sense will dictate how to act in every circumstance for the greatest advantage to the State.

In your letter of 1798 you wrote that Shields had handed over a Kolosh [Tlingit] lad to the English, but did you discover why he did that? Do you have any information about this and about anything else pertaining to Shields? If there were no adverse consequences to that action, then as noted above, do your best to stir him to greater effort for the general good. Most importantly, you are to preserve and strengthen, among all the peoples under your jurisdiction, the good rapport so essential to the realization of the great undertakings which the Company has entered upon in this auspicious period.

IV.

Your reports have been forwarded to the Main Administration directly, not through Okhotsk, because the Company is not under the jurisdiction of the gubernia administration. Now

---

discovered Sitka Island (now Baranov Island) in 1796. Because of the tremendous distances and slow passage of correspondence between Irkutsk and Alaska, the Main Administration at the time of this document was as yet unaware that Shields had died in 1799 when the *Feniks* was wrecked en route from Okhotsk to New Arkhangel. *See* Fedorova, *Russkaia Amerika*, II, p. 297.

Nikolai P. Rumiantsev, forceful head of the College of Commerce, joined Admiral N. S. Mordvinov in supporting Krusenstern's proposal for a Russian circumnavigation (similar to earlier European voyages) to be undertaken with Lisianskii. N. N. Bashkina, *The United States and Russia, The Beginning of Relations*, (OHS neg. OrHi 82937)

is the time to organize a number of governmental institutions in America. This should be kept in great secrecy; you alone, as Chief Administrator, are entrusted with this. Consequently there is no reason to send these dispatches to the administration of the Irkutsk gubernia, where it would not be possible to keep them secret. The enclosed travel journal of Grigorii Ivanovich Shelikhov can serve of proof of this to you. It is the journal which he submitted to the late Governor General Iakobii. When Iakobii was replaced, it was stolen from the office of [his successor] Governor Pil, and without the approval of the late Shelikhov, was published in Moscow. To gain financial reward ignorant persons revealed state secrets. Thus you can see that the [bronze] plates [claiming land for Russia] must be moved. We give you the authority to do this in timely fashion. In regard to the plates without numbers, which you still have, you may emplace them wherever you think best, but do not let anyone know except for the Main Administration. Further, anything pertaining to political subjects or to navigation, you are to send as a special dispatch marked Secret.

V.

Regarding medals and the like, to be distributed as rewards, you will receive these with the first transport because they could not be procured this year.

VI.

The execution of all of this, on behalf of the Empire, is entrusted to you as the Chief Administrator of the American districts, with the full understanding that through your zeal and hard work you will attract the Imperial attention of Our Gracious Sovereign to yourself, and you will make your name henceforth famous in the annals of Russia.

Director Mikhail Buldakov
Director Evstrat Delarov
Director Ivan Shelikhov

Reference: United States National Archives. *Records of the Russian American Company, 1802, 1817–1867*. Vol. 1, No. 190, Folios 2–7. Manuscript.

6

AN IMPERIAL DECREE FROM ALEXANDER I TO COUNT NIKOLAI P.
RUMIANTSEV, MINISTER OF COMMERCE, PROHIBITING THE IMPOR-
TATION OF FUR SEAL PELTS INTO RUSSIA FROM FOREIGNERS TO
AVOID COMPETITION WITH THE RUSSIAN AMERICAN COMPANY

Count Nikolai Petrovich! Acceding to the request of the Russian American Company, which states that the local customs office, in accordance with the decision of the College of Commerce, allows the importation of grey beavers from a certain Kapskii Island, which pelts Russian merchants consider actually to be fur seals, I hereby decree that the importation of such furs from foreign lands be prohibited, because this fur trade is a hindrance to the fur trade of the above mentioned Company in America. Those furs which have already been registered, or which are in the Customs warehouses, are to be sent back under supervision during the current sailing season, in accordance with the 1793 ukaz regarding the importation of prohibited goods. These furs, however, are not to be confiscated, nor are they to be available for public sale. Beginning with the new year, if these furs are again imported, you are to treat them as goods prohibited by ukaz.

Reference: *PSZ*. First Series, Vol. 27, No. 20,387, 232.

OCTOBER 26, 1802

A CONTRACT FOR SERVICE TO THE RUSSIAN AMERICAN COMPANY INVOLVING THE RUSSIAN NAVY AND THE KRUSENSTERN-LISIANSKII EXPEDITION

In an application which I have submitted to the Main Administration of the [Russian] American Company, the first point states, "If the ship's cargo is not ready, or if the entire cargo from the previous voyage is not unloaded in time, the sailing of the vessel is to be delayed until it is feasible to depart. Further, if the commanding officer of the ship is dispatched to describe and explore unknown places, or to stop at previously discovered locations, I will be required to serve at sea as long as the interests of the [Russian] American Company require my services. If the commanding officer of the vessel becomes ill or incapacitated for some other reason, I am to assume command of the Company vessel and act in all the best interests of the Company and the Fatherland."

1. In reference to this provision, I request that when we reach our settlements in North America and report under the command of Baranov, the Company inform us as to how long we will be there and where and on what duty we will be assigned.

2. [I also request] that all documents issued to the Captain, and any others pertaining to our expedition should not be kept secret, but made known, not only to the officers but to every sailor, so that in case of a misfortune resulting in the death of the Captain, his second could readily assume command of the ship.

3. In all places where we may have to anchor, the names of [Company] agents should be made known to us, so that in case of unusual circumstances every crew member could turn to him for assistance.

To the second clause I have said that "I should receive salary as of taking over the ship."

4. Since each of us will be absent from the Fatherland for such a long time, without receiving any news, we feel it is quite

necessary that before we depart we are allowed to put our personal and family affairs in order. For that reason we feel it necessary that we be received into Company service as of December 1 of the present year [1802].

5. In regard to salaries, considering our basic needs, and operating on advice from persons who have spent several years on such expeditions, we have concluded that the proposed compensation is inadequate. For that reason we request that the Company increase [salaries] by 1,000 rubles per year, and allow each member of this expedition to decide for himself whether or not he wishes to become a shareholder of the Company.

The third clause states that "the Company assumes responsibility for providing board and all necessary food."

6. We request that the Company inform us how it proposes to fulfill this responsibility. If it plans to supply each person on a yearly basis, then frequent changes of location should not subject us to a cut in rations. For that reason we believe that if we are to have the same rations as those issued to every member of the Navy of His Imperial Majesty, the minimum cost of such rations will be 1,200 rubles per person per year.

7. We ask that the Company offer us assurance that when the expedition is completed we will not have lost any time in His Imperial Majesty's service in regard to decorations, promotions and the like.

8. If any officer or member of the lower ranks should come down with a contagious disease and have to be taken ashore, he should be treated in the same manner as prescribed in the service of His Imperial Majesty: he should be provided with quarters, a servant, food and care, and a physician should be engaged to treat him. As soon as he has recovered he should be put aboard some ship or sent back to St. Petersburg at Company expense.

9. If for some reason officers and crew should have to live on shore, they should be provided with living quarters at the expense of the Company.

10. We ask to be informed: in what currency, and where, are we to be paid?

11. If we return successfully to Russia, having brought benefit to the Company and glory to our Fatherland, we trust

Admiral Adam Johann (in Russian Ivan F.) von Krusenstern,
a Baltic sailor in British then Russian service, was the first
Russian circumnavigator (1803–1806). Although this expedition was responsible to Baranov while in the settlements of
the Russian American Company, after Baranov's retirement
in 1817, all subsequent Chief Administrators were themselves Russian naval officers. *Memoirs of the celebrated admiral
Adam John de Krusenstern*. (OHS orHi neg. 82020)

that the Company will reward each of us with a lifetime pension.

12. In conclusion, each of us swears on his honor as an officer in the service of His Imperial Majesty that if, by some chance, he should be unable to take part in this expedition, he will return to the Company any funds he has received in advance.

While on this voyage each of us promises to do everything within his power to benefit the Company and bring glory to Russia.

In the absence of Captain-Lieutenant Ivan Fedorovich Krusenstern, this document is signed by his senior officer,

Lieutenant Fedor von Romberg

Reference: Library of Congress. Manuscript Division. Yudin Collection, Box 2. Unpaged.

JUNE 7, 1804

OBSERVATIONS ON THE HAWAIIAN ISLANDS BY GEORG HEINRICH
VON LANGSDORFF, GERMAN NATURALIST WITH THE KRUSENSTERN-
LISIANSKII EXPEDITION, 1803–1807 ABOARD *NADEZHDA*

On June 7 [1804] we sighted the eastern extremity of the
island of Hawaii (19° 34″ northern latitude), which was
some 36 sea miles from us. This island, the largest of the group
called the Sandwich Islands, became widely known as the
place where the greatest navigator of our time [James Cook] lost
his life. Several years after Cook's death, his distinguished dis-
ciple, [George] Vancouver, drew up a detailed map of this
group of islands.

Captain [Ivan F.] Krusenstern planned to reach Nagasaki,
the major trading city of Japan, before the end of September,
and he hoped that by accelerating his voyage he would escape
the period of change of the northeasterly monsoon which frequently occurs in the middle of September. Consequently, in
order to gain time, he did not anchor in Kealakekua Bay on the
island of Hawaii, but followed the example of other navigators
who lost no time in carrying on a profitable barter trade with
the inhabitants of the island, and by moving along the coast in
this manner, within several days he managed to acquire a suf-
ficiency of pigs and every other kind of provision.

With this aim he cruised along the southern coast of the
island until the tenth [of June]. To our great misfortune, however, during that period only a very few inhabitants of the island came to us, and they demanded such high prices for the
produce they brought out to us that Captain Krusenstern decided to refrain from further attempts to secure provisions, the
success of which was doubtful. He left the island and without
stopping anywhere, set out for Kamchatka. This goal was
accomplished thanks to the excellent state of health of the
entire crew.

The inhabitants of the island whom we had the opportunity to observe were naked, dirty, poorly built and of medium
stature. Their skin was a dark dusky brown color and was cov-

Georg H. von Langsdorff, a German-trained naturalist with
the Imperial Russian Academy of Sciences, established a remarkable record of observations in Brazil, the Northwest
Coast of America and the Sandwich Islands. N. N. Bashkina,
The United States and Russia, The Beginning of Relations. (OHS
neg. OrHi 82933)

ered with rashes and sores, probably caused by a drink called
kava, or by venereal disease. Most of the men had lost their
front teeth during fights when they would throw rocks at one
another. On many, the navel protruded so much that it looked
swollen and about to erupt.

The people are fine swimmers. On their arms and along the
sides of their bodies they had tattoos depicting lizards, goats,
guns and diamond-shaped forms. In contrast to the tattoos we
had seen on Nuka Hiva, these did not adorn the body, but
actually disfigured it. The unfavorable impression these persons made on us was all the more pronounced since we had

such a short time prior to that (May 17) left an island whose inhabitants, by virtue of their physique and build, are without doubt among the most beautiful people on earth [Nuka Hiva].

In other respects the inhabitants of the Sandwich Islands, probably because of their more frequent contacts with Europeans, appear to be brighter than those on Nuka Hiva. Cabri, our Frenchman, was so disenchanted with these island men and women that he decided not to remain among these disgusting people. He earnestly pleaded with Captain Krusenstern, who had intended to put him ashore here, that it would be better to take him to Kamchatka, which the captain did. Cabri understood the language of the people of Nuka Hiva very well, but he could not communicate with the people of Hawaii. Sometimes we had better success with the help of a few English words.

These people go out into the open sea for many miles in canoes which are light and both beautifully and skillfully made. This precision indicates that these people have made much greater progress in navigation than the people of Nuka Hiva.

The coast along which we sailed is pleasing to the eye. We saw a great variety of plantings, and an enormous number of coconut and banana groves. Our attention was particularly drawn to the majestic view of the mountain Mauna Loa. According to previous observations its peak was estimated at 2,578 *toises* [1 toise = 6.39 feet] high, but our diligent astronomer, Dr. Horner, calculated that the height was only 2,254 toises. This towering mountain, which is 300 to 400 toises higher than the peak of Tenerife, rises so gradually from its base barely above sea level, to the summit, that it has a remarkable appearance and is a most pleasing sight. Of course nowhere else is it possible to climb such a height so easily. The mild climate facilitates this because even in spite of its considerable height, the peak barely reaches snow level at the equator, and we observed that at this time of year the peak was completely free of snow.

How many unknown plants may yet be discovered here, and what a great contribution could be made to geography and the natural history of the local vegetation! It would be desirable

The ship-choked Port of Honolulu as drawn by Louis Choris.
Voyage pittoresque autour du monde. (OHS negs. OrHi 82059)

for some naturalist to be sent here to this island to spend at least a year studying this.

On June 10 we left Hawaii, so I was unable to collect any information on the present condition of the island. When in 1805 and 1806 I wintered on the Northwest Coast of America, I had the opportunity to gather information about it which I would like to relate here briefly.

The Sandwich Islands are very well suited for anchoring all ships which sail along the Northwest Coast of America, to the Aleutian Islands or to Kamchatka. There are many safe bays and the islands abound in pigs, breadfruit, bananas, coconuts, taro, sweet potatoes, salt, wood, water and the like. The islands are a wonderful place for relaxation. Seafarers from the free United States of America visit them annually on their way to the Northwest Coast, and from the islanders they obtain sea otter pelts in exchange for items made of iron, cloth, knives, axes, kitchen utensils, rice, molasses, sugar, gunpowder and firearms. The pelts are very highly valued by the Chinese, so they take them to Canton. This trade has been carried on quite successfully since the English and the Spanish have left Nootka Sound and have abandoned their former settlements there.

The trade must be exceedingly profitable, since almost every year from six to eight ships cruise between 50° and 57° northern latitude in the region of Nootka, the Queen Charlotte Islands and Norfolk Sound. If they do not manage to acquire a good cargo of sea otter pelts for Canton in one year, then in October or November they will set out for the Columbia River, or more frequently for the Sandwich Islands, where they spend the winter and put back out to sea at the beginning of March with such a load of goods that they again begin their barter trade on the Northwest Coast.

The large number of ships which come to Kealakekua Bay and the constant trade with the natives, have already had such a great influence on the culture of these islands that their inhabitants have moved along the route to civilization with seven-league strides; more rapidly than any other people on islands in the South Pacific they are becoming a civilized commercial country.

King Kamehameha [I, 1737?–1819], thanks to the constant contact with seafarers from the American states, and especially with Mr. [John] Young and Mr. [Isaac] Davis, who have lived there for many years and seem to be his ministers, has introduced European customs, the English language and English habits to such a degree that a large and very active part of the people on this island now speak English.

Kamehameha has managed to bring all the islands in this group under his control, and appears to be their only ruler. Thanks to the constant trade and exchange of goods, within a year or two he understood the value of silver, and preferred to sell products from his country to ships who would pay cash in the form of thalers or Spanish piasters. As soon as he had accumulated a sufficient sum of money, he bought a ship from an American and manned it with a crew made up partly of his own men and partly of foreign sailors, many of whom even now live in Hawaii.

King Kamehameha, a larger than life figure in Hawaiian history, appears in the earliest Russian accounts as well as in the reports of most European explorers. All attested his monarchical power and sagacity during his reign of thirty years. Louis Choris, *Voyage pittoresque autour du monde*. (OHS OrHi neg. 82092)

Sailors from the United States so much like the bountiful gifts of nature, the easy work and the beautiful young women that almost no ships sail away from there without leaving behind one or more crew members on the island. The king allows only persons of good conduct to remain on the island; they

Louis Choris accompanied von Kotzebue to New Arkhangel in the brig *Riurik* in 1815. His drawings such as this one of women dancing, delineated the attractions of the Islands. Louis Choris, *Voyage pittoresque autour du monde*. (OHS negs. OrHi 82058)

must have good recommendations from their captains. Meanwhile the local people have become so accustomed to sea life that they have become excellent sailors.

On the Northwest Coast of America I had the opportunity to talk with people from that island who were serving on Bostonian ships which had come in from the Hawaiian Islands. They were hired as sailors and received a salary of 10 to 12 piasters per month. They make such good rope and twine for nets and tackle (probably using fibers from *Phormium lenax Forts*) that sailors already can obtain all such supplies here. They consider that the tackle made by the Sandwich Island people is much better than that made by Europeans.

In everything he does, Kamehameha shows great understanding, insight and energy. In a short period of time he built up his naval forces so much that by 1806 he had at his disposal 15 ships, among which were several three-masters, brigs and cutters. That same year he sent word to the Russian American

Company representative, Baranov, who was in New Arkhangel in Norfolk Sound. He said he had learned from the accounts of people who had visited the Northwest Coast that the Russian settlements on that coast were sometimes experiencing great shortages of food and other things. Therefore he proposed to send a ship every year with salt, pork, sweet potatoes and other provisions, even products from Europe, if in exchange [Baranov] would give him sea otter pelts at a fair price, which [Kamehameha] would then send to Canton for resale.

In addition to other matters, the king is much involved in questions pertaining to shipbuilding. It is said that he can very accurately point out the merits or shortcomings of one ship or another. Therefore every instrument or tool needed for ship construction is a most useful item of exchange. Sailors who can also work as shipwrights find an especially cordial welcome here. They are allotted land and receive other privileges.

Several years ago in Hawaii an especially remarkable discovery was made. Wood was found there which was suitable for shipbuilding; the woodboring worm (*Teredo navalis Linn.*) which causes great destruction to ships in those waters, does not attack this tree at all. If this discovery is verified, it will render completely obsolete the usual necessity of sheathing vessels with copper.

Among other vegetation in this group of islands, sugar cane also grows. If this were to be cultivated, and a large amount planted, in time Kamchatka and all of Siberia could be supplied with sugar from here.

The war and political conditions in Europe in the last years have turned the attention of enterprising merchants away from these places to Europe alone. But when freedom of the seas is reestablished for ships of other nations, then the benefits of trade with these regions will not be forgotten, benefits which were so clearly pointed out by Cook, La Pérouse, Meares, Portlock, Vancouver, le Marchand, Broughton, Krusenstern and many others.

On June 10 at 6:00 in the evening we shouted "Hurrah" three times and parted from our companion ship *Neva*. Captain [Iurii] Lisianskii was ordered to proceed aboard that ship to Kodiak and to the Northwest Coast of America. He was not in as much of a hurry as we were and for that reason decided to anchor for a few days in Kealakekua Bay to give his crew some rest.

However, since in the course of four days we had not been able to lay in a store of provisions from shore, Captain Krusenstern considered it necessary to make the firm decision not to lose any more time and not to anchor in that bay. He proceeded directly to Kamchatka.

See: Georg Heinrich Freiherr von Langsdorff. *Bemerkungen auf einer Reise um die Welt in den Jahren 1803 bis 1807*. Vol. 1, (Frankfurt am Main: 1812), 163–169. Russian translation in N. N. Bashkina et al., eds. *Rossiia i SShA: stanovleniie otnoshenii, 1765–1815*. (Moscow: 1980), 262–266.

9

A REPORT BY IMPERIAL RUSSIAN NAVY LIEUTENANT NIKOLAI A.
KHVOSTOV CONCERNING THE CONDITION OF THE SHIPS OF THE
RUSSIAN AMERICAN COMPANY

[Following are questions put to Lieutenant Khvostov, and his replies, upon his return to St. Petersburg in 1804 from a business journey to Okhotsk on behalf of the Russian American Company.]

What is needed for safety on ships sailing between Okhotsk and America?

1. Strong, durable ship construction is needed. At present ships are being built by inexperienced carpenters, following designs drawn up by [Russian American] Company apprentice shipwrights.

2. Adequate armament.

3. Experienced naval officers.

4. Reliable servitors.

In short, everything necessary for proper and safe sailing.

How should Admiralty vessels be built, and by what shipwrights?

I believe that for the Company's prosperity and the substantial advantages, it is most important to devote its efforts first of all to transferring its port, and rebuilding it in a more favorable place. Second, the Company should locate and establish a [new] route from Iakutsk to the new port. Third, it should put the present shipyards and seagoing vessels into better condition. To accomplish this it is necessary to find an experienced, reliable naval officer. He should be made the commandant of the port, and authorized to draw up detailed tables of organization for all port facilities which are necessary to fit out ships with equipment and supplies. He should be in charge of all persons, regardless of their positions, who are involved with navigation. Together with the administrator of the office he should be empowered to command the entire marine part of the Company's activity. He should have an assistant selected from navy officers, a boatswain, an assistant navigator, an apprentice shipwright, a naval gunner, a master shipwright, four to six experienced ship carpenters, two caulkers, two blacksmiths, a ropespinner and a master tacklemaker. These persons should be chosen from among the most experienced in their professions so the promyshlenniks belonging to the Company can learn from them.

How many vessels in all does the [Russian] *American Company have?*
Seven, and an eighth is under construction.

How many ships are seaworthy?
Three. *Mariia* is still on the ways; *Elizaveta* is in Okhotsk, and *Aleksandr Nevskii* is in America. The rest, *Petr, Pavel, Dmitrii, Ekaterina* and *Olga*, because of age and poor construction, cannot be considered seaworthy.

What is their cargo capacity?
Mariia, Elizaveta, Aleksandr, Dmitrii and *Pavel* 6,000 puds; *Ekaterina* 4,000; *Olga* 1,000.

How many ships are presently under construction, or in the planning stage?
Mariia is completely finished, but still on the ways. Last fall [1803] they laid the keel for one other ship 45 feet in length which will perhaps be ready in June of this year, 1804.

How many ships are needed to sail in those waters to transport the entire annual cargo of the Company? What kind of cargo is it, and what kind of vessels would be best suited?
At the present time the entire shipment of cargo from Okhotsk to America consists of goods intended to be exchanged for furs. This cargo includes provisions such as flour, gunpowder, firearms and the like, necessary for supplying this distant and barren region. From America to Okhotsk, the cargo is furs. Consequently, for this single item of trade, if other kinds of trade are not developed, in my judgment two ships, from 60 to 70 feet in length, will be adequate. However they should be built with very sharp keels so that when laden they would draw 13 to 14 feet. The advantages of the sharp keel over the flat bottom are well known to every naval officer, and for that reason I consider it unnecessary to expand on this.

Ships of the United States may serve as evidence of this. It is said that sharp-keeled ships cannot pick up the amount of cargo that flat bottoms can, and that the depth of the Okhota River will not permit the passage of such vessels, which ride deep in the water. To the first, I respond that it is better to transport a smaller cargo speedily and reliably than a larger one over a longer period of sailing, and with hazard. Furthermore, one can build ships ten feet longer with a sharp keel. To the second, I suggest that the port be located on the Ulia River, which does have adequate depth.

The Company should order that every year a ship be dispatched from America at the end of May bound for Okhotsk, and from Okhotsk for America at the end of June or early in July, in order to strengthen its holdings in America every year, and to bring in goods from there.

Two or three naval commercial vessels of 16 guns should be permanently stationed in American waters: one to protect our possessions, and the one or two others to prevent Bostonians from entering into trade with the American savages. Further, every effort should be made to persuade the Bostonians to trade with us rather than with the savages.

Ships dispatched from Kodiak to the coast of America could deliver supplies of food to our settlements, as well as other needed items, while carrying on trade with the savages in the manner of the Bostonians. When these republicans have been prevented from carrying on trade in our possessions, we will be able to obtain goods from the savages at moderate prices, which will be beneficial for us as well as for them, because they have already developed the desire for European goods.

One ship of 50 to 60 feet will be adequate to deliver goods to the Aleutian archipelago, and from there to Okhotsk, since the distance is short enough so the ship could make a round trip in the course of a single summer.

For the Kuril Islands and Petropavlovsk harbor, again, one ship of 40 to 50 feet will be enough. The one essential thing is that all of them should have sharper keels than those at present.

It is also necessary to have a tender or filibuster vessel of 45 feet for reconnaissance and unforeseen assignments.

In regard to fitting out these vessels, I believe it would be best to do this along the same lines as naval brigantines, so they would have standing and running rope of adequate strength and gauge. Aboard merchant ships which sail in small seas, all the rigging, especially the running gear and the sails, is usually light-weight so a smaller crew can handle the ship. But ships of the Russian American Company must sail great distances and therefore their rigging should also be reliable and durable.

There should be no problems with insufficient numbers of crew, and unnecessary expense, because it is necessary to send as many as 60 men every year from Okhotsk to America as replacements for any who do not wish to remain there or who are being sent back to Okhotsk because of illness or injury.

In my judgment the Company may reorganize as follows, in the present circumstances. The ships *Mariia* and *Elizaveta*, although their construction is not of the desired quality, should be used to sail between Okhotsk and America. The ship *Aleksandr* should be designated to sail in the Aleutian Islands, after her galiot rigging is replaced; it is not appropriate for sailing in heavy winds. *Ekaterina*, although she is already unreliable, can sail between the Kuril Islands and Petropavlovsk harbor, until a new ship is built. It would be a good idea to use the ship under construction for exploring and new discoveries. The completely unseaworthy *Petr*, *Pavel* and *Dmitrii* should be disposed of however possible.

How many officers, navigators and servitors are needed?
Aboard each of the two or three naval-commercial ships which are proposed for America, there should be a lieutenant, a midshipman, a navigator with the rank of a non-commissioned officer, or a navigator's mate, and up to 80 servitors, including a boatswain, two non-commissioned officers, six gunners, 12 sailors, 50 Russian promyshlenniks and 10 hired American natives.

Aboard the ships which will be used to transport goods from America, and from the Aleutians to Okhotsk and back, there should be a lieutenant, a midshipman, a non-commissioned navigator or mate, one military guard and five sailors. There must be plenty of promyshlenniks.

On the ship to sail to the Kuril Islands, there should be an experienced midshipman, a non-commissioned navigator, a military guard and five sailors.

What are the disadvantages of the port of Okhotsk, and what are the advantages of the Ulia River?

The disadvantages of the port of Okhotsk have been noted for a long time. This is evident from many personal ukazes [from Russian rulers] ordering the use of all possible means to find a new and more suitable harbor. But since I have never seen a written description of the details of these disadvantages, I consider it appropriate to explain them here.

1. The town of Okhotsk is built on a rocky ledge which is not more than three *sazhens* [one sazhen = seven feet] above water. This ledge is a peninsula two and a half *versts* [one verst = .633 miles] long and 100 sazhens or slightly more wide. The isthmus which links it to the mainland of the Okhotsk coast was formed as the result of the constant action of the Okhota River, which in some places is not more than three sazhens wide, so that [even] in low tide, water from the sea flows into the Okhota River.

This description makes it easy to visualize how precarious the location of the town of Okhotsk is. First, the Okhota River can easily break through the isthmus and surround the entire town with water. Second, there are frequent storms out of the east here, with high tides and heavy rain which not only threaten the town with disastrous floods and deluges, but also possibly with total destruction and washing away of the whole rock ledge on which the town is built.

These are not imaginary fears, but conclusions drawn from fact. We know that in 1733, 1742, 1755, 1777 and 1783 there were such great floods that many large parts of the coastline were torn away and swept into the sea. In 1749, 1759, 1768, 1782 and 1786 many private and government structures were destroyed, and two streets were cut off. The result is that at present the town is so crowded that in a room of one square sazhen as many as fifteen men are billeted. There have been times when there was such a shortage of living quarters that people had to live in the churches.

This crowding causes health problems in Okhotsk which

have often led to epidemics. Furthermore, because of the rocky foundation and the small area of the town, there is no suitable place to keep any kind of livestock, either in winter or summer. All of these circumstances together create a situation that leads one to say the location of this town is one of the most disastrous in the world.

2. The Okhota River has no place where an artificial harbor could be built, even with tremendous effort.

3. Even at high tide the bar at the mouth of the Okhota River, which ships have to cross, is no more than 12 feet deep. Consequently ships coming in from the sea have to wait for high tide, even in heavy winds, and meanwhile they must stand at anchor in the open sea, on a sandy bottom.

4. The mouth of the Okhota River is subject to constant change. Frequently banks and shallows will appear where previously there had been adequate depth; and the opposite may occur: there may be a deep place where before there had been sandbanks and shallows. For this reason the channel is unpredictable for ships coming in from the sea. This is caused by the fact that the Okhota River has a swift current by the time it reaches its mouth, and the bottom is flat or gently sloping. Rain washes sand down from the mountains and from the banks of the river, and [because of the nature of the bottom] it is easily swept to the bar in the middle of the estuary, where it reaches the first and only barrier.

Thus the sand creates a hindrance to the flow of the river, and the river, rushing over the obstacle here and there, washes it away and thus causes the changes in depth.

5. Finally, a serious problem with the port of Okhotsk is the fact that the route there from Iakutsk is terrible and it is thus extremely difficult to supply the port with goods and cargo of any sort. There is no known water route between Iakutsk and Okhotsk. All attempts to find a new passage via the Aldoma, Maia, Iudoma and Urak rivers have been futile because of the low water in the Urak. Thus there is only one means of supply. Trade goods and all other supplies must be brought overland on packhorses. The track from Iakutsk to Okhotsk passes over mountains and there are three especially difficult areas to cross: Chegdalsk, Iunikansk and Semikhrebet, which extend over a distance of 250 versts.

The tremendous problems associated with this route have from time to time become even worse, but the problems of the port of Okhotsk and the hope of finding a better port site have forestalled efforts to make the necessary efforts to improve the Iakutsk-Okhotsk track.

At the present time this route is in the worst possible condition. First, it is hourly ever more undercut by the small streams which flow along it. Second, in many places the trail is blocked by trees which have fallen because of rot or high winds, or which were deliberately felled by the Iakuts so they could shoot the squirrels which had taken refuge in them. Third, the heavy snow that falls there in winter causes slender young trees to bend down to the ground, where they become entangled in undergrowth and create a barrier in the track. Fourth, the horses travel in strings with their packloads, and all step in the same places; this has created such a deep trail that it is extremely awkward to walk in it, especially since it is always filled with water. All of these factors taken together make this route not only slow and difficult, but indeed, nearly impassable.

As noted above, all of these disadvantages associated with the port of Okhotsk have long been perceived, and for that reason there has always been an effort made to find a better place for a new port. The Ud, Urak and Kukhtsa rivers have been searched for such a site, as well as the area near the Aldoma bay, but eventually all of these places were found unsuitable, and half a century has been spent in futile attempts.

Long ago many persons thought and maintained that the mouth of the Ulia River was suitable for a port, but this assertion was based only on the fact that the mouth of the Ulia has greater depth than that of the Okhota. They did not take into account other requirements for a good port site, and thus there are questions that should be asked. Are there woodlands near the Ulia River with timber suitable for ship construction? Are there as many fish in the Ulia as in the Okhota? Is the entry into the river satisfactory? Is there a natural harbor? Will it be too narrow? Will it be possible to accommodate the anticipated number of ships without great expenditure to make it appropriate? Can one anticipate finding a suitable [overland] route to the new port site?

These and other questions remain unanswered, in part because so much attention has been devoted to the other sites just mentioned, and in part because the pursuit of answers to some of these questions has been attended with difficult and potentially dangerous travel.

However, fortunate circumstances and my own dedication to the good of the nation have given me the means of obtaining a great deal of information, which enables me to conclude very truthfully that the Ulia River is superior to the Okhota.

In 1803 when I arrived at Okhotsk from the island of Kodiak, the Chief Administrator of the Russian American Company office in Okhotsk, [Aleksei Evseevich] Polevoi, informed me by letter that he had instructions from the military governor of Irkutsk and from the Main Administration of the Russian American Company to survey the mouth of the Ulia River that summer. He asked that I undertake this voyage and make every possible effort to find a suitable site to build a new port, which is such a vitally important matter. Already more than 40 years have gone by, and enormous sums of money have been spent trying to find such a place, but to date no one has succeeded. In the meantime the port of Okhotsk is falling into ever worse condition. I feel it is my prime duty to dedicate my life to the service of the Fatherland, and thus I willingly agreed to his request, and immediately set out on that voyage.

On September 6 [1803] I sent a navigator's mate and ten oarsmen in a *baidara* [large open boat], with orders to proceed along the coast. I took a Iakut [native] with me and went on horseback along the coast to inspect the track which was about ten versts long; the first part went through gravel and then it became a dirt trail covered with grass. We spent the night at the mouth of the Urak River, some 24 versts away [from Okhotsk].

At high tide the next morning there was an east southeast wind, and I sent the navigator's mate with the baidara to continue along the coast. After a short time he returned and reported to me that because of the high waves and heavy surf he could not get out of the mouth of the river. This really surprised me, because according to my observations I thought that when the wind was that strong at the mouth of the Okhota River the waves would not be so great. For that reason, doubting him, I wanted to see this for myself. I sent the Iakut on ahead with the horses and I climbed into the baidara and ordered the men to paddle. In a short time I saw that the wave action and surf really were extraordinary and quite unpredictable, from all sides. The baidara was half full of water, and the oarsmen lost their paddles, so we could go neither forward nor backward and were in grave danger. It seemed there was no way to save ourselves in this desperate situation. However, I realized, peering between waves, that the shoals where the surf was most violent did not extend far out into the sea. I felt that if we held to our course we would get out of this heavy surf. I decided to raise the sail immediately, and ordered the crew to paddle as hard as they could with the oars we had left. In this way we managed to get up enough speed to make our way through the fearful abyss, and suddenly, we found ourself in calm and peaceful water.

This experience convinced me that the mouth of the Urak River is completely unsuitable for ships to enter, especially if the incoming ship has to be kedged or towed. In such a case the ship could easily lose its weigh and would be wrecked. This happened in 1802 when the ship *Aleksandr* sank in the mouth of the Urak.

At midday, having managed to reach shore, I continued my journey on horseback. The roadway continued to be dirt covered with dense grass, and with great piles of driftwood. From the Urak River almost all the way to the Ulia, the trail goes along lakes which are connected by small creeks and streams. On the other side of these lakes a small forested area and shrubs were visible. About 45 versts from the Urak a small river called the Marikanka empties into the sea. At all times of the year except in spring the mouth of this little river is so filled with sand that there is no indication of the river itself.

Since it was dark, we stopped there for the night. The situation of that place is very like the previous one. Iakuts come here from Okhotsk with their packloads to graze their horses, sometimes with as many as 15,000 or more horses. They divide them into two herds; one herd they drive beyond the Marikanka to the Inia River; the other they take to the Ulia River. All of them say that the grass along the Ulia is very fine.

About ten versts from this place there is the small Nelba

River which flows to the southwest, and about four versts from the Ulia it falls into the Nelbar. The Nelbar rises in the mountains and flows some 30 versts, then gradually widens and joins the mouth of the Ulia. The depth at its mouth increases to two and a half or three sazhens. Between these two rivers is low land which is under water during high tide so that these two rivers flow together and form a sizable bay.

When I reached the mouth of the Ulia River on September 8 I spent two days trying to measure the depth of that river, as well as of the Nelba and a tributary called the Tangaiakh. I then sailed across to the south bank, where sometime previously a lighthouse had been built and is still standing. The situation of this place is similar to that on the opposite bank, but much more extensive, and the grass on it is much denser. Also, it is covered with an incredible amount of driftwood. My people found a good deal of *sarana* [Kamchatka lily] there. It is very nutritious and quite flavorful. Russians in America use it to take the place of bread.

In my judgment a harbor could well be built along this bank, as can be seen better on the appended map which I have drawn up.

Toward evening some Tungus natives who had been living there for many years came to see me. I wanted to learn about many things pertaining to the environs from them, but I realized they were not willing to talk very much. They would keep replying that they did not have any information. I finally managed to gain their confidence through kindness and small gifts.

Their information is not altogether reliable, but some of it appears to be quite accurate when it is compared with other news and some of the information gives a basis for drawing inferences. I base my opinion concerning the suitability of the mouth of the Ulia River for a port site on the following:

1. What I have seen with my own eyes.

2. What I have heard from the Tungus.

3. The comparison of both of the above with earlier pertinent information.

In reference to what I have seen personally, I find that:

1. The southern bank of the mouth of the Ulia River is firm ground, seven sazhens above water level. It is not littered

with gravel and therefore the area is immeasurably larger, better and safer for a settlement than the rocky outcrop on which Okhotsk is built.

2. The ground there is covered with grass, and a large amount of driftwood is brought in by the sea; thus one can heat dwellings and graze livestock, which is not possible in Okhotsk.

3. Although the mouth of the Ulia, like the mouth of the Okhota, is filled with sand, nevertheless the sand there is along the banks, and the center is clear. The reason is that although the Nelbar and Tangaiakh rivers, which enter from opposite sides, carry a great amount of sand, nonetheless the Ulia flows between them and has a more rapid current than they do and so the Ulia carries the sand off, and maintains a constant depth. Thus I believe that the bottom of this river mouth may not be subject to such changes as those at the mouth of the Okhota. Proof of this is the existence on the southern bank of a lighthouse built there probably at the end of the first half of the eighteenth century. It follows that the channel then was the same as it is now.

4. Ships entering from the sea into the mouth of the Ulia may move either to the right or left and will find water of adequate depth in the Nelbar and Tangaiakh rivers. These two areas will provide calm anchorage for a number of ships so they may come alongside, lower a gangplank, anchor safely and spend the winter. If the space is not large enough to accommodate the desired number of ships, it would be easy to conceive ways of enlarging the natural harbor of the Tangaiakh River. It would require a certain amount of work, but not a great deal, and there is no doubt that it would be possible to accommodate 30 ships or more. The expense could be greatly minimized by using the 180 men presently sentenced to hard labor in the Okhotsk saltworks who are not usefully employed in that port. I am certain that it costs more to maintain these criminals than it would to bring in from Iakutsk the amount of salt they produce, and the salt would be of better quality.

5. The entry into the mouth of the Ulia, both at high and low tide, is convenient and safe. Consequently there is no need to anchor out in the open sea when there is a heavy wind, as is often the case at the mouth of the Okhota.

These are the questions I put to the local Tungus, and their answers:

Does the mouth of the Ulia River change?
They could not observe that it does.

Where is the source of the Ulia?
Along the Ud route there is a river called the Uiu which empties into the Aldoma, and not far from where those two join, the Ulia rises, in the mountains.

How far upriver have they gone?
To its very source.

Is it far?
Ten days travel on good horses.

Can one go far upriver in lodkas [flat bottomed boats]?
One can sail to the rapids in large lodkas, but the river is so swift that no Tungus boat can go above that.

Do trees grow along the Ulia?
They do.

Are the trees big and tall? What kind are there?
There are trees thicker than the body of a man and so tall that the Tungus could not kill a squirrel in them with a bow and arrow. There are larch and poplar trees.

At what distance from the mouth of the Ulia does the forested area begin?
About 20 versts.

Does the forest extend far in various directions?
In one direction it extends about 25 versts, and in the other they did not know. Sometimes they have gone into the forest for an entire day and have not reached the end of it.

Is the source of the Nelbar River far from there?
About 30 versts.

Are there trees along its banks?
Yes, but not large.

Are there other rivers that empty into the Ulia? How far away are they?

From the north a creek called the Gorba or Ulku empties into it. It is located about two days' travel away.

Does forest grow along its banks?
A large forest grows, with both large and small trees, which could be floated down the river in high water.

What is the name of the high place on the southern bank?
It is called Kunkul.

Is there a small river beyond it?
There is the river Chirgirika, located about a day's journey from here, and there is forest along its banks.

Does it join with the Ulia River?
They do not know.

How early do fish enter the Ulia River, and what kind are there?
They come somewhat later than in the Okhota River, not in the same amount, and they stop about the same time.

Do they prepare a large amount of iukola [dried fish]?
Quite a bit, and they trade it with the reindeer-herding Tungus.

What is the name of the river which enters the mouth of the Ulia from the south?
The Tangaiakh, but it is not a [separate] river, it is a branch of the Ulia.

Where does the construction timber found on the banks of the Nelbar come from, and where was it cut?
Some of them recall that it was cut by the [Russian] government men along the banks of the Nelbar River, but they do not know how long ago.

By whom and when was the lighthouse built on the southern bank of the river mouth?
They were told by their elders that it was built long ago, but they do not personally remember this.

From these accounts of the Tungus it is evident that in the area around the Ulia River one can find a sufficient quantity of timber for building ships. These accounts were also borne out by other information. In 1772, for example, Captain [Timofei

Ivanovich] Shmalev, who was here then, dispatched an apprentice sloop builder, Kozmin, to look over the forests. When Kozmin returned he made a written report stating that he had surveyed the forest and found suitable timber for ship construction. Further, as noted above, from the mouth of the Urak River almost all the way to the Ulia, there are lakes which are connected by streams. Thus even if we were not to believe all the above testimony, and were to assume that in the area around the Ulia there is no timber suitable for ship construction, there would still be a way to float logs down through these lakes and streams, procuring them from the Urak River, which, as is well known, has a great many of them.

In regard to the question of fish, according to the Tungus as well as by my own observations, they must be abundant in the Ulia and sufficient to provision a large number of people. Moreover it would not be necessary to prepare as much there as in Okhotsk, because since there is no forage in Okhotsk they have to use dogs instead of horses, and dogs need a great deal of food.

It still remains to consider the important problem of the condition of the track from Iakutsk to this port [site on the Ulia]. Regarding this I will state:

First. The distance from Okhotsk to the mouth of the Ulia River, compared to the distance from either of these places to Iakutsk, is so slight that the route from Iakutsk to either of these two places should be approximately the same. Consequently, even if the difficulties are not avoided, at least they are no greater. The expense and labor necessary to restore the route from Iakutsk to Okhotsk will be the same as to the mouth of the Ulia.

Second. There is the strong probability that the route from the mouth of the Ulia to Iakutsk would not go along such difficult places as does the route from Okhotsk to Iakutsk. An example from 1787 offers the reason for reaching this conclusion. In the fall of that year the Iakuts were for some reason delayed in Okhotsk, and the snow fell very early that year and was so deep it could not be measured, as was true again in 1803. The Iakuts tried, but learned from their own attempts and from previous experience and the accounts of their predecessors that there was no way they could travel in snow that deep. So they moved on to the mouth of the Ulia, and from there went to the Maia River and along that river to the Aldoma. They managed to reach their settlements safely, near Iakutsk. They assured everyone that the Stanovoi mountain range along that way is not as rugged nor as high as the mountains on the present route from Okhotsk to Iakutsk. I feel I must mention that Captain Shmalev also described this route as much better.

See: V.A. Bilbasov, ed., *Arkhiv Grafov Mordvinovykh*. Vol. 3, (St. Petersburg: 1902), 571–587.

10

AUGUST 1, 1804

A REPORT TO THE HOLY GOVERNING SYNOD OF THE RUSSIAN
ORTHODOX CHURCH FROM MISSIONARIES IN RUSSIAN AMERICA
DETAILING COMPLAINTS AGAINST ALEKSANDR A. BARANOV

When Ioasaf, our Bishop in Kodiak, departed to assume a post in Irkutsk, he left four of us [missionaries] in Kodiak: *ieromonk* [priest-monk] Afanasii and *ierodiakon* [priest-deacon] Nektarii in charge of spiritual matters and the monks Herman and Ioasaf in charge of domestic matters. We are responsible not only for tending and instructing the orphans who live with us in our quarters; each of us is also, as able, trying to instruct the local native people. To do this we need to have friendly relations with these people. However, the administrator of the Company, the Kargopol merchant Aleksandr Baranov, has imposed a heavy burden on all the natives, both men and women, through [forced] Company labor and excessive demands, because he is so jealous of the love the natives have shown toward us. Through the tremendous power he wields over them he reveals his anger toward us.

First he wrote to the monk Herman in extremely abusive language forbidding any of us from having any contact with the natives without first informing him. In that same letter he also announced that he has full authority here. He ordered that all the natives be kept away from us and that we were not to have any important contacts with them without his permission as the administrator here.

It is impossible for us to describe in detail the excesses, the pillaging and murder perpetrated against the natives here by Baranov and the local promyshlenniks.

In the year 1800 the first indications of a shipwreck came from debris which washed up on shore. This came from the wreck of the ship aboard which our Bishop Ioasaf had departed. We realized that a disaster had happened, but at the present time we do not know where it happened or how. We do not know whether the Company has information, because it does not reveal to us any news of ship departures.

In accordance with the Imperial decree of 1796, all the [loyal] natives were to be brought here to swear the oath [of allegiance], but there was not enough time to do this before our bishop left. Since his departure, the fact of the apparent disaster and the fact that the Company dispatches the natives to far off places to hunt for the Company, and because they have been transferred, we have been unable to begin to teach the natives the Holy Faith. Neither have we been able to tell the natives about the tragedy which has befallen our bishop, because in the above mentioned order from Baranov to our monk, Herman, we are prohibited from maintaining contact with the natives.

The ieromonk Afanasii asked Baranov to allow the natives to be brought to swear allegiance. Baranov's response was to ask why Afanasii is called ieromonk. Then, using abusive language, he ordered Afanasii to leave and not to visit his quarters in the future. He also ordered that some 20 bold natives [who had kept in contact with us] be rounded up secretly and put in a dark cell like a dungeon. Other natives were pursued with firearms. Baranov took hostages from all the natives who had already sworn allegiance, and so to date we have been unable to baptize.

Baranov also wanted all of us to be put in chains, and he wanted to seal off our quarters so neither could we leave nor could anyone come to us. He threatened terrible things if we tried to make a public reading of the text of the manifest and bring the natives to swear allegiance at any time.

This is why we cannot hold services in the church or in our quarters, and why all attempts to baptize natives have been postponed. None of the natives dares to come to us except for one who was previously permitted to do so by Baranov.

Two Treasury officials, the interpreter Osip Prenishnikov and the navigator Lieutenant Gavriil Malin, are constantly threatened by Baranov and the promyshlenniks. They have been subjected to terrible harassment and mortal threats.

But we cannot describe the problems in detail here.

Baranov will not let us speak out about our complaints to government authorities nor will he let us make known rumors about the Company [problems]. Likewise he intercepts government instructions to us. For example, rumor has it that this year Baranov received sixteen packages for the spiritual mission; these had come from various places and were brought in by promyshlenniks who had just come to Kodiak from Unalaska. However, we did not receive a single one of these. Baranov tries to belittle us in front of the natives by saying that in the opinion of government authorities, polygamy is a legal form of marriage. He also says that we should not try to prohibit native games, or even shamanism (which he considers a form of worship), as this may impose a burden on the natives. He says our attempts to teach them will alienate them and make them hate us.

We humbly bring these matters to the attention of the Holy Governing Synod.

Ieromonk Afanasii
Ierodiakon Nektarii
Monk Herman
Monk Ioasaf

Reference: Library of Congress, Manuscript Division. Archive of the Holy Synod, Box 643, 1–5.

11

A REPORT FROM NIKOLAI P. REZANOV TO EMPEROR ALEXANDER I CONCERNING EVENTS THAT OCCURRED DURING HIS VOYAGE ABOARD *NADEZHDA* WITH IVAN F. KRUSENSTERN ON THE FIRST RUSSIAN CIRCUMNAVIGATION

The ships of Your Imperial Majesty which were entrusted to my command have completed a major part of their assigned circumnavigation. We left the coast of Brazil near St. Catherine Island on January 23 [1804]. We had favorable winds and in three weeks reached the Strait of Le Maire, which we passed on the right, and rounded Cape Horn in 60° southern latitude. Here a fierce storm separated us from *Neva* and we had to contend with heavy weather and violent winds for the next three weeks. We were often very alarmed and our ship took the full brunt of the storms. The ship began to leak and endangered us to such a degree that Captain Krusenstern was forced to give orders to sail to Kamchatka instead of Japan, in part because he was afraid the provisions and other goods would be ruined. In accordance with the wise decision of this experienced officer, I willingly set aside my mission and we held to our course for Kamchatka. Since we had no fresh provisions, we put in at the island of Nuka Hiva, one of the Mendocino [Marquesas] Islands. For two days we anchored in the bay of Anna Maria or Taiohae. We were much relieved at the arrival of *Neva*, for the rendezvous had been set for this location. We remained there nine days but were not able to take on fresh provisions. We took on fresh water and continued our voyage.

Near the island of Hawaii, one of the Sandwich Islands, we parted from *Neva*, which in accordance with Your Imperial Majesty's instructions set course for Kodiak while we hastened on to Kamchatka. On the fourth of July we safely put in at Petropavlovsk harbor. Here Lieutenant Captain Krusenstern unloaded our cargo, careened the ship, caulked it and had other repairs made. Having ascertained that the underwater parts are sound, we are now making preparations to sail to Japan, and hope to embark from here about August 20.

The ship's crew are well, although the voyage was very difficult. We sighted no land at all between Brazil and Kamchatka except for the island of Nuka Hiva where our sailors, under the protection of armed guards, managed to obtain water from the savages. For nearly four months we had no fresh food and no provisions but hardtack and salt pork.

We crossed the equator, and all during our voyage we continually experienced rapid changes of climate. But through all of this, the meticulous attention of our captain saved the men. We lost only one man, a hired cook from Courland named Nieland. He was in poor health and could not stand the changes of climate. He died during a storm.

While we were on shore here a serious case of stones incapacitated Academician Kurlantsev and prevented him from continuing the voyage with us. It has deprived us of a devoted companion, since I found it necessary to send him to St. Petersburg. I have been extremely worried about his serious condition and the fact that there are no medical personnel here. Since there was no one to help, I made the decision to send a medical student, Brikin, with him.

I have also sent Count Tolstoi back, and now I have on my mission only Court Councillor Fosse and Major Friederits. Although the former suffered several epileptic seizures on the voyage because of the hot weather, he never shirked his duty in the service of Your Imperial Majesty.

Although I have experienced a shortage of official personnel for my mission, I have found volunteers here whom I can use. These include two qualified officers, Adjutant Koshelev and Captain Fedorov, of the Kamchatka garrison. I have decided to take them with me, since their knowledge of local conditions may be useful in establishing trade in this area. And since the number of our sailors has also been reduced by eight promyshlenniks who are [now] serving in Kodiak, Major General Koshelev has given me volunteers from among the soldiers who are willing to undertake this voyage. I am taking six men and a noncommissioned officer and a drummer to act as guards to add a special distinction to Your Imperial Majesty's embassy. This is quite necessary in order to gain the respect and achieve success with the haughty Japanese.

I must send Kiselev back to Irkutsk; he is [a Japanese native, officially identified as] a registered clerk, who was as-

These contemporary woodcuts illustrate the conversations
between the Krusenstern expedition's spokesman, P. I. Rikord, and the Japanese. Rezanov's report on the failure of the
Japanese mission in which he emphasized that he held authority over Krusenstern and his officers, holds much interest
for its description of the long voyage from Brazil to Kamchatka and the details of the harrowing life in Petropavlovsk
and it environs. V. A. Divin. *Povest o slovnom moreplavatele.*
Moscow, 1976.

signed to me as a Japanese interpreter. Throughout the entire
voyage he has quarreled with the [other] Japanese and this has
caused bitter hatred and animosity. The other Japanese swore

that he would be appropriately punished, both for having accepted Christianity and for having betrayed his native land. Since I perceived this trouble at the very beginning of their enmity, I had to start to learn to speak Japanese myself, and I hope that now I may be able to manage without the help of this interpreter, thus avoiding an insult to the Russian Empire, for in accordance with a strict observance of Japanese custom, they would put the interpreter to death if he had the rank of an officer.

After I have concluded my mission in Japan, I hope to return here in June of next year, and submit my most humble report to Your Imperial Majesty. That same month I will depart for Kodiak and send a ship to Canton, and from there around the Cape of Good Hope to St. Petersburg.

I hope to remain in America through the winter and carry out the responsibilities Your Imperial Majesty has entrusted to me, regarding reorganizing this region. After I have effected the reorganizational plan, I will return to Kamchatka in 1806 aboard a brig which is to be built there. At that time I will sail around the entire peninsula and prepare a topographical and statistical description of Kamchatka. Then I will journey overland in order to draw up an accurate report about the Chukchi and other subject peoples in Kamchatka. I will also inspect the Okhotsk route. I will be in a position to ascertain first hand the possibility of obviating the difficulties. Meanwhile I will issue all necessary instructions regarding trade with Japan, because otherwise that trade will not achieve the desired success.

I feel it is my duty to report to Your Imperial Majesty that Petropavlovsk harbor can be the focus of all the trade of the Russian American Company, especially when trade with Japan has been established. It will develop into an important city. I have already begun to organize a factory here and I have instructed the Okhotsk office to hire 20 men to build warehouses, initiate various enterprises and develop cattle breeding here. For this latter purpose I have requested that cattle be shipped here, for this region has abundant meadowland.

I venture to assure Your Imperial Majesty that Kamchatka is by no means a poor land. On the contrary, I find that the abundance of natural resources attracts settlers. The amount of fish is incredible; there are vast numbers of marine animals; and the Koriaks have an immense number of reindeer. These, then, are three inexhaustible resources for the beginning of trade with Japan: fish, fat and hides. In addition there is a great quantity of game such as wild sheep which are not inferior to the domestic variety; and there are bears, foxes and multitudes of sables. There are also wolves, wolverines and ermines. There is an unusual abundance of grass everywhere, plenty of forest, water communication within the peninsula, and in addition to these, agriculture can be developed to a very satisfactory degree. But even with all these riches of nature, everything is extremely expensive here, primarily because of the shortage of labor.

In accordance with the authority which the Company has given me, I have lowered the prices on many goods here to such a degree that the inhabitants cannot remember a time when everything was so inexpensive. I humbly submit to Your Imperial Majesty a comparison between the prices I found here, and those which I have ordered.

Further, in accordance with special authority from the directors of the Company, I have supplied the battalion, the hospital and agricultural workers with various necessities, without charge. This relief for the settlers is made possible primarily by the successful arrival of our ship here, and I state unequivocally before the throne of Your Imperial Majesty that the credit for carrying out my task belongs to Lieutenant Captain Krusenstern, whom I recommend to Your Imperial Majesty for recognition. I have instructed him to prepare a report for Your Imperial Majesty on his observations on navigational matters, as well as on related affairs.

In regard to agriculture, I have discovered that the concern and efforts of the local administrator, Major General Koshelev, would have had greater success if he had been provided with necessary items at all times. The shortage of cattle and horses, and even more, the small population, are a hindrance to the development of agriculture here. At the suggestion of the commanding officer, I have decided to recommend that Shishliakov and Zamaratskii, two outstanding military servitors who have made distinguished contributions to agriculture, be awarded silver medals.

I must also report to Your Imperial Majesty my observations about the conspicuous decrease in population here.

1. The inadequate number of medical personnel leads to

outbreaks of smallpox, yellow fever and other epidemics which ravage entire settlements. Such diseases can spread rapidly from one island to another. Many are completely devastated, and there is no way to end such disasters. And in addition to this, venereal disease is rampant.

2. There is a real shortage of food.

3. There is also a shortage of salt. In spite of the abundance of fish, the poor people here have no means of preserving it. They ferment it in pits as food for sled dogs, and in case of famine, they resort to eating it themselves. They even eat birch bark. This causes the outbreak of scurvy and other diseases. The Company has supplied bar iron here for use in evaporating salt, but it is actually heavy sheet iron which is needed for this purpose. We obtained some salt from our own crew to help the inhabitants.

4. A shortage of gunpowder makes it impossible to take advantage of the abundant wild fowl and game here; thus the people are deprived of delicious and nourishing food and are forced to eat half-rotted fish. Even a robust person's health is undermined by this. Many die before begetting children.

5. Even more serious, there is a shortage of women here, and thus an impediment to increasing the population. At present there are more than 30 men here for each woman. Young men despair, while the women, through circumstance, are drawn into licentious behavior and become sterile.

When I have had time to inspect the oblast, I shall report in greater detail to Your Imperial Majesty.

Hot springs located close to the settlement of Malkinsk offer an opportunity for building a hospital there. Merciful Majesty, forgive your ambitious subjects! In order to mark our arrival in a manner worthy of Your heart, [and in thanks for] the lowering of prices, the people of the Kamchatka oblast and we, presuming to carry out Your Most August wish, in our mutual delight and loyal gratitude, have taken the liberty of naming these salubrious hot springs "The Springs of Alexander." We have collected some 5,000 rubles here to develop them and to build a home for the care of the sick. We submit this humble plan to Your Merciful Imperial Highness for review, through the head of the oblast, Major General Koshelev, as the initial co-sponsor of this helpful facility.

When I sent Your Imperial Majesty a report from Brazil concerning disagreements which had arisen between certain naval officers and myself, I worried all during the voyage that this unpleasant news might give Your Imperial Majesty a bad impression of us, that such trivial personal problems could prevail over the interest of the state. I admit to Your Imperial Majesty the cause of this was the intense desire for glory, which blinded the minds of all to such a degree. This enthusiasm unfortunately influenced Lieutenant Count Tolstoi, a youth of tender years, and when at last the desire for our common good triumphed and inspired in everyone a mutual respect even greater than previously, he fell victim of his own actions. In reassigning him back to his post, I humbly beg Your Highness to forgive him, because severe punishment might diminish the glory of a great achievement.

Your Imperial Majesty's mercy is the only refuge for all of us. I consider myself guilty, and in my hasty report I prostrate myself at Your Imperial Majesty's feet and humbly beg forgiveness for myself and all my naval officers. All merciful Sovereign! We willingly offer our lives for You, as we have done in the past, and will continue to do in the future.

See: P. A. Tikhmenev. *Istoricheskoe obozrenie obrazovaniia Rossiisko-Amerikanskoi kompanii i deistvii ee do nastoiashchego vremeni.* Vol. 2, (St. Petersburg: 1861–63), Supplement, 187–192.

12

FROM THE JOURNAL OF CAPTAIN IURII F. LISIANSKII, ABOARD THE SHIP *NEVA* DURING HIS 1803–1806 CIRCUMNAVIGATION.

When I reached Kodiak, I supposed that my voyage had ended for this year, but I was mistaken. The day after our arrival, Bander [Ivan I. Banner] gave me a message from the Administrator of the Russian American Company, Collegiate Councillor [A.A.] Baranov, in which he informed me of the seizure of the Sitka settlement by local natives and requested my assistance. I knew that Baranov had gone there in the spring with four sailing vessels and 120 Russians, as well as 800 Kodiak natives and 300 *baidarkas* [kayaks], and I realized how significant it was to Russian trade that the Sitka settlement had been taken; therefore I lost no time and immediately began to prepare to put back out to sea. I ordered that the rigging be inspected as quickly as possible and that all necessary preparations be made. If the rains and prevailing east winds had not hindered us, we could certainly have put back out to sea in ten days. But the winds were so constant that the United States ship *O'Cain*, which we found in the harbor, had been detained for six weeks.

During our stay in the harbor of St. Paul I sent my navigator to Chinatsk Bay to survey it. Whenever possible I personally made astronomical observations, according to which it appeared that we were then in 57° 46′ 36″ northern latitude. We also had an opportunity to check the compass and chronometers. Number 136, instead of losing 42″ 2, as I had supposed, from the Sandwich Islands, lost 48″ 4; number 50 lost 13″ instead of 10″.

15 August 1804. Precisely at noon the *Neva* was towed out of the harbor of St. Paul, and at 3:00 p.m. was under sail. When we raised anchor there was a brisk wind out of the west. As we moved into the bay between the coast of Kodiak and Lesnoi islands we were becalmed; however, we soon had a light northwest wind on which we moved out into the open sea. The water through which we passed is called the Northern Strait.

It has a great advantage over the Southern in that it is possible to sail southeast on a northwest wind, almost on a single course, especially if one has the ship's oars in readiness.

During our voyage to Sitka Bay nothing remarkable occurred. For the most part the winds were out of the east and the ship sailed quite rapidly. We were also helped by the southwest flow of the current, which is constant.

19 August. At 6:00 A.M. we sighted land to the north northeast. But since the horizon was still dark, it was impossible to have a good look at the land which had been revealed to us. According to our calculations, at noon we were in 57° 08' northern latitude and 136° 46' western longitude. At this time Cape Edgecumbe was about 25 miles northeast of us and clearly visible. I therefore had to conclude that either my chronometers were registering 15 miles more to the west, or that the cape must be located in 136° western longitude. The wind was light all day so that *Neva* could not come opposite Mount Edgecumbe until 10:00 P.M. Even more troubling to me was the fact that we could not catch up with a vessel we sighted to the south and assumed to be the *O'Cain*.

20 August. All during the following night the weather was mild and at 9:00 A.M. a brisk west wind came up. Taking advantage of that and of the rising tide, we reached Cross Harbor and anchored in 55 sazhens of water with a bottom of silt.

From the time we entered Sitka Bay until we anchored, there was not a single person to be seen anywhere, nor was there even the slightest indication of a dwelling there. To our eyes there were forests everywhere. The entire coast was covered with trees. I have had occasion to see many uninhabited places but, none can compare with this for being wild and deserted. In the sound itself it is possible to tack almost everywhere, except for the spit southeast of the first prominent cape on the eastern side of Mount Edgecumbe and the middle islands, and it is not difficult to find an anchorage.

The ship which we had seen the previous day had anchored near the shore beyond the second cape from Edgecumbe. As soon as we dropped anchor four men in a small boat came out to us. At first they approached very cautiously, but then, realizing I was signalling for them to come out to us, they came alongside.

Iurii F. Lisianskii separated from Krusenstern in the Hawaiian Islands, sailed north to Kodiak Island and reached Pavlovsk ten months and twenty-two days out of Kronstadt. He
then proceeded to Sitka Island where he provided critical assistance to Baranov, fiercely engaged with Kolosh [Tlingit]
Indians who had overrun New Arkhangel. N. N. Bashkina,
The United States and Russia, The Beginning of Relations. (OHS
neg. OrHi 82931)

I wanted to encourage one of them to come aboard the ship,
but none dared to do this. I gave them several brass buttons
with the intention of striking up an acquaintance with them,
but when they saw two large boats come out from the islands,
they immediately left and moved off toward shore. These two
boats were Company baidaras. When our navigator Petrov
went aboard he reported that they belonged to the Russian

American Company vessels *Aleksandr* and *Ekaterina*, which had been here for the past ten days. They had come from Yakutat and were waiting for Baranov and his party who had gone out to hunt under the protection of two sailing vessels, *Ermak* and *Rostislav*. To my dismay I learned that the inhabitants of Sitka had congregated in one place and had resolved to do everything in their power to prevent the Russians from reoccupying their settlement. I hoped, however, that this affair would be resolved without bloodshed.

About sunset the previous boat appeared, but with other people who invited us to come to them. I told them they should come to Cross Harbor. These guests were armed with firearms and asked me to trade them some guns, for each of which they would give two sea otter pelts. Their faces were painted red and black. One of them had made a black circle like a half mask from his forehead down to his mouth. His beard and other parts of his face were also smeared with a shiny black. Since I wanted to be completely prepared to ward off any sudden attack, that night I ordered half our cannon to be loaded with round shot and the other half with canister.

23 August. The wind would not permit the ship to enter the harbor under sail, and therefore we had to kedge it in with anchors. But since the depth was great everywhere, that day we could only reach an anchorage, where we dropped anchors from bow and stern.

25 August. The ship approached us which on the 20th had anchored at the second cape from Edgecumbe; this was the *O'Cain*. The reason for her coming to this country was that her captain believed the Sitka natives were carrying on large scale trade with us in sea otter pelts, of which we had actually seen none at all here.

26 August. The next day a boat went out to *O'Cain*; in it were a young man and two grown boys. I invited them to come aboard, but in vain. One of the Kodiak people who had recently escaped from captivity at the hands of the Sitkans came to us from the *Aleksandr* and informed me that he believed the young man in that boat to be the son of the Sitka leader, our prime enemy. However, since he was not absolutely positive of this, I sent him to make certain and meanwhile I prepared an armed yawl. As soon as the boat left the *O'Cain* we set out in

British-schooled Lisianskii surveyed the treacherous waters around Kodiak Island and later Sitka's waters. That same month he sailed in the *Neva* with a cargo of furs, bound for Canton. His lively description is recorded in his *Voyage Round the World in 1803.* . . . (OHS neg. OrHi 83211)

pursuit of it, but in vain. The three young men paddled with such vigor that our yawl could not overtake them. Not only were they not afraid of pursuit, they fearlessly returned our gunfire.

The same day I arrived I went aboard both Company vessels and found they had serious shortages. Each had two six-pound cannon and two four-pound cannon. They had no gunpowder, however, nor rigging enough to accomplish their plan. I was amazed at how these two ferry boats (for they could not be called ships) in such sorry condition could have set out against natives who, once they had committed their crime, used every possible means to defend themselves and had accumulated a sizable collection of firearms. For this reason I entered into a practical arrangement with these vessels and told their leader to request everything he needed. I meanwhile gave each vessel two more cannon and a goodly number of balls.

31 August. Until the 31st we did not see any natives except for those on the previously mentioned boat; but today at about noon a large boat came into sight carrying twelve men, each of whom was painted and had his head decorated with down. They came round the cape of the harbor and then stealthily made their way along the shore. We had sent two baidaras out to fish that morning, and I feared the Sitkans would seize them, so I opened cannon fire on the Sitkan craft. It was impossible to damage them, however, because they rapidly escaped in the strait opposite us.

At that time the *O'Cain*'s captain had taken his barge and gone beyond the forest; as he was returning, the Sitkans attacked him from the shore. I immediately sent out a barge to pursue the Sitkans, but it was not possible to overtake them because they managed to drag their boat over the shallows into another large bay which we could not do with our barge. After this I sent the same vessel together with the cutter to help the men who were fishing, in case the Sitkans tried to attack them; but by sundown all our oared craft had returned safely. Although the fishermen had also seen an enemy boat that morning, they did not encounter the one that had passed us.

We therefore concluded that when the natives were frightened by our cannon fire they had quickly decided to make for home. However, I do not know what to think about how the Sitkans behaved today. If they had no hostile intentions they could have come right out to our ship. Instead, when they came alongside they fired several shots, one of which pierced the cutter which we were just then lowering into the water. They did similar minor damage to *O'Cain's* barge, but not a single man aboard was killed or even wounded.

On the morning of September 8 the *O'Cain* put out to sea. Taking advantage of the clear weather, I made astronomical observations and found that the longitude here is 135° 18′15″′ west, and the latitude 57° 08′24″, north. Ever since our arrival we had not simply been waiting for our fishermen, the other workers and Baranov. But during the previous new moon I had observed high and low tides, and determined that the tidal hour* was at 1:10 A.M. We could of course have busied ourselves making a detailed description of the strait which separated us from the next archipelago, but because of the hostile activity of the Sitkans it would have been dangerous to go out in rowing vessels, and so we had to spend our time in tedious inactivity.

On September 19 the wind was out of the southeast, with occasional squalls and rain. This foul weather continued from 8:00. In general I can say that from the time we arrived, with the exception of a few days, the weather was windy, rainy and occasionally foggy.

At 5:00 P.M. Baranov arrived aboard the vessel *Ermak*. There is no need to describe the joy with which we witnessed his arrival. Suffice it to say that we had been awaiting him for more than a month in this miserable climate and had had no news whatsoever. I confess I had begun to doubt he was still alive.

According to Baranov the foul weather had continued almost the entire time he was at sea. He had sailed in Cross Sound and all the nearby straits and had been in Khutsnov

---

*Lisianskii refers here to the interval between the time of the moon's transit across the meridian and the next following high water on days of the full or new moon. It is usually referred to in contemporary English references as the time of High Water Full and Change; for a full definition *see* The Mariner's Handbook (Taunton: 1979).

with his hunting party, which separated from him on the third day because of heavy winds. Thus they would soon be coming here too. He had made his voyage in order to punish those who had routed our people at the time of the destruction of the fort at [New] Arkhangel, and also to hunt sea otter, of which, in spite of many vicissitudes, he had managed to take 1,600. He had not had much success with the first part of his plan because the Kolosh [Tlingit], upon learning of his arrival, immediately ran off.

20 September. The next day Baranov came to me and brought various Kolosh items and masks which were quite artistically carved from wood and decorated in various colors. These masks are worn during festivals and represent the heads of animals, birds or some kind of monster. They are all so heavy that a ball fired from a considerable distance cannot penetrate them.

Of the things he brought the most important, an item of more than usual interest, was a flat piece of native copper (like a shield) hammered and drawn into a shape. This piece is three feet long, one foot ten inches wide at one end and eleven inches wide at the other. The upper surface is decorated with various drawings. Such pieces are so rare and so valuable that they never belong to any but wealthy persons. Each such piece is worth from 20 to 30 sea otter pelts. We are told that during festival rites these pieces are carried in front of the hosts, and sometimes they are beaten to make a sound as a substitute for music. However, the real importance of such pieces is that they are made of native copper. A similar piece made of our metal is worth no more than a single sea otter pelt.

23 September. Having no news of the whereabouts of the party that had separated from Baranov, we dispatched the *Ermak* to search for the men. Meanwhile we busied ourselves preparing a suitable place for them on shore. At 8:00 p.m., to our great delight, the vanguard of the party appeared. This consisted of 60 baidarkas and more than 20 Russians under the leadership of [Ivan] Kuskov, who fired a salute as he approached the *Neva*. We set off two rockets in response. Although it was still light I ordered a lantern to be hung on each mast, anticipating that other baidarkas would be arriving all night long.

24 September. The next morning no more than half the hunting party had assembled, but for 150 sazhens the shore was teeming with people. By the time the sun came up the sky cleared. But since many of the Kodiak [natives] still were not here, I sent out the barge armed with four falconets, and gave orders for them to be in the strait and if necessary to protect the rest of the party against Sitkan hostility. At 9:00 I went ashore.

It would require a great gift of eloquence to describe adequately the scene that met my eyes when I descended from the sloop. Some families had already managed to build huts, others were just beginning to build them, and all the while great numbers of baidarkas pulled into shore. Everywhere there was intense activity. Some people were spreading out their things to dry, others were cooking food, a third group were building fires, and the rest, exhausted from their labors, were trying to recover their strength through sleep.

When I stepped off the sloop about 500 Russian Americans [natives under Russian sovereignty] gathered around me, among whom were the *toions* [leaders]. Several hours later as I was about to return to the ship, the baidarkas that had come in from the sea suddenly informed us that the Sitkans were attacking the Russian Americans. The armed promyshlenniks immediately went to their aid and for my part, I sent the ten-oar cutter and the yawl under the command of Lieutenant [Pavel P.] Arbusov, and within half an hour the entrance to the harbor was dotted with oared vessels.

At 5:00 P.M. our forces returned and Arbuzov reported that he had gone to our destroyed Arkhangel fort but saw none of the Sitkans. He only heard from the Kodiak natives that the enemy had come in a single boat, seized our baidara and killed two oarsmen.

25 September. Finally, on the 25th the entire hunting party with the exception of thirteen baidarkas had come together in one place. If they had not been accompanied by the *Ermak* we would undoubtedly have supposed they were enemies. It was astonishing that the Sitkans had not captured at least a quarter of the hunting party because the previous day the party had been so spread out that nowhere were there more than three baidarkas together.

Our Americans [natives] were so audacious that at night they went alone right up to the enemy dwellings. In the morning I went ashore again. Our forces had already established themselves in the inlet and each family group was building a shelter. These shelters are made in the simplest possible way. First the baidarka is turned on its side, then four or five feet in front of it they drive into the ground two sticks the diameter of a pole. Both ends of the baidarka paddles are fastened to the sticks. This [form] is then usually covered with seal hide, and the ground is carpeted with grass and then matting. In front of each of these shelters a fire is built where food is kept boiling or roasting all the morning.

The Baranov hunting party was made up of Kodiak natives, Alaskans, Kenaits and Chugach. When they started out from Yakutat there were 400 baidarkas and about 900 men, but now there are no more than 350 baidarkas and 800 men. This loss of people is ascribed to a catarrhal illness from which a number of persons have died. Others have been sent back to Yakutat to recover from it. There are 38 toions in the party who rule over their people and communicate on all matters with the Russian promyshlenniks. Usually the hunting party's weapons are long spears, arrows and other equipment which is made for hunting marine animals but which is sometimes also used for protection. This time they were issued a large number of firearms; however, even these were apparently very little feared by our Sitkan enemies.

27 September. Today, as yesterday, our ship was filled with these Americans. I deliberately gave orders to let them all come aboard, which they were most eager to do. They had never had an opportunity to see such a ship and they were amazed by it. Our cannons, cannon balls and other armaments astonished them. I treated the toions to spirits in my cabin. Of course they went away with the notion that I had gathered all my most precious treasures on board the ship, since the chairs and tables and my berth were beyond their imagination.

After dinner the Chugach entertained us on shore with their dancing. They were arrayed in their very best attire, which only they possess. Some wore a pullover top without any lower garments; others wore cloaks and parkas (like a sarafan with sleeves). They had all decorated their heads with feathers and down. They sang songs, drawing near to us, and each of them carried an oar except for the toion who wore a red fabric cloak and a round hat. He came forward with an air of importance, a little to one side of his men. The whole hunting party came up to us and stood in a circle. At first they sang slowly, then gradually the song became more spirited. They accompanied their singing with body movements which became subdued at the end.

The dancers also provided the music, which consisted of their voices and an old, broken tinned kettle which they played like a drum. When they ended their celebration, I gave each of them several leaves of tobacco and went back aboard my ship.

Toward evening the *Ermak* appeared, and with it the same baidarkas we thought had been wrecked. Thus all the vessels were now gathered together except for the *Rostislav*, which had separated from Baranov when they left Khutsnov Strait. Without losing any time we prepared to attack the enemy and force them to bow to our demands, which were that they not hinder us in rebuilding our hunting settlement in their land.

At dawn on September 28 our ships began to assemble for the attack on the Sitkan settlement. The entire party moved out of Cross Harbor at 11:00 A.M. When we left there was no wind so the sailing vessels had to be towed. At 10:00 P.M. we arrived at the appointed rendezvous. All night the voices of the Sitka people could be heard. From their frequent shouting we deduced that they were involved in shamanism (a kind of witchcraft), probably having to do with our arrival.

September 29. The next day the weather was fair. At 10:00 A.M. we approached the old Sitkan settlement which they had deserted. One Sitkan toion whom we saw at the cape announced that the natives wanted peace and were very willing to halt the discord without bloodshed. We wanted nothing more than to have a peaceful conclusion to the matter and invited the toion to come aboard the ship for further discussions. However, he was unwilling to do this, which led us to conclude that the Sitkans did not have the slightest inclination toward peace, but only wanted to play for time.

Baranov went ashore with a certain number of armed men and raised the flag on a high hill in the middle of the abandoned settlement. At the same time the *partovshchiks* [the Russians in the hunting party] covered the entire slope of the hill with their baidarkas and disposed themselves in the Sitkan dwellings. We set up six cannon in the fortress—four brass and two cast iron. By its very siting the fort could be considered impregnable. Baranov had intended to occupy this site for his first settlement, but since the Sitkans had been very friendly toward him at that time, he did not want them to feel he was trying to oppress them and so he settled for the same site which the Sitkans have been attacking for the past two years, and where they have killed some 30 settlers.

Before we went ashore we fired a volley into the bushes in order to discover whether any of the enemy were hiding there. Meanwhile Lieutenant Arbuzov left the barge to survey the shore. At noon I reached the fort, which had been named Novo Arkhangelsk, and had several volleys fired from all the guns.

Soon after this, in the distance there appeared a large craft which I ordered the barge to attack. The barge engaged it near the last island. After a considerably prolonged skirmish, involving guns and falconets with which the barge was armed, one cannon ball hit the gunpowder on the enemy boat which they had gone to Khutsnov to fetch. The main Sitka toion, Kotlean, was aboard, but when he saw our ship he quickly went ashore and made his way through the woods to the fort. If he had fallen into our hands this warfare would quickly have ended in peace without any bloodshed.

The barge brought six prisoners, of whom four were seriously wounded. It was amazing that in such condition they could have defended themselves for so long and at the same time wield their paddles. Some of the prisoners had as many as five wounds on the thighs from our gunfire.

Toward evening an envoy came to us from the Sitkans. There were three other men with him, but they found it necessary to go back. The envoy announced that his fellow tribesmen wanted him to conclude peace with the Russians and were waiting to hear that we would agree to this. He was informed through the interpreter that since the Sitkans had destroyed our fortress and killed many innocent people without any reason, we had come to punish them. If they repented their crime and sincerely wanted peace, they must immediately send their toions to the fort and the conditions would be explained to them. When these had been accepted, in spite of our anger, we would be very fair and would be ready to accede to their request and conclude the affair without bloodshed. With this reply the envoy departed for his settlement.

30 September. The next day the same men, upon our request, came to us in a boat, but without the toions and with only one hostage. When they approached the fort they were singing something in a long drawn out way, and as soon as the boat reached shore, the hostage threw himself flat on his back into the water. We immediately sent men as an escort. They raised up the hostage and brought him to the fort. Baranov gave him a marmot skin parka, and the Sitkans sent us a gift of a sea otter pelt.

At that time a white flag was flown both on our fort and on the enemy's. In spite of that, the envoy must have come back without any success, since without the toions we did not intend to enter into any peace negotiations. At about noon some 30 armed men appeared, went around the fort at the distance of a gunshot and then stood in formation and began to speak.

Baranov gave orders to tell them that he was completely ready to forget their terrible crime if they were willing to give him the two hostages he wanted and if they would return all the Kodiak natives they had taken captive. The envoys did not accept our proposal, but gave another hostage in place of the one who was already in our fort. In this manner the negotiations, which went on for about an hour, were concluded without the desired success. Seeing that the enemy were trying to draw out the time, we let them know in no uncertain terms that at the first opportunity, without delay, armed ships would appear at their stronghold. One ship was anchored in a bay 1½ versts from our fortress. When they heard this, the whole group reacted, shouting "Oooo!" three times (according to the interpreter, this should mean the conclusion of the affair) and they immediately returned to their settlement.

On October 1 in the morning we began to kedge our ship with the anchors, up to the enemy stronghold, which we reached at about noon. Immediately upon our arrival the Sitkans raised a white flag. We responded with the same and waited an hour for negotiations to begin. However, when we saw no indication of this we decided to frighten the enemy with a little gunfire. Meanwhile I sent the barge into shore with several sailors, and the yawl with the four-pound brass cannon, under the command of Lieutenant Arbuzov. Their assignment was to destroy the enemy boats and set fire to the warehouse which was not far from them, if they had a chance to do so.

Arbuzov put his men ashore and took one of the cannons with him and approached the enemy fortress. Baranov set out after him with two cannons and shortly afterward another two cannons were brought, so that by about 5:00 P.M. we already had a good supply of artillery on shore and about 150 guns. In spite of incessant gunfire from the enemy fort, our men approached boldly.

By nightfall the assault was launched. Arbuzov employed his cannons against some of the gates, and Povalishin fired on the others. The artillery was carried over a small river. The attackers, losing no time and shouting "Hurrah!" broke into the fortress. But the enemy, who had long since prepared a strong defense, opened fearful gunfire. Our cannons were totally successful and the fort would certainly have been taken if the Kodiaks and some of the Russian promyshlenniks had not run off under cover of the artillery fire.

Taking advantage of this opportunity, the enemy intensified their fire against our sailors and in a short time wounded all of them and killed one. Arbuzov and Povalishin, seeing that their attack was unsuccessful, decided to retreat. At that time another sailor was killed and the Sitkans hoisted his body up on a spear.

Realizing that the enemy was making a sortie with the intention of pursuing those in retreat, I ordered gunfire from the ships in order to hold back the Sitkan advance and give cover to those in retreat. Arbuzov put all of his men in the oared vessels and took the artillery with him. He returned to us in the evening. According to him, if everyone had comported himself with as much courage as the sailors had demonstrated, the fort could not have held out for long. The cannons were already right at the gates and a few shots would have given us victory. But the cowardice on the part of the Kodiaks ruined everything. Baranov, Povalishin and all the sailors who took part in this affair were wounded. One sailor died the next day.

2 October. In the morning the enemy, encouraged by their success, fired on our ships from their cannon but inflicted no damage. Baranov informed me that his wound prevented him

from coming out to the ship and he asked me to take whatever measures I felt necessary to end this matter. I ordered the ships to harass the enemy with cannon fire at every possible opportunity, but not to put any of our men ashore. This order had the desired success. The enemy were forced to ask for peace. I accepted their proposal, but with the condition that they send hostages to us and return all the Kodiaks they had taken captive. The envoy at first tried to talk his way out of my conditions with eloquence, but when he found that unless he complied we would not leave the fortress, he sent us his grandson as a hostage and gave his word of honor that all the other requirements would be met the following day.

I suspected that he might have some sudden change of mind and so I gave orders through the interpreter that not a single man was to leave the fort and not a single boat was to pull out until peace had been firmly concluded. Meanwhile, having had much experience with the perfidy of the Sitkans, we prepared for a new attack. I treated our hostage kindly and learned from him how many toions they had, how much gunpowder, guns and cannon, how much provisionment and where the women lived.

3 October. At dawn the Sitkans raised the white flag on the fort and began to send hostages, but this was done so slowly that by evening I had received only nine. Meanwhile we had to fire on the fortress repeatedly because many people were coming out of it onto the shore in order to pick up our cannon balls. Even with all of this, however, we still expected there would be peace, since we were holding the toion's closest relatives.

4 October. In the morning the Sitkans sent us one man and two Kodiak women from whom we learned that there were still some toions who were not well disposed toward us; therefore we demanded they also send us hostages. Baranov came out to me in the afternoon and stated his firm intention of demanding the surrender of the fort, without which it was impossible to conclude peace. We made this demand in the evening so the enemy would have enough time to consider it. Meanwhile I ordered my ships to move in toward shore. Right from the time our ships came to this place our partovshchiks had spread out through the island. In the evening the Kodiaks managed to find

such a great quantity of iukola that they loaded 150 baidarkas with it.

5 October. In the morning another hostage was brought to us, as well as a young Kodiak girl. She told us that our enemies were not confident of their own strength and thus had sent to the Khutsnov people, their kinsmen, to ask for help. This news forced us to send the interpreter to the Sitkans with the demand that they immediately leave the fort if they wanted to avoid being totally annihilated. The entire day was spent in negotiating. Finally the head toion himself asked us to let them spend the night in the fortress, and he gave us his word of honor that at dawn all the inhabitants would leave.

6 October. In the morning we hoisted the white flag on the ship and asked whether the Sitkans were ready to leave the fort. We received the reply that they were waiting for high tide. Around noon the tide was near its high mark but the enemy showed not the slightest indication of carrying out their promise. The interpreter was ordered to hail the fort again, but there was no response, so we had to fire on them. We did not capture any boats this day.

Seeing no progress in negotiations, I advised Baranov to order a raft to be made so that at high tide the cannon could be placed on it and taken in right under their walls. In the evening the same person came to me who had brought us all the hostages. He asked that we return his boat which we had taken; he said that he was just about to leave when his boat was taken out of the water. I refused his request and advised him to urge his fellow tribesmen to get out of the fortress as quickly as possible. He promised to do this and said that if his people agreed to our demand he would call out three times that night, "Oooo." And in fact at 8:00 P.M. we did hear a voice calling "Ooraa!" three times. After this the Sitkans through their singing let us know that only now did they consider themselves completely safe.

7 October. The next morning, seeing no activity, I concluded that the Sitkans were busy preparing their departure from the fortress. After some time I noticed there were a great many ravens everywhere, so I sent the interpreter ashore. He soon returned with the news that there was not a single person in the fortress except for two old women and a young boy.

Fearing that when they came out in their boats we would fire on them, the Sitkans had decided to abandon everything and escape into the woods, leaving some 20 boats for us, of which many were still new. Thus for all their evil deeds they inflicted a very harsh punishment on themselves.

On the 8th the fate of the Sitkan fortress was decided. When I went ashore I saw the most barbaric sight which would have made even the hardest heart shudder. Fearing that the cries of the infants and the dogs would lead us to find them in the woods, the Sitkans had killed them all.

The form of the Sitkan fortress was an irregular triangle, with the longest side extending about 35 sazhens toward the sea. It was made of heavy logs in a form similar to a palisade. There were two inside rows of spars below, and three rows outside. Between these were heavy timbers about ten feet long which were braced against the exterior. At the top they were joined with similar heavy timbers and below they were held up by supports. One gate and two embrasures faced the sea and two gates faced the woods. Within this broad enclosure were fourteen *barabors* [dwellings], all crowded together.

The palisade was so stout that not many of our cannon balls had pierced it. Therefore we attributed the flight of the Sitkans to their having an inadequate supply of powder and shot. In the fortress we found about a hundred of our cannon balls. I ordered these to be taken out to the ship. In addition to these we fell heir to two small cannon left by the enemy. We found a certain amount of dried fish in the barabors as well as salted roe and other foodstuffs, and also a quantity of empty boxes and some plates. All of this led us to conclude that there had been at least 800 men in the fortress.

9 October. Having concluded our campaign against the Sitkans, on the 9th we returned to the New Arkhangel fortress.

15 October. The weather continued to be rainy from the 10th on and was a great hindrance to our work, which involved several construction projects. In regard to the Sitkans, we have had no news of them as yet, although every day some 100 of our fishermen have gone out into various straits. For some time we have been unable to obtain any freshwater fish here in the rivers and have caught only halibut. Some of these weigh as much as eight puds. People fish here in November, and from

then until March go out to very deep water. Thus it is necessary to prepare food ahead of time for the winter.

21 October. The next week our marksmen killed five sea lions, the largest of which weighed about 70 puds and the others from 40 to 60 puds. The meat of these animals is similar to beef and makes good food. The kidneys and tongue are delicious. Today a baidarka went out on the river for fish, not far from our old fort. One of the oarsmen was shot by a person in the forest. This led us to believe that the Sitkans do not want to live in peace with us.

23 October. Today an old man came out to the *Neva*, bringing Sitkan hostages to us. At present he appears to be an envoy from the Khutsnov people, assuring us they do wish to live in friendship with the Russians. He brought us two sea otter pelts as a gift. Baranov and I reciprocated with various presents and gave him full assurance of our desire to preserve good relations with our neighbors.

After this the envoy asked us for permission for the Khutsnov people to take the Sitkans under their rule, maintaining that the Sitkans do not merit our trust. To such a strange request Baranov replied that he had no intention of intervening in their domestic affairs, but wanted to have friendship with all. Then he instructed the interpreter to tell about the killings that had taken place three days previously. When the old man heard this, he reiterated his request that his fellow tribesmen be allowed to take charge of the Sitkans.

After this he related the following account of the origin of the Sitkans:

"In a bay not far from our old fortress there lived two young brothers, but no one knows where they had come from. They had everything they needed. But as they were walking along the seashore, the younger one, whose name was Chash, found a plant similar to a cucumber with prickles, and he ate it. The elder one, seeing this, told his brother that they had been forbidden to eat that plant and that having committed such an offense they would now have to work to find their food. Previously they had had plenty of everything, but now all that would cease.

"After this they began to weep. After some time the Stakhine people appeared from the strait beyond Admiralty Island

and wanted to take both brothers captive. But the brothers told about their orphaned condition, their youth and poverty, and begged the strangers not to deprive them of their freedom, and to furnish them with wives and with advice on how to live in the world.

"Their wish was granted. They had many children and established the beginning of the Sitkan people."

2 November. On the third day the weather began to change. The mountains around us were covered with snow and we felt the morning cold very keenly. That morning great numbers of swallows passed on both sides of the ship. This seemed strange to us, since they usually come to these shores in spring to catch herring.

After our passage to the New Arkhangel fortress we had no cause to complain about the weather. We noted that the tide was at its height at 12:11 p.m.

During the previous week we often saw northern lights at night and the weather was so cold the thermometer did not rise above zero.

See: Iurii F. Lisianskii. *Puteshestvie vokrug sveta na korable* "Neva" *v 1803–1806 godakh*. (Moscow: 1947), 142–163.

13

A SENATE DECREE INSTRUCTING THE MINISTER OF COMMERCE TO
ORDER THAT THE RUSSIAN AMERICAN COMPANY HIRE FOR MARI-
TIME SERVICE ONLY PERSONS HOLDING PASSPORTS VALID FOR
SEVEN YEARS

The Governing Senate reviewed the following:
1. Your report that Governor General Selifontov of Tobolsk and Irkutsk requests an order that the [Russian Ameri-
can] Company hire for maritime service to America [only]
persons who have first received from their home units special
seven-year official transfer documents. He cited as an example
[of problems] the case of a man named Shutov from Tomsk
who took goods worth 1,436 rubles from various persons, and
then squandered it all and decided to [escape and] take a sea
voyage aboard ships of the [Russian] American Company. But
since the Governor General's request departs from a decision
made by the Governing Senate in 1801, you have submitted
copies of two memoranda concerning this from the Governor
General, together with a report from the Main Administration
of the [Russian] American Company for review by the Governing Senate. You have noted that if there were orders stipulating
that the Company could only hire persons for its business who
could receive seven-year passports from their gubernia administrations, the number of available persons would diminish.
The reason is that working people of other gubernias [than Ir-
kutsk] will not be able to secure such passports, since they will
have no prior guarantee of being accepted by the Company.

2. Two memoranda to you, Minister of Commerce, from
Governor General Selifontov of Irkutsk, Tobolsk and Tomsk,
and a report from the Main Administration of the Russian
American Company.

3. A report from the Main Administration of the Russian
American Company which submits, in accordance with Point
Two of the ukaz of the Governing Senate to the Irkutsk Gubernia Administration of March 28, 1784, that in issuing passports to workers who are dispatched on voyages, on the one
hand this should not in any way interfere in the hunting which

supports the Kiakhta [fur] trade, and on the other hand, since they often spend several years on islands without any news and are deprived of any opportunity to receive passports at an appropriate time, for these reasons they should be issued passports valid for seven years.

In Point Three, reference is made to the provision that managers of the Company who hire these workers must pay the state taxes for all workers whom they send out to sea, when they return those workers to the port of Okhotsk. In case a worker deserts, the manager must pay the taxes for the runaway until a new census is taken [not done on a regular basis].

Because of this, and on the basis of Imperial privileges granted to the Russian American Company on July 8, 1799, Point Six, as well as by virtue of the ukaz of the Governing Senate of February 16, 1801, which was sent to the Irkutsk Gubernia Administration, up until the present time the Company has not had a problem in obtaining seven-year passports for its workers whom it hires for work at sea. Such persons come to the Company from their own home regions in search of work, carrying the usual travel papers and passports. They must hand in these papers to the authorities when they request the seven-year passports. The Company has always taken on the obligation of paying state taxes for these persons, and is paying these at the present time, without deductions.

Now, however, the Irkutsk Gubernia Administration asks that in the future, promyshlenniks who are hired by the Company, in addition to travel papers and passports, have a legal document confirming that they will be hired by the Company. As a result, if the Company is prohibited from hiring people to hunt who have only the usual passports and travel papers as legal evidence that they are not fugitives or under suspicion, it will [in effect] be deprived of hiring workers for service, and its extensive enterprises in America, which require a constant resupply of labor, will come to ruin.

For this reason, the Company has requested the right to issue, without hindrance, seven-year passports to persons it hires who have the usual passports and travel papers. However, people belonging to the pomeshchiks must have specific permission to be hired as promyshlenniks. [The Company requests] that the earlier decree of the Governing Senate be reaffirmed, which will obviate the difficulties which the Company is encountering. Then the Company, in addition to paying state taxes, will assume responsibility for any of its hired promyshlenniks found to have debts or to have committed some crime. In such a case as soon as there is a request from any office, the Company will return that person from America on the first available transport. For this reason the Company will also publish in newspapers the names of workers it hires for service.

The Company humbly requests a favorable resolution to its request.

We have decreed as follows:

The Imperial decree of His Imperial Majesty [Paul I] of July 8, 1799, granted privileges to the Russian American Company, Point Six of which stipulates that the Company may hire for voyages, hunting and enterprises any persons belonging to free categories who are not under suspicion, who have legal evidence of their status. Because of the great distances they were being sent, gubernia authorities were instructed to give state settlers and other classes of free persons passports valid for seven years. The Company may not hire pomeshchiks' peasants and household serfs without permission from their pomeshchiks. The Company must pay state taxes for all persons it hires.

The ukaz of the Governing Senate, dated February 16, 1801, to the Irkutsk Gubernia Administration ordered that the Administration was not to interfere in any way whatsoever, nor to cause any obstacle to the hiring procedure, or to the dispatch of free workers to hunt for the Company in accordance with the privileges granted to the Russian American Company by His Imperial Majesty. Further, at the request of the workers, the Administration is instructed to issue them seven-year passports without exception and inform all other Gubernia administrations from where they had come and assume responsibility for seeing to it that in the future any hindrance to trade will be eliminated, on the basis of the privileges granted by the Emperor [to the Company]. Any officials causing difficulties are to be severely punished.

If workers are hired by the Company who in the future may be sought by authorities, before their seven-year passports have elapsed, the Russian American Company office is to be contacted, and the wanted person returned to the place from which he came without delay.

If there are any doubts concerning the issuance of seven-year passports to persons hired by the Russian American Company, the following procedures should be implemented.

In accordance with the privileges granted to the Company by His Imperial Majesty of July 8, 1799, Point Six, and the ukaz of the Governing Senate of February 16, 1801, the Company may hire for sea duty only persons who have been issued seven-year passports by the Irkutsk Gubernia Administration. The Irkutsk Gubernia Administration must provide seven-year passports for such voyage to free persons who submit the usual passports and travel papers from their gubernia administrations, without demanding special documents authorizing the voyage. Persons belonging to pomeshchiks, and peasants who have permission from their pomeshchiks, are also to be issued passports, but the names of those hired by the Company are to be sent to their respective gubernia administrations.

In this manner the Russian American Company will not encounter any problems or shortages of hired workers. By taking on the obligation of publishing the list of names of hired people in the newspapers, and by returning criminal suspects or debtors to their original places by first available transport from America, upon request of authorities, no worker with debts, or one who may be guilty of a crime, will escape lawful punishment.

Reference: *PSZ*. First Series, Vol. 28, No. 21,705, pp. 972–975.

14

A REPORT FROM NIKOLAI P. REZANOV TO EMPEROR ALEXANDER I
CONCERNING INSUBORDINATION DURING HIS EXPEDITION, AND
THE PRESENT CONDITION OF AFFAIRS IN KAMCHATKA

Most Gracious Sovereign! A subject of Yours who has been insulted and greatly offended makes bold to appeal to the throne of the just and merciful Monarch and open his soul. Sovereign, please spare me precious time to hear my problems patiently.

When I was chosen to achieve great deeds for Your Glory, I willingly accepted the challenge, not in expectation of rewards or personal gain, but only to benefit the Fatherland. Your Imperial Majesty entrusted me with the leadership of an expedition around the world, with the particular aim of promoting trade. You gave me instructions, the Russian American Company gave me its full authority, and I was entrusted with the responsibility for all of its enterprises, ships and capital goods. So strongly bolstered with such flattering responsibilities, how could I have anticipated a disaster arising from disorderly conduct and insubordination?

Most Merciful Sovereign, I do not ask for justice for myself. The situation was a disgrace to Russia, and especially since it occurred on Your Name Day, which is such a joyful time for us. I only want Your Majesty to know the truth so as not to blame me, but to see my sacrifice. This is the only thing that can assuage my despair and reinvigorate my depressed strength, the last vestiges of which I offer up to Your Will. I want to emphasize that I am guided not by vengeance; in fact, Sovereign, I request favor for my enemies. They are evil men and therefore they are more unfortunate than I. But they overcame obstacles to carry out such a glorious voyage. Sovereign, I only want You to be informed of their moral weakness, which in distant regions results in disaster.

Without enumerating the many unworthy details bearing on the entire affair, I will present here only the main outlines. Captains Lieutenant [Ivan] Krusenstern and [Iurii] Lisianskii signed a contract with the [Russian American] Company for

5,800 [rubles] per year, with a bonus of 10,000 rubles apiece. The Company also planned to put Krusenstern in charge of trade, but when Your Majesty appointed me, the Company empowered me to be its sole representative. This precipitated malice and envy. Even before we raised anchor I sensed the ill feeling, and so I informed Krusenstern of the contents of Your instructions. There was no need for me to read them formally because everyone knew the content, even though this was not a published document.

We reached Copenhagen. They wanted me to replace the prikashchik Shemelin with another man from Reval whom they had selected; they said Shemelin was not qualified. I responded politely that I would like to oblige them but that would be contrary to the intentions of the Company. It is true that Shemelin does not speak other languages, but he is a sober-minded person and he understands trade. Please examine his qualifications in the appended statement he has submitted. This was a failure in their calculations, and the source of my disaster!

During our voyage we met Sidney Smith. Krusenstern did not mention to him that I was aboard the ship, but that is beside the point. When we met with the *Virginia* he [Krusenstern] advised me to transfer to that ship and then proceed to England by land in order to purchase the necessary maps and instruments. I perceived his self interest in this, since in that way he would be the commanding officer when the ship arrived in Falmouth.

Finally we proceeded en route to Tenerife. [The officers] also planned to stop in Madeira. I politely told them the winds were favorable in Tenerife and that it would be unnecessary to put into harbor there. We arrived and gained time. It was here that open hostility developed. [However] I kept silent about many things and we proceeded to Brazil. There the activities of Count [Fedor] Tolstoi are well known to Your Majesty. We spent six weeks there and replaced the masts. This work was contracted at 300 piasters, but on the day of departure they paid 1,000 piasters. All this time they treated me as an outsider. I am ashamed to describe their coarseness and disorderly conduct. They thought they would exhaust my patience so I would leave the ship and return to Russia, but they were mistaken.

Once we left Brazil the angry encounters continued, one giving rise to another. I was not informed about the rendezvous or the stopover. I became the butt of their jokes and laughter! Without my consent they partitioned off my cabin on the ship. Academician [Stepan] Kurlantsev [the Academy artist] was deprived of mess hall privileges and was kept on the forecastle for six weeks because he had made a formal complaint to me against Tolstoi. When I asked the reason for his exclusion, Lieutenant [Makarii] Ratmanov shouted that the naval officers had made that decision and it was none of my business, that I was nothing but a passenger. But this is a minor matter.

When we approached the Marquesas, the sailors told me there was a plot against my life and that if I valued my life I should not go ashore. However, I went with them, since I would have persons around me whom I trusted. Then there was an attempt to kill me in my cabin, but the sailors protected me by organizing a constant guard. I slept with loaded pistols.

I had proposed collecting rarities for the Academy, but they gave me no opportunity to do this. They greedily filled their own cabinets. I endured this, but when they had the gall to take axes away from the clerk, many of which were meant for barter, I was compelled to ask the captain [Krusenstern] if he was not ashamed to act in such an immature way.

He immediately shouted at me asking how I dared to say such a thing!

[I said,] "I dare to say even more, as your superior!"

"You, superior!" [he retorted].

I withdrew into my cabin. He dashed up to me in a fit of anger and shouted that he would deal with me in a way I had never anticipated.

I asked him to spare me his shouts.

He then went aboard *Neva* to Lisianskii, his second in command. They agreed that the officers of both ships would be my judges. The officers of *Neva*, however, except for [Vasilii] Berkh, did not take part in this.

When they returned they summoned the crew and demanded that I hand over Your Majesty's ukazes. I refused to comply with this insulting request. These demands were relayed through Lieutenant [Fedor] Romberg, who was often drunk to the point of unconsciousness even while on watch. I remained silent. They decided to take me by force. Tolstoi lunged toward me but was stopped. The foul language continued. In order to halt this disorderly conduct I stepped forward and revealed Your Imperial Majesty's personal instructions. The captain always wore his cap, so I ordered him to remove it in respect for Your person. Then I read the instructions to him.

Laughter broke out! They asked, "Who wrote these?"

I replied, "Alexander, your Sovereign, signed these."

"We know that, but who wrote them? He will sign anything."

Then Lisianskii said, "Our commanding officer is Krusenstern."

Ratmanov shouted, "He [Rezanov] is a runaway public procurator. That son-of-a-bitch should be locked up in his cabin!" He supplemented this with all the rich vocabulary of a carriage driver, which I had often heard used by the lower classes, but never like this. He assumed an even more patronizing attitude.

Lisianskii interjected, "I have a rather useful prikashchik named [Petr] Korobitsyn."

Ratmanov said, "We will make him the master of his berth."

I went back to my cabin and became insensible. Illness sapped my strength. The cursing continued constantly, but sailors secretly brought me food. The doctor never once came to see me; I was given no medications. When we crossed the equator I was overcome by the terrible heat and humidity. I stayed in my little enclosure almost until we reached Kamchatka, never once venturing out onto the quarterdeck.

It appeared that my death would be the only thing that would satisfy them. When I slept they deliberately rapped on the bulkhead by my head. When I asked to bathe they poured dirty water over me. The only one who did not take part in this harassment was Lieutenant [Petr] Golovachev. He was always quiet and considerate.

In short, even criminals would not devise such tyranny. Sovereign, this is what I have endured!

When we reached Kamchatka everything went on in the same way. At that point I should have asked for help from General Major Koshelev, and I should have set out to return to

Your Majesty. My eyes were filled with tears and I grieved, [but] I forgot all [my problems] and departed for Japan.

Meanwhile they had persuaded the naturalist Tilesius that I had no authority to give him orders, that this would be contrary to Krusenstern's contract. Tilesius believed this, and I gave up on him. When we reached Japan they appeared to be meek, but secretly they persuaded Tilesius, shortly after we reached Japan and during my audience with the Japanese officials, to reveal to them our intentions in Nagasaki. I was stunned. When I reprimanded Tilesius and asked why he had done this without talking with me, he replied that I was not his leader!

Sensing new jests in the offing, I took strong measures to put an end to them. But when we left Japan there were new pranks! Through interpreters I had obtained 2,000 small sacks of salt for Kamchatka. The captain, in an effort to placate the sailors who had witnessed his misconduct, gave orders that the salt be given to them. The crew were pacified.

The [Japanese] Emperor gave the officers and me 25 boxes of silk wadding. Seeing their greed, I took nothing for myself, but I kept out three boxes for the Court and divided 22 among them. New complaints! Why were three kept out?

After I arrived here [Kamchatka] I gave instructions to set out for Sakhalin. They refused to put out from port; they cavilled at the prikashchiks; they took the vodka [intended] for rations and sold it here, to the detriment of the [Russian American] Company. I decided to leave them and proceed to America aboard a vessel [*Mariia Magdalina*] which leaked all through the lower part and has barely been able to reach this present destination. I traveled in very unhealthy circumstances, in stifling close quarters with 30 promyshlenniks.

Here they hoped to find cover by involving me in a quarrel with Major General Koshelev over the fact that Your Majesty had instructed me to review conditions in Kamchatka and my report was that I found it in worse condition than before. The previous year he [Koshelev] had bombarded me with words, but the fact is that a year later there was not the slightest improvement in agriculture. The soldiers here are young lads, but hard drinkers. The weather has been hot for three weeks and the grass is growing, but they have not even started to plant

Alexander I repulsed Napoleon and in 1814 conferred with
William I of Prussia and Francis of Austria in Prague. (OHS
OrHi neg. 82970)

gardens yet. They catch furbearing animals for which each soldier receives 200 rubles or more, but they spend it all on drink.
They are so spoiled the officers do not venture to reprimand
them. We desperately need someone to take charge here.

Soon the Kamchadals will be annihilated. The naval officers [Nikolai A.] Khvostov and [Gavriil I.] Davydov, who
spent the winter here, have confirmed the accuracy of these
rumors to me. They have told me that this year all the dogs
and native people living between the harbor [Petropavlovsk]
and Verkhnekamchatsk are in pitiful condition, and dying.
The soldiers have transported provisions with their dogs at a
fee of 4.50 rubles per pud, but it was the Kamchadals who had
to feed them without being reimbursed. Every native had to
provide 900 fish to make iukola to feed the soldiers' dogs. How
could the natives fish for their own needs? Then all winter they
had to deliver the post.

I took the brother of Adjutant Koshelev to Japan in order to verify his information, but in spite of his ability he is not suited for this region. Rumor has it that he has a different interest. He commands 500 cossacks here, all of whom fear him. One can say that this young man administers the entire oblast. He travels with his people to ostrozheks carrying vodka, which our officers have now enabled him to buy from the sailors.

Everything here is in a state of collapse. Everything that exists here was built in the past by Major Shmalev; nothing is new. In short, the battalion here in its present condition will be completely detrimental to the native inhabitants. I am glad, however, that I have been able to use the salt I brought from Japan to fill the needs of the inhabitants for a year or more. I have also brought them chickens, pigs and seeds, but I believe this is useless.

Most Merciful Sovereign, decree that someone [else] inspect this region, and conceal my name. I most humbly entreat You to reward my zeal by keeping my name out of the report. I say this because during Your most illustrious rule, tears flow in rivers here, whereas with the great abundance of nature there should be prosperity.

Last year we contracted to set aside 5,000 rubles for the construction of an infirmary, but the year has gone by and nothing has been done. When even a century passes, still nothing will be done. My deep concern will obviously turn everyone against me, but I will never give up the cause to which I am committed.

> Your Imperial Majesty's most loyal subject,
> Active Councillor Rezanov

Reference: Library of Congress, Manuscript Division. Yudin Collection, Box 2.

15

A LETTER FROM NIKOLAI P. REZANOV TO THE DIRECTORS OF THE
RUSSIAN AMERICAN COMPANY REGARDING RUSSIAN ORTHODOX
MISSIONARIES IN ALASKA

My dear Sirs. . . .
In regard to the religious mission I will tell you that the members have baptized several thousand natives here, but literally just that, baptized them. Seeing the dispositions of the Kodiak people somewhat more tractable, I attribute this not so much to the work of the mission as to the passage of time and the natives' own efforts. Our monks have never followed the methods of the Jesuits in Paraguay; they have never tried to understand the beliefs of the savages; and they have never understood how to become part of the larger policies of the government or of the Company.

They baptize the American natives and then when the natives imitate the monks for half an hour and can make the sign of the cross properly, the missionaries are proud of their success and do not develop the natives' greater capabilities. The monks simply return from their work thinking that the whole matter was accomplished with a nod and a wink. Because the missionaries have too much time on their hands they have interfered in civil aspects of administration, referring to themselves as a governmental body. The disgruntled officer group has used them as a weapon against the Administrator, which has caused bitterness and imperils the entire region.

I will cite one example for you. When the Sovereign [Alexander I] ascended the Throne, the monks, without informing the Administrator, sent messages to all the settlements saying that the natives were to gather on Kodiak to swear the oath of loyalty. There were no provisions on Kodiak, and if the Administrator had not managed to send his own people to prevent them from gathering there, several thousand of the natives assembled would have died of starvation.

Further, without informing the Administrator [the monks] set out for any place where they took it into their heads to make converts. On the Alaska Peninsula near Iliamna Lake, now Lake Shelikhov, trade had been developed with mountain natives and offered great potential. The monk Iuvenalii immediately hurried there to proselytize; he conducted forced baptisms and performed marriages, taking young women away from some [men] and giving them to others. The American natives tolerated all this madness and even put up with beatings for quite a while, but finally decided they had to get rid of this depraved person. They took counsel among themselves and solved the problem by killing the priest. There is no need to grieve over him, but in their rage the natives also killed the entire artel of Russians and Kodiaks; not a single one of them survived.

Since then the natives feed on vengeance. They fear Russian settlement. And although the Russians have made some mistakes, they now are being given no quarter; last year five Russians were killed. I have warned the Holy Fathers that if they make a single move without approval from the Administrator, or if they interfere in any civil matter, I have authorized the Administrator to send any transgressors back to Russia where they will be defrocked and punished for endangering public safety. When they heard this, they wept and fell to their knees and said officials had instructed them and they promised to conduct themselves in the future in such a manner that the Administrator would always make favorable reports about them. I reprimanded them privately in the presence of Father Gideon, but afterward I treated them with the respect due their religious rank. My monks realize they have used bad judgment and are very eager to give their services to the Company through agricultural work and in education of the young people.

Father Nektarii is especially able in this regard. I have assigned him to be in charge of the school and have promised him official financial backing which he certainly deserves for his work. I have entrusted twenty young lads to Father Herman to be taught practical agriculture. I took them with me to Elovoi Island so they could learn how to plant grain, potatoes and garden produce, gather mushrooms and berries, tie fishing nets and prepare supplies for fishing and the like. They will be brought to school for the winter so they will learn to read and write and study their catechism. In this way I hope to prepare the first twenty young families to be farm workers for you. I believe that once these young lads become accustomed to working they will be trustworthy and able farmers for the Company.

I further explained to [the missionaries] the responsibilities of the mission. I chided them for not having learned any of the dialects of the American natives so far; I told them they must do this not only to be able to pray, but to be able to deliver a sermon in the language of the American natives.

I have instructed them to compile a dictionary so they will not always have to depend on an antagonistic interpreter; they must be like bears in every new venture. Meanwhile I have personally begun to compile a dictionary, with a great deal of work. I am appending it to this report, and I humbly ask that it be published for the benefit of the American schools, and once it is printed, be sent here. Everyone assigned to Company service in America should take a copy with him, and all literate persons already here will want a copy. Copies should also be available in all offices of Siberia. I hope that because of its novelty the dictionary will be used throughout Russia, and that a percentage of the sales receipts may be set aside to educate young natives. Please note that the purpose of the mission is based on proper and solid rules. . . .

See: P. A. Tikhmenev. *Istoricheskoe obozrenie obrazovaniia Rossiisko Amerikanskoi kompanii i deistvii eia do nastoiashchago vremeni*, Vol. 2, (St. Petersburg: 1861–1863) Appendix, 197; 214–216.

16

A LETTER FROM NIKOLAI P. REZANOV TO THE DIRECTORS OF THE
RUSSIAN AMERICAN COMPANY REGARDING THE CHARACTER OF THE
CHIEF ADMINISTRATOR, ALEKSANDR A. BARANOV

M y dear Sirs. . . .
Concerning [A.A.] Baranov I can tell you that the loss
of this man from this region would be a loss not just for the
Company but for the entire Fatherland. Believe me that he
values his honor above his life. If we lost Baranov we would be
deprived of the means to realize the sweeping plans for which
his work has paved the way. The name of this distinguished
elder is known in the United States of America, but unfortunately it has not yet reached the same status among his own
countrymen; while he receives praise from other nations he
drinks from the cup of bitterness of his own people. And Oh
God! He accomplishes everything with such successful management! When the Most Gracious Sovereign [Alexander I]
gave him the rank of Collegiate Counselor he shed tears of
gratitude as he realized the Monarch's esteem for him in the
distant regions where he was trying to carry out his assignments. He was on Kodiak then and was overwhelmed with
terrible grief upon receiving news of the loss of Sitka. His devotion to honor strengthened his resolve. "No!" he shouted, "I
have been rewarded but Sitka is lost and I cannot live! I must
either die or bring it back into the lands of my Illustrious
Benefactor!"

He grabbed a handful of men who had been loyal to him
and rushed to carry out his intention, but the late autumn
weather hindered him. When he reached Yakutat he left Kuskov there to complete the fort which he had already started,
and instructed him to build two ships by the next spring. That
same fall, 1803, he returned to Kodiak where his presence was
necessary and after spending the winter there he returned to
Yakutat where his distinguished associate launched the ships
Rostislav and *Ermak*, which he had built without shipwrights.
(*Ermak* has presently been sent to the Hawaiian Islands).

Immediately thereafter [Baranov] left for Sitka and recaptured it. He settled there and in that new place laid the foundation for trade with the Bostonians, from whom he obtained through barter as much of the supplies needed to reinforce his people as his resources would permit. This is a tale worthy of a true Russian. If the value of his great effort is generally felt, the Company should unanimously request a new reward for Baranov from the Throne. At the very least the Company must defend him against any criticism.

Gracious Sirs, do not forget that he is almost 60 years old, and that during the last encounter with the American natives he was wounded in the arm by arrows. While I was there two bone [arrowheads] had to be removed. Because of his earlier wounds and his hard work, his strength has been sapped so much that in spite of all his determination, sorrow and illness in part drive him to despair. Glory is his element, and since the success of his undertaking has already brought him a reward, in all fairness his fellow countrymen should do likewise, so they will not be reproached by posterity.

Gracious Sirs, do not suppose that I speak of Baranov with partiality. Not in the least. I have witnessed the difficulties here and I know what a tremendous effort is required for him to hold America. But no matter how much I value his accomplishments, I am aware of his shortcomings. Yet I will tell you frankly that if he is sent away from here at this time it will be extremely difficult for the Company because thanks to his rare knowledge there is no better man to manage the promyshlenniks. But when the region is reorganized and takes on a different aspect, [we must ask ourselves] without slighting Baranov's great service and his virtues, will he be qualified then to administer the region?

First, his age and the diminution of his strength will not enable him to meet the challenge. Second, in spite of his ambition, selflessness and other rare qualities, fate will put him into the midst of wild thinkers. He will have to gain their approval and obedience, and of necessity he will have to accommodate himself to their way of life and thereby humble himself to such a degree that it would be contrary to his intellect and his heart. He is accustomed to pay no attention to weaknesses in persons whose behavior is incompatible with morality. Since

Interior view of a Kolosh establishment. *La Corvette Senavine.*
(OHS OrHi neg. 82971)

our Company must enter into more important pursuits, it is
necessary to prepare people for a different way of thinking.

The outline of my plan also characterizes the qualities
needed in a Chief Administrator. These include good morality,
strength enough for the task, exemplary behavior, firmness of
spirit, patience, farsightedness, resoluteness and profound intelligence. These are the characteristics essential for the position of Administrator here. In regard to knowledge of local
conditions, each official in the regional administration to be
established should immediately familiarize himself with his
duties and the Company's interests.

Concerning [Ivan A.] Kuskov, I will say to you that in the
present situation of the Company he is essential here. His

ability, selflessness, enterprising spirit and practical knowledge make him extremely useful, but he is not like Baranov in having the passionate spirit and farsightedness essential to carrying on widespread trade. In zeal and honest adherence to rules he will always be an exceptional administrator. But because he lacks political perceptions he cannot be the leader. Nonetheless I ask that you secure the rank of Collegiate Assessor for him, not so much to protect him from abuse, but in some small measure to guard him from bodily violence with which he is often threatened.

I have no doubt but that the Sovereign Emperor will graciously grant him this. Such a just Monarch of course will wish that there were more frequent opportunities to reward such achievements which bring great glory. I am not submitting his name to His Imperial Majesty at the present time, because I will speak of it when I submit my plan. I believe that I will delay my request until the shareholders approve my personal tribute to him in its present form and will support me in this.

Meanwhile, I will say that more than once I have found Baranov in bitter tears caused by a Bostonian captain [John D'Wolf] who is wintering here. My doctor has found a republic of drunkards here, right at the time when the Sovereign, as they know, is trying to introduce administrative reorganization here and has sent me as his Plenipotentiary.

For God's sake please act with all possible speed on this matter. Be assured it is none to early to do it, for if there is no determination to control this violence, we will lose America.

See: P. A. Tikhmenev. *Istoricheskoe obozrenie obrazovaniia Rossiisko Amerikanskoi kompanii i deistvii eia do nastoiashchago vremeni*, Vol. 2, (St. Petersburg: 1861–1863). Appendix, 197, 218–220.

17

A LETTER CONCERNING TRADE FROM NIKOLAI P. REZANOV TO THE
VICEROY OF NEW SPAIN, JOSÉ ITURRIGARIA

My dear Sir:
The agreement which has been concluded between our two countries, the proximity of our settlements in the new world, and the great mutual advantages which may result from trade are all factors which have compelled me to come to New California to talk with the Governor [Arrillaga] about how beneficial the results [of our relationship] can be for regions located such a vast distance from their mother countries. This, my dear Sir, is the sole purpose of my trip. It has brought me the pleasure of visiting this land; I am so pleased it is under your jurisdiction, and especially since it is being administered by such a distinguished person as Señor Don José de Arrillaga. Neither any of my compatriots nor I have found anyone to compare with him in stature or the warm hospitality he has extended to us.

New California has an abundance of various kinds of grain and livestock; it may market all its surplus produce in our settlements and may very readily have help in acquiring its necessities through trade with our region. It appears that the best way to provide for the well-being of the missions and to bring the country into prosperity is to exchange surplus produce for goods. There is no need to pay cash and there will be no difficulties regarding importation. It is only necessary that we receive in good time the products we need, shortages of which now hinder the development of [our] crafts and industry. In this regard the short distance [between New California and Russian America] will make it easier for our settlements in the North to exist. At present they import from great distances all those things which they are deprived of by the severe climate.

Nature itself, my dear Sir, has created the ties which may make the subjects of both lands even more fortunate, and may forever maintain friendship between these two countries which control such extensive territories.

I felt it was a duty of honor, my dear Sir, to give Your Excellency a true account of the success in spreading the Gospel which may benefit thousands of people. This truth will be confirmed by all the inhabitants of the land which I am presently leaving to return to Russia where I will present a report of my journey for the review of the Emperor, my August Sovereign.

I hope, Your Excellency, since you are so magnanimous, and know what comprises the happiness of the people in possessions entrusted to you, that you will be favorably inclined toward the region which is the subject of this correspondence, and that you will devote your heartfelt good will to help bring about these favorable results, if this [proposal] should be realized.

I would be most pleased, my dear Sir, to have the honor of suggesting to you a person in whom you could have confidence, who, upon completing his journey would consider coming to Mexico to discuss these mutual interests in greater detail if they are approved by our governments.

I humbly beg you, my dear Sir, to accept here my expression of the most heartfelt gratitude for the cordial reception extended to us in the possessions of His Catholic Majesty.

See: Ministerstvo inostrannykh del SSSR. *Vneshniaia politika Rossii XIX i nachala XX veka: Dokumenty rossiisskogo ministerstva inostrannykh del*. [Hereafter *VPR*] First Series, Vol. 3, 692–693n.

18

JUNE 17, 1806

DISPATCH FROM NIKOLAI P. REZANOV TO EMPEROR ALEXANDER I
REGARDING TRADE WITH NEW SPAIN AND INVESTIGATION OF THE
KURIL ISLANDS

M ost Merciful Sovereign! During the blessed days of Your reign, all seas are open to the Russians for extensive voyages. This new freedom, but also circumstances which endanger Your Majesty's throne with the loss of the American territory compelled me to go to New California. I completed this voyage in three and a half months and on June 8 of this year returned to New Arkhangel with supplies of provisions and the conviction that this distant land of Your Imperial Majesty's is now safe from disaster.

I submitted to the Spanish government an extensive trade proposal which was accepted with satisfaction and now only needs Your Majesty's approval. Its success will resuscitate America, Siberia and Kamchatka. It will encourage domestic industry in Russia, open new vistas to the glory of the Empire, and create abundance everywhere. I am presently going to inspect the Kuril archipelago. The volume of official business does not permit me to burden Your Imperial Majesty with extensive dispatches. I have written to the Minister of Commerce [N.P. Rumiantsev] at length. I explained in that communication my innermost feelings as Your Majesty's most humble subject. . . .

See: Ministerstvo inostrannykh del SSSR. *VPR*. First Series, Vol. 3, Doc. 81, 208–209.

19

JUNE 17, 1806

A CONFIDENTIAL REPORT FROM NIKOLAI P. REZANOV TO MINISTER OF COMMERCE NIKOLAI P. RUMIANTSEV, CONCERNING TRADE AND OTHER RELATIONS BETWEEN RUSSIAN AMERICA, SPANISH CALIFORNIA AND HAWAII

Confidential
Gracious Sir, Count Nikolai Petrovich.

From my latest dispatches to Your Excellency and to the Main Administration of the Company, you are well aware of the desperate situation in which I found the Russian American territories. You know of the famine which we experienced all last winter. People barely managed to stay alive on the provisions we bought along with the ship *Juno*. You also know about the illnesses and the miserable condition which affected the entire region, as well as the resoluteness with which I made a voyage to New California, putting out to sea with an inexperienced and scurvy-ridden crew and risking everything to save the region or die. Now, with the help of God, I have carried out this arduous voyage and I am pleased to submit to Your Excellency this report concerning the initial ventures of the Russians in that land.

We left [from New Arkhangel] on February 25 [1806] aboard the ship *Juno* which I had bought from the Bostonian [John D'Wolf], but my men soon fell ill. Scurvy incapacitated them so that barely half the crew could man the sails. Our miserable condition forced us to slow our pace.

I had intended to survey the Columbia River in spite of all this; since I have sent a good deal of information on this matter to the Main Administration of the Company, I will not repeat myself here, but will only refer to my last dispatch. We sighted the mouth of the river on March 14 [1806], but head winds forced us to stand off. We held to a course to the south and returned the next day, intending to enter the river, but our observations indicated we were in a different latitude [from the river mouth] and we realized that because of the strong current we had been carried nearly 60 miles away and that we were now opposite Gray's Harbor. Its northern shore very much resembles the mouth of the Columbia.

The wind from shore allowed us to anchor, and we sent Dr. [Georg von] Langsdorff into the harbor in a baidarka. The sounding lead indicated to him that the depth of the water at low tide was between four and five sazhens at the bar. Subsequently he reported that it is not as difficult to cross the bar as has been supposed. It is possible that since the earlier descriptions were made the tides may have increased the depth of the water. He observed many smoking fires at the end of the bay and concluded that the area is inhabited. The place [where we anchored] is good, with protection from the winds, and with a sandy bottom. I am repeating here for Your Excellency what the doctor told me, but I personally observed that the shore sloped gradually, was sandy and forested. That night we made use of the wind and moved out from shore. From then on strong winds kept us at sea. Every day more and more of the crew fell ill; one died, a victim of our wandering course. Scurvy spared no one, including the officers and me. We tried to enter the Columbia River in order to recover our health, since it is the only harbor north of California. We approached it in the evening of March 20 and dropped anchor. We planned to enter the river the next day, but the tremendous current and the great breakers in the channel hindered us. The Indians lit fires on the hills to bid us to enter, but the heavy winds prevented us. Finally we decided to seek shelter and sailed into such turbulence that we barely managed to anchor in four sazhens of water. Here I observed the ability of Lieutenant [Nikolai A.] Khvostov, who deserves much credit. Thanks to his steadfastness we saved ourselves and managed to sail out of there even though we were surrounded by reefs.

A brisk north wind, and especially the illness of the crew compelled us to sail on. Thanks be to God we had a favorable wind. At last, on the night of March 24 [1806], ashen and half dead, we reached San Francisco Bay. We dropped anchor in the fog and waited for dawn.

The next day a favorable wind and the current allowed us to enter into the harbor, and we took advantage of this. Aware of the distrustful nature of the Spanish authorities, I considered it pointless to ask for permission to enter, because if they

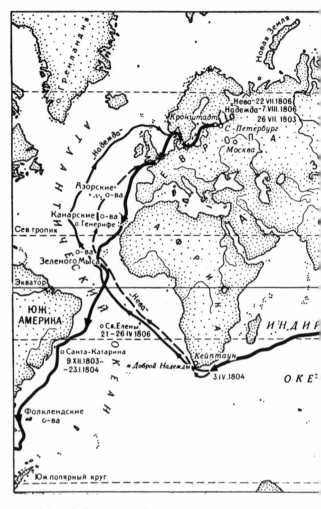

Affairs in Europe claimed Rumiantsev's energies, but the possibility of a strong triangular trade pattern between food-short Russian America, Spanish California and lush Hawaii intrigued the Count. Some of the vexing problems spawned by distance and remoteness might be ameliorated by such a development. The Krusenstern voyage (above) suggests the immense geographical problems which persisted until the end of Russian America. D. M. Lebedev and V. A. Esakov. *Russkie geograbicheskie otkrytie i issledovaniia*. (OHS OrHi neg. 82031)

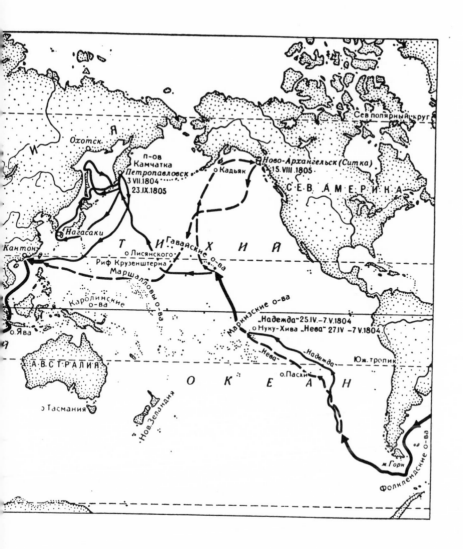

Север полярный круг

Охотск.

п-ов
Камчатка
Петропавловск
3 VII 1804
23.IX.1805

о Кадьяк

Ново-Архангельск (Ситка)
15.VIII 1805

СЕВ.АМЕРИКА

Нагасаки

Т И Х И Й

Кантон

о.Лисянского
Гавайские о-ва
Риф Крузенштерна
Маршалловы о-ва

Каролинские
о-ва

о.Ява

Маркизские о-ва

"Надежда" 25.IV.–7.V.1804
о.Нуку-Хива "Нева" 27.IV –7.V.1804

"Нева"

"Надежда"

Юж.тропик

АВСТРАЛИЯ

О К Е А Н

о.Пасхи

э.Тасмания

Нов.Зеландия

м.Горн

Фолклендские о-ва

115

had refused we would have died at sea. I therefore judged that two or three cannon shots would be of less import to us than a refusal, and I decided to sail directly toward the gates near the fort because our situation was so perilous. We raised all sails and made for the harbor.

As we approached the fort we noticed that there was great ferment among the soldiers within the fort. When we came abreast, one of them used a speaking trumpet to ask what ship we were. We replied that we were Russian, whereupon they shouted several times that we should anchor at once, but we simply responded, "Sí, Señor, sí, Señor!" Then, pretending that we were trying [to comply], we passed the fort and sailed into the harbor beyond their line of fire, where we acquiesced to their orders and anchored.

Soon some twenty men on horseback, including the Commandant and a missionary, rode up and demanded our ship, but we were now a little bolder since their horsemen were within range of our guns. I sent midshipman Davydov to advise them that I was the person who I hoped their authorities had informed them was en route to Monterey, but that heavy storms had damaged our vessel and forced me to seek safety in the first harbor. I said that once we had made necessary repairs, we would be on our way. They replied that the King had already sent orders that they were to assist me, and they informed me that the Commandant was inviting me to the Presidio to dine with him and that they would supply me promptly with everything I needed.

Gratitude inclined me to go ashore, where I was greeted by Don Luis de Arguello, the Commandant's son, who in his father's absence was taking his place. We were provided saddle horses, but since the presidio was not more than a verst from shore, we proceed on foot in company with the Commandant and a missionary, Father José de Uria. The Commandant's very kind family received us courteously. They were our hosts for dinner, and we remained with them until evening, when we returned to the ship. Meanwhile they sent meat, vegetables, bread and milk [to our ship], and after the crew had recovered their exhausted strength, they felt as grateful as we did.

Don Luis told me most courteously that he was obligated to send a courier to the Governor to inform him of my arrival, and therefore he had to ask me where the ships *Nadezhda* and *Neva* were. He had already been informed about them. I replied that I had sent them back to Russia; I told him that the Sovereign Emperor had given me authority over all [our] American regions and that I had inspected them the previous year; I said I had wintered in Norfolk Sound; and, finally, I said I had resolved to meet with the Governor of New California in order to discuss our mutual interests with him, as the head of the neighboring territory.

Gracious Sir, please do not think that it was from vanity, but rather to instill in the Spaniards respect for our northern territories, as well as to give my mission importance, that I announced myself as the Commandant General of the territories. It was to our national benefit that I did this. However, this was not a misrepresentation, because I actually do have that authority, by the will of the Sovereign, and the trust of all the shareholders [of the Company]. I will not misuse that authority, but shall constantly devote myself to the public weal.

I sent a letter to the Governor with the courier, in which I thanked him for his hospitality and informed him that as soon as we had repaired our ship we would depart for Monterey.

The next day the missionaries invited me to San Francisco to dine with them. The mission was about an hour away from the presidio. I went there with my officers. We talked of trade and their strong desire for it was very apparent.

At an appropriate time I will have the honor of explaining to Your Excellency the situation of all the missions, presidios, trade, and the surpluses and shortages of this province. But for now, permit me, Gracious Sir, to burden you with matters perhaps less important in order to show you how I attained my goal without their realizing it although I was in such a critical situation, and the means I used to accomplish this.

When we returned from the mission I sent handsome gifts to the Commandant and to the missionaries. In both instances I was very generous so as to conceal our poverty from the Spaniards, and to cover up our shortages, which, to our detriment, they had heard of from the Bostonian ships. I was fully successful, for everyone received something he valued, and their general satisfaction warmed their hearts to us. Favorable rumors about the Russians attracted missionaries from far away, and those who were nearby had already offered to help supply me with grain.

When I realized that it was possible to be provisioned with grain through this port, I decided to travel overland to Monterey, some 80 miles away. I dispatched a courier to the Governor with a letter in which I explained that since the ship's repairs might detain me for some time, I would like his permission to meet with him. His response was most courteous; he said he was sorry he had not previously been able to allow this. The next day he approved my request. He assured me he was ready to assist me in every way, and was sending the Commandant to welcome me ceremoniously in his name and to wish me well.

I recognized that the Spanish authorities were suspicious everywhere and were trying to prevent foreigners from becoming familiar with the interior of their land and perceiving the weakness of their forces.

Meanwhile the superb climate of California, the abundance of grain, California's surpluses as contrasted with our shortages, and the prospect of continued famine [in New Arkhangel] were the constant subjects of discussion among our men. We sensed they were quite eager to remain in California and so took appropriate measures to deal with this. The third day after our arrival three Bostonians and a Prussian who had entered Company service as seamen when we purchased the ship *Juno* informed me they wished to remain there. I told them I would discuss the matter with the Commandant, and when he refused permission, I ordered they be put on a barren island [Alcatraz?] where they were to remain for the duration of our stay.

Meanwhile we placed sentries on shore, organized watches, and the Spanish provided horse guards. But in spite of all these measures, two of our best men, Mikhailo Kalianin and Petr Polkanov, went to a creek to wash their clothes and ran off, disappearing without a trace. Later the Spanish authorities gave me their word that they would send the men back to Russia through Vera Cruz, but I asked that they be punished and returned to [Russian] America permanently. Unless we deal harshly with these traitors, we will not be able to make others understand.

While we awaited the arrival of the Governor we spent every day in the home of the hospitable Arguello family and soon became quite well acquainted. Of the lovely sisters of the Commandant, Doña Concepcion is the acknowledged beauty of California. Your Excellency may well understand when I say that we were well compensated for all our [previous] suffering and had a most enjoyable time. I hope you will forgive me, Gracious Sir, if I include a little romance in such a serious letter. Perhaps I should be more reserved.

All during this time the favorable news of us which constantly reached Monterey from the port inclined the Governor to be favorably disposed toward me. Fortunately for us, ever since his youth he has been very close to the Arguello family.

At last on April 7 Don José de Arrillaga, Governor of both Californias, arrived. The fort fired a nine-gun salute in his honor and a battery which was out of sight behind the cape in back of our ship fired a salute of the same number of guns.

Although the Spaniards are weak, their artillery has increased since Vancouver's time. Eventually we secretly inspected this battery. It has five twelve-pound brass cannon, and it is reported that there are seven guns in the fort. We do not know whether that figure is correct, because I never went there myself and I would not permit the others to do so, in order to avoid any possible suspicion.

Immediately upon the Governor's arrival I sent an officer to greet him and received his response, with the explanation that he had a painful leg problem and was fatigued from his journey, but hoped to meet with me shortly. This grey-haired old gentleman was very tired from his horseback journey, but there is no other means of transport in California.

The next day while I was waiting for him, or at least for a message from one of his officers, I noticed a great deal of activity among the soldiers in the presidio. It was close to noon when two missionaries came out to the ship to tell me that the elderly Don José de Arguello, who had arrived with the Governor, was inviting me to dine with him. I was grateful to him for his kindness, but told the missionaries that courtesy required me to thank him for the daily hospitality of his family, but now he was entertaining the Governor in his home as his guest, and since I had a political relationship with the Governor, I was obliged to ask to be excused for declining his invitation.

One of the missionaries, with whom we had become closely acquainted, explained to me, "You have misunderstood. The Governor himself is also inviting you. Everyone in the presidio is dressed in his parade uniform in order to receive you properly."

I suggested they should have sent an officer [rather than a missionary to deliver the invitation]. But the merry Pedro retorted, "Are holy fathers beneath officers? We live in America, and here we acknowledge no [protocol] but sincerity."

I felt that perhaps they considered they had complied with protocol several days ago when they sent a Commandant [to me], and so as not to upset matters, I decided to go. Horses were brought and we set out.

I fell behind with Father Pedro and asked him whether they had been given permission to sell grain to us.

"I will tell you in confidence," he replied, "before the Governor left [Monterey] he had word from Mexico that if we [Spain] are not already at war with you, we will be soon."

"What nonsense!" I laughed. "If that were so, why would I come here?"

"We said the same thing," he replied.

This episode revealed that they were more apprehensive of us than we of them, and that they suspected we had come with intentions different from those we stated; they perhaps supposed that the two other vessels which they had been expecting would soon arrive.

Meanwhile, pretending I had forgotten my handkerchief, I sent a note to the ship ordering that no one be allowed to go ashore, and I quietly continued my journey. We entered the presidio. Officers met us beyond the gates. A picket was posted on guard and the Governor, in parade dress, came out to meet us in the courtyard. As we crossed the square and saw the smiling Spanish beauties my worries vanished, for if they had planned hostile action they would certainly have kept the ladies away.

After I had been presented to the Governor, and had thanked Arguello for his family's kindness, I explained to them candidly that the missionaries had extended the invitation to me on their behalf, and that since I did not know what the relationship with these holy fathers was, I did not feel I should delay, but rather I was consigning manners to a secondary place and was giving priority to the goal which had brought me to this region, and was very anxious to become acquainted with the authorities.

The Governor spoke French quite well. He was puzzled and apologetic for the precipitousness of the missionaries. "It is true that I wanted to have the honor of inviting you," he said, "but I did not venture to do this before arriving, for although everything here in California is under my jurisdiction, my right leg [is not, and] has been troubling me." And indeed he could barely walk because of it. "As a result," he continued, "the missionaries who were already acquainted with you took it upon themselves to invite you, but they did not precisely carry out my instruction."

"In that case," I said, "I am even more grateful to the missionaries for managing to bring us together."

The Governor's openness of character, our exchange of compliments at the dinner table and my intimate acquaintance with the Arguello family soon established a genuine rapport between us.

The Commandant of Monterey, Don José de la Guerra y Noriega, an artillery officer and several cadets who had come with him were most courteous to me, and from that day on I became well acquainted with the principal California authorities.

I asked the Governor for an appointment to discuss my affairs with him. He set a time for the next day, but I persuaded him not to delay, and as a result, we began our discussions that very evening.

"Do not be surprised by my impatience," I said. "I hope that you have realized from my correspondence that time is very valuable to me."

I told him about myself and then went on to say that my voyage there was for the purpose of promoting the well-being of the American territories belonging to both our nations. Then, having introduced the subject, I tried to show him how all the shortages of California and the needs of our settlement could only be met through mutually beneficial trade. This alone would forever strengthen an alliance between our Courts. The colonies of both would prosper, the coast that forms a mutual bond between us would forever be equally protected by both powers, and no one would dare to settle in the lands located between us.

I further affirmed that the possessions of His Catholic Majesty in the New World are so extensive that it is impossible to defend them, and that when [foreigners] perceived the weakness of their forces, sooner or later their possessions would fall victim to enterprise. I said that, it was possible that war in Europe was saving them; and that if by reason of the long held suspicion of their Court they supposed that we wanted to establish ourselves in their possessions, I could assure him that even if they were to give us California, the cost of maintaining it would be so high [for us] that it would not bring us the kind of benefits we might realize through trade. I told him to put aside any such false notions [of Russia's intentions].

"The domains of my Monarch in the North hold inexhaustible sources of wealth in furs, and there is such an increasing demand for this luxury and a willingness among northern peoples to spend money for this, that we will never give up those territories which are enriching us and which are so vast they cannot be exhausted for centuries. Thus both Russia's location as well as her profits should reassure you that she has no need for the southern regions of America. If this were not so, you will agree that such a powerful empire [Russia] would not hide her intentions, and you would be in no position to forestall her.

"I will tell you frankly that we need grain. We can obtain it in Canton, but since California is closer to us and has a surplus of grain which it cannot dispose of, I have come here to discuss this with you, as the highest authority in this area. I am certain we can make preliminary arrangements which can then be sent to our respective Courts for review and approval. This is the real reason I have come here, and I humbly ask you to make a decision quickly in regard to my proposal so I will not be spending time in vain."

I perceived that the Governor was listening to me with considerable pleasure.

"We have already been informed of the trust your Monarch has placed in you regarding America," he said, "and we also know of your assignments concerning all matters of trade, and for that reason I am personally very pleased to know you. But my [official] position is quite a different matter, and for a number of reasons I cannot give you such a rapid decision. But let me ask you whether you have recently had letters from Europe?"

"Ten months ago," I replied, and this was a lie, for by chance, thanks to the missionaries, I had been able to obtain new political information before he arrived.

"Do you know that you are at war with Prussia?" he asked.

"That is possible," I replied, "because of the purchase of Pomerania."

"But according to my most recent information from Europe, some five and a half months ago, I hear that Russia's relations with France and thus with the other nations allied with France, are not amicable?"

"That is possible," I responded, "but threats by European powers should not always be taken literally. You will agree that we are now in such a remote corner of the world that by the time we hear of war it is possible peace has already been concluded."

"That is true," he said, "but I think you are accepting this news too coolly!"

"Men like you and me who are accustomed to every kind of danger should not pay much attention to rumors."

I returned to the previous conversation, and he asked me to give him time to consider it until the next day. Meanwhile, he courteously informed me that although he had no doubts about my character, nonetheless the formalities required that I submit to him my papers which granted me plenipotentiary powers, so that he could send them on to the Viceroy.

"Of course," I said, "and so we will discuss this more seriously tomorrow morning."

The next day, through my connections in the Arguello household, I learned word for word everything that had been said after I left. The Governor liked my candid explanation.

He acknowledged the merits of my analysis about the short-comings of their land. He also consulted with the missionaries, who were completely favorable to me, and they informed him about the antagonistic positions of our European governments. He admitted that he was extremely eager to rid himself of such guests [the Russians] in any way he could, because no matter whether he was favorable or unfavorable toward them, he could suffer for it because of the suspicion of his Government. He spent the entire evening writing down my remarks.

When I appeared [the next morning], the Governor received me courteously. I immediately engaged him in conversation about my business affairs. I presented him with the papers from various countries, which I had in duplicate, which stated that I had given the Spanish language copies [of my documents] to the ships which were returning to Russia, since at that time I had not intended to go to California. He copied the document from the French Court and the letter of credit from the [Russian American] Company, and returned all the papers to me.

"I was very much interested in your remarks yesterday," he said. "I admit that I would wish you success with all my heart, but I will not hide from you the fact that I am hourly expecting a complete rupture between our two countries. For that reason I tell you sincerely that I do not know how to deal with your proposal, but I would be most pleased if we were to part on amicable terms before I receive any news from the courier I am expecting."

"I am astonished by your haste," [I said]. "You have instructions on how to receive me, but even if you [subsequently] receive different orders, it seems to me that since I come with good intentions, you are legally entitled to part with me on friendly terms. Simply set the time for me to leave."

"Oh, you may be certain I will do that."

"In that case," I said, "let us put aside any unfriendliness, since nothing at present prevents us from discussing matters which are beneficial to both empires."

"You wish to purchase grain here. Please tell me how much you need. For sea rations you do not need a great deal."

"I will explain my situation to you right now. First, my ship needs repairs and will have to have her ballast unloaded.

In place of her ballast I would like to reload with grain. Second, I would like to buy enough grain in order to take some to all of our settlements in America and to Kamchatka. I need to ascertain whether the price will be reasonable. Then, once I establish the needs of each area I will be able to determine more precisely how much we need in all, now that I have some idea of what provisions California can provide for us. And you yourself will admit that 5,000 puds of cargo does not really represent much trade."

"I agree with that," he said, "but we have heard that you have also brought some goods [to trade]."

"No, but my ship's commissar does have some goods," I replied. "I let him bring these goods with him and I will not deny that with your permission of course I would be pleased to exchange these for grain."

The Governor replied, "The only thing I can do to help you is to allow you to buy grain for cash in piasters. But in regard to trading, I am sorry, but I cannot agree to this because of strict instructions from my government. So I ask you, please give me a note on what you need, without going into great detail, and in the note please give me a brief account about your voyage from St. Petersburg."

I said, "I am sorry that you cannot make a decision regarding [trade]. I hear that your people need certain goods, and I would be very pleased to let my commissar sell them things so we would have more cargo space on the ship. It doesn't matter to me whether we pay the missionaries for the grain in cash, or whether our commissar is paid in cash for his goods. I am only sorry that while I am here the missionaries will not be able to obtain the things they need. You could easily give your consent [to this arrangement]: the missionaries will bring grain; I will pay in piasters; I will take their promissory notes; you will submit the originals [of the notes] to the Viceroy; and then neither you nor I will concern ourselves with how the holy fathers use the money."

"No, no," he said, "that would be trade. And since I have lived for 60 years without blame, I cannot do this."

"But this is not greed, just a desire on your part to provide benefit for your compatriots. You would be justified in doing this as a duty. You are better positioned here to know the needs of the region than officials in Madrid are. I really do not see any culpability in this," I said with a smile, "especially since all the clergy will go down on their knees to pray for you."

"Oh!" replied the governor in amusement, "I see very clearly that they have already gone down on their knees for you! But all joking aside," he continued, "you cannot imagine what a strict prohibition there is against carrying on any trade here. I will give you an example. Five years ago a ship from Boston spent the winter here. It ran up a debt, and since it had no cash, I decided to accept some needed goods in payment. But first I reported the matter to the Viceroy. I received the reply that this time I had made an acceptable decision, but I should never permit any such arrangement in the future because that would give foreign vessels grounds for visiting our ports."

I said, "In order to convince you that the last thing I want is to cause you any problems, I will end this conversation. I only ask you to give me some indication of whether I may obtain the amount of grain I need?"

"You will receive it."

"And in order not to lose time, I will order that my ship be disarmed."

"Go with God," replied the Governor.

While I was still with him I sent orders to the ship [to disarm]. I was grateful to have made a start and I decided to let time resolve the matter of trading transactions, being certain this would work out.

The next day I delivered the statement, but five days elapsed without any grain being delivered. Meanwhile rumors of war between us and the French increased day by day. A frigate from San Blas was expected; it was to cruise along the coast. I discovered that part of the Monterey garrison had been assigned to the mission of Santa Clara, which was a distance of one day's travel by horse from the port. The inclination of our men to become disloyal to us, and the fact that two of our men had already deserted, made our position still more critical. Meanwhile, however, the Spaniards continued to hold me in respect. I always had dragoons as a guard of honor, the Spanish picket would present arms, and the Governor personally met me every day and saw me off. The general courtesy allayed my worries.

Every day, although the Governor did not realize it, the kindness of the members of the Arguello household drew us more closely together. He apologized for the fact that he had not yet visited me aboard my ship.

"Let us dispense with meaningless formality," I said. "I know the customs of your government, and I am certain that if your heart had its way you would long since have visited me. That is the reason that I come to you every day."

"You have gained our esteem ," said Don José de Arrillaga, and I can vouch for the fact that the family of my good friend Arguello takes great pleasure in having you in their home. He is very grateful for your good influence."

Now here I must reveal my personal affairs to Your Excellency. I realized that my position was not improving and that every day the possibility of unpleasantness increased, and I had little confidence in my own men. So I decided to progress from courtesy to a posture of more consequence. As I daily courted the Spanish beauty [Concepcion], I noted her enterprising nature and boundless ambition, which in spite of her age of fifteen years had already made her the one member of her family who was not satisfied with her homeland. Always in a facetious manner she would speak of it as "a beautiful land, warm climate, lots of grain and cows and nothing more."

I portrayed Russia for her as a land with a more rigorous climate, but one which abounded in all things. She was eager to live there, and at last, imperceptibly, I engendered in her an impatience to hear something more serious from me, so I proposed marriage to her and received her consent to my proposal. My proposal overwhelmed her parents, who had been raised in extremely strict religious conditions. The difference in our religions, and the prospect of the future separation from their daughter was a thunderbolt to them. They rushed off to the missionaries, who did not know how to handle the situation. They took poor Concepcion to church, had her confess and tried to persuade her to refuse me, but her steadfastness finally reassured everyone. The holy fathers left it to the Throne of Rome to make a decision, and if I could not finalize my marriage, at least I had made a conditional act and forced our betrothal, which was agreed to, with the proviso that the matter be kept secret until the Pope had reached a decision.

From that time on I established myself as a close relative of the Commandant and already I was managing the port of His Catholic Majesty to benefit my own interests. The Governor was dumbfounded, since he realized he had inadvertantly vouchsafed for me in the warm hospitality of [the Commandant's] home, and now he found himself my guest, as it were.

His 30-year close friendship with the Commandant led him to consult with the Commandant on all matters. Every official paper he received passed through the hands of Arguello, and thus also through mine. Soon the Governor became confident of me. He came to trust me and finally he did not keep even the slightest of secrets from me. As time went on I spoke more and more Spanish. I was in Arguello's home from morning till evening, and his officers observed that I was becoming half Spanish. They vied with each other to bring every piece of information to me, so I was no longer apprehensive about the arrival of a courier with dangerous news.

But meanwhile I was puzzled that the missionaries were not bringing grain, and I expressed my dissatisfaction to the Governor. He told me openly that the holy fathers were waiting for a courier and thought they might obtain the ship's entire cargo free by delaying. I told the Governor just as candidly that he was the reason for the delay. Why was he holding the garrison in Santa Clara? As soon as he ordered it to return to Monterey, all the rumors would vanish.

The Governor was surprised that I knew even his secret orders, but he laughed it off and immediately sent an order to the unit to return. The missions were informed that those wishing to deliver grain could do so, and that otherwise he would have to take other measures. At the same time, at my request, he called in the invalided [veterans] from the Pueblo where, with the assistance of Concepcion's brothers, the grain was being prepared for the first shipment for me. As soon as that shipment was moved, the missions were in eager rivalry to deliver it in such quantities that I had to ask them to stop shipping because with the amount of ballast, artillery and trade goods cargo, my ship could not take on more than 4,500 puds, which included 470 puds of tallow and butter and some 100 puds of salt and other items which I had received.

Our account was figured in piasters, but since I knew the prices in California which were set by the government, I concluded my transactions without error. I will discuss this elsewhere, but I wanted to carry out this trade experiment without delay. I used every means at my disposal to persuade the Governor, and promised him the good will of my Sovereign. The old gentleman wavered for some time, but finally he asked me for my candid advice as to how he could grant my request but at the same time remain above suspicion.

I said, "It is very easy. Allow the missionaries and the inhabitants to submit requests to you, then hand these over to me. Order your officers to verify the quality of the goods and ascertain the prices, which I will make as favorable to the inhabitants as possible. However, you will have to order that I be allowed to see the original invoices for the goods you receive and then I will order payment in piasters which I will transfer to my commissar. You will receive the goods from him and distribute them to the people, according to their needs."

This plan was carried out. The goods were verified, the transfer was made, and my name did not enter into the transactions at all, except for my signature on the general invoice of the goods they purchased, attesting that these goods belonged to Commissar Panaev, and that to fulfill the needs of the inhabitants of California, as well as to oblige the Spanish Government, I had given him permission to sell these goods. They kept this statement in the port office as an official document.

This, my Esteemed Sir, is our initial experiment in trade with California, which may amount to at least a million rubles per year. Our American territories will not suffer shortages. Kamchatka and Okhotsk may be provisioned with grain and other foodstuffs. The Iakuts, who are currently burdened with having to haul grain, will have respite from this. The Treasury will have reduced expenses for the maintenance of soldiers. The high prices for grain in Irkutsk will be reduced, when a substantial part of the grain that has annually been delivered to distant provinces becomes available for its own use. Custom collection points will produce new revenues for the Crown. Russia's domestic industries will benefit substantially because the California trade alone will call for an increase in the number of factories. Meanwhile ways will be found to promote trade with India, via Siberia. Your Excellency may be certain that with a sound and well conceived beginning, all of this can be accomplished in a short time.

I have written extensively in my recent dispatches to the Main Administration concerning the means of raising trade here to a level worthy of a great empire. I will simply make mention of this here. Once again I will state my sincere opinion that it is too soon for us, or rather, not to our advantage, to send ships back to Russia via Canton.

I believe first of all that we should strengthen New Arkhangel, then dispatch ships from there to Canton, thence to Siberia and to America, so their sailings will be faster, safer and more profitable. Ships should be sent from St. Petersburg with necessary goods, but only with the understanding that they will remain here. In this way [Russian] America will be fortified and its fleet strengthened. Siberia will come to life through trade. When it is no longer possible to sell all the goods [here], a time will come when it will be profitable to undertake circumnavigational trade. Otherwise I tell you that it will be all show and no profit.

But forgive me, Gracious Sir; I have started to philosophize again and am departing from the matter at hand. I must give Your Excellency an accurate description of the California trade. I will begin by explaining the measures, weights and coins of California. . . . [material excised by Tikhmenev]

But all jesting aside, Gracious Sir, if you could obtain permission to develop trade with California, the Company could build granaries in conjunction with it, and through kind treatment of the savages, who are no longer so numerous in the projected southern colonies, we could also develop agriculture and livestock production. When we had established trade with Canton, we could even settle Chinese people there. Your Excellency may laugh at my long term plans, but I must emphasize that my proposals are completely feasible if we have enough personnel and resources. With no great expenditure from the Treasury this entire region could be brought permanently under Russian control. When all the circumstances are carefully reviewed and their interconnection is understood, you yourself will agree that trade will make significant and gigantic strides.

All ambitious plans appear ludicrous on paper, but when they are carefully prepared, the results can be astonishing.

Only in this way, not through petty trade, have major trade enterprises achieved greatness. If [our] Government had given its attention to this part of the world earlier, if it had had proper respect for it, or had persistently pursued the sagacious visions of Peter the Great, who with the small resources of his time dispatched the Bering Expedition on its voyage of discovery, one may be certain that New California would never have become a Spanish possession. It was not until 1760 that Spain turned its attention there and secured that region permanently, thanks to the enterprising efforts of the missionaries. A part of the territory is still unoccupied, which could be so beneficial and vital to us. If we let it fall from our grasp what will future generations say? I know that I will not be the one to blame.

We must assume that the Spanish, fanatical as they are, will continue to move [northward], in spite of the fact that I tried to divert their suspicions of us. Their government will hardly believe my reassurances. I am firmly convinced we could succeed in occupying these parts, but I am equally certain that if this does not happen during the reign of Alexander I, we will never accomplish it. The time for success will have passed by, and then it will be apparent that the Russians, despite all their national character and enterprising spirit and ability to surmount obstacles, have fallen into apathy, and finally our spirit of ambition and grandeur will be snuffed out. In short, we will be like a worn out flint, from which one tries until one's hand is weary to strike a spark; but even if the spark is struck it is too small to ignite anything. Yet when that flint had the power to strike fire, it went unused.

In God's name I beseech you, Gracious Sir, to look carefully, in a spirit of patriotism, at the circumstances of this territory which offer the Fatherland such great commercial opportunities. Your Excellency is our only intermediary with the Throne to present to the Sovereign Emperor these concepts which will be immortalized in centuries to come. Queen Elizabeth of England was responsible for its present greatness, and her name is revered by her people. The name of our Monarch will be even more revered if during his fortuitous reign the Russians rid themselves of the yoke of foreign nations and reap a bountiful harvest from their great enterprises.

In my last reports to the Company I explained that my experiences will justify these proposals. All nature has so rightly beckoned us in this direction for a long time. My voyage to California, it seems, has not only verified this, but should convince Your Excellency that there is nothing of the impractical visionary in the other parts of my goals.

I have already had the honor of explaining to Your Excellency that once the Governor unexpectedly became my close friend, he did not conceal anything from me, since he realized I could find out everything from Arguello. He told me candidly that their Court fears Russia more than any other power and that Shelikhov's settlements led them to expect further encroachments; however, the last twenty years have completely allayed their fears.

"Please dismiss all suspicions on the part of your Court," I said, "and explain to the Court the conversation I have had with you regarding this matter."

"You do not need to ask me to do this," he said. "It will be my personal pleasure to inform the Viceroy of your friendly and sincere assurances. This will be all the more helpful to us in establishing closer commercial ties. Show me how the people entrusted to me will benefit, and you will see my sincere pleasure in being ready to assist you."

And, in fact, every day I had new evidence of that friendship. Everything was completely at my command. The garrison was constantly trying to expedite the grain delivery, their people supplied us with water, and in short, they vied with one another to oblige us. Since I had no difficulties, I only gave orders. Although I heard many rumors of war, I hosted the Spanish at festivities and dinner parties and paid attention to everyone in the presidio after returning from my official assignments. The Governor, as evidence of his sincere feelings, and in spite of his weak legs, danced [aboard our ship], and we were not sparing of gunpowder either on shipboard or in the fortress. Spanish guitars mingled with Russian singers, and in spite of all my inadequacies, the Californians, I believe, will long remember the coming of their gift-bearing Russians, for I confess to Your Excellency that I spared nothing to establish the important position the Russian nation deserves in this part of the world.

The Governor and I often discussed trade. I was surprised that California needed so many things, since it had so many ways close at hand of satisfying those needs.

"It appears to me," I said, "that with a slight encouragement of trade, all your needs here could be fulfilled."

"Do not be surprised that we have neglected trade," he replied. "At the present time although the Government is opening its eyes to this matter, it still perceives it through a fog. The differing powerful voices at Court and the interference by private interests do not afford the means to settle everything for the benefit of the general public. It is true that trade has received great support. The class of people engaged in it at present is respected, and the King, in spite of the rights of the nobles, has conferred on many persons the title of Marqués, which has never before been done in Spain.

"The Caracas Company, for example, was in complete disarray, but three years ago it was strengthened in an unprecedented manner. The directorate is located in Madrid; suddenly 15,000,000 piasters were paid in. The King himself was among the shareholders and bought 6,000 shares for 1,500,000 piasters. He granted the ships the right to fly the royal flag, as well as the right to recruit officers and servitors from the navy, as needed. The company carries on trade with the East and West Indies, but poor California is forgotten. I regret to tell you, but it is in fact true that our Government is too indifferent, and therefore it does not have any clear understanding of this situation, nor does it wish to have any.

"When the company expressed a willingness to assist [national interest] by means of trade, certain private interests who had long been sending Manila galleons to Acapulco, protested this support as a violation of their rights. They persuaded the King to prohibit the company from establishing contact with the west coast of America.

"The Manilans continue to send their galleons. Part of their cargo consists of Chinese goods, and although it reaches us, we have to deal with the Mexicans who send two naval corvettes from San Blas every year to cruise along our shores. They supply our needs, but at unreasonable prices. We have to pay in a year in advance, for the things we need and cannot live without."

I turned his attention to the Philippine Islands and asked him with which nations they carry on trade, and whether it is true that the Manilans will lend money [to Europeans] at 2% or 3% in order to transfer their piasters to Europe.

"Manila is our free port," he replied. "It is possible that this lending practice used to exist, and still does, and that the cupidity of the English and other nations who trade in India has increased prices to the benefit of the Manilans. But I know very well from one of our San Blas officers that the English paid them at least 25%. And even at that, believe me, the English enriched themselves, because they made more than a 200% profit on goods they bought with borrowed money in Canton, Bengal and other places. However, I now believe that the Bostonians will benefit as a result of the breach in our friendship with [the Manilans], because after the declaration of war with England they renewed their earlier request for permission to trade in our American possessions.

"The government refused them, but when the United States Minister left Madrid in anger, the critical situation was so evident to our Court that the Court was compelled to send a favorable reply when the Minister departed. Subsequently four ports on the east coast have been opened to them: Buenos Aires, Vera Cruz, Caracas and Cartagena. They have secured the New Orleans territory from France, and because of the proximity of New Mexico to Pensacola, they have already begun to trade there even without government permission. Santa Fe is already beginning to use their goods.

"I have personally witnessed the enterprising spirit of this republic in our waters and I am not surprised at its success. It flourishes on trade and recognizes its value. Who but us does not presently recognize this? We pay dearly with our purses for this neglect, and while the world pursues the prey, so to speak, we are the only ones who are content with iukola.

"I will tell you honestly," the Governor continued, "the only thing necessary is for your Emperor to be more insistent, and the whole matter will be resolved speedily. Otherwise the procrastination of our government will cause problems for you.

The Bostonians are an example. For a long time they pleaded, without success. But finally their determination forced an agreement, and the same ministers who for several years would not give their consent, found it useful to carry on trade, and realized that in wartime the establishment of trade with a neutral power always offers the safe transfer of piasters from America to Europe.

"Be assured," I said, "that when my Monarch professes interest in my project, I will consider it already carried out. But you must make the same strong presentation of the matter to your Viceroy."

"Of course," he replied. "I will reveal my plan to you. Three missions have already submitted their requests [for goods] to me. When I return to Monterey, I will receive more requests from others. I will submit all of them in the original to the Viceroy, with my recommendations, in which I will explain all the benefits you have so clearly laid out. I will only add those things I feel in my heart, that this proposal would resolve all the needs of the territories, to which I have dedicated my entire life. In the meantime, I beg you to strengthen my argument in your letter to the Viceroy."

"Absolutely," I responded. The next day I gave him the letter.

All during this time, by means of the missionaries and his friends, I tried in every way to instill greater enthusiasm in the old gentleman, so his report would be more persuasive. My daily power of suggestion had already turned his attention frequently to this matter.

"I am very grateful that you have come," he told me one day. "It has given me an opportunity to resume my repeated reports concerning the necessity of trade, which never received proper attention because this place is so remote. Sometimes I would become bitter when my friends reported unfavorable responses from the ministers [who would say], 'This cursed land of California! It is nothing but trouble and expense!' Did they think I was responsible for the unprofitability of the establishment?"

"Tell me," I asked. "How much does it cost to maintain it per year?"

"At least half a million piasters."

"And what revenue does it produce?"

"Not a single reál."

"But did you not once tell me about a tithe on grain?"

"That is collected only from the invalided veterans, and even that is set aside for the benefit of the missions in case they have a crop failure. That is why they have sentries on guard at their warehouses. In a word, the King maintains the garrisons, naval vessels and missions, and also provides funds for the construction and beautification of the churches, because his principal goal is to propagate the faith, and keep the people happy. As a true defender of the faith he bestows all his privileges on religion."

As I listened to this outburst I could hardly refrain from laughing.

"This is very commendable, and salutary for the soul," I said piously, "but unfortunately we see so much moral corruption that there are already entire nations who do not profess the goal of true beatitude and who are so deluded that they seek temporal pleasures rather than eternal salvation. The noble intentions of your heart and the fervor of your prayers are powerless to protect your religion, or even yourselves, from such outcasts of the human race."

"You are right," he replied, "and I have several times requested that our military forces be increased, but when your presence in the north involved such a limited number of men, our people's fears were calmed and my requests evoked only promises. However, at the present time the boldness of the Bostonians has awakened us. This year the authorities have promised to send me a naval frigate to put a stop to the vessels of the American states which are constantly smuggling along our coast and carrying on illicit trade. But that is a relatively minor problem. Sometimes they leave ten or fifteen men among us who are hardened criminals, and because our garrison is so small this creates a very bad situation here and corrupts our morals. They even put women ashore. They try in every possible way to settle here among us permanently.

"Some time ago I spoke of the Bostonian, Captain O'Cain," the Governor told me one time. "In 1803 he brought 40 [native] islanders from Unalaska with their baidarkas, and they hunted sea otters all winter long. We do not know where he concealed himself. I will be much obliged if you will repeat this story, which I perhaps should report to the Viceroy."

Here I feel I must inform Your Excellency about this situation. Captain O'Cain came to Kodiak aboard a ship of the same name. He contracted with Baranov for 40 baidarkas to hunt sea otters on an equal share basis on a new island he had discovered. He promised that if he happened to anchor in a place where he could provision, he would allow the prikashchik to purchase supplies for the [Russian American] Company. He was not to participate in this transaction. When he obtained the [Kodiak] people he went directly to California and put them ashore. Whether he deceived Baranov, or whether Baranov was to have profited from this fraud, I leave it to Your Excellency to decide. I will only add that at the time [Baranov's people] were starving to death and their lives were saved by several barrels of flour which O'Cain brought.

At the present time a similar contract has been negotiated with [John D'] Wolf, to which I could not object. Having bought his ship I did the same thing, without any censure and in a large way. However, I gave the Spanish the following account of this matter.

"I am very glad that you have reminded me of this incident," I said. "The Bostonians harm us more than they do you. They put people ashore in your territory, but they abduct them from ours. In addition to carrying on trade in our waters, this scoundrel of whom you are speaking seized a departing hunting group of our American natives from Kodiak, 40 men and their families. The next year young Captain [Henry] Barber, the same kind of knave, returned 26 of them to Kodiak, saying he had paid ransom for them in the Queen Charlotte Islands and that he would not hand them over to us unless we paid him 10,000 rubles. We had to do this out of humanity, but we still do not know what O'Cain did with the others.

"The ones who were returned testified that they had been in various places on different vessels, but which vessels, and where, we could not ascertain because they themselves did not know. I venture to assure you that this and other such things the Bostonians have done have taught us to be more careful.

We are now also taking measures to disassociate ourselves from these intruders. However, because of the many straits in our waters, we do not have the necessary means to do this."

"I can tell you," he said, "that I have drawn up orders which should probably drive them away. I have ordered mounted patrols to ride along the coast. As soon as they sight a ship on the horizon, from their height on horseback, they are to report to the nearest presidio. They are not to lose sight of the ship's course, and as soon as it puts a boat ashore, I am confident it will be seized."

And in fact, about five days later the Governor showed me a notice he had received from the port of San Diego reporting that an Anglo-American brigantine, *Peacock*, 108 tons, 6 cannon, 4 falconets, Captain Oliver Kimball, had approached the coast and landed a boat with four men; the boat was captured but the ship managed to escape. The navigator, Bostonian Thomas Kilvain, second quartermaster Jean Pierre from Bordeaux, and two sailors were captured. They testified that they had left Boston in September of 1805; they reached the Sandwich Islands on February 12 [1806]; only fourteen of the crew were left; their cargo was arms and various items which they were taking to the Russian American possessions to exchange for furs; and they had put ashore only to take on fresh supplies. The following day a letter to the navigator was found on shore; in the letter the ship's captain assured the navigator he would sail along the coast for several days and that he should try to escape. But the men [from the ship's boat] were shackled and taken to San Blas.

I congratulated the Governor on how successfully his orders had been carried out, and the old gentleman was very pleased.

Finally dispatches came in from Mexico, and although they were threatening, I no longer feared them. Newspapers were also sent with the news that Napoleon had decisively defeated the Germans and that our forces had returned. One very unwelcome article from Hamburg dated October 4, 1805 reported that an unexpected revolution had occurred in St. Petersburg, but the newspaper would not venture to give details until concrete information had been received. This news disturbed me, and no matter how I tried to conceal my anxiety, it was apparent to others.

The Spaniards all said this couldn't possibly have happened to a man such as the Sovereign who is beloved not only by his own subjects, but by all other peoples as well, and that all [foreign] newspapers emphasize his good heart and make [foreigners] envy the good fortune of his subjects. No matter how often I heard such impartial praise from strangers, I was always especially pleased, but this time I was even more touched.

"Good Lord," I thought. "What has happened in my fatherland?"

I could not be calm, and because the Governor did not show me the letter from the Viceroy, I thought the most recent newspaper was being kept from me. However, since nothing was being concealed from me, I was soon given the letter. The Viceroy described to the Governor in detail the fierce conflict between their allied fleet and the English. He sent the Governor four issues of the newspaper and supplemented this with excerpts from letters he had received from France which reported that Napoleon had seized Vienna and had forced the [Holy] Roman Emperor to retreat into Moravia. The letter closed with a bitter joke at the expense of the Allies. I found nothing more, and it appeared that the newspapers were not trying to conceal any secret.

I asked the Governor how often he received news from Europe.

"Officially I receive reports once a month aboard a special packetboat that brings them in from Cadiz, but commercial vessels bring news more often. Also, in addition to the usual monthly courier, special messengers bring urgent news to all the important places."

I envied this system and thought how ill-served our possessions are in this regard in this unfamiliar new world. As a result of expanding our trade, we might receive news twice a year.

"But in wartime if your packetboat were to be seized by the enemy," I asked, "would not your dispatches fall into their hands?"

"No, never," he replied. "The dispatch box is always fastened to a heavy lead weight and in case of attack it is thrown overboard. The same news will be brought with the next vessel, because in wartime dispatches and letters as well are sent in duplicate and even in triplicate. If you should wish to write to Europe," he added, "you may be certain your letters will reach their destinations safely."

I accepted his offer and sent a report to His Imperial Majesty, a copy of which, together with my letter to the Viceroy, I have the honor of including here for Your Excellency. . . . [Material excised by Tikhmenev.]

These, my Gracious Sir, are all of my comparisons and observations on this land, made during my six-week stay in California for Your Excellency. Forgive me if I have in some places been too candid in expressing my personal feelings; ascribe this to human weakness. As I observe conditions here [New Arkhangel] I cannot speak of them with indifference, especially since I have had to expend so much effort and sacrifice on them. I make bold to assure Your Excellency that there is hardly a man to be found who will venture to accept this challenge in the future. I have made a good study of the ways of the native inhabitants and also of the visitors who have come to them.

I have observed both groups, I have devised a plan to reorganize this territory, and I have shown the means of ending evils which are shameful in our time. I have discussed trade, the economy, industry, overcoming shortages, organization of law and order, discipline and charity. I have expounded on the fruits the remote oblast of Siberia could derive from such reorganization, and I have not left a single topic untouched. I have traced the steps by which commerce should be organized to benefit our political aims, I have fought prejudice, emphasized the obvious. Perhaps not in the best way, but at least with my soul and heart I have presented reams of papers and have sent them to the Main Administration [of the Russian American Company], and if all of this does not merit their attention, what does?

If my assessment of matters, both present and future, in both negative and positive aspects, does not prompt their attention, I will be bitterly disappointed with my work, and I will have an even more painful feeling that unfortunate results will force them to acknowledge that I was right, but [by then] the opportune time will have been lost . . . [material excised by Tikhmenev].

Forgive me, Gracious Sir, that in my letter I have included many matters just as I encountered them, and with these I have also included my personal affairs. I do not have time to put each in proper order, and to write special letters to Your Excellency, and therefore I am frankly describing here all developments just as they happened.

Fate may decree a happy ending to my romance. Ardent passion should have no place in a man of my years, but my motives are quite otherwise, perhaps as much a result of still having emotions which in former times brought happiness into my life. At first I entered into this very carefully and conditionally, in consideration of the circumstances, the remoteness of the area and my responsibilities. If Fate does so decree, I will be in a position to render new service to the Fatherland. I will be able personally to inspect the harbor of Vera Cruz, Mexico, and travel through the entire interior of America. Thus I will be able to avail myself of an opportunity open to no one else because of the suspicion of the Spanish government, and I will bring you news of their trade, surpluses, shortages, needs and other detailed information. I will be able to obtain new benefits for my compatriots and when I become acquainted with the Viceroy I will be in a position to secure the entry of our ships into American ports on the east coast. For Russians living in the reign of such a gracious Emperor I will open trade from Petersburg in such surpluses of natural resources and manufactured goods of ours as are used by foreigners. At the same time I will be able to examine the trade of the American states, visit them, and establish business connections with our Company.

Here, Gracious Sir, is a new offering for you of a man who has dedicated himself completely to the service of his fellow man, and who wishes nothing more in life than that his strength may be equal to his zeal.

But I must also report to Your Excellency about our voyage from California and about all local matters here.

We left the port of San Francisco on May 10 at 6:00 P.M.

The Governor and all our friends went to the fortress to see us off. We saluted them with seven guns and they responded with nine. Upon leaving, we set out along the longitude, and after crossing 10 degrees we encountered a favorable wind which took us to the island of Kaigan [Dall Island, Alexander Archipelago]. For ten days we were becalmed there. At that time many of the shrouds had given way, and by cutting cables we had just managed to repair them with stoppers when a great storm came up which would certainly have broken all our masts [if repairs had not been made].

We reached Norfolk Sound on June 8 and saluted the fort, but the responses were slow. We saw no baidarkas, no men anywhere, and so we were worried. It was fresh in our memories that we had left almost all of them on their deathbeds. Having ten good cannon, we began to prepare for action, but at night the baidarkas arrived and we were relieved to hear the good news that New Arkhangel was safe. That night we were towed into harbor and dropped anchor at 9:00 the next morning. Our return voyage was quite successful except for illness. Fevers developed, and a terrible rash from sarampion. Even I came down with sarampion, but thanks to God we all recovered and arrived here safely.

Thus far I have had the honor of writing to Your Excellency about all the events as they appeared to me, as I felt about them prior to my return. Now I will supplement that with news of local developments.

When we left here scurvy was rampant both here and on Kodiak. Seventeen Russians died. In the port of New Arkhangel 60 men were incapacitated. Our American natives were also stricken with this illness and many died. Fortunately, on March 22 the herring run began. People then had fresh food and began to recover. At present only six men are in danger, and five walk with crutches. We are trying to strengthen them by giving them vegetables and grain foods. More than 1,000 Kolosh came here to fish during the herring run. Some of them had guns and we doubled our security measures against them. They remained here until April 1 when a three-masted vessel from Boston, the *O'Cain*, arrived, under the command of Captain [Jonathan] Winship, an old friend of Baranov's. He recognized the critical situation and refused to trade with the

Kolosh. He let them know he was a friend of the Administrator's, and forced them to disperse more quickly through the straits. Thank God they did not dare to make any decisive attempts [to attack] while we were most undermanned. They fear Baranov greatly, and frankly, his name holds the entire region in fear. But I must tell Your Excellency that he will not remain here after May of next year. He has been very firm in asking me to tell the Main Administration about this. It is too bad, a genuine shame to lose this worthy man, because when he leaves, all the best men will also leave.

Since then the Kolosh have been constantly sending groups of ten or fifteen men here to observe our fortifications. Meanwhile, rumors have been spreading that the Chilkat and the Khutsnov people want to unite with the Sitkans and take possession of the port. Baranov has surrounded his elevated site with a stockade, within which he has made embrasures for cannon and maintains a strong guard. In truth, our fort is more like an island, but this precaution is adequate against the Kolosh, because no matter how bold they are, they will not dare attack the hill. Our people do not dare to go to the wharf unless they carry loaded guns. The same is true of venturing into the forest to cut wood and burn charcoal. And these precautions also apply to all other work. The Kolosh now seem more friendly, and our people have begun to go about more frequently; but one must not place faith in these monsters. There are no people more treacherous.

On April 26 the ship *Aleksandr* arrived here from Kodiak with a great deal of bad news. The savages captured Yakutat in October. They burned the fortress and killed everyone except for eight men, two women and three young boys who were not in the fort at that time, but in a meadow, and who managed to escape. They are presently being held prisoner by the Aglegmiut, who are demanding ransom. This is being sent from Kodiak. The Aglegmiuts committed this crime with *kaiurs* [native slaves, in this context] who had apparently been bought by Kolosh living on Akoi.

We have also had word from Kenai and Chugach bays and from Nuchek that the Chugach and Mednovsk are threatening to kill the Russians. The Kenaits have already begun to manifest a cold attitude, complaining that they are receiving too little tobacco. Malakhov and Pernin, who are in charge of these two strongholds, have requested assistance. Ten men have been sent to them from Kodiak; no more could be spared. But what good will this do? It will only increase the number of victims!

On Kodiak the people have suffered great adversities while transporting provisions and furs. Many have drowned during storms. Everywhere there is a need to build seaworthy vessels for transport. They cost more than baidaras, but since human lives are at stake, this proposal should be adopted. . . . [material excised by Tikhmenev]

Captain Winship has told Baranov that last fall 60 [American] men were sent overland to the Columbia River [Lewis and Clark Expedition] to establish a settlement there, but we could have occupied that region more easily. The American states claim their right to this coast, insisting that the headwaters of the Columbia River rise in their territory. But using this same argument they can claim their possessions also extend over all territories where they do not encounter European settlements. However, I believe they will be prevented from settling, because the Spaniards have currently granted them [access to] four ports on the east coast of America, and there is a provision in their commercial agreement that the Americans are not to intrude on the west coast of America. This happened after Winship left Boston, and the American ships are not aware of it.

Four Bostonian ships are presently cruising and trading in our straits here: Captain [Samuel] Hill on the brig *Lydia*; Captain Porter (whose brother [Lemuel] was killed) on the ship *Hamilton*; Captain Brown aboard the ship *Vancouver*; and Captain [John] Ebbets aboard the ship *Pearl*. We know that a number of vessels come to trade at Kaigan: *Model*, *Hazard*, *Peacock* and others. When and how will we evict these guests if we do not plan to build our flotilla? I have spoken of this in my reports to the Main Administration, and I refer Your Excellency to these reports. There you will find the reasons why I do not find it to our advantage to enter into negotiations with the government of the American states concerning the coastal region here. If we strengthen this region they will leave it alone. I will be disappointed if the Ministry does not do this.

The ship *Peacock*, which I have mentioned, has been sent from O'Cain to Baranov with goods, with the understanding

Imperial Chamberlain Nikolai P. Rezanov fell from his horse and died en route home across Siberia. One can only wonder from his reports what might have happened otherwise, for this brilliant, guileful man, the bane of Krusenstern and his officers, possessed deep insights and bitter animosities. As an Imperial Chamberlain and son-in-law of Shelikhov, his powers were as impressive as his ambition, but his waspish complaints would have palled. N. N. Bashkina, *The United States and Russia, The Beginning of Relations*. (OHS Neg. OrHi 82929)

that O'Cain will also sell the ship to Baranov, at which time the entire crew will enter Company service. [Benjamin] Swift told Baranov that he has not forwarded the cargo he had promised because he had word that *Nadezhda* and *Neva* had supplied him, but in the meantime he has dispatched the ship *Hazard* which rounded the Horn in company with *Peacock* and then separated from it.

Swift and other friends have invited Baranov to Boston. Baranov asks permission to go there aboard an American ship next year, and from there perhaps to proceed to St. Petersburg. I am waiting for *Peacock* and hope to buy it.

Although I have tried as much as possible to condense my letter, my conscience would bother me if I kept silent on any matter of interest, and although I may incur Your Excellency's displeasure, nevertheless I will carry out my responsibility to you.

The king of the Hawaiian Islands, Toome-Ome-O [Kamehameha] has offered his friendship to Baranov. Your Excellency may find this rather strange, but let me tell you about the Tsar of the savages and then tell you how this came about.

Captain Winship says that Kamehameha attracts Europeans from all over; they have begun to settle on his islands and they are introducing agriculture and livestock with great success. He grants settlers freedom to leave his land whenever they wish. He also allows his subjects to sail on foreign vessels without pay, in order to have them return as experienced sailors. He bought fifteen single masted vessels, and has hired a shipwright from Boston. He is organizing an Admiralty office, and he has recently bought a three-masted ship from the Americans. [George] Clark, a navigator who had sailed with Winship, has been settled in the Sandwich Islands for the past two years; he took a wife there and has children and various enterprises there. Several times he has visited local places [in Russian America] and has been well received by Aleksandr Andreevich [Baranov]. He understands the needs of this region. He has spoken a great deal about this to his king, who sent him to negotiate trade. If this is permitted, since the distance is not great, Kamehameha wishes to come to New Arkhangel in person to lay foundations of trade. He promises to send us fruits and vegetables such as breadfruit, coconut and taro, as well as swine and grain, whenever there is a surplus. From here he would receive ticking, canvas, iron and lumber for shipbuilding. He plans to make the preliminary arrangements for this unusual trade next year, and it is too bad that we will not have Baranov here then. The vessel *Ermak*, which Baranov built here and later traded for the ship *Juno*, made the voyage to the Hawaiian Islands in 42 days, in spite of its late fall sailing. The shipwright Moorfield wrote to his partner [John D'] Wolf that few of the small ships he is familiar with are its equal and that he would be quite willing to sail it to Canton, and from there around the Cape of Good Hope to Boston. The builder is elated. Another vessel which he built, *Rostislav*, is presently sailing to Okhotsk. Although D'Wolf and his navigator Podgash have praised it highly, I did not dare to entrust him to forward all my dispatches. Moorfield writes that seven of his crew from Boston have become citizens of the Sandwich Islands.

Along with the bad news that awaited me here, I did have some satisfaction in finding that every one of my recommendations concerning the economy had produced some results. In spite of the fact that our people here have been ill and in weakened physical condition, I found twice as many kitchen gardens have been planted with vegetables and potatoes and are doing very well. Aleksandr Andreevich obtained seed from the Bostonians. I am all the more convinced that proper organization of this region can eliminate all shortages.

Forgive me, my Gracious Sir, that since I do not have time to write separately to the Main Administration, I must humbly ask Your Excellency to read my letter to the Committee, and to give them a copy, for the letter includes information necessary for them and will serve as a supplement to my reports. If the Committee can be trusted with government secrets, I think it can certainly be trusted with my views as a private citizen. I expect nothing from them except that they take note of my sacrifice, and not reject my suggestions out of hand. If my efforts have not merited this, I will leave it to each member to judge. I will be content to know that I have done my best to work for my country everywhere I have been. I am convinced that I have not done one thing that could be detrimental to or detract from the honor of my compatriots.

I beg you most humbly to submit the brief report to His Imperial Majesty. You will see its content in the copy under letter "B."

With great respect and devotion I have the honor to be forever, most Gracious Sir, Your Excellency's most humble servant,

Nikolai Rezanov.

New Arkhangel
June 17, 1806

Reference: AVPR, f. SPb. Glavnyi arkhiv, I-7, op. 6, 1802 g., d. 1.

See: P. A. Tikhmenev. *Istoricheskoe obozrenie obrazovaniia Rossiisko-Amerikanskoi kompanii i deistvii eia do nastoiashchago vremeni*, Vol. 2, Supplement, 253–283.

Manuscript translations of this material are to be found in The Bancroft Library [by Ivan Petroff] and the University of Washington Northwest Americana Collection [Dmitrii Krenov]. Both have been published in limited editions: the Petroff version [*The Rezanov Voyage to Nueva California in 1806*] in San Francisco in 1926; and the Krenov version, improved and edited by Richard A. Pierce, and with additional material from Langsdorff and Khvostov [*Rezanov Reconnoiters California*, 1806], published by the Book Club of California in 1972. Dmytryshyn and Crownhart-Vaughan have used their own translation for the present volume.

20

A REPORT FROM THE MAIN ADMINISTRATION OF THE RUSSIAN
AMERICAN COMPANY TO EMPEROR ALEXANDER I, REGARDING THE
FUR TRADE.

Yesterday a courier traveling by horse from Irkutsk brought news to the Main Administration of the [Russian American] Company informing them of the following:

1. Last August the Company brigantine *Maria* reached Okhotsk safely with a cargo of furs. The Main Administration of the Company humbly submits with this report a list of the number of furs and the prices for which the Company believes the furs can be sold. This brigantine, under the command of Lieutenant [Andrei V.] Mashin, was dispatched in 1806 from the port of New Arkhangel on the island of Sitka.

2. Two other Company vessels arrived in that same port of Okhotsk: one was the large three-masted *Juno*, under the command of Lieutenant [N.A.] Khvostov; the other was a smaller vessel, the tender *Avos*, under the command of midshipman [G.I.] Davydov. Both vessels spent the winter of 1806 in the port of Petropavlovsk on Kamchatka, and were selected by Privy Councillor [N. P.] Rezanov for some kind of secret expedition. Since the Main Administration of the Company has not been informed about this, it does not know what those two ships were doing. There was no Company cargo aboard them.

3. On June 14 a fourth Company vessel, *Rostislav*, also arrived at the above mentioned port. In 1806 it was sent from Sitka Island to Okhotsk with the naturalist [G. H. von] Langsdorff who had been on an expedition around the world, and the Bostonian [John D'] Wolf, from whom Councillor Rezanov and Administrator Baranov on Sitka had bought the vessel *Juno* and all of its cargo, which contained provisions essential for the Company. This vessel reached St. Petersburg last week. It had not been able to reach Okhotsk and so had wintered in the harbor of Petropavlovsk on Kamchatka, from where it set out on May 25. This vessel also carried no cargo.

This vessel was handed over with all its rigging and armaments for government service because of the urging of the

Okhotsk harbor commandant, Captain of the Second Rank Bukharin. There are very few government transport ships. In exchange, Bukharin promised to supply the Company, using government ships, with all necessities for Kamchatka and other locales, and to provide support for ships that sail there and need rigging and weapons.

From America the local administrator [A.A.] Baranov informs us via these ships that:

In April, 1806, after Councillor Rezanov sailed to California, a North American ship from Boston, *O'Cain*, under the command of her captain and owner, [Jonathan] Winship, came to Sitka. Baranov bartered with Winship for some needed supplies for the Company.

In Bering Strait near Yakutat Bay where a Company fort had been built and there was a good settlement with agricultural settlers, a misadventure occurred. It is surmised that 22 Russian settlers from there, and loyal island [natives] who were with them, had neglected to take necessary precautions and were attacked by hostile American [natives] who lived nearby. They burned the settlement and the fort and killed fourteen Russians and many islanders. Although four promyshlenniks and four settlers with two women and three children managed to escape by running off, during their flight to another fort, Konstantinovsk, in Chugatsk Bay, they were captured by other bellicose Aglegmiut people. One of these unfortunate captives was allowed to go to Baranov carrying the demand for ransom for the rest. Baranov is taking the necessary and appropriate measures to deal with this.

Finally, Baranov informs us that he plans to move from Sitka to Kodiak where he has not been for three years and where he must tend to certain Company matters. He will leave Commercial Counselor [I. A.] Kuskov behind on Sitka as his deputy; the Main Administration has already appointed Kuskov to be Baranov's successor. Baranov doubts whether he will return to Sitka because his years and poor health are taking their toll.

The Main Administration of the Company has the honor of humbly informing Your Imperial Majesty about all of these developments.

Principal Director and Cavalier [M. M.] Buldakov
Director [I. A.] Shelikhov
Chancellery *Pravitel* [Administrator] [I. O.] Zelenskii

INFORMATION ON THE CARGO OF COMPANY FURS
BROUGHT IN ON THE BRIGANTINE *Maria*

NUMBER OF PELTS	ANIMAL	VALUE IN RUBLES
2,520	Various qualities of Kamchatka sea otters	176,400
372	Yearling sea otters	3,720
4,250	Sea otter tails	21,250
39	River beavers	390
586	Black brown fox	8,790
1,325	Grey fox	9,275
994	Red fox	3,976
430	Otter	6,450
2,989	Blue fox	29,890
109	White fox	109
324	American sable	486
46	Mink	46
168	Wolverine	840
84	Black bear	2,520
72	Lynx	720
12	Wolves	120
61,814	Fur seals	92,721

TOTAL   357,704 rubles

See: Ministerstvo inostrannykh del SSSR. *VPR*. First Series, Vol. 4, Doc. 40, 105–106.

JANUARY 28, 1808

A REPORT FROM MIKHAIL M. BULDAKOV, PRINCIPAL DIRECTOR OF
THE RUSSIAN AMERICAN COMPANY, TO EMPEROR ALEXANDER I,
CONCERNING TRADE BETWEEN RUSSIAN AMERICA AND SPANISH
CALIFORNIA

M ost Generous Sovereign! The late Active Councillor Rezanov was given the honor by Your Majesty of inspecting
the North American Russian settlements and establishing useful projects there, and was also empowered by the Russian
American Company to act in its commercial dealings. He was
in that region and made many useful discoveries and observations to improve Russian trade, which brings important benefits both to the American settlements and to the entire eastern
part of Siberia. His papers and diaries give clear evidence of
this. One of his observations, based on his personal experiences
in California, is so important that I, as a representative of
the entire Russian American Company, humbly make bold to
bring it to the attention of Your Imperial Majesty.

California abounds in grain, but since there is no outlet for
it, more than 300,000 puds of it are left to spoil. In contrast,
the [Russian] American settlements only have access to grain
brought overland across Siberia for more than 3,000 versts.
This transport costs the [Russian American] Company more
than 10 rubles per pud. This figure does not include salaries to
the commissioners, nor the loss of horses [through overwork
and accident] by the Iakut overland transporters, who in time
will have no horses left.

California abounds in domestic cattle and horses, which
roam without any supervision in the forests, and spread in
great herds all the way to the Columbia River. The Spanish
government, in order to prevent their livestock from causing
damage to agriculture, has decreed that every year between
10,000 and 30,000 head are to be slaughtered. In contrast, the
Okhotsk and Kamchatka regions have a desperate need for
these cattle because they often suffer widespread famine. During Rezanov's stay in California several hundred head of cattle

were killed just in order to have the hides in which the Russians could wrap the grain they had bought from the Spaniards; the meat was discarded.

California has a great shortage of all kinds of textiles and of iron. Instead of iron they use leather belting in the construction of homes. They even use it to hold up ceilings and everything else that must be suspended, no matter how heavy. In Russia not only is iron abundant, but so also is fabric. Without impoverishing herself Russia can well supply other countries with these.

In regard to these goods, Councillor Rezanov had a discussion with Don [José] de Arrillaga, the Governor of California who was visiting in Monterey. The latter emphasized the fact that the Spaniards cannot get by without trade with the Russians, who are their closest neighbors in America; however, this trade is prohibited to them. For that reason he agreed to submit his views to his superior, the Mexican Viceroy, who apparently would refer the matter to the Spanish Court. This was all the more likely since during the time Rezanov stayed there, several provinces asked the Governor to let them enter into trade with Russia.

All that now remains, really, is to be in contact with the Court in Madrid, if Your Imperial Majesty might deign to read my humble explanation of this, which is taken from the papers and diaries of the late Rezanov. When he discussed this problem with the Governor of California, [Rezanov reported that the Governor] said, "If only the Court in Madrid knew the needs of this country, it would certainly enter into mutual trade relations with Russia, which would bring mutual benefit. Then the Bostonians would not be able to incite the wild savages, especially if the two countries would protect their new subjects by sending a frigate or a naval corvette to cruise along these shores."

The suggestion of the California Governor has previously been made by Russia: in 1807 a naval sloop was sent to Company settlements, and the Company instructed its ship *Neva* to cruise in those waters. With respect to Russian trade with the California provinces, if Your Imperial Majesty were to agree to seek an agreement with the Court of Madrid, the Russian American Company would be most grateful for Your august

In the midst of the grand Imperial designs along the Western American coast and to the south seas, Paul's successor, Alexander I, established himself as a European intellectual and military leader. He made an official visit to the "Public" library, today the renowned Saltykov-Shchedrin Library in Leningrad. *Imperator Aleksandr Pervyi.* (OHS negs. OrHi 82972)

protection. It would commit itself to provide for the mutual benefit of both nations, and especially for the Kamchatka and Okhotsk regions and for its possessions in America, by sending two ships each year to the California ports of San Francisco, Monterey and San Diego. These ports were in fact specifically discussed by Rezanov and the Governor himself.

I remain, Most Merciful Sovereign, Your Imperial Majesty's Most Loyal Subject,

Principal director and Cavalier [Mikhail M.] Buldakov

See: Ministerstvo inostrannykh del SSSR. *VPR*, First Series, Vol. 4, Doc. 65, 163–164.

22

INSTRUCTIONS FROM N. P. RUMIANTSEV, MINISTER OF COMMERCE AND FOREIGN AFFAIRS, TO G. A. STROGANOV, RUSSIAN MINISTER PLENIPOTENTIARY TO MADRID, CONCERNING TRADE BETWEEN RUSSIAN AMERICA AND SPANISH CALIFORNIA

The late Councillor [N. P.] Rezanov, to whom the Sovereign Emperor assigned the task of inspecting the North American Russian settlements, upon reaching [his destination] immediately recognized the needs of this new land. He sought the means of supplying the needs of Kamchatka and eastern Siberia [as well], and so resolved to travel to California where he hoped to find the means of carrying out his intentions. When he reached Monterey he proposed to the Governor the establishment of trade between the colonies of both powers. Everyone hopes that our Court will exert itself in this matter, because the American states, through firm insistence, have opened four ports on the coast of [South] America for their trade.

During meetings between Councillor Rezanov and the California Governor who was visiting in Monterey, it is apparent that the Governor himself urged the necessity of this trade with the Russians, their closest neighbors in America. He agreed to submit this matter to his superior, the Mexican Viceroy, as well as to relate to him the fact that during Rezanov's visit, several of the provinces of which California is comprised implored the Governor for permission to trade with Russia.

The eagerness of the California inhabitants to open trade with Russia is based on the following situations. California abounds in cattle and horses, which are spread out in countless herds even as far off as the Columbia River. In order to prevent these animals from damaging crops, the Spanish government has decreed that between 10,000 and 30,000 cattle be killed each year. By way of contrast, the Okhotsk and Kamchatka regions have a great need for these cattle.

California also abounds in grain, but since they have no way of marketing it, more than 300,000 puds of it goes to waste

The "Gibraltar of the North," headquarters for the Russian American Company in New Arkhangel (now Sitka), This superb 1805 painting by von Langsdorff shows the settlement in its earliest years. The Bancroft Library.

each year. In contrast, the [Russian] American settlements have to obtain grain through Siberia, via an overland route of more than 3,000 versts. This costs the Company some 15 rubles per pud. Likewise, grain that the government transports to Kamchatka for local military needs costs more than 10 rubles per pud.

California has a very great need for all kinds of fabrics and for iron. In contrast, Russia has a surplus of these commodities.

With such mutual needs, and mutual means of satisfying them, to the equal benefit of both parties, the Sovereign Emperor instructs Your Excellency to request from the Spanish Ministry that permission be given for not more than two Russian ships [at a time] to stop in the California ports of San Francisco, Monterey and San Diego, with the proviso that no other ships of ours would come there until the first two had departed. In return for this we suggest that in regard to the need of California for iron and textiles, His Imperial Majesty is ready to permit [Spanish Californian] ships to come not only to Russian American ports, but to Kamchatka as well. Through this means, trade relations will develop which are mutually advantageous. I am proposing that only two of our ships come at any one time to open California, since such a modest request will be more likely to incline the Spanish government [to agree to it]. However, if Your Excellency should manage to obtain permission for more of our ships, this would of course be even more advantageous for our trade.

If your oral explanation of this is received favorably, you may handle this problem officially and reach a mutual agreement as to whether it will suffice to have the conditions written out only in official notes to be exchanged between you and the Spanish minister, to which both governments will consent in order to put this into being; or whether the Spanish government will want to set up such an agreement through a special convention. I will expect you to notify me about this so I may report to the Sovereign Emperor.

The full measure of your sincere inquiry into all matters for the service, my Dear Sir, assures us that you will make every effort to see that this new assignment is carried out in accordance with the will and expectation of His Imperial Majesty.

I remain . . .

See: Ministerstvo inostrannykh del SSSR. VPR, Series I, Vol. 4, Doc. 102, 235–236.

23

APRIL 21, 1808

A STATEMENT FROM DIRECTORS OF THE RUSSIAN AMERICAN COM-
PANY REGARDING PROBLEMS CAUSED BY THE INCURSION OF BOS-
TONIANS INTO WATERS AND TERRITORIES CLAIMED BY RUSSIA

In the northwestern part of America the Russian American Company has established trade, set up hunting operations, built forts and settlements, constructed ships and undertaken every possible kind of enterprise. Above all, it has persuaded many savage native tribes to accept the sovereign power of Russia over them, and to profess their [Russian Orthodox] religion. The Company constantly attempts to improve and expand these programs; it even hopes to establish educational facilities for native children and charitable homes for impoverished and orphaned girls. But all of these efforts are encountering serious obstructions.

The single most important reason is that ever since 1792, every year ten to fifteen merchant ships come to that region from the North American United States. On these ships come [American] citizens who trade not only with the [Russian American] Company, but with American savages who live in various places on the islands and mainland. The Americans trade for furs to sell in Canton; every year they obtain as many as 15,000 sea otter pelts and 5,000 beaver pelts, in addition to other furs. And in exchange for these they bring various goods but especially firearms such as cannon, falconets, guns, pistols, sabers and other instruments of destruction; they also bring gunpowder; and they even teach the savages how to use these weapons.

The harm to Russian American Company trade in this land, caused by these American citizens includes the following:

In regard to trade: Every year the Americans carry to Canton the above mentioned number of sea otter pelts. They sell the sea otters to the Chinese for 50 rubles apiece; beaver pelts fetch 5 rubles each. The Americans take half in cash and the rest in tea, which they obtain for 40 rubles per pud in our currency. If we assume this price, then the sale of this number of sea otters and beavers brings 775,000 rubles; and this does not include the sale of furs of other land animals. They snatch this profit right out of the hands of Russian subjects, and right under their eyes. They make a huge profit both from the sale of tea in Europe and from the barter of their goods with the savages. They give the natives a firearm (certainly not the best quality) and ten cartridges and bullets in exchange for one sea otter.

The Chinese, for whom these furs and others from land animals have become indispensable, and who obtain so many of them in Canton [where Russians are prohibited from trading], give us a much lower price for our furs in Kiakhta, which is the only place we can sell them. Further, they buy few from us; each year they buy no more than 2,000 to 3,000 sea otters and between 80,000 and 100,000 fur seals. And in addition to this problem, in Kiakhta we have to pay duty on these furs as well as on the goods we buy from the Chinese. This expense is a severe impairment to our trade, and because of it we have to resell the Chinese goods at much higher prices each year.

In regard to political and moral matters: The North American republicans expand their operations in places occupied by the Company and induce in the savages actions contrary to the goals of the Company. They instill among them the notion that they should not consider the Russians their oldest, most dependable and best friends, with the natural right to be their protectors not only against foreign nations but in intertribal quarrels. Such disputes have long been customary among them, and have led to their mutual destruction, with one tribe constantly warring with another over trivial insults. The republicans encourage this depravity by bringing all manner of firearms to exchange with these savages, who by their very natures and lack of education are craven and brutal.

As a result of this the savages have caused a number of unfortunate situations for the Russians who had been friendly and had had commercial relations with them. In addition to the many successful attempts they have made to destroy the Russians in their settlements, in 1801 the Sitka Islanders, reinforced by groups of mainland natives, came in great numbers and attacked our Mikhailovsk fort on that island. They killed the people in the fort with fire, and with swords killed the garrison of Russian promyshlenniks who had been there.

On the basis of explanations by some of the savages themselves, the local Chief Administrator, Baranov, believes the Bostonian ships and crews of skippers Crocker [*Jenny*] and [William] Cunningham [*Globe*]* were responsible for this disaster, for they not only incited the islanders but gave them gunpowder and guns. After the Russians had been killed the Bostonians took from the savages all the furs the Russians had obtained, which amounted to 3,700 sea otter pelts and others, with a value of more than 300,000 rubles. They also burned the Company vessels, and were brutal toward any natives who asked a high price for a sea otter or some other pelt during the barter negotiations.

Another incident occurred in 1805 in Yakutat Bay on the mainland where the Company had established a settlement called Slavorossia. Several families lived there, both men and women; they were farmers, artisans and hunters. They had for some time had friendly relations with the savages, and were confident of their security; however, the savages obtained firearms from the Bostonians, and being inclined to battle and violence, they took the Russians by surprise, as well as Aleuts and other American natives who were loyal to us. They killed them all, burned the settlement and destroyed the entire enterprise.

That same year the Russians built a settlement for the second time on the island of Sitka. This time by chance they found the savages had a wooden fortress equipped with guns and other small weapons traded from the Bostonians. They inflicted considerable harm on us, and if the crew of the ship *Neva* [commanded by Iurii Lisianskii] had not come to our help when they stopped there during their circumnavigation, it would still be in doubt whether that island belonged to us.

Indeed these lawless people, because of a shift [in attitude], suffered the same consequences they had caused us. In 1805 skipper [O.] Porter [*Atahualpa*] was in Milbanke Sound bartering with the savages to acquire some 6,000 sea otter pelts. He let the savages who had brought the pelts come aboard his ship, but as soon as they were aboard they shot Porter and several of his crew with pistols obtained from Porter himself. The natives threw the bodies overboard. If it had not been for the bold

---

*Cunningham, the mate, took command of the ship after her skipper, Bernard Magee, was killed by natives at Skidgate in the Queen Charlotte Islands in October 1801.

decision of the navigator, Adams [who took command of *Ata-hualpa*] and the arrival of another Bostonian vessel [*Lydia*] under the command of skipper [Samuel] Hill, who put down the insurrection, Porter's ship and entire crew would have been taken by the savages.

For these reasons long ago the Company administrator on Kodiak undertook to explain to the Bostonians who came there the forceful instructions he had from his government; he advised them they were not to come to barter with the savages for furs in places that belonged to Russia, and especially they were not to bring them firearms. They were to do all trading with the Company. But even in the face of this advice, the Bostonians would simply reply that they were merchants, free to seek their profit. In regard to any prohibition against trading with the savages, they replied they had not heard of any such prohibition either from their own government or from the Russian government.

These circumstances lead to the conclusion that in order to establish permanent [Russian] settlements in that land, to maintain and increase various institutions in the future, as well as to develop enterprises based solely on the hunting and trade of the dependent peoples, it is necessary that Imperial authority issue a statement that foreigners, and especially the North American republicans, are prohibited there. A similar situation exists in all other European colonies, in both Indies, where no [foreigner] may trade with the savages, but only with the [colonizing] company. This would only apply to Kodiak, the main Russian factory site. They [foreigners] could enter into commercial relations with the Company, and if there is mutual agreement, local trade could be set up with any republicans who wish. This could be established on mutually advantageous terms. Without such a statement, all of the Company's concern about that land will not be sufficient to produce the desired result.

Principal Director and Cavalier [M. M.] Buldakov
Director Benedikt Kramer

See: Ministerstvo inostrannykh del SSSR. *VPR*, Series I, Vol. 4, Doc. 104, 241–243.

24

A MEMORANDUM FROM THE MINISTER OF COMMERCE AND FOREIGN
AFFAIRS, N. P. RUMIANTSEV, TO ALEXANDER I, CONCERNING THE
INCREASE IN POPULATION IN THE RUSSIAN AMERICAN COMPANY
SETTLEMENTS

The Main Administration of the [Russian] American Company has charged me with presenting to Your Imperial Majesty its most humble report. This report states that there are shipyards, fortifications and households in its settlements on the islands and mainland, which have been built by persons hired by the Company on the basis of their passports. Because these persons have stayed for a long time in those places they have not only acquired homes, but have married savage women and begotten children with them. But the Company can never attain its goals in its business enterprises because those people who have settled there may return to Russia upon termination of their contracts. For this reason the Company requests of Your Imperial Majesty permission for those who are now in the settlements who have expressed the desire to remain there permanently to do so; it also requests that others who may wish to become permanent settlers in those places be freed from the taxes imposed on them in their previous settlements [in Russia].

In my own view I recognize that a settled way of life for persons employed in the enterprises of the American Company is related to advantage to the State. It would therefore be my judgment that they should be given such permission in order to enable free persons to settle there: merchants, petty bourgeoisie, state and economic peasants, iasak paying people, retired military men and the like. Regarding [serfs] belonging to pomeshchiks, the Company can do nothing without the consent of the pomeshchiks themselves. If persons who have settled there are freed from the taxes imposed on them in their previous places of residence, in order that the Treasury not lose its revenue from this, I would like to suggest that these taxes be imposed on the Company, since it will be to its benefit to have those people settle there. However, this would not include

This winsome view of Sitkan natives, perhaps overly roman-
ticized, nonetheless conveys reasons why some men chose to
remain the in easternmost outpost of empire. Drawing by
Kittlitz. *La Corvette Senavine*. (OHS OrHi neg. 82053)

taxes designated for social services which were established by
choice, since they are not included in government revenue.

In bringing this to Your Imperial Majesty's attention I ask
Imperial permission to present my opinion for review by the
State Council.

Minister Count Nikolai Rumiantsev

See: Ministerstvo inostrannykh del SSSR. *VPR*, Series I, Vol. 4, Doc. 120,
270–271.

25

INSTRUCTIONS FROM ALEKSANDR A. BARANOV TO HIS ASSISTANT,
IVAN A. KUSKOV, REGARDING THE DISPATCH OF A HUNTING PARTY
TO THE COAST OF SPANISH CALIFORNIA

My dear Ivan Aleksandrovich:
Because of the present unsatisfactory progress of our hunting efforts on Kodiak and in this area, and the substantial diminution of common assets because of various unforeseen expenditures, we are compelled to seek sources of revenue in regions other than those which have been assigned to us in order to improve and enlarge our fur trade and other activities. This will benefit our current shareholders whose interests are inseparable from the benefits of the entire Company, and the future goals of the Empire.

I have invoked God's assistance in this endeavor and have adopted what I consider to be a good plan to dispatch a hunting party to the coast of the American New Albion with the Company vessels *Mirt Kadiak* and *Nikolai*. These ships and their commanding officers, navigators of the 14th rank, are to protect the hunting party as well as to survey and describe the entire coast from the strait of Juan de Fuca to California, with complete accuracy placing on the charts plans of important sites such as harbors, bays and straits where there might be suitable anchorage, provided they have the means to carry out this assignment. The experience of previous groups of our men aboard foreign vessels, in regard to the undisputed profits of that region, gives considerable hope, because in a very short time a number of small groups have discovered and attained substantial trade possibilities. For this reason a small vessel, the *Nikolai*, has already been sent there under the command of [Nikolai I.] Bulygin on September [date missing] of this year, with instructions to make a full description of these shores and to discover harbors, bays, straits and islands with anchorages for large vessels. Enclosed are copies of the instructions I gave Bulygin and the ship's supercargo, [Timofei] Tarakanov.*

---

*For a complete account of the fate of this voyage, see *The Wreck of the* Sv. Nikolai: *Two Narratives of the First Russian Expedition to the Oregon Country,*

Since the importance of this matter requires very sound and careful attention to the selection of sites for settlements and enterprises and to the problems of supply, as well as great care and patriotic zeal in regard to all the details of the venture, I felt I should go there personally, first aboard the *Aleksandr* and then aboard *Neva*, from Kodiak. Unfortunately various unforeseen circumstances have prevented me from doing this, including the following:

1. I am waiting for Captain O'Cain to come from Sanak, because I am the only one who can resolve the important question of the Company's capital.

2. I am also waiting for the naval frigate from St. Petersburg, which was to have arrived here long ago with official instructions for me from the Main Administration of the [Russian] American Company. This is just as important as the above.

3. The ship *Neva* remains idle here, under the supervision of local authorities, awaiting instructions to be brought by the same frigate or via Okhotsk on a transport vessel, which will inform us whether trade with the Chinese is permitted in Canton. *Neva* is to be sent there as the primary destination for her voyage. This lack of information is now preventing me from making decisions, and for that reason I cannot leave this port, since the burden of issuing instructions and administering the region still falls on me alone. This may be incompatible with my poor health and advanced years, but I am determined to use whatever strength and years I have left to do everything in my power to work for the benefit of this country. I challenge Your Excellency to distinguish yourself through this illustrious deed as proof of your loyal devotion which you owe to our generous Monarch and to our Fatherland. You have a duty as a subject of the Empire to do this, and even more because you have been granted great favor by being elevated from a middle level to a high level staff position.

Although I trust your good judgment and many years of experience in organizing successful hunting and commercial profit ventures, and providing for the men entrusted to your

1808–1810, edited with an introduction by Kenneth N. Owens; translated by Alton S. Donnelly. Portland, 1985. North Pacific Studies, No. 8.

command, nevertheless I do feel I must advise you of my views pertaining to hunting, trading and politics in regard to that region.

1. From the instructions I have mentioned, for navigator Bulygin, who is being dispatched aboard the brig *Nikolai*, you already know that his first rendezvous is set for the coast of Albion in the port or bay of Gray's Harbor, located in 47° northern latitude and 236° 3' longitude from London. You are to proceed there directly with the vessel *Mirt Kadiak*, and if you find him there or if you receive information about him as per his instructions, then depending on local circumstances, weigh the potential of the hunt there and remain for some time to give the hunting party an opportunity to gain experience in this area.

If the results are unsatisfactory, leave the place and proceed south to Trinidad Bay located in 41° 3' northern latitude and 236° 6' longitude from the London meridian, which is the place designated for the second rendezvous with Bulygin. You are to stop there without fail. Do not enter the Columbia River; I foresee no need for this, for it is far above the channel located on Vancouver's maps. It is possible Bulygin will anchor there to make his observations. The mouth of the Columbia River and the channel are surrounded by many sandy reefs and banks, and therefore the entry is dangerous for large vessels. There are many [native] people living along the shores and it is possible the American Bostonians have already supplied them with firearms. Their goal is to settle and establish a colony there, as you know. For that reason it is doubtful whether our hunters should be put to work there, even if marine animals are seen. Indeed it is doubtful that there are furbearing animals in the river there, except for river beavers and mountain animals. I wish you a safe arrival at Trinidad Bay.

2. Whether or not you meet Bulygin there, or receive news of him, make all preparations to hunt there. First, send Slobodchikov to a bay which is not more than 20 miles south along the coast and learn from him whether Bulygin is there. If he is not, and has not been there, explore and make careful measurements of the entrance and the interior of that bay, and if the entry seems suitable and your ship *Mirt Kadiak* can enter, immediately move your ship there for safe anchorage, because the

Trinidad roadstead is not safe. Then give instructions for hunting in various locations.

The experience of the hunting group led by Tarakanov is very encouraging because there, where Kimball anchored, and also near Bodega and Drake's bays, a goodly number of animals were sighted, and although the hunting party was small, it nevertheless was very successful. For that reason it would be appropriate to establish a main camp there, selecting one of three sites: in Slobodchikov Bay, or where Kimball anchored, or Bodega Bay, if it is possible for ships to enter there.

Periodically send promyshlenniks to Trinidad and farther south to hunt, gain knowledge of the area and of the people who live there, especially in those places where the brig *Nikolai* may not have the chance or opportunity to go. However, at the present time it is not necessary to build large structures there while the whole coast from San Francisco harbor in California to the strait of Juan de Fuca remains completely unsurveyed and we do not have formal permission from our government to occupy it and settle there. However, at the most suitable place, you are to build a fortress with proper living quarters for secure temporary housing for yourself and your men.

Do not dissipate your energies on things not absolutely necessary. Your only objective is to hunt and determine where all the most advantageous places are along the coast of Albion. For this reason if there should be danger from the natives, you are to employ more Russians on hunting expeditions. However, you must strictly prohibit even the slightest exploitation of the local natives either by Russians or by members of the hunting groups; they must not be either insulted or abused. You personally and your subordinates must make every effort to win their friendship and affection. You must not use fear because of the superiority of your firearms, which these people do not possess. Rather, seek to attract them through kind gestures based on humanity, and occasional appropriate gifts to win them over. Do not neglect any opportunity to gain future benefits.

Even in their natural weaknesses, their predilection for theft and deceit, you should pardon minor transgressions due to animal thoughtlessness which circumscribes their comprehension and morals. However, even while you forgive minor transgressions, let them know your displeasure, and little by

Langsdorff's view of Kolosh women dancing. Von Langsdorff, *Voyages and Travels*. (OHS OrHi neg. 82041)

little teach them to understand the difference between good and bad, and to see how they bring destruction upon themselves through harmful and evil deeds. When you become better acquainted with them try to secure from them, by purchase if necessary, two or three young lads from among their prisoners. When you have clothed them decently, teach them the Russian language. As soon as they can understand the words for things, in your free time write down useful vocabularies so that in the future you can use them as interpreters. Also, you may gain some understanding about the meaning of basic concepts.

You are strictly to forbid anyone from accepting even the most trivial item from them as a gift; not even a bit of food is to be accepted. Pay a little something for everything, using our goods and trinkets which they may desire. Entertain their respected leaders and give them food to eat every time they visit, if you have enough food to do this. In short, teach them to view all Russians and partovshchiks as benevolent friends who pose no danger to them. Obviously you should on these and all other occasions take all precautions necessary for your safety.

3. According to Tarakanov, Bodega Bay, up to now, more than any other known place along that coast, offers the best prospects for hunting, because with the incoming tides a mul-

titude of sea otters enter the bay to feed; the bay is narrow, has a sandy spit with a clay bottom, and remains calm in all storms. It probably has plenty of shellfish, which is the principal food of the sea otter.

The entrance to the bay is very narrow and well suited to the use of nets for trapping. If the high and low tides are similar to those of Yakutat Bay, one can anchor farther off the mouth of the bay and send the hunting party to the interior of the bay to drive the sea otters out into the net. Near the mouth the sea otters are so abundant that in one hour [Tarakanov], while sitting quietly on shore, was able to kill five with his gun. It is always possible, even if there are breakers at the entrance to the bay, to enter it [by portaging] across the spit, as well as from Drake's Bay, from where there is a portage of less than two versts according to Tarakanov. The interior of the bay is possibly quite similar to San Francisco Bay; the northernmost Spanish fortress, with the same name, is at the entry to the bay. It would be useful for future political considerations to explore the area between those two bays very cautiously, so as not to give the Spanish the slightest reason for suspecting our intention to hunt in such close proximity. For that purpose you should dispatch a group of your most dependable and unassuming men. Although they should be properly armed as a precautionary measure, they should be strictly ordered that at no time during their expedition are they to fire at a single animal or bird, unless a member of the expedition is in great danger.

You should definitely appoint Tarakanov to head the hunting party unless it is possible to detach one of the leaders from the vessels, someone who could fulfill this assignment more faithfully, that is, to use the compass to chart the isthmus in the narrowest place between these bays, especially the location of San Francisco Bay, where the route to Bodega begins and ends. Describe this with annotations indicating the distance from the river fort. But if by some unforeseen chance this should arouse the curiosity of the Spaniards from the fort, order the group to return at once. Likewise, if it is impossible to send a navigator to do this, and it is left to Tarakanov to carry out this assignment, in that case you are personally to move temporarily to Bodega and Drake's bays, proceed north either to the harbor where Kimball anchored, or to Slobodchikov or Trinidad bays where our vessels are to be anchored at that time. This procedure is especially important to follow if any naval vessel is sighted at the Spanish fortress. If there is no naval vessel, anticipate no danger because the Spaniards have no rowboats there.

4. While you and your ships or detachments are near the Columbia River, determine whether there are any American Bostonian vessels there, and whether their government is trying to establish colonial settlements there. If this is the case, and if you happen to encounter [Bostonians] or explorers from other European nations, or Spaniards themselves, if you have an opportunity to enter into conversation with them, do not embark on any negotiations concerning the allocation of occupation rights in local places. You are only to say that the Russians have the same right as other nationals to hunt marine animals and seek profits along all coasts and islands, from the port of New Arkhangel south to California, where other nations have not established claims in accordance with natural law. This does not apply to places already occupied by other enlightened powers. Tell them you are sailing with a group of promyshlenniks from place to place, where it is profitable, solely to hunt.

5. If by some chance you should have an opportunity to negotiate or discuss matters with the Commandant of the above mentioned Spanish fort of San Francisco, [Don] Luis, the son of the former Commandant, Señor Aksenii [sic; Arguello] with whom our late representative, His Excellency Nikolai Petrovich Rezanov in 1806 had a gratifying meeting and friendship, and to whom the beautiful daughter of the latter and the sister of the former, Concepcion, became engaged, you should first inform them of the death of Rezanov in accordance with the letter given to Shvetsov, a copy of which has been given to you. Then send fitting gifts from among the things you have taken with you and ask their kind permission for our hunting parties to operate in the oft mentioned bay of San Francisco. At the first opportunity promise to pay one piaster's worth of any of our goods they wish for each large sea otter, except for a *koshlok* [half grown] or *medvedka* [young, suckling]. Also suggest that you have a list and samples of such goods. For these

goods you will ask to receive the same value in food supplies which the deceased general [Rezanov] received, at the same asking prices, but more flour, if the prices are lower than those quoted to the general. Do not hesitate to bargain, even if they ask twice as much as the going price for wheat.

You are fully aware of other aspects of the situation: what is available, what the prices are, and what we need most. But above all you are to try, if you have a chance, to establish future mutually advantageous, amicable trade and hunting relations, so we can freely supply them with our goods in exchange for their products. Do not make sea otters an item of trade, nor take them at any price, until such time as you make the Spanish more inclined to allow our hunting parties to hunt without interference along the coast of California in places where there are most animals and where hunting is more desirable. For this, offer to pay them a specified amount each year, or an amount for every 1,000 pelts, counting only the *bobrs* [adult males] and *matkas* [adult females], [and secure for us] permission to obtain provisions freely through voluntary trade with church missionaries.

6. After wintering on the coast of Albion, early in the spring, around March, when you ascertain that it is safe to settle in inhabited places and that you may hunt with profit, but no longer need one of the ships for protection, it would be a good idea to send it with a small group of men farther south to search for islands off the coast of California, islands which have not been located on maps, and to explore the island of Guadeloupe which is located at some distance off the mainland in 29° 17' northern latitude and [missing] degrees longitude from the London meridian. This detachment should ascertain whether there may be potential for profitable hunting of sea otters or fur seals on that island or others similar to it which are located at some distance from the mainland.

However, this sailing and searching should be undertaken with the greatest caution because of the danger from Spanish royal vessels and French privateers who may be in those waters looking for the English, although this is not anticipated. Nevertheless we have long been unaware of European developments, so order your men to avoid contact as much as possible.

7. If the Benevolent Peacemaker gives you bountiful success in your hunting by May or June of 1809, but you believe there may be still greater profits to be made by leaving a group of Russians and hunting parties behind in a secure position in those or in other newly discovered places, and if you personally decide to stay there, and then if these hunting opportunities and dangers come to an end, you should decide about our future course of action and when to return there with the entire party of hunters and with the vessels. Finally, if you should feel it advisable, send back a small vessel, bringing part of the furs and news about everything that has happened up until then. I entrust that decision to your good judgment, in the hope that you will not let any opportunity slip by which might secure profits for the Company, for our public and for the Fatherland.

If you chance to encounter the American Bostonian Captain [George W.] Ayers in those waters, negotiate with him. I made a special contract with him on Kodiak regarding hunting and provisioning from California. He has been assigned 26 baidarkas, under the command of Shvetsov, with my nephew as his assistant. If necessary, draw up an agreement in conformity with the contract, a copy of which is being sent to you, but with new terms if there is an opportunity anywhere for joint hunting. Make your plans, taking into consideration local prospects for success. Try in every possible way to move him away from the coast of Albion, even if you do make a joint agreement, so that neither [the Bostonians] nor other foreigners will discern our directions and intentions.

9. In the detachment of this expedition which is entrusted to you, be as humane as you possibly can and have the greatest regard for all peoples, Russian and Aleut, who make up the hunting party. If it is within your power, anticipate all necessities, potential shortages, and physical exhaustion which may enervate the men. Show special compassion toward the sick and spare no effort to restore them to health and to their previous strength. This concern, along with precautions for safety, must be your prime consideration in new settlements. For that purpose ten *vedros* [pails] of rum and one barrel of molasses have been provided for you.

In conclusion, I recommend that you not forget that orderly habits among all enlightened people require that you keep a daily journal of events which may happen from the time of your departure from here. In particular you should not omit from this journal any noteworthy information deserving attention, even if it is heard from native inhabitants of the area. Remember also to inquire around Bodega and Trinidad whether it is true, as the California missionaries told the general [Rezanov], that cattle and horses are already widely spread out along the coast of New Albion. You and your people should try to learn whether it is possible that detachments will be sent farther inland from the coast, especially to little known places where pasture lands suitable for grazing livestock and for shelter may be found.

I am also appending a copy of the instructions I gave to navigator Petrov regarding the orders for his first voyage.

Written October 14, 1808 in the American port of New Arkhangel.

Administrator, Collegiate Counselor
Cavalier Aleksandr Baranov

Reference: Manuscript Department, Lenin Library, f. 204, 32.34, 1. 27–32 ob.

See: N. N. Bashkina et al., eds. *Rossiia i SShaA: Stanovlenie otnoshenii 1765–1815*. (Moscow: 1980). Doc. 276, 344–347.

26

OCTOBER 7, 1809

A LETTER FROM ANDREI IA. DASHKOV, RUSSIAN CONSUL GENERAL
IN PHILADELPHIA, TO ALEKSANDR A. BARANOV

My Dear Sir, Aleksandr Andreevich.
Last year, by virtue of the Imperial will of His Imperial
Majesty [Alexander I], I was appointed Plenipotentiary and
Consul General in the United States of America, and I have
been residing in this republic since July of this year.

In accordance with the instructions I received from our
Minister of Foreign Affairs and Commerce, His Excellency
Count Nikolai Petrovich Rumiantsev, I have been directed to
devote all possible attention to supporting and defending the
commercial interests of the Russian American Company in its
relations with citizens of the United States. In case of necessity, I am to intercede on its behalf with this government, and
to inquire whether the Americans wish to continue their trade
with the savages who live in the vicinity of, or within the limits
of, the Russian settlements, a trade which is deleterious to the
Russians' hunting, trade and indeed their actual physical safety
there.

At the time of my departure from St. Petersburg last September, the Russian American Company paid me the honor of
naming me its correspondent, and informed me at length about
the political and commercial situation of its settlements on the
Northwest Coast of America. The Company empowered me
to enter into correspondence with you, and to inform you at
the earliest opportune time of all circumstances which are germane to you and about which you should have information. I
therefore have the honor and pleasure of advising you of the
following:

1. My appointment, rank and future sojourn in the United
States of America; the instructions I have received from offi-
cials of the Company indicating all its support for the Russian
American Company on commercial matters, and regarding its
relations with the government or with citizens of the United
States; and the confidence with which the gracious Company

has favored me, having revealed to me its situation and aspirations, so I can assist as much as possible in the realization of those aims.

2. The views of this government on the Northwest Coast of America and how it regards our settlements in that region.

3. Discoveries made by the American government along the Columbia River and a rivalry that may develop between our settlements and those of the Americans, if the latter intend to establish themselves in our vicinity.

4. How best to halt or avert the trade of these republicans with the savages of that region, a trade which is detrimental to the Company.

5. The means of establishing permanent trade with citizens of the United States, to supply our settlements in the most beneficial manner with their basic needs, and to avert the injury caused by the republicans' hunting and illegal trade with the savages on the Northwest Coast of America and on the islands.

I will try, my Dear Sir, to elucidate each point with such information as I have been able to secure during my three months here, in addition to other activity related to my position.

Although the first point does not require any clarification, nonetheless since I have not had the honor of becoming personally acquainted with you, I feel I should state that I am personally very determined to do everything that can benefit my country and therefore extend the success of the Russian American Company as much as my attention and work will permit, in accordance with the instructions I received from officials of the Company. Thus I beg you, my Dear Sir, to call on me for assistance in all instances where my efforts may be helpful for the esteemed Company.

Regarding the second point. Although the activity of this government cannot be secret, and every action is fully public, nevertheless some of its intentions and objectives are not always revealed to the people. I consider one such objective the views of the United States toward the Northwest Coast of America. In its discourse about this, it appears that the present government is playing down its interest; however, on the basis of many facts I feel justified in concluding that it is taking a considerable interest in the condition of that area, and if one detects a certain slow pace in carrying out its intentions, I can only ascribe this to the single fact that the government here cannot undertake anything on its own authority, but must win over private persons who depend on the government, by giving them aid—and all of this requires time.

The opinion of certain local merchants who sometimes consider trading in that region is that our settlements extend to 57° northern latitude and 135° western longitude. On the basis of instructions which I have received from the esteemed Company, and in accordance with its desire to establish permanent and firm trade between our settlements and the local populace, I felt that the best means of doing this was to inspire in Mr. [John Jacob] Astor the desire to develop direct and permanent trade with our settlements, on mutually agreeable terms, and to convince him of the advantages accruing to him from this. I found Mr. Astor very favorable to this, as if he had come to these conclusions himself.

Our conversation expanded and focused on business. Each of us posed many questions to the other. I tried to answer in an indirect manner in all instances where it was not to our advantage to disclose the conditions of our settlements or the intentions of the esteemed Company. From Mr. Astor I learned the following:

1. It is the intention of his projected company [Pacific Fur Co.] to establish a colony on the northern shore of the mouth of the Columbia River.

2. Such a settlement, if it were founded for the purpose of mutual advantage and if its relationship to Russian settlements were agreed upon, could be of definite benefit to the Russian American Company. As Mr. Astor says, when the Russian settlements—which are still far from the Columbia River at the present time—spread to the south, and when the American settlements extend to the north, and these eventually approach one another, the English, who already have intentions toward the same territory, at least in regard to trade, will have no right to settle between them.

3. The projected new settlement of the Canadian English company [North West Company] in the upper reaches of the Columbia River is the first step in that direction. Its intention

is to turn the trade with local savages to its own advantage. (From this it is obvious the Americans are more apprehensive of the proximity and competition of the English than of the Russians). You will further realize, my Dear Sir, that Mr. Astor's view on the second point is founded in part on his desire to undertake this enterprise on his own, not for the company, and that perhaps it would be better for the Russian settlements not to mention the place where his settlement will be, north or south of the mouth of the Columbia. There is no doubt but that Mr. Astor is much more enthusiastic about this undertaking than his government is, and this being the case, one can use his proposal and turn it to the advantage of the aims of the Russian American Company. With his capital, enterprise and knowledge of business, Mr. Astor can avert from us the competition from any other company which would be to our disadvantage.

When he posed the question to me whether the Russians have any intention to move farther south or to settle along the Columbia River, I continued to respond that I did not know to what latitude [how far south] our settlements have spread, and that I considered the Columbia River too far from our settlements to organize such a venture.

Regarding point three, I believe that you already know, my Dear Sir, that this government sent Captain [Meriwether] Lewis to the western parts of America to make further explorations, and that Mr. Lewis was the next person after [Alexander] McKenzie to reach the Columbia River and the Pacific Ocean. The government rewarded him by appointing him Governor of Upper Louisiana, but his travel account, which was to have been published a year ago, has still not appeared in print. *I do not know why*.

Meanwhile, I have learned from very trustworthy persons that the English Canadian company not long ago established a settlement, although still quite small, in the upper reaches of the Columbia, in the foothills of the mountains where it has its source, an event of which not many persons here are aware. But I have not heard that there is at the present time any settlement at the mouth of that river, or near the place where it empties into the Pacific Ocean. Nevertheless I am convinced that several American citizens are thinking of establishing a company with a joint capital of between $2,000,000 and $5,000,000, and that they intend to ask the government for a charter and will settle near the mouth of the Columbia, I believe on the north bank. This venture appears to be backed by the government, but the company has not yet been organized, and they are not in a hurry to do so.

Regarding the fourth point. Following the request of the Russian American Company to our government to suppress forbidden trade along the Northwest Coast of America by citizens of the United States who supply the savages with various weapons and provide them the means of pillaging Russian settlements and endangering the lives of the settlers, I have been instructed that this government should prohibit Americans from continuing this trade, and should try to convince them to deal only with the Russian American Company, not with the savages.

When I made a thorough study of the Constitution of this republic, and the powers of the executive branch of government, I learned the following:

1. The government cannot prohibit Americans from carrying on trade with any people, civilized or savage. (The current embargo against England and France is an exception to the rule because of dire circumstances, and was approved by Congress).

2. There is no legal prohibition against trade in weapons, that is, military contraband. Thus such weaponry can be delivered anywhere, just as any other goods. But it is public knowledge that international law does not permit a neutral state to supply military contraband to powers who are at war; and that a neutral ship sailing to the port of a power at war, with such a cargo, will rightfully become the prize of an enemy who may halt and seize her. Therefore the United States does not depart from this general rule, and does not intercede on behalf of American ships that may be seized as prizes, nor does that government consider it necessary to warn its citizens against entering certain ports with military contraband. But even if the American government, in deference to ours, were to proclaim such a prohibition, it would not serve us unless we had naval vessels cruising in those waters, which could check the venturesome Americans.

Consequently, I believe it is necessary to look for means of preventing unrestrained American trade from harming our settlements, not so much through the American government as through our own, or from a special form of trade between our settlements and the United States. I will explain this more fully in the next point. However, I will not fail in my efforts with this government, through certain legal methods, to make it as difficult as possible for the enterprises of the Americans who enter into this trade which is so detrimental to us.

5. I have devoted considerable effort to finding out who the persons are who are planning to organize the [American] company, and have learned that John Jacob Astor is one of the most active members of that company. He lives in New York and is respected there not only because of his wealth, but also because of his character. Consequently, when I learned that he is trying to send a ship to the Northwest Coast of America, I went to New York in order to meet with him and ask him to take my letters to you, since his ship plans to visit our settlements.

Although I know that the Russian American Company is trying to convince the Americans to trade exclusively with its settlers, and not with the savages, it was difficult to persuade the Americans to trade with only one company, not, as is their custom, each man for himself, competing with each other which would eventually put the trade of this land solely in our hands.

Since I want the information which I have gathered to be of advantage to the Russian American Company, I have the honor now to inform you of Mr. Astor's proposals.

1. He wants to enter into a contract with you for at least a three-year period during which time he would supply necessary goods for our colony. He is willing to furnish goods at established prices, either for cash or for checks drawn on the Russian American Company in St. Petersburg; or he would barter the goods for furs. He can send two or three ships to you every year, depending on your needs. Please note that it is understood that he will not carry on trade with the savages. We did not discuss the question of whether you will have the right to enter into an agreement with another supplier during this period.

2. He offers the use of his ships to carry your goods to Canton, either together with his own cargo, or separately.

3. He offers the services of his agent in Canton, whose sole activity, if the Russian American Company wishes, would be to sell furs for himself, Mr. Astor and the Russian American Company on an equal basis.

Although by virtue of your position as administrator of the region, and your experience, you are the only person who can truly judge whether Mr. Astor's proposals are of value, and whether or not they are advantageous to the Russian American Company, I cannot resist suggesting to you, my Dear Sir, how they could be of benefit to our settlements.

1. Every American who dispatches a ship from here to the Northwest Coast of America and intends to trade with the savages always has to rely on trade with our settlements because the Americans cannot be absolutely certain of profiting from trade with the savages. If they did not have the possibility of trading with our settlements they would not take such a risk. They have learned that our settlements deal with one or more reputable business firms. These American speculators will not venture to trade only with the savages. Thus without great effort, the trade of United States citizens with savages, which is so detrimental to our trade, will be restrained.

2. Our settlements can be supplied on a regular basis, at established prices, with everything they need to be successful in their own ventures.

3. Prices on furs in Canton will be higher because the trade will be in the hands of one person, and this will certainly impact our trade in Kiakhta.

In addition to the above proposals, Mr. Astor asked me to inquire of you whether you could anticipate how it might be to our mutual advantage if he personally, not his company, were to establish a settlement on the northern shore of the mouth of the Columbia River. Could new commercial relations with the Russian American settlements be established? Even though he knows that every nation and every individual has the right to settle there, it would be better for both sides if the Russian settlements were favorably inclined toward [such a settlement]. I did not reply at all on this question except to say that I would inform you about it, my Dear Sir. Meanwhile, along with my letter I will send a copy to the esteemed [Russian American] Company.

Mr. Astor is dispatching his ship *Enterprise* from New York

Ivan A. Kuskov served as Baranov's assistant for many years, working successfully to develop cooperative sea otter hunting parties with American ship captains. A possible successor to Baranov, he was superseded by naval Captain Leontii Hagemeister. Kuskov continued to run Fort Ross in California until 1821, an assignment he may have preferred. This portrait by an unknown artist is held in the collections of the Kraevedcheskii Muzei, Totma. (OHS neg. OrHi 82936)

with John Ebbets as master, and is authorizing him to talk with you and negotiate an agreement. He wishes that such agreement not take effect until Mr. Ebbets returns and there can be general consent between Mr. Astor and me, providing you feel it beneficial for the Russian American Company to authorize me to do this. I humbly beg you, my Dear Sir, to write to me in detail regarding this, instructing me as to what I may do and how to proceed in regard to amending terms of such an agreement, if you foresee the necessity for this.

In regard to Mr. Ebbets, I doubt that Mr. Astor has given him the right to conclude a final agreement with you, and he has not yet begun to negotiate with me. Consequently I ask you to write to me about anything you may not wish to reveal to them, although I cannot be certain they will not become privy to the content of your letters, which after all will come to me through their hands.

Mr. Astor asked me to give him a list of items that would be most necessary for the settlements so he could prepare his cargo on that basis and this I have done. I drew up the list from the instructions which the esteemed Company gave me. I hope, my Dear Sir, that if you do not take exception to the prices and other considerations, you will be so kind as to give preference to the goods Mr. Astor will bring, over those which some other vessel might offer.

I also feel it important to inform you that I have learned from certain persons whose information I trust that several months ago a certain Englishman in Canton planned to arm a ship to attack and pillage our American settlements, but a shortage of manpower prevented him from carrying out this plan. I have not been able to learn his name.

Europe is still in the heat of battle. Bonaparte has almost destroyed Austria. Every day I expect to hear the Russian forces have occupied Turkey [Russo-Turkish War, 1806–1812]. The war with Sweden has not yet ended [Russo-Swedish War, 1808–1809]. The English have not inflicted any damage on Russian ports. Their expedition against Antwerp [1809] failed, and the men returned home, leaving Flushing behind. Trade is in a miserable condition. It looks as if the United States and Russia will enter into a commercial relationship.

Reference: TsGAOR SSSR, f. 907, op.1, d. 55, 11. 3–10.
See: *VPR*, First Series, Vol. 5, Doc. 132, 270–274.

27

NOVEMBER 12, 1809

A REPORT FROM COUNT NIKOLAI P. RUMIANTSEV, MINISTER OF
COMMERCE AND FOREIGN AFFAIRS, TO EMPEROR ALEXANDER I

I n submitting to Your Imperial Majesty the most respectful
reports of the [Main] Administration of the [Russian] American Company, and of Collegiate Councillor [Aleksandr A.] Baranov concerning our American settlements, I venture to give
a brief review of the contents of these, as well as of other documents which the Administration has given to me.

1. In 1808 some five ships from the American States came
to the [Aleutian] Islands to corner the fur trade by bartering
firearms, powder and shot with the savages for furs.

2. Baranov heard from Bostonians who had come from
Canton that French privateers from Ile de France were plotting
to ravage our settlements. These rumors, however, did not ma-
terialize. Baranov hopes to defend the area from attack by small
vessels with the armed ship *Neva*, but he must put himself into
the power of Providence against attack by large vessels, since
the government sloop *Diana* which was ordered to cruise in the
vicinity of the Company settlements was held by the English
at the Cape of Good Hope, according to last year's information. However, the captain of the *Diana* [Vasilii M. Golovnin],
hopes to obtain free passage because the voyage has a scientific
rather than a military purpose.

3. The American States had planned to establish a settlement in New Albion at [the mouth of] the Columbia River
during the summer of 1808, if the Russians had not already
settled there. In order to forestall them, Baranov dispatched a
party of Russians and savages who were loyal to us, under the
leadership of Commerce Counselor [Ivan A.] Kuskov, to occupy a site for a settlement between Trinidad Bay and the fortress of San Francisco. He ordered Kuskov to trade with the
savages there for precious furs, a trade which only the Bostonians had taken advantage of previously. In addition he sent a
Bostonian vessel with a group of Russians and island natives to
California to buy necessary provisions; although this is strictly

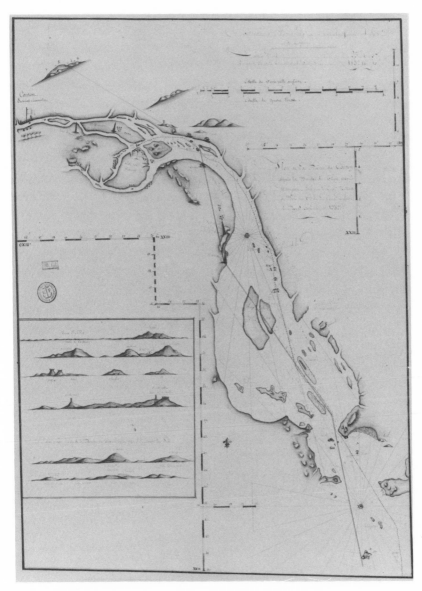

A superb French map of the Pearl River, with Canton at the
flag in the upper left. Biblotheque Nationale, Paris.

forbidden by the Spanish court, local authorities and the missionaries in particular find it profitable to sell these things
secretly.

4. [Sysoi] Slobodchikov, the leader of a group of Russian
promyshlenniks, sailed to the Sandwich Islands in 1807 aboard

Watercolor by Tinqua shows later view of the Whampoa (Pearl) River filled with the ships of five nations. Peabody Museum of Salem. Photo by Mark Sexton.

a small vessel which had been purchased from the Bostonians. He became friendly with the local king, and brought Baranov a gift from him as a sign of friendship, a helmet decorated with varicolored feathers. Baranov speaks of Slobodchikov as an efficient and energetic man who brings honor to the Russians, although he is illiterate.

5. When the ship *Neva* arrived, in order that it not be idle, Baranov sent it to the Sandwich Islands in an effort to establish trade with the islands. Lt. [Leontii A.] Hagemeister, the commander of that vessel, arrived in the islands in January of the present year. There he learned that the islands of Maui, Hawaii, Molokai, Lanai and Kauai are led by King Kamehameha and that the local produce has become extremely expensive because the Bostonians refresh themselves there en route to Canton and obtain various necessities by bartering their goods for mere trifles. The king of these islanders has taken over this trade for himself, and many of these European goods are moldering in his warehouses. Finally, Hagemeister learned that not only will the king not oppose Russians settling on the island of Molokai, which is very fertile, although less so than the other islands, but in fact he needs such a settlement in order to defend himself against the king of other Sandwich Islands. Hagemeister believes that twenty men would be enough to establish a settlement there and to defend it, with one cannon.

He remarks that these islands, which have a superb climate, are well situated to supply all of Asiatic Russia abundantly with their produce—coconut, breadfruit, a sweet root from which good rum is distilled, sugar cane, millet, wild tobacco, pineapple, from which excellent wine is made, sandalwood and other woods similar to lignum vitae, wild cattle and swine.

6. Russian promyshlenniks, who were sent aboard a Bostonian vessel as American prikashchiks to Canton to trade, brought a letter to Baranov from the Swedish consul [Anders Ljungstedt] in Canton, in which he appended a decree from the Chinese Emperor concerning the prohibition against Russian vessels entering Canton. This was issued at the time when the *Nadezhda* and *Neva* arrived in Canton. [The Swedish consul] proposes that we carry on trade in Canton under the flag of the American States or of Sweden; if the latter, we must request permission from the Swedish court. He also proposes serving as commissioner for the Company for 10,000 rubles for each cargo.

7. The decree of the Chinese Emperor includes an order for the head of the customs office in Canton to give an explanation as to why and how permission for those two vessels to trade there was granted. He is reminded that Russians had never come to Canton before, and that since this was a new development he should have asked higher authorities for permission to allow these vessels to enter. The decree also stipulates that if the ships have not yet departed, information should be secured about both of them, and that in the future no vessels from countries which have not previously visited Canton are to be permitted to do so without permission.

The following items in these papers require a decision from Your Imperial Majesty:

A. The Administration of the [Russian] American Company is ready to invoke strong measures against Bostonians who continue to sell weapons to the island natives, in spite of having been censured for this. But the Administration cannot act without specific permission from Your Imperial Majesty.

B. Concerning the projected [Russian] settlement in New Albion, the American States will undoubtedly be jealous of it, and the Administration places itself under the gracious protection of Your Imperial Majesty. Baranov believes that because of a shortage of personnel, except for those who are employed

Watercolor by Tinqua shows the factories of Canton and the English Church on the Pearl River. Peabody Museum of Salem. Photo by Mark Sexton.

as seasonal promyshlenniks, the Company is not strong enough to build a permanent colony and protect it with a fortress. He maintains that for Imperial benefit this settlement must be a government project, if this proposal receives Imperial consent.

C. Baranov considers Lieutenant Hagemeister a man of excellent qualifications, knowledge and zeal for the goals of the Company and solicits awards for him in rank and decoration.

My conclusions on these matters are as follows:

1. Concerning the admonition to the Bostonians regarding the sale of firearms to island natives: it will suffice to authorize Count [Fedor P.] Pahlen to demand the suspension of such harmful commerce. I myself will definitely bring up this matter with the American minister here, [John Quincy] Adams.

2. Regarding a [Russian] state settlement in Albion: since the government in the present instance is unable to provide financial support to such an undertaking, I propose leaving it to the Administration of the Russian American Company to

establish this settlement at its own expense. However, in case of need they may expect the gracious protection of Your Majesty.

3. Concerning the awards requested by Baranov for Lieutenant Hagemeister, I myself make bold to ask Your Imperial Majesty to grant this distinction to such a worthy officer, from Your special grace.

4. Finally, regarding the decree from the Chinese Emperor: it contains no severe measures directed specifically against the Russians; and because this is a new situation, since the Russians have never previously visited Canton, it orders that vessels of powers that have not previously visited Canton not be allowed to do so without permission. I will transmit a copy of the Chinese decree to the Governor General of Siberia, and will append to it the instructions which Your Imperial Majesty gave to the Civil Governor of Irkutsk, [Nikolai I.] Treskin, on the occasion of the renewal of our embassy in China.

Count Nikolai Rumiantsev

Reference: TsGIA SSSR, f. 13, op.1, d. 287, 11. 78–84 ob.
See: N. N. Bashkina et al, eds. *Rossiia i SShA: Stanovlenie otnoshenii 1765–1815*. (Moscow: 1980). Doc. 312, 388–391.

28

A REQUEST FOR ASSISTANCE IN ESTABLISHING TRADE BETWEEN RUSSIAN AMERICA AND CALIFORNIA, FROM MIKHAIL M. BULDAKOV, CHAIRMAN OF THE BOARD OF THE RUSSIAN AMERICAN COMPANY, TO NIKOLAI P. RUMIANTSEV, MINISTER OF COMMERCE AND FOREIGN AFFAIRS

In January, 1808, thanks to Your Excellency, I had the honor to submit to His Imperial Majesty my most humble statement concerning the opportunity and means for establishing commercial relations between the Russian American Company and inhabitants of California. The latter desire this trade because they experience shortages of many items of natural and manufactured goods in which Russia abounds. In contrast, California is rich in certain things which are either in short supply or completely unobtainable not only in the [Russian] American settlements, but in the Kamchatka and Okhotsk regions as well.

The California Governor in Monterey has already written to the Mexican Viceroy concerning a petition for permission to establish such ties; he did this while the late Rezanov was visiting there. The Viceroy has undoubtedly submitted this to the court in Madrid. All that is now necessary is for the Russian ministry to submit a proposal and request, and according to Your Excellency's assurances, this was done in 1808. However, to date there has been no result. We must hope the reason is the great change which is presently taking place in the Spanish government, and the rising unrest there. Since the chances for this proposal appear to be favorable at the present time, I am taking this opportunity of submitting the request to Your Excellency, and I most humbly ask in the name of the entire Russian American Company for your gracious assistance in soliciting trade with California.

Reference: *VPR*, First Series, Vol. 5, Doc. 156, 327.

29

SEPTEMBER 22, 1810

A REPORT FROM THE MAIN ADMINISTRATION OF THE RUSSIAN
AMERICAN COMPANY TO EMPEROR ALEXANDER I

To the Most Illustrious Reigning Great Sovereign Emperor and Autocrat of All Russia, a most respectful report from the Main Administration of the Russian American Company.

The Main Administration of the Company is pleased to report most respectfully to Your Imperial Majesty that the following news has been received by couriers from Kamchatka and Okhotsk, and from the Chief Administrator, Collegiate Councillor and Cavalier [Aleksandr A.] Baranov in America.

The ship *Neva*, which has made its second circumnavigation to America, again sailed from the island of Sitka to Petropavlovsk harbor on Kamchatka, where it successfully anchored on May 28 [1810]. The ship brought the Company a substantial cargo of furs from America, the value of which is appended to this report.

This ship will remain in Kamchatka for continued Company use because it cannot proceed to Canton, although it was sent to Kamchatka for that purpose; it is not yet possible [for Russia] to trade in Canton. Furthermore, it would be dangerous for the ship to return around the world because of the present European situation. For that reason the commanding officer, Lieutenant [Leontii A.] Hagemeister, and his officers and entire crew have left Company service and are returning [overland] to [European] Russia, and in fact have already moved on to Okhotsk.

The small cutter *Rostislav* also put in at Petropavlovsk this past year, with a cargo of furs sent from the island of Unalaska. This year the vessel will be dispatched to Okhotsk to take on as much of the *Neva's* cargo as possible. We do not have information as to whether it has reached Okhotsk.

We have had no news of any problems involving the local native inhabitants or foreigners on the island of Sitka or in any of the other Company enterprises. Everything has been peaceful and calm, with the exception of an unfortunate plot conceived by two Russian promyshlenniks, who conspired with some of their associates to do what [Mauritius A.] Benyowsky, a Polish or Hungarian exile, did in Kamchatka at one time [1771]. But because the conspirators were not well informed and did not understand how to go about such matters, and because that kind of person is extremely inept, the plot was soon discovered. After a careful investigation of the background of the situation, and of the confessions of the plotters, they were put aboard the *Neva* and sent to Kamchatka where they were put into the hands of the courts of that oblast administration.

Baranov informs us that Bostonian merchants and seafarers are visiting [Russian] America much less frequently than previously. With the exception of one vessel, there have been no Bostonians there since 1808. The reason for this may be their fear of being captured by the English.

One of the fourteen seagoing vessels, both large and small, owned by the Company, the small tender *Avos* was dispatched in September, 1808, from Unalaska to the island of Sitka, under the command of Lieutenant Sukin; the vessel was wrecked off Sitka on October 11. All of the crew were rescued, and part of the cargo as well. The same fate befell the Bostonian [Joseph] O'Cain, who under the terms of an agreement with Baranov, had sailed his three-masted ship *Eclipse* to Canton to sell furs and buy Chinese goods. When he completed this mission in 1808 he brought the Chinese goods to Kamchatka for resale; but when he set out from there en route to Baranov on Sitka, he had a shipwreck near the island of Unalaska. He built a small vessel from the wreckage of the *Eclipse*, set out in it in 1809, but was again wrecked between the islands of Umnak and Sanak. Although the ship was lost he managed to survive the night by using ice floes to reach shore; however, both he and a young Sandwich Island woman eventually succumbed. The rest of the crew survived.

Your Imperial Majesty has already been informed, in [a report of] November 5, 1809, of the expedition Baranov dispatched in 1808 to settle in New Albion at the Columbia River. Baranov has not yet reported to us whether that expedition was successful. The only information we have comes from Kodiak Island, that the head of the expedition, Commerce Counselor Kuskov, sent Baranov a dispatch with the ship *Kadiak* and then returned safely to Sitka with a valuable cargo. The vessel *Ni-*

kolai was left behind, and we know nothing of its fate at the present time. [See footnote, Document 25]

According to Administrator Baranov, Lieutenant Hagemeister, commanding *Neva*, made no new discoveries. The Main Administration of the Company reported most respectfully to Your Imperial Majesty on November 5, 1809, that when Hagemeister first returned to Kamchatka from Kodiak, he had intended to proceed to the Komandorskie Islands and then south to 45° to search for undiscovered islands. There had been many conjectures about the possibility of the existence of such islands by earlier seafarers. However, heavy fog and contrary winds prevented Hagemeister from sighting them, although he noted many indications that they do exist.

In 1808 and 1809 Administrator Baranov built two new vessels on Sitka, in addition to the existing fourteen Company vessels. The first is the three-masted *Otkrytie*; the second is a schooner, the *Chirikov*, named for the Russian captain [Aleksei I.] who was the first to touch America, at Cape St. Elias.

The decision was made not to build more ships because since Canton has not been opened to [our] trade, they are not needed. [Baranov] expressed his deep heartfelt sorrow, out of patriotism, that trade with Canton still has not been opened. Without it Company activity cannot reach full fruition. He also regrets that the Company has been unable to develop close contacts with California, which would provide necessary provisions for which the Company enterprises suffer a great need. These provisions are presently delivered there via Okhotsk at great cost, and are not always fresh, nor available in the amounts required.

Finally, we report that the government sloop *Diana*, which was dispatched around the world to Kamchatka, reached there and this year has set out for [European] Russia. The vessel delivered various supplies to the Company's enterprises in America, for which the Company paid four rubles per pud.

INVENTORY OF FURS TAKEN BY THE VESSELS *NEVA* AND *ROSTISLAV* IN 1809 AND 1810 TO KAMCHATKA [from America].

Sea otters	5,414
Immature sea otters	377

Sea otter tails	3,976
Red foxes	2,556
Cross foxes	936
Black brown foxes	707
Blue foxes	2,527
River otters	521
Minks	29
Bears	139
Beavers	8
Wolves	4
Wolverine	1
Seals	39,678
Walrus tusks	98 puds

The Company Administration appraises this entire cargo at average prices for a total of 778,521 rubles.

Reference: Library of Congress, Manuscript Division. Yudin Collection, Box 1.

30

OCTOBER 11, 1811

A LETTER FROM ANDREI IA. DASHKOV, RUSSIAN CONSUL GENERAL IN PHILADELPHIA, TO ALEKSANDR A. BARANOV, CHIEF ADMINISTRATOR OF THE RUSSIAN AMERICAN COMPANY.

Gracious Sir, Aleksandr Andreevich.
Your esteemed letter of July 28, 1810 reached me in June [1811], three days before an American ship left for the port of St. Petersburg. I took advantage of that opportunity to inform the Russian American Company of all the circumstances it needed to be aware of. This time too (as usual) I encountered the inconvenience of not being able to send a large packet because the captain refused to take any papers which looked as if they might be official government matters. I had to make an abstract of your letters, which I sent to St. P[etersburg] with my report. I will keep the various records I received from you until I have a better opportunity to send them.

I made certain to inform the Main Administration of the content of your letter to Mr. A. [John Jacob Astor], concerning your agreement with [John] Ebbets about delivering your furs to Canton and purchasing other goods for you. I also informed them of your arrangement to receive from Mr. A. a cargo of goods which you had ordered, at set prices. Mr. A. found, however, that almost all of your prices were so low it was impossible for him to agree to them. He demonstrated this to me, using various examples which were mutually agreeable to him and to me. He definitely wants to enter into commercial relations with you. This is quite obvious, because in spite of the substantial difference in prices, he is sending you a large part of the goods you want, with a statement of the present prices of each article. He is leaving it completely up to your own judgment to decide what the markup for freight and for his profit should be. Judging impartially, this should be at least 20% to 25% on the total cargo.

By sending you the goods you have ordered, Mr. A. wishes to enter into business relations with you, not just to make a profit from the goods he is sending. Moreover, he would stand

Alexander saw his troops encamped on the Champs Elysees in Paris in 1814. His chief concerns were in Napoleonic Europe and the Caucasus, but there was always time for the far Pacific ventures. From Schilder, N. K. *Imperator Aleksandr Pervyi*. (OHS neg. 82973)

to suffer a loss if his main purpose in dispatching the ship were not to establish his settlement on the Columbia River, where he is sending all the goods necessary for an initial settlement, and where he has already sent some 70 workmen overland and by rivers across the United States.

Last March Mr. A. sent Mr. [Adrian] Bentzon (who is married to his daughter) to St. Petersburg, where he is presently negotiating with the Company about various matters with which you are familiar.

I am very sorry to have to inform you that I have not received any news from the Company since I came here, nor have I had any replies to letters I have been sending in duplicate and triplicate for more than a year.

However, I am able to append a list of prices which are

current in various places. When I sent in my first dispatches, I forwarded several of these printed sheets to you, but they have not reached you. One should not rely on the prices printed here, however. Political circumstances and news reports are constantly forcing them to change. For example, if war were to break out between the Americans and the English, or if the transport of provisions to Lisbon or Cadiz were to be cut off, [certain items] would fall 30 or 40 percent, while the prices of Russian goods would rise.

I am much indebted to you, my dear sir, for all the news about your region which you sent to me; I am most interested in it. In my latest dispatches I advised the Main Administration of the most important items, and those most deserving of their attention.

Mr. A. showed me a letter from Mr. Eb[bets] in which he tells of his stay in New Arkhangel and mentions that he stopped in the Queen Charlotte Islands where he carried on trade, but on a very small scale, no more than 3,000 dollars, including goods which he gave to certain American skippers who asked for them, men he had met on his voyage. Mr. A. wanted to use this information to impress on me the fact that Mr. Eb. had not been trading prior to the time he reached you.

The voyage of his son-in-law to St. P. will settle the question of whether the Company will want to enter into some agreement with Mr. A. That news may reach you next spring.

I feel it my duty to inform you that I suggested to Mr. A. that he give me an inventory of the goods he sent you, with the above mentioned prices he suggested, or the cost of the goods to him, so I could note my comments. He did send me the inventory of goods and quantities, but not prices. For this reason I have found it necessary to send you the various prices, even though they are not absolutely firm. The quality of goods, and the time when they are bought, causes an increase or decrease in price.

I have no reason to suspect that Mr. A. intends to take advantage of you. On the contrary, I am convinced that in business he is direct and sincere. I do not anticipate that he will increase prices over and above the current ones, and what he himself pays. For that reason he hopes that you will add at least 25% for freight and his commission, and that you will impose this sum on the entire cargo of goods.

Reference: TsGAOR, f. 907, op. 1, d. 55, 11. 17–18 ob.

See: N. N. Bashkina et al, eds. *Rossiia i SShA: stanovlenie otnoshenii, 1765–1815*. (Moscow: 1980). Doc. 398, 491–492.

31

A REPORT FROM THE OKHOTSK OFFICE OF THE RUSSIAN AMERICAN
COMPANY CONCERNING TROUBLE WITH THE JAPANESE

On November 8, 1811, we received from the Okhotsk office its Report No. 373, dated August 12. Among other pieces of information it contains the following news.

There is concern [in Okhotsk] about news from Japan. The news concerns the sloop *Diana*, which reached port on the 3rd of this month, having sailed along the coast of the Kurils and the Japanese islands. The report states that the commanding officer of the ship, Captain Lieutenant [Vasilii M.] Golovnin, was captured by the Japanese military force who live on one of the nearest islands, the island of Matmai. The naval sloop *Diana* was armed with 24 guns, but because of the great number of armed [Japanese], the crew could not offer enough resistance to prevent the capture of the commanding officer, and the ship had to return without him. Midshipman Mur [Moore?], navigator Khlesnikov and four sailors were also captured along with Golovnin.

This news and rumors attest to the fact that the Japanese are well armed and live in a state of constant vigilance on all the islands near Sakhalin. This has forced the Okhotsk office to postpone the Sakhalin Expedition. This is possibly also due to the late arrival of the ship *Finlandia*, or her failure to arrive at all—which of these two possibilities is the case, remains a mystery.

The small vessel which the [Okhotsk] office has at its disposal does not have an adequate crew: most of them are new and inexperienced at sea. In addition it does not have an adequate complement of guns and other necessary equipment. This is the opinion both of the office and of [Iakov A.] Podushkin, the leader of the expedition, under these new and unexpected circumstances.

The office believes that since the behavior of the Japanese could interfere with the plans of the expedition now, this situation will not improve in any way next year, because in the

The English artist J. A. Atkinson spent many successful years at the court of Emperor Alexander I painting the heroes of 1812. He was attracted to the exotic, as witness this Russian presence in Nagasaki, with possibly the Dutch entrepot in the background. Krusenstern, *Voyage Round the World.* (OHS OrHi neg. 82029)

spring [the Russians] will have no large ship available except for the *Finlandia*, nor will they have any more men or weapons than they presently have. Consequently, to ensure success, the office has decided to follow the advice of the local administrator and of Podushkin, and to send the navigator Vasilev and all the men to winter over at Petropavlovsk harbor. Then as early in the spring as possible they will proceed under Podushkin's leadership to sail aboard *Neva* to Kodiak or Sitka.

Since they do not have their own vessel, the local commander is lending them a state owned vessel with officers and the necessary number of sailors, on the condition that these people are to receive only Company provisions in Kamchatka, and that the money [for their wages] and for the entire cost of transporting and maintaining them at the harbor will be paid to higher authorities. That decision was immediately put into effect on September 1, in spite of the fact that no one knows the whereabouts of *Finlandia*, and that *Rostislav* is also urgently needed: the former, to be sent to Atka, and the latter, to remain here in accordance with the decree of the Main Administration.

See: Library of Congress, Manuscript Division. Yudin Collection, Box 2.

32

NOT BEFORE JANUARY 16, 1812

A REPORT FROM OSIP P. KOZODAVLEV, MINISTER OF INTERNAL AF-
FAIRS, TO COUNT NIKOLAI P. RUMIANTSEV, MINISTER OF COM-
MERCE AND FOREIGN AFFAIRS

Gracious Sir, Count Nikolai Petrovich.
Your Excellency is undoubtedly aware of the present situation regarding the affairs of the Russian American Company and its colonies. The settlements which the North Americans are planning to establish at the mouth of the Columbia River threaten to put an end to the Company's enterprises, and the [Russian] colonies are at hazard because these same Americans have supplied the Indians with firearms and have instructed them in their use.

Although Your Excellency has informed the Main Administration of the Russian American Company of the proposal of the New York-based company of [Adrian] Bentzon, [to halt the sale of firearms to natives and to export furs to Russia], the Company finds this proposal inimical to its business affairs and feels it should not be adopted. It hopes it will have support from the gracious patronage of His Imperial Majesty.

Before any decisive action is taken concerning this, I feel obliged to submit my thoughts, Gracious Sir, based only on general observations.

I believe that any means which uses force or firearms to deflect the attempts of the North Americans, even though such means would undoubtedly be successful, would not be appropriate in this case. I firmly believe that any action which would breach governmental relations for the benefit of a private company would be ill-conceived. Thus I believe it would be better to utilize the efforts of our Chargé d'Affaires in the United States to end the ventures of the Americans [detrimental to the interests of the Russian American Company]. If all arguments and importunities on our part are ineffectual in persuading the Americans to do this, then Bentzon's proposal, especially with some restrictions, would be a most plausible means, because it would establish a balance in the fur trade and raise a barrier to monopoly, in case the Russian American Company had it

Signs of disorder are seen as Napoleon and remnants of La Grande Armée leave Moscow. The city gates on the Kaluga Road emphasize the smoking ruins behind, where the frustrated Emperor has ordered the Kremlin towers leveled. Russian American Company concerns would seem far away to Alexander I during this fateful invasion period. N. K. Shilder, *Imperator Aleksandr Pervyi*. (OHS OrHi neg. 82985)

in mind to establish a monopoly there. By conducting a large part of its fur trade with Kiakhta, the Company would lose much less profit than by permitting settlement on the Columbia River.

In submitting this opinion for Your Excellency's attention, I find that I must turn your thoughts away from important Imperial concerns, and I most humbly request, my Gracious Sir, that you briefly review these circumstances. Because of your long administrative experience and skill in handling foreign affairs, you are much more familiar with procedures. Kindly honor me with your gracious advice, which will guide me in this matter.

Reference: TsGIA, f. 18, op. 5, d. 1201, ll. 12–15.
See: N. N. Bashkina et al, eds. *Rossiia i SShA: Stanovlenie otnoshenii, 1765–1815*. (Moscow: 1980). Doc. 407, 814–815.

33

AFTER DECEMBER.16, 1813

A REPORT TO EMPEROR ALEXANDER I FROM THE RUSSIAN AMERI-
CAN COMPANY COUNCIL, CONCERNING TRADE WITH CALIFORNIA
AND THE ESTABLISHMENT OF FORT ROSS

To the Most Illustrious Reigning Great Sovereign Emperor and Autocrat of All Russia.

A most humble request from the Council of the Russian American Company, organized through permission of Your Exalted Imperial Majesty on December 16, 1813.

Article Two of the authorization for the Council states, "All matters which are urgent or which because of political considerations require secrecy, as well as matters concerned with the extension of trade and navigation, and instructions concerning the same from the [Russian American] Company, are inseparable; these and any other matters that may pose difficulties for the Directors, or which are beyond their competence, must come to the attention and under the jurisdiction of the Council, together with the Main Administration of the Company."

In accordance with this, the Council has carefully reviewed the document submitted by the Directors of the Company concerning the inauguration of trade between the Company and Spanish California. The Council has found the following facts.

1. The reason for desiring this trade is the acute shortage of basic necessities which the Company colonies experience, whereas California, which is in relative proximity, abounds in these items. Although the Company has made a determined effort for many years to introduce agriculture in its colonies, the harsh climate has constantly hindered these efforts. While livestock breeding is progressing, it is nevertheless still in a condition where one cannot expect great increase. The livestock can be used for food, but only in extreme cases. Consequently all foodstuffs as well as tackle and sails must be brought from Russia and Siberia by the Company over a very long route. Such transport is exceedingly expensive, and frequent shipwrecks deprive the colonies even of that delivery.

2. Although California abounds in the production of grains and other foodstuffs, and although cattle are to be found in great numbers in forested areas, none of these can be procured through trade because the court in Madrid, on the advice of the earlier missionaries, has declared such trade with any foreigners illegal. Nonetheless North American skippers who sail to that region secretly buy everything they need from the Californians.

3. When Active Counselor [Nikolai P.] Rezanov visited the California port of San Francisco in 1806, the local governor allowed him to sell several items of Russian production such as linen fabric, work clothing, articles made of iron and the like; and he was permitted to buy various foodstuffs for our colonies. This permission was only granted because the Spanish had had favorable reports from all the foreign courts about this expedition, which had been sent around the world with the highest approbation of Your Imperial Majesty. Rezanov strongly urged future trade with Russia, and the Governor assured him that he would intercede with the Mexican Viceroy so permission might be obtained from the court in Madrid. He recognized the great benefit from mutual trade relations between the Russians and the Californians, and advised Rezanov that it would be useful for the Russian government also to make this request.

4. From that time on, the American company began to request that such trade become reality. As a result, we submitted a most humble request to Your Imperial Majesty, asking Your approval that such trade be inaugurated and that permission for the same be obtained from the court in Madrid, using the services of our Ambassador to Madrid, Baron [Grigorii A.] Stroganov. However, this request was not made a reality because of excesses and changes that were occurring in Spain. Consequently Your Majesty authorized the State Chancellor, Count [Nikolai P.] Rumiantsev, to inform the Company that until peace is restored in Europe, the Company should try to realize its objectives through its own efforts.

5. By reason of this, the Company continued to submit requests, whenever and however the opportunities presented themselves, through its own relationships and those of the Chief Administrator of the colonies, [Aleksandr A.] Baranov,

with the California missionaries and commandants. There has been favorable response because the Californians have a strong desire to establish this mutually profitable trade with the Russians. But because California is still subject to the [royal] prohibition, neither the Governor nor the Viceroy of Mexico could resolve this problem personally. Further, no news has come from Mexico regarding the request which had been submitted to the Viceroy. Consequently, the Californians advise that the Company submit its own request to Your Majesty, asking such permission, and that Your Majesty request the court of Madrid to act favorably on this matter.

All of these matters are clearly detailed in the copy submitted for Your Monarchial review; the Company Administration gave this copy to the State Chancellor on May 15 of this year.

6. The Administration of the Company is unaware of any action taken on this matter by the State Chancellor. Meanwhile, it has received a second communication from the colonies, from Baranov's island; it is dated June 3, 1813 and comes from a California missionary who has influence on local authorities. The strong content is the same as that of the earlier response and carries a promise to supply our colonies with various necessities, without publicizing the matter, whenever our ship docks at the port of San Francisco. A translation of this letter is hereby humbly appended to this petition, for Your Most Gracious review.

Most Merciful Sovereign! The Council of the American Company, in reviewing all of the above, concludes that only one thing is necessary to establish trade with California: Your Monarchial permission and the concurrence of the court of Madrid. This would allow our ships to put into all ports of the Spanish colonies, such as Manila on the island of Luzon, if the Company should decide to send its ships there. And the Spaniards, for their part, could come to our colonies

Therefore, believing that this situation is completely possible at this present favorable time; and since the Company needs to supply its colonies with sufficient provisions which are available relatively nearby and are abundant and inexpensive; and since the Company can benefit by exchanging Russian products for those provisions and thus inaugurate that trade; therefore last year the Company sent a substantial cargo around the world aboard the ship *Suvorov*. It would please the Californians themselves to establish mutual trade. We therefore make bold, on behalf of the entire Company, to request Your Most Merciful approval.

If the Company extends its ties with that country, in time we may expect that the Company will be able to obtain more than enough to meet its own needs, and will be able to forward the surplus to Kamchatka and Okhotsk, which have a great shortage of provisions and other goods, except for furs.

The Council also feels bound to report humbly to Your Imperial Majesty concerning the information which we have received from the colonies dated April 16 of this year. The Main Administration of the Company reports the start of a new [Russian American] settlement in 1812, some 40 versts from the port of San Francisco in a small bay called Bodega. This settlement [Ross] has been organized through the initiative of the Company. Its purpose is to establish a [Russian] settlement there or in some other place not occupied by Europeans, and to introduce agriculture there by planting hemp, flax and all manner of garden produce; they also wish to introduce livestock breeding in the outlying areas, both horses and cattle, hoping that the favorable climate, which is almost identical to the rest of California, and friendly reception on the part of the indigenous people, will assist its success.

Although we have not yet had any official word about this from the Commercial Counselor [Ivan A.] Kuskov, who has been entrusted with this expedition, nevertheless North American skippers who have visited that location have assured the Chief Administrator [Baranov] of the colonies that the Spaniards of California have received Kuskov and all the other Russians favorably, and have already supplied our settlement with livestock and grain.

As a result of this fortunate development, the Council hopes that with the establishment of trade with California, the organization of a regular Company settlement there, and the introduction of agriculture, livestock breeding and various other economic enterprises and manufacturing operations, it will be possible to have more people there to build ships, and to have enough of all goods not only for the colony's own needs, but a surplus to be sent to Kamchatka and Okhotsk, which will thus have to rely less on the delivery of necessities from [European] Russia and Siberia.

Reference: Library of Congress, Manuscript Division. Yudin Collection, Box 3.

34

A REPORT FROM THE MAIN ADMINISTRATION OF THE RUSSIAN
AMERICAN COMPANY TO OSIP P. KOZODAVLEV, MINISTER OF IN-
TERNAL AFFAIRS, CONCERNING LOSSES DUE TO SHIPWRECK AND
RUINED PELTRY

In compliance with Your Excellency's instruction Number
193, dated September 11, the Main Administration of the
[Russian American] Company has the honor of submitting
herewith a report on the balance of its capital for three two-
year periods (in accordance with Paragraph 11 of the Imperi-
ally confirmed Regulations of July 8, 1799, which were granted
to the Company). The three reports are for the years 1808,
1810 and 1812. Balance sheets for previous years have already
been submitted to Your Excellency in our report of December
22, 1811, at which time information about the business activity
of the Company was appended.

In examining the balance sheets herewith submitted, it may
be useful for Your Excellency to know why there was not only
no increase in capital prior to 1812, but indeed some decrease,
as compared with the stock issued. The Administration of the
Company has the honor of explaining that there were some
gains in those years, but they were offset by losses from various
causes, namely: the loss of ships with their cargoes, nonpay-
ment of debts by debtors and the like. However, there were
two most significant events which exerted tremendous influence on all the years from 1800 to 1810.

The first of these involved the frigate *Feniks* [Phoenix],
which was dispatched to the colonies in 1799 with 90 new promyshlenniks and a cargo worth more than half a million rubles
which was sent to strengthen these colonies. The ship was
wrecked. The Company did not learn of the wreck until 1803,
and could not immediately dispatch a new cargo of supplies
because of the loss of Baranov Island (Sitka) [to the Tlingit
Indians], including the fort which has been built there and
various economic enterprises. There were so few promyshlenniks left that they were either killed or taken captive by the

savages who had been incited by the Bostonian [British] skipper [Henry] Barber prior to the establishment of the fort in 1801.

As a result of this, in addition to the losses just mentioned, the Company lost 4,000 sea otter pelts (valued at 400,000 rubles) which had belonged to the promyshlenniks. For the next five years the Company had no significant hunting success. Although the island was retaken [by the Russians] in 1803, and a new settlement established opposite the previous one which had been destroyed, the loss of the earlier settlement had a great impact on the Company until 1806, because not until then did the Company begin to take enough pelts to hold sway in those waters.

The second circumstance is that because of inexperience on the part of the promyshlenniks and their desire for a large and quick profit (promyshlenniks receive half the pelts taken in return for their labor), in 1800, 1801 and 1802 they killed some 900,000 fur seals on the northern islands of St. Paul and St. George. They could not process and dry such a number of pelts in the open air, so they tried to dry them in hot bathhouses. The result was that a huge number of pelts were ruined; almost all were quite worthless. They sent about 600,000 of the pelts to Okhotsk and Irkutsk for the Company, who tried every possible means to dispose of them by selling at the lowest prices possible; but they had to burn more than 111,000 because they were not usable. In addition, they had to destroy more than 180,000 that had been left on those islands. They then had to issue a prohibition against hunting fur seals for the next five years, lest the seals become aware of the decimation and begin to avoid these islands because of the terrible slaughter.

These furs are in great demand by the Chinese, all the heathens who inhabit Siberia and Russia, and Russians of the lower classes throughout the country. If the pelts had not been ruined, the value according to prices at that time would have been from four to eight rubles apiece (and at present prices, from six to ten rubles apiece), which would have created a substantial profit for the Company. However, this loss deprived the Company of profit for eight years, because the hunt was again prohibited until 1810. Since then the hunt has been reopened, with the stipulation that no more than 150,000 to 200,000 be taken per year, even though it is possible to take as many as 300,000 per year. This rich and inexhaustible resource is the surest hope of the Company for making substantial profits.

These developments involving the loss of *Feniks* and the fur seal pelts made it impossible to attain growth prior to 1812. At the present time, with these problems behind us, as is apparent from the balance sheet for 1811, not only has the capital of the Company stabilized, but it has increased to the point that the value of every share has increased 50%. The shareholders have decided that this be divided among them, a fact which the Main Administration of the Company had the honor of bringing to Your Excellency's attention. It is likewise the case that the period ending in 1814 will also turn a significant profit.

Chairman of the Board of Directors
and Cavalier Mikhailo Buldakov
Director Benedikt Kramer
Director Andrei Severin
Chancellor Zelenin

Reference: *VPR*, First Series, Vol. 7. Doc. 421, 396–397.

35

MAY 15, 1814

A REPORT FROM THE MAIN ADMINISTRATION OF THE RUSSIAN
AMERICAN COMPANY TO NIKOLAI P. RUMIANTSEV, MINISTER OF
COMMERCE AND FOREIGN AFFAIRS, CONCERNING TRADE WITH
CALIFORNIA

Your Excellency is undoubtedly aware of the fact that the inhabitants of the region of California, which is part of the Spanish New World, have been prohibited by the Madrid court from trading with foreigners. Because of this the local people have had to sell or trade secretly any surplus of goods they may have to the North American skippers who sail all over the world and also come to them. For the same reason, the Russian American Company, although it is California's closest neighbor by virtue of its location in the Baranov Island colony (Sitka), and because of the almost constant friendship between the two nations, has not dared to send its vessels there, even though it has often had to maintain communication with that land [using non-Russian vessels] because its colonies have a shortage of the basic necessities of life such as grain, livestock and the like, which are abundant and inexpensive in California.

The Californians cannot sell their grain anywhere and thus do not plant as much as their favorable climate and fine soil would permit. Their domestic livestock has increased to such an extent that herds run wild in the forests over several hundred versts with no supervision or account. In order to prevent them from ruining the fields, the local government has had to reduce the number of these ranging beasts by decreeing that every year 10,000 to 30,000 head be slaughtered, the carcasses buried and any hides than cannot be tanned, destroyed.

In 1806 when the late Active Councillor [Nikolai P.] Rezanov was on Baranov Island to review all the colonies and their enterprises, there was such a desperate shortage of basic provisions that he resolved to go to California personally to look into the possibility of supplying the colonies with their primary needs, and if this were successful, to establish commercial ties with the Californians for the future. With this intention in mind, he took with him a quantity of various items, especially those of Russian manufacture such as iron, iron utensils, work clothing, linen and the like [to trade]. On February 25, aboard the Company frigate *Iunon* [*Juno*], he entered the port of San Francisco where there is a fortress with seven cannon and a battery of five field pieces.

The Spaniards knew of his around-the-world expedition because Your Excellency had informed all foreign governments about it. Thus they received Rezanov cordially, especially Don José Arguello, the commanding officer of the fortress, and his son, Don Luis. At Rezanov's request, the Governor of California himself soon came there from the gubernatorial town of Monterey. Rezanov was able to establish very friendly rapport with this distinguished elder gentleman, Colonel and Cavalier Don José de Arrillaga, who was a close friend of the commanding officer, Arguello. But Arrillaga could not make a decision on regular commercial relations with the Russians because of the above mentioned decrees prohibiting trade with foreigners, even though he acknowledged such a relationship would be beneficial not only to himself, but to all the other inhabitants as well, especially those who had befriended Rezanov, the local missionaries Martin de Landosta and Ramon de Avella. However, he gave permission for the frigate *Iunon* to sell its goods at that time and to buy the items Rezanov needed for the colonies, particularly grain, garden produce, salted meat, poultry, butter, tallow and the like.

In regard to regular trade in the future, he gave his word to Rezanov that he would present the matter to the Mexican Viceroy. He explained the problem to Rezanov in this manner:

"If the Madrid court knew the needs of this land, it would certainly establish mutual trade relations with Russia. In this manner both would benefit, and the Bostonians would not be in a position to incite the savages against the inhabitants, especially if the two powers, in order to protect their new subjects, would allow a frigate or a corvette to cruise along the coastline."

With such welcome statements on the part of the Governor, and the desires of all the Californians, Rezanov returned to the colonies with all he had been able to procure for them in California. He informed the Main Administration of the Company of this and recommended that it resolve the problem. For this reason the Main Administration of the Company, in the person of the Chairman of the Board of Directors, submitted to His Imperial Majesty, through your kind assistance, a humble petition, of which a copy is appended for your reference, as well as another [petition] addressed to Your Excellency.

Your intercession on behalf of these petitions has so far had only the result that the Russian Minister, Baron [Grigorii] Stroganov, who had just arrived at the Madrid court, was asked to request permission for our trade with California, but there was no resolution to this situation because Spain was in the midst of very troubled times: King Ferdinand VII had been taken prisoner by the French. For this reason Your Excellency, upon the Emperor's instruction, directed the Chairman of the Board of Directors of the Company that the Company itself should seek means to establish commercial ties with California.

In 1810 this was referred to the Chief Administrator of the colonies, Collegiate Counselor [Aleksandr A.] Baranov, with instructions to outfit a ship with cargo appropriate for [California] send the ship there, and give either the California inhabitants or the administration a letter sent in the name of the Company administration, written in Russian, Spanish and Latin. Baranov carried out this assignment. In 1812 he sent a letter with one of his promyshlenniks, Bakadorov, who acted as his agent. Bakadorov went aboard a Bostonian ship. Baranov instructed Bakadorov to try to establish friendship with any of the local missionaries through gifts, in order to bring the letter to the attention of the local administration. If possible, he was to arrange an agreement concerning trade relations which would open the way to further negotiations on the subject.

Bakadorov adroitly established friendly relations with the missionary Don Manuel Luis, and from him he received a response to Baranov's letter, in Spanish, dated May 2, 1812. The response stated that the letter presented by Bakadorov had been sent on to the Mexican Viceroy. It stated that although the Californians were very willing to trade with the Russians, their laws were such that they could not make a decision on the matter without permission from their beloved monarch, Ferdinand VII, and from the present government in Spain. Therefore the Viceroy could not presently give permission for trade, but suggested that the [Russian] American Company bring the matter to the attention of their monarch, and then with his permission the Company could request permission to trade from the Madrid court. An exact copy of this response is being submitted for Your Excellency's attention.

In like manner the Spanish Consul [De Zea] Bermudez, who is visiting here [St. Petersburg], because of the rapport he has with the Company Director [Benedikt B.] Kramer, has now agreed to submit a proposal to his government concerning establishing commercial relations between the Company and California. He has requested a note which would set forth this matter, and has been given just such a note, as is evident from the copy appended.

Thus it appears that at present, with the current favorable attitude of the Madrid court, which is obligated to be generous to Russia, the only thing lacking is a request from our government for favorable trade relations with California. In view of this, the Main Administration of the Company has decided to present all of the above to Your Excellency in the hope that the Company will have your gracious consent, and your advice.

[Mikhail M.] Buldakov
[Benedikt B.] Kramer
[Andrei I.] Severin

Reference: *VPR*, First Series, Vol. 7, Doc. 280, 695–697.

36

OCTOBER 16, 1814

A LETTER FROM THE DIRECTORS OF THE RUSSIAN AMERICAN COM-
PANY TO ANDREI IA. DASHKOV, RUSSIAN CONSUL-GENERAL TO THE
UNITED STATES, CONCERNING JOHN JACOB ASTOR, TRADE AND
THE COLUMBIA RIVER

Gracious Sir, Andrei Iakovlevich.

[Aleksandr A.] Baranov, the Chief Administrator of our colonies in America, has forwarded to us his correspondence with you. In perusing your most recent letter to him, dated February, 1813, we have realized that thanks to your devotion to national goals and interests, you have justified our expectations concerning the position of the Company's diplomatic agent, which position you graciously accepted upon your departure from here. All of this gives us the pleasant task of thanking you most cordially for all your work for the benefit of the Company.

When Baranov received your other letters and reports, including this last letter, they were so wet and torn he could not separate them or pull them apart; your letters had been sent aboard [John Jacob] Astor's ship, which was wrecked near the Sandwich Islands. Even your most recent letter, of which Baranov sent us a copy, met the same fate, but at least we were able to make it out. But the content of your other letters remains unknown to us.

At the present time, as you know, there is no war between any countries in Europe, for even the Norwegian affair [Swedish-Norwegian War, 1814] was quickly settled. Only England and the North American States are at war and it cannot be expected to end soon, if one considers that the English, who now have a larger fleet than ever before and a goodly number of land forces who have even been on the mainland and fought with the Allies, will certainly not choose to remain inactive. This is all the more likely since by virtue of her politics England cannot manage without action and is now taking vengeance on the Americans at her own pleasure without interference.

A reasonable likeness of one of the greatest fur entrepreneurs in world history, John Jacob Astor, ensconced in his New York City office about 1825. His predictably sharp trade practices were ill-regarded by Baranov and St. Petersburg officials. The Russian American Company eventually reached an accommodation with Hudson's Bay Company with long term favorable results. From an engraving by Alonzo Chappel. N. N. Bashkina, *The United States and Russia, The Beginning of Relations*. (OHS neg. OrHi 82932)

Will the Congress of Vienna, presently meeting, with six imperial monarchs participating, propose some denouement to this war, which threatens all American seafaring merchants, even those who visit our colonies? Baranov writes that eight ships are seeking shelter in the Sandwich Islands, and that one, Astor's *Pedlar*, commanded by [Wilson] Hunt, has come to the port of New Arkhangel on Baranov (Sitka) Island for that purpose.

This ship is the only one left from Astor's expedition, which established a fur company factory on the Columbia River. The factory and all other enterprises of that company were destroyed by the English and thus there is no longer a settlement or any activity in Astor's company. What an ending.

Another ship of Astor's, *Lark*, which carried the previously mentioned letters you wrote to Baranov, was wrecked; her cargo which was sent on the account of the American Fur Company was a total loss, and our Company received nothing. We are extremely sorry for Astor's loss, but at the same time we must admit that the cargo would have been disastrous for the [Russian American] Company; it contained a huge amount of rum and other items which were useless to the Company. Baranov did not want them, and had not ordered them, but they were sent, in great quantities, and at prices we could not have agreed to. If Baranov had accepted the cargo, Astor would have been the only person to profit; our Company would have suffered substantial losses. For example, Astor had submitted a figure of 24,000 piasters for freight alone, (the piaster here is worth 5 [rubles]). Such necessary items as sailcloth, cable, rope and the like were either not included at all, or were sent in small quantity.

We cannot imagine that the real reason the [Russian] American Company concluded its well known agreement with Astor's Fur Company has escaped you. If the Company could have avoided it, obviously they would not have made the agreement. However, it included prices for goods which the fur company would supply, which were to be agreed upon jointly by Baranov and the person who delivered the cargo. They would also decide what goods were to be delivered. But Astor, on his own, and of course not to the benefit of our Company, apparently tried to reap the profits he craved, from us, for useless items which it would have been shameful for Baranov to accept. If Baranov had taken the rum which was sent, his supply would have been enormously increased, because the rum previously delivered is still in the warehouse and is evaporating. [Most unlikely.—Eds.]

For this reason we humbly request, Gracious Sir, that you tell Astor, if you have an opportunity, not to send our colonies the kind of cargo he sent on *Lark*. He should seek more advice, and he should always send provisions, materials for clothing and footware for our workers, ship rigging, sailcloth, and other things which Baranov specifies.

Further, if the English do not intervene, Astor's company will scarcely be in a position to put an end to the Americans' custom of calling at our colonies. And even if he did manage to do this over a period of several decades we would still refuse to accept unwanted goods, and he would have to do with them the same thing his countrymen do.

In short, our reluctant link with the Fur Company does not promise anything useful, if they try to impose on our Company cargoes such as those sent previously. We have nothing to say about Canton. This is our sincere acknowledgment to you, as a Russian, a patriot, a diplomat and a benefactor of our Company; and we are convinced that you, Gracious Sir, will consider this confidential. Please encourage Astor to hold as good an opinion of our Company as possible.

We are thinking of requesting our High [Imperial] Protector, when he returns to the capital, to order a naval vessel to cruise in the straits of our colonies. If this is done, His Imperial Majesty himself has already suggested that each year a sloop be sent around the world. The war, however, has interfered with this. Then American interlopers will cut off their trade in gunpowder and firearms with the savages.

From local public news reports you have undoubtedly already noted that last year we sent the ship *Suvorov* around the world to the colonies. It carried a cargo of goods needed there. It has already put in at Rio de Janeiro, and has left but we will not be able to learn anything further until it reaches the colonies. Next summer we plan to dispatch another vessel with the

A very approximate view of fort Astoria located well up on the south bank of the Columbia River, identified today inside downtown Astoria, Oregon. Belcher, *Voyage Around the World*. (OHS OrHi neg. 82086)

same cargo and therefore hope that the services of Astor will come to an end and not burden the Company.

From the enclosed two copies please note that the Company is most pleased to have the honor of having another special Council to give additional guidance on political and commercial matters. We are its spokesmen, and for that reason we are acting in accordance with the Council's advice. We hope this news will please you, because as we perceive, you are well disposed toward the Company.

Gracious Sir, we hope that you will continue to be favorably disposed toward us in the future, and will advise us, and especially Baranov, as to the best interests of the Company. Baranov especially needs your support, because he lives in such a remote place that it is pleasing for him to read even a single word in Russian. The news you sent him about the French penetration into the heart of Russia, and about their humiliating retreat, reached him before our information did; the two ships he sent to Okhotsk, and which he expected to return, failed to do so because they were wrecked.

Mikhail Buldakov
Benedikt Kramer
Andrei Severin

Reference: TsGAOR, f. 907, op. 1, d. 55, 11.25–27 ob.

See: N. N. Bashkina et al., eds. *Rossiia i SSha: Stanovlenie otnoshenii, 1765–1815.* (Moscow: 1980). Doc. 550, 666–668.

37

DECEMBER 23, 1816

A REPORT FROM THE MAIN ADMINISTRATION OF THE RUSSIAN
AMERICAN COMPANY CONCERNING CURRENT TRADE WITH THE
NORTH AMERICANS

Although Russia had no navy until the early part of the eighteenth century, her people are enterprising, resolute and courageous, and long before that time they had made many important discoveries sailing in small boats. By the seventeenth century the Russians who sailed in the Arctic Ocean had rounded the Chukotsk Cape, a feat which is very difficult even now.

The state archives contain information and evidence that long ago Russia had knowledge of the northwest part of America opposite Russia's Asiatic coast, information which was still unknown to all the rest of the world; Russians were the first to step on the mainland, and on almost all the islands from Bering Strait to the Columbia River in 46° northern latitude.

The world is familiar with the geographical expeditions sponsored by the Russian government in 1728, 1733, 1740, 1741, 1764 and 1785, which discovered and described that region. Those places they found to be unoccupied by any European nation, they made an appurtenance of Russia. Russia's emblems have been planted there; Russian flags wave over the fortresses and settlements; the Greek [Russian Orthodox] religion has been adopted by the natives; Russian educational institutions have been established; and beneficial and economic enterprises attest to the fact that from that point and on to the south, the entire expanse of Northwest America and its islands are Russia's possessions. None can deny her right to these, on the basis of first discovery and settlement prior to other Europeans, who acquired their possessions in both Indies in the same manner and by the same right. Are not the possessions of European powers in the Indies considered their colonies?

If some of them have the right to claim these possessions by virtue of state treaties, this stemmed from force of arms. But in contrast, there has been neither conflict nor disagreement concerning Russia's settlements.

The Russian American Company, by virtue of privileges granted to her, carries on trade with the islanders in the colonies she established in the northwestern part of America and on the adjacent islands, and she also conducts hunting enterprises for marine and land animals. Her right to this, or to put it another way, the right of the entire Russian nation, is based on this right of first discovery and occupation of settlements. Hence on her own territory, she may forbid trade and hunting to merchants of other nations.

But during the brief period of time [it has held these possessions] and even more, a shortage of manpower due to the impossibility of having a large number of reliable and capable Russian promyshlenniks there (there are only 400 in an expanse of 4,000 versts), and the small number of hunters who journey to such distant regions—all of these are reasons the [Russian] American Company does not yet control all these places in such a manner that foreigners would be denied trade contacts with the native Americans and native islanders, with whom only the Russians should deal.

Having perceived this weakness, the English, and especially the citizens of the North American states, as republican people, in 1792 began to visit our colonies in their vessels, which now sometimes number as many as fifteen. They exchanged their own goods as well as those of foreign countries with the American and island natives, and this included all manner of firearms and cold steel, gunpowder and shot. They instruct [the natives] in the use of these weapons to the detriment of our promyshlenniks. They also set their prices so low that the [Russian] American Company goods have to be more expensive because of the rigors and cost of transport across Siberia to Okhotsk. Consequently they not only undermine our trade, but indeed they harm it considerably by introducing such activities in places not far from us, and in fact sometimes even within sight of our colonies. They obtain furs from the savages, including as many as 10,000 to 15,000 sea otters per year, and take the pelts to Canton to sell there, and in exchange obtain Chinese goods such as tea and other items. They sell all of this during their return voyage or in their own country upon their return, and make enormous profits.

The consequences of their trading firearms, powder and shot with the savages have on many occasions threatened the Russians, who prior to that time had maintained amicable and friendly relations, as well as commercial ties, with the savages. The natives killed our promyshlenniks who sailed through various bays and straits, and they often still do when they have a chance. Here are some concrete examples of such occurrences:

1) In 1800 the Russians established a settlement and a fort called Mikhailovsk on the island of Sitka. The following year the native islanders, reinforced by groups from the mainland, suddenly attacked it, set it afire and eventually destroyed it, as well as a seagoing vessel. Some of the Russians who were there were killed and the rest were taken prisoner. The natives appropriated all the Company property except for 3,700 sea otter pelts. An investigation by Chief Administrator [Aleksandr A.] Baranov disclosed that the savages had been incited to carry out this evil deed by the Bostonian ship skippers Crocker and [William] Cunningham, who had given them firearms, powder and shot in return for their trade goods, and then, with the help of their crews, seized everything the natives had looted. In 1804 this island, presently called Baranov Island, was again under the control of the Company. Another fortification, New Arkhangel, has been built at the harbor.

2) In 1805, a settlement called Slavorossiia was established in Yakutat Bay on the coast of the mainland. There were several families there, both men and women. There were farmers and artisans and also savages, who had long since, through friendly relations, provided a sense of security. But once they received firearms and powder from the Bostonians, the savages suddenly attacked the settlement, killed everyone, and burned the settlement and a seagoing vessel which was anchored there.

As a result of this Chief Administrator Baranov requested instructions on what to do in regard to foreigners carrying on trade [in our colonies], and suggested that the only way to deal with this would be to issue a warning so they would stop trading firearms and powder with the savages.

In 1804 a committee was organized in the [Russian] American Company by order of His Imperial Majesty [Alexander I]; it authorized the Main Administration of the Company to instruct Baranov that "he was to try through peaceful means to prevent the Bostonians, if possible, from selling firearms [to the natives]; meanwhile here [in St. Petersburg] they would endeavor to discuss with [representatives of] the United States measures to put an end to this trade, and to insist that the natives trade only with the Company." A report about this was made to His Imperial Majesty.

Subsequently, however, Baranov wrote repeatedly that his reprimands to the North Americans about trading firearms to the savages, and in fact trading with them at all, were met with laughter. The Americans said they had no such instructions from their government. For this reason, since Baranov had no means to acquire great amounts of furs in that vastness, which these foreigners could utilize to their own benefit, he had to enter into agreements with them. He signed contracts with them and sent his own promyshlenniks aboard their ships, gave them baidaras (made of hides, patterned after Aleut lodkas capable of navigating between rocks) and goods to enable them to hunt marine and land animals. The catch was to be divided equally [between the Bostonians and the Russian American Company], and Baranov was fully aware that this would cause a negative balance of trade in Kiakhta on the Chinese frontier where Russian merchants and the Russian American Company had to pay a high duty on the goods it obtained in exchange for its furs.

But as the Company has previously reported, even this method affects the Kiakhta trade very little, because the North Americans bring their ships to Canton every year with as many as 15,000 sea otter pelts which they obtain around our colonies. Since they obtain these furs inexpensively, they sell them at a low price and thus satisfy the needs of the Chinese for this commodity. This in turn allows the Chinese to force us to lower our prices on this fur in Kiakhta. Otherwise the Chinese would have to pay more because sea otters are found only in the waters which wash the shores of our colonies.

These developments, however, have not halted the zeal of the American Company in carrying out the privileges given it for the benefit of the fatherland. Upon receipt of new information from the colonies concerning the decline of hunting caused by the North Americans, and the harm they have caused through trading firearms to the savages, the Main Administration of the Company has tried to forward that information in its humble reports to the Sovereign Emperor, and has also turned to the Imperial Chancellor with a request to end this problem. Thus the Consul General in Philadelphia, [Andrei Ia.] Dashkov, has been instructed to conduct negotiations with the United States government and obtain a resolution aimed at halting that harmful trade.

However, there has been no successful resolution to the problem, for in a communication of July 9, 1810 to the State Chancellor, from the Minister Plenipotentiary Count [Fedor P.] Pahlen, the statement is made, "From the reports of Mr. Dashkov, His Imperial Majesty directed that, in spite of the many proposals submitted to the United States government concerning the illegal trade carried on by certain of its citizens with Indians living in Russian possessions, it was impossible to reach an understanding that the United States government should take measures to terminate the disorders which threaten the very existence of our possessions. Having examined everything pertaining to this matter, I have ascertained that the government of the United States does not have either the desire or the power to put an end to this illegal trade."

Many persons who have influence in the eastern part of this country, and are not at all well-disposed toward the present government, share in the profits from this trade. The government is afraid to anger them by acting contrary to their interests. Furthermore, no prohibition will create the desired result, because even at the time the "non-intercourse" act was proclaimed, in almost all the ports of the United States people violated the resolution right under the eyes of the government. How, then, can one hope that a prohibition pertaining to such distant places as the Russian settlements would be respected? A government that does not have enough authority to compel adherence to its laws in its own territories cannot expect compliance beyond its jurisdiction.

Subsequently, reasoning that to resubmit this subject for new consideration would not be consonant with the dignity of the Imperial Majesty, and that it could not attain the desired result, the Russian government decided it might achieve its goal without the cooperation of the government of the United States in the following way. Since that government had given one of its fur companies, headed by the very wealthy New York merchant [John J.] Astor the privilege to establish a settlement on the Columbia River, almost in the vicinity of our colonies, and since that company, through the intercession of Mr. Dashkov, proposed and pledged itself to carry out the intent of our Court without any mediation by the United States, he believed, possibly mistakenly, that if the Russian American Company were to enter into a mutual agreement with that fur company, it could protect itself from vicious attacks by the savages.

Following this report, Astor's son-in-law, the Danish councillor [Adrian] Bentzon immediately came here to propose a general convention. The State Chancellor informed the Main Administration of the Company of this, saying that His Imperial Majesty approved the idea that the Russian American Company if it wished might benefit by negotiating the matter.

This unexpected opportunity was not ignored. The Main Administration of the Company did enter into negotiations with Bentzon and soon discovered that the purpose of the authority Astor had given him was not primarily to conclude a trade convention between the two companies, but through this trade to secure permission to bring bearskins, raccoon pelts and other furs to Russia without paying duty on them. (According to the tariff at that time such furs were prohibited but are now permitted.) The Main Administration of the Company, by virtue of its firm principles, did reach an agreement on May 20, 1812, as to how much was possible. The agreement, valid for four years, contained the following provisions.

1) In areas occupied by our Company, Astor's company would not carry on hunting and trade. Our Company would do the same in places occupied by him.

2) Both companies would absolutely not sell any sort of firearms, cannon, pistols, sabers, bayonets, large knives, lances or any other weapon or powder or shot to savage Indians in areas belonging to either Company. Each party agreed that violation of this provision would entitle either side to submit a

grievance to its own government and the guilty party must be punished.

3) To prevent the importation of foodstuffs and other goods into our colonies by other North Americans, the Astor fur company pledged itself to deliver only all the items the colonial administrator actually orders, at prices mutually agreed upon.

4) For the general profit and good of both companies, both agreed that if anyone tried to introduce hunting and trade into areas belonging to either company, both would act jointly and unanimously to halt such an enterprise.

5) Astor pledged to deliver our furs to be sold in Canton, carrying them as freight on his ships.

A sixth point was introduced which would allow this convention to be renewed, if the Astor company operated properly, neither losing its profits nor mistreating our Company. The State Chancellor was informed of this.

However, subsequent events revealed that this agreement, which was aimed at preventing other North American traders from bringing contraband goods, especially firearms and gunpowder, into our possessions, had no success whatsoever. In fact, such persons increased their activity, which in the future was bound to cause harm and be a detriment to our Company. This happened for the following reasons.

1) Astor never showed any intention of informing other traders not to voyage to our possessions.

2) He was more concerned with establishing his own colony (which seemed rather insignificant) on the Columbia River. However, during the war between the United States and England, English persons living in Canada took possession of his colony; in fact, it seems certain he sold it to them.

3) Although he had sent a certain amount of goods to our colonies even before that convention was approved, the cargo consisted of mostly useless items. The goods the Administrator had asked him to send immediately were either delivered in small quantity or not at all, and everything was at a price so high it was impossible to pay. One shipment which he sent had been marked up 125 percent. The term of the convention expired and Astor did not request renewal. Even if he had, it would have been impossible for us to agree without precise and firm limitations, for the above mentioned reasons, and also be-

cause one of Astor's agents, Wilson Hunt, skipper of the ship *Beaver*, came to our colonies in 1812 with Astor's cargo and while receiving our furs as payment for the goods, resorted to trickery and low arguments and objections, which forced our people, in order to restore quiet, to make reductions of more than 2,000 rubles on the value of their furs, which he subsequently sold at great profit in Canton. This was the last time we traded with him.

Subsequently Hunt went to Canton and to the Sandwich Islands where he sold the ship entrusted to him and bought another, *Pedlar*. He hired crew members from other European ships, men who were every sort of riffraff whom the English were pursuing. In 1814 he showed up again in New Arkhangel, but without any goods. We did not know what he intended. According to him, he needed to repair his ship, which request was granted him through the hospitality and good will of Collegiate Counselor and Cavalier Baranov, the Administrator of our colonies. Hunt said that Astor was to send him another ship with goods to be sold to our Company, but sixteen months passed without any such ship appearing. Subsequent events revealed that he had come with the same intention as others of his countrymen, to carry on contraband trade with island natives by any means, obtaining trade goods from others of his fellow countrymen who came there.

Baranov perceived this but did not have clear grounds to put an end to it. In order to divert this greedy, cunning and restive intriguer from his plans in as seemly a manner as possible, and at the same time to ascertain the condition of our new settlement at Bodega Bay, Baranov decided to take Hunt's suggestion and send 6,000 sea otter pelts there on Hunt's ship; he would also send other goods and some of his men. This was done, but at great loss to the Company, which was to be expected as a result of dealing with Hunt and his countrymen. Finally, in December of 1815 Hunt returned to the port of New Arkhangel.

One would suppose that after his ill-favored behavior and Baranov's generosity, Hunt would have been grateful to the Company. But any such feeling was alien to his nature. In May of 1815 [sic] Baranov ordered the ship *Suvorov* to return to Europe. Her cargo of furs, including fur seal pelts, was already being loaded, destined for sale in Macao. At that point Hunt claimed the cargo on the grounds that Baranov had committed the cargo to another English skipper [William J.] Pigott, with the proviso that if Pigott did not claim this commitment in New Arkhangel in time to receive payment for the fur seals, he would be paid in St. Petersburg with bank notes. Pigott was not in the port, but Hunt, acting in his name, requested payment on the last day of the agreed time, when the cargo of fur seals had already been loaded aboard the vessel. What was to be done? Should Baranov have the cargo unloaded from *Suvorov* and give the pelts to Hunt as payment for the obligation, with Hunt acting as proxy for Pigott? Hunt, in the four and a half months he had been staying at New Arkhangel had not given the slightest indication he planned to do this.

It is clear that the honor of the Company must be upheld, but the resulting loss would be substantial, because *Suvorov*, due to make a return voyage here at the most favorable time of the year, would have to spend an additional three months for a voyage to the Seal Islands to take on a new cargo. For that entire period the Company would have to pay the salaries of the officers and crew for no reason. Later, when the ship was on its return voyage, because of the late season and the constant winds it would have to forego its intention to put in at Macao and other places where the Company had planned [to sell cargo]; and as a result, the Company would lose its profit.

This intrigue, as well as Hunt's impossible character and ill-intended activities forced Baranov to inform him that once he had received payment in seal pelts he and his ship must leave our harbor. But Hunt replied contemptuously that he would not take the seal pelts because of the war between England and our country, nor would he leave the harbor unless a shot was fired across the bow of his ship, in which case he would surrender as a prisoner of war.

Baranov did not know what to do. The necessity to preserve the alliance between our government and that of the North American states forced him to be as patient as possible, especially since this republican [Hunt] had lived with the officers of the *Suvorov*, and had become such a friend of theirs that at his instigation they joined with him in proposing a very deleterious plan to Baranov, that *Suvorov*'s first lieutenant, [Semen

Ia.] Unkovskii, be appointed to command Hunt's ship under a Russian flag, take one of *Suvorov's* men, a Captain Northrup who had lost his ship, and proceed together to the Sandwich Islands to procure sandalwood to sell at great profit in Macao.

Baranov could not agree to this, or to other plans which were suggested. He considered them reprehensible and rejected all. His instructions from the Main Administration of the Company were to avoid close commercial ties with foreigners as much as possible.

In spite of all this Baranov resolutely readied *Suvorov* for her return voyage in accordance with the intentions and instructions of the Main Administration. Hunt was emboldened by his friendship with *Suvorov's* officers, and by having his own ship in the harbor. He and some of his crew, without permission, went ashore to live in tents a short distance from the fort, and while there, very much in character, he insulted a number of our people. He went into the forest and secretly traded gunpowder for furs from the island natives, thinking this would go unnoticed. He prolonged his stay under the guise of repairing his ship. Meanwhile Pigott arrived and personally accepted the payment which was due him, in seal pelts, which were unloaded onto shore.

All of this happened prior to July 18 of last year [1815], at which time Pigott put out to sea. Officers from *Suvorov* and Hunt accompanied him for some distance. When they were about to return in small boats Pigott put a small keg of powder weighing one and a half puds or more on one of our small boats; he entrusted it to an English navigator, [John] Young, at that time in our Company's service, instructing him to deliver the keg to Hunt's ship, which Young did, without informing Baranov. Baranov learned of this through a report from our clerk, Terentev, who had been aboard the small boat on which the powder was transported.

This was open defiance on Hunt's part of even the most elementary courtesy. His actions could be harmful to the Company, not only his secret trading with the natives, but also the fact that the gunpowder could be used maliciously to blow up the wooden fort some night. His character led one to expect anything. It could lead to the islanders using the powder and firearms he had furnished them to attack the fort, just as had happened with the previous Sitka fort. Furthermore, the keg of powder had been transferred in a neutral port by persons of a nation which was at war with another country, of which Hunt was a citizen. All this forced Baranov to resolve to make an immediate inquiry into the matter. He sent Terentev and *Suvorov's* assistant supercargo, the *meshchanin* [townsman] Krasilnikov, to Hunt to demand an explanation as to why he had dared to accept the powder from a foreigner, right in the harbor, without prior notification. They were also to [confiscate and] send the keg to Baranov so the powder could be compared with some which had recently been found in the possession of armed island natives, so as to ascertain whether the two kegs of powder were the same. Baranov suspected that the keg had been transferred from *Suvorov.* But instead of explaining and carrying out the demand [for the keg], Hunt harrassed our men to the point that they had to ask for reinforcements from our ship *Otkrytie,* anchored nearby, aboard which all the officers of the *Suvorov* were visiting. But not only did the officers refuse help, they remained silent as if they had heard nothing.

When a terrible shout was heard a boat had to put out from shore with four Russians aboard. Skippers and sailors from other foreign vessels, seeing this, set out for Hunt's ship, some twenty of them. They met our men with fists and a general fight broke out.

As soon as Baranov learned of this he decided to go out personally; accompanied by Dr. [Georg A.] Schäffer and [Herman] Molvo, *Suvorov's* supercargo. Baranov went without any weapon, with only his cane to support his infirmity. When Baranov boarded the ship and asked why they were fighting our men, Hunt did not reply a single word, but stormed off into his cabin and shouted that he would surrender his ship as a prize. He took most of his men and went onto another American vessel.

In order to undermine any secret nefarious attempts Hunt might make, Baranov spiked his cannon, threw some of his firearms overboard and took ashore four kegs of powder, including the one from Pigott. Baranov put these in a warehouse for safekeeping, and for security ordered that guards be posted both at the ship's cabin and the hold. Baranov then went with Schäffer and Molvo to the ship where Hunt was taking refuge in order to take a statement from him in the presence of his countrymen. Hunt, however, failed to appear after twice being summoned. The third time he came to the cabin in a very resentful mood, a pistol in his hand half hidden under his shirt. He went up to Baranov as if he meant to fire. This shocked Baranov, but he did not lose command of himself. With his cane he hit Hunt on the hand holding the pistol so he could not fire. Hunt's countrymen grabbed him and dragged him out of the cabin. For the time the affair was over.

The next day Hunt sent Baranov a biting letter in English in which he charged that Baranov had seized his ship. In response, Baranov sent a letter in Russian in which he clearly stated the fact that he had no need or desire to seize Hunt's ship, but had only needed to ascertain from where and from whom Hunt had obtained the gunpowder. However, if he wished to give up his ship to Baranov, Baranov would report this to his superiors.

Baranov's precautions were altogether necessary. The Russians were surrounded by savages and by vicious and very hostile island natives. They were in an area too remote to have any help beyond their own vigilance and constant alertness. Furthermore, they were in the presence of several foreign ships and their crews. And as Count Pahlen noted in the above mentioned dispatch to the State Chancellor, when North American skippers and crews are sent to our coast, they receive no pay. Instead they receive a certain share of the profit from anything they may obtain on such a distant and prolonged voyage. For this reason they try to sell, buy, barter and deal for profit. A sailor who is in desperate need of money will not stop at anything to enrich himself. Experience has shown that in trade of that nature even crime is permitted.

Upon inspection it was found that the powder in the four previous kegs and in the one which had caused the problem bore the same mark. It was also identical to the powder which the islanders had traded for, and which some of them were using in their firearms. They would conceal themselves in places where our promyshlenniks had to stop. It followed that all this powder was English and had been given to the North Americans by an Englishman at a time when England and the United States were at war. From all of this one can conclude that in the matter of trade, both had the same intention, to harm the Company.

Hunt twice returned unopened the letter Baranov had written in response to Hunt's letter, which threatened to seek satisfaction through his [diplomatic] minister. Baranov then decided to ask Lieutenant [Mikhail P.] Lazarev to go to Hunt and translate the contents of the Russian letter for him. Lazarev was on friendly terms with Hunt and with other officers would often visit him. When Lazarev returned he reported that Hunt was holding to his previous position and considered himself under arrest. Baranov appointed a commission to make an inventory of Hunt's ship and cargo; the group included Lieutenant Cavalier [Iakov A.] Podushkin, commander of our ship *Otkrytie*, Lieutenant Unkovskii of *Suvorov* and others from the North American crew.

Meanwhile several of the Englishmen serving aboard foreign vessels told Baranov that some of the North Americans were so angry about Hunt that they were saying they would like to go ashore at night, go to the warehouses and blow up the powder. Although Baranov did not believe this, he had to take every precaution appropriate for a vigilant administrator in such a barren and unprotected place, surrounded by a multitude of foreigners, some of whom were hostile. He therefore doubled the pickets and guards and gave written instructions to Lieutenant Lazarev of *Suvorov*, which was anchored out in the roadstead, to come in closer to the fort in case there was need to defend it against hostilities. If necessary, Baranov could rely on his compatriots in service to the Company.

The inventory of Hunt's ship was made by Lieutenant Podushkin, Dr. Schäffer, [assistant] navigator Samsonov and Second Lieutenant Balashov. Hunt was asked to submit a statement but refused. In the ship's cargo they found several bales of cable, four lengths of sailcloth from *Suvorov* and 5,000 fur seal pelts which he had not received from us. We do not know where he obtained them.

Three months after this incident Hunt agreed to take back his ship and cargo and departed from the port of New Arkhangel. Nevertheless Chief Administrator Baranov asks the Main Administration of the Company for instructions on how to handle such a matter if it arises in the future.

The Main Administration of the Company, having set forth all this evidence, requests advice on what to do in case North Americans continue to carry on contraband trade in our possessions by furnishing dangerous weapons to the savages, and in case any foreigners behave as Hunt did.

In this regard would it not be desirable for the council to review the appended draft of a resolution which all foreign vessels should observe when they come to our colonies? It might forestall and prevent any future incidents similar to the one involving Hunt. If this proposal is also approved by higher authorities, it might be published in the two most widely used European languages and be sent to our colonies.

Signed: Mikhail Buldakov, Chairman of the
Board of Directors
Cavalier Director Benedikt Kramer
Director Andrei Severin
Office Administrator Zelenskii

Reference: *VPR*, Second Series, Vol. 9. Doc. 120, 378–386.

38

MARCH 14, 1817

A REPORT FROM DMITRII P. TATISHCHEV, RUSSIAN AMBASSADOR
TO MADRID, TO COUNT KARL NESSELRODE, MINISTER OF FOREIGN
AFFAIRS, DETAILING SPANISH REACTION TO RUSSIAN ACTIVITY IN
ESTABLISHMENT OF A RUSSIAN COLONY IN CALIFORNIA

My dear Sir, my dear Count!
A report from the Commandant of the port of Callao to
the Minister of the Navy has attracted the attention of the
Spanish government concerning the success of the [Russian]
outposts on the Northwest Coast of America. According to
this report, the [Ross] settlement at the port of Bodega located
in 38° 15′ latitude may encroach upon the area which has previously separated our possessions from those of Mexico. The
Commandant of the port of Callao elaborates his reports with
details from the log of the ship *Suvorov* and with statements
which the Governor of San Blas received from certain deserters
from our colonies.

The new Russian settlement located between the port of
San Francisco and Cape Mendocino appears like a new mani-
festation of the determination of our outposts to spread to the
south. It is reportedly surrounded by a palisade, is much better
built than other outposts, and serves as the most important
depot for the fur trade. According to this information, communication by sea from the port of Bodega with our other
colonies may be easily undertaken and may develop into a
flourishing enterprise.

The Minister of the Navy forwarded this dispatch from the
Governor to the port of Callao for review by one of the departments under his jurisdiction. It is probable that as a result of
this review there will be precise instructions on controlling
how far to the east and south our settlements may go.

The Department of the Navy at the same time received
news of a settlement at the mouth of the Columbia River, identified on some Spanish maps as *l'entrada d'Eceta*, in 46° 16′ latitude. The information, however, is imprecise. It is not known
definitely whether this settlement was founded by Americans
from the United States or by the English.

Sr. Pizarro spoke with me in a very muddled manner about our outposts on the Northwest Coast of America. He had confused information recently received from the Naval Ministry with some vague reports he had apparently heard concerning negotiations in 1806 between [Nikolai P.] Rezanov and the Spanish commandant in San Francisco. While Rezanov made a brief stay in San Francisco during his voyage to Japan, he tried to persuade the Governor of San Francisco and California to accept in good faith a proposal to establish commercial relations between the Spanish and the Russian colonies and permit the Russians to enter the harbors of Monterey, San Diego and San Francisco. It is not known however, what the results of Rezanov's action were.

It is probable that our government has now established a policy regarding America, and Your Excellency will undoubtedly send me instructions in the near future so I will know how to respond to this matter.

Reference: United States National Archives. *Records of the Russian-American Company*, M11, Roll 1, Vol. 1, Folios 135–136.

39

MARCH 22, 1817

A DISPATCH FROM THE MAIN ADMINISTRATION OF THE RUSSIAN
AMERICAN COMPANY TO ALEKSANDR A. BARANOV REGARDING
TRADE EXPEDITIONS TO CALIFORNIA

I n last year's dispatches you reported that it would be desirable for the Main Administration of the [Russian American] Company to request permission from our Government to establish trade with Canton and California. This has been done, but no response has yet been received. There is no doubt that both of these areas will become acquainted with us. However, it is unfortunate that at this time we cannot cheer you by giving you this permission you so earnestly desire. But at least the Company is constantly bringing the matter to the attention of the responsible people. Until a decision about this has been reached in one place or the other, or in both places, you should outfit expeditions to go there, not under the supervision of foreigners, but under your own people.

Until then you must be patient, which is necessary in all difficult situations. Meanwhile, as last year's dispatches noted, you may carry on trade with California to the fullest possible extent, even if the Ross settlement should be in a position to completely provision the colonies, because any surplus can be sent to Kamchatka and Okhotsk.

Reference: United States National Archives *Records of the Russian American Company*, M11, Roll 1, Vol. 1, No. 184, Folios 45–46.

40

A DISPATCH FROM THE MAIN ADMINISTRATION OF THE RUSSIAN
AMERICAN COMPANY TO ALEKSANDR A. BARANOV INSTRUCTING
HIM TO DISCHARGE DR. GEORG SCHÄFFER, AND NOT TO BUILD
SCHOOLS IN CALIFORNIA

In a dispatch of last year, a copy of which is appended, you were informed as to why Dr. Schäffer is to be considered of no help to us, having left the ship *Suvorov* because of personal disagreements with the officers and because he was displeased that the ship did not anchor in every place where he wanted to collect natural history specimens, which were not for the Company, but for himself and for foreign countries. We now reemphasize the problem. When he has carried out the expedition to the Sandwich Islands which you have entrusted to him, dispatching him aboard the ship *Otkrytie*, he is no longer to be entrusted with any expedition at all. He is a foreigner who is not making his acquisitions for the Russians.

If, however, you still have a use for him you may keep him on as a doctor, but do not let him establish a school or a distillery at the Ross settlement. It is too early to do either of these things, and will continue to be until the Russians have become firmly entrenched there and the Spaniards accept us as their neighbors.

This is especially true since in California for the most part the monks dominate the entire local administration. If we established a school they would view our enterprising settlement with entirely different eyes than is now the case. And since Sitka Island is now the main gathering place, it follows that all beneficial institutions, especially an infirmary, should be established and developed in New Arkhangel. You will certainly agree with this.

Keep the Ross settlement in such condition the Spanish will have no reason to consider it anything more than a simple promyshlennik outpost. Meanwhile, under this cover, build up agriculture, livestock breeding, poultry raising, the planting of

Pomo Indian boys drawn by the artist Tikhonov. L. A. Shur,
K beregam novogo sveta. (OHS OrHi neg. 82007)

fruits and vegetable and establish plantations. Improve the
settlement itself with necessary buildings.

Reference: United States National Archives. *Records of the Russian American
Company*, M11, Roll 1, Vol. 1, Doc. 196, Folios 67–68.

41

A DISPATCH FROM THE MAIN ADMINISTRATION OF THE RUSSIAN AMERICAN COMPANY TO CHIEF ADMINISTRATOR ALEKSANDR A. BARANOV ADVISING ON PROBLEMS OF PERSONNEL AND ADMINISTRATION OF THE COLONIES

We have received your two reports, Number 22 dated August 26, 1815, and Number 18, of September 4, 1815, which you sent via the sloop *Konstantin* with Herman Molvo, the former supercargo of the ship *Suvorov*. Molvo delivered your reports here in person on October 12, 1816. Thus more than a year passed between the time when you sent them and we received them.

Konstantin left New Arkhangel on September 10, [1815] but because of strong contrary winds during the late fall period had to seek shelter and winter near Kodiak. She set out from there on April 23, 1816 and reached Okhotsk on June 27. The ship needed repairs, and thanks to the zeal and efficiency of the Okhotsk office these were made quickly so the vessel could return to you. She departed Okhotsk on August 1 [1816] under the command of assistant navigator Samsonov. God grant she will reach your part of the world safely, even though she carries only a rather small cargo of provisions and relatively few persons.

Along with *Konstantin*, another vessel wintered near Kodiak, *Mirt Kadiak* which you had previously sent to the Sandwich Islands with *Otkrytie* under the command of Dr. Schäffer. She was also forced to seek shelter there for the same reason as *Konstantin*. Do you have news of these two vessels?

The brig *Finlandia*, which brought you new personnel and which you dispatched to Atka last year, came to Okhotsk and wintered there. Presently she is being outfitted for her return voyage, but we do not yet know whence, whether to Atka or to you. The supposition was that she would be sent to you in case you did not send a vessel to Okhotsk last year, as you had intended. At present no such vessel has even reached Kamchatka. We do not know whether the purpose was to send you as many new people as possible to strengthen your position. It would be best to have a special ship, however, to carry personnel, because there are now in Okhotsk more than 60 men, plus goods, supplies and provisions, all destined to be sent to you.

The 7,000 fur seal pelts you sent to the Company aboard *Konstantin* have been received; thank you. Other items in the cargo aboard that vessel were either dispersed on Kodiak or used up en route.

You know that the Company sent to you a fourth expedition around the world last year, consisting of the ships *Kutuzov* and *Suvorov*. The ships themselves informed you of this. You have also been sent dispatches with advice on maintaining order. These were sent this year via Okhotsk, and were forwarded to you aboard *Konstantin*. You should refer to these dispatches and pray God to strengthen you in health and force so these instructions can be carried out. When Leontii Andreevich Hagemeister reaches you, probably in July of this year, he will take over part of your responsibilities.

The circumstances you described in your dispatches sent with Molvo, concerning the unwarranted behavior of officers from *Suvorov*, and the insolence of the American [Wilson P.] Hunt, have been submitted: the former to the Minister of the Navy, who has ordered a court martial for Lazarev which is already in session at Kronstadt; the latter to the Minister of Foreign Affairs, with a request that the American government prohibit such misconduct in the future. Hunt has been forbidden to go to our colonies again. The Main Administration will inform you promptly of the outcome of these two situations.

As early as 181? [illegible] in this harbor a regulation was drawn up for all visiting skippers and their ships. The Main Administration of the Company is sending you ten printed copies of this regulation: in case visiting foreigners cause some new disorder in your port, you may use this regulation to take action. It is written in both Russian and German. When a foreign ship comes, a pilot boat should [take someone out to] read this regulation, and inform the foreigners they are there at the pleasure of the Russian government and must conduct themselves strictly in accordance with this regulation. After it has been read to the skippers, you should retrieve the copy. We are also sending you a form on which every skipper must write what is required of him. In case of a violation, you are to conduct yourself as the administrator of the area, empowered both by the Company and by the government.

News was brought with *Konstantin* that the elderly [Ivan I.] Banner died, and that according to his instructions, his duties have been assumed by Grigorii Potorochin. Since you are familiar with Potorochin's qualifications, we leave it to you to decide whether to leave him in this post or to replace him with another person. In addition to [Kyrill T.] Khlebnikov, supercargo aboard *Kutuzov*, who has promised to remain with you, we are also sending three commercial prikashchiks: Mikhail Ivanov Nosov, Mikhail Afanasiev Sukhanov, and Prokhor Dmitriev Ivanov. Whichever of these seems most capable should become the administrator of Kodiak. Before you send him off on his own, keep him with you for a time so you can assess his abilities. You may also be able to choose one of these men to be the office administrator for the Unalaska and Sitka offices. It would be good to have them as assistants, especially in the Sitka office. Organize this however God may guide you. It would also be good if someone were sent to Ross as administrator of the office there to assist [Ivan A.] Kuskov and to put affairs in better order there.

We have now informed you of all of the above, but have responded to just some of the questions raised in your dispatches, because special papers are being sent to you in regard to other matters. So now it remains only to say that all is going well throughout the Company. This year dividends for the year 1814–1815 will be distributed. The balance sheet for this period is appended for your information. The gain on your shares and of other persons in your region, in accordance with the plan, is being set aside in a special account and will draw a small rate of interest.

Regarding affairs in general in our country, Europe and other countries, you will find information in the enclosed newspapers and journals which we have gathered together and have dispatched via Okhotsk with the expedition.

Reference: United States National Archives. *Records of the Russian-American Company*, M11, Roll 1, Vol. 1, No. 182, Folios 14–16.

42

INSTRUCTIONS FROM THE MAIN ADMINISTRATION OF THE RUSSIAN
AMERICAN COMPANY TO ALEKSANDR A. BARANOV CONCERNING
EDUCATION FOR CREOLES

You will note from the enclosed article taken from a periodical which was sent to the Main Administration, that the *creole* [person of mixed Russian and native parentage] Burtsov has completed his course of study of shipbuilding and is being sent back to his native land under your jurisdiction, with the rank of shipbuilder-carpenter, a rank which he has been officially assigned. A creole woman, Matrena Kuznetsova, is returning with him. She came here with the other creoles you sent, but she is the only one still alive. She is married to Burtsov. Try to set them up in as good a situation as possible. Burtsov appears to be a reliable young man. He has conducted himself well here, and his wife has had good supervision. They have been provided here with everything they need.

It would be desirable to encourage other creoles, especially young island natives, to come here to study. They would be more useful to the Company. A proposal has been made to grant Burtsov 14th degree rank. The Main Administration hopes this rank may attract volunteers. You will have in him a new, and hopefully an educated, citizen who may become an example to others. In your previous dispatch you suggested that such persons be included in the current census of Russian citizens, so that while they are living on the islands they can assume obligations and pay taxes. We do not yet have permission from the government to transfer them into that category and therefore the Main Administration of the Company believes that when the appropriate time comes, we should request permission to create a special class of island citizens for all the creoles. They would be independent of all but local administration.

It would be a good thing if you were to send two or three more bright young lads here to study medicine, pharmacy, bookkeeping, and the like, but do not send them until they have been vaccinated against smallpox. Sergei Kolobov, the Kolosh [Tlingit] you sent here, was a bright healthy young man, but because he had not been vaccinated against smallpox, he fell victim to it.

The following creoles are already students of navigation: Andrei Khmamov, Gerasim Kondakov and Ivan Chernykh. The first is now working in Okhotsk on the *Finlandia*, and by order of the Okhotsk office is receiving a salary of 1,200 rubles. He appears to be working well. Consequently the Main Administration will attempt to secure the rank of officer for him. However, he was very foolish in Okhotsk. For some reason he asked to be assigned to some position and be issued a passport. This was refused by the Company administration. Inform all the creoles not to worry about their rank. They will have rank under the special laws drawn up for them.

P.S. If the wife of the priest who has been sent to you is able to provide education in household management even to only a few orphaned creole girls, and if perhaps Matrena Burtsova can also do this, please build a schoolhouse for these women and help them as much as you can. It would be desirable to assign several young females from among the *kaiurs* [native worker for the Russians] to assist them.

Reference: United States National Archives. *Records of the Russian American Company*. M11, Roll 1, Volume 1, No. 188, Folios 52–53.

43

15 APRIL, 1817

A STATEMENT FROM DE ZEA BERMUDEZ, SPANISH AMBASSADOR AT
ST. PETERSBURG, TO COUNT KARL V. NESSELRODE, MINISTER OF
FOREIGN AFFAIRS, PROTESTING RUSSIAN PRESENCE ON THE COAST
OF UPPER CALIFORNIA

The Mexican Viceroy has submitted to the Spanish government a report prepared at the end of 1812, which states that there are some 100 men on the shore of Upper California. They have established a settlement five or six miles north of the port of Bodega and about 30 miles from the port at the mission of San Francisco; they have built dwellings and a redoubt along the coast, and have fitted it out with a number of pieces of artillery.

When information first reached the Viceroy concerning these men who had come there on a ship flying the Russian flag, he did not know how to interpret this unusual development. In analyzing the situation he was concerned lest Bonaparte's emissaries or American insurgents might have taken this illegal method of establishing themselves there in order temporarily to conceal their true purpose. He gave local officials explicit instructions to inspect this post immediately, which had been established by foreigners, and to invoke martial law against them if they proved to be enemies of the state. If, however, contrary to that initial supposition, they proved to be Russian subjects, and exactly the kind of men they purported to be, the officials were not to deal harshly with them but inform them in a friendly manner that they were violating territorial rights. After that they should be allowed to remain, taking into account the friendship and close alliance which exist between our two governments. As evidence of this good relationship, the Viceroy sent four copies of an agreement concluded in Velikie Luki, to indicate that the government in the present circumstances was limiting its response and would later send him a formal reply.

The Viceroy subsequently issued an order to inspect the settlement with a detachment of royal forces. After some discussion, the officer who commanded the detachment confirmed the fact that these people actually were mostly Russians and that a man named [Ivan] Kuskov was their leader. Kuskov told him that this settlement had been organized in accordance with the direction of the agents at the factory of the Russian American Company of Unalaska or Kodiak. The Mexican Viceroy ordered that friendly relations be maintained; this was relayed to Kuskov but was not altogether successful.

When the Regency Council, which administered the monarchy in the absence of His Majesty Ferdinand VII, learned of these developments, it wished to act so as to avoid the disapprobation of His Majesty, the antagonism of the participants of this expedition, and any unpleasantness which might develop. Thus the Council instructed the Viceroy that he must adopt firm measures and give the Governor of California all necessary instructions, in the name of the Spanish government, to persuade Kuskov and his men to heed the valid and friendly advice already given to him. He must leave the settlement; it was incompatible with maintaining peace and friendship between Russia and Spain. In case there was a complaint, this could be submitted to a just sovereign such as Emperor Alexander, who is much dedicated to law.

The undersigned [Bermudez] must state with considerable regret that all the proposals and correspondence which took place after the fact on numerous occasions as part of his responsibilities, have produced no results. Solely as a result of obstruction by those persons unwilling to relinquish this settlement to Spanish jurisdiction, His Supreme Highness authorized his minister to sign the document to be formally submitted to the attention of His Imperial Majesty. This is a formal complaint against [the Russians] stating that the entire problem has been caused by them.

The undersigned is firmly convinced that he could not better carry out his obligations than by being completely sincere; he has limited himself to presenting this simple outline of what happened on the basis of correspondence received from his government; he has tried in every possible way not to present any explanations.

However, he feels compelled to add that His Catholic Majesty is fully convinced that this action came about because of a misunderstanding on the part of a few persons who had no real reason other than commercial greed to come to us. As a result they have violated every feeling of justice, and every respect for the sovereign of a friendly nation. The King is most regretful that these enterprises intended to spread and increase their commercial activities and enterprises, and that these persons have adopted means which are so illegal and unrealistic. [The King] represents the law in his relationship with them; he is exercising great restraint because of the respect he has for His August Ally [Alexander I], but since [the King] is convinced that His Imperial Majesty cannot permit such violations on the part of His subjects,the King believes that His Imperial Majesty will indicate His supreme disapproval of such actions by ordering that measures be taken which in His wise judgment will result in their leaving this place they have taken.

I beg His Excellency the Privy Councillor and State Secretary Count Nesselrode to bring this note to the attention of His Imperial Majesty. De Zea Bermudez takes this occasion to convey to Your Excellency his respects.

Reference: United States National Archives. *Records of the Russian American Company*. M11, Roll 1, Vol. 1, n.n., Folios 133–134. From a Russian translation of the French original.

44

APRIL 18, 1817

A REPORT FROM LEONTII A. HAGEMEISTER, COMMANDING OFFICER
OF THE RUSSIAN AMERICAN COMPANY SHIP *KUTUZOV*, TO THE
MAIN ADMINISTRATION OF THE COMPANY

Last March 17 the Russian American Company ship *Kutu-zov* successfully reached the roadstead of the city of Callao. The ship *Suvorov*, which had parted from us at Cape Horn, reached there twelve days later. As soon as I received permission to put in at Lima I hastened there with the ship entrusted to me and explained my purpose, which was to take on water and other supplies and await *Suvorov*.

During conversation I complained a good deal about the weight of *Kutuzov*. She was carrying too much iron, which caused her to pitch and roll heavily when we rounded Cape Horn. I was apprehensive about undertaking further sailing with the ship in such condition. By making this explanation and revealing the amount of iron she was carrying, I hoped to receive permission to sell part of the cargo, especially since I had heard that Chile was in the hands of insurgents and that the delivery of cable and hawser had been interrupted so that the Admiralty was suffering shortages of these. I expressed my wishes to Señor Abadia when we saw each other upon his return from the countryside where he had been spending a short time. He presented my request to the Viceroy and promised to do everything he could to help me.

Following this promise, he took me to various important officials, to whom he spoke about reloading *Kutuzov*'s cargo. The Intendant Arietta, a friend of Abadia's, taking advantage of the Viceroy's trust, took it upon himself to convey the message about the need to reduce the weight of the vessel, and asked that permission be given to sell some part of the cargo. The kindness shown to the former Viceroy encouraged the present General, Don Joaquin Pesuelli, to receive me in a proper manner, and after dinner to drink the health of the Sovereign Emperor. But although he welcomed us and gave us his assurance that he would be glad to help us, he instructed Abadia and Arietta to contact the Commerce Office to make certain there would be no record in his report that he had allowed foreigners to trade, at the same time he was burdening local merchants with enforced contributions for the war with the insurgents.

Meanwhile the Easter holiday came and all business came to a halt. I had to be patient traveling from Lima to Callao and back by ship. Realizing that our affairs were going well, I felt it necessary to ask Abadia to give me some idea as to what price I could sell each item for, and what duties I would have to pay. To my great surprise I received an accounting, which I am appending in translation under letter "A." This indicates that although prices may seem high at first sight, the duties are exorbitant.

I did not intend to conceal my disappointment, so I announced that as soon as *Suvorov* arrived we would depart and that there was no way I could sell at such prices. *Suvorov* did arrive, and I requested a reply. Abadia assured me that the prices listed were in order. He gave me to understand that my request to ask the government that the prices be modified would be granted if my ship could be listed as under Spanish registry, coming from Cadiz. I would be able to take the money if, in return for a modification of the rules, I would sell part of my cargo to private individuals at a lower price. This brought some positive results, and at last, on April 1 it was decided that I should submit a formal request for the approval of the Viceroy. The profit from the sale of goods and the payment of duties would be substantial, compared to Abadia's account, especially since one can expect better profits from trade with private individuals. Woolens, wax and canvas, which comprised the bulk of the goods I had brought, are not profitable. But we must sell wax here and will do so as opportunity arises even though the profit will be small, because wax will not bring even that amount in California or in Manila.

At the present time in the harbor, in addition to Spanish ships which sail from one place in America to another, they are expecting two more ships to arrive at any minute from Cadiz, carrying rich cargoes. There are also three ships here belonging to the United States of America, two English, one French and one Portuguese. The inhabitants joke that it looks as if the port of Callao will soon be open to all nations. This may mean that they expect the Insurgents to come. Chile is lost. There has been no news of action between the 4,000-man royal army and the insurgents in upper Peru.

Matters in Mexico are a great mystery to the public. One must suppose things are not going very well. I have been assured that except for the capital and the principal maritime towns the entire country has gone over to the opposition, and that small areas often pass from the hands of one to the other. The weakness is further demonstrated by the fact that all the Spaniards, even including the Viceroy, are indifferent about the new settlement of the Russian American Company, Ross. In fact, they even commend its organization. I professed complete ignorance of this, saying that if our people had occupied any such point, they probably did it in order to prevent Americans or English from settling there. Both of these groups try to establish settlements in various places, and impede both our trade and that of the Spanish. By extending a helping hand to each other in the New World, we may strengthen the friendship which was firm in the Old World, and with cooperative efforts we will be in a position to expel unwelcome guests. Their hatred of Americans and English, because of the aid they have given the insurgents, leads them to feel that our proximity is a lesser evil.

Suvorov will not have the opportunity to sell her cargo and then to barter part of her goods for local items. Because of this I plan to order her departure for New Arkhangel in ten days. While sailing from Cape Horn she had the misfortune to lose two sailors overboard during a storm. One of the sailors aboard *Kutuzov* broke his arm and was very badly hurt, but thanks to God and the diligent efforts of Court Counselor Kerner, he is now almost completely recovered.

Taking advantage of the rules for Spanish ships which arrive from Cadiz, according to Abadia and others, we will not have to pay more than 25 percent of the duties in silver.

In the appended copies of the account, under letter "B," please note the prices suggested for the Treasury, and the amount we hope to sell to lighten *Kutuzov*. We will sell to private individuals everything the [Spanish] government does not need. Abadia assures me that the Treasury is short of cash and will not buy much, and that we should be able to sell the rest at better prices. We could not persuade anyone to buy the wax, woolen fabrics and canvas goods. We must sell these in some other way. It seems to me that if private persons would pay 20 percent to 30 percent aboard this ship, we could dispose of everything our colonies do not need. One cannot expect large profits in America. Much will be sold on credit or will find no market and the Company will not even recover its own money. Instead, we now find that we can sell part of our goods for cash, some for a fairly good profit, and another part for a small profit—better than one might expect throughout the world in neighboring places.

After I had prepared this report, I waited for the Spanish vessel which had been dispatched to Cadiz, but it was delayed, and in the meantime our own affairs took another turn. The arrival of two vessels from Spain created many problems for us, and the [local] Commerce Board refused to give its consent for us to sell our cargo here. I transferred many goods from *Suvorov* to *Kutuzov*, and kept those which might be in short supply in Sitka. We are preparing to sail together with *Suvorov*, and will separate near 3° 15′.

On the fifth of this month I had the honor of sending a report, Number 63, to the Main Administration, by way of Panama. I hope that my subsequent reports will be sent from the [Russian] American colonies, but in all likelihood that will be early next year. I will then submit a detailed report about everything that God may help us to do and to build.

Fleet Captain Lieutenant and
Cavalier Hagemeister
Ship *Kutuzov*,
in the roadstead
of the city of Callao

P.S. I have the honor of adding, for the information of the Main Administration, that on April 13 I received notice that my request had been denied. The Viceroy seemed to be dissatisfied with it, but since I made good use of my time in Lima, I found another way to protect the Company's interests, even though it is more difficult. Among other things, I hope to bring some 1,000 puds of lump sugar to [Russian] America; it is presently selling for about 50 kopecks per pound.

A

APPROXIMATE ACCOUNT OF SALES AND PRICES FOR ITEMS LISTED
BELOW, PREPARED BY ORDER OF LIEUTENANT HAGEMEISTER.

100 *Quintals*	Iron anchors, bar iron, etc.	@ 13 piastres	1,300
100	Cast copper kettles	1.5	150
100 Quintals	Iron nails	30	3,000
100 *Varas*	Flemish cloth; 2½ lengths	26	65
100 "	Sailcloth; 2½ lengths	30	75
100 Quintals	Tarred rope	18	1,800
100 "	Liquid tar	15	1,500
100 "	Boiled tar	15	1,500
100 "	Wax	100	10,000
100	Guns	17	1,700
		TOTAL SALES	21,090

Duty and Expenses

Import duty in Cadiz; export and import in Lima	5,200
Expenses for unloading and transfer to custom house and warehouses	400
Commission on sale, 4 percent	803
TOTAL EXPENSE	6,403
TOTAL SALES PROCEEDS	14,687

In order to take the above 14,687 piasters from the port of Callao, one must pay 25 percent. Thus proceeds from this amount of goods sold actually came to 11,016 piasters.

B

The bill presented for the amount of iron and other heavy goods which I wanted to have offloaded from *Kutuzov* to lighten her, which was proposed to go to the treasury for the aforesaid against each article of cost, plus loading goods onto my ship from the Spanish ship that had come from Cadiz, and for unloading silver, and for Abadia's assurance, in all came to less than 25 percent. There did not appear to be enough of the provisions the Admiralty is ordering, which, by my suggestion, should be taken on over and above the amount I ordered.

	Middle anchor, per quintal		18 piastres	
1200 Quintals	Bar iron		8	
	Bolt iron		10	
50 "	Iron ingots		16	
150	Iron nails for shipbuilding, 4–8 quintals		21	
150	Pitch			
100	Boiled tar		12	
1500	Hawser and cable		18	
150 Lengths	Flemish cloth, each		27	
125	Sail canvas		30	
1000 Pairs	Boots, low and high	high	3	
		low	2.25	
1000	Shoes		1.125	
200	Guns with bayonets		15	

Since we are now not taking the goods on shore, we cannot hope for the prices indicated in Account "A;" but expenses will also be less.

The most useful goods are *ravenduk* [coarse linen], teak and cable. But for the present market they need rope of a lesser quality than ours which can sell on the ship for a 33⅓ percent markup, or about 18 piasters, that is, a profit of 100 percent. It is too bad there are not more looking glasses and candelabra made of cut pieces of wire. If your ship comes here a second time, perhaps if Peru is not in a state of enmity with Spain and the requested letter has been received, one might come here for *nalivka* [a fruit liquer]. In order to do more, it is absolutely necessary to exercise the greatest of care and show a desire to be useful.

Reference: Library of Congress, Manuscript Division. Yudin Collection, Box 2.

45

APRIL 26, 1817

INSTRUCTIONS FROM THE MAIN ADMINISTRATION OF THE RUSSIAN
AMERICAN COMPANY TO LEONTII A. HAGEMEISTER TO SEARCH FOR
POSSIBLE SURVIVORS FROM ALEKSEI I. CHIRIKOV'S SHIP DURING
THE SECOND KAMCHATKA EXPEDITION, 1741

From the appended memorandum which was received from a certain person who serves in the Ministry of Foreign Affairs, you will learn of a matter the government should have attended to long ago. Catherine the Great would undoubtedly have cared for it if she had not been involved in war at that time. Subsequently her ministers lost sight of it and thus this matter has remained forgotten until the present time, buried deep in an archival box. Unfortunately whoever prepared this memorandum could not make a more detailed extract because of the immensity of the situation. We have brought this to the attention of Count Nikolai Petrovich [Rumiantsev] who was astonished by this situation which had for so long been hidden from the government. He assumed direction over the problem and requested all the details so he could pass them on to us. We do not know how soon these details will reach us. But in the meantime, so as not to let time pass without informing you, we have decided to bring this brief memorandum to your attention, with our own commentary.

You will recall that in the year 1741 Captain [Aleksei I.] Chirikov sent navigator [Avraam M.] Dementev ashore [on the Northwest Coast of North America] between 57° and 58° of northern latitude for purposes of reconnaissance. Neither Dementev nor the sloop and twelve oarsmen sent with him returned. Subsequently a second detachment was sent in a yawl under the command of boatswain [Sidor] Savelov, but he too failed to return. In all, some sixteen men were left on the American shore. But now we have information from a Spaniard named [Gonzalo Lopez de] Haro, who sailed in the region between 48° and 49° northern latitude, and probably also near Georgian Bay in the same parallel as Nootka [Sound] above the Columbia River. [He reported that] there was correspondence regarding this matter between Empress Catherine and the Spanish king; the latter stated that although these Russians were on land belonging to him, he would permit them to settle there as his subjects.

Think how important this matter is now! It is essential to search for these people, and find them; and it is even more important to determine, on the basis of their knowledge, the boundary of the Russian possessions which are presently delineated only up to 52°.

In our judgment you are better qualified than anyone to carry out these assignments. Consequently, once you have consulted with Aleksandr Andreevich [Baranov], to whom we are sending a communication regarding the matter, you are to take on this task and set out to find these Russians. We feel it unnecessary to give you any specific details for this expedition; we trust that you will carry it out prudently and carefully, gain true glory for yourself, and give the Company the opportunity to take advantage of your discoveries. We expect detailed information from you so we may inform higher authorities about this. Until that time we will keep the matter a deep secret.

We also hope the Almighty Creator will give you His blessing. With this sentiment, we have the honor to remain your most humble servants.

Reference: United States National Archives. *Records of the Russian-American Company*, M11, Roll 1, Volume 1, Doc. 222, Folios 87–88.

46

SEPTEMBER 4–28, 1818

FROM THE DIARY OF FEDOR P. LÜTKE DURING HIS CIRCUMNAVI-
GATION ABOARD THE SLOOP KAMCHATKA, 1817–1819: OBSERVA-
TIONS ON CALIFORNIA

September 4 [1818]*

On this day the fog began to dissipate somewhat and at 1:30 P.M. we saw several puffs of smoke on shore directly ahead of us, and the flag of the Russian American Company. We were much gladdened by this sight. We immediately fired two salvos to inform our countrymen of our arrival, and shortly after, two more. We soon saw three baidarkas coming out to us from shore, for which reason we heaved to under the main topsail. At 2:00 P.M. the baidarkas came alongside, and in one of them we recognized the head of the [Ross] settlement, Commercial Counselor [Ivan A.] Kuskov. As soon as he learned who we were he sent his baidarkas to shore to bring us fresh provisions. Meanwhile we continued to tack opposite the settlement not more than three cable lengths [one cable = 185.2 meters] off-shore. During this time we fired our cannon several times in order to hasten those who had gone for fresh provisions, but in spite of this they did not return until 8:00 P.M. They brought us two steer carcasses which amounted to 44 puds of meat, four large pigs and twelve large rams, as well as potatoes and cabbage.

It is unnecessary to add that they took no payment for any of this. Kuskov apologized for not being able to provide us with pumpkins and watermelons, because in that particular year they did poorly, in contrast to the usual harvest.

When it was completely dark we had a very interesting spectacle: a certain extent of land near the settlement was all afire. The Indians who live in this area eat a wild plant which resembles rye, for which reason our settlers call it *rozhnitsa* [*rozh*, rye]. When the kernels of the rozhnitsa have been harvested, the straw which remains is generally burned. This procedure makes the next year's crop bigger and more flavorful. The fires continued throughout the night. At 9:30 P.M. we

---

*Naval dates are from noon to noon. [Eds.]

bade farewell to our obliging Kuskov and put out to sea. At that time the Ross settlement was 50° northeast of us at a distance of three Italian miles [1 Roman mile = 5,000 feet]. According to our calculations this point was located in 38° 32′ latitude and 122° 51′ longitude.

The Ross settlement, or Slaviansk, is built on a level stretch of ground, on the slope of a hill, some [missing] versts from the shore. In regard to the ocean, it would be impossible to find a location with fewer advantages. The coast is very straight; there is not even the smallest bay or curve. This is the reason that one can rarely approach the Ross settlement in an ordinary rowed vessel without danger. When there are moderately brisk winds from the south, southwest, west or northwest, the breakers are so strong it is impossible even for baidaras to land. The depth is quite unfavorable for anchoring. The depth at one mile from shore is 30 sazhens, it increases as one goes out to sea, and beyond three miles it is more than 80 sazhens.

The bottom, it is true, is silt everywhere, but one can hardly anchor in the open sea for more than one day even under the best of circumstances. There is no fresh water at all near the settlement. And, furthermore, the place has no distinguishing landmarks. In a fog, or without several days of observations, it is very difficult to come directly onto it. In clear weather several white rocks close to shore, a little north of the settlement, can serve as a tolerable landmark, and also there are fewer forested areas around the settlement, so it appears to lie on a sandy plain. But with an error of more than ten minutes in latitude, these landmarks are completely worthless. Either urgent need or total ignorance must have served to select this site for the settlement of a maritime trading company.

From Kuskov we learned that *Kutuzov* anchored at Little Bodega some time ago, and is now in Monterey. This information decided our captain to go straight to Monterey.

September 5. A very strong head wind continued all day and the weather remained fair. At 7:30 A.M. we sighted the Farallon Islands lying off the entrance to the port of San Francisco. These islands, or more accurately, rocks, are located in SW½W to the right of the extreme end [of Point Reyes] and extend over a distance of about fifteen miles. There are four or five of them, in two groups, lying SE and NW of one another.

They are white and are visible from a distance of 25 or 30 miles. The southernmost is the largest. Hunting parties of pro-myshlenniks live there at the present time. They hunt fur seals between the islands and the mainland. But it should not be concluded from this that the Farallons have any intrinsic value. They are nothing more than completely barren rocks. If there is a long period without rain the promyshlenniks do not even have water and must go to Point Reyes.

At 3:00 P.M. we were three miles from the southern group of the Farallons, in 67° SW. We took soundings but at 120 sazhens had not reached bottom. The wind gradually calmed and finally stilled. At 9:30 the next morning a small sloop was put to sea so our navigator could go in it to measure the current. A drum was let out for 50 sazhens but no current could be discerned.

At about 10:00 A.M. we spotted a sleeping sea otter not far away. Since the sea was absolutely calm, we put the little sloop into the water again and sent [Antipart] Baranov* (who to our great delight has now completely recovered from his illness), and the naturalist [Morten] Wormskjold [a Danish botanist] to capture it. They did not succeed because the sea otter kept diving and would not let them come within firing distance. Instead of catching the sea otter they hooked a very strange fish. Wormskjold could not determine precisely what species it was because he did not have the proper books, but he thought it belonged to the shark family. It very much resembled the sea-angel [*Krotenhai Meerengel*], but differed in that it has a small mouth and a hind belly fin. Its tail had been bitten off, undoubtedly by another shark, and therefore no accurate comment can be made about that portion of its anatomy nor about its total length.

September 7. At midday we were located in SW 41 1/2°, 23 miles from the southern group of the Farallons. At 4:00 P.M. a gentle wind came up from the NW. By evening it had shifted to W by N and was so brisk that we had to sail at night under fore-topsail. In the morning, however, the sea was again

---

*Antipart Baranov was the creole son of Aleksandr A. Baranov, the Chief Administrator of Russian America; he had been taken aboard *Kamchatka* in New Arkhangel for a voyage to Russia.

calm, the skies were overcast and we regretted having shortened sail the previous evening. At 6:30 A.M. we sighted the shore NE by E and supposed it was the northern extremity of Monterey Bay. At 9:30 we sighted Cape Pinos to ES½E (which is also called Cape Kaparis on the La Pérouse map). At 11:15 we sighted a three-masted ship to the NNW, but at that distance we could only make out the masts. We had many reasons to suspect this was our vessel *Kutuzov*, and we had to decide whether to sail toward her and not enter Monterey Bay today, or go directly to port and miss a rendezvous with *Kutuzov*. Both alternatives were bad. First, however, we confined ourselves to hoisting our flag. We soon noticed that the other vessel had a flag with three stripes. There was no longer any doubt. We immediately hauled up and fired our guns. In response *Kutuzov* proceeded toward us under full sail. We then proceeded along our earlier course, letting her know we would rendezvous with her in Monterey. However, soon after that, she turned into the wind and also fired her guns. Supposing she wished to communicate with us, we lowered sail and lay to. She, under full sail as before, proceeded toward us.

[September 8]. At 2:30 p.m. *Kutuzov* approached us at a distance of not more than half a cable's length and gave us a seven-gun salute (to which we responded with the same) and then lay to. The captain ordered me to go to Hagemeister and tell him to delay no longer but go together with us to Monterey, because we had business with him which could not be concluded in an hour. Just then we realized that he was coming over to us in person. The visit was very brief. He left very shortly, after which we went together to the roadstead where we moored at 5:00 p.m. Soon *Kutuzov* dropped anchor near us. . . .

Our first concern was to send an officer ashore to present passports and request a salute. Midshipman Wrangell was received by the Governor [Pablo Vicente de Sola] very correctly, and on the question of a salute received a satisfactory response. As a result, immediately upon his return we saluted the fort with seven salvos and they responded with the same. His interpreter was a Spanish skipper with whom we had become acquainted in Lima and whose ship, *Hermosa Mexicana*, was presently anchored here. As soon as Baron Wrangell went ashore the man approached him and in broken French expressed his joy that he had met an old acquaintance, and offered his assistance. If Don Gaspar was happy to meet Baron Wrangell, one may be certain the latter was even more pleased to meet the former.

In the morning the commandant of the presidio, Don José Maria Estudillo, an army lieutenant who is about 50 years old, accompanied by our acquaintance, Don Gaspar, visited us. We were busy all day transferring Company goods we were carrying to *Kutuzov*, while the captain conversed with Hagemeister.

September 9. In the morning we prepared to travel to the mission of San Carlos, accompanied by Vasilii (William) F. Bervi, a doctor aboard *Kutuzov*. We had already mounted our horses when suddenly throughout the presidio we could hear drums, which caused anxiety. The children of the commandant and of several other officials asked several of us very politely to lend them our horses for a moment, and they galloped off to the fort. We could not understand what all this alarm signified. Finally we learned that a ship had appeared in the bay. If an entire enemy fleet had suddenly appeared in front of some fortress, it could not have created more agitation. At first we thought several ships had come, and perhaps large ones; but when we looked, we realized that the cause of this commotion was our friend Robson [skipper of the English merchant brig *Columbia*.] The Spaniards meet every ship in this fashion. The whole garrison stands at arms; the fort goes into defensive condition and the only thing missing is the retreat of the people and their belongings into the forest. This reminded me of the fear created by the sudden arrival of the ship *Nadezhda* into Petropavlovsk harbor [first Russian circumnavigation under I. F. Krusenstern] in 1805 where the poor inhabitants naturally supposed the ship had gone half way around the world to capture their barren little corner, whereas *Nadezhda* had simply arrived several weeks ahead of schedule.

Robson himself was no calmer than the Spaniards when he entered the bay, or at least so it seemed. Without dropping anchor he sent a letter to the captain in which he explained that his only purpose was to speak with Captain Hagemeister. He asked the captain to intercede on his behalf with the Governor to obtain permission for him to anchor, in case Robson himself could not secure this permission. To that end our captain sent Baron Wrangell to the Governor. He readily gave permission, although he made it clear that he did so only because of our captain.

Robson then anchored and saluted the fort with eleven salvos, to which they responded with only five. Subsequently Robson complained a good deal about the Spanish. Not only would they not permit him to trade, and he was highly indignant over this, but they would not even allow him to buy provisions. He said that one Spaniard who was very friendly with him advised him, after we left, not to stay long in Monterey. This was apparently all due to the Lima ship. The Monterey Governor and the inhabitants might perhaps have traded with him, but they were afraid that Don Gaspar would reveal this when he reached Lima, and this would have had unpleasant consequences for them. However, only God knows whether one should believe everything Robson says. It is possible that he is discouraging the Spanish from trading with anyone else, such as us, although Robson even refers to us as his protectors against the Spanish; this may all be a pose on his part.

September 10. In the morning *Kutuzov* put to sea. Hagemeister obtained an entire cargo of 18,000 puds of wheat and a number of hides, but only with considerable effort and expenditure. He had to give the Governor a gift of 500 piasters, and a like amount to other officials. Then when it was all done, the Governor announced he must pay duty on the transfer. Hagemeister would not agree to this at first, and asked by what right such an order was given. The Governor replied that he yields to necessity; for some years he has received no [financial] support from Spain, his soldiers have been serving without pay, and that he saw no other means of securing monies properly.

Hagemeister had to agree to accept this tax, which in truth was quite modest, but one could not suppose that such a prudent man as he would not take exception to it. After he had bought some 7,000 puds of wheat in Monterey he set out for the mission of Santa Cruz on the north side of Monterey Bay, where he bought the remaining 11,000 puds without having to pay any duty. He could have bought a much greater quantity, but his ship could not hold any more grain.

All this while the Governor treated him very well and they parted friends, although he did reveal that he hoped this would be the last Russian ship to come to Monterey to trade; he said he had permitted Hagemeister to trade this time only out of personal respect for him. Of course this reply had a double meaning. Not only personal gain, but necessity forces the Spanish to want foreign ships to visit; therefore one may hope that after this last ship, permission will be given to one more, and so on. Obviously all of this must be accomplished with skill and calculation.

Hagemeister left four Aleuts and two baidarkas with us to be delivered to the Ross settlement. He should have stopped there himself to do this, but it would have meant a considerable loss of time, which is very important this late in the season.

After [noon] dinner we went on horseback to the mission in company with the son of the Commandant, the cadet Don José Joaquin [Estudillo]. The prefect of the mission, Father Juan Amoros, received us very cordially. Our interpreter was an Irishman who had deserted from an American ship and had a position of some responsibility here. The mission of San Carlos is located some [missing] versts from Monterey, along the Carmel River which empties into a small bay of the same name. The road from Monterey to the mission is sandy and passes through the hills which are not very high here. Along both sides one finds lovely groves and meadows, which at this time of year do not have the same pleasing appearance as in other seasons; the summer heat scorches the grass and now one sees nothing but the unrelieved yellow surface.

The mission is built of stone, plastered over. All the buildings are roofed with tiles, so that from a distance it has a far more pleasing appearance than it has from the inside. It is built in a square, around which are placed several rectangular buildings. Inside the square are a church, living quarters for the administrators, and warehouses. The outer buildings are dwellings for Indians, of which there are about 450 at this mission. Married persons have special quarters. All unmarried men live together in one part, unmarried women in another. The eye is struck by the filth in which they live. It is impossible to enter any of their huts without being immediately covered with hordes of fleas. These huts have floors of bare earth, but they are completely black with filth. The huts for married persons have a place for a fire in the middle which comprises the entire kitchen. The interiors of these dens really differ very little from Kamchadal or Kodiak iurts, although the exterior gives no hint of this. Unmarried men and women have access to a communal kitchen which supplies their daily food. The mission church is an oblong rectangle without any precious decor. The paintings are rather good. Mass is served every Sunday to the accompaniment of an organ and several violins which the Indians have been taught to play. We could not stay in the church very long because we did not want to be exposed to the frenzy of the fleas which have spread here from the Indian dwellings.

The mission has a fairly large garden, kitchen garden and plowed fields which are worked by the Indians. In the garden there are many flowers and fruit trees such as apple, pear and peach, but according to our interpreter they do not do at all well here; he attributes this to the fact that the land is near the sea and is quite salty. However, this should not be thought to apply to usual harvests in Northern California, which one can say is one of the most productive lands on earth. There are many lands in the same latitude as San Carlos which would produce a larger harvest. Garden vegetables grow very well here, as does wheat, the only grain this mission produces.

Until this year there were nineteen missions in Northern California. Recently one more has been established, seven versts north of the port of San Francisco and twenty versts in from the coast: this is the mission of San Rafael. In all, there are some 15,000 baptized Indians in these missions. The missions are administered by brothers of the Franciscan Order; they are called prefects, and there is a bishop of the same order who supervises them. At the time we were there this position was filled by Father Vincentio Francisco de Sarria. He has no permanent residence, but moves in his official capacity from one mission to another to inspect them, and from one presidio to another. But he appears to spend most of his time in Monterey.

These spiritual fathers are very important persons, especially in California, as is true in all Spanish possessions. In

Headresses of native Californians. Louis Choris, *Voyage pittoresque autour du monde*. (OHS OrHi neg. 82057)

addition to the fact that they have great influence in affairs, the outward respect shown to them is very great. I. A. Kuskov told us that he had on two occasions seen the Governor bring the Bishop's horse to him, and guided his feet into the stirrups once he had mounted. However, this authority which the clergy has taken unto itself does not stem from prejudice or superstition; position and circumstance provide this. Here, as everywhere, the Spaniards do nothing because of their inherent laziness. They value every step, and "mucho trabajo" may disincline them from any undertaking, no matter how beneficial it might be for themselves or others. Here the missionaries are the only persons who are not idle. If California benefits at all, and if Spain receives any good from California (about which I have my doubts), it is exclusively thanks to them.

But even the missionaries' work can be termed such only

Native Californians dance in front of the mission of San Francisco. The mission buildings were far more impressive than the missionaries' conversion rates. Louis Choris, *Voyage pittoresque autour du monde*. (OHS OrHi neg. 82013)

by comparison. Their only work consists of seeing to it that the Indians work. Obviously it was an effort, and perhaps a great effort, to bring the Indians to the mission at first. But at present the replacement of those who leave is an everyday occurrence. I could not learn precisely whether this is done by force or not. Some say they manage by giving presents to the Indians who come, and in this way attract them to remain in the mission. It seems to me, however, that this may have been true only at first, when an Indian thought that by staying in the mission he could improve his status. Now they run off from all contact with the Spanish, as even the Spanish themselves admit.

I know there are a number of the Monterey soldiers who make their living just by going on an *Indian Hunt* (!) three or four times a year. It is obvious this is for no other purpose than for the missions, since the ones who are stationed at the presidios are there because their bad conduct is unacceptable at the missions. The Indians are hunted like animals, and kept like animals. They have no belongings. Everything they have is from the mission; everything they do is for the mission. They are roused at sunrise and driven to prayer, then to work. About noon they eat and then go back to work. At sunset they are driven into their sheds. Men do all the agricultural work; women spin wool and sew. Their only garment is a piece of cloth or a blanket (which they make here in the mission) which they wrap around themselves.

Their food is better than one might expect in such circumstances, but for this they can thank only their own land for its bounty. Every Saturday several head of cattle are slaughtered; the cattle graze in great numbers in the areas around the mission without any supervision; there is plenty of pasturage all year long. Indians with families are given enough meat for a whole week, and salt to preserve it so it will not spoil. Food is prepared for unmarried men and women in a communal kitchen. Meat and maize comprise their entire diet.

The missionaries teach children to sing and to play on some instrument, but nothing else. Not one of the Indians is literate. They are treated now, apparently, just as they were before. Although we did not hear whips cracking while we were at the mission, as Jean François La Pérouse did, our interpreter assured us Indians are beaten for any transgression. To prove his point he showed us a whip which he, as one of the overseers, always carries with him. However, he described the Indians as good-natured people, and assured us they are not as stupid as some would like to make them seem. If they were treated better, they would be useful in many ways. It is not difficult to imagine how they feel about those who treat them in such a manner. They sometimes try to free themselves. But the lack both of means and of unanimity of thought deprives them of success. Their oppressors cruelly force them to regret any such attempts. If one of them does run off, they immediately send soldiers in pursuit, and woe to him if he is caught. However, if he does manage to escape, they will try to capture others to take his place, and they nearly always succeed.

September 12. We were invited to a dinner by Governor Don Pablo Vicente de Sola. No matter how hard he tried to make it gala, and perhaps even sumptuous, it could only compared to a dinner given by a meshchanin or more likely a provincial nobleman. We dined in the garden (as it is called) under a canopy which they probably call a summerhouse or a gallery or some such, but by our standards it was simply a tent. The weather was quite inappropriate for an outdoor dinner. It rained all the time and was quite cold, so that we would have been very pleased to have been inside the Governor's house, but there was not enough room. When we entered the garden we saw a long table set with utensils, and another table beside it which held a number of plates of cakes and fruits, rather lacking in variety. There were two flags on each plate, Spanish and Russian, made of paper, which made for a considerable diversity of colors. To keep up this *ponderous* compliment he gave each of us from his own hands a small cake. This was the beginning of a banquet, about the refinement of which nothing can be said. We could not anticipate a delicious dinner. The wine was unfit to drink. Instead of music for dining, we heard the sounds of chained Indians working in the neighboring enclosure, often walking through the garden. The Spanish were so accustomed to this they were too lazy to hide from us even this unpleasant spectacle, not supposing some would react to it as we did.

The Governor spoke quite a bit about the relationship between our sovereigns, stressing that there are no other two monarchs in Europe so closely allied. It would have been strange to do anything but agree with this. After dinner he had intended to entertain us with the spectacle of a fight between a bear and a bull. For this purpose he had been sending hunters into the forest for several days to capture a live bear, but unfortunately (as he said) they were not successful. Immediately after the dinner, which went on much longer than we would have wished, we departed for the ship.

This day was remarkable because of the success of our Aleuts. Every morning they put out to sea to fish, and always return for dinner. Thanks to them, we have had fresh fish every day. But today, contrary to their usual practice, they did not return for a long time. The wind was brisk and we began to fear that something had happened to them. However, at 5:00 P.M. they returned. They came alongside and very cautiously asked if any Spaniards were with us. When they heard there were none about, they brought out from their baidarkas four sea otters which they had caught: one large and three small.

One was still alive. We were all very pleased with the live otter because if we could take it back to Russia alive, it would be a novelty that had never happened before. The first day there was very little hope. It ate nothing and cried constantly. But the next day it ate fish, meat and everything offered with good appetite. This made us less pessimistic about being able to bring it back alive. But it could not long endure a kind of life to which it was unaccustomed. It was still a suckling, used to being nursed by its mother, and it is well known the mothers are very tender with their young. It died five or six days later.

The passion of the Aleuts for hunting sea otter transcends any description and can only be compared with the zeal of a cat for catching mice. During the two weeks Hagemeister was at the mission of Santa Cruz, those four Aleuts in their two baidarkas caught 42 sea otters, 22 of them on one outing. But it should be noted they put to sea before sunrise and returned by noon so as not to create any suspicion among the Spaniards, since we only had permission to catch fish. When a sea otter appeared in daytime, they all ran up on deck and without saying a word stood poised with a net and would not take their eyes from the animal until it disappeared.

September 16. The Governor paid us a visit. With him were the Commandant; Father Pedro, the prefect of the mission of San Antonio, some distance from Monterey; and Don Gaspar. But if we had had very little pleasure at the Governor's, he had even less with us; in fact he suffered a good deal of torment. However, we were not responsible for this. At first everything went well. When the Governor arrived we saluted him with nine salvos, and the fort responded with the same. This is customary among the Spaniards. We all ate in the captain's quarters. At the table we toasted the health of King Ferdinand VII and the eternal alliance between Russia and Spain (to which the Governor somehow added in passing the health of our sovereign) accompanied by a 23-gun salute. The fort again responded shot for shot. It is a long time since I can remember so much powder being expended in such a short period of time.

About noon the wind came up from the northwest and grew stronger as time went on. A heavy swell developed in the bay, which caused the ship to roll so heavily that the guests who were unaccustomed to the sea were seasick. Most recovered by staying up on the deck, but the Governor had to be taken to a berth. Around 7:00 P.M. the wind subsided enough so we could take them back to shore, but then a new suffering began. The sloop pitched and rolled to an extraordinary degree and the Governor became terribly ill. Near shore the breakers were so heavy it was difficult to land. The poor Governor tried to jump out of the sloop and almost fell into the water, but at least this was the end of all his suffering. If he remembers the Russian frigate without pleasure, at least he will not forget it for a long time. . . .

September 18. Our affairs were now completed and the captain intended to set sail after dinner, but the Commandant announced that the accounts could not be settled by then, so the captain decided to postpone our departure until the next day.

Robson, following advice given to him, raised sail in the morning and began tacking, saluting in front of the fort with a six-gun salute (perhaps so it would not be possible, as had happened earlier, to respond with less than six), but the result was that the fort answered with five.

September 19. Around noon a brisk wind came up from the southeast, and not wishing to lose such a favorable circumstance, we asked the Commandant to hasten the final accounting, which he did, with the result that we did not have to postpone our departure any longer and just after 3:00 P.M. we cast off from the moorage.

During this while the shore was blanketed with fog. This was hard to believe, because the sky was completely clear and there was no sign of foul weather. But when this supposed fog drifted nearer us, it was apparent that it was smoke which we imagined was coming from a forest fire somewhere. However, when the Commandant arrived shortly afterward, he told us it was not a forest fire, but grass, which had caught fire for some unknown reason, not far from the presidio. The grass was so dry the fire rapidly spread over a great area. Within a short time the smoke spread all along the bay, and completely hid the shore and even the sun from us. This rather accelerated our departure because it was uncomfortable to choke every moment on the acrid smoke engulfing us. At 3:30 we raised anchor but had to heave back because the Commandant and Don

Gaspar were still aboard our ship. At 4:00 we parted from them, bagged the sail and put to sea.

The Monterey Presidio is nothing more than a square white stone and stucco structure, of which each side is 100 sazhens long. This description is very accurate and gives a true picture of the presidio. There are no windows or chimneys on the outside which could make this description inaccurate. In a word, this structure is entirely similar to the square of the Lima Pantheon, with the exception that the pantheon houses the dead and the Presidio here, the living. The only thing that breaks the complete symmetry inside is the church which has somewhat higher walls, and is ornamented a bit. Outside, the scene is rather more diverse and livelier because there are groves of trees around the Presidio, and in amongst them one sees herded livestock, and sometimes strolling people or galloping horsemen. Inside, absolute silence reigns and not a word is spoken. The silence is only interrupted by the deep-toned tolling of the bell, which makes one think he has come upon some sort of monastery. Even Petropavlovsk harbor, with all the disadvantages of its location, is twice as lively as Monterey. Monterey is located on the coast in a broad valley which could be beautiful if even the slightest effort were made to cultivate and plant it. If Monterey were in the hands of any other nation for three or four years, this valley would be transformed into a most beautiful English garden, in which one could revel in full measure in the elegance of this climate, as one sat in the shade of cypress trees, but such an undertaking far exceeds the abilities of the Spanish. Their *inertia* prevents them from caring for even their basic needs, to say nothing of those things needed for the enjoyment of life. There is not one flower garden in the entire Presidio, for what we saw at the Governor's [residence] does not deserve to be called a garden, just as Monterey cannot be termed a city. [The yard] is a square space about 30 paces on each side where some bushes and flowers grow. The Commandant's kitchen garden is quite like those which our children make when they are at play. With this exception, there is not one blade of grass in the entire Presidio and vicinity which the Spanish would make any effort to help grow.

If, in spite of all this, they eat and drink well, this is due to the beautiful climate, which enables the livestock to graze all year long, and to the lesser laziness of the missionaries, who provide the Presidio with everything else, without exception. With such an opportunity here, who would not regret that one of the most blessed countries in all the world would fall into the hands of such lazy, listless people, with such mediocre political virtues as the Spanish. Lands that could be transformed into a source of wealth and prosperity for millions of people stand idle, while such industrious persons as the Japanese have to live on sea cabbage!

Don Pablo de Sola is the Governor of New California. He has no dealings with the missions, and if he has any influence over them, it is very minor. He is in charge only of the military personnel and the presidios, each of which has its own commandant. But this command is quite insignificant. Monterey is the capital of New California and its chief military port; and it has a garrison of no more than 100 men, according to the Spanish themselves, who naturally did not underestimate the number, and more likely exaggerated it. The other presidios probably have even smaller garrisons, which would indicate that the entire military strength of the Spanish in New California is slightly more than 200 men. The fortifications are also inconsequential. Monterey is protected by a fort which has no more than fourteen guns; it is simply a square surrounded by a stockade. It is located several sazhens in from the coast on an elevation, and is more than a verst from the Presidio. The fort thus offers little defense for the Presidio, or against entry into the bay, and therefore it is difficult to understand its significance.

Furthermore the garrison could not be concealed within it, and probably could not even take cover in it, because the fort is in no condition to withstand even the lightest attack by cannon. But aside from all that, it could not defend itself even against the savages, if it had such neighbors as our Kolosh. Sitka is a Gibraltar compared to Monterey. But for all that, the Spanish would not permit us to enter the fort, or indeed to go near it. There was no need for this, however, since the entire fort could easily be seen from the ship.

California does not carry on trade with anyone, at least it is not supposed to. This potentially fertile country could carry on a very profitable trade in all kinds of grain, lumber and even wine. Grapes grow and do very well in some of the missions, and they would grow everywhere very well if an effort were made to plant them. Sea otter pelts alone could bring great profit. A multitude are to be found along the coast, but ever since California has belonged to the Spanish, not one Spanish ship has been used to hunt them. The Spanish forbid ships of other nations to hunt the sea otter, although some American vessels and our own [Russian] American Company have agreed to pay them substantial sums of money for permission to hunt. The Spanish government acts precisely as if it were afraid that California might in some way bring some sort of profit to someone.

Monterey is quite a safe harbor because, as they say, there are never any very strong winds there. . . .

It is quite profitable to acquire all manner of provisions (except water) here. Meat is very inexpensive; a beef carcass, regardless of weight, costs six piasters. Those we purchased weighed about 20 puds each, which means that one pud of meat costs less than four kopecks. Lamb and pork are also inexpensive, but there are no domesticated fowl. Vegetables and fruits are plentiful. All of this is available for cash and is inexpensive, but it is even less expensive if one can pay with some commodity instead of cash. For example, an arshin of wool which was purchased for sixteen shillings a yard in England sold here for sixteen piasters. Everything else is in proportion to this example.

Water is a bad problem. One must dig a well and fill casks with water, then carry the casks some 150 sazhens to a place where a ship can come alongside. Water thus procured is often dirty and tastes bad. Officials who live in Monterey use this water only for washing clothes. For cooking and drinking they bring water by oxen from the little Carmel River which flows near the San Carlos mission. One can quite easily provide oneself with wood, because the forest is not far from the coast. . . .

The poor quality of the water in Monterey and the difficulty of procuring it, as well as the necessity of seeing what the Company is doing in Little Bodega harbor, persuaded the captain to proceed there, where the water was reported to be good and more accessible. For this reason Captain Hagemeister assigned our captain to go to the Ross settlement. . . .

September 21. At 1:45 P.M. we sighted the Farallon Islands just south of us. At first the captain intended to pass them to the seaward, but then decided to proceed between the islands and the shore because it was closer, and the wind was such that we could proceed in either direction. When we approached, we noted that our promyshlenniks were living on the southeast side of the largest of the Farallons. At 4:00 P.M. we fired a salute and raised our Russian commercial flag, because it was more familiar to them than our naval flag, which they might even misinterpret as the flag of a foreign vessel. Soon thereafter we saw six or seven men running from their shelters to the east side of the island. We thought perhaps they had baidaras and were running to them in order to come out to us, but they quickly hid between rocks and were seen no more. Since we had no need for them, and presuming they had no need of us, we proceeded on our way without stopping. The roar of the sea lions was clearly audible. It made a dismal hollow sound with the noise of the breakers. At night on the shore we saw a bright glow which probably was due to the same cause as the one we saw in Monterey; however, here it did not cover much of the shore, and it reached a definite height, for which reason it was possible that it came from a forest fire.

At 2:00 A.M. we sailed close to the wind which came from the southwest, and at dawn found a bottom of thin silt at 80 sazhens and proceeded directly to Bodega. At 7:45 A.M., having come close to shore, we heaved to and sent our Aleuts directly to the Ross settlement to notify Kuskov of our arrival. We lay to the southeast in order to avoid the shallows which extend out from a small island at the entry to the bay. At 9:00 A.M. we raised the flag with a gun salute, and at 9:30 came to a depth of six sazhens. The bottom was sand, and we lay to at the moorage with our port and starboard anchors. . . .

Our first concern, of course, was the business for which we had come, to take on water. Consequently, wasting no time, we put as many empty casks as we could aboard two rowboats and sent them to shore. Meanwhile, we also sent a launch, which we used on this kind of occasion.

Toward evening Kuskov sighted us and delighted us with an unexpected visit. We had not anticipated he would come out, because the Aleuts whom we had sent could not have reached him so soon. But they had met him halfway as he was traveling to Bodega on business.

September 22. We went ashore to an Indian settlement some distance to the north. I believe it would be difficult to find a people who have less political comprehension than these Indians. Their living quarters are more like beehives or anthills than human habitations. They are made of sticks stuck in the ground in a semicircle about one and one-half arshins high; these are fastened together and then covered with dry grass or tree branches. These dwellings do not give them shelter from rain or foul weather, which, fortunately for them, is quite rare in the area where they live. They lead wretched lives in these huts; they seem to have no pleasure except such as animals might have. They are completely indifferent to things unfamiliar to them. Our arrival aroused not the slightest attention. Not more than two or three of them visited our sailors who were taking on water and washing their linen on shore. When we anchored they first of all examined the items around us. Two Indians came out of the hills down to the shore. We followed them with our binoculars until they again hid, and not one of them turned back to look at our ship. It seemed as if this did not deserve their attention, any more than the shrubs through which they passed. When we entered the settlement, not one of them left off what he was doing, or even left his place to look at us. Not even those with whom we started to converse would turn to look at us.

Our interpreter was a Kodiak Aleut who had run off when Kuskov first went to the port of San Francisco. [The Aleut] had lived with the Indians for nearly a year, but when the next group came to hunt, he reappeared and began hunting sea otters with the others. From his accounts we must conclude that these Indians have a quarrelsome nature, but are not evil. He said they quite often quarrel and fight with one another, but that they never bothered him.

There is no evidence that they revere God, and in general it seems that not only do they have no understanding of God, but that they never even wonder how and for what purpose they and everything else around them were created. Such people obviously can have no laws. Nevertheless there was one among them who called himself their leader, and whom our people by custom refer to as a toion. But we could not determine how extensive his power is over all the others. We did not even see any exterior indications of respect shown him by the others, and he would not have looked any different from the others if some of our people had not given him two shirts the day before, both of which he wasted no time in putting on. It appears that this position is hereditary, because his father was also a toion.

In spite of the fact that they have dwelling places, their lives are almost nomadic, because in this settlement there are sometimes more than 50 of them, and at other times no more than ten. This is not surprising because what they have here they can also find elsewhere. There is no shortage anywhere of sticks and dry grass for making habitations. Their food consists only of acorns and rozhnitsa, and in the summer, whatever the sea provides. They grind acorns as we do coffee, beat it up and mix it with water and heat it. This sweet porridge comprises their main food. In place of a saucepan they use reed or grass baskets, into which they put heated stones. There is no intermediary between these baskets and their mouths except their fingers, which they dip into the porridge and lick, and thus satisfy their hunger. Although this form of eating does not arouse an appetite in others, I decided to try it and found that this provision is a bitter, rather unpleasant tasting blend. We did not have an opportunity to observe how they prepare rozhnitsa. It is probably not available at this time of year, because we did not see anyone who had any. However, fields in many places were burned, probably for the same reason mentioned earlier.

Aside from this they eat all sorts of shellfish and some fish, but not much of the latter because they have no means of catching them. However, we did see one family eating small broad fish about two inches long, which can probably be taken along the coast. The only preparation was to bury them in hot ashes for a while; they were then eaten whole, including the skin and the ash clinging to it. Although this does not indicate their brilliance, nonetheless so as not to be without this, they always make their habitations near the shore. The settlement we saw was near the bay, or more accurately, near a lake connected to the bay. They only drink water which they obtain from a pit about 1-1/2 arshins deep. The water is dirty and has a foul taste.

Industry among these Indians is still in a state of complete infancy, or to state it better, it is nonexistent. They walk around stark naked. Some of them make a kind of shirt for themselves from blankets the Spanish or the Russians give them, which garments, however, do not cover their private parts. But there is very little of this kind of clothing, because the Spanish do not like to give them anything for free, the Indians have nothing to give in exchange, and there are few Russians here. We saw some Indians who had a kind of cloak made out of seagull skins, but this covered no more than half the back. Considering the type of clothing with which they attempt to cover the back, rather than any other part of the anatomy, one can conclude that they have no conception of modesty. This refers only to the men. The women wear the pelts of wild sheep which they fasten around the waist and allow to hang down below the knees. We saw very few objects of their own handiwork. I have already mentioned the baskets made of grass. Of all the items they make, these deserve special attention because they are so tightly woven that water does not seep through.

Their only weapons are the bow and arrow, which are rather crudely made. Although they live for most of the time near the sea, they have no boats whatsoever. On the shore near their settlement there was something resembling a raft, which consisted of a few bundles of thin reeds fastened together. This contraption, which cannot possibly hold more than two persons at a time, and which in all fairness one can term unseaworthy, they use if they have to cross a stream, or in some other such circumstance. Small nets, crudely plaited of grass, conclude this list of their handicrafts.

These Indians have skin of a dark copper color; their hair is completely black and very disheveled. They are somewhat less than medium height and have generally a rather clumsy build. Their eyes, however, without exception are full of life. In addition to this, one may say that the women are not bad looking. Their full round faces are quite well-proportioned, with a small mouth, a not too large nose and lively eyes, which gives them a quite pleasing appearance. The color of their skin is apparently due to the filth in which they live, rather than from nature; they assured us that if they were to wash they would be quite white

Some of the promyshlenniks and Aleuts have married these Indian women. Our interpreter, whose wife is one of these people, told us that she had learned his language very quickly and well, and that she had also learned Aleut handicrafts, such as sewing the whale gut *kamleika* [waterproof outer garment] and other things. In one hut I saw a rather comely young woman preparing food, and when I approached her I was surprised that she spoke easily and in clear Russian. She invited me to eat her acorn porridge, and then complained about the rain. When I inquired I found that she had lived for some time in the Ross settlement with a promyshlennik, and then had returned to her people. Something could still be made of the women but these unfortunate creatures seem to comprise the lowest class among their own tribesmen, as is true with nearly all savages. Women have no rights which would attract them to return to their previous status. An Indian takes as a wife an Indian woman whom he likes; he keeps her as long as he wishes and discards her whenever he chooses. Women do all the work. In the entire settlement we saw only one man at work—he was weaving a net—and perhaps he was doing that out of boredom. All the rest either play or do nothing. It was a rare woman who was not occupied with some work.

These Indians use a special kind of bathhouse which is really just an underground iurt. An opening is made on one side, through which one must crawl. There is a smoke hole in the top. When the bathhouse is heated, they enter and play. Their play is similar to that of the Kolosh and the Kodiak Aleuts. There are several marked sticks which one person mixes up, concealing the marks; the other person must guess which is which. Idleness has created a situation where persons who have almost nothing to lose have a passion for the game. It is quite remarkable and amazing that among peoples who inhabit the entire Northwest Coast of America, from Kodiak to the 38th parallel, this game of chance is one and the same, even though they have no other relationship, nor the slightest similarity, nor do they have any communication with one another at all. However, one can make almost the same observation about the peoples of Europe—diverse languages, diverse religions, diverse customs—but identical card games. Some philosopher or other will perhaps find in this an indication of one of the major shortcomings of human nature, and conclude that human beings are more accustomed to adopt something bad than something good.

Their language is quite pleasant to the ear, and that is all that can be said about it. It has no sounds that are rough or heavy on the ear, and they speak very rapidly.

Little Bodega Bay, or as our settlers call it, Rumiantsev Bay, and as the natives say, Chokliva. . . . has an entry no more than 40 sazhens wide and is a fairly large bay about ten miles in circumference. On the shore there is an Indian settlement which has been described above.

This bay would be the most wonderful harbor in the world if ships could enter it, but the depth permits only small rowing vessels to enter. A large part of it beginning from the *koshka* [shallows] and extending nearly to the middle is dry during low tide. Thus it is of no use for seafarers. From the end of the koshka a sand bar extends southeast almost parallel to the shore. The shore itself at this point has a rather deep area and thus makes it possible to have a small but rather good anchorage where two or three small vessels can anchor safely. But there are many disadvantages. The entry into it between the end of the sandbar and the shore of Cape Rumiantsev is narrow and winding, and furthermore the depth in this channel during low tide is no more than four feet, and at high tide between ten and eleven feet. At full and change, it rises to fourteen or fifteen feet. Thus this harbor can be used only by small vessels, but in order to enter the harbor, even small vessels must choose a time when the water is high and ideal circumstances prevail. Large ships have to anchor in the outer bay, which is almost completely closed from SW to N, and almost to the E. From SW to S by W, it is protected by an island SE by S from Cape Rumiantsev, and by reefs which extend from this island to the sea, and others abutting the cape. From E to SSE it is protected somewhat by the mainland, which turns slightly to the SW and terminates at the end of Point Reyes. From the remaining three *rhumbs* [compass points] it is open. This description indicates to all that Rumiantsev Bay is a rather poor harbor. In summer months the risk is not great, but in winter only the greatest necessity would force a ship to seek refuge there. . . .

From the sea Rumiantsev Bay has few landmarks. The most distinctive part is Cape Rumiantsev, which is high, treeless and sandy, while the adjacent shore is low, gently sloping and covered with verdure. It is this, and the fact that it juts out into the sea somewhat, that from a distance makes it look like an island. A small island SE of it is also a rather good landmark if one is already quite close to it.

From the inner part, as much as from the sea, Cape Rumiantsev differs from the surrounding coastline. From the sandy low shore that has a width of about 40 paces, it suddenly rises straight up to a height of about 70 feet, then, less steeply, another 100 feet. The opposite or eastern shore rises in a moderate slope to low hills, beyond which lies a vast tundra. The entire vicinity is treeless, and only in the mountains beyond the tundra are trees visible in some places. Close by there is nothing but small shrubbery. The grass was all burned over, as in the area around Monterey, but the soil is very rich chernozem. Taking this into consideration, along with the beautiful climate of this place, one can truly say that every conceivable fruit and vegetable would grow here as well as anywhere else. This is also evident by the astonishing fertility of the land around the Ross settlement, not more than eighteen miles from here. There all vegetables are grown to produce two crops a year. They are planted in November and harvested in April, then planted again in May and harvested in October. As an example of the fact that everything grows there very well, suffice it to say that Kuskov once picked a radish from his garden which weighed one pud and fourteen pounds. One might consider this a cock and bull story if Kuskov were not a man who does not prevaricate about anything. This region would have no need for anything in the world, if only it had a population.

At the present time a seafarer can find nothing in the Rumiantsev port but water, which is pure, delicious, and empties into the interior harbor from a small creek which flows from the hills. It is very easy and convenient to obtain water. All one needs is to build a trough from the water to a cask, and wait until it fills up. Although this is very important there is really no other reason to come here. In the inner part of the bay there are of course many snipe which can be taken in any number for daily use. There are very few fish, and wood is difficult to obtain, even for everyday use.

Poor as this port is, nonetheless it is not without use for our [Russian] American Company. It is the only harbor in which vessels that bring items for the Ross settlement can be unloaded, and for this purpose there is even a warehouse here, actually just a shed, which was completely empty while we were there. In addition Kuskov has built a shipyard in the Ross settlement where vessels are built and brought to this port for fitting out and loading with cargo. We found the first of the vessels he had built; a schooner of some 80 tons, *Rumiantsev*. It was being readied to hunt in the Farallon Islands. Another ship, *Buldakov*, was still in the building slip in Ross, but was already in its final stages. The plans for these ships were made by an English shipbuilder who was in Company service; however, we did not meet him. The vessels are built by a simple promyshlennik, one of those from an Irkutsk merchant [Vasilii Grudinin], who had previously never seen a ship, and who only knew how to use an ax. Further, his only prior training came when he evidently had a chance to help repair Company ships. When the plans were sent to Ross, he examined them and first tried to build models, and when these were approved, he undertook to build the ships.

Rumiantsev, which we saw, was very well built, judging by its outward appearance, and it certainly did not look as if it had been built by a simple promyshlennik. The unfairness of the Company is reflected in the fact that this talented man receives a salary of only 400 rubles. How can the Company expect that honest men will serve it, if it rewards them so poorly?

Having examined the disadvantages of the location of the Ross settlement, naturally the question arises as to why the Company did not establish the settlement on the shore of the port of Bodega, which, while not ideal, at least is more advantageous than Ross. The Company would have done this if it had had permission, but although the Spanish authorities permitted the Company to have a settlement, they seem to have been afraid to give it too many advantages. Even though they were willing to have the Russians as their neighbors, they preferred a distant to a close neighbor. We must remember that all of this was arranged, as it were, without the knowledge of either government.

The Company acted in accordance with its charter, and did not consider itself obliged to ask prior permission from the government. The Spanish Governor had a different motive. This all took place in 1812 when news reached here of the overthrow of Ferdinand VII from the throne, and the accession of a new dynasty. It is well known that its rights in all of Spanish America were repudiated and the Governor of California [José Joaquin Arrillaga] and others did not consider themselves subjects of the then government, but rather that the Governor had the right to act in the name of the legitimate king, Ferdinand VII. The Company, having received permission to settle, immediately sent Kuskov with a group for this purpose, who upon arrival at the designated place, quickly began to build dwellings, warehouses, and in other words, started to *settle*. They bought from the Spaniards the necessary domestic animals which were driven to the settlement by officers from the presidio of San Francisco personally. Furthermore, as Kuskov related, the officers supposed the Russians did not know how to milk cows, and sat down under the cows to demonstrate the process.

After Kuskov had become well established, he began to build the fort, which now has [missing] guns and is thus stronger than Monterey. The Company considers all these factors, including the last two, as sufficient evidence of its rights to this place.

Once the legitimate king was returned to power, the Spanish government received news of this [Ross], and since this had been done without its knowledge, reprimanded the former Governor who has since then gone to eternal bliss (and according to Kuskov's assurances, he certainly must be in paradise). His successor, de Sola, was given strict orders to send the Russians out of California. However, such matters are only decided in government offices. The Spanish government, thinking perhaps that our government would intervene on behalf of [the Company], makes no statement, and for the same reason, ours is also silent. But in the instructions to our captain, one of the most important points is an explanation of all this, and an examination of the rights of the Company. Our Emperor is not disposed to acknowledge as legal anything which is not legal. Thus now that he is familiar with the entire matter as it now stands, at the slightest protest from the Spanish government he will not hesitate to order the Company to pull out of this area. One can be even more certain of this if one knows how His Majesty usually views such matters.

In the meantime the Company is adding new rights to its previous rights. Kuskov concluded a pact with the elder of the Indians who live in his vicinity, by virtue of which the Indian cedes to him all the land he occupies (nearly all of California), into the jurisdiction of the Russian Emperor; he himself submits as a subject to the Emperor's government. (Hagemeister asked our captain to take this document with him and to give it to appropriate persons when he reaches Russia.) However, a pact made with a person who is illiterate and has not the slightest understanding of what a treaty means, may only serve as a point to be argued, not a well-founded right; probably it will serve no purpose at all.

At present everything continues as before. Kuskov continues to complain that they are *indulging* the Spanish (!), "so it is very likely they will come to force us out." The Spanish Governor continues to express hope that Kuskov will voluntarily leave this place, for he does not have the forces to drive him out. (It is possible this may serve him as a pretext to let Kuskov remain there so he can be utilized as a neighbor.) The Russians and the Spanish remain friends. Many years may pass before matters take some other direction, because Spain does not see a threat to itself from this. Revenues do not decrease, because even without this the Spanish receive nothing from California. Likewise the governors will not be too stubborn. This neighbor provides them the advantage that ships will come to them more often, and will bring them everything they need. On the other hand the Company also receives little benefit from this settlement. Its main hope was that it would be permitted to hunt sea otters, but the Spanish are stubborn about this and now the Company's only advantage is that its ships which come here or pass here may enjoy fresh provisions. Of course this is worth something, especially since it costs the Company nothing to maintain the settlement.

In regard to the Indians, some of the men had tattoos on the chest, straight lines and zigzags which extended from one shoulder to the other; they also pierced their earlobes and placed small bits of feather shafts in the orifices. The women wore no ornamentation at all.

September 24. We completed all our business in two days. On the 24th a brisk wind came up from the WNW. Toward night it quieted, and at 6:00 A.M. the next morning we began to cast off from the moorings. At 9:00 A.M. we weighed anchor and proceeded with a light NW wind to the SE. The captain had to go to the Ross settlement once more to take the document from Kuskov, and if possible, to go ashore in person to inspect the settlement. Kuskov set off at dawn in a baidara in order to precede us, and so as not to detain us in case we had a favorable wind and could go there quickly. He left two Aleuts and a baidarka with us. . . .

September 26. . . . The baidara came out to us [from Ross] empty-handed, so to speak. It may as well not have come at all. The captain immediately dispatched it back to Kuskov with a note which probably asked him to send the document out quickly. We continued to tack.

September 28. . . . While we were hove to, we had the pleasure of seeing the honorable Kuskov again. He apparently realized that he was detaining us and that we were eager to set out, because his face revealed an embarrassment we were not accustomed to seeing in him. It is possible his late arrival was nothing more than a desire to be as helpful as possible to us, because he brought us so much in the way of pigs, sheep, two live steers and a quantity of various greens that we scarcely had room to stow it all. It had taken him some time to put all of this together. He did not even forget our naturalist, and brought him some trees he was not familiar with. Wormskjold could not identify them either, because there were only leaves and twigs, no flower or fruit, so it was impossible to make an identification.

At 6:00 P.M. we bade farewell for the last time to this distinguished man whose good nature and helpfulness will never be erased from our memories. I could not help remembering that because of his eagerness to help we almost mistook him for a fool. Departing from him, we set out under full sail and proceeded SSW, at this time four miles from Ross, SW 45°.

Reference: TsGAVMF, f. 15, op 1, d.8.

See: Leonid A. Shur. *K beregam Novogo Sveta: iz neopublikovannykh zapisok russkikh puteshestvennikov nachala XIX veka* [To the Shores of the New World: From Unpublished Notes of Russian travelers of the Early Nineteenth Century]. (Moscow: 1971), 135–163.

47

AUGUST 13, 1817

INSTRUCTIONS FROM ADMIRALTY TO CAPTAIN VASILII M. GOLOV-
NIN CONCERNING HIS VOYAGE ABOARD *KAMCHATKA* TO RUSSIAN
AMERICA

During your first around-the-world voyage in 1807 the Admiralty gave you instructions with detailed directions on how to conduct yourself during the voyage, determine the route, keep a journal and what useful information to enter into it. The Admiralty is confident of your knowledge, experience and skill and does not find it necessary to repeat these instructions at the present time. It will rely on your ability and good judgment in all matters.

You may set your voyage from Kronstadt to Kamchatka, depending on the season and circumstances, either via Cape Horn or the Cape of Good Hope. En route you may put in anywhere you find it necessary and convenient to take on fresh provisions and water.

When you sail across the Pacific Ocean it would be useful if your voyage were to take you to places where no other seafarer has yet voyaged, or to such areas where earlier seafarers have noted the possibility of the existence of land, in the hope that that you will have the chance to discover new lands. For your information, a map of all previous voyages is appended.

In accordance with the decision of the Supreme Council concerning the reorganization of Kamchatka, which the Emperor has confirmed, Part IV, section 86 states that you are to put in at the Sandwich Islands if circumstances permit, to obtain salt if you need it and if you can load it aboard the sloop. You may also obtain fresh provisions and water there for the rest of your voyage to the harbor of Petropavlovsk. When you leave the Sandwich Islands, if winds permit, you are to proceed WNW along the chain of islands to ascertain whether this archipelago extends farther in that direction and is part of the same archipelago recently discovered by [Iurii] Lisianskii.

When you approach Kamchatka, try to cut across the course taken by the ship *Slava Rossii* in 1790 [Billings-Sarychev

Russian naval captain Vasilii M. Golovnin sailed the St. Petersburg-built brig *Kamchatka* to the North Pacific. Earlier he had accomplished a successful circumnavigation in the 16-gun sloop *Diana*, sailing from St. Petersburg-Kronstadt to Japan and Petropavlovsk, an historic expedition. This engraving on wood is by the Russian artist Soloveichik. N. N. Bashkina, *The United States and Russia, The Beginning of Relations*, (OHS neg. OrHi 82935)

Expedition], at 170° longitude east of Greenwich and 50° northern latitude; at that time they noted some indications of land.

The document from the Governing Senate, Part IV, Section 86, assigns you the task of trying to locate more accurately on naval charts remote places, and if possible, to discover new islands. In addition, in accordance with the intent of the instructions in the same section, you are to take an inventory of the inhabitants of the Aleutian Islands and of the American mainland who are Russian subjects. For that reason you are to sail across the entire expanse of the ocean from Kamchatka to America. During your voyage there it would be useful to sail north and south of the Aleutian Islands, at a distance of between 180 and 200 Italian miles. At that distance one might expect to find unknown islands whose existence is suspected because of the presence there of fur seals and sea otters, who come every year from the southern part of the ocean, through the entire Aleutian archipelago to the north; then in October they return from the north, through the same archipelago, and proceed south. From this one must conclude that these amphibious creatures spend the entire summer on islands in the north, where they give birth to their young, then in winter proceed to islands in the south.

In order to improve the maps of these seas it is necessary to survey the hitherto unexplored part of the American coast from Bristol Bay to Norton Sound. Captain Cook could not continue his voyage off this coast because of the existence of a large offshore reef. For that reason this coast should be surveyed from rowed boats, for which purpose you will need to have a large hide-covered baidara. When your sloop reaches the cape of Bristol Bay in the northwest, send the baidara with the surveyors to proceed along the coast to the north. Instruct them to survey the coast as far as Norton Sound, where the sloop should proceed at a like distance from shore, as the depth of the water permits, so that when you arrive at Norton Sound you will take up the surveyors and the baidara aboard the sloop.

In Bering Strait, on the American coast opposite St. Lawrence Bay, Chukchi accounts indicate there is a large deep bay inhabited by certain people not related to American natives. According to the Chukchi these people have books and icons to which they pray. Captain [Gavriil A.] Sarychev intended to survey this bay at the time of Captain [Joseph] Billings' expedition, but it was too late in the season, and head winds prevented him from doing this. For that reason it would be desirable, during your visit to those places, if time permits, to carry out Sarychev's intention.

On your return voyage from the north you are to approach St. Matthew Island, and from there search for another island which Lieutenant [Ivan] Sindt sighted, and which he located on the chart as being 70 Italian miles southwest of St. Matthew Island.

The entire east coast of Kamchatka from Avacha Bay north, and continuing along the coast of Asia to Bering Strait, has never been properly surveyed, and this should be done. It could best be accomplished from a baidara outfitted and dispatched from Petropavlovsk harbor early in the summer. The surveyors should be instructed that while proceeding along the coast they should survey it to St. Lawrence Bay, where a large seagoing vessel will pick them up and return them to Petropavlovsk. If they are sent from Petropavlovsk the same summer you are in Bering Strait, you may take them on your sloop and it will not be necessary to send another ship out for them.

> Vice Admiral Sarychev
> Acting State Counsellor A. Labzin
> Ober-Berg-Hauptman 4th Class Loginov
> Fedor Shubert.

Reference: Vasilii M. Golovnin. *Sochineniia i perevody Vasiliia Mikhailovicha Golovnina*. Vol. 3, (St. Petersburg: 1864), Part 2, v–viii.
Also: *VPR*, Second Series, Vol. 9. Doc. 194, 649–651.

48

AUGUST 17, 1817

A REPORT FROM THE MAIN ADMINISTRATION OF THE RUSSIAN
AMERICAN COMPANY TO THE MINISTER OF FOREIGN AFFAIRS,
KARL V. NESSELRODE, CONCERNING THE HAWAIIAN ISLANDS

A few days ago the Main Administration of the Russian
American Company had the honor of sending Your Excellency certain information on the [Russian] establishment on
the coast of California. The copy herewith appended, of a report received since then from Dr. [Georg] Schäffer, from the
island of Kauai, describes the danger which this establishment
presently faces from the Spanish.

This report primarily concerns the news that the king of
the islands of Kauai and Onecheo has not only given the
Russians a cordial reception but that he has made certain commercial arrangements, and has submitted himself unto the sovereignty and protection of His Imperial Majesty. As testimony
of this he has presented a formal document to Dr. Schäffer, a
copy of which is enclosed. Schäffer reports that he sent the
original [to Russia] on a Russian ship.

When this news is submitted to the attention of His Imperial Majesty, it may lead to a superior order and may reach the
sloop *Kamchatka* before her departure. If this should be the
case, the Main Administration of the Company humbly requests permission to send certain dispatches to its employees.

The English newspaper *Courier* of July 30 [1817] reports
this news in an article, which is appended.

> The Main Administration of
> the Russian American Company
> Benedikt Kramer
> Andrei I. Severin

[Dr. Schäffer's report:]
The ship *Bering* which belonged to the [Russian American]
Company was wrecked on the island of Kauai in the Sandwich
Islands, as a result of the malicious deeds of Captain [James]
Bennett. I was sent here by Collegiate Counselor Baranov in

the capacity of plenipotentiary to investigate this matter and demand the return of the cargo which the Indians salvaged. To my great satisfaction, I carried out this assignment in 24 hours. Thus 20,000 Spanish piasters worth of goods were saved for the Company.

Baranov also wanted to build a factory in the Sandwich Islands, but King Kamehameha, whose activities were guided by an old English seaman, [John] Young, and by several Americans, firmly rejected this proposal. However, King Tamara of Kauai not only agreed to the establishment of the Russian factory, but even requested protection from the Russian Emperor. In a very solemn ceremony, in a written document he entrusted supreme authority over his island to His Imperial Majesty, the Russian Emperor Alexander Pavlovich. I am sending herewith a copy of this document. The original will be sent via Sitka and other points to the Main Administration in St. Petersburg, so it will be presented at the foot of the throne of His Imperial Majesty. [The Company] should request Imperial all-gracious approval and immediately inform me here, via Sitka, by reliable means.

In the name of the Company I concluded a commercial agreement with King Tamara, under the terms of which the Company secures the exclusive right to purchase sandalwood. Further, the King transferred into Company ownership for all time the entire area of Kauai, with a population of some 400 Indian families. We can use the land for plantations, factories and the like. The place also has a maritime harbor called Honolulu. I will send the principal documents to St. Petersburg with a Russian ship, or via Okhotsk. The documents contain the most detailed account of everything.

My only desire is to have dispatched from St. Petersburg to here two good ships with full crews and appropriate armaments. There is not a single reliable ship in Sitka, nor any experienced navigator with the exception of Lieutenant [Iakov] Podushkin. There is everywhere a shortage of labor and of artisans.

Russian settlement in California is threatened with complete destruction by the Spanish. I know very well that the Governor of Monterey has asked permission from the Viceroy of Mexico to do just that. Quite recently he took some 30 baidaras and Aleuts and many Russians including Dr. Elliot [John Elliot de Castro] into the interior, as captives.

Perhaps His Majesty the Emperor will send a frigate to the Pacific. It will render substantial service and be very important for the Russian Empire. I would like to have two 400-ton ships from the Company. The Company ship *Otkrytie*, which brought me here, lost two masts, and we barely escaped with our lives.

Georg Schäffer

[Original in German]
Reference: *VPR*, Second Series, Vol. 1, Doc. 195, 651–653.

49

INSTRUCTIONS FROM THE MAIN ADMINISTRATION OF THE RUSSIAN
AMERICAN COMPANY REGARDING ITS EXPEDITION TO THE ISLAND
OF KAUAI

An event has occurred which is important not only for the Russian American Company, but for the entire Fatherland. The Collegiate Assessor, Doctor of Medicine and Surgery [Georg] Schäffer; has reported that the king of the island of Kauai, Tamara Taeevich, with all the islands and peoples under his control, has submitted to the mighty scepter of our Sovereign Emperor and Autocrat of all Russia, and gives to the Russian American Company to hold in eternal possession [for Russia] an entire region, whose inhabitants number some 400 Indian families. [The king] has concluded with [the Russians] in the name of the [Russian American] Company, a commercial treaty for the exclusive trade in sandalwood.

As a result of these developments, although we still do not have detailed and complete information about these islands, the inhabitants, and much more which Schäffer has promised to provide, the Administration of the Company, until further policies have been promulgated, assumes the duty of issuing brief temporary instructions on how the person who will be in proximity to this new acquisition should conduct himself until further notice. The following directions are to be observed.

1. Since it is quite likely that King Tamara submitted to the protection of the Russian Autocrat because he is not the king of the other islands, or may suffer from being oppressed by them, the leader of the [Russian] detachment on the island of Kauai should endeavor to protect the king and his people from attacks by other island rulers as much as possible. If an attack is supported by any European power, however, or even is influenced by such, the Company should not interfere until further notice.

2. King Tamara himself should be respected as a ruler who is friendly to us and who is subject to the protection of our Sovereign. As such, he should be given as much respect as

possible, within the framework of his simple and primitive way of life.

3. If some discord should arise between our people and his Indian subjects, or if there is some other kind of affair that requires factual investigation, all such matters are to be handled by the commander of the expedition. His Russian subordinates are not to interfere. Such matters are always to be brought to King Tamara, with the request that he be the judge. If any member of the families which he made subject to or entrusted to, the Company should be found in some transgression, the commander of the expedition is not to pass judgment or punish such person. Rather, he is to seek advice from this king, who will decide the punishment. All of this is to be strictly adhered to until new instructions are sent for that expedition.

4. Above all, under threat of certain and severe punishment, members of the expedition are not to cause even the slightest offense or oppression to the islanders. They are not to appropriate property and especially they are not to have relations with the women without their consent. All such ignoble conduct always redounds to the detriment of the newcomers, and the Company does not wish to be associated with such behavior in any way. In fact it has always prohibited such actions, because of the losses thus caused. Such crimes are generally committed by persons who do not understand the consequences to the Company in our colonies, or by persons who have no regard for the Company.

5. Likewise, the islanders are not to be used [as laborers] by the Company, not even those who may belong to the Company. They are not to be forced into service or forced to work as slaves. They should be encouraged and taught to have an interest in service, in accordance with local circumstances. They are to be adequately rewarded for any work they do. Commercial contact should be skillfully established with them; gradually they should be attracted to this.

In a word, treat the islanders as one would treat fellow countrymen, as friends, as Russian subjects. Otherwise you will never succeed in befriending these children of nature, nor will you ever manage to unite them to us. On the contrary, you will only create barriers which will eventually take over.

6. Since detailed information about Kauai Island is expected but has not yet been received we do not know what sources of profit are there, or what commercial advantages, or what kind of trade might be introduced. Because of this, no specific instructions are being given to the leader of the expedition. He is to be guided by personal familiarization and experience, and by the instructions Baranov originally gives him. In time, when the Main Administration of the Company has studied all the details, appropriate instructions will be issued.

Director Benedikt Kramer
Director Andrei Severin

Reference: United States National Archives. *Records of the Russian American Company*. M11, Roll 1, Vol. 1, No. 472, Folios 173–176.

50

SEPTEMBER 22, 1817

A "TREATY" BETWEEN THE RUSSIAN AMERICAN COMPANY AND THE KASHAYA POMO INDIANS, CEDING LAND FOR FORT ROSS

On September 22, 1817, the Indian chiefs Chu-gu-an, Amat-tan, Gem-le-le and others, appeared at Fort Ross by invitation. Their greeting, as translated, extended their thanks for the invitation.

Captain Lieutenant Hagemeister expressed gratitude to them in the name of the Russian American Company for ceding to the Company land for a fort, buildings and enterprises, in regions belonging to Chu-gu-an, [land] which the inhabitants call Med-eny-ny. [Hagemeister] said he hoped they would not have reason to regret having the Russians as neighbors.

Having heard [what was] translated for him, Chu-gu-an and a second, Amattan, whose dwelling was also not far off, replied, "We are very satisfied with the occupation of this place by the Russians, because we now live in safety from other Indians, who formerly would attack us and this security began only from the time of [the Russian] settlement."

After this friendly response, gifts were presented to the toion and the others; and to the Chief, Chu-gu-an, a silver medal was entrusted, ornamented with the Imperial Russian seal and the inscription "Allies [*soiuznye*] of Russia" and it was stated that this [medal] entitles him to receive respect from the Russians, and for that reason he should not come to them without the medal. It also imposes on him the obligation of loyalty and assistance, in case this is needed. In response to that he and the others declared their readiness and expressed their gratitude for the reception.

After the hospitality, when [the Indians] departed from the fort, a one-gun salute was fired in honor of the chief toion.

We, the undersigned, hereby testify that in our presence the chief toions responded in exactly this way.

Navy Captain-Lieutenant and
Cavalier Hagemeister

Pomo Indian woman of Northern California by the Russian artist Mikhail Tikhonov. Tikhonov took part in the circumnavigation aboard the sloop *Kamchatka* under the command of Captain V. M. Golovnin. His superb portraits of natives are considered ethnographic as well as artistic treasures. L. A. Shur, *K beregam novogo sveta*. (OHS OrHi neg. 82006)

Staff doctor and
Court Counselor Kerner
Commerce Counselor and
Administrator of Fort Ross, Ivan Kuskov

Assistant Navigator 14th class [Ivan M.] Kislakovskii
Company Agent Kyrill Khlebnikov
Commercial Navigator Prokofii Tumanin

Reference: *Arkhiv Vneshni Politiki Rossii* [Hereafter *AVPR*]. Fond RAK, del.
308, 11. 11 i 11 ob.

51

A REPORT FROM THE MAIN ADMINISTRATION OF THE RUSSIAN AMERICAN COMPANY TO THE MINISTER OF FOREIGN AFFAIRS, KARL V. NESSELRODE, CONCERNING THE HAWAIIAN ISLANDS

In the middle of August last year the Main Administration of the [Russian American] Company had the honor of submitting to Your Excellency for review by His Imperial Majesty a summary of an official document by King Tamara Taeevich, which was brought here by a foreign ship. In that document he placed himself, his people and the islands belonging to him, under the mighty protection of His Imperial Majesty, and he swore [loyalty] on behalf of himself and his descendants. The original document has been promised to be sent via a Russian vessel.

The Administration of the Company, taking advantage of the departure from Kronstadt of a government frigate bound on an around-the-world voyage, at that time inquired through Your Excellency whether it would be advantageous for His Imperial Majesty to issue some sort of guidance concerning this matter. We were pleased to receive from you word of [The Emperor's] intention, that until we receive the original document of King Tamara's and other information Dr. [Georg] Schäffer has written about, no action should be taken.

Now the Administration of the Company has received the original document from the Administrator of the Russian colonies in America, Collegiate Counselor and Cavalier Baranov, and we have the honor of transmitting it to Your Excellency to bring to the attention of His Imperial Majesty.

The information received consists of the following:

Baranov sent Dr. Schäffer to the island of Kauai aboard a foreign vessel to retrieve a cargo from the Russian American Company ship *Bering*, which the subjects of the aforementioned King Tamara had looted. Dr. Schäffer stopped first at the island of Hawaii, which was under the control of another powerful king, Kamehameha, and stayed there until two of our ships which Baranov had dispatched arrived there.

Schäffer needed the assistance of this king in case the Kauai inhabitants refused to return our cargo. For that reason Baranov sent with Schäffer to King Kamehameha a large silver medal to pin on his chest, in the name of the Russian Autocrat, with the ribbon of the order of St. Vladimir. Such medals were given to Baranov to use by the late Councillor Rezanov, who visited the Russian colonies.

In spite of this, King Kamehameha received Dr. Schäffer very badly and even threatened his life. The cause for this was either agitation by foreigners or the severe character of the king himself. However, through subsequent circumstances, the king and Schäffer became closer. The king developed a chest affliction and Schäffer cured him, with the help of his first and favorite wife, Kachuman. After this Kamehameha pledged to force the Kauai people to comply, if they were unwilling to return our cargo. In addition, as a token of his gratitude, he granted Schäffer both people and land on his island of Hawaii to establish a settlement there, for his eternal possession, and he built three homes for Schäffer. Meanwhile, three of our vessels arrived at Hawaii and Schäffer left with them for Kauai.

There he seized the cargo without any difficulty, for King Tamara had not consented to the pillage. It had been perpetrated primarily at the instigation of the inhabitants by the First Minister, a relative of Tamara's. Subsequently this matter, as well as future trade with the Russian American Company, was resolved by a special act drawn up between him and Schäffer, a copy of which is appended to this report. By this act King Tamara allowed the Company to build its factories in all places it wishes. He also assigned his people to help the Company establish plantations. Finally, he promised always to prepare provisions for [visiting] Russian vessels. During this period another document was drawn up, under the terms of which this king was brought under the suzerainty of His Imperial Majesty [Alexander I]. The commander of the Company ship, Lieutenant [Iakov A.] Podushkin, writes in his journal that this took place to the accompaniment of the following ceremony. On May 21, 1816 the king was on the deck of the ship *Otkrytie*, and presented Dr. Schäffer with this act of submission. In return for this evidence of his submission he asked that

Podushkin give him the flag from the ship and his uniform with all its insignia. Then he left for shore to a seven-gun salute from the ship. When he reached shore he immediately raised the flag at a prepared place, to a fourteen-gun salute from cannon which had been especially emplaced there for the occasion. The people assembled around the king, he revealed his submission, and they all shouted "Hurrah!"

The next day the king invited Dr. Schäffer and Lieutenant Podushkin to dine, and met them at his home with his entire family. Thirty chosen men comprised his honor guard and stood on parade; in all there were about a thousand people. Only the men sat at the table; the women withdrew. There were drums instead of music. The king proposed a toast to the health of the Sovereign Emperor, to the thunder of cannon and shouts. Then a toast was drunk to his health.

As a result of the second commercial act, of which Baranov was informed by Company prikashchiks who had sailed aboard *Otkrytie*, one factory was built on Kauai, but the precise location is not clear. Schäffer himself reports that at the factory on the land which the king had granted, he has planted a substantial amount of all kinds of garden produce, tobacco, cotton and sugar cane. He has also planted coconut palms, bananas, taro, potatoes, watermelons, pineapples, grapes and orange trees. He will soon take steps formally to accept this territory and its people, which King Tamara has given to the Company. In addition he also granted to Baranov, in absentia, a royal village on the island of Oahu, with the rank of First Minister for all eternity. In token of this Dr. Schäffer was given a special document.

All these developments, as is evident from the proceedings, resulted from the good will of the independent ruler Tamara. There was only one thing Dr. Schäffer should not have agreed to, which causes considerable problems because Baranov never empowered him to do it, and that is the third act concluded with King Tamara, which is appended to this report, which promises to give him arms and to assume the obligation to lead his army in subduing the islands which had been taken from him, and to purchase at Company expense a naval vessel for that expedition.

The Main Administration of the Company much regrets

that neither it nor Baranov, because of the distance and the short time involved, could prevent or foresee this, and will not be able to know what consequences may result from it. But meanwhile the Administration is sending instructions to Baranov to recall Schäffer, and thus forestall if possible any actions which may be detrimental to the activities of the Russian American Company.

In conclusion, the Administration of the Company herewith submits for review by Your Excellency, historical, climatic and statistical information on the Sandwich Islands, prepared from information which it has in its possession from naval officers serving with the Company, who have been on these islands. From them it is clear that all of these islands are completely free from the influence of European powers.

Finally, the Administration requests that Your Excellency bring all of the above information to the attention of His Imperial Majesty.

Baranov advises that the Monarch [Alexander I] be asked to grant this ruler [of the Sandwich Islands] special medals, a saber and a uniform appropriate for that climate, if the loyalty of King Tamara is viewed favorably by His Imperial Majesty.

All of this information has been reviewed by the Supreme council of the Russian American Company, and it has been decided to bring this to the attention of the Emperor, through Your Excellency as intermediary.

> Chief Director and Cavalier Mikhail Buldakov
> Director Benedikt Kramer
> Director Andrei Severin
> Secretary of the Office Zelenskii

Reference: *VPR*, Second Series, Vol. 2, Doc. 54, 173–175.

52

A MEMORANDUM FROM KARL V. NESSELRODE, MINISTER OF FOR-
EIGN AFFAIRS, TO OSIP P. KOZODAVLEV, MINISTER OF INTERNAL
AFFAIRS, REGARDING THE HAWAIIAN ISLANDS

On September 13, 1817, Your Excellency transmitted to me for review a copy of a letter from Dr. Schäffer, presently in the service of the Russian American Company. The letter concerned King Tamara's voluntary consent to come under the sovereignty of His Imperial Majesty [Alexander I], with two of the Hawaiian Islands under his jurisdiction, Kauai and Hawaii. This was based on a written document approved by that king, which was appended [with your letter] to me.

The Sovereign Emperor believes that the acquisition of these islands and their voluntary consent to come under His Sovereignty not only cannot bring any substantial benefit to Russia, but on the contrary, in many ways may cause extremely serious problems. Consequently, His Majesty feels that King Tamara should receive every possible courtesy and that friendly relations with him should be maintained, but this act [of submission] should not be accepted. Future relations should be limited to the maintenance of friendly ties similar to those which he has with other independent states, and efforts should be made to extend trade relations between the Hawaiian Islands and the [Russian] American Company, as long as such are in accord with business practice. This single rule must guide the Company in its enterprises in that area. In consequence of this, my dear sir, do you not think it wise to send the Company written instructions so it will not deviate from this rule?

Reports which Your Excellency subsequently received from Dr. Schäffer indicate that his rash actions have already given rise to certain unpleasant results. Consequently, without taking any measures to resolve these problems, Your Excellency should await further instructions concerning this matter.

I have the honor . . .

Alexander I: So be it.

Reference: *VPR*, Second Series, Vol. 2, Doc. 78, 258.

The famed Russian Minister of Foreign Affairs, Count Karl V. Nesselrode. N. N. Bashkina, *The United States and Russia, The Beginning of Relations*. (OHS neg. OrHi 83210)

53

NOVEMBER 3, 1818

A REPORT FROM THE MAIN ADMINISTRATION OF THE RUSSIAN AMERICAN COMPANY TO EMPEROR ALEXANDER I CONCERNING CONDITIONS IN THE RUSSIAN COLONIES IN ALASKA AND CALIFORNIA

On October 16, 1817 the Main Administration of the Company had the pleasure of bringing to the attention of Your Imperial Majesty information about the successful voyages of two of its vessels, *Kutuzov* and *Suvorov*, which had been dispatched from Kronstadt to the Russian American colonies under the leadership of Captain Lieutenant [Leontii] Hagemeister. Their last rest stop was in Lima's port of Callao. At the present time we report most respectfully that these vessels separated along the coast of Peru. *Suvorov* set her course directly for the colony on Sitka Island, the port of New Arkhangel, where she arrived on July 22. *Kutuzov* entered the bay of Guyaquil and from there proceeded to the shores of California where our colonial settlement of Ross has been established. After a stay in New California in the port of San Francisco, she reached New Arkhangel on November 22. Both vessels and their crews were in good condition. All during the voyage the crew kept vigil without the slightest fatigue, thanks to the most watchful care on the part of their commanding officers, Hagemeister and Lieutenant [Zakhar] Panafidin.

According to available information, they found the colony of New Arkhangel and all of our other possessions in sound condition. In order to give the Company a quicker turnover of the cargo sent there, on January 12 of this year *Suvorov* was sent from there back to Russia with Company furs and a part of the goods from South America, such as cocoa and sugar, purchased from foreigners who come there. On this return voyage Lieutenant Panafidin put in at the Washington Islands, and following Krusenstern's voyage, at Port Chichagov. In that place he took on fresh provisions and then set out for Brazil, for the port of Rio de Janiero, where he arrived on June 6. There he rested and attended to minor matters for 32 days, and then set out for Europe.

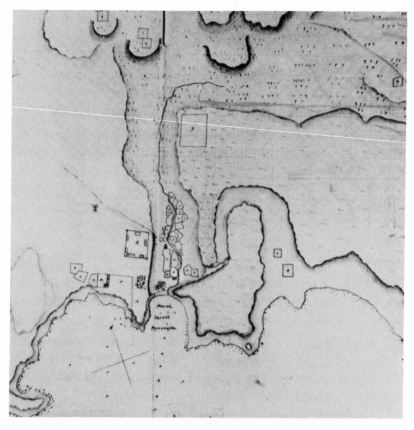

Diagram of Fort Ross made in 1817 by an unknown Russian artist. The diagram clearly indicates the favorable siting for the fort. N. N. Bashkina, *The United States and Russia, The Beginning of Relations.* (OHS neg. OrHi 83213)

In 79 days he reached the Copenhagen roadstead where he took on fresh water. There he anchored for thirteen days because of contrary winds, and reached the Kronstadt roadstead on October 18 with both crew and vessel in good condition.

Aboard that vessel the Company received goods, which at even the most modest appraisal are worth more than 1,000,000 rubles.

In reports he submitted from the colonies, the Main Administration of the Company was informed of the following:

1. The Chief Administrator, Collegiate Counselor Baranov, is as of now relieved of his responsibilities. He is an elderly man of 70 who has spent 27 years in Company service; he

has been left in distant, savage places, deprived of association with family, friends and cultured society, and burdened by constant cares and concerns; he has many times requested to be replaced so he could spend his old age and infirm state in peace. His obligations in regard to colonial matters are for the time being assumed by the above mentioned commander of the expedition, Hagemeister, whose instructions, based on reports to the Main Administration of the Company, must be approved. His straightforward approach, honesty, care for every economy, and his foresight earn him the gratitude of the Company. On the basis of such outstanding traits, he recommends his colleague, the commanding officer of *Suvorov*, Lieutenant Panafidin [for recognition]. During his return voyage Panafidin demonstrated that he is capable of sailing a ship without supervision from anyone. Hagemeister asks the Main Administration of the Company to submit the name of this officer for Your Imperial Majesty's all gracious consideration. This is done all the more willingly because from the reports from the fleet we have personally learned a great deal about Panafidin's fine qualities.

2. While Hagemeister was at Rumiantsev (Little Bodega) Bay, at our Ross settlement which was established in 1812, he wanted to learn about the attitude of the local inhabitants, the Indians, toward our settlement there, and of our people toward them. From among natives living nearby he invited to the settlement a head toion, Chu-su-oan, and another, Gem-le-le, and many of their fellow tribesmen, who unanimously expressed their satisfaction that the Russians had settled among them, thereby creating a barrier against attack by distant Indians who live near the Spanish presidio of San Francisco. [They further stated] that the resulting peace and friendly relations shown them by the Russians obligates them willingly to cede all the land our settlement now occupies, and they said they could yield more land if need arises.

Finally, Hagemeister, a person who does not like to deal with matters in a superficial fashion, but rather to treat specific situations, was convinced of the sincerity and beneficial mutual relationship between the Indians and the Russians, especially since many of the Aleuts whom the Russians employ as promyshlenniks have married daughters of the Indians and have

Painting of Fort Ross made in 1817 by an unknown Russian artist reveals the location prone to heavy fogs. This proved unfavorable to large scale agricultural production, which the Russian American Company urgently desired. N. N. Bashkina, *The United States and Russia, The Beginning of Relations.* (OHS neg. OrHi 83212)

established family ties. In recognition of the fidelity of the chief toion, Hagemeister bestowed on him a small silver medal with the Russian seal and the inscription, "Ally of Russia," which he accepted with genuine pleasure. To commemorate the time and circumstances of this development, Hagemeister also drew up an act which he and all the staff and senior officers of his ship signed. It was also signed by the administrator of the Ross settlement, Commerce Counselor Kuskov, whom Hagemeister gives an excellent recommendation because of the order found in all the departments Kuskov heads. [He was also commended] for his outstanding zeal in watching over the colony, his work and concern for introducing and developing, thanks to the favorable climate there, agriculture, kitchen gardens, livestock breeding and every possible economic activity. This settlement already supplies substantial amounts to the colony of New Arkhangel, which lacks many needed things because of the adverse climate. Hagemeister also recommends that the Main Administration of the Company submit to Your Imperial

Majesty for consideration the name of this man who has devoted more than 20 years to Company service, so that he might be favorably considered for reward.

When *Suvorov* reached the Kronstadt roadstead she was quarantined for thirteen days because she had failed to bring with her a certificate of quarantine from Copenhagen. The Main Administration of the Company received information from Okhotsk that on August 13 the Company schooner *Chirikov* arrived there, commanded by navigator Klochkov, one of the officers of *Kutuzov*. *Chirikov* carried a cargo of furs which the Main Administration of the Company conservatively values at more than 1,000,000 rubles. The dispatches brought on that ship dated from March 25 to May 4, in addition to accounts and information on capital assets; these repeat the information received with *Suvorov*, that until a suitable replacement is named, the present temporary Chief Administrator of the Company, Hagemeister, has appointed Lieutenant Ianovskii as the Chief Administrator of the local colonial office. [We are also informed that] Hagemeister will undertake his return voyage on *Kutuzov* to Russia, and while sailing around the world will try to discover some new place. Until that time he will try to spend some time in our northern islands near Bering Strait, in order to inspect local matters there.

Chief Director Mikhail Buldakov
Director Benedikt Kramer
Director Andrei Severin
Office Administrator, Collegiate
Counsellor Zelenskii

Reference: *VPR*. Second Series, Vol. 2, Doc. 166, 574–576.

54

AUGUST 12, 1819

INSTRUCTIONS FROM THE MAIN ADMINISTRATION OF THE RUSSIAN
AMERICAN COMPANY TO CHIEF ADMINISTRATOR LEONTII A. HAGE-
MEISTER REGARDING RELATIONS WITH THE HAWAIIAN ISLANDS

Via the ship *Borodino*, which is presently departing from the port of Kronstadt, sailing to the colonies, you will receive a dispatch from this Administration dated March 15, 1818, No. 121. This was written in accordance with the expressed wish of His Imperial Majesty the Emperor [Alexander I], and concerns the relationship the Russian American Company is to maintain with the Hawaiian Islands. This dispatch was to have been sent to you from Okhotsk this year aboard the brig *Chirikov*, but the local office made a mistake and it was returned to us with other mail; thus we have decided to send these items aboard the ship *Borodino*.

When Dr. Schäffer, the former commissioner on those islands, came here, he submitted a project to the government which was extremely bold and audacious, like his actions. He was presumptuous enough to hope to induce the government to occupy the Hawaiian Islands through force, and through his efforts. You will see his plan in the copy appended to this, and you will see the view of the Main Administration of the Company, which the government requested, also in an appended copy. Finally, the last item is an Imperial decree given to the Administration of the Company through the Ministry of Internal Affairs, dated July 15, item No. 206. This Imperial statement does not require any explanation or additions from this Administration; it is to be carried out literally, just as written.

Zakhar Ivanovich Panafidin, commanding officer of *Borodino*, has been instructed to stop at the Hawaiian Islands en route to you, if possible, and ascertain the true situation there, and the reason our people have been expelled from there.

On the basis of his information, our directive, and any information you have, the Main Administration of the Company authorizes you to outfit and send a special expedition to those islands as quickly as possible, if you are able. The expedition is to go to the ruler Tamara, who lives on the island of Kauai.

First. Establish contact with him in order to explain to him that His Imperial Majesty, the Emperor, in regard to Tamara's request and petition and the oath he has already sworn, has not deigned to accept him into suzerainty, solely on the basis of his philanthropic and kindly spirit, because He already has an extensive domain which occupies almost one-eighth of the entire world. He hopes Tamara will maintain ties of friendship and trade with His Imperial Majesty's Russian subjects, on precisely the same terms he maintains ties with other European nations who come to his islands.

This Imperial decision is to be explained to him through the Russian American Company, which is under His Imperial Majesty's personal patronage. [The Company] has dispatched this vessel to Tamara on his island of Kauai, and has entrusted this mission to an honest and reliable man, who in the name of Our Great Sovereign, is to assure him that if he will again receive the good Russian subjects who have come aboard that vessel; if he agrees to have ties of friendship and trade with them, which he has already agreed to in many written documents which have come to the attention of His Imperial Majesty; and if he renews these acts now, he will now receive, in the name of His All Gracious Majesty, rich gifts which have been selected for him and will give him great honor and will assure him the gracious disposition of His Imperial Majesty in the future.

It is also to be conveyed to him on behalf of the Company that if he maintains the ties of friendship and trade with the Company which have already been established through his good will and confirmed in writing, but which have been abrogated mainly through unfriendly action by certain envious persons, he will receive great benefits. The Company can supply him with many goods, and through the import of economic products the Company will introduce many benefits and much practical knowledge to his subjects.

The person selected to undertake this mission should be instructed to explain this to the ruler Tamara in the most flattering language. That person's relations with Tamara and his family and other persons who influence him should be exemplary, and abound in those deeds which can promote close relations. That person should strive to obtain consent for Russians to settle, primarily on the island of Hawaii. It would be best of all if he were to sell this island to the Company; as you know the Main Administration of the Company has designated a sum of 10,000 rubles or more, and an even larger amount should be proposed. The acquisition of this island is especially important for the Company because it is the one closest to the colonies, and since it is sparsely populated, it presents less danger from the arrogance of the inhabitants.

Second. As soon as there is reason to hope that Tamara will consent to the Company's proposals, and if he does approve this in such a way that no doubt remains, so that the agreement will not be abrogated again by his treachery, he should receive the gifts from the most gracious Sovereign Emperor which are listed in a special document, written in the name of the Russian American Company, in both Russian and English, which is appended to this. Add to these gifts the Company's presents which were sent aboard the sloop *Kamchatka*, which include various items made of glass, porcelain, mirrors and the like. These gifts should be used to entice his household advisers and other persons who influence him to affirm the agreement with the Company, depending on how hopeful or hopeless these negotiations may seem.

Impress on them at the same time that if Tamara has any thought of using the Russians to make conquests for him, he is to be disabused and informed that such assistance is contrary to the peaceful disposition of the Sovereign Emperor.

To carry out this plan you should select a person whose judgment, steadfastness, resourcefulness and other good qualities can attain the desired result. With the exception of his crew, his associates should at first consist of no more than 50 men, so other Company intentions will not be revealed by sending large numbers of men. Half of the men you send should be engaged in enterprises and the others in providing security. The latter should be kindly, businesslike, sober, and above all, good shots. It is advisable at first not to try to cover too great an area if the expedition is to be successful. It should not try to make acquisitions in many places as Schäffer did.

View of the Port of Honolulu. Louis Choris, *Voyage pittor-esque autour du monde*. (OHS neg. OrHi 82054)

The best thing at first would be to try to build in a likely place a large tower right at the anchorage, which would impress the islanders and others. The tower should be fitted out with several cannon, and the men should have small arms in case of unexpected attack by the savages. For that reason strict discipline must at all times be maintained. If natives from other islands appear in large numbers, they should not be permitted to rendezvous anywhere. The atmosphere everywhere in this fort should be one of military caution. This advice is not based on personal observation of the situation; local circumstances will be a better guide for the man in charge as to how to organize his security to attain his goal.

It will be difficult to select the person to carry out this assignment, but the Main Administration of the Company has great hope that through your zeal and insight you will choose a person who will be a reliable advisor, and thus your assistant in this important matter. He should observe details and follow rules and vital instructions wisely; he should be kindly and cautious in supervising the men entrusted to him, as far as the islanders are concerned. He should never completely trust the islanders because of their barbarism, and he must always maintain unflagging caution, yet treat them in an open, gentle and friendly manner. All his men must be prohibited from engaging in any discord with the islanders; and the islanders must not be forced to do anything against their will. A good example of this approach is the policy of the Company on Kodiak and

Sitka, where we have been able to establish ourselves by using gentleness and caution rather than force.

There will be no shortage of agricultural implements and gifts to use to carry on trade and hold the people on those islands; these items are from earlier cargoes taken there as well as from the present cargoes. It appears that it is always necessary to have vessels specifically assigned to be near these islands, especially in places where we have established ourselves; such a vessel would eventually be replaced by another.

You will undoubtedly order the commanding officers of the ships in the establishments to give assistance if necessary, in full force, and you will instruct them as to precisely how they are to conduct themselves.

The return of the goods seized earlier, and the property which was later taken from Schäffer, but not the things taken as a result of the last [debacle], should be negotiated by using very unpretentious political negotiations, and not too hastily. This should be accomplished through friendship with Tamara, or with some other powerful persons, or through the introduction of trade in sandalwood, which Tamara, in written agreements with Schäffer, promised as reparation [for the pillage of cargo].

All of this is just an outline. You should prepare an actual plan of the scope of the action on the Hawaiian Islands on the basis of your best information, and in accordance with the Imperial will.

For your further success in many relationships, in securing proper influence in these islands, you would do very well to send a young man on that expedition, one who is able to learn the language of the Hawaiian Islanders, so he could eventually write and speak in their language and explain to the islanders the importance of the Christian religion, in the same manner that Bible societies and fraternal orders explain matters to various peoples in different languages.

It is equally important to use a reliable method for success: to try immediately to develop family ties with the islanders, in a manner similar to that used to secure control of Kodiak Island. This may more quickly establish the foundation for our settlement there if properly used.

Finally, if you can think of a better plan, be certain to implement it.

Chief Director and Counselor Mikhail Buldakov
Benedikt Kramer
Andrei Severin
Office Administrator,
Counselor Zelenskii

Reference: *VPR*, Second Series, Vol. 3, Doc. 33, 104–106.

55

NO DATE

INSTRUCTIONS FOR COMMANDERS OF SHIPS BELONGING TO THE RUSSIAN AMERICAN COMPANY

First. Upon taking command of a ship entrusted to you, you are to accept all items and materials belonging to the ship in accordance with the manifest, and give a receipt for them. Register them as having been received, according to the proper form in the book with ties and fasten the book with the seal of the Main Administration of the Company.

2. All items and materials which are used are to be entered as expenditures according to the proper form in the other book of expenditures with ties, with a specific indication of when, for what purpose, and on what occasion each item was used.

3. The Company prikashchik is to be in charge of food supplies of all kinds designated for the ship's crew. He is to register the provisions he obtains and distributes to the crew in the revenue and expense books, according to the proper form. As the ship's commander, nothing is to be done without your knowledge. Upon each acquisition of provisions entered into the revenue book, and every week when provisions have been consumed, you are to sign your name in the expense book, under provisions, as testimony that a given quantity of provisions actually has been consumed.

4. In provisioning your crew, you are to act in accordance with the instructions of the Company administrator in the place from whence you are setting out on your voyage; you are not to deviate from his instructions in any way, except in an extreme emergency. If circumstances compel you to deviate from his instructions, you are to record the reasons in the Ship's Log, and in your instruction to your prikashchik which concerns the change [you have made] and provisionment of the crew.

5. You are to issue written instructions to the prikashchik regarding every issue of provisions over and above the amount stipulated by the [Company] Administrator.

6. The ship's cargo or goods are to be under the jurisdiction and care of the prikashchik; you are only responsible for their proper distribution aboard ship so they will not spoil. If possible, order that they be frequently inspected and aired or dried out. Further, you are not to allow the prikashchik to unload them on shore or aboard other ships in any place other than the designated port from whence you set out. If circumstances and need force you to use any of the goods from your cargo while you are en route, you are to do this only with the counsel of the prikashchik. His counsel, and the reasons, are to be entered into the Ship's Log.

7. You are to keep a journal in the special bound book, in accordance with the set form. In addition to the usual incidents encountered at sea you are to enter the following: how many persons are ill each day, who they are and what the illness is; what provisions and the amount the crew receive each day; if anyone is punished that should be entered, stating the reason and the form of punishment. If anything spoils or is broken or lost, that is to be entered, with a statement of what happened, when, and how it was replaced.

8. If any provision or item is ruined and is not usable, it should be thrown overboard. Before doing this, however, you are to consult and receive acknowledgment from the prikashchik and from three senior crew members; assemble them for this purpose and enter this into the journal. Any ruined thing which is thrown overboard should be discarded in the presence of the entire crew.

9. Nothing registered in the tied books is to be erased or crossed out. If a mistake is made, enclose the mistake in parentheses and above, write the word "mistake."

10. When the ship reaches a port where there is a Company office and an administrator, you must immediately give him your tied journal and the books, in which he signs his name and notes the date of receipt. This will serve as evidence that your journals and books are kept correctly and always ready for inspection.

11. When you set out from port, all instructions to you from Company administrators are to be in writing. You are not to accept nor are you obligated to carry out oral instructions.

12. If you consider any instruction from a Company administrator detrimental to the Company, you may submit your opinion to him in writing. However, if he does not respect your objection, you must carry out his instruction. You may submit your objections about the matter, and the circumstances, to the Main Administration in St. Petersburg when you return. If your objection is found to be substantive, you will be thanked and even rewarded, depending on the importance of the matter.

13. If you discover malfeasance in any matter affecting Company business, you have the right to submit a secret report about it to the Main Administration so measures can to taken to correct the problem. But do not reveal this, because in that case the Main Administration would lack the means of punishing the guilty and restoring order.

14. If you should happen to discover theft of Company funds, either anywhere in the colonies or in Company offices, and if you apprehend the guilty person and have clear evidence of his guilt, in such a case, in addition to earning the regard and gratitude of the Company for correcting the matter, the Company will give you for your own personal use half of the retrieved monies which the Company would otherwise have lost.

15. During your stay in foreign ports, when you must purchase certain items or provisions for your ship, you are to make such purchases only with the agreement of the Company prikashchik. Give the authorities of the place a list of all the supplies you need, at existing prices. From the local administration as well as from the vendors, you are to obtain written receipts indicating costs; on the basis of laws and custom of all civilized peoples they cannot refuse to give this to you.

16. In addition, concordant with your obligations and honor, you must devoutly guard all secret matters entrusted to you by the Company administration. You are not to reveal to foreigners any matters pertaining to the Company, nor any information which could be detrimental and prejudicial to its well-being, which is inseparably linked to the benefit of the entire Fatherland; neither are you to listen to and spread, as certain persons of ill will do, rumors intended to besmirch the Company. On these matters your own conscience, honor and good judgment should be your guides.

17. While in command of the ship which has been entrusted to you, until [you receive] the Regulations currently being prepared for Imperial approval, you are to be guided by the Naval Code of Emperor Peter the Great, insofar as this corresponds with the rules of commercial navigation; that is, you are to adopt it as the basis for determining subordination and order among the crew, safety measures during voyages and while at anchor or at any other time.

18. Nothing helps to maintain order and proper subordination in any group so much as the fear of God, honesty and knowledge of law. Therefore, you are to consider it an inviolate obligation to assemble the entire crew in front of the ship's icon every Sunday morning and on mornings of other holidays observed in our Fatherland, especially when good weather and freedom from essential work permits. If there is no priest, have one of your subordinates read prayers. Periodically, at least once a month, in front of the officers of the ship read the articles of the Naval Code concerning maintenance of order and obedience to the commander.

19. During time free of ship's duties and other Company work, you are to instruct the crew on how to use the guns and other weapons. Periodically have the weapons loaded, but do not use any more gunpowder in these exercises than the Main Administration of the Company sets aside for such purpose for a year's time. There is no need to remind you that the benefit of the Company, as well as your own personal honor and safety, require that your command be experienced in using weapons, and be able, in case of need, to repel not only savages who are hostile to Europeans, but also Europeans themselves, should any of them attempt to perpetrate acts hostile to the Company and its possessions.

20. Supplies which are allocated provisionally for you, may be taken a year in advance if you feel it necessary, or even more than a year, considering the distance of your voyages. However, in regard to cash for salaries, when you assume command of your ship you may receive these monies for six months in advance, but subsequently you are not to receive advances except that due for the period of one year, half a year or a third of a year, whichever is most useful for you.

When you request your salary at any Company office, or

from the administrator or commissioner of the Company, you are to submit to him your expense book and the Ship's Log. If he finds that your request is properly entered, he will issue the funds to you. At that time he will append his signature and the seal of his office, and give you a certificate which will serve as a voucher for you to receive future salary payment in some other place where you may be, and where you will submit this voucher. But if you receive additional salary owed to you in that same office, you are to return the earlier voucher and be issued a new one. You are never to have two vouchers in your possession.

21. In regard to the objectives of your voyage, your conduct in regard to natives of neighboring lands and in regard to foreign ships encountered, as well as your conduct in all other circumstances which may be influenced by local situations and political climate and will change from time to time, you will have special instructions, either from the Main Administration of the Company or from the [Chief] Administrator of the colonies. In accordance with Article 4 of this agreement, you will be obligated to carry out these instructions with absolute fidelity.

22. If another person is appointed commanding officer of the ship entrusted to you, you are to hand over to your replacement all equipment, items, tied [fiscal] books and the Ship's Log with an accurate inventory; you will receive a receipt from him for all of this.

23. You are to protect and guard with all possible zeal all materials and equipment on the ship entrusted to you, as well as any other items issued to you, if circumstances permit, as provided in the regulations for Company ships. If some item is unuseable, you are not to destroy it unless absolutely necessary, nor are you to alter it for any other purpose until it has been examined by the Administrator of the Company office in a harbor, or by someone appointed by him. If some item is needed for use at sea, or if there is no [Company] office in the vicinity, you are to describe the use to which you have put the item in the expense book as well as in the Ship's Log.

24. Upon your arrival in a port where there is a Company administrator, you are to submit to him an accurate report on any deficiency in your ship, and a list of unuseable items. On

the basis of these an inspection will be made, repairs will be carried out and unuseable items will be replaced.

25. You are to conduct yourself with decorum and with the courtesy expected of a nobleman toward administrators of Company offices and toward all persons in charge of Company affairs or who have the trust of the Main Administration in places where you are. Submit your requests to them in an unassuming manner; never be insolent, rude or coarse.

26. If you should be shipwrecked, God forbid, try to save your Ship's Log and your dispatches, if the disaster occurs on our own coast or along a friendly coast. However, if it occurs elsewhere [in a hostile situation], try to sink all of this so it will not fall into foreign hands. The same must be done if you should be forced to surrender your vessel to the enemy.

27. Without the consent of the administrator of the office where your ship may be located, you are not to allow any of your crew to go ashore or to accept replacements for themselves. You are not to leave any crew member behind in a foreign port. In case of desertion you must insist that authorities there have a diligent search made for the deserters and return them to you. Also, you personally are to make every effort to find such persons.

28. You are not to issue anything to crew on your ship on the Company account which they are not presently entitled to, or will be entitled to in the future, because any such issue, if necessary, is to be determined by the Administrator of the office. However, if you should be on a long voyage, away from contact with the Administrator of the office, and if the crew has dire need of clothing and footwear, using your own judgment you may then use Company stores or funds to provide them these necessary items.

Reference: Library of Congress, Manuscript Division. Yudin Collection, Box 2, No. 2.

56

JANUARY 12, 1820

INSTRUCTIONS TO CHIEF ADMINISTRATOR MATVEI I. MURAVEV ON
GOVERNING RUSSIA'S COLONIES AND CONTINUING EXPLORATION
IN THE NORTH OF ALASKA

Your voluntary agreement to devote several years to administer the distant region, which is in need of so much, requires the Main Administration of the [Russian American] Company to give you a detailed account of all the matters which are an integral part of your obligations and responsibilities. These were defined in general instructions of March 31, 1811 from the Main Administration and the offices under its jurisdiction, as well as in individual instructions. Consequently you may adopt these instructions as general rules, with later additions and supplements prepared by the former Chief Administrator [Leontii] Hagemeister, and also with the November 10, 1818 orders for the project issued by then Chief Administrator [Semen I.] Ianovskii. You are to resolve all other matters pertaining to local circumstances and periodic activities through your own judgment.

The Main Administration of the Company is confident that when you assume your responsibilities you will instruct all the offices and officials to provide you with information about capital and inventories of various items associated with your administration, and that you will incorporate these into a report which you will send to the Main Administration of the Company for its review.

The Main Administration is also confident that you will choose an appropriate time personally to inspect all affairs and enterprises on Kodiak, Unalaska and the northern islands, and that you will instill everywhere the same order which has been introduced into the New Arkhangel colony; further, that you will put all other matters into a condition that will provide sound benefits for the Company and the Fatherland, if all the plans Hagemeister started have not yet been fully carried out.

The Main Administration of the Company wants you to implement all Hagemeister's instructions for a northern exploring expedition. You will learn the details of this when you reach the colony. This expedition may very well discover new sources for hunting furbearing animals, which would relieve the present shortages in all hunting areas.

The Main Administration of the Company may send you a dispatch only once a year; it will send a duplicate the following year in case the original might be lost. Thus we will send you copies of all instructions that were sent to Ianovskii and to the New Arkhangel office; these copies are being sent to you aboard the ship *Borodino*. If you have not already done so, you are to attempt to carry out the instructions contained in them.

The Company trusts you to administer the Russian American regions and expects you to devote work and concern to the well-being of those regions to provide the real benefits that will accrue to the Company and to the Fatherland.

Reference: United States National Archives. *Records of the Russian American Company*, M11, Vol. 2, No. 34, Folios [2]–3.

57

JANUARY 16, 1820

INSTRUCTIONS FROM THE MAIN ADMINISTRATION OF THE RUSSIAN AMERICAN COMPANY TO CHIEF ADMINISTRATOR MATVEI I. MURAVEV CONCERNING POLICY TOWARD SERVITORS WHO WISH TO LEAVE THE COLONIES

In a dispatch dated May 1, 1819, No. 346 from [Semen I.] Ianovskii, [Chief] Administrator of the colonies, we are informed that 37 persons have this past year expressed a desire to leave the colonies. It is not clear whether these persons are indebted to the Company, whether they are permitted to leave because of illness or incapacity to work any longer or because they are parasites. Among these are four who had become settlers: Shchukin, Krylatskii, Podomarev and Sokholov. On the basis of an earlier ukaz given to Shelikhov to establish crafts and agriculture [in the colonies] these persons should only be released by permission of the authorities.

When you reach New Arkhangel if you find those settlers are still there, please prevent them from departing. Other servitors who are indebted to the Company should also be refused permission to leave, unless they have intolerable vices. In the future, follow this rule for your guidance: do not allow any servitor to leave, to the detriment of the Company, unless an urgent matter of justice demands that he be allowed to do so.

Reference: United States National Archives. *Records of the Russian American Company*. M11, Vol. 2, No. 54, Folio 10.

58

INSTRUCTIONS FROM THE MAIN ADMINISTRATION OF THE RUSSIAN AMERICAN COMPANY TO CHIEF ADMINISTRATOR MATVEI I. MURAVEV TO RESUME TRADE WITH THE HAWAIIAN ISLANDS

In a dispatch dated August 12, [1819], No. 487, which is being sent to you with the ship *Borodino*, you will note the desire of the Main Administration of the Company to resume trade relations with the Hawaiian Islands. [Former] Chief Administrator [Leontii] Hagemeister was assigned to do this; it is unfortunate that this desire of the Sovereign Emperor has still not been carried out by [Semen] Ianovskii. Consequently the Main Administration of the Company is giving this assignment to you and asks that you carry it out, insofar as local circumstances permit.

Reference: United States National Archives. *Records of the Russian American Company*. M11, Vol. 2, No. 90, Folio 34.

59

APRIL 29, 1820

A DISPATCH FROM THE MAIN ADMINISTRATION OF THE RUSSIAN AMERICAN COMPANY TO CHIEF ADMINISTRATOR MATVEI I. MURAVEV, CONCERNING THE SUPPLY ROUTES TO KAMCHATKA AND TO OKHOTSK

The Minister of Finance on the 10th of this month posed the following questions to the Main Administration of the Company.

a) Is there a way in which communication can be established between Iakutsk and Okhotsk without burdening the Iakuts?

b) Could the Company supply the ports of Petropavlovsk and Okhotsk with provisions, especially grain and salt, through its contacts with California or the Philippine Islands? For this purpose there should be one ship in those places, which would be used for that purpose each year. A decision would have to be made whether the estimated cost of the upkeep of the ship which would carry the provisions should be increased.

c) Could the Company send to Kamchatka and Okhotsk articles which are needed for the maintenance of the local inhabitants, which are presently supplied from Irkutsk at tremendous cost, and which do not meet the needs because of heavy spoilage?

The Main Administration of the Company responds to these questions as follows:

a) The best means of supplying all these areas is by sea from Kronstadt, around the world, which the Company is doing. A sixth such expedition is presently being dispatched so that all colonial provisions for ships and people, as well as for the maintenance of the Okhotsk office and the Kamchatka commissariat are to be sent to Okhotsk.

The result and implementation of this response here presented for your attention, for the present Governor General of Siberia, strongly maintains that the use of the Okhotsk route for government provisioning should either be completely eliminated or at least greatly reduced. You will receive information from the Okhotsk office indicating what it will receive this year from Iakutsk and what additional goods it will still need to make up the deficiency. Perhaps it would be possible next year to fill these needs from the surpluses in your Department and from the cargo you will receive aboard the ship *Borodino*. The Main Administration of the Company believes that Okhotsk should be supplied every year as requested by the local office.

b) If, at the urging of the Main Administration of the Company, our government should apply for and obtain free trade privileges in California and Manila, the Company will not only voluntarily, but indeed as an obligation, supply Kamchatka and the Okhotsk region with grain and other provisions, as well as supplying its own colonies. Our Ross settlement does not yet have any hope of settling enough persons permanently to obtain land there as their own property, and to work the land in order to produce grain to be sold to the Company. In time there may be hope for this, but not before the Ross settlement belongs to us, as is evidenced by recent correspondence between our government and that of Spain; when that happens, we can choose several creole families to settle there. It would be a good idea to begin to make preparations for this soon.

c) We have already replied to this under point "a."

Consequently you must carry out this proposal when you have a surplus of grain purchased in California in the same way Hagemeister obtained a fairly large cargo of it there. No doubt you will give this problem your attention, especially since there is now nowhere else to procure grain.

There is one more consideration. If you are able to ship grain, by what means will you do so? One large ship could supply Kamchatka with grain and other goods; or two vessels, one of which would be smaller, could sail to the Okhotsk port, load a cargo to take back to you, but could not supply you with anything from Kamchatka; thus a large ship would sail empty from Kamchatka. If a ship destined for Kamchatka were also to put in at Okhotsk to unload cargo, there is the question of the risk of the Okhotsk roadstead to consider.

Thus the better solution would seem to be to use two vessels of the same size, one sailing in the summer to Kamchatka and the other to Okhotsk. The two ships would not use an overly large number of men of which you always have a shortage.

In short, you will have to resolve this situation for the best interests of the Company. Use your common sense and consider the local situation. But keep this in mind: do not become known as a carrier of contraband under the guise of trade goods or "provisions for this ship's crew," because the Okhotsk port authorities are always on the lookout for problems. They confiscated a cask of rum which the late Baranov had sent to his brother, declaring it contraband. It is permissible to carry rum aboard foreign ships, but not on Russian ships.

Reference: United States National Archives. *Records of the Russian American Company*. M11, Vol. 2, No. 275, Folios 78–80.

60

APRIL 29, 1820

A DISPATCH FROM THE MAIN ADMINISTRATION OF THE RUSSIAN AMERICAN COMPANY TO CHIEF ADMINISTRATOR MATVEI I. MU-RAVEV REGARDING WHALING

A proposal has been made by [Petr Ivanovich] Rikord which would allow foreigners, under the guise of whaling and fishing, to penetrate all the possessions of the Russians in the Pacific Ocean. Without asking the government, he concluded a ten-year contract with an Englishman, [William H.] Pigott, which gives exclusive rights to himself and three American associates: [William H.] Davis, [John] Ebbets and [Thomas] Meek. Without approval of the government he began to implement this arrangement, which permits foreign ships to fly a Russian flag, and to try out oil from all marine animals (obviously sea otters and seals) all along the coast of eastern Siberia, in bays, harbors, and on all the islands.

Higher officials considered this such a threat that they resolved not only to evict all foreigners from Okhotsk and Kamchatka, but also to refuse them access to our colonies, so they could not bring in contraband firearms, gunpowder and the like. To enforce this they decided to send two naval vessels each year to our colonies. You will see all of this from the appended records. You may also note that whaling is not profitable now because if the oil is designated only for the people of Kamchatka and Okhotsk, the population is so small that a very small amount of oil is needed and the cost is so great that the price will be higher than anywhere else in the world, and there is no other place where it could be sold.

Thus, while the foreign vessels made no apparent profit, they needed the guise of whaling to carry on the hunt for sea animals such as sea otter and seals, and perhaps also land animals whose pelts provided them with great profit. They even managed to entice good Petr Ivanovich [Rikord] into their scheme. Meanwhile, in that ten-year contract period they would settle our islands and take them from us because they would bring many of their own people there. They would also

329

Early view of Okhotsk, on the Sea of Okhotsk. Private collection.

have a monopoly on fishing, which they would procure in waters off Kamchatka, and they could export 30,000 puds of salted fish per year, which would take the last bit of needed provisions from the Kamchadals. What a disaster for those poor people! It is incredible how such things are decided, and so boldly, without the approval of the government, or even its instructions.

However, the Main Administration of the Company has decided to undertake whaling itself, and for that purpose will purchase a ship in Holland, which it will outfit, staff with harpooners, and send around the world.

Reference: United States National Archives. *Records of the Russian American Company*. M11, Vol. 2, No. 276, Folios 82–83.

61

NOT AFTER DECEMBER 20, 1820

AN OFFICIAL REPORT FROM THE MAIN ADMINISTRATION OF THE
RUSSIAN AMERICAN COMPANY TO EMPEROR ALEXANDER I

On May 10 of the present year the sloop *Konstantin* was sent from the colonial port of New Arkhangel (on Sitka Island) on a three-month voyage. She safely reached the port of Okhotsk on August 10, with a cargo of various furs valued at approximately half a million rubles. This sloop was prepared for the return voyage and on September 5 was ready to sail and waited only for a fair wind.

The latest news from the port of New Arkhangel includes the following.

All the colonies are in good condition. Last year Fleet Lieutenant [Semen] Ianovskii, who administers them, inspected all the colonies, sailing from Sitka to the islands of St. Paul and St. George, located to the north in Bering Strait.

In June of last year a [foreign] schooner was sighted out at sea from the fort on Sitka. A pilot was immediately sent out to board her, and then a launch was sent to take her in tow. The next day she was brought into the roadstead. When she arrived, to the astonishment of everyone, it was apparent that there was not a single European aboard, and that the only ones aboard were seven Sandwich Islanders. They were in agreement in stating that Bushard, captain of the Spanish insurgent frigates *Argentina* and *Santa Rosa*, had taken them on as seamen from the Sandwich Islands. These frigates sailed from there directly to New California, where they set fire to the port of Monterey, the headquarters of the Governor, and to San Francisco. They then sailed to the island of Seros, and returned to Monterey where they found this schooner which they claimed as a prize.

Judging by her construction and equipment, she is not a Spanish vessel, but must be North American. Her former captain and the Spanish crew went ashore. Three Europeans and the Sandwich Island people were put aboard to sail her to some port under insurgent control, but a mutiny occurred aboard the frigates. Captain Bushard and other officers were killed, but a few managed to escape ashore. The rebels chose new captains. Then the Europeans aboard the schooner transferred to the frigates, taking with them whatever they could from the cargo, and ordered the Sandwich Islanders to follow the frigates. The frigates put to sea.

One of the Sandwich Islanders, who had earlier sailed on American vessels but barely knew how to read a compass, served on the schooner in place of the captain. In this manner they sailed after the frigates. But the frigates did not want to have to wait for the schooner, so the Sandwich Islanders chose another course. Instead of following the frigates, they proceeded [supposedly] to the Sandwich Islands with the thought that they would hand over the schooner to their king, Kamehameha. They sailed for 82 days in all, but instead of reaching the Sandwich Islands, they appeared at Sitka. On board they only had enough provisions for another two days and half a cask of water. Everything in the hold was in disorder and the schooner was leaking badly.

At the present time she is in Sitka and her small cargo of cotton has been taken to the local warehouses. The Sandwich Island captain of the schooner and his assistant are likewise being detained on Sitka, while the rest of the crew have been sent to the Sandwich Islands aboard a Company ship.

A Company promyshlennik, a native of the island of Kodiak by the name of Kykhklai, who had been taken prisoner by the Spaniards in 1815 and returned to our settlement at Ross and then to the headquarters of the colony on Sitka Island in 1819, gave the following account of inhuman treatment by the Spaniards of one of the Company promyshlenniks.

In 1815 a Company servitor named [Boris] Tarasov was on Ilmen Island, which did not belong to any nation. He was the leader of a group of promyshlenniks who were there to hunt. Since they were unsuccessful there they decided to set out with fifteen dependent islanders from our Kodiak colony to go to other islands, Santa Rosa and Ekaterina [Catalina?]. During the voyage his baidara began to leak, and he had to proceed to the coast of California. They stopped at the bay on Cabo San Pedro, where bad weather detained them until the next day. While they were there a Spanish soldier came to them from the mission of San Pedro and informed Tarasov that in exchange for some gifts, he would bring to him two of our Kodiak men who had previously run off from another such hunting party and were presently in the mission.

When the soldier left, although the weather was calmer and they could proceed on their projected route, the desire to see and to free their fellow islanders persuaded them to remain there longer. On the fourth day of their stay they were suddenly attacked by some 20 armed horsemen, who tied up all of our people and wounded many of them with their sabers. One of the Kodiak islanders named Chunagnak was wounded in the head. The attackers looted all their possessions and all the Company trade goods. The prisoners were then taken to the mission of San Pedro where they actually did find the two Kodiak islanders who had fled from the island of Clement from another party of partisans. When they reached the mission, a missionary who was head of the mission wanted them to accept the Catholic faith. The prisoners replied that they had already accepted the Greek Christian religion and did not wish to change. Some time later Tarasov and almost all the Kodiak people were taken to Santa Barbara. Only two of them, Kykhklai and the wounded Chunagnak, were thrown into prison with the Indians who were being held. They suffered for several days without food or drink.

One night the head of the mission sent the runaway Kodiak islanders with a second order for them to accept the Catholic faith, but again they remained steadfast in their own faith.

At dawn a cleric went to the prison, accompanied by Indians. When the prisoners were brought out, he ordered the Indians to encircle them. Then he ordered the Indians to cut off the fingers from both hands of the above mentioned Chunagnak, then to cut off both his hands; finally, not satisfied with this tyranny, he gave orders that Chunagnak be disemboweled.

Tortured in this manner, Chunagnak breathed his last after the final procedure. The same punishment would have awaited the other Kodiak, Kykhklai had it not been for the fact that the cleric received a timely piece of paper. When he read it, he ordered that the man who had been killed be buried, and that Kykhklai be returned to prison; several days later they sent him to Santa Barbara. There was not one of his comrades there who had been taken prisoner with him. All of them had been sent off to Monterey. Khykhlai was assigned to the same work as other Company promyshlenniks who had been taken prisoner by the Spanish.

Wanting to escape from a life of such torture, Kykhklai and another man conceived the idea of breaking away. They stole a baidarka and went in it to the bay on Cabo San Pedro, and from there to the island of Catalina, then to [Santa] Barbara [Island] and finally to *Ilmen*, where one of them died and where Kykhklai was taken aboard the Company brig *Ilmen*, which had come to the island and then went to the Ross settlement. The others who had been taken prisoner at the same time were freed on the insistence of our captains Hagemeister and Kotzebue.

This incident, just one of many, is a striking example of the inhuman way in which the Spanish treat Russian promyshlenniks. Many who had previously been in their captivity were so exhausted with labor and so abused from beatings that they will carry the results with them to the grave. The suffering inflicted on the poor Indians is impossible to conceive without shuddering. Not only do they not consider the Indians human beings, they consider them below animals. The Spanish take great pleasure in beating innocent Indians and then bragging about it to other Spaniards.

At the request of the Main Administration of the Company an expedition was organized in 1818 to go by baidarka to make a reconnaissance of the coast and interior of America north of the Alaska Peninsula. This expedition, led by the Company servitor [Petr] Korsakovskii, reached the cape which Captain Cook had named Newenham and by sailing along the coast discovered several islands and rivers and became familiar with the people living in that area. From Cape Newenham the expedition returned via the west and northwest, ascending rivers and lakes and crossing portages to the Milchashna River, north of Kenai Bay.

In 1819 the vessel *Konstantin*, under the command of navigator Pometilov, was sent to provide a detailed description of the islands, bays and rivers, while the expedition members in baidarkas kept in contact with *Konstantin* and built a fort on the

Nushagak River which they named for Your Most August Imperial Majesty [Aleksandrovsk]. They went as far as Imakhpichuak Bay in 59° 09' northern latitude.

Over a period of two years they gathered information about the natives who live far to the north, but it appears that a good deal of that information needs to be corroborated. One of the most interesting pieces of information was that the crew of the ship *Konstantin* encountered the Kust-kokhontsy Indians and learned from them that there are two quite large islands north of their settlements, and that on these islands live people with beards and white complexions. They claim that these people pray in our fashion. Certain items the natives have obtained from them—a small bronze bell, a Iakut *palma* [a large knife], a Chukotsk lance and a piece from a clock—definitely suggest that these bearded white people are our fellow countrymen. They may perhaps be descendants of the promyshlenniks who sailed under the leadership of Fedor Alekseev from Kholmogory.

They went aboard seven *koches* [small river boats], setting out from the Kolyma River and sailing around Chukotsk Cape, proceeding through Bering Strait to the south to explore. They became separated in a storm. One koch put in at Nizhnekamchatsk, and the other six sought safety opposite, on the American shore. There our people were stranded, either because they had lost their vessels, or for some other unknown reason.

In 1779 the Kamchatka *cossack sotnik* [commander of 100 cossacks] [Ivan] Kobelev received information about these bearded white people from the natives of Imovlin Island. On the basis of these stories from the islanders he concluded that these people really were Russians, and he planned to search for them, but the Imovlin people refused to take him there. For that reason he wrote a letter and asked the islanders to take it to the white people. This information is taken from the reports the sotnik Kobelev made to the government which were published in 1790 in *Ezhemesiachnye Sochineniia* of the Academy, Part v, pages 370–374.

Since many of the Kust-kokhontsy had visited the bearded white people, and had traded with them, the commander of the sloop invited two of them to go with him to New Arkhangel, and from there the administrator of the colony specially outfitted the brig *Golovnin* to search for the white people with the help of the two Indians. That expedition was entrusted to the navigator [Khristofor M.] Benzeman, who was given prudent instructions and a letter to those people, urging them to send one or two of their number to express their submissive allegiance to His Imperial Majesty The Main Administration of the Russian American Company has the honor of reporting most humbly to Your Imperial Majesty about these matters.

Reference: *VPR*, Second Series, Vol. 3, Doc. 206, 681–684.

62

A DISPATCH FROM THE MAIN ADMINISTRATION OF THE RUSSIAN
AMERICAN COMPANY TO CHIEF ADMINISTRATOR MATVEI I. MURA-
VEV REGARDING ALEUTS WHO WISH TO BE RETURNED TO THEIR OWN
ISLANDS FROM ST. PAUL AND ST. GEORGE

In a dispatch of February 27, 1820, No. 43, [Acting] Chief Administrator [Semen] Ianovskii wrote that the Aleuts who have been living for a long time on the islands of St. Paul and St. George have urgently requested him to transfer them back to their families. As a result, he promised that he would transfer the old and infirm this year, but he persuaded the young to remain there for two more years. He has asked the Main Administration of the Company what to do when the two years are up. He says he cannot persuade the inhabitants of Kodiak or the Fox Islands to provide replacements for them, but he does not state why this is not possible. He intends to ask the *baidarshchik* [overseer] of Kenai Bay and Nushagak River to talk to local people in order to persuade some of them to settle there if possible, but it would be far more advantageous for the Company to transfer savage Indians there from California or from the Sandwich Islands.

This proposal which has been drawn up in the briefest manner, does not prevent the Company Administration from making a final decision in accordance with actual local circumstances. It only suggests that it is necessary for you to take cognizance of the fact that elderly Aleuts, no matter where they may be, should be returned to the bosoms of their families and relatives. Younger ones who have already been in Company service for a sufficient length of time should not be taken from their families and relatives for long periods. Justice demands that they be replaced by others.

But to refer to Ianovskii's statement, who will be their replacements? Are there not healthy young Aleuts in the Fox Island group? Explain to them that they have an obligation to serve the Company because they are Russian subjects, and the work of the Company is inseparable from the good of the

An unfinished drawing of the Pribilof Island of St. Paul, made by the Russian naturalist I. G. Voznesenskii in 1843. On the right above the Aleut dwellings (iurts or barabors) is the 1821 wooden chapel dedicated to saints Peter and Paul; one also sees the administrative quarters. All lumber had to come from New Arkhangel, for these islands are completely devoid of trees. Institute of Ethnography, AN SSSR, Leningrad. (OHS neg. 27005)

Fatherland. Inform them that when they have been supervised in their Company service for a stipulated period of one, two, three or four years, they will be released from service, and will not be held beyond that time. Have people already been taken from the Fox Islands? It would be good if the Kenaits could also be induced, using these same arguments.

In reference to using Californians and inhabitants of the Hawaiian Islands, it would be ridiculous to consider them because the Company has no authority over them, and furthermore they have lived in a warm climate and could not endure the cold.

Ianovskii's proposal and the opinion of the Main Administration of the Company are presented for your consideration, and your implementation, if possible, depending on what the local situation is. It is expected that you will inform the Main Administration of your intentions.

Reference: United States National Archives. *Records of the Russian American Company*. M11, Vol. 2, No. 10, Folios 129–130.

63

AN IMPERIAL UKAZ PROHIBITING FOREIGN MERCHANT SHIPS FROM
TRADING IN THE RUSSIAN COLONIES IN THE NORTH PACIFIC

We have observed, from reports submitted to Us, that the trade of Our subjects in the Aleutian Islands and along the coasts of Northwest America which belong to Russia, is subjected to certain constraints and impediments because of constant illegal trade. We find that the primary cause of these difficulties is the lack of regulations to establish the limits of navigation along these coasts, as well as the order of maritime relations, both in those places and in general along the east coast of Siberia and in the Kuril Islands. Therefore We recognize the necessity of defining these relations by means of special resolutions which are appended.

In forwarding these regulations to the Governing Senate, We direct that they be published for general information, and that appropriate measures be taken to enforce them.

THE ENACTMENT OF REGULATIONS CONCERNING THE LIMITS OF
NAVIGATION AND THE ORDER OF MARITIME RELATIONS ALONG THE
COASTS OF EASTERN SIBERIA, NORTHWESTERN AMERICA, AND IN
THE ALEUTIAN, KURIL AND OTHER ISLANDS.

1. Commercial whaling and fishing and all trade on the islands, in ports and bays, and in general along the entire Northwest Coast of America is hereby assigned to the exclusive use of Russian subjects, beginning from Bering Strait to 51° northern latitude; in the Aleutian Islands; along the east coast of Siberia; also in the Kuril Islands—that is, from Bering Strait to the southern cape of the island of Urup in 45° 50' northern latitude.

2. Accordingly, no foreign vessel may anchor on the coast or islands belonging to Russia, described in the previous article, nor may such vessel even approach closer than 100 Italian miles. Any vessel violating this prohibition will be confiscated with its entire cargo.

3. This regulation does not apply to vessels which have been carried to such places by storms, or to those in genuine need of provisioning which must put in at shore and can find no place to do so except the coast belonging to Russia. In such case a vessel must present proof of the reason for having done this. Vessels sent from friendly powers solely for the dissemination of knowledge are also exempt from the foregoing regulation; but in such case they must previously obtain passports from the Russian Minister of the Navy.

4. Foreign merchant ships which come to the above mentioned coasts for reasons stated in the preceding article must attempt to find a place where there is a Russian settlement; they must conduct themselves in accordance with the following article.

5. If time permits, a pilot is to be sent out to meet a foreign merchant vessel as it approaches. The pilot will designate the anchorage for the ship. A captain or skipper who disobeys the pilot and anchors somewhere else without giving local authorities a satisfactory reason for his action, will pay a fine of 100 piasters.

6. Rowing boats from foreign merchant vessels must anchor at shore at a designated place where a white flag will fly during the day, and a lantern at night. An overseer will be stationed there permanently; he is to see that there are no illegal imports or exports of any goods or commodities.

Any person who anchors in a place other than that designated, even without intending to carry on trade in contraband goods, will pay a fine of 50 piasters. The fine will be 500 piasters for anyone who puts goods ashore, and all such goods will be confiscated.

7. Commanders of vessels in need of provisions and navigational or other equipment in order to be able to continue their voyages must inform the [Russian] commander of the area, who will indicate where such necessities can be obtained. Subsequent to this the ships' commanders may without hindrance dispatch their vessels to procure their needs. Persons violating this regulation will be fined 100 piasters.

8. If it is actually necessary for a foreign merchant vessel to unload her entire cargo in order to make repairs, her commanding officer must request permission from the local admin-

istrator. In this instance the captain of the ship is to provide local authorities with a detailed inventory of the offloaded goods, specifying the contents and quantities of such goods. Anyone who fails to report any part of his cargo will be under suspicion of intending to carry on contraband trade and will pay a fine of 1,000 piasters.

9. Expenses which these vessels incur during their stay in Russian lands are to be paid in cash or written acknowledgements of debt. In case the captains of these ships have no cash, and no one will give collateral, the local commanding officer may, upon the request of the ship's commanding officer, permit the sale of an amount of goods, provisions or supplies required to defray only the amount of the debt. Such sale, however, can be made only by the Company, with the local commanding officer acting as intermediary. This transaction cannot exceed the sum needed by such ship, under penalty of seizure of the cargo and a fine of 1,000 piasters.

10. As soon as a foreign merchant vessel is ready to reload her cargo, goods, supplies and commodities, she must do so immediately. After an inspection of the reloaded cargo and verification of the invoice, indicating that nothing has been left behind, she is to set sail without delay. The same immediate departure at the earliest opportunity also applies to a vessel that has not unloaded her cargo, as soon as she is in condition to put to sea.

11. The commanding officer or other official of such foreign vessel, whoever he may be, is prohibited from taking on goods, provisions or supplies in the place the ship has anchored, except as provided in Article 7, under penalty of confiscation of ship and cargo.

12. Such foreign vessel is also prohibited from taking on board any Company servitor or foreigner living in a Company settlement, unless there is specific permission from the local authorities.

13. No foreign merchant vessel may buy, sell or barter with personnel in service to the Company. This prohibition extends also to personnel on shore or working on Company ships. Any ship violating this rule will pay five times the value of articles, supplies or goods which were intended to be part of this prohibited trade.

14. Further, foreign vessels are prohibited from any purchase or barter with native peoples of the islands and and mainland of all parts of Northwest America. Any ship engaged in such trade is subject to confiscation.

15. Articles, supplies and goods found on shore in ports or harbors, which belong to Russian subjects or to foreign ships, and are involved in this prohibited trade, will be confiscated.

16. Foreign commercial ships anchored in the port or roadstead cannot under any pretext send out their sloops to vessels at sea, or to ships which have already arrived, until the ships have been questioned and inspected in accordance with existing customs. If a foreign vessel flies the yellow flag signaling a contagious disease aboard, the symptoms of a disease or some other dangerous condition of which the ship wishes to rid itself, in such case all communication with that ship is prohibited until the flag is lowered. This prohibition does not apply, however, to persons specifically appointed, whose sloops carry the flag of the Russian American Company. Any vessel violating this rule will be fined 500 piasters.

17. Ballast may only be disposed of in places designated by local authorities. A ship which violates this rule will be fined 500 piasters.

18. No foreign merchant ship may anchor in port or roadstead while its cannon are loaded with round shot and canister. There will be a fine of 50 piasters for every such offense.

19. No foreign merchant ship in port, in the roadstead or standing at anchor may fire cannon or guns without previously informing the local commanding officer of the place or the settlement, except to signal the need for a pilot. In such a case the ship will fire one, two or three shots and hoist a flag to signal this need. Anyone violating this rule will be fined 100 piasters for every shot.

20. Immediately upon the arrival of a foreign ship in port or roadstead, a sloop will be sent out to meet her to deliver a copy of this written regulation to the captain, who is to sign a special book indicating receipt. He must also provide all information required of foreign vessels, in accordance with the example below. Any ship refusing to comply may not approach the port or roadstead, or anchor offshore.

Name and value of ship	Nationality	Name of owner of ship	Name of captain	Number of crew members	Number of cannon	Cargo
Place from which ship was dispatched		Destination of ship				

21. The captain of a foreign merchant ship anchored in port or roadstead must upon his arrival submit a statement concerning the health of his crew. If a contagious disease later breaks out aboard the ship, the commanding officer must immediately inform the local authorities. Depending on the circumstances such a ship will be sent out or put under quarantine in a specially designated location where the crew can be treated without exposing the local inhabitants to the disease. Any captain who deliberately hides such information will have his ship and entire cargo confiscated.

22. At the request of local authorities the captain of a [foreign] vessel must submit a complete list of crew and passengers. If any name is omitted, the fine is 100 piasters for each name omitted.

23. Captains of ships must be responsible for the behavior and orderly conduct of crew on shore and in port, and must prevent any trade or barter with Company personnel. Captains are responsible for the behavior both of sailors and other subordinates. A violation of trade regulations by a sailor will be treated as if the captain had personally committed the violation, because otherwise it would be possible for captains to carry on contraband trade without punishment by blaming the

sailors. Any article carried on the person of a sailor when he leaves the ship, which cannot be concealed from his superiors in his pockets or under his clothing, and which he then sells or brings on shore, will be considered contraband goods from the ship, and will be subject to the established fine.

24. Foreign military vessels must also comply with the regulations for foreign merchant vessels regarding the protection of the rights and privileges of the Company. If there are violations, complaints will be made to their respective governments.

25. If a ship of the Imperial Russian Navy or a ship belonging to the Russian American Company encounters a foreign ship along the previously described shores, or in the harbors or roadsteads of this expanse, and the commanding officer finds the foreign vessel subject to confiscation in accordance with the provisions of this decree, he is to proceed as follows.

26. The commander of the Russian ship who suspects that the foreign vessel is subject to seizure is to question [the captain] and inspect the vessel; if his suspicion is confirmed, he is to take possession. If the foreign vessel offers resistance, the [Russian] commander is first to use persuasion, then threat, and finally, force. He is, however, to do this with the least amount of harm, and with all possible humanity. If the foreign vessel responds to force with force, [the Russian] is to treat [the foreign captain] as an overt enemy and force him to surrender in accordance with Naval Regulations.

27. After establishing the necessary order and security aboard the foreign vessel, the commander of the Russian ship or the officers sent out by him, will demand the Ship's Log from the captured vessel and immediately make an entry in it specifying the day, month, year, hour and place said vessel was encountered. He will also make a brief written account of all the circumstances, the pursuit and seizure. He is to sign this and have the captain of the captured vessel confirm it with his own signature.

If he refuses to sign this, the officer of the Russian ship is to repeat his request in the presence of all other ranks. If he continues to refuse, and no other person in authority will sign it, the Russian officer will record this circumstance as well and attest to it with his signature.

After completing this procedure he will gather all of the following materials into one packet: the Log, list of crew members, passports, invoices, account books and all other papers relating to the purpose and voyage of that vessel; also personal papers such as the journals of the officers and their correspondence. This packet is to be sealed with the seals of the officer of the Russian ship and the seals of the skipper and a senior officer of the foreign vessel. This packet is to be kept by the commanding officer of the Russian ship, with seals unbroken, until he reaches the harbor of Petropavlovsk where the packet will be handed over to a commission as described in Article 33 of this ukaz. Also to be sealed with the seals of the commanding officer and the skipper are all other items not necessary for continuing the voyage to Petropavlovsk harbor, except for items for personal daily use of the crew, which are not to be taken from them.

28. Once all necessary security measures are taken, the officer sent to seize the foreign vessel will immediately report on everything to his commanding officer and await his instructions.

29. If for the reasons stated in Articles 2, 11, 12, 14 and 21 of this Regulation, a foreign vessel in any harbor near a settlement of the American Company is subject to confiscation, the commanding officer of that settlement is either to request assistance from a Russian vessel if there is one, in which case its commanding officer upon receiving this written request must immediately seize the vessel, taking all the security measures detailed above; or, if there is no Russian naval vessel in the harbor or vicinity, and the commanding officer of a settlement believes he can seize the foreign vessel with the help of his own people, he is to proceed to do so in accordance with the intent of Articles 26, 27 and 28. He is to put ashore the skipper and everyone else in order to prevent the ship from escaping, and he is immediately to use every possible means to inform the Main Office of the Russian American Company or the commanding officer of a Russian naval vessel, if the whereabouts of such are known.

30. When the administrator of the Main Office receives such information and dispatches a Company vessel or requests a naval vessel, the head of the settlement is to hand over the

seized vessel to the Russian vessel, with all of its belongings, and submit a detailed report concerning all the reasons for the confiscation and an account of everything that has transpired.

31. The commander of the Russian ship which takes over the seized vessel and its inventory is then and there to verify the circumstances described in the report of the administrator of the settlement, and request of him any additional information.

32. All vessels detained by Russian naval ships in accordance with these regulations are to be taken to Petropavlovsk harbor where a special commission designated for this purpose will decide what is to be done with them.

33. The commander of Kamchatka will preside over this commission, which will consist of three of his senior officers and a commissioner of the Russian American Company.

34. As soon as the Russian vessel brings the seized foreign vessel to Petropavlovsk harbor and anchors at the designated place there, the commanding officer is to report immediately to the commander of Kamchatka in brief, informing him what vessel he has brought, the number of its crew, how many are ill and with what illness, whether the ship has adequate provisions and whether it carries goods, cannon or other firearms, gunpowder and the like.

35. Upon receiving this report the commander of Kamchatka is immediately to dispatch two officials with an appropriate number of personnel to board the seized ship.

36. These two officials, together with the officer commanding the Russian ship who has brought the seized vessel into the harbor, will board the ship at the request of the commander of Kamchatka. Once aboard, they will ask the skipper and two senior navigators or assistants jointly to verify all the sealed documents. Once the seals are broken they will together examine the detailed inventory to ascertain what was aboard the ship.

37. Upon completion of examination of the inventory the document is to be signed by all officials of both sides who were present when it was prepared. The commander of Kamchatka is to make every effort to preserve intact and undamaged everything that belonged to the seized vessel.

38. The crew of the seized vessel is to be ordered to go ashore

to a location designated by the commander of Kamchatka; they will remain there until the investigation is completed.

39. The commanding officer of the Russian vessel within two days after bringing the foreign ship to Petropavlovsk harbor is to submit in detail to the commander of Kamchatka a report about all events pertaining to the seizure of the vessel, and hand over to him the vessel and the sealed packet containing the vessel's papers, as described in Article 27.

40. If for some reason the Russian vessel which brings the foreign ship to Petropavlovsk harbor cannot remain there until the investigation is complete, but must put back out to sea immediately, the commander of Kamchatka is to expedite all matters set forth in these articles which require the presence of the [Russian] ship, so that ship will not be detained.

41. As soon as order is completely restored aboard the seized vessel and the crew has been put ashore, the Commission is to commence deliberations, and as quickly as possible attempt to settle the question of whether the vessel was seized legally.

42. In order to resolve that question the following information is necessary:

1) Was the vessel encountered within the territory indicated in Article 2 of this regulation? Was its presence there due to reasons other than those in Article 3?

2) Was the vessel actually subject to seizure in accordance with Articles 2, 11, 12, 14 and 21 of this ukaz, and with the instructions for officers commanding naval vessels?

43. In order to verify either of these points, the Commission is to examine the documents which have been submitted and to it, extract any evidence of guilt and eliminate any doubts which might justify the presence of the foreign vessel. The Commission is to request the testimony of the commander of the Russian vessel and all supplementary and necessary clarifications. Once all the evidence incriminating the foreign vessel has been obtained, the Commission is to draw up a full explanation for the confiscation.

44. If, in preparing the charges, the Commission discovers that the foreign vessel was seized without cause, the Commission is immediately to determine any appropriate compensa-

tion for losses caused by the seizure. The Commission will inform both parties of this and give them copies of the decision, sealed with the official seal.

45. Within two days each side must express its satisfaction or dissatisfaction with the Committee's decision. If they do not agree, their views must be presented in writing.

46. If both sides are in agreement concerning the findings of the Commission, the commander of Kamchatka will immediately free the seized vessel, return to the skipper everything listed on the inventory and give him the adjudicated recompense for losses, taking this from the party who was at fault.

47. If by the third day there is an objection to the Commission's findings, there is to be an immediate review. If the Commission finds the objection valid, it may change its original decision. However, if it finds the objection invalid, it is to reaffirm its decision and inform both parties of this. Thereafter it is to accept no further objections. It will summon both parties, allow each side to submit a written protest setting forth reasons for objecting, and then order its decision to be carried out.

48. If on the basis of the charges the Commission finds the vessel was seized rightfully, it will summon the skipper of the foreign vessel and two of his senior officers and inform them of all the reasons for the seizure and give him a certified copy of the indictment.

49. Not more than three days later the Commission is to receive a response from the skipper. If this is not submitted on time the Commission will again summon him and his two associates and inform them that their silence is taken as an indication that the indictment is just.

50. In such a case the Commission, having made its final determination, will inform the entire crew of the foreign vessel the next day. During this phase of its inquiry the Commission is to obtain the signature of every crew member of the foreign vessel. After that the commander of Kamchatka will carry out the sentence as handed down by the Commission.

51. If the [foreign] skipper submits his response in the designated time, however, the Commission will review it with all possible impartiality, gather any further testimony necessary,

enter it into the records of the deliberations, and then pass judgment, which it will issue as set forth in Article 47.

52. If the decision of the Commission is that the seized foreign vessel should be freed and compensated for the detention, if the vessel was taken by officials of the Russian American Company, and if the compensation is not to be more than 5,000 rubles, the commander of Kamchatka will request the Company office to pay this sum immediately. However, if the sum is greater than that amount, the commander of Kamchatka will inform the Company office, and issue the foreign vessel a voucher for this amount. The Company can only pay the funds after the review, however, and upon the direction of its Main Administration.

If the foreign vessel was seized unlawfully by a Russian naval vessel, and if the compensation does not exceed 5,000 rubles, the sum will be paid by the Treasury, and [the commander of Kamchatka] will report about this to proper authorities. If the sum is greater than 5,000 rubles, the commander of Kamchatka will issue a voucher to enable [the foreigners] to receive the funds upon the approval of higher governmental authorities.

53. Reimbursement for damages suffered through unlawful detention must be obtained from the commander of the naval vessel and from all officers with whom he consulted who had agreed that the foreign vessel should be seized.

54. When the verdict is that the foreign vessel is to be seized, the commander of Kamchatka must issue all necessary instructions to send her crew to Okhotsk and from there via Irkutsk to one of the Baltic ports so that each may return to his own country. The confiscated ship and cargo, however, are to be treated as a prize taken in wartime.

55. After this the commander of Kamchatka is immediately to appoint a commission to establish the value of the ship and its cargo. This commission will consist of one member appointed by the commander of Kamchatka, one member from the naval vessel and one from the Russian American Company.

56. The Commission is to draw up a detailed inventory and price list for every item, and in this it is to be guided by the following rules:

1) All provisions, rigging, iron, powder and firearms are to be priced on the basis of their cost to the government there.

2) Goods which can be used in Kamchatka or in the colonies, and which are sometimes brought there from Russia, are to be appraised on the basis of prices current there.

3) Goods which are not imported from Russia to those regions but are needed there are to be valued on the basis of those brought from Russia which are most similar and according to their utility.

4) Goods not used in Kamchatka or in the colonies are to be sent to Irkutsk where they will be sold in public auction by the gubernia authorities.

57. The Commission will submit its findings to the commander of Kamchatka for his approval. He may supplement these findings with his own observations and if he should find that the report has been prepared incorrectly, he will appoint other officials to examine items that were incorrectly valued.

58. If the Commission later insists on its own appraisal but the commander of Kamchatka finds it impossible to agree with them, he will make a preliminary approval of the findings of the Commission but leave any final decision to another higher governmental authority.

59. After a value has been established, the commander of Kamchatka will designate the items he feels must go to the Treasury. The rest he will distribute to officials of the Russian vessel of the Russian American Company.

The Commission will also appraise the value of the ship which is to be reported immediately to the Minister of the Navy, with an inquiry as to whether that vessel is needed for government service.

60. The entire sum of the value of the confiscated vessel and cargo is to be divided in the following manner: first, expenses are to be deducted which are necessary for sending the crew to one of the Baltic ports. The rest of the sum is to be divided in such a way that if the ship was seized by officials of the Russian American Company and brought to Petropavlovsk harbor by its own ship without the participation of a naval vessel, then one-fifth of the sum would go to the Treasury, and the other four-fifths will go to the Russian American Company.

If the vessel was seized in Company settlements by Company officials, and brought to Petropavlovsk harbor by a Russian naval vessel, after one-fifth goes to the Treasury, two-fifths go to officials of the naval vessel and two-fifths to the Russian American Company. Finally, if the foreign vessel was taken by a naval vessel without any participation by Company officials, after setting aside one-fifth for the Treasury, the rest is to be given to officials of the naval vessel. If, however, the foreign vessel was taken or seized by a joint force of naval and Company vessels, the prize must be divided between them in proportion to their efforts, considering the number of cannon each had.

61. The sum that officials of the naval vessel will receive will be divided among them in accordance with rules which exist for the distribution of naval prizes of war. However, in every case the officers who took part in seizing the foreign vessel, which has been convicted of intent to violate the privileges that were most graciously granted to the Russian American Company, may expect to receive tokens of Imperial good will, especially when their part of the prize sum will be trifling once various expenses for crew transport are deducted.

62. If a foreign vessel which has been seized by a Russian and commanded by a Russian officer, is wrecked before reaching Petropavlovsk, the following procedure should be observed:

a) If only the foreign vessel is lost, and the Russian vessel accompanying her manages to reach Petropavlovsk, when the latter arrives there the Commission is to be convened and examine whether, in accordance with the preceding articles, the foreign vessel was seized legally or illegally. In this case the Government will assume the expense of sending the crew who are saved from the shipwrecked vessel to a Baltic port.

However, if it is discovered that the vessel was seized illegally, then these expenses plus the value of the vessel are to be established and submitted to higher authorities for whatever payment may be deemed just.

An inquiry is to be made into the reasons for the shipwreck, and the officer in command, if he has been saved, will be tried in accordance with Naval Regulations.

63. The commander of Kamchatka is to report in detail

on all matters concerning the foreign ship to the Governor-General of Siberia, submitting to him copies of all the documents, logs and Commission findings, and in general, all of the papers which relate to this matter.

Reference: *PSZ*, Vol. 37, No. 28,747, 903–904; 825–832 [sic].

64

A PERSONAL IMPERIAL UKAZ FROM ALEXANDER I TO THE SENATE
RENEWING THE PRIVILEGES OF THE RUSSIAN AMERICAN COMPANY
AND APPROVING REGULATIONS FOR ITS ACTIVITIES

The Russian American Company, which is under Our patronage and enjoys privileges most graciously granted to it in 1799, has completely fulfilled Our expectations by mounting extensive successful voyages, expanding the profitable trade of the Empire, and bringing significant benefits to the immediate participants. Because of the importance of this, wishing to continue and consolidate its existence, We hereby renew the privileges which were granted to it, with necessary additions and changes, from this time for the next 20 years. Having approved new regulations for it, We are forwarding to the Governing Senate [this Imperial intent], instructing it to prepare an appropriate document embodying these privileges and to bring it for Our signature and issue appropriate decrees pertaining to it.

PRIVILEGES GRANTED TO THE RUSSIAN AMERICAN COMPANY FOR
THE NEXT TWENTY YEARS.

The Company is most graciously granted the following rights:

1. This Company, chartered for hunting on the mainland of North America and on the Aleutian and Kuril Islands, will henceforth, as previously, be under the patronage of His Imperial Majesty.

2. The Company will have exclusive rights along the shores of Northwest America which have belonged to Russia from of old, beginning from the northern cape of Vancouver Island in 51° northern latitude to Bering Strait and beyond, as well as on all islands adjacent to that coast, and others located between it and the East Coast of Siberia, and likewise on those Kuril Islands where the Company has enterprises, to the southern cape of the island of Urup in 45° 50', they will have exclusive hunting and fishing privileges, unhindered by any other Russian and foreign subjects.

3. It will have the use of all resources in these parts, both above and below ground, which it has previously discovered or may in the future discover, without interference from anyone.

4. It may make new discoveries beyond the above delineated regions. These newly discovered places, if they are not occupied by and subject to any European nation or [settled] by citizens of the United States of America, and have not become dependents of them, may be occupied by the Company in the name of Russia; however, it cannot establish permanent settlements there except with Imperial permission.

5. The Company has permission, as its requirements and judgment may dictate, to establish new settlements within the boundaries set forth in Article 2, and fortifications where necessary to protect dwellings. It may expand and improve earlier settlements and dispatch ships carrying goods and promyshlenniks to those regions without any interference.

6. For the greatest assurance that the Company will be able to enjoy the exclusive rights granted to it, with no hindrance or interference by either Russians or foreigners, regulations are hereby established for dealing with those who deliberately or through unfortunate circumstance violate this prohibition against entering the areas described in Article 2 of the privileges. These regulations must be strictly observed both by the Company and by those authorities to whom the regulations pertain.

7. The Company has the right to maintain maritime and commercial relations with all neighboring peoples, pending the consent of their governments, with the exception of the Empire of China; Company vessels are not to sail to those shores. The Company must be absolutely certain that its vessels have no commercial or other relations with people whose government is opposed to this.

8. The Main Administration of the Russian American Company has the right to establish offices in appropriate places to administer the affairs of the Company. Matters under its jurisdiction relating to the Company which may be brought to court are not to be handled by any of the partners of the Company, but by the Main Administration.

9. The Most Gracious [Emperor] entrusts to the Administration of the Company an extremely broad expanse of land

and a considerable number of persons inhabiting it. In order to give the Company greater ability to carry out the aims of the government to stimulate its servitors in all domestic and overseas factories and warehouses of the Company, and to staff the positions of administrators, bookkeepers, cashiers and assistants, supercargoes, ship prikashchiks and others, the Company is granted the following advantages:

A. If the person appointed to the post of Chief Administrator is an official serving in either military or civil capacity, upon appointment he will have the right to enjoy the privileges stated in the ukaz of March 21, 1810, which applies to all posts in the Siberian gubernia.

B. In accordance with the ukaz of April 9, 1802, servitors whom the Company employs on a temporary basis will be considered on active service, in regard to their recompense. This does not apply to ranks who are promoted on the basis of seniority and favor from their present positions. Such officials will receive half of their salary and daily rations on the basis of this ukaz.

C. Retired officials who are assigned to a [Company] position will retain their rank and be considered on active service again. This also applies to persons who served the Company in various capacities when Imperial approval of the Privileges was given in 1799. However, any persons who are members of classes which are entitled to enter service, but who have never served at all and have no rank will receive the rank of Collegiate Registrar two years after entering Company service, with the approval of the Main Administration of the Company. They will be promoted to appropriate ranks on the basis of general rules. Upon retirement they will retain rank only if they have held it for five years and if the Administration attests to their ability and merit.

D. Company servitors who do not belong to a class entitled to enter government service will not be accepted on an equal basis with those persons referred to in point "c" above, until the former have been moved out of such categories. However, if such a person is appointed as an office administrator, he will enjoy the privileges of the ninth rank, Titular Councillor, for the duration of his service. Depending on the qualifications and merit of those working as bookkeepers, cashiers and assistants, supercargoes and others, the Main Administration has the right to assign to them the specific rank between the fourteenth and the ninth to which they will belong. But when these servitors are released from obligations and service, they may retain the prerogatives of the class in which they were registered, if they come from that category, carry out all the obligations specified in the applicable public laws, serve the Company at least twelve years, and upon retirement are attested to as worthy and able.

10. On the basis of the ukazes of the Governing Senate of February 16, 1801, April 6, 1805, and March 20, 1808, the Company has the right to recruit men into service from all the gubernias of the Russian Empire. They may take free persons of all classes who are not under suspicion, and who have valid passports or ration papers; these persons may be recruited to voyage, hunt and engage in various enterprises. Gubernia administrators are ordered to furnish such persons, whom the Company hires, with passports valid for a period of one to seven years, upon request by the Company. The Company is responsible for paying the taxes for those persons, and fulfilling their other obligations.

11. When the period of the contract has expired, if servitors of the Company wish to return to America, in service to the Company, or if they are indebted to the Company, the Company is not obliged to return such persons to Russia. Upon the Company's request, prior to their departure, they are to be issued new passports; however, it should be noted that such a request is to be accompanied by a written statement testifying to the consent of the servitor to continue to live there, with the reason for the decision. The person himself must sign this, or if he is illiterate, the statement must be witnessed and signed by two other persons.

12. Company servitors must carry out all orders and instructions of their superiors precisely, and they are answerable to the Company for damage or dereliction of duty. The administrative offices require that every person be accountable. Upon request of the Main Administration of the Company, any person [responsible for loss or negligence] will be subject to a legal inquiry, and discipline in accordance with the decision of the Administration. However, when a verdict is issued, no one is

to be denied the opportunity to submit a protest to the Governing Senate; such protest must be made no later than six months after the decision is handed down.

13. No work place or administrative office in a town established as a Company office or agency is to remit payment to anyone for any reason whatsoever without first obtaining the required documentation. If the Main Administration of the Company has not authorized the office or agency to make payments, all demands for payment must be referred to the Main Administration.

14. If a shareholder of the Company incurs a debt to the government Treasury or to a private individual, and is unable to pay it from his assets aside from his stock in the Company, such stock will become either completely or partially the property of the Treasury or the creditor, depending on the size of the debt, along with all accrued dividends undistributed as of that date. The Company, in accordance with this action, upon notification of the government or upon judicial decision, will transfer such assets from the debtor to the Treasury or the creditor.

15. Shares issued by the Company in accordance with the decision of the Committee of Ministers on September 19, 1814, will be accepted as security by the Treasury at half their value. If certain shares have been appropriated to pay a debt, and the person who owned them is not able to repurchase them after he has repaid the debt with the shares, the shares are to be sold in public trading. Once sold, any money remaining after the debt has been paid will be returned to the original owner. However, if at the time of the sale the offered price is less than the asking price, the Treasury may keep the shares if it feels this course to be preferable; or the Company may immediately pay the Treasury the amount of the debt and take the shares into its own holdings.

16. If a difficulty which cannot quickly be resolved equitably arises between the Company and a shareholder regarding settling accounts in mutual business transactions, such account is to be brought to a general meeting of shareholders with voting rights, with the shareholder himself present, and decided through mediation. The decision is to be put into effect immediately; however, if the shareholder is still not satisfied, he

may appeal to the Governing Senate no later than six months after the other shareholders have made their decision

17. The Most Gracious [Emperor] grants permission to the Russian American Company to send ships carrying Russian and foreign goods, on which cargo duties have already been paid, from Kronstadt around the world and from Okhotsk to our colonies. The Company may also unload from ships returning from these colonies goods consisting of local products, furs and other items, without delay, after the Main Administration has submitted the appropriate documents to the customs office in Kronstadt and the Company commissioner has presented the proper documents pertaining to the cargo to the local authorities in Okhotsk. Since both cargoes are sent from one Russian port to another, no duties are to be imposed on them, provided a general law does not impose special internal duties on furs.

18. Although Imperial ukazes prohibit the cutting of trees anywhere in government forest lands without a permit from the Forestry Administration, nevertheless, because of the distance [from St. Petersburg] of the Okhotsk oblast, where the Company must repair and overhaul vessels and sometimes build new ones, the Company is permitted to use the lumber they need in that oblast, cut in suitable places, provided the Company immediately informs local forestry officials where they have cut, the amount and the nature of the timber cut.

19. If Company communication with the colonies by sea should be cut off from here [St. Petersburg], the Company has the right to use its own funds to purchase, at regular prices, 40 to 80 puds of gunpowder per year from the government artillery depot in Irkutsk, and up to 200 puds of shot from the Nerchinsk factory; these will be used for the purpose of shooting animals, making signals at sea and for any unforeseen situation which may arise.

20. In order for the Company to conduct its affairs freely and with security, all of the structures that house its factories are exempted from billeting.

Finally, in granting these privileges to the Russian American Company, [We decree that] all civil and military officials, and various local officials, are forbidden to interfere with the Company regarding these privileges. However, they are to warn the Company of any potential danger, and if requested by the Company's Main Administration or by Company officials in offices or agencies, they are to render the Company every assistance, defense and protection.

[The first 34 articles, pertaining to general rules and administrative structure, are omitted.]

GENERAL OBLIGATIONS OF THE COMPANY.

I. *Company obligations to the Government.*

35. The Company must make every possible effort to merit the trust given to it: preserve intact the colonies granted to the Company exclusively for its use; avoid anything which might disturb relations with neighboring powers; organize all its enterprises for the benefit of the entire country; and keep strictly within the limits of the privileges and these regulations which have been granted to it.

36. The Company will report to His Imperial Majesty through the Minister of Finance on matters pertaining to its own orders, successful activities, propitious accomplishments and the amount of its capital. On other matters, including its own administration, the Company will report directly to the Minister of Finance. If necessary he will add his own remarks, and if the Company does not agree with certain of the Minister's suggestions, he will report to His Imperial Majesty.

II. *Company obligations to Russian subjects living in areas entrusted to Company administration.*

37. In addition to the obligations imposed on the Company by these regulations, the Company is to see to it that the colonies under its jurisdiction have an adequate number of priests and clergy, that there are places of worship or appropriate places to conduct religious services wherever there are enough persons to warrant this, and that these structures are maintained in good condition.

The Company is also to see to it that priests have everything they need to live decently and that local administrators always give them all possible assistance in carrying out their assignments. Company servitors are to be able to fulfill all the requirements of God's commandments and have all the help and strength to do this which they have the right to expect from servants of the church.

38. The Company is strictly obligated to see to it that administrators of their offices who enter Company service from various backgrounds carry out all their instructions meticulously. If the Main Administration eventually finds it necessary to make some change in the present regulations, this must be submitted to the Minister of Finance. Depending on the importance he will either make a decision personally, or he will submit the matter to higher authorities.

39. The Company must use every means to build needed living quarters for its inhabitants. These are to be in places which are salubrious and convenient in both summer and winter. The Company must provide all necessary food and clothing appropriate for the local climate. Finally, in case of illness among its servitors, the Company must do its best to provide necessary medications and experienced doctors who will be assigned to duty in those colonies.

40. If there are Russian-born servitors of the Company in the colonies, or if in these distant places native women are married to Russians, when the Company receives annual reports of this it must notify appropriate authorities of the number of births to these women, and list those who are enrolled in the category of the father, as well as any who die before leaving the colonies. The survivors of legitimate marriages are to return to Russia immediately, with their families.

41. Creoles [those of mixed Russian and native parentage] who, according to most recent information, number 180 males and 120 females, and all who are born in the future, must be registered in the [census] lists of the main colonial office. Such persons will henceforth comprise a special category and will be subject to the following rules:

A. Creoles are subjects of Russia. In this category they have the right everywhere to the legal protection of the government, just as all other subjects do who belong to the category of *meshchanstvo* [town dwellers]. However, they do not have the rights of other categories, either through service or for other reasons.

B. Creoles who live in the colonies will not be subject to any government tax or obligation until a new decree is issued regarding this.

c. To protect these rights the Company is to authorize the Chief Administrator of the colonies to act as an official in government service, so that he will work with officials of the colonial offices under his jurisdiction to exercise watchful concern and supervision over the persons and property of creoles.

D. Creoles who have entered Company service and have distinguished themselves through hard work and ability, may, upon review by authorities, enjoy the privileges granted to other Russian subjects who have entered Company service from the meshchane category.

E. Creoles who receive professional training in science or arts and crafts in Russia at the expense of the Company are awarded the status of student or medical assistant upon graduation from institutions of higher education. They will have all attendant rights established for universities and the Academy. They must agree to serve in the colonies for at least ten years, to be of service to native inhabitants. They are to receive appropriate wages and maintenance expenses from the Company. When the set period has expired they may leave the colonies if they desire and be employed elsewhere, depending on their occupations.

42. The following peoples live in regions administered by the Company: Islanders, Kurils, Aleuts and others . . . and the following tribes live along the American coast: the Kenait, Chugach and others.

Concerning Islanders.

43. The government considers these people equal to all other subjects of Russia. They comprise a separate category as long as they live in the colonies, and until by virtue of their service or other opportunities they are transferred to another category.

44. As Russian subjects they are subject to all State laws, and they are protected by the same.

45. Since their status has not yet been formalized, the government does not require from them either duties or *iasak* [tribute paid in furs] or other obligations. The Company is likewise prohibited from imposing any obligations on them other than those set forth in Article 51 below.

46. The Company must keep a record of the inhabitants of the islands and their current dwelling places, also an account of the number of inhabitants of both sexes, births, deaths, bap-

tisms and conversions. That information is to be reported to the government.

47. Islanders are administered by tribal toions under the supervision of *starshinas* [elders] appointed by the Company from among its best Russian servitors.

48. These starshinas, together with the toions, are responsible for caring for and supervising the islanders entrusted to them. They are to resolve conflicts, arguments and dissatisfactions, and assist the islanders in their needs.

49. The Company is to furnish islanders with land adequate for their needs in places where they presently live or where they will settle in the future. The Company is to strive to acquaint them with the benefits of community life, and will provide them with the means to profit from it.

50. Everything an individual islander obtains through his own labor or through inheritance, purchase or barter is his own inalienable property. Anyone who tries to take it from him, or secure it through personal injury, must be prosecuted by law.

51. Islanders and others have an obligation to the Company to hunt sea animals. For that reason it is decreed that half of all males between the ages of 18 and 50 may be required for Company service.

52. For this purpose, every year at a time designated by the Company, the toions, at Company request, will assign the required number of males (but no more than as set forth in Article 51). The toions will see to it, however, that wherever possible those selected will come from families where there is more than one male member, so the women and children in that family will not be left without help and subsistence.

53. The Company is to provide appropriate clothing, food and baidaras for islanders assigned to serve the Company; they are to be paid for animals they take, an amount not less than one-fifth of what the Company previously paid Russians. Those chosen to serve the Company will perform these duties for no more than three years; after this time they will be replaced by others.

54. However, when islanders complete their three-year period of service, and wish to continue to serve the Company, they will not be prohibited from doing so.

55. If the Company should find it necessary to utilize in

some form of service island women and young people under eighteen years of age, this will only be permitted if there is mutual agreement and an established rate of pay.

56. Islanders not in Company service are permitted to fish along shores where they live for their personal and family sustenance, but they are not allowed to go to neighboring areas without special permission from the Company. They may likewise hunt sea and land animals on those islands and in places where they live; everything thus procured is their own property. But if they wish to sell any of the furs they obtain in this manner, they may only sell to the Company, at a price which the Company Administration must report to the government.

III. *Company obligations to native peoples inhabiting the coasts of America where the Company has its colonies.*

57. The prime objective of the Company is to hunt sea and land animals; it has no need to extend its possessions into the interior of these lands, along whose shores it carries on its hunting; it is not to attempt to subdue native peoples who inhabit these coasts. For this reason, if the Company sees some advantage in establishing factories in certain places on the American mainland in order to provide security for their commercial operations, it may do so, with the consent of the native inhabitants of those places; but it must use every possible means to maintain good relations there, and avoid anything that might arouse their distrust and suggest that the Company intends to violate their independence.

58. The Company is forbidden to impose tribute, iasak, levies or any other form of taxation on these people. Likewise in time of peace the Company must not take by force anyone from a family whose members are presently being held hostage. Hostages must be kept decently; Company officials must take special care of them and not abuse them.

59. However, if it should happen that some of the native people on the American coast express a desire to settle in Russian colonies, the Company may give permission, provided it will not compromise the security of our colonies.

New settlers will be accepted as islanders and will enjoy the rights and prerogatives of the category granted to them.

IV. *Company relations with neighboring foreign powers and their citizens.*

60. The trust which the government places in the Company by giving it the right to administer such extensive frontier lands imposes on the Company the obligation to avoid anything which might disrupt good relations with neighboring powers. In this regard the Company must strictly obey all decrees of foreign powers regarding the relations of their subjects with foreigners, and also all provisions of treaties with the Russian Court, especially those pertaining to relations with the Chinese Empire.

61. In all instances where the Company will have contact with a foreign government on matters transcending the authority of the colonial administration, the Company must submit the matter to the Minister of Finance beforehand, and through his mediation await the decision of higher authorities.

62. Special regulations have been drawn up to guide the Company in the colonies on how to handle foreign vessels which go there either through some unexplained chance, or in direct violation of the privileges granted to the Company by the Emperor. These regulations are entitled "Regulations Concerning the Limits of Navigation and Procedures for Maritime Relations Along the Coast of Eastern Siberia, Northwest America, the Aleutian and Kuril Islands."

GOVERNMENT SUPERVISION OF THE ACTIVITIES OF THE COMPANY

I. *Supervision by the Ministry of Finance.*

63. The Minister of Finance is empowered to supervise the activities of the Company regarding its obligations to the government.

64. For this reason he is to exercise vigilant supervision so the Company will not undertake any action contrary to the privileges and regulations regarding it. If a violation occurs, the Minister of Finance must immediately take appropriate measures to correct it.

65. From other ministries or offices or individual persons within his jurisdiction, the Minister of Finance will receive information about all events which may influence Company activity. He is to warn the Company and take appropriate measures to guarantee the Company necessary support and protection.

II. *Supervision of activities of Company servitors in Siberia and the colonies.*

66. Civil and military authorities who receive complaints of improper activity (excluding criminal acts) against Company offices presently established in Siberia, or offices which may in the future be established there, are to obtain from the implicated offices clear responses, with supporting evidence.

If on the basis of the evidence the administrator of the office is seen to be responsible for the problem, the authorities are to inform the Main Administration of the Company so legal processes may be begun. The authorities are also immediately to report such matters to the Minister of Finance.

67. The government does not consider it necessary at the present time to have its own official in the colonies in order to ascertain 1) whether the general decrees of the government pertaining to Russian subjects are being observed in all cases, and 2) whether any parts of the privileges and regulations are being violated. The government feels it is sufficient to entrust responsibility for this to the Chief Administrator of the colonies who is always to be chosen from among the naval officers. He is to be fully responsible to Supreme Government Authority and to the Company. To ensure this, the Chief Administrator of the Company will be selected and sent to the colonies only upon the approval of the Sovereign Emperor, from among the candidates submitted by the Main Administration of the Company. His term of office there is to be set at a maximum of five years, unless he wishes to spend more time in the colonies.

68. The government and the Main Administration of the Company must have reliable information on the following:

A. Are any of the Company's servitors being held in Company settlements by force?

B. Do Company servitors receive everything due them, in accordance with the terms of the agreement under which they serve?

C. Does the Company render them the assistance they are entitled to? Are they treated well?

D. Are native inhabitants, creoles and nondependent neighboring peoples treated as specified?

E. Do they carry on secret and unlawful relations with foreign ships or foreign powers? The government holds the Chief Administrator of the colonies responsible for strictly supervising these matters.

F. Finally, the Chief Administrator is not to participate in any trade whatsoever; he is to be limited to the salary established for him by the Company.

69. If commanding officers of naval vessels receive complaints of persecution from anyone, they must try to ascertain the facts and report to the Chief Administrator, who is to assemble evidence and prepare a report. The report will be taken to Supreme Government Authorities by the commanding officer of the ship. If the authorities do not find the report satisfactory, they will arrange for a review when the Chief Administrator returns to Russia; otherwise an official designated by the government and the Company will conduct the review and will be sent to the colonies by the next available transport.

70. A naval vessel which visits Company settlements and also straits where foreign merchant vessels are known to anchor and carry on illicit trade with native peoples, will winter over wherever instructed by Supreme Government Authorities; however if the Chief Administrator of the colonies wants the vessel to winter at a certain place in the colonies, the commanding officer of the vessel will have appropriate instructions regarding this.

Commanding officers of naval vessels are empowered to seize all foreign vessels they may encounter within the boundaries of Russian possessions. They will likewise reaffirm the existing naval regulations which strictly prohibit any such trade by naval personnel. The Chief Administrator of the colonies and those in charge of Company offices are responsible for ensuring that measures prescribed by the government are followed. If there is any violation the Chief Administrator is to lodge a formal complaint with the commanding officer of the vessel. If he does not receive a satisfactory response, he is to report to Supreme Government Authorities through the Main Administration of the Company.

Reference: *PSZ*, Vol. 37, No. 28,756; 842–854.

65

A DISPATCH FROM COUNT KARL R. NESSELRODE, MINISTER OF
STATE FOR FOREIGN AFFAIRS, TO PETR I. POLETICA, COUNSELOR
OF THE RUSSIAN DELEGATION AT WASHINGTON, REGARDING CON-
TRABAND TRADE ON THE NORTHWEST COAST OF AMERICA

Sir:
When the Privileges of the Russian American Company are
renewed, and the Regulations concerning its commercial operations are submitted for revision, the Government should
pay particular attention to complaints which have more than
once been occasioned by the activities of foreign smugglers and
adventurers along the Northwest Coast of America which belongs to Russia. It is recognized that these activities are aimed
not only at fraudulent trade in furs and other articles reserved
exclusively to the Russian American Company, but these
[smugglers and adventurers] often even seem to exhibit a hostile attitude: some of them, without permission, have furnished
arms and ammunition to natives in our possessions in America
and have used various means to arouse them to resist and revolt
against authorities established there.

It has therefore been necessary to use stern measures to
oppose these activities and to protect the Company against the
substantial losses which have resulted. It is in reference to this
that the attached regulation [the ukaz of 1821] has just been
published. The Imperial envoys are requested to bring it to the
attention of the governments to which they are accredited, and
to make clear to them the motives which have dictated it, in
accordance with the following explanations:

The new regulation in no way forbids foreign vessels from
navigating in the seas along the Russian possessions on the
coasts of Northwest America and Northeast Asia. A similar
prohibition, which would not have been difficult to carry out
with an adequate naval force, would actually have been the
most efficacious means of protecting the interests of the Russian American Company, based on incontestable rights. On
the one hand, to forbid foreign vessels once and for all from

navigating along the above mentioned shores would be to bring an end forever to the criminal activities which the regulation seeks to prevent. On the other hand, considering the Russian possessions which extend along the Northwest Coast of America from Bering Strait to 51° northern latitude, and along the opposite coast of Asia and the adjacent islands, from the same strait to almost 45°, it cannot be denied that the stretch of sea for which these possessions form the boundaries includes all the elements which the best known and best accredited publicists have attached to the definition of a "closed sea," and that consequently the Russian government would be perfectly within its rights to exercise its sovereignty over this sea, forbidding foreigners to approach it.

Nonetheless, however important the considerations which justify such a measure, however legitimate this measure might be, the Imperial government does not wish on this occasion to exercise a right which the most sacred titles of possession assure it, and which, moreover, irrefutable authorities confirm. On the contrary, it confines itself, as one has reason to realize through the newly published Regulation, to forbidding all foreign vessels from landing at Russian American Company establishments such as the Kamchatka Peninsula and the shores of the Sea of Okhotsk, and also, in general, from approaching within a distance of 100 Italian miles of such coasts.

Ships of the Imperial Navy have been dispatched to enforce this resolution. To us, this seems both legal and urgent. For if it has been shown that the Imperial government should have had the power, strictly speaking, to close completely to foreigners that part of the Pacific Ocean which borders our possessions in America and Asia, there is even greater reason that the right, in virtue of which it has just adopted a measure much less generally restrictive, must not be called into question. This right is, in effect, universally admitted. All maritime powers have used it to a greater or lesser degree in their colonial systems. Finally, the decision which the Imperial government has recently made in favor of the Russian American Company, will not endanger the interests of any nation, it being understood that there is no reason to suppose that aside from specific exceptions in our regulation, a foreign vessel can have real and legitimate reasons for putting into port at Russian establishments.

We now hope the powers to whom this new regulation will be communicated will recall the major considerations which have served as a foundation for it, and that through the series of peaceful and harmonious relations which exist between them and Russia, they will not hesitate to impose upon their respective subjects the duty of conforming strictly to this in order to prevent the inconveniences which contravention on their part would necessarily give rise to.

His Majesty the Emperor desires that His envoys obtain this result, in carrying out the communication which the present circular prescribes.

Be assured of my most estimable regard.

Nesselrode.

P.S. In preparing the instructions for officers commanding Russian ships of war, which have been instructed to patrol the Pacific Ocean to enforce these newly concluded decisions regarding Russian American Company establishments, the Imperial government supposes that a foreign vessel which would have sailed from one of the ports of Europe after the first of March 1822, or from one of the ports of the United States after the first of July of the same year, could not legally pretend ignorance of the new regulation. Our sailors have now received the order to regulate their conduct accordingly, in regard to the time reckoning from which they will carry out the above mentioned orders.

We believe we must communicate these additional thoughts to the Imperial envoys, and instruct them to bring them likewise to the attention of the governments to whom they are accredited, in order to complete the information enclosed with today's circular.

Ut in litteris.
Nesselrode.

Reference: J. Franklin Jameson, ed. "Documents. Correspondence of Russian Ministers in Washington, 1818–1825, I." in *American Historical Review*, Vol. 17 (January 1913), No. 2 . 329–331. Original in French.

66

NOVEMBER 30, 1823–JANUARY 12, 1824

FROM THE JOURNAL OF ANDREI P. LAZAREV, CAPTAIN-LIEUTENANT
OF THE SLOOP *LADOGA*, DESCRIBING CONDITIONS IN CALIFORNIA
IN THE REGION OF THE PRESIDIO OF SAN FRANCISCO

On November 30 [1823] in the morning we sighted the shores of California. By our calculations we were 35 miles distant. At noon, taking a bearing on the western island of the Farallon group, and according to the known latitude, we were some 42 miles from the entrance to the port of San Francisco, although our chronometers when last verified 35 days previously, showed it 13 miles farther west than on the map. (On the Arrowsmith map this coast is located according to the determination made by Captain [George] Vancouver.)

Gradually decreasing wind delayed our entrance into the port; at 11:30 P.M., because of a lack of wind and a contrary current we anchored at a sand bank some miles from port. The depth there varied between seven and four sazhens, with a bottom of sand. The tumultuous currents in many places are alarming to a navigator who has not experienced them, and the strong current caused by the heavy tides directly off the entry to the bay stretches for six and a half knots and demands careful attention in handling the rudder.

The next day, December 1, we sighted the frigate *Kreiser*, which was standing at anchor, having arrived just a few hours before we did. At 2:00 P.M. on the change of the tide we cast off anchor and began to tack into port. Somewhat after 6:00 P.M. we passed the fort on our right beam, and without delay dropped anchor in 5 sazhens. The fort was WSW⅓W, at a distance of 1½ miles. On this roadstead we encountered the sloop *Apollo* which had come in from the port of New Arkhangel for repairs, and the brig *Golovnin*, which had been sent down to purchase wheat for the Russian American Company.

The entry into the San Francisco roadstead is about 2½ miles wide, and there are rocks along the shore on both sides. When entering it is best to hold to the northern shore and anchor about a mile from the southern shore, just short of a building of which just the roof is visible from the roadstead. I do not advise sailing any closer to shore because it is rocky at low tide. The bottom is generally quite good, but the current is difficult at times because of the swift thrust of water against the cable.

Three shots were fired from the fort, which was flying a flag completely new to us (the red, white and green flag of the new Mexican Empire: on the white stripe there is a single-headed eagle perched on a rock in the middle of a lake, and the eagle is devouring a snake); this signaled a great celebration among the local people in honor of Our Lady of Guadaloupe, the patron saint of the entire region. This feast day is celebrated with a great pilgrimage. The civil dating in this place is one day later than ours because we reached it sailing east, while the Spaniards who settled here were sailing west.

On the next day of our stay, after the sloop was moored, we saluted the fort with a seven-gun salute, and they responded with the same. Toward evening we put up tents on shore and built a place to verify our chronometers. The next day we set to work. We began by mending the sails, preparing casks for water and repairing many pieces of iron equipment and tackle. The thought of returning to our beloved Fatherland spurred us on. The clear warm weather which prevails here at this time of year was very favorable. We needed considerable amounts of fresh water and firewood, but these were only obtainable at some distance from us, and the swift currents hindered us. Group effort overcame this problem, however, and in 40 days we were ready to depart, but were delayed for another two days by a wind from the southwest.

On the southern shore there was a square with dirty, tumble-down structures. In one of these live the Commandant of the fort and the Administrator of this place, which for this reason is called the Presidio of San Francisco. There are about 25 ragged soldiers who have not received any government pay for a long time; they comprise the garrison and entire force protecting this coast.

The mission of San Francisco is seven versts from the Presidio, and there are few other such missions within an area of some 100 versts circumference. Priests administer these missions, which house savage nomadic Indians who have been

371

William Smythe recorded the vaqueros near the San Francisco mission in 1831. Lazarev reported lassoes were also used to capture Indians, who were then taken to the missions to be forcibly instructed in religion. Beechey, *Voyage to the Pacific*. (OHS OrHi neg. 82030)

captured with lassoes, and who, without any preliminary explanation of religious dogma or even the slightest instruction in language, are forced against their will to accept the Catholic faith. The harsh treatment they receive at the hands of these fathers, which is reinforced by a number of soldiers, forces them to attend church services on holidays; they understand nothing of religious teachings, or even of the Mass itself, and only with their eyes can they follow the outward manifestations of ceremonies they are unwillingly required to imitate. They have no relaxation, for the rest of the time they work the land and serve the selfish wishes of these overseers, who grow fat through laziness and sated through greed. After a few years, under the guise of illness, the clergy leave here with enough piasters to lead a quiet life in their homeland. Not only do they not attempt to spread Christianity among the various tribes of these people, they do not try to teach the responsibilities of citizens even to those who become accustomed to their way of life. The long-term presence on this coast by the Spanish has taught some of the American natives to understand the Spanish language and to serve as instruments to carry out the wishes of their mentors. Toward that end the priests have several bodyguards or followers called *bakers* [vaqueros].

The church and dwelling adjacent, where the church servitors live, are made of whitened stone and comprise the main structures of every mission. Sheds made of unbaked brick without windows, floors or ceilings occupy most of the square and serve as living quarters for the oppressed American natives, who by nature are weak-minded. The dirt and dreadful stench in these sheds are extraordinary and probably are the primary cause of the premature deaths of those who inhabit these dwellings. The staple of their diet is maize, peas, beans, and on holidays, meat (of which there is no shortage because of the propagation of wild cattle), issued in frugal amounts from the communal kitchen. They make their own outer garments from the wool of sheep, and this is the extent of their scanty clothing.

The environs of this place are quite varied and pleasant. Two fresh water lakes filled with wild ducks and sea birds often attracted us for outings and provided delicious food. The moderate temperature, clear weather and multitude of various wild birds, of which the partridge are the most beautiful and flavorful, lured our hunters for considerable distances. Weariness often forced us to turn to the nearest mission, to which the road was easily recognized by cattle skulls and bones and whole carcasses of horses, scattered about everywhere. The terrible smell from these, and the flocks of jackdaws, seagulls and various kites which devour this carrion usually signalled the proximity of a settlement. I think this region is obliged to these feathered creatures for being the only protection against contagious and epidemic diseases.

More than once I took part in outings and in hunting. I sometimes visited a mission and was always grateful for the hospitality of the priests. Food, wine and fresh milk were willingly offered to travelers, and in spite of the reserve of the missionaries, our conversations on those occasions gave us a better understanding of the locale. I feel it is germane here to make some mention of the mission of San Francisco, because it was built on the coast before the others. This place is a most convenient anchorage for our ships on their return voyage from New Arkhangel to Russia. Two priests, José and Tomas, ran the mission. Before our arrival they had separated; José, a zealous proselytizer, received permission to establish a new post. This mission was established in 1777. It is almost completely surrounded by water, and during high tide the water sweeps in from the west so high that at mid-tide our long boat could easily come up to the mission.

The land belonging to the mission of San Francisco is about nine miles in circumference. Although that land is not everywhere equally suitable for farming, it produces enough to feed 6,000 men. In addition there is extensive pasture land. Unfortunately these places are not watered by rivers, and consequently the inhabitants do not have good drinking water; they dig wells but only get dirty water with a bad taste.

Based on information I gathered, the population of the mission of San Francisco is 958: 490 adult male Indians, 286 women and 182 children of both sexes. There are 4,049 head of cattle, 8,830 sheep and 820 horses.

I am including a table of the various grains planted and harvested in 1823.

GRAIN	AMOUNT PLANTED	AMOUNT HARVESTED
Wheat	300 *fanegas* [1.5 bushels]	2,800 fanegas
Barley	20	386
Peas	4	100
Beans	4	103
Kidney beans	5	110
Maize	5	600

While I do not dispute the information I received about the harvest of grain, nor do I question the stewardship and ability of the local farmers, I do reserve the right to make several observations here. I often had an opportunity to visit the mission of San Francisco and hear Mass on holidays. The church is quite well decorated, and on those days it is filled with local Indians. Judging by their numbers, one must accept the large number as shown above for population. The harvest of grain as shown in the table, however, is unusual because the land is poorly cultivated and immense flocks of birds nest in the fields from planting time until harvest, and the spikes of grain are threshed by horses hooves. All this gives reason to doubt such

Voznesenskii portrayed Don Garcia, a Spanish rancho owner, in vaquero garb in 1841. Institute of Ethnography, AN SSSR, Leningrad. (OHS neg. 26992)

[claims of] great fertility, which [if true] would in a few years fill all the warehouses; during our stay there were only small reserves in the warehouse. The sale of grain is insignificant, in spite of the fact that not long ago it was exported to Lima because internal problems there caused a total failure of the crop; they also make an annual shipment to the New Arkhangel region. These conditions cannot relate only to the mission of San Francisco and its extensive environs, because both shipments came mostly from missions near Monterey and other coastal places. The Indians, except for the priests, have not developed a taste for wheat.

The large number of horses gave us no small pleasure and benefit. All the officers and I, and even the lower ranks who went ashore on holidays, hired horses very inexpensively and galloped off for fifteen versts without fearing the dire consequences of not knowing how to ride, for the stirrups and saddles were so well made that even the worst rider could hardly fall off, and the horses have such strong legs they never stumble. Their natural caution when descending hills and avoiding dangerous places always justified our daring, so no one could complain of unpleasant consequences.

There was another equally entertaining spectacle. Every two or three days they would give us several head of cattle to be used for food. The cattle were lassoed and were generally fastened by their horns to much stronger domestic cattle. With considerable effort they were brought in and herded by mounted vaqueros to our tents. Here the domestic steer was forced down with its horns on the ground, which compelled its companion to do the same. This gave the man with them time to put a rope around the hind legs of the wild animal and force it to the ground. Then they untied the domestic animal and to the horns of the wild one they attached a wooden plank about five sazhens long, with an eight- or ten-pud weight and then freed its legs.

It is amazing that such a powerful beast, in a furious rage, could never rid itself of such a relatively insignificant burden, even when it hurled itself savagely at people who approached. When this wild prisoner tired, our sailors amused themselves by throwing lassoes at it and tying its legs, then threw it on the ground and killed it. This ended the Spaniard's favorite spectacle.

After the overthrow of the legal government in Mexico, the people elected their man Don Augustin Iturbide as Emperor. He had previously been a general in the Spanish army. At the beginning of his administration he was called Augostino Primo. Later, by the will of the same elected authority, he was deposed; however, he managed to make off with a great haul of

Soldado de Monterey

Drawing of a soldier on duty in Monterey, made by Jose Cardero during the Malaspina Expedition (1791–92). (Private collection)

treasures augmenting his imperial title to Augostino Ultimo. The government was then transferred to a junta authority, but because it was weak and suffered internal disorder, now every region seeks independence.

During our stay in Monterey at the headquarters of the

Governor of Upper California a junta was convened by popular will. It consisted of local missionaries and several retired old Spaniards who had settled in the region. They decided to sever all their connections and establish this part of California as a region independent of all others which had previously comprised such an extensive and rich possession of Spain.

At the present time California is administered in accordance with earlier laws and Don Luis Arguello, an army captain and Provisional Governor of this country, has claimed the right of self-government, along with the clergy.

During our stay at the port of San Francisco the brig *Golovnin* took on wheat in exchange for trade goods and set out for Santa Cruz where she was to take on the rest of her cargo. [Kyrill T.] Khlebnikov, prikashchik of the New Arkhangel office, recognized the opportunity for taking an entire cargo of wheat aboard the brig *Riurik*, and operating on the instructions of the Chief Administrator of the colony, [Matvei] Muravev, he sent the brig *Golovnin* to the Hawaiian Islands to purchase rum, sugar and other items which our colony needed very much. Khlebnikov came to San Francisco aboard *Riurik*. [Adolph] Etolin, commanding officer of *Golovnin*, was instructed to make the purchase on the basis of previous years, through an exchange of fur seal pelts for goods from ships from the United States which presently anchor with various goods in those islands. According to regulations approved by the Emperor [Alexander I], naval cruisers are sent out to our colonies on the Northwest Coast of America every year and merchant vessels from the United States have almost entirely halted their trade with the Kolosh [Tlingits]. Instead, they go to the Hawaiian Islands where they have expressed the desire to exchange their goods for fur seal pelts brought there by ships from the [Russian] American Company. In fact there have even been proposals to sell their ships [to the Russians].

The usual price for a fur seal pelt is 1¾ Spanish piasters. This is presently the main item of trade of the Company. Sea otter trade is very slight, so in order to make a profit for the Company Khlebnikov made use of the troubled conditions in the government of California and managed to conclude an agreement with the Governor which permits us to hunt sea otters in San Francisco Bay. For that purpose 25 baidaras were dispatched from the Ross settlement, with Aleut hunting parties who moved about the bay in search of sea otters. At the end of an established period of time they divided the catch in half. During the two months Khlebnikov was there they managed to take about 300 sea otters, of which half were turned over to a schooner sent by the Governor under an American flag; the pelts were to be sold in Canton. It is worthy of note that sea otters, and the schooner itself, belong to the present administrator of California. This coincidence is in accord with the maxim, "Catch fish in roiled waters."

The port of San Francisco is the only place in this region where the weary mariner can seek repose after a prolonged stay along the Northwest Coast of America. In addition to the fact that it provides protection from the winds and a calm anchorage, for the most part the clear weather provides an opportunity to make necessary repairs to ships for new voyages. The abundance of livestock, fresh bread, and the complete freedom for the crew on shore, restores their earlier enthusiasm, and a sailor again puts out into that vast ocean with complete readiness to overcome new difficulties.

During the entire period of our stay here, in accordance with our arrangement with the commanding officer, Don Ignacio Martinez, we received plenty of fresh meat, paying four piasters for a nine-pud wild steer; we bought wheat from the priests for three piasters per fanega. We baked delicious healthful bread in ovens which we set up on shore, thanks to the thoughtfulness of Captain [Mikhail N.] Vasilev, leader of the expedition sent to Bering Strait, who was here in 1820, and also thanks to Lieutenant [Stepan P.] Khrushchev, commanding officer of the sloop *Apollon*.

The only thing a visiting seafarer might wish is that the missionaries would stop being so lackadaisical about breeding domestic fowl. There is such a shortage it is difficult to obtain fowl from the priests. One might also wish that they would set an example for the settlers to produce garden vegetables, because in spite of the ideal growing conditions they still have no vegetables but pumpkins.

It is quite appropriate here to refer to the remarks of Ogievskii concerning the vegetation, temperature, animals and minerals [of California]:

379

"The environs of the port of San Francisco consist of moderately high hills and mountains which terminate in lovely slopes interspersed with picturesque valleys cut by small streams and clear little lakes. Insignificant trees and shrubs cover the slopes, while the valleys have various grasses.

"There is no lumber suitable for building near the port except for *chag* [Sitka spruce] which in girth exceeds even our century-old pines, but is very soft and weak. There is only one shrub worthy of mention; in size and appearance it resembles the *kalina* [white hazel]. It grows in great abundance and causes an unusual reaction: when one carelessly touches it, one suffers unbearable itching, pain and swelling in whatever part of the body comes in contact with it, and also parts nearby. The natives treat this nuisance by making a poultice of cows milk and white bread or maize flour. Russian physicians who treated the many cases our sailors suffered found that a lotion of lead is very helpful, but even better is a preparation made of boiled linseed and other oils. The symptoms last two or three weeks. The Spaniards call this shrub the hydra. It had no leaves while we were there, so we could not obtain information about all its parts [probably poison oak].

"From November on, when the sun departs for the southern hemisphere, the temperature here changes. The nights are cold but never below 0° on the Réaumur thermometer. Small vegetation dries up, and the more tender trees and shrubs drop their leaves; however, this is caused not so much by cold weather as by lack of rain, which does not begin again until the sun returns at the end of December. By early January one can see flowering currant and field violets. Such is winter here! Ungrateful native inhabitants complain of its severity, but the Russian sailors considered this the most pleasant time. However, the Spaniards who live here do not have heating stoves or fireplaces in their dwellings, and glazed windows are found only in the living quarters of monks and military officials.

"In addition to large livestock and horses, there are abundant range and mountain sheep. Pigs are very rare. In the category of wild animals there are many bears, wolves, wolverines, foxes, wildcats and others. Among reptiles, lizards and various snakes are known to exist here. One cannot say anything about fish, because the abundance of excellent meat from the livestock gives the lazy inhabitants little incentive to fish.

"There has been little prospecting for minerals. It is only known that the mountains of California, especially around Monterey and Santa Cruz, abound in silver ore. Mining began in those regions in 1820. The Spaniards, however, considered this unprofitable and abandoned the operation. Near the port of San Francisco one finds varieties of serpentine, asbestos, colored sandstones, jasper, horneblend and others."

On December 31 the crew were excused from all work and had permission to visit other vessels. Countrymen and friends separated for a long time by service met and had friendly chats about events that had taken place, and in the evening the convivial ones formed a carousel and their games and singing enlivened the festivity.

Midnight January 1 witnessed the moving parting from these good sons of the Fatherland. On the morning of January 1, 1824, we fervently offered thanks to God for saving us from past dangers at sea, and prayed for His blessing and protection and for success in the future in carrying out the desires of our Great Monarch. We pressed on to hasten the moment when we would return to our beloved Fatherland.

By January 10, 1824 we were completely ready to depart. We brought out tents from shore, and after collecting all our provisions onto the sloop we waited only for a favorable opportunity to proceed under sail, leaving behind as testimony to our stay there a sad memorial to midshipman Tulubev who died there last year; he had served aboard the sloop *Apollon*. A fellow servitor and friend of the dead man, Lieutenant Kiukhelbeker, took on the responsibility of erecting a square pyramid-shaped [monument] on a high hill opposite our ships; he enclosed it with a very nice fence.

Clear weather gave us a chance to verify Chronometer No. 991, which on January 11, the last day of observations, was behind by 5° 46, 40″ 23 [sic], meridian San Francisco, and was daily behind 22′19 according to the longitude observations in the Norey tables of 237° 57′30″ East. It differed from the Arrowsmith map by 7 minutes to the West.

At 8:00 on the 12th of January a northwest wind ended our

wait and the two sloops, *Ladoga* and *Apollon*, raised anchor and began to tack out of the bay. Our former companions came to bid us farewell. Rejoicing in our forthcoming return to our Fatherland, we tried to project our readiness for new assignments, while [those remaining behind] made much of the difficulties which lay ahead. The argument was not prolonged, however, for the obligation and zeal for service immediately pacified us and we parted with mutual wishes for success.

Upon our departure from the port of San Francisco I was required, because our cannon was small caliber, to change some of our nighttime signals. I instructed Lieutenant Khrushchev, commanding *Apollon*, that in case he suddenly became separated from me he was to bring his ship into the wind and cruise for two days on short tacks in the area where he had last sighted our signal.

Reference: Andrei P. Lazarev. *Plavanie vokrug sveta na shliupe "Ladoga" v 1822, 1823 i 1824 godakh*. (St. Petersburg: 1832), 117–199.

67

APRIL 5, 1824

THE RUSSO-AMERICAN CONVENTION CONCERNING THE PACIFIC OCEAN AND NORTHWEST COAST OF AMERICA

In the name of the Most Holy and Indivisible Trinity.

The President of the United States of America [James Monroe] and His Majesty the Emperor of all the Russias [Alexander I], wishing to cement the bonds of amity which unite them, and to secure between them the unvarying maintenance of perfect concord, by means of the present convention have named as their Plenipotentiaries to this effect, to wit:

The President of the United States of America, [names] Henry Middleton, a citizen of said States, and their Envoy Extraordinary and Minister Plenipotentiary to His Imperial Majesty; and His Majesty the Emperor of all the Russias, his beloved and faithful Charles Robert, Count of Nesselrode, Actual Privy Councillor, Member of the Council of State, Secretary of State directing the administration of Foreign Affairs, Actual Chamberlain, Knight of the Order of St. Alexander Nevskii, Grand Cross of the Order of St. Vladimir, First Class, Knight of the White Eagle of Poland, Grand Cross of the Order of Saint Stephen of Hungary, Knight of the Orders of the Holy Ghost and St. Michael, and Grand Cross of the Legion of Honor of France, Knight Grand Cross of the Orders of the Black and of the Red Eagle of Prussia, of the Annunciation of Sardinia, of Charles III of Spain, of St. Ferdinand and of Merit of Naples, of the Elephant of Denmark, of the Polar Star of Sweden, of the Crown of Württemberg, of the Guelphs of Hanover, of the Belgic Lion of Fidelity of Baden, and of St. Constantine of Parma; and Pierre de Poletica, Actual Councillor of State, Knight of the Order of St. Anne of the First Class, and Grand Cross of the Order of St. Vladimir of the second;

Who, after having exchanged their full powers, found in good and due form have agreed upon and signed the following stipulations:

ARTICLE I.

It is agreed that, in any part of the Great Ocean, commonly called the Pacific Ocean or South Sea, the respective citizens or subjects of the high contracting Powers shall be neither disturbed or restrained, either in navigation or in fishing, or in the power of resorting to the coasts, upon points which may not have already been occupied, for the purpose of trading with the natives, saving always the restrictions and conditions determined by the following articles.

ARTICLE II.

With a view of preventing the rights of navigation and of fishing exercised upon the Great Ocean by the citizens and subjects of the high contracting Powers from becoming the pretext for an illicit trade, it is agreed that the citizens of the United States shall not resort to any point where there is a Russian establishment, without the permission of the governor or the commander; and that, reciprocally, the subjects of Russia shall not resort, without permission, to any establishment of the United States upon the Northwest Coast.

ARTICLE III.

It is moreover agreed that hereafter there shall not be formed by the citizens of the United States, or under the authority of the said States, any establishment upon the Northwest coast of America, nor in any of the islands adjacent, to the north of fifty-four degrees and forty minutes of north latitude; and that, in the same manner, there shall be none formed by Russian subjects, or under the authority of Russia, south of the same parallel.

ARTICLE IV.

It is, nevertheless, understood that during a term of ten years, counting from the signature of the present convention, the ships of both Powers, or those which belong to their citizens or subjects respectively, may reciprocally frequent, without any hindrance whatever, the interior seas, gulfs, harbors, and creeks, upon the coast mentioned in the preceding article, for the purpose of fishing and trading with the natives of the country.

ARTICLE V.

All spirituous liquors, firearms, other arms, powder and munitions of war of every kind, are always excepted from this same commerce permitted by the preceding article; and the two Powers engage, reciprocally, neither to sell, nor suffer them to be sold, to the natives by their respective citizens and subjects, nor by any person who may be under their authority. It is likewise stipulated that this restriction shall never afford a pretext, nor be advanced, in any case, to authorize either search or detention of the vessels, seizure of the merchandise, in fine, any measures of constraint whatever toward the merchants or the crews who may carry on this commerce; the high contracting Powers reciprocally reserving to themselves to determine upon the penalties to be incurred, and to inflict the punishments in case of the contravention of this article by their respective citizens or subjects.

ARTICLE VI.

When this convention shall have been duly ratified by the President of the United States, with the advice and consent of the Senate, on the one part, and on the other, by His Majesty the Emperor of all the Russias, the ratifications shall be exchanged at Washington in the space of ten months from the date below, or sooner if possible.

In faith whereof the respective Plenipotentiaries have signed this convention and thereto affixed the seals of their arms.

Done at St. Petersburg the 5/17 of April, of the year of Grace one thousand eight hundred and twenty-four.

Henry Middleton
Le Comte Charles de Nesselrode
Pierre de Poletica

Reference: William M. Mallory, comp. *Treaties, Conventions, International Acts, Protocols and Agreements between the United States of America and Other Powers, 1776–1909*. Vol. 2, (Washington, D.C.: 1910), 1512–1514. Spelling slightly modified.

68

1829

FROM NOTES ON CALIFORNIA BY KYRILL T. KHLEBNIKOV, MANAGER OF THE NEW ARKHANGEL OFFICE OF THE RUSSIAN AMERICAN COMPANY

California is a province of Mexico. It is divided into two parts, Lower and Upper, or Old and New. . . . Old California was discovered by Cortez in 1536, and New California was discovered by the end of the sixteenth century. Admiral Biskaiko [*sic*, Sebastian Vizcaino] described the coast and bay, and named it Monterey after the then Mexican Viceroy. The Jesuit [Eusebio] Kino crossed this territory in 1634 and found that Old California is a peninsula. In 1769 two ships were dispatched from Mexico to build forts.

Both regions comprising California border on the north with the Russian settlement of Ross in 38° 30′ northern latitude, on the east with Indian settlements and the Colorado River, and on the south and west with the Pacific Ocean.

In Old California there is one fort, Loreto, on the east coast of the peninsula. In New California four fortresses or presidios have been built and are administered by commanders. They house infantry garrisons and some cavalry. These presidios are:

San Francisco; in 37° 48′ northern latitude, founded in 1776
Monterey; in 36° 48′ northern latitude, founded in 1770
Santa Barbara; in 34° 22′ northern latitude, founded in 1786
San Diego; in 32° 39′ northern latitude, founded in 1770.

Monterey was previously the main town of both Californias and the headquarters of the Governor. However, in 1825 when a Mexican administrator for both regions was appointed, he established his headquarters in San Diego for greater convenience in administration.

There is still an artillery command in Monterey, and a commissar for both regions.

The term mission here refers to an institution whose purpose is to convert Indians to the Christian faith. These institutions were initially founded by the Jesuits, but later taken over by other monastic orders. It must be noted that they did not always use force to convert the savages. Many of the Indians came to the missions voluntarily, sometimes to visit relatives, sometimes because of famine, and they remained and accepted Christianity. The missions in New California are under the administration of the Franciscan monks, and in Old California, the Dominicans. The former are headed by a Padre, a President and Padre Prefects. Below is a list of all the missions in New California, with their divisions, and the approximate number of Indians living in each.

In New California

REGION	MISSION	NUMBER OF INDIANS
Presidio of San Francisco	1. San Francisco Solano	600
	2. San Rafael	1,000
	3. San Francisco	400
	4. Santa Clara	1,400
	5. San José	1,700
	6. Santa Cruz	500
Presidio of Monterey	7. San Juan Bautisto	1,100
	8. San Carlos of Monterey	370
	9. La Soledad	500
	10. San Antonio	500
	11. San Miguel	500
	12. San Luis Obispo	400
	13. La Purissima	500
	14. San Inez	400
	15. Santa Barbara	500
	16. San Fernando	600
	17. San Gabriel	1,000
	18. San Juan Capistrano	800

19. San Luis Rey	2,800
20. San Diego	1,750

NOTE: The number of Indians in many of these missions is not exact, only an approximation. The compiler, as a foreigner, could not personally verify the information furnished him by the Spanish missionaries.

In Old California

MISSIONS

1. San Miguel	8. Santa Gertruda
2. San Tomas	9. San Ignacio
3. Santa Catalina	10. La Purissima
4. San Vicentio	11. San José
5. Santa Rosalia	12. El Rosario
6. San Fernando	13. San Francisco Xavier
7. San Francisco de Borgia	14. Loreto

NOTE: To the south, at Cabo San Lucas, there are the following missions:
15. San José de San Lucas
16. San Domingo
17. Todos Santos.

NOTE: The missions in Old California have very few Indians, and some of them have been completely abandoned . . . .

Padre Filip Arroyo has been at the mission of San Juan Bautisto for the past eighteen years. He has learned two of the Indian dialects very well and has written a grammar. He explains the Christian dogma to the Indians in their own language, and for that reason has gained their special respect and affection.

After the overthrow of the temporary emperor, Augustin de Iturbide, the new republic demanded that the monks swear allegiance to the Constitution, but the Padre President and the Padre Prefect refused, and most of the monks followed their example. In 1825 the Governor of California reported this to the Mexican Government, and it has now been decreed to desist from this practice, but to deport the Padre President. There is a rumor that the Government intends to replace the monks of the Franciscan order with white [secular] clergy in all the missions. Because of this the monks have neither the incentive nor the inclination to draw in the savage natives. All of them are most desirous of leaving for Europe or Manila.

Many missionaries had substantial amounts of hard cash in their possession, but since the Government has used various pretexts to demand the money from them, they have had to hand it over. Now they have decided not to keep any cash at all in the missions, but to keep gold bullion so that if they leave it will be easier for them to conceal it on their persons. In 1825 two monks left California aboard whaling vessels bound for Europe.

There are somewhere between 500 and 3,000 Indians of both sexes at these missions. . . .

The mission buildings are all similar, built in the form of an enclosed rectangle. In some of the missions all the structures are of brick, and in others of unbaked brick held together with clay. In still others the buildings are made of stone suitable for construction. The church and a large number of related rooms are under one roof. There is neither floor nor ceiling. In the better rooms the ground is covered with brick, or very rarely with wood.

In addition to living quarters, there are storehouses near all these buildings; these are for the purpose of storing grain and other supplies. All the buildings are generally roofed with tiles and are whitewashed both inside and out. There are from two to six soldiers at each mission, and the most trustworthy is given the title of Major Domo; under the jurisdiction of the Padre, he gives orders to the Indians and is in charge of the livestock and of all supplies.

The Major Domo receives as much as twelve piasters per month from the mission as salary, along with two head of cattle, some lard and grain. The rules of the Franciscan order prohibit monks from accumulating wealth, especially gold and silver. . . .

Each mission has gardens and fruit trees which are suitable for the climate. The trees are planted in precise order and the gardens are irrigated. Many of the orchards, such as those in Santa Cruz, Santa Barbara and San Gabriel, are kept in splendid condition.

Previously the Indians received very poor maintenance, but after the declaration of independence it was necessary to reorganize the administration of the Indians and [improve] their maintenance. At the present time each mission provides the Indians daily rations of frijoles, maize, barley and dried meat; on feast days there is fresh beef, wheat, lard and fruits.

Indians who are married and have families live in dwellings or grass huts near the mission. Unmarried adults live in common quarters, men separated from women. Every evening the room or shed for the women is locked and reopened the next morning.

They have also ended the practice of capturing free Indians. In fact, they are freeing elderly Indians. But since these have become unaccustomed to nomadic life, they rarely return to their tribal lands. The government plans to make them citizens and settle them throughout California will probably not come to pass, or if they do, not for a long time.

Those who have been set free from the missions by order of the Governor, as well as those who live in the presidios, are not forced to work, are quite unwilling to work, and live by thievery. Generally speaking, all the Indians who live in the missions have been converted to Catholicism. The missionaries have trained some of them to be musicians, and although there may not be any great virtuosos among them, almost all instruments are used. The better missions have organized workshops; although these are not perfect, they fulfill the needs of the mission.

All the officials feel the mission of San Luis Rey is the best in all California. They credit the missionary there with having all the most commendable qualities and feel he is the most enlightened and active of all the brothers.

It is worthy of mention that if it were not for the introduction of additional Indians, the mission population would decrease by reason of disease, for although women have eight to ten children, most of them die in infancy. We are told that many women deliberately abort the fetus.

Venereal disease has spread to a great extent all through

California. Padre Filip Aroyo maintained it is transmitted from savage Indians who live in the interior. . . .

The four presidios previously mentioned have as settlers military personnel, both active and retired. Monterey, the most populous, has at most 700 persons; others have fewer.

In 1826 the Monterey military garrison consisted of 70 men of which 30 were infantry and about 25 artillery; there were thought to be some 400 women.

In addition to these establishments in New California, there are three more settlements where retired [military] persons live, as well as those who have never been in service who are descended from the first settlers of California or who have moved from various regions of Mexico. One such region is the Pueblo of San José, near the mission of San José in the vicinity of the port of San Francisco. A second is a small settlement, the Villa de Branforte, near the mission of Santa Cruz; a third is the Pueblo de los Angelos, not far from the mission of San Gabriel located near the bay of San Pedro. This last settlement is very populous with more than 1,000 persons of both sexes. It is located on a plain about two miles from a mountain range, and some twenty miles from the sea. They claim the the climate in this area is the best in all California; since it is some distance from the sea, there are no more than five or six days a year when it is foggy. These settlements are administered by alcaldes, selected from among the older citizens, who decide all minor matters. Criminals are transferred to presidios where deputies and fort commandants pass judgment; the Governor then confirms those decisions.

During the past ten or fifteen years when foreign vessels have begun to put in at California, first for contraband trade and later for legitimate reasons, several sailors from various European nations and several negroes have deserted from these ships. All have settled at missions or in other establishments. Some have accepted the Catholic faith, have married, engage in farming or livestock breeding, and live better than native Californians; but those who are lazy and vagrant barely manage to make a living.

A few Russians have also fled from our settlement of Ross, both in the early days and later; but none of these has remained in California; they all left, some to go to Mexico, and others on various merchant vessels bound for Europe or the United States of America. . . .

Farther back from the coast there are lovely valleys with exceptionally rich chernozem soil which abound in fertile pasture land. One such valley is near the missions of Santa Clara and San José; there is a large one near the mission of San Juan Bautisto; and there are many between the missions of San Gabriel and San Diego. The hills, foothills and areas close to the sea are sandy and not cultivated. Grass grows on some of them, however and provides pasturage for livestock. The mountain peaks are rocky and unproductive, but compared to the advantages of the area, this is unimportant. The location of the mission of Santa Clara in a broad valley is very interesting. . . .

PRODUCTS

The northern part of California, that is, the area around San Francisco and Monterey, has a considerable amount of forest land in which the most important trees are oak, pine, alder, laurel and spruce. There are also all manner of shrubs such as rose willow, hazel and a variety of small brush willow called poison willow [poison oak]. It grows in vast stretches along the shore of San Francisco Bay and in Monterey. There is a poisonous reaction if one touches the sap or the leaves, or even smells it. Whatever part of the body touches it becomes swollen, the swelling spreads all over the body, but subsides after two or three months. There are no forests near the sea in the south, except in distant mountainous areas. . . .

In April and May all the grasses are in bloom and the valleys have a perfumed aroma. In June and July vegetation dies back and the land is devoid of charm. Fruits are abundant all through New California. There are apples of various kinds, pears, peaches and figs native to the entire country; and in the southern part, from Santa Barbara on to the south, grapes, lemons, oranges, bitter oranges, pomegranates, citrons and bananas grow in abundance. Orchards are abloom with shrub roses, carnations and stock; there are many medicinal herbs and garden vegetables such as squash, watermelons, pumpkins, garlic, onions, potatoes, various cabbages and salad greens. But this produce is only seen near the missions.

They grow the following grains: wheat, barley, peas, beans, frijoles, garbanzos, lentils and maize. There are productive valleys in all regions. A good harvest of wheat will yield 60 to 70 times the amount planted. There are reports of one fanega yielding a harvest of more than 100 fanegas. But years of such abundant harvest do not often happen. Sometimes winter rain-caused floods prevent it, or drought, or fog. In such cases the harvest is only ten- to fifteen-fold, and there are even times when they harvest barely as much as they plant. They consider a harvest good if it produces 20, 25 or 30 times the amount planted. In 1823 the mission of San Diego planted about 400 fanegas of grain and harvested 11,000 fanegas of wheat and 4,000 of barley. But the next four years were not productive. In 1826 the mission of San Luis Rey planted 1,000 fanegas and harvested only 700. That year rust spoiled all the grains. Maize yields 300, 400 or 500 measures for each one planted, and comprises the main item of food for the inhabitants. . . .

Of all the fruits, grapes produce the most significant benefits. Each mission from Santa Barbara to San Diego produces some 100 casks of brandy and wine, and in the Pueblo de Los Angelos, in a good year they will distill up to 150 casks of a spirit similar to Russian fortified wine, which is very detrimental to one's health.

They produce both red and white wine; it is sometimes quite good, especially in the mission of San Luis Rey, but usually is of low quality. A cask of spirits sells at the site for 40 to 50 piasters. Wine sells for 15 to 20 piasters. Foreign vessels buy apples and other fruits at two piasters per *arob* [about 25 pounds]; onions sell for three piasters per arob. In the southern missions they salt olives and sell them for eighteen to twenty piasters per cask. The mission of San Diego produces a good deal of fine quality cotton. Some missions raise flax and hemp, but not on a regular basis.

POPULATION

The population of the four presidios and three villages consists of descendants of the early Spanish settlers in Upper California, and military personnel and civilians who later moved there from various provinces of Mexico. In all there are no more than 2,000 men or about 4,500 of both sexes. There are no more than 50 European men, even including the monks. In all the missions of Uppers California there are about 20,000 Indians of both sexes. There are about 100 foreigners, English, Americans, negroes and others. The population of the entire province does not exceed 25,000, which number does not include the independent Indians who are quite populous in the interior of California.

California women are amazingly fertile; almost every household has at least ten children, and many have fifteen or eighteen. There are various opinions about their faithfulness, and in fact they even related the following anecdote.

In San Francisco a certain foreigner visited the home of a well known resident who had a large family. Looking at the children, the foreigner inquired with amazement how it happened that some children had blonde hair, others red, brown, or black. "There is no need to be surprised," the father of the family responded in a matter-of-fact manner, "for you know that this is a port, and vessels of various nations anchor here, and our home has been visited by Englishmen, Americans, Russians and Frenchmen." The mother, who was present, covered her head with her shawl at that moment. But of course this anecdote concerns only one family.

The Californians, generally speaking, are lazy, ill-kempt and do not look ahead. Their simple attitude makes them seem like children. At present the Mexican authorities are trying to introduce European customs among them, beginning with dress, dancing and food. The young people often dress in the European manner, drink tea and coffee, and have become accustomed to table ware and other novelties. The older people still adhere to their earlier customs. Their clothing consists of short breeches which button at the knee, and at the bottom are trimmed with gold braid about an inch wide. [They also wear] a long camisole of brightly colored silk or cotton which is fastened at the bottom with two or three buttons. Over this they wear a blue jersey with a red collar, lapels and cuffs. And atop this they wear a red sash, sometimes with tassels. They have low deerskin boots, and those for the well-to-do are decorated with gold and silk thread. Above the boots, from knee to heel they wrap their legs in ochre-colored suede in which various designs have been cut. Below the breeches they wear an undergarment and leggings which extend all the way down into the boot, if the legs are not wound about with suede. Around the neck they wear a kerchief which is not tied, but twisted once, and then the ends are pulled through a ring or hoop which gleams on the chest. They cover their heads with silk or cotton fabric, and when they prepare to go out either on foot or on horseback, they put on a hat over the fabric. Instead of a coat they wear a piece of fabric like a blanket, with a slit in the middle. This is called a *serape*. They put it on over the head and wrap it around the body. Many people have serapes made of a thin blue fabric with a velvet square in the middle decorated with fringe and tassels. Generally they make these of brightly colored wool, of good quality, produced at the missions.

The older women wear a skirt and cover the torso with a shawl called a *rebozo*, made of Mexican cotton. They usually wear this shawl over the head in such a way that one can see only half of the face. The new style for women for the most part is to wear long dresses of muslin or silk. They wear their hair in ringlets and fasten it with a comb which is decorated with various artificial flowers. The shawl is worn only over the shoulders. Simpler people have neither floors nor ceilings in their dwellings, and because of the dirt there is an enormous number of fleas.

The food of the California inhabitants consists of maize, frijoles and meat. The maize is cooked in water to which slaked lime is added so the maize will swell up as it cooks. It is later ground into flour on a rock. After they dissolve the flour in water they bake it in a skillet in flat cakes called *tortillas* which resemble *blinis* [small thin pancakes]. This takes the place of bread. They do not prepare the tortillas until meal time because the hotter they are, the better they taste. Frijoles are cooked with beef suet which is used year round, often in place of butter. Meat is usually cooked in a sauce with a huge amount of red pepper, or else it is just cooked until it falls apart and then is eaten with a pepper sauce.

Among vegetables, they are fond of a squash called *calabasa* and a fruit which the Spanish call *tomato* and the English refer to as *love apple*; this is prepared in a sauce.

Even if there are ten people at the table, only one or two

knives are used, and no forks at all. Men of all ages smoke tobacco wrapped in paper, and many of the older women follow this custom. The men drink a vodka called *aguardiente*, while women and even young girls drink wine. Many women of lower standing eagerly drink vodka and rum, but not to excess. In general one may say that the Californians are sober people, and very rarely does one see a person intoxicated.

It was not more than ten years ago that the missionaries began to introduce tableware, and the more influential officials used table linen, chairs and tables. In the homes of the older people there is usually a couch or a bed on which the lady of the house sits with her daughters, having taken off her shawl, and wearing just her blouse and skirt. But when strangers are present, they will sometimes wrap their shawls about themselves. Children are dressed rather carelessly and are extremely rowdy and mischievous.

Californians are excellent horsemen. From the time they are children they ride horses, and by the time they are adults they are superb riders. They very skillfully throw their lassos over the horns of cattle and the heads of horses when they have to catch them. Those who are hunters ride out after bear with their lassos. They throw one rope over the bear's head, and two over its legs, and drive it some distance. Often two men, with no weapons, just with lassos, will go out after this dangerous game. Children also go out with lassos, and learn how to hunt with them from the time they are very young, by throwing the lasso over pigs, chickens, and in mischief, sometimes over horses.

The men do almost nothing. If they can get Indians from the missions to work, they simply cross their arms and show the Indians what to do. There is not a single master craftsman among them. With the introduction of free trade some inhabitants have begun to farm arable land, plant wheat, and have become industrious, but they are very very reluctant to give up their indolence.

When they greet one another in the morning they will usually inquire about health, which requires at least three or four answers, and then they begin to converse about the weather. . . .

Californians always carry a large knife on their person,

which they wrap in something and strap to the leg. They use it for eating. In arguments they become insane with anger. Sometimes, when one of them is unable to prove his point, he will grab for his knife and without a word, stab his opponent. Often in the past, and now too, they will inflict deadly wounds without the slightest cause, and indeed, a person may be killed right then and there. Suicide, however, is unheard of.

Thievery is frequent among people of the lower class. If you invite them into a cabin aboard ship, you must watch carefully and put tempting items out of sight. . . .

Most of the Californians are tall and strongly built. The color of their skin is swarthy; their features are regular with straight or hooked noses; the hair is black and tied in a long braid. They have long side whiskers and rarely shave the beard. Their faces reflect the rigorous habits stemming from the conquerors of Mexico.

Hospitality is a virtue alien to them, but they love to be entertained. If you invite two or three men for dinner, they will very likely bring ten or more of their friends with them, without considering whether there is space to entertain them all aboard a ship.

The disorderliness of the inhabitants is apparent when one approaches a settlement. All around the dwellings are scattered horned skulls and legs of cattle. They will drive these cattle toward their dwellings every Saturday, kill them, remove the meat and hide, and then discard the head, legs and entrails. They have no appropriate place to dispose of all this, so the filth is never cleaned up, but just left lying around everywhere. One can only imagine what the air is like in these settlements.

The chief form of exercise is horseback riding. The women have a special kind of saddle. They sit on one side, and in this way they ride very skillfully, and fast. Their wagons have two wheels of solid wood four or five inches thick. Axels are made rather primitively. The body of the wagon is made of poles fastened with withes. The wagons are harnessed to two or four oxen for hauling heavy items such as twelve to twenty fanegas of wheat, an amount equal to 50 to 80 puds. But aside from the wagon, almost no inhabitant has any other transport equipment, except for some of the missionaries, who use European wheeled vehicles.

Most of these observations relate to the older residents who are deeply entrenched with the old customs. Young people, especially those who have come from Mexico, where education is being introduced, are very courteous, cordial and might even become hospitable, if they could learn economy and thrift.

Californians incur their major expenses in clothing for their wives and daughters. It is not for me to pass judgment on the caprices of women, which are excited for various reasons. Women everywhere have their weaknesses and whimseys, the Californians, the Kamchadals, Europeans and those along the Northwest Coast of America. In the latter place, blue shells in the ears of one woman arouse envy in another, in the same way a shawl does in a Mexican woman. . . .

Reference: Kyrill T. Khlebnikov. "Statistika. Zapiski o Kalifornii, sostavlennyi Khlebnikovym." In Syn otechestva i Severnyi arkhiv. Vol. 2 (1829), 208–227, 276–88, 336–47, 400–10.

69

APRIL 2, 1835

AN OFFICIAL DECREE CONCERNING THE STATUS OF RUSSIAN AMER-
ICAN COMPANY PERSONNEL WHO DECIDE TO SETTLE PERMANENTLY
IN THE RUSSIAN AMERICAN COLONIES

The Governing Senate has heard the report of the Minister of Finance, which notes that from the time of the founding of the Russian American Company, promyshlenniks, hired Russian townspeople and peasants have visited the colonies of the Company. Many of them have married there and have children and have returned to their homeland. Others, however, because of large families, poor health and advanced years, have remained there. Since there are now a good many of the latter who are no longer able to work, they are a burden on the Company, in whichever department of the colonies they are living. It is not practical to resettle them in Russia because they would be a burden to society there.

Consequently, the Main Administration of the Company, wishing to improve the lot of these people and to organize them on a proper and secure basis for their families' well-being, has proposed to the Ministry of Finance that they be settled permanently in the Russian American colonies. These proposals are very useful, and accord with the views of the government concerning increasing the extent of the Russian settlements there. Therefore, the Minister of Finance has submitted a proposal concerning this matter to a committee of the Council of Ministers. His Imperial Majesty, in accordance with the report by the Committee, on April 2 decreed the following.

1. Willingly hired Russian townsmen and peasants who are presently in the Russian American colonies as hired personnel of the Company, who have married creoles or [native] American women, and those who are in poor health, advanced years, who have lived there for a long time and have become accustomed to the climate and way of life there, or those who have been so long away from Russia that they no longer have any close relatives there, [will be allowed to settle there]. They are to submit to the Company a statement of their desire to

remain permanently; the request is to be submitted in writing. They will be allowed to settle along the Kenai coast of America, or wherever the Main Administration of the Company designates, within Russian possessions. The Company must build adequate living quarters for them and supply them with the necessary equipment for hunting and farming, and with livestock, domestic fowl and seed grain. It must also provide them with provisions adequate for one year, and further, the Company must see to it that these persons are not in want in the future.

2. The Company is to notify local authorities [in Russia], after which the names of these persons are to be removed from the registers of their previous classification in Russia.

3. These persons will continue to be in the same rank as previously. There is a soul tax obligation for them, but no other levies. These taxes will be paid by the Main Administration of the Company in accordance with rosters which the Company receives from its Chief Administrator in the colonies.

4. The Main Administration of the Company will submit the names of these townsmen and peasant settlers to the Ministry of Finance in its annual reports.

5. Children of these settlers will be accepted into Company service, upon their own request, at the established rate of pay.

6. The Company may purchase surplus produce from these settlers at the going rate, but furs and animal products will be purchased at established prices.

7. Creoles who have left Company service and wish to become farmers may also settle there on the same basis as above.

The Minister of Finance will instruct the Main Administration of the Russian American Company to issue appropriate rules based on this Imperial authorization, and he will report it to the Governing Senate so the action may be officially published.

Reference: *PSZ*, Second Series, Vol. 10, No. 8018, 292–293.

70

MARCH, 1836

A REPORT FROM BARON FERDINAND P. WRANGELL TO THE MAIN
ADMINISTRATION OF THE RUSSIAN AMERICAN COMPANY CONCERN-
ING HIS NEGOTIATIONS IN MEXICO

England, France and some of the secondary powers in Europe have formally recognized Mexico's independence and the government of the Republic: and Prussia, which has a Consul General in Mexico, has concluded a commercial agreement. National pride, bolstered by diplomatic relations with the governments of these powers, determines the affairs of the Republic in many relationships. Because of the fear of losing prestige in public opinion, the government does not seek recognition where it is not ready to enter immediately into proposals for political rapprochement. The ministers of England and France in Mexico use their influence with the present government more to prevent their competitors from trading with Mexico than to bring other nations into a fruitful relationship with the Republic.

In consequence, it is very natural that the government in Mexico not only did not display the slightest inclination to listen to a proposal from the commercial agent of a nation which does not recognize the independence of the Republic, but would be insulted if I were to make such a proposal without any diplomatic intermediary.

I had hoped to obviate all these difficulties by using two letters of introduction to the Vice President, General [M.] Barragan, from persons well known to him. General Barragan, however, was ill when I reached Mexico and died two weeks later. The newly elected Vice President, [José Justo] Corro, was quite unwilling to enter into so sensitive a relationship as receiving a military official from Russia who had no credentials from the Russian government to present. Thus it seemed there was no way to carry out my assignment.

Then I decided it would not be detrimental to the commercial interests of Prussia and this Republic, if Russia and Mexico were to have close ties; on the contrary, such a bond would strengthen the power of the present Prussian diplomatic agent here. And so I turned to the Prussian Consul General, Herr [Friedrich] von Gerolt, and proposed that he assist me by informing the Minister of Foreign Affairs of my desire to meet with the present government while I was in Mexico, to discuss matters of mutual interest.

Herr von Gerolt declared himself eager to render me any possible assistance with my affairs. After many fruitless attempts, he finally managed to obtain a reply from Señor [José Maria Ortiz] Monasterio that he would accept a written statement from me, and would subsequently see me personally.

I composed my letter to Señor Monasterio on the basis of a memorandum from the Vice Chancellor [Nesselrode], which was to serve as my instruction. Letters from General José Figueroa of April 11 and July, 1833, and his death, gave me the opportunity to refer to the government of Mexico and explain to the Minister why I had decided on this course of action. [I stated that] I had no instructions from my government in this matter, and was acting solely as the agent of a commercial company. The memorandum about the proposed commercial relationship with our colonies may mollify him and assure him that our wishes fully correspond with the interests of the subjects of the Republic, and will not burden the government.

A week after sending my letter I was invited to present myself to the Vice President, Señor Monasterio and von Gerolt, with the latter serving as interpreter.

Señor Corro responded to my letter in noncommittal terms, and it seemed to me he did not even know the contents, or had forgotten. Finally he said I would receive a reply to it the next day. I expressed my readiness to give him information on conditions in Upper California, the relationships various nations have with that country, and in general about subjects which I imagined might be interesting to him and might also serve my affairs. Señor Corro and Señor Monasterio, however, declined to listen to me. I then said that when a new Governor was appointed in California, I would want to know whether he would interfere in any way with Russian American Company ships which visit California for commercial purposes, be-

Captain of the First Rank Baron F. P. von Wrangell was one of the ablest negotiators for the Russian American Company in North America in the 1830s, but his undertakings for Count Nesselrode gained little. He served as Chief Administrator for 1830–1835. Shur, *K Beregam Novogo Sveta*. (OHS OrHi neg. 82008)

cause if that were the case our colonial ships would go to Chile [instead], and our relations with California would be cut off completely, to the obvious detriment of the Californians themselves.

The Vice President replied that the new Governor of California will use every means to establish friendly relations and maintain contacts between the Russian possessions in America and California, and there should be not the slightest reason for any misunderstanding. Señor Monasterio later emphasized the same thing. After this I took my leave of the Vice President and did not see him again.

Instead of hearing anything further the next day, it was exactly one week later that I received a response . . .

It is important to note at this point that my meeting with the Vice President and the Minister of Foreign Affairs was not kept secret from other diplomatic agents, and for some reason the editor of the Mexican government newspaper published more articles against Russia during this period than ever before; the articles were taken from English newspapers.

It is appropriate to mention opinions here concerning our establishment at [Fort] Ross. These opinions greatly exaggerate our forces and reveal an astonishing lack of knowledge of local conditions; this exaggeration arouses fear. No one understands or believes that a small Russian settlement located between the possessions of England, the United States and Mexico, is not only not dangerous to Mexico, but on the contrary may serve as an impediment to the aggressive attempts by the citizens of the United States of America to occupy all of Northern California. I believe that if the Mexican government will view our settlement from this point of view, it will not be difficult for the diplomatic agent from St. Petersburg to persuade this government to make formal recognition of our occupation of the lands around Fort Ross and the area of Bodega Bay and the valleys of the interior, some twenty miles to the east.

I also have reason to believe that in a relatively short time the United States of America will take advantage of the favorable circumstances to support Upper California to separate from the Republic of Mexico and join the Northern Confederation. Should England seize the Sandwich Islands (as many believe she will), the trade of United States citizens will suffer a significant loss, and in that case every means will be used by the Northern Republic to seize the bay of San Francisco as the only place which may compensate for the loss of the Sandwich Islands in regard to the vital commerce between China and the West coast of America and whaling in this ocean.

I shall submit additional information on this matter upon my arrival in St. Petersburg.

Captain of the First Rank F. Wrangell
To the Main Administration of
the Russian American Company.

Reference: TsGIA ESSR,f. 2057, op. 1, d. 343, 11. 14–15.
See: L. A. Shur, ed. *K beregam Novogo Sveta*. (Moscow: 1971), 260–263.

71

1838

A REPORT ON THE NATIVES OF THE NORTHWEST COAST OF AMER-
ICA BY BARON FERDINAND P. WRANGELL, FORMER CHIEF ADMIN-
ISTRATOR OF THE RUSSIAN AMERICAN COMPANY

T he Cape of St. Elias can be considered the northwest
boundary of habitation of the coastal Kolosh people.

THE UGALENTS

Farther to the west live the Ugalents, a rather small group
of only 38 families. In winter they live in a small cove east of
the island of Kayak; in summer they move east to the mouth of
the Copper River to fish. The territory which they inhabit is
some distance from the coast and has more river otter than the
area around Yakutat. They take between 500 and 700 of these
animals each year. In order to sell the pelts they travel by
boats similar to the ones used by the Kolosh to Konstantinovsk
redoubt, the administrative unit which has jurisdiction over
them. These people are peaceful and have been subjugated.
They live in communal log structures built above ground, in
which each family has its own space along one side of the structure. In the middle is a fire for common use. From two to six
related families live in each of these structures.

The intellectual level, beliefs and way of life of the Ugalents are similar to those of the Kolosh of the Yakutat region,
with whom they have intermarried. Although their language
differs from that of the Kolosh, it nevertheless stems from the
same root; these two peoples are two branches of the same
tribe. The adjacent Yakutat Kolosh and the people of the Copper River region refer to them by the same name as they are
known in the colonies.

THE MEDNOVSKS

This small group of about 60 families at present lives along
the banks of the Atna River, and call themselves Atnakhtians.

They are peaceful and live in harmony with all neighboring tribes. They have trading relations with the Chugach, Ugalents, Kolosh, Kolchans and Kenaits. From the time the Europeans arrived, the land of the Mednovsks became known to all of these people because of the copper deposits there. The natives have made axes, knives and armor from that metal for their own use and for sale to the Ugalents, Kolosh and other neighboring tribes. At present they are the only metal workers who know how to forge iron, which they obtain from the Russians. Neither the Kolosh nor other natives in the colonies are familiar with this skill. The Atnakhtians call the Russians *Ketchetnai*, from their word for iron, *ketchi*.

The primary occupation of the Mednovsks is the caribou hunt. In spring when the ice on rivers and lakes is still strong, they drive the caribou herds that come at that time into a specially built enclosure in the shape of the Roman numeral V sidewise. The opening sometimes stretches for as much as ten versts. When the animals come to the point of the V and begin to crowd, the savages slaughter them. Another caribou hunt takes place in the fall when the animals migrate back to their wintering grounds. At that time the natives drive them into the lake and kill them from boats.

The very existence of the people depends on the success of the caribou hunt. The caribou supplies them with both clothing and food. The Mednovsks do not catch enough fish for the entire winter. Because of this, if the caribou hunt is unsuccessful the people will suffer terrible famine and entire families will starve to death. This happened in 1828, when more than 100 adults and children died of starvation.

To make their own garments, and to sell furs, the Mednovsks also hunt elk which wander in, and they kill marmots, ground squirrels, foxes and black bears; however, they do not kill beavers even though such animals are to be found in their land. They consider beads to be their most precious wealth. The more prosperous collect as many beads as possible, bury them in the ground and bequeath them to their descendants, who in turn try to increase the amount of this treasure.

Like the Ugalents, who belong to the same tribe as the Kolosh, the Mednovsks resemble the Kolosh in their beliefs, customs and language. Generally speaking their language is easy and more melodious than that of the Kolosh.

The Mednovsks divide the year into fifteen months; they do not have names for the months, just first, second and so on. There are ten months of fall and winter, and five of spring and summer. The more prosperous have *kalgas* [slaves] which they purchase from the Kolchans, but unlike the Kolchans and Kolosh, they do not put the kalgas to death when a starshina dies.

However, like the Kolosh they burn the corpse, collect the bones, wrap them in a sueded caribou hide from which the hair has been removed, and keep the bundle in a small box on a post or in a tree. Feasts for dead relatives are celebrated every year.

The Atnakhtians, like the Kolosh and other branches of the same tribe, believe that the earth and human beings were created by a raven which stole the elements, one by one. Tales about a mighty bird which created the universe are embroidered in poetic memories among the Knisten, Chippewas and other savages of the eastern plains of North America, and have been reduced along the West Coast into a simple tale about the raven. They have no legend about a worldwide flood.

THE KOLCHANS AND GALTSANS

The Mednovsk people call the tribes along the northern and eastern rivers and streams tributary to the Atna, and those people who live still farther off, beyond the mountains, Kolchans, or "alien people." They distinguish between the near and the distant Kolchans. They carry on trade with the former, receiving pelts of elk, lynx and beaver; they only know of the distant Kolchans through hearsay. The near Kolchans frequently come to our Mednovsk *odinochka* [trading post] to sell beaver pelts and other furs. They come down the rivers in small boats covered with dried caribou hide, with the hair on the inside, into which they load all the furs they have taken during the summer in the mountains and on lakes. When they reach the odinochka they take apart the little boats and sell the caribou hides as such, or make them into suede, also for sale. The savages then return home on foot, carrying the beads and tobacco they have obtained.

The various branches of the Kolchans battle each other. The distant branch is described as very ferocious, and in time of famine are reputed to be cannibalistic. The near Kolchans belong to the same tribe as the Mednovsks and Kenaits, and although they speak a different dialect, can understand one another.

The Kenaits call them Galtsans, "guests," and the tribal branches who roam the headwaters of the rivers that empty into the Bering Sea are known to them by the same name. They come together with these and other Galtsans at the time of the caribou hunts in early summer, on the lakes beyond the mountains. They trade elk hides with the Mednovsk Galtsans, and obtain sable and beaver pelts from the others. The Galtsan settlement closest to the northern Kenaits is called Titlogat. From there it takes ten days to cross the mountains to Lake Knytyben for the caribou hunt. The Kenaits also come to that lake to meet and trade with the Titlogat savages. The Kenaits hunt caribou on Lake Khtuben, which is six days south of Knytyben. It takes fourteen days to travel from Lake Khtuben to the northern part of Kenai Bay.

The closest settlement of the Mednovsk Galtsans to the Kenaits is Nutatlgat; its inhabitants sometimes travel to Lake Khtuben to trade with the Kenaits. They reach it after ten days of very rapid travel over the mountains. From Nutatlgat the Galtsan Kenaits sometimes obtain English-made weapons, copper coins and beads, but nothing of Russian origin. They say such items are received third-hand, from people who live near a fort. The Kenaits believe that beyond the distant Galtsans there are people with tails.

THE KENAITS

These people call themselves Tnaina, from "Tnai," human beings. The Kodiaks know them as Kina-iut, which name the Russians have also adopted. There are about 460 families who live along the shore and in the environs of Kenai Bay (Cook Inlet) and near the lakes of Iliamna and Kyzzhakh. They belong to the same tribe as the Galtsans, Kolchans, Atnakhtians and Kolosh. This is obvious not only through similarities in certain words (barely noticeable in the Kolosh language; the similarity has almost disappeared), but also in like beliefs and rituals. This view is supported by the division into two main branches which are subdivided into families known by different names.

The Kenaits of the raven clan are considered relatives by the Galtsans, Mednovsks, Ugalents and Kolosh of the same clan or tribe, even though they may not understand the same language. There are no general distinguishing marks to identify the clan to which one belongs; savages always accept claims of membership on faith.

According to the Kenaits, the raven created two females from various substances, and each founded a tribe. One tribe comprised the six clans of one woman; the other, five clans from the other woman. The first six clans are called: Kakhgia, croak of the raven; Kali, fish tails; Tlakhtan, grass mat; Montokhtan, back corner of the dwelling; Chikhei, a color; and Nukhshi, falling from the sky. The second five clans are called: Tulchin, desire to bathe in fall's freezing cold water; Katlukhtan, hunters who string beads; Shshulakhtan, a ravenlike creature who constantly tried to deceive while the earth and humans were being created; and Puchikhga and Tsalytan, from the mountains near Lake Skiliakh near the headwaters of the Koktna River. According to ancient tradition, men of the six-clan tribe cannot marry within their own clans, but must choose wives from other tribes. Thus they must always select a wife from a friendly tribe, but not from among their own relatives. Children belong to the same clan and tribe as the mother. This rule is not presently firmly adhered to, so one may marry within one's own clan, but the old people believe this intermarriage poses grave danger to the Kenaits. The heir is the child born of a sister. A son inherits a very small amount from his father, because while his parents are alive he must provide his own food and clothing.

Courtship ceremonies are very simple. Early one morning the suitor appears in the home of the young woman's father, and without speaking a word, heats the bathhouse, draws water, prepares food, and this continues until he is asked who he is and what he wants. He responds, giving his desire; once he has revealed his intention he remains in the home for a year as a worker. At the end of the year the father of the young woman gives the suitor some pay for his work, and the savage takes his young bride into his barabor. There are no marriage ceremonies. Prosperous men have three or four wives. Although the wife works industriously in her family, she is not her husband's slave. She has the right to return to her father's home, and in such a case the husband must return the pay he was given for his work during the courtship. The wife has full ownership of items belonging to her, or which she has acquired; often the husband will buy such items from her. If he has more than one wife, each has a separate dwelling place, apart from the other wives or members of the family.

The entire tribe mourns a death. They gather with the closest relative of the deceased, sit around the fire and wail. The relative who is the owner of the dwelling dresses in his best clothing and wears a headdress of eagle feathers. He inserts an eagle feather through a slit in his nostril, and appears before the assembled relatives, with his face painted, to weep. He holds in his hands rattles beautifully made from the toes of a sea bird called a *toporka* [*alca arctica*] and shakes the rattles as he sings a funeral song in a firm voice. He uses his entire body, especially his legs, to make strong movements, stamping the ground, but not moving out of place. He recalls the brave achievements of the deceased. His words then become the text of a verse which the entire group composes and sings in unison, accompanied by drums. At the end of each verse all weep loudly together. Meanwhile the host bows his head, lowers his head to his chest and takes a deep breath until he again feels the need to weep. This ceremony is an expression of the deep grief of the gruff, undemonstrative savage, an inhabitant of the North, who is endowed with strong, enduring, unfeigned emotion.

I will cite the text of one such song which I personally heard:

CLOSEST RELATIVE: He was a great hunter.

TRIBAL CHOIR: He was the bravest; he chased belugas.
He never returned home without a catch;
When he went to the mountains for
caribou

His arrow flew straight into the heart of
the beast.
If he encountered a bear in the forest
He would not let it go, neither black nor
brown.

CLOSEST RELATIVE: He was generous and merrier than the
others.

TRIBAL CHOIR: He always shared his catch.
Whether it was a catch from the sea or
from the mountains,
He shared everything and helped the
poor.
And when he worked in his home,
He sang, danced and made merry.

After the singing, the host distributes the clothing and
other belongings of the deceased among the relatives who have
taken part in the funeral ceremonies. The closest friends of the
deceased from the other tribe come uninvited to this ceremony
and bring various furs to the closest relative, but they do not
sing or weep. Immediately after the death they burn the
corpse, gather up the bones and bury them, not permitting any
member of the tribe to delay this rite. The closest relative of
the deceased tries for a year or more to acquire as many caribou
hides, sueded caribou pieces and other hides as possible; he
then celebrates the memory of the dead person by holding a
festivity. He calls in his own friends and those who buried the
bones, and provides a feast, offers them gifts for their earlier
contributions and for the work of burial, and distributes his
own belongings, which brings him great glory. Each tries to
outdo the other. The relatives dance, sing mournful songs and
try for the approbation of the other guests.

The name of the deceased must not be mentioned again in
the hearing of the closest relative, who will even change his
own name, by which the deceased used to call him. Anyone
who violates the rule and speaks the name of the deceased will
be challenged to fight by the closest relative if the culprit belongs to a friendly tribe, and he must buy himself out of this

situation with gifts. Retribution is not practiced among one's own relatives; an apology is sufficient.

An impoverished person will often lead a wealthy friend into temptation, and the latter, realizing the intent, will quickly mention the name of the deceased in order to humor, with prideful generosity, the awakened anger and grief of the poor person.

The Kenaits use various means to alleviate sadness. For example, a poor person will wait until a little pond where he lives is completely frozen over in winter, so no water is available. Then he will call on wealthy friends in another tribe to invite them to a feast, and he will serve them melted snow. Meanwhile his own relatives note the amused grimaces of the friends, listen to them talk, and tell the host. He immediately runs from his hut, puts on his best clothing, takes up his bow and arrow, and angrily appears before the guests and challenges the guilty one who dared to make fun of him. He then stabs his own cheek or lip with an arrow as evidence of the fact that he prefers death to having his name insulted. Of course those present have anticipated this response. The wealthy person who insulted him expresses his desire to pay him, and in this way satisfies the hurt, vain, sly speculator, the likes of whom would probably be found in other countries, too.

Festivities such as dancing, singing, entertainment and gift-giving, are done for various reasons. When a person recovers from a serious illness he organizes a festivity for those who were concerned for his health, who came to visit him, wept, expressed their concern, brought him the best food and doctored him. Anyone who can amaze his fellow tribesmen by the scope of his generosity during these festivities is held in the very highest esteem not only in his own settlement, but throughout the entire tribe. Others seek out his advice, and will not contradict him in anything he says. This is the beginning of toionship, a respect for that person. The authority of the *kyshka* [elder] is not based on family, although it is generally handed down to one's heir. Nevertheless the authority is conditional, and either one willingly acknowledges the authority of the elder or moves to another settlement where he may do as he pleases, or else lives isolated from others.

There is a subtle competitive spirit between these two tribes, even in the merest trifles. Murder or insult perpetrated against one's own tribal member is avenged by the insulted person or his nearest relatives through killing or beating, without any intervention on the part of those outside the family. But if such a situation involves a friend of the other tribe, then all members of the family stand ready to defend the honor of the insulted family. In major issues, such incidents result in internecine wars. They try to put down such wars, however, and do not take prisoners as slaves, but return them for ransom. Prior to the occupation of this country by the Russians, both tribes joined forces to battle the Kodiak people, who had to beat off their attacks. The prisoners were made slaves, and for that reason the Kenaits called the Kodiak natives "Ulchna," which is taken from their word for slaves, "ulchaga." At present the quarrels are over. Disagreements among families or tribes are turned over for settlement to the administrator of the Nikolaevsk redoubt who tries to resolve each problem peacefully.

The Kenaits are of medium stature, well built, and their facial features and the color of their skin indicate their direct origin from [native] Americans. Many are tall, but I have seen more hunchbacks among them than in the other colonies I have visited. They have cheerful dispositions; they begin all their work with a song, and at the end, dance for relaxation.

Their winter dwellings are similar to those of the Ugalents and the Mednovsks. They are wide, tall wooden structures with an opening in the center. The sides are divided into as many compartments as there are families who have decided to live together. Each such dwelling has two or more bathhouses, at the ends of the structure. The natives spend a great deal of time in the winter in these bathhouses. They resemble the Aleut *zhupans* [dwellings] but are neither as spacious nor as light; they are more like bears' dens, completely covered with earth, so that there is only one small round opening from the dwelling, and a person enters with considerable difficulty. The bathhouse is heated with burning hot stones.

Since I have previously mentioned some of the customs of the Kenaits, I will note here that the shamans (who are here called *lykyn*) teach that the Kenaits are descended from a raven who took special pleasure in forever deceiving man, its own creation. They believe that after death a person continues to live under the earth, where it is neither dark nor light, and that they live a life similar to that above ground with the sole difference that they sleep while people above ground are awake, and vice versa.

It is likely that the Kenaits came to their present areas from beyond the mountains. They were nomadic mountain people who subsequently became semi-settled coastal people. They still use the small birchbark boats which they formerly used on rivers and lakes. They use *lavtaks*, that is, cured skins of sea animals, to cover their baidarkas and baidaras, a usage they probably adopted from the Kodiak or Chugach people. However, the Kenaits cannot in any way compare to the others in craftsmanship and in the bold skill in maneuvering their baidaras. The Kenaits' favorite occupation is hunting land animals across the mountains.

The Kenaits set up their fishing camps at river mouths or along the edge of the bay, at tidewater. *Chavych* [king salmon], *krasnaia* [blueback], *gorbusha* [humpback], *golets* [loach], *kizuch* [silver salmon] and other varieties come into the bay from the sea in great numbers, and into all the rivers and streams, from spring until fall. These savages use a very simple method to catch fish as they swim upstream. They make baskets out of roots, tie them to a long pole and let them float in the water. As soon as a few fish swim into the baskets, they pull them out of the water. Old men and children use this method. To catch larger amounts of fish, they make a net weir several sazhens long, which looks rather like the railing of a coachbox. During the fish migration men use long-handled spears to stab the fish [as they are trapped by the weirs]. The women dry iukola, prepare fish roe, gather berries and sarana, and try out oil from small fish called *sak* here, or from *beluga* (*Delphinus leucas*), which the most skillful fishermen catch in the following manner. The men emplant posts in places where beluga go in search of small fish, such as low water close to shore or in streams. The men sit near these posts and watch the fish. As soon as one comes close to a post, the Kenaits will shoot an arrow at the fish, or actually, an arrowhead, which is fastened to a cord 1½ sazhens long, with a bladder attached to the other end of the cord. The arrow becomes embedded in the beluga, which quickly thrashes off; the bladder shows its location; another fisherman in a baidarka pursues it, grabs the cord, stabs the beluga several times and pushes the dead creature ashore.

The Kenaits do not hunt whales, but whales do come into the bay, and if one is stranded on shore, the natives will use the meat and the oil.

These activities last until the end of July. By early August everyone except the weak and the sick go over the mountains to breathe the mountain air of the ancient Fatherland, hunt land animals, and visit the Galtsans. They take their wives and children who hunt marmot and ground squirrel while the men hunt caribou. Those who live in the central and southern parts of Kenai Bay go beyond the mountains where they hunt mountain rams instead of caribou. Those from the more northern settlements of Knyk and along the Sushitna River take a much more distant route. From the northernmost corner of the bay they go northeast, following the mountain passes which they reach in seven days of rapid travel or ten days at a normal pace, until they reach the crest. There they leave their wives, children and the less skillful hunters. The best hunters cross the mountain crest, and in seven days reach a small lake called Khtuben located in a forested meadow in the mountains near the headwaters of the Sushitna River. They spend the winter here, where the caribou abound in vast numbers. The hunters chase the herds from the forest into the lake, and kill them in the water from small birchbark boats.

The Mednovsk Atnakht people also come here, traveling for fourteen days from Lake Mantylban; and the Mednovsk Galtsans come across the mountains in ten days of rapid travel to visit and to trade with the western Galtsans. The Kenaits travel for another six days to a small lake where they rendezvous with the others. All of these people are very much accustomed to bartering items they have made, and their own knowledgeable experts identify the items of best quality. For example, porcupine needles used to decorate kamleis are considered best quality if they come from the Atna River, and those dyed red are especially valuable. The Mednovsks use cranberries for this dye, and the Kenaits use red bilberries.

Ivan Veniaminov, the Alaskan missionary who eventually succeeded to the highest office within the Russian Orthodox Church, Metropolitan of Moscow and Kolomna. As Innokentii, the "Apostle of Alaska" he worked zealously and with great love for the natives whom he served. *The Pacific: Russian Scientific Investigations.* (OHS neg. 56340)

When the hunt ends in late September or early October they travel down the swift Sushitna River in boats covered with untanned caribou hide. It takes them four days to reach Kenai Bay. Those who were left in the mountains return by their previous route. Because of the strenuous work of travel and hunting, when these people return from the mountains they are exhausted and thin. Even so, if the weather is not yet too cold they will rapidly hunt beaver in their own environs. By the time winter sets in they spend their time in celebration and relaxation. They play games, squander the fruits of their summer and fall labors, and in the end suffer from a shortage of food; but the advent of spring and the new runs of fish save them from prolonged famine.

This, then, is the way of life of the great majority of the natives. They consider any attempt to change the ancient customs of their forefathers a first step into a sinister abyss.

THE CHUGACH AND KODIAKS

The Chugach are newcomers from Kodiak Island, driven off by tribal strife to the areas they presently occupy along the coast of Chugach Bay (Prince William Sound), and west to the entry into Kenai Bay. There is no question but that they come from the same stock as the Kodiaks, speak the same language, and have similar beliefs and customs. They differ from them in two basic ways: they believe they are descended from the dog rather than the raven, and they are not divided into two main tribes, as are the Kolosh, Ugalents, Mednovsks, Kolchans, Galtsans and Kenaits. In addition, the Chugach and Kodiaks are exclusively coastal people. Using their lavtak-covered baidarkas, they incessantly hunt all sea creatures: sea lions, seals, whales and sea otters. Their garments are not made of caribou hide, as are those of all the other people of this region; rather, their parkas are of bird skins, and their kamleis are made of the intestines and throats of both sea and amphibious creatures. According to their accounts, they came here from the north, and even to this day they encounter fellow tribesmen all along the coast from Bristol Bay to Bering Strait.

At the present time the Chugach, Kodiaks and the inhabitants of the entire Aleutian chain, because of their long relationship with the Russians, have changed in their customs, and have lost native traditions. For this reason I will not describe these people here; [G. A.] Sarychev, [G. I.] Davydov and [Georg von] Langsdorff have described them in their original [pre-contact] condition. I will only observe that the Chugach and Kodiaks have intermixed with other American natives whose wives they have taken captive. As a result of this, and because of the moderate climate, in their outward appearance they much more resemble the American natives of the mountains [of Alaska] than the Eskimos of the North. The Chugach call themselves Chugachik, and there are about 100 families of them at present.

THE INKIULIUKHLIUATS

On the river Khulitna, at the headwaters of the Kuskokvim and Kvikpak rivers, lives a tribe who are known at the Aleksandrovsk and Mikhailovsk redoubts as Inkiuliukhliuats. They are described as closely resembling the Kolosh, both in appearance and customs. [I. F.] Vasilev described the Khulitnovsk Inkiuliukhliuats in the following manner: "When they dance they fluff swans' down over themselves and paint their entire bodies red. Their songs and dances are very similar to those of the Kolosh. The dancers, like the Kolosh, hold spears or knives in their hands, which they twirl over their heads and make feints with them, all the while shouting 'Kha! Kha!' and 'Ogol! Ogol!'"

The weapons of the savages consist of arrows, bows, lances and knives. Their arrowheads are made of iron and red copper; they obtain the former from the Kenaits and the latter from the Tutnovs. They wear parkas, trousers and winter boots made of sea otter and muskrat pelts; kamleis are made of fish skin, primarily chavych.

Their household utensils are wooden cups and small clay bowls. Their dwellings are built of logs and are similar to those of the Russians, but they are very low. Many are covered with sod. Some have a real Kolosh barabor with a round opening instead of a door. They do not have baidarkas, but use small boats which can carry only one or two men, and which are so light they can be carried in one hand if necessary. The Inkiu-liukhliuats are bellicose and brave. They have no more than 100 men on the Khulitna River, but they are not at all afraid of the extremely populous Kuskokvims. . . .

THE INKALITS

This name applies to the people who live along the Kvikpak and Kuskokvim rivers and their tributaries. They comprise the middle link between the coastal people and the mountain inhabitants. [Andrei] Glazunov made the following observations about the Inkalits:

"They speak a language quite different from that used along the coast, which is the tongue of the Kodiak Aleuts. The dialect of the Inkalits is a mixture of the Kenaits, Kodiak, Unalashkints and Mednovsk languages.

"These people have large bones and dark complexions. They have coarse hair, black lips which they slit, and into the

The Valaam Monastery in European Russia was the training ground for a number of the Russian Orthodox missionaries who went to Alaska. This serene and contemplative scene little suggests the tempestuous conditions the missionaries would face. Schilder, *Imperator Alexander Pervyi*. (OHS OrHi neg. 82056)

slits insert small stones and beads. The women have clean faces, and only under the chin do they have two narrow blue tattoos. Their long hair is braided on each side and decorated with colored beads. The men shave their heads down to the skin using a sharp stone.

"Men's clothing is sewn almost entirely from beaver pelts— parkas, trousers, head covering, mittens, boots and even bedding. When it rains they wear kamleis and overboots of fish skin. Women's parkas are of sable, muskrat and rabbit fur.

"Domestic utensils are made of bent wood; the workmanship is extremely skillful, and the items are decorated with varicolored clays in red, green and blue. They use fired clay pots to cook their food. In summer they travel on rivers and lakes in small birchbark canoes of very fine workmanship, and in winter they travel by dogsleds.

"Their main settlement is on the Kvikpak River. Their neighbors speak the coastal language, are called the Anilukhtakhnaks, and number about 700. The Anvigmiuts and Magimiuts are also considered Inkalits."

PEOPLE WHO SPEAK THE COMMON LANGUAGE OF THE COASTAL DWELLERS, WHICH IS QUITE SIMILAR TO THAT OF THE KODIAKS

The Aglegmiuts at the mouths of the Nushagak and Paknek rivers number some 500 persons. The Kiiatents or Kiiataigmiuts along the Nushagak and Ilgaiak rivers number about 400 persons. The Kuskokvilts along the Kuskokvim River and its tributaries and along lakes south of that river, according to Vasilev, are about 7,000 in number.

The Kvikhnakts and all of their subdivisions such as the Magmiuts on the Kyzhunak River, the Agulmiuts on the Kvikhliuvak River, the Pashtuligmiuts on the Pashtul River, the Tachigmiuts near Mikhailovsk redoubt, the Malimiuts near the shores of Shaktulakh or Shaktol Bay, the Aklygmiuts in Golovnin Bay, the Chnagmiuts north of the Pashtuligmiuts and west of Cape Rodney, and the Kuvikhnagmiuts on the Kubikhnal River all speak the same language and belong to the same tribe, which also extends north along the coast of America, up to 71° 4′ latitude, according to the information of Captain [F. W.] Beechey. Beechey considers 60° 4′ northern latitude the southern limit of the west coast people he calls the Western Eskimos. In language, facial appearance and customs he sees a very close tie to the Eastern Eskimos of Hudson Bay, Greenland, Igliulik, and in general, the northern coastal areas of America. He has also noted the similarity of the Western Eskimos to the Chukchi, and suggests they are descended from the Chukchi. Cook thought the Chugach and the Aleuts of Unalaska Island originated from the Greenland Eskimos.

The inhabitants of Kodiak speak almost the same language as the Chugach and the people of the coastal region between Bristol Bay and Norton Sound. Consequently we encounter the Eskimo language from Bering Strait south along the coast of America as far as the Chugach, and east to Greenland and all through the Aleutian chain, including Kodiak.

When we examine the dialects of these people more carefully, however, and compare their customs, beliefs and facial features, we discover striking differences. For example, the island people of the Aleutians differ in many ways from the Kodiak and Chugach. There are some similar words in their languages, but these are few. An inhabitant of Unalaska does not understand a person from Kodiak at all.

When one first looks at an Aleutian islander, one sees the ancestral characteristics of the Asiatics, Mongols or Manchus. The Japanese who were in New Arkhangel as a result of having been shipwrecked in the Sandwich Islands remind one of the people of Unalaska. But by contrast, the Kodiak people more closely resemble the American tribes, and in their outward appearance they are not at all like either the Eskimos or Asiatic peoples. They have probably intermixed with American tribes, and although they have preserved some language, they have lost the Asiatic cast of face and body. According to popular lore, the Kodiaks, Chugach, Kuskokvims and others close to them came from the north to the places they presently occupy, while those of Unalaska came from the west.

If we were to assign all of these peoples to the one basic tribe of Eskimos, then based on differences in dialect, external appearance and lore, we could make the following divisions:

The Eskimos of Bering Strait and the inhabitants of the entire northern coast of America all the way up to Greenland we will call Northern.

Eskimos living south of Bering Strait from near Cape Rodney to the Alaska Peninsula, on Kodiak Island and in Chugach Bay, we will call Southern. The Aleutian Islanders we will call Western.

The Northern Eskimos, especially those from the eastern part who live in the coldest and least productive country, and who live in small communities, have remained at the very lowest level of intellectual development. The Southern Eskimos possess an area which is somewhat forested, where there are not only foxes and wolves, but also beavers and otters. These people have left the mountains and have come down to the coast where they have acquired many new concepts and have intermingled with other people.

The Western Eskimos have come from a different part of the world, and in the general movement of the Eskimo tribes to the east, have not touched on polar lands. They least resemble the other branches. Their mental abilities and spiritual qualities make them very receptive to education, much more than the Kodiak people.

A highly esteemed and industrious priest, Ioann Veniaminov, learned the language and understood the character of the Unalaska Aleuts, and compiled a grammar and a dictionary of their language which is to be published. Father Ioann has given the public the most accurate information about these people, and for that reason I will not describe them here.

The Northern Eskimos are known through the descriptions made by Krantz, [M. C.] Perry, [A.] Ross, Beechey and others. Davydov, [I. F.] Lisianskii and Langsdorff have described the Kodiak people. What now remains to be done is to supplement this with information about the Kuskokvims, Kvilpolkakhs and the people from Bristol Bay and Norton Sound. I will describe only the Kuskokvims, with whom Vasilev became acquainted, and I am taking most of the following information from his journal.

THE KUSKOKVIMS

The Kuskokvims inhabit the land between the watersheds of the Nushagak, Ilgaiak, Khulitna and Kuskokvim rivers, all the way to the coast. The majority of them live along the Kuskokvim River west of the nexus of the Kuskokvim and Anigak rivers. Vasilev states that there are at least 7,000 of these savages, including both sexes and all ages. They are also known as the Kushkhkkhvakmiuts, from Kushkukkhvak, which means Kuskokvim.

The Aglegmiuts and the Kiiataigmiuts or Kiiatents in no way differ from the Kuskokvims; the latter are considered one with the others. The Aglegmiuts and Kuskokvims are hostile, because the former were forced out of their original homeland along the banks of the Kuskokvim River. They have adopted their present name from a settlement called Agolegma, where they lived during the siege. One part of their people retreated to the island of Nunivok, and the other part to the mouth of the Nushagak River, where they are under the protection of the administrator of the Aleksandrovsk redoubt and no longer have to fear attacks by the Kuskokvims. However, even to the present day they sing songs of lament about their ancient homeland. The Aglegmiuts in turn expelled the native inhabitants from the mouth of the Nushagak River, who resettled on the eastern part of the Alaska Peninsula and are now known to us as the Severnovsks and the Ugashents.

One cannot call the Kuskokvims either nomads or wanderers. In winter they always assemble in permanent settlements along the rivers. In summer they spread out to procure food. They have a very strong attachment to the places where their forebears lived, and they consider those lands where their ancestors hunted and carried on other activities as tribal possessions.

Every settlement has one communal structure called a *kazhim*, which is large enough to accommodate all the males of the settlement. Around the walls of the structure are several tiers of benches, and a hearth in the middle. Light comes from an opening above the hearth. These kazhims are built of boards set into the ground and covered over with earth, in similar fashion as their living quarters are constructed. All the people in a settlement gather in the kazhim to consult on important matters such as war, peace, tribal festivities and the like. Usually the kazhim serves as a communal dwelling for all the males in the settlement except for the old men and small boys. This custom is quite interesting in regard to the daily occupations of the Kuskokvims and other tribes of the same origin.

At sunset all retire, the adult men to the kazhim, and the women, children, old people, invalids and shamans to their iurts. Early in the morning before sunrise a specially assigned young lad lights the oil lamps in the iurts. The women immediately arise and begin to prepare food for their husbands and families. They crush berries and mix them with fat, caribou blood and a particular kind of grass. The shaman dons his attire, takes up his drum, and then with his assistant goes to the kazhim where the men are dressed and ready to receive him. Then the shaman conducts the religious ceremonies for the entire group.

When the ceremony is completed, the women bring food to their husbands and families in the kazhim. After these have eaten, the other members of the family eat in their iurts and afterward all, including young girls and small children, go out to gather enough wood for the whole day for the kazhim and each iurt. When the sun rises, the men leave to hunt wherever they wish, using their baidarkas. In winter they use dogsleds. Some, however, remain in the settlement. When a hunter returns, he leaves his baidarka or sled without securing it in any way, and goes directly to the kazhim to sit near the fire. His wife, sister or mother takes his catch, unharnesses the dogs from the sled or pulls the baidarka upon shore and hurries to feed this new arrival and dry his clothing.

Married men visit their wives during the night, but not before everyone else in the kazhim is asleep; then they quietly leave the kazhim, and return before the others awaken.

The men hang their bows, arrows, spears, knives and all other weapons along the walls of the kazhim.

Festivities called *igrushkas* take place in the kazhim. When the winter cold sets in and the hunt is over, each settlement conducts an annual festival without fail. The purpose of the celebration is to prepare great tribal displays of hunting achievements, and the prowess of each hunter, showing quarry ranging from the smallest to the most impressive. This desire for glory causes great excitement.

Each mother carefully collects all the birds, nestlings and little mice her small sons have shot [with arrows] or trapped throughout the entire year. She stuffs them, suspends them on a cord fastened to the middle of a bark image of a bird in flight. This decoration is hung in the kazhim, and an oil lamp is lighted on the floor, below the bark bird. There are quite a few of these in the kazhim. A fire of dry wood burns on the hearth in the middle of the kazhim. The men and women gather and take their places on the benches according to seniority. Then one of the best hunters steps forward into the middle of the kazhim, where his relatives join him. All stand in a row and then begin to dance, to the accompaniment of drums and songs sung by all present at the meeting.

At the conclusion the dancers return to their places and the hunter distributes his catch among those present. He gives each person something, a pelt, a lavtak, a garment, some food, adornments and the like. He offers these gifts especially to the older men and women and to those in need. The daring and wealth of the hunter are determined by the quantity and value of the goods he distributes, and by the number of relatives who join him in dancing to proclaim his fame.

After the distribution of gifts, his wife places huge containers of food in front of everyone as evidence of his skill as a provider, and she treats the guests with great hospitality.

Then a second hunter steps forward, then a third, and eventually all appear on the scene, one at a time. Sometimes an unmarried hunter with no close relatives steps into the arena and stands alone, but the natural instincts of these savages will not let him remain in this situation for long; usually one of the old women will step forward, or perhaps several; they will recall some distant family tie with the hunter and stand with him, indicating they will help him while he is alone.

Of course such festivities must continue for several days in the large settlements. It should also be noted that although the original aim of this custom is commendable, nevertheless people everywhere are the same, and during these tribal feasts the Kuskokvims squander their property and provisions out of boastfulness, so that by the end of winter they suffer famine. However, their hunger does not shame them; rather, their lavish hospitality elevates them to a high level of regard, and hence the vanity of the savage in giving away his wealth is in fact his salvation from want.

In addition to the tribal festivities there are private celebrations for various kinds of occasions. For example a skillful hunter may be killed by enemies in a hostile settlement. His closest relative calls all the men from his own and from all friendly neighboring settlements into the kazhim, gives each a gift of some sort, entertains them all, then describes the insult to his family and asks them all to join with him in seeking revenge. Immediately strife begins, and only ends with the killing of the enemy who caused the quarrel. Of course vengeance is not always limited, and often several men will die. When that happens the war sometimes becomes a dynastic struggle between two clans, and ends with the expulsion of an entire clan from its land. It is noteworthy that the savages never kill the old people or the children. They take women into slavery and kill the men. They smear the faces of their children with the blood of those killed so the children will not be afraid of death.

As we know, the Kolosh enslave their captives, and in peace negotiations with other tribes, exchange hostages. These customs are alien to the Kuskokvims.

They do not allow women to take part in council meetings in the kazhim, and in tribal ceremonies the only women who may participate are those who have previously been initiated by the entire assemblage. The ceremony of initiation of a woman into the kazhim is carried out after she has lost her virginity, even though she is not married. A close male relative assembles the people, presents gifts, feasts them, and then presents his relative. On this occasion there is an offering to the shaman of beads, tobacco and fine clothing, which is then offered to the spirits who are believed to make it possible for the young woman to give birth to bold warriors for the tribe. The shaman declares that, out of respect to the parents of the young woman, he is obliged to become her first lover so she will be worthy of appearing before the assembly. The ceremony ends with dancing and singing. Of course, the poor maidens are excluded from the kazhim assemblies because they are not admitted into this sanctuary.

Every Kuskokvim who has killed a living creature keeps some sign in memory of it; he may paint an image of the animal on his bow, or more frequently will take one of its teeth and fasten it to his belt, along with a large number of teeth from caribou he has killed. He wears this belt during ceremonies with considerable pride, as a sign of distinction.

The Kuskokvims are ardent bathers. In winter they bathe three or four times a day. Some bathe in the kazhim and others in small bathhouses built near each iurt. These are heated by scorching hot stones. No one has secret conversations anywhere except in the bathhouse, when they are sweating from the fierce heat. If a father is displeased with a grown son he says nothing to him, but will invite a close friend to his bathhouse, and there reveal to the friend his problem, and ask him to tell the son to mend his ways because his father is unhappy with him. . . .

Generally speaking, the Kuskokvim are of medium stature; they are well built, agile and often strong. For the most part they have dark skin, but there are a number who have light skin and resemble Europeans. Most have dark hair, but some have brown or even reddish hair. The men are better looking than the women. They pierce the lower lip and insert beads, bones or pebbles. Some also pierce the nostril. The usual illnesses are broken bones, lung problems and boils. The shamans and old women know many cures. Among a number of medications, they greatly value the oily matter from two small glands near the anal opening of the beaver. They use this to treat rheumatism, wounds, blood spitting and lung problems. In the latter case, they cook the glands over a fire and use the inner part, having the afflicted person eat a pair for each dose.

I will conclude with these observations. We have only very superficial information about their beliefs and religious outlook, so it is impossible to make any positive statements about this very important and worthwhile subject. I am not including a description of their clothing, domestic utensils and weapons, because these are similar to those of other savage tribes of the north and are not significantly different.

Reference: Baron Ferdinand P. Wrangell. "Obitateli severo-zapadnykh beregov Ameriki" [The Inhabitants of the Northwest Coasts of America], in *Syn Otechestva*, 1838, Vol. 7, 51–82

72

AN IMPERIAL DECREE TO ESTABLISH A SPECIAL BISHOPRIC FOR THE RUSSIAN ORTHODOX CHURCHES IN RUSSIAN AMERICA

The Holy Governing Synod has heard a report approved by His Imperial Majesty [Nicholas I], and presented by the *Ober-Prokuror* [official in charge of Holy Synod]. The report is as follows.

First. The Sovereign Emperor, in accordance with the most humble report of the Ober-Prokuror of December 1, approved the proposal of the Holy Synod concerning the formation of a special bishopric for the [Russian Orthodox] churches in the Russian American settlements and nearby regions, on the basis of suggestions in a report of November 29, [1840]. The Emperor ordered that the bishop of that diocese be named the Bishop of Kamchatka and of the Kuril and Aleutian Islands.

Second. On December 1, 1840 a personal decree of His Imperial Majesty ordered, in accordance with the most humble proposal of the Synod, that Arkhimandrit Innokentii, who has previously served as a missionary in Russian America, be named Bishop of Kamchatka and of the Kuril and Aleutian Islands.

Third. The Emperor has approved an amendment to the November 29 report of the Synod, which directs the following:

1) Establishment of a bishopric for the churches in Russian America, which bishopric would also have jurisdiction over the churches in Kamchatka and Okhotsk, removing these from the bishopric of Irkutsk.

2) This bishopric will comprise three classes.

3) The bishop will reside in New Arkhangel. The Holy Synod directs that the orders of His Imperial Majesty be made known to all clergy through printed instructions, and that the Governing Senate be advised of this.

Reference: *PSZ*, Second Series, Vol.15, No. 14,073.

JANUARY 4, 1841

AN IMPERIAL DECREE TO PERMIT THE RUSSIAN ORTHODOX CHURCH TO ADMIT BAPTIZED NATIVES AND CREOLES FROM KAMCHATKA AND THE KURIL AND ALEUTIAN ISLANDS INTO RELIGIOUS TRAINING TO BECOME CLERGY

The Holy Governing Synod has respectfully maintained that in order to recruit native clergy in Kamchatka and the Kuril and Aleutian bishopric it is necessary to admit local tax-paying natives into the religious calling, without prolonged correspondence about the matter. It has also maintained, in its resolution of December 21, 1840, point 25, concerning the organization of that bishopric, that the bishop should be permitted to accept into religious calling capable and reliable persons from among newly baptized tribes and from the creoles currently under the full authority of the Russian American Company, in consultation with the [Chief] Administrator, from whom he is to receive approval, since these persons are under his jurisdiction.

On January 4, 1841, the Sovereign Emperor approved this most humble decree which had been submitted to Him by the Ober-Prokuror of the Holy Synod.

Reference: *PSZ*, Second Series, Vol. 20, No. 14,156a.

DECEMBER 20, 1841

INVENTORY AND BILL OF SALE TRANSFERRING POSSESSION OF
RUSSIA'S CALIFORNIA PROPERTIES TO JOHN SUTTER*

Inventory of structures and chattels located at Port Bodega, the Ross settlement, and the Russian American Company ranchos.

STRUCTURES

The structures are in the following locations: "A," at Ross; "B," at the Kostromitinov Rancho; "C," at the Khlebnikov Rancho; "D," at the Chernykh Rancho; and "E," at Bodega.

A. AT THE ROSS SETTLEMENT.

A square fort, surrounded by a row of posts 172 sazhens** long by 2 sazhens high. There are turrets in two of the corners.

Inside the fort are the following structures:

The old house for the commandant, two stories, built of beams, 8 sazhens long by 6 wide, covered with double planking. There are 6 rooms and a kitchen.

The new house for the commandant, built of square beams, 8 sazhens long by 4 wide. There are 6 rooms and a vestibule.

The house for Company employees, which has 10 rooms and 2 vestibules; 10 sazhens long by 3½ wide.

The barracks with 8 rooms and 2 vestibules; 11 sazhens long by 4 wide.

The old warehouse, two stories, built of beams, 8 sazhens

---

* The original document from which this translation is made is in French. A Spanish version also exists, but to date no Russian version has been found.

** The French term is *toise*, the Spanish, *braza*. In the absence of a Russian version, Glenn J. Farris, State Archaeologist with the California Department of Parks and Recreation, has applied the archaeological research at Fort Ross to determine that the correct translation is the seven-foot Russian *sazhen*. See his study, "Fathoming Fort Ross," in *Historical Archaeology*, Vol. 17 (1983), No. 2, pp. 93–99.

long by 4 wide. It is surrounded by an open gallery with pillars.

The granary, built of planks, 7 sazhens long by 4 wide.

A kitchen, 4 sazhens long by 3½ wide.

A storehouse for provisions, planked, 6 sazhens long by 4 wide.

An attached jailhouse.

The chapel with a cupola.

A well, 2⅓ sazhens deep.

Outside the fort there are the following structures:
A forge and blacksmith shop, built of planks, 5⅓ sazhens long by 3⅔ *arch.* [arshins?] wide, with 4 partitions.

A tannery, 5 sazhens long by 3 wide.

The public bath, 5 sazhens long by 2½ wide.

A cooperage, 10 sazhens long by 5 wide.

A shed for the baidarkas, on beams, 10 sazhens long by 5 wide.

Around the fort:
A public kitchen 5 sazhens long by 3 wide.

Two byres built of beams, 20 sazhens long by 3½ wide.

A corral, 28 sazhens long by 20 wide.

A shed for ewes.

A shed for swine.

A dairy built of planks, 6 sazhens long by 3½ wide.

A storehouse for cleaning wheat, 7¾ sazhens long by 3½ wide.

A wooden threshing floor 8 sazhens in diameter.

A windmill with a grindstone, which can grind up to 20 fanegas per day.

A windmill (old) with one stone.

A horse-powered mill with a grindstone.

A machine for making cordage.

A carpentry shed, 7 sazhens long by 3 wide.

A planked floor for winnowing wheat, 6¾ sazhens long by 5 wide.

A well, 1½ sazhens deep.

In addition, there are 24 dwellings around the fort:

4 dwellings, 5 sazhens long by 2½ wide.

5 dwellings, 4⅓ sazhens long by 2½ wide.

9 dwellings, 3⅓ sazhens long by 2 wide.

3 dwellings, 2 sazhens long by 2 wide.

At almost every dwelling there is an orchard enclosed by palings, and there are 8 sheds, 8 bathhouses and 10 kitchens.

All these houses are covered with double planking; they have glazed windows and each has a floor and a ceiling.

Located 500 sazhens from the fort there are the following:
A planked threshing floor 10 sazhens in diameter, with an adjoining shed 5 sazhens long by 3 wide.

An orchard 54 sazhens long by 2 wide, enclosed by a hedge. There are more than 260 fruit trees, including:
207 apple trees
29 peach trees
10 pear trees
10 quince trees
8 cherry trees

In the orchard there is a new four-room house 4½ sazhens long by 4 wide, covered with planking. The house has a kitchen 2½ sazhens square.

A small garden 4 sazhens long by 10½ wide, in which there are some 20 fruit trees. At Ross there is as much as 70 *arpents*

[1 arpent = 1.5 acres] of arable land, most of which is enclosed by fences.

A fruit garden enclosed by a fence, 70 sazhens long by 20 wide, with a small orange grove.

B. THE KOSTROMITINOV RANCH.

A barracks 8 sazhens long by 3 wide, covered with planking, with 3 rooms and a vestibule.

A warehouse 7 sazhens long by 3 wide, covered with planking. There are seed storage compartments inside. Next to this, the land slopes down to the river.

A house 3 sazhens long by 2 wide.

Two wooden threshing floors: one 8 sazhens in diameter, and the other, planked, 10 sazhens.

A wheat-winnowing floor, 12 sazhens square, built on posts.

A shack for Indians, built of planks, 7 sazhens long by 2½ wide.

A kitchen 2 sazhens square, with 2 stoves.

A bathhouse 3 sazhens long by 2 wide.

A boat for crossing the Slavianka [River].

There are more than 100 arpents of arable land here [suitable] for sowing up to 250 fanegas of wheat.

C. THE KHLEBNIKOV RANCH.

A 3-room adobe house, 3½ sazhens long by 2½ wide, covered with planks and surrounded by a hedge. Next to it is a sundial.

A barracks 10 sazhens long by 3½ wide, divided into 3 sections, covered with planks.

A storehouse 7½ sazhens long by 3½ sazhens wide, covered with planks, with compartments for storing seed.

A large wood threshing floor 12 sazhens in diameter.

A kitchen and a forge 6 sazhens long by 3½ wide, covered with planks.

I. G. Voznesenskii made this unfinished sketch of Fort Ross from the sea during his 1840–42 visit to California. We see the high palisade and the octagonal shore bastion; the Russian American Company flag would have flown from both flag-poles. Institute of Ethnography AN SSSR, Leningrad. (OHS neg. 26989)

4 shacks for the Indians and for storing provisions. These are of various dimensions.

A horse-powered mill with one stone, which can grind 4 fanegas per day.

A large corral for the livestock.

The arable land is enclosed by a fence. The fields here produce very good fava beans, maize, tobacco, watermelons and other things.

D. THE CHERNYKH RANCH.

A 6-room barracks 7 sazhens long by 3 wide, covered with planks.

A kitchen 4 sazhens long by 2 wide.

A bathhouse 3 sazhens long by 2 wide.

A storehouse for provisions 7 sazhens long by 3 wide, covered with planks.

A floor for winnowing wheat, 18 sazhens square.

Two shacks for supplies.

A threshing floor 10 sazhens in diameter.

Two hothouses made of planks, each 8 sazhens.

The arable land is enclosed by a fence. There is as much as 20 arpents of land on which 50 fanegas of wheat can be

The Chernykh rancho, as seen by Voznesenskii shortly before the sale of Russia's California possessions to John Sutter. Fenced cattle stockades are in the foreground, cultivated land on the slope beyond. Institute of Ethnography AN SSSR, Leningrad. (OHS neg. 26997)

sown. The fields here produce very good fava beans, maize, onions and other things, and the land is suitable for an orchard.

E. BODEGA.

A storehouse with an open gallery surrounded by columns, 10 sazhens long by 5 wide, covered with planks, well-suited for storing seeds and merchandise.

A house 3 sazhens square, with 3 rooms and a stove.

A bathhouse 4 sazhens long by 2 wide.

A corral.

A boat.

The following should [also] be considered as belonging to Bodega:
   A cottage on the grazing ground.
   A large corral.
   A shack and a corral.
   The boats:
      A copper-covered smallboat, well suited for navigating all along the coast of California. 25 tons.

Two hide-covered launches; one has 16 oars, the other, 18.

A baidarka.

A longboat.

Machinery and agricultural equipment:

A cast iron *ecopaise* [?] for threshing wheat.

A Fogh Harrow.

27 ox-drawn plows.

24 horse-drawn plows.

26 pairs of plowshares.

21 harrows.

24 harnesses *en lais* [?]

30 horse harnesses.

21 bridles.

29 saddles.

8 bridle bits.

20 shadracks.

16 saddle blankets.

5 4-wheeled carts.

10 2-wheeled carts.

15 pairs of wheels.

Furnishings:

14 laurel wood chairs.

4 armchairs.

1 couch.

1 oval table.

1 square table.

1 armoire.

1 ordinary square table.

2 counting tables.

4 sofa pads.

8 pads.

1 bed mattress.

3 mattress cases.

3 cushion cases.

2 bed sheets.

8 chairs covered with hide.

11 wood chairs.

3 armoires with windows.

4 ditto.

6 spring-roller shades.

Livestock:

1,700 head of horned beasts, namely:

Plow oxen	70	
Medium size oxen	174	
Small oxen	111	355

Large cows	777	
Medium cows	409	
Small cows	159	1,345
		1,700

940 horses and mules, namely:

Large mules	53	
Small mules	2	55

Large stallions	20	
Medium stallions	30	
Small colts	50	100

Large mares	320	
Medium mares	70	
Small mares	90	
Horses	305	785
		940

About 100 of the horses have been broken to the plow and wagon, and some 20 mules to the harrow.

900 ewes and wethers, namely:

Medium wethers	100	
Small wethers	35	
Large ewes	540	
Medium ewes	217	
Small ewes	8	900

TOTAL: 3,540 head of livestock

(Signed) P. Kostromitinov   (Signed) J. A. Sutter

Received from Mr. Sutter in the month of December, 1841, in Spanish piasters	$400.00

Due from Mr. Sutter to the Russian American Company as of January 1, 1842	33,468.16
TOTAL	33,868.16

(Signed) P. Kostromitinov

Port San Francisco
19 December 1842 v.s. [old style]
Current Account
Russian American and Mr. Sutter   San Francisco

According to the stipulated contract, for the sale of the structures and chattels at Ross	$30,000.00
By another current account for various merchandise, provisions and materials	3,868.16
TOTAL	33,868.16

(Signed) J. A. Sutter

The undersigned, agent of the Russian American Company, Petr Kostromitinov, and the inhabitant of Upper California, the Chargé de justice and Representative of the Government on the frontiers of the Sacramento River, Captain J. A. Sutter following preliminary agreements, have drawn up the following articles:

ARTICLE 1. It is agreed that the Russian American Company, in evacuating Ross, upon the consent of His Majesty the Emperor of all the Russias [Nicholas I], cedes to Mr. Sutter all its establishments located on the coasts of New Albion at Port Bodega and North of that port to Ross, *with the exception, however, of the land*, according to the inventory signed in order by the two above mentioned persons.

ARTICLE 2. It is agreed that as the price of all these establishments ceded by the Russian American Company, Mr. Sutter is obliged to pay the sum of 30,000 piasters within four years, reckoning from the year 1842.

ARTICLE 3. It is agreed that the payment of the said sum will be made in produce of the land during the first and second years, in the amount of five thousand piasters ($5,000), and in the third year in the amount of ten thousand piasters ($10,000). For the last, which is to say the fourth, year, Mr. Sutter will pay in cash the sum of ten thousand piasters ($10,000).

ARTICLE 4. It is agreed that Mr. Sutter will prepare produce in the following amounts within the appointed time (Article 2) during the first two years:

1,600	fanegas of wheat @ $2	$3,200
100	fanegas of peas @ 2¼	225
25	fanegas of frijole beans @ 3	75
50	quintals of soap @ 14	700
200	*arrobas* [1 arroba = ¼ quintal] of lard @ 2	400
250	arrobas of tallow @ 1½	375

The third year this quantity must be doubled, that is, to equal the sum of $10,000. It is understood that all these commodities must be of the best quality, the wheat and peas fresh, the soap dry, the tallow and lard fresh and clean. Five and one-half Spanish arrobas are equal to one fanega.

ARTICLE 5. It is agreed that Mr. Sutter is obliged to have the produce ready by the first of September during the three years, n.s. [New Style; see Editorial Principles], reckoning from 1842, the time established for the arrival of the Company vessels at Port San Francisco.

ARTICLE 6. It is agreed that the Russian American Company will dispatch its ships to the port of San Francisco to take on the goods during the time established by Article 5, and Mr. Sutter, upon the arrival of the vessel, will make the necessary arrangements to load the prepared goods through his own means, so the vessel will not lose time.

ARTICLE 7. It is agreed that if the shipment of goods is not ready upon the arrival of the Company ship at the designated time, and if the vessel must return to Sitka without having loaded its cargo, Mr. Sutter will be personally responsible, without rejoinder, for all expenses incurred by the ship from Sitka to Port San Francisco; that is, the maintenance of the crew and the cost of freight; or, in place of the produce, he must pay cash, reckoning the sum which must be paid this year as per Article 4.

ARTICLE 8. It is agreed that the vessels of the Russian American Company, which will come to take on the commodities mentioned in ARTICLE 4, will enter without paying customs fees or tonnage dues. If necessary Mr. Sutter will pay fees for tonnage and for anchorage, according to the size of the vessel.

ARTICLE 9. It is agreed that although the Russian American Company is fully confident of the integrity of Mr. Sutter in regard to payment, nevertheless as guarantee of the agreement, and in case of unforeseen circumstances, for repayment of the above mentioned sum, his establishment on the Sacramento River, which is called New Helvetia, founded in accordance with the government of California and in accordance with legal documents, with all the structures and chattel existing there, will serve as guarantee. Likewise, all the establishments at Port Bodega and at the Khlebnikov and Chernykh ranchos, which Mr. Sutter intends to keep intact and in his own possession, will [also] serve as security so that in the event of nonfulfillment of this obligation we will nevertheless be able to enter our claims as the owners of Port Bodega and of Ross. This same stipulation extends to the heirs of Mr. Sutter in the event of his death, if such mischance should occur before the formal fulfillment of the agreement, and if they should refuse the payment as per ARTICLE 4.

ARTICLE 10. It is agreed that if, in the event of war between Russia and any other nation, the Mexican Republic were to join the enemies of the Russian Empire, and thus be unable to dispatch vessels to accept the produce at the time established above, the sanctity of this contract will remain inviolable, and as soon as peace is reestablished, it will resume in full force.

ARTICLE 11. It is agreed that the Russian American Company, desiring to render assistance to Mr. Sutter, is ready to transport to Bodega from Ross, structures which are not too cumbersome, such as window frames, doors, and all other small items which can be transported in our hide small boats and the large launch. The transport will begin from the present time, and continue until the arrival of the vessel from Port New Arkhangel at Bodega or San Francisco. At that time any persons who have remained here should be put on board without delay, and Mr. Sutter will take possession of everything and continue the transport by his own means.

To give this contract full force and weight, we sign below and affix our seals.

(Signed) J. A. Sutter   (Signed) P. Kostromitinov

[In Spanish]

[I am] Francisco Guerrero, Justice of Peace of this place. Don Pedro Kostromitinov and Don Juan Sutter, with whom I am acquainted, have come before me and stated their intention to sign an agreement written in French regarding the structures and chattels of the Ross Establishment, and each of them has affixed a red wax seal beside his signature.

I have signed below, and in ratification they have signed with me, and with the other witnesses, to which I hereby attest.

(Signed) J. J. Vioget   (Signed) Francisco Guerrero
                                                              J. A. Sutter
                                                              Jacob Leese

[In English:]

I hereby certify that the above is a true copy of the original received at the Legation from the Foreign Office.

Julian A. Mitchell
Secretary of the Legation

Reference: Bancroft Library, Manuscript Division. J. A. Sutter Correspondence and Papers, 1846–1870. MS C-B 631. We have made our own translation.

CIRCA 1840–45

INSTRUCTIONS FROM ARVID A. ETHOLEN, CHIEF ADMINISTRATOR OF THE RUSSIAN AMERICAN COMPANY, TO TOIONS WHO ARE TO BECOME STARSHINAS IN ALEUT SETTLEMENTS IN THE KODIAK DEPARTMENT

The Kodiak office, with the approval of the Chief Administrator of the colony, will select starshinas from among Aleut toions who have come to the attention of the office and of local officials because of their exemplary behavior, industry and zeal in projects which are beneficial to the Company. Thus, the starshinas will influence the Aleuts over whom they have jurisdiction and this will assure that the Aleuts pay proper respect and obedience to these starshinas.

The starshinas know the Aleut way of life, their needs and their weaknesses. They are to direct their people toward a better standard of living in every possible way, and thus facilitate the desire and concern of the administration to improve living conditions for the Kodiak Aleuts by consolidating them into [larger] communal settlements, as is presently done in other departments of the colony. In addition to supervising the Aleuts and taking responsibility for their needs, as fathers do for their families, a starshina who fulfills his position well must constantly set an example for them in all aspects of hunting in the Kodiak department; and through his work on behalf of the Company he will try to justify in full the trust and distinction which the colonial administration has conferred upon him.

In order to carry out his duties properly, each starshina who is initially entrusted with supervising four Aleut settlements will receive a salary of 500 rubles per annum, in addition to other remuneration which he is entitled to expect for zealous service on behalf of the Company. (At present there are nine settlements on Kodiak Island and several small communities. Each toion receives 250 rubles in paper currency per year. If he is the leader of a hunting party he also receives a share of the overall catch).

The primary obligations of the Aleut starshinas are as follows:

1.

The starshina must be firm in having the Aleut men and women fulfill their Christian obligations and carry out all tasks assigned to them by the priest. Toward this end, each settlement is to try to build a chapel, through its own effort, where the priest can conduct worship services when he visits. They should build the chapel when time and circumstances permit, after the settlement has been organized and put into order.

The starshina must also always see to it that there are sufficient supplies of food and clothing for winter. In regard to health, in order to prevent epidemics and the like, he is to notify promptly the officials of any signs of disease he observes among the Aleuts. Seriously ill persons are to be sent for treatment to the infirmary at Pavlovsk Harbor as quickly as possible. The starshina is to take careful note that any indisposed persons who remain in the settlement follow the physician's orders explicitly. The physician will visit the settlement periodically, as required, to examine the Aleuts of both sexes and of all ages.

2.

Upon orders from the Kodiak office or from the administrator, the starshina is to appoint Aleuts for the hunting parties. In summer they are to hunt sea otter; in winter they will trap and hunt small game. They are also to hunt whales and birds, as well as sea lions, seals and other such animals to obtain pelts for lavtaks. When the starshina receives all the necessary hunting equipment from the baidarshchik or other agent from the Kodiak office, he is to distribute it to responsible promyshlenniks, using his own judgment. At the end of the hunt he will collect this equipment and return it to the baidarshchik. While the hunt is in progress, the starshina is to supervise everything closely so the promyshlenniks will hunt as zealously as possible for the Company's benefit and their own, and so they will not waste time through idleness and inactivity.

Indolent Aleuts are to be reported to the office administrator, and when needed, should be assigned to temporary work at Pavlovsk Harbor or with various artels. The starshina is to assign each promyshlennik his own place to hunt, where no one else will have hunting rights, and the starshina is always to have spare parts to replace damaged lasts, harnesses or trap jaws.

3

The starshina is to organize hunting parties for the mutual benefit of the Aleuts and the Company; each Aleut is to be assigned to the kind of hunt for which he has the greatest aptitude, and in which he has the greatest experience. The starshina is also to make certain that when he assigns the hunting parties, there are enough males left in the settlement to prepare the necessary amounts of food and supplies for the colony for winter. He is to equip the necessary number of Aleuts to perform Company work, both seasonal and permanent. In order to ease the burden on Aleuts who go on hunting parties or who work to prepare food and supplies for the colony, the old men, women and young boys and girls can be put to work. They are to carry out the tasks the starshina assigns to them, without arguing, for the general benefit of the settlement.

Only persons of advanced age, those who are infirm, and women close to giving birth may be excused from work.

4.

The starshina is to see to it that the old and infirm, and any orphans assigned to the settlement, always receive sufficient food from the communal supplies in the settlement. He is to take special care that young orphans are trained by the most reliable Aleuts, who will teach them the true Aleut way of life, instill in them a sense of morality at an early age, and oversee the lawful marriages of the young people.

5.

The starshina is responsible for seeing to it that the people entrusted to his care are in good health. It is absolutely necessary that these persons frequent the bath houses more often, that healthy persons do not bathe together with those who are ill, and that the baraboras in the settlement are constantly inspected to insure that they are clean and that all objects which might rot and befoul the air are immediately disposed of in the sea.

Persons who die are not to be buried just where they happen to be; rather, the local official is to take the bodies to a special burial place, some distance from the settlement. Bodies must be buried as deep as possible, and a cross should immediately be erected on each grave.

The starshina is to watch over the Aleuts and repeatedly

Native chief of Port Mulgrave. Belcher, *Voyage Around the World*. (OHS neg. OrHi 82081)

warn them not to eat meat from decayed whales washed up on shore, or from any other toxic substance they may come across. Through inexcusable lack of prudence the Kodiak Aleuts have often died prematurely from this cause. The starshina should also warn them against putting out to sea in their baidarkas in heavy storms and other dangerous weather conditions.

6.

The starshina is at all times to keep an accurate census of all men and women who have been assigned to his settlement, and he should keep a roster of all Aleuts and promyshlenniks capable of performing work for the Company so that when he goes to Pavlovsk harbor in March every year, upon the request of the office administrator he can submit this roster for the immediate assignment of persons to hunting parties and Company work projects. Toward this end if the starshina is illiterate, he should be assigned a creole who knows how to write.

7.

When the sea otter hunt is concluded, the groups of baidarkas should not disperse, but instead, proceed to Pavlovsk harbor to be paid for the hunt. Aleuts who have used their own baidarkas and kamleikas during the hunt will be [additionally] recompensed. The Aleuts are then to proceed from the harbor directly to their assigned settlements and report to the starshina. Under no circumstances are they to travel about at will.

If the starshina of some settlement notices that an Aleut from another settlement has come to live in his settlement, as soon as possible the Aleut is to be transferred back to his own place; if not, the starshina of the other settlement must be informed. In general, every starshina should exercise firm control so none of the Aleuts under his supervision will roam about or venture to leave the settlement without permission from the starshina.

8.

Any furs the Aleuts obtain through the use of traps and firearms with the consent of the starshina must be brought back to the local baidarshchik and handed over to the Company at the established price. In exchange, the Aleuts will be provided with everything necessary for the way of life. They are not to wander freely from their settlement to Pavlovsk Harbor, under the pretext of delivering their furs there—a catch which often consists of only a single fox or sea otter pelt. Through such profitless journeys the Aleuts lose men needed for their work in the settlement for the benefit of the Company as well as for their own advantage.

9.

Once the hunt is over the starshina is to collect all the traps and turn them over to the local baidarshchik or to any other person the Kodiak office designates. From the baidarshchik he receives Company firearms for the hunt; he distributes these to the most reliable promyshlenniks. Upon completion of that aspect of the hunt, all the firearms are to be returned to the baidarshchik. The starshina must maintain strict supervision so none of the Aleuts who may have weapons of their own will resort to shooting animals during the season closed to hunting. It is especially important that no one frighten off the sea otters in this manner.

10.

The starshina of an Aleut settlement is completely dependent and subordinate to the Kodiak office and its administrator, and is always to refer to the local [Russian] baidarshchik as the person whom higher colonial authorities have appointed over him. For nonfeasance of the prescribed rules, for any disorder in his settlement, and for neglect of duty or unjust actions against the Aleuts entrusted to his care, the starshina will be subjected to strict discipline and removal from his position.

The baidarshchiks of artels or odinochkas absolutely must not interfere in the starshina's sphere of responsibility, but nonetheless they are accountable for seeing that the rules pertaining to starshinas are carried out. Every baidarshchik must know the obligations of the Aleut starshinas, and in case of neglect of duty or abuse of power on the part of a starshina, the local baidarshchik must immediately report this to the Kodiak office. The administrator of that office is to investigate the matter personally and immediately, not relying on the word of the baidarshchik.

11.

In order to improve the organization of the settlements and to teach the Aleuts how to be productive, it is necessary to try to plant potatoes near the settlements; these will be available for regular use by the inhabitants, and in case of necessity, can be a source of sustenance. Livestock breeding is to be introduced wherever local circumstances permit, but the animals should be used to produce milk, and not be slaughtered for meat. The starshinas are to see that milk is distributed to the sick, and to nursing infants whose mothers are ill and cannot nurse the babies themselves; milk is also to be provided for orphans, or for children who have lost their mothers. The Kodiak office should set aside several head of cattle for this beneficial purpose. This arrangement is to be considered a loan to the settlement from the Company, for their mutual benefit. The livestock are to be returned when the herd is sufficiently increased.

12.

After listing the above primary responsibilities of the Aleut starshinas, it only remains to hope that as individuals who have been favored with the special attention of the higher colonial administration, they will try to use every effort to justify fully the trust placed in them, and that once they have carefully studied the reason for establishing these settlements, they will understand how this measure will be of great benefit to the Kodiak Aleuts. As guardian fathers of families, the starshinas should be taken into the confidence of all the persons over them, and realize that all practical suggestions for improving the living conditions of the Aleuts will be given the full attention of the authorities.

Native chief of Sitka. Belcher, *Voyage Around the World.* (OHS neg. OrHi 56316)

Once the Aleuts are grouped into these settlements and have agreed to the general structure, it is advisable that each year they donate a certain percent of the furs they have obtained to be used for the benefit of these settlements, to make improvements, so that in time they will have their own tidy small sum under the supervision of the Kodiak office, which can be used in case of some unforeseen emergency in the settlements, or for some further improvements. With a constant and settled way of life they can forever end that unhappy condition which, in spite of the efforts of the authorities, has been the lot of the Kodiak Aleuts to the present time, as opposed to Aleuts from other departments of the colonies. They have faced constant suffering and impoverishment from the unsettled and disorganized aspects of their lives; and the intractable customs and prejudices of their forefathers have brought so many disasters upon them.

May the Almighty send down His blessing from heaven to consummate the organization which has been introduced for the benefit of the Kodiak Aleuts.

Reference: P. A. Tikhmenev. *Istoricheskoe obozrenie obrazovaniia Rossiisko-Amerikanskoi kompanii i deistvii eia do nastoiashchago vremeni.* Vol. 2, (St. Petersburg: 1861–63), Supplement, 74–79.

76

THE RENEWAL OF THE CHARTER OF THE RUSSIAN AMERICAN COM-
PANY FOR TWENTY YEARS: RIGHTS AND PRIVILEGES

Chapter I. The Rights and Privileges of the Company.
1. The Russian American Company, organized to hunt on
the mainland of Northwest America and on the Aleutian and
Kuril islands, as well as all through the [North Pacific] Ocean,
is under the patronage of His Imperial Majesty.

2. The limits of navigation and hunting for the Company
along the coast of the mainland and among the islands of
Northwest America are located in the following delineated area
between Russian, English and American possessions. Beginning from the southernmost point of Prince of Wales Island,
located in 54° 40′ northern latitude and between 131° and 133°
western longitude (from the Greenwich meridian), that line
proceeds north along the strait known as the Portland Canal to
the point of the mainland where it reaches 56°, northern latitude. From there the line of demarcation follows the crest of
the mountains extending parallel to the coast to its intersection
with 141° western longitude (from the same meridian); and finally, from that intersection, the same meridian, 141°, represents in its extension to the Arctic Ocean the frontier of
Russian possessions on the mainland of Northwest America.

3. In all of these places which belong to Russia according
to this delineation, the Company has the exclusive right over
all Russian subjects to engage in the hunting of all animals and
fish.

4. The Company is permitted to utilize everything it has
discovered to the present time, or may discover in the future in
these places, both surface and below ground, without any [con-
flicting] claim on the part of others.

5. Within the limits set forth in Paragraph 2, and based on
its own judgment and needs, the Company will be permitted
in the future to establish new settlements and fortified posts
where it considers them necessary to provide secure living conditions. It also has the right to enlarge and improve previous

enterprises, and to dispatch ships with goods and promyshlenniks to those regions without the slightest hindrance.

6. The Company is permitted to dispatch its ships to all neighboring peoples and to carry on trade with them, upon receiving permission for this from their governments.

The Company is also permitted, as it may desire, to dispatch its ships to trade in the following Chinese ports: Canton, Amoy, Fuchzhou-Fu, Ninbofu and Shanghai, with the proviso, however, in accordance with Article 2393 of the Customs Regulations (Code of Laws, Volume 6, 1842), that these ships are not to carry any opium whatsoever for sale in China.

7. All [government] offices are to acknowledge the Main Administration of the Russian American Company as the principal agent designated to administer the affairs of the Company; requests from such offices concerning matters relating to the Company are not to be directed to any partners of the Company, but rather to the Main Administration.

8. In order to provide the Company greater opportunity to comply with the aims of the Government, which has entrusted to the Company the administration of such a vast extent of land inhabited by a considerable number of persons, the Emperor grants the servitors of the Company the following rights regarding the fulfillment of their assigned responsibilities.

A. Those who belong to categories with the right to enter into service, but not exclusively in service to the Company, are considered actually to be in government service, and have the right to advance in rank and to wear the full dress uniform of the Ministry of Finance. They are subject to civil regulations in promotions, and enjoy the same rank and rights as all other civil servants. Their advancement in rank is determined upon the recommendation of the Main Administration to the Minister of Finance, who, in the case of medical personnel, confers with the Ministry of Internal Affairs.

B. The Company has the right to offer work, and hire for naval duty and for service in other departments, officers, noncommissioned officers, sailors, gunners, medical personnel and *feldshers* [medical assistants], both for service aboard ships sent out from Russia to her colonies and for service within the colonies and in Okhotsk. During their time of service with the Company, these persons are considered to be on active service in regard to all recompense, except for [promotion in] rank, to which they are entitled on the basis of seniority and designation by their appropriate superiors. Officers retain the right to receive half pay and have batmen. Medical personnel of civil rank are appointed to Company service by the Ministry of Internal Affairs.

c. Retired officials, upon assignment to a permanent position with the Company retain their rank and previous status and are considered on active duty, enjoying all the privileges set forth in Paragraph 1.

D. Company servitors from categories not having the right to enter government service enjoy the status of categories to which their assignments entitle them. However, if they retire from Company service in less than ten years they return to their previous status.

E. Those who serve for ten years with special benefit to the Company, upon retirement from Company service, with the recommendation of the Main Administration of the Company, will be granted the status of personal distinguished citizenship. Such persons are removed from their original social status, and as a result of their special service, the Main Administration of the Company has the right to request for them the status of hereditary distinguished citizenship.

9. When officials who have been in Company service continue in government service, they retain the right of receiving pensions for their service with the Company, and a medal for outstanding faultless service.

10. Officials of the Company who serve in the colonies are entitled to receive the Order of Saint Vladimir, Fourth Class, for service; this order is granted after a shorter period of service than is usual, which also applies to those serving in Siberia.

11. For service in navigation, or as artisans and other skilled employment, the Company may hire anywhere in the Russian Empire persons of any condition who are free, above suspicion and have the usual passports or travel papers. Upon the request of the Main Administration, gubernia authorities must issue to these persons hired by the Company passports good for one to seven years. Where applicable, the Company

must pay taxes and obligations for such persons, and deduct these costs from their pay.

12. When the agreed term of service has expired, the Company is not obliged to send back to Russia any servitors who desire to remain in America or are indebted to the Company. Upon the request of the Company such persons [who remain] are to be issued new passports; however, it is obligatory that such requests be accompanied by a written statement. Servitors who express the desire to remain in the colonies for any of the above reasons are to sign this request personally, if they are literate; if they are illiterate someone else must write the request on their behalf and two witnesses must attest to it. If the servitor is indebted to the Company, the Chief Administrator must sign the document requesting the new passport.

13. All Company servitors must fulfill their obligations and carry out the instructions from the Main Administration and orders from their superiors that accord with the statute of the Company and with laws pertaining to hunting and trade and the accompanying instructions.

Dereliction of duty or the detection of abuse are subject to investigation according to the rules pertaining to government service. Local officials are to have servitors make an account, and if the Main Administration requests it, there is to be an immediate legal investigation.

When a decision has been handed down, there is no prohibition against presenting a petition of complaint to the Governing Senate but this must be done within six months after the decision. In such cases military and medical personnel are to address any complaints to their superiors. . . .

16. Ships dispatched around the world from Kronstadt, or from Okhotsk or other Russian ports, to the Russian colonies, are permitted to take on cargoes of Russian as well as foreign goods on which duties have previously been paid. Upon their return from the colonies they may unload the cargos of furs and other goods and products without hindrance, upon presenting notification from the Main Administration to the customs officials; if in Okhotsk, this should come from the office of the local authority. Since these and other goods are dispatched from one Russian port to another, duties should not be

levied on them unless some special decree is issued imposing internal duties on furs.

17. Because of the remoteness of the Okhotsk oblast, where it may be necessary to repair or refit a vessel or even to build a new vessel, the Company has the privilege of using lumber without hindrance, in places convenient for them. The Okhotsk office is immediately to inform the local forestry authorities of where the lumber is being cut, how much, and of what nature.

18. For the purpose of shooting animals, firing naval signals, arming ships, ports and redoubts, and for other needs on the American mainland and islands, the Company may use its own funds to purchase from the Kronstadt port supply depot gunpowder, arms, shells and other armament which cannot be obtained in the colonies at unrestricted sale.

All the above items are to be sold to the Company at the same prices paid by the Navy, with a markup of ten percent to cover warehouse expenses. If there is no maritime communication between St. Petersburg and the colonies, the Company may obtain 40 to 80 puds of gunpowder per year from the Irkutsk government arms depot, on the same basis, and up to 200 puds of lead shot from the Nerchinsk ammunition works.

19. In order that the Company may act without restriction and with security in its affairs, all structures where its factories are located are hereby exempted from billeting. . . .

21. All civil and military authorities and local officials are expressly forbidden to interfere with the privileges granted to the Company, and in case of potential loss or danger to the Company, they are to give warning. They must also render assistance, security and protection, upon request from the Company's Main Administration, its offices and agents.

22. These rights and privileges are granted to the Company for a period of twenty years beginning January 1, 1842. . . .

Chapter II. Company Obligations to the Government; Government Supervision of Its Activities.

24. The Company must use all possible means to try to justify the trust placed in it, protect all the colonies over which it enjoys a monopoly, avoid any action which could disrupt

concord with neighboring powers, establish all its enterprises for general benefit to the state, and strictly observe the boundaries as established in this Statute.

25. The Company reports directly to His Imperial Majesty concerning its affairs, instructions, progress, improvements in Company enterprises, and the amount of its capital.

In regard to other matters involving the government the Company is to report directly to the Minister of Finance. If he offers suggestions with which the Company cannot agree, the Minister will report this to His Imperial Majesty.

26. The Minister of Finance is responsible for supervising Company activities as they relate to the government.

27. The Minister of Finance is to exercise vigilant supervision so the Company will undertake nothing contrary to the privileges and regulations decreed for it. Should there be any violation, he must take immediate measures to correct it.

28. The Minister of Finance receives from other ministers or from other offices or individuals within his jurisdiction reports on everything that may relate to Company activities, and therefore he will warn the Company [of any impending problem] and take appropriate action to make available to the Company any necessary protection and assistance.

29. Any civil and military authorities who receive complaints of improper activity (with the exception of criminal matters) on the part of Company offices presently operating in Siberia, or others which may be established in the future, must have clear responses and documentation; the administrator of each office bears the responsibility for such activities. The [civil and military] authorities will investigate the matter and report to the Main Administration of the Company in order to set into motion legal procedures. They are also to make an immediate report to the Minister of Finance.

30. In order that the Minister of Finance may have precise information on all the activities of the Company and the status of its business, the Main Administration of the Company must report the balance of the Company's capital to the Minister of Finance, giving him the same figure to be reported to the general meeting of the shareholders of the Company. They must also furnish him with a detailed account of the condition of the

colonies, the population, the condition of charitable institutions and other enterprises, the amount of goods exported, the method of disposing of exported goods in Kiakhta and in Russia, and, finally, a general account of all matters undertaken for the improvement of the colonies.

Reference: *PSZ*, Second Series, Vol. 19, 1844. No. 18,290, 612–617.

77

OCTOBER 10, 1844

THE RENEWAL OF THE CHARTER OF THE RUSSIAN AMERICAN COM-
PANY: COLONIAL ADMINISTRATION

Chapter VII. The Establishment of Administration for the Colonies: The Chief Administrator

143. The Chief Administrator is appointed by His Imperial Majesty from a list of candidates presented from the Main Administration of the Company. These candidates are definitely to be selected from among senior naval officers, with the prior approval of the supreme naval authorities. Staff officers lower in rank than Captain First Rank, upon appointment as Chief Administrator will be promoted to the next higher rank.

144. The term of service for the Chief Administrator in the colonies is five years from the time of his appointment until he hands over his command to his successor.

145. If he desires to administer the colonies for a longer period of time, he may do so with the prior approval of the naval authorities and with the consent of the Main Administration of the Company.

146. With respect to military personnel originally from European countries now serving in the colonies or aboard Company ships, the Chief Administrator has authority over them corresponding to that of Port Commandant. In the case of military personnel not in Company service, but on temporary assignment in the colonies, the Chief Administrator's relationship to them is determined by rules corresponding to the relationship between junior and senior officers.

147. Because of the lack of courts in the colonies, the Chief Administrator is granted the following authority:

A. Criminal matters: on the basis of his own investigation he is to transfer these matters to the Council of Colonial Administration, or to a commission especially organized by him to ascertain the facts. Upon investigation he is to send both the facts of the case and the criminals to the nearest authority in Russia. The same procedure is to be followed in regard to military personnel in Company service, when the matter of crime falls within the jurisdiction of a military tribunal.

B. Lesser matters normally under police authority: the Chief Administrator will either decide the manner of punishment himself, on the basis of existing laws, or he will transfer the matter to a special commission whose decision, upon his confirmation, will be carried out then and there. A report is to be forwarded to the Main Administration of the Company.

148. For minor offenses which often occur among workers, such as idleness, drunkenness and fighting, the Chief Administrator will determine the manner of punishment on the basis of police regulations.

149. All disputes over property which arise in the colonies between Russians and creoles, creoles and natives, or between natives and their toions and starshinas, are to be settled by the Chief Administrator, with the advice of the Council of Colonial Administration, or through a special commission organized for that purpose.

150. The Chief Administrator has the right to use his discretion in the following matters:

A. Appoint and replace commanding officers of Company ships.

B. Submit to the Main Administration of the Company for confirmation or rejection his choices for administrators of the colonial offices.

C. Appoint and dismiss bookkeepers, secretaries, warehouse supervisors and other servitors under his jurisdiction.

D. Appoint settled natives to the rank of toions, and dismiss them from that rank.

E. Designate amounts of pay, without overstepping the guidelines presently set by the Main Administration, or to be set in the future.

F. Distribute cash compensation once a year, without exceeding the sum designated by the Main Administration.

151. The Chief Administrator has the right to require that all persons under his jurisdiction in the colonies carry out his orders and instructions.

152. The Chief Administrator has the right to demand an accounting from the administrator of the Okhotsk office on all matters having a direct bearing on the colonies. The latter must carry out all orders from the Chief Administrator.

153. The Chief Administrator is responsible for all Company servitors in the colonies who have been negligent or have

failed to safeguard the Company's interests. Depending on the degree of guilt, he is to use the following means of punishment: reproof, reprimand, docking of pay, demotion, dismissal or expulsion to Russia before expiration of contract. The Chief Administrator is to report on all of these matters to the Main Administration of the Company; the latter must bring such matters to the attention of the Naval Ministry and the Ministry of Internal Affairs if the punishment involves naval officers or medical personnel.

154. The Chief Administrator cannot personally change or limit existing decrees and instructions from higher authorities or from the Main Administration. He may only submit reports about local problems and difficulties, but in especially important cases, while awaiting a decision, he may suspend the punishment and take personal responsibility for any problems which may result.

155. The Chief Administrator has no jurisdiction over frontier matters established by treaties.

156. The Chief Administrator, in establishing the amount of money to be paid to the Aleuts for hunting, in trading with foreigners, cannot exceed the sum determined by the staff and by the instructions of the Main Administration of the Company. Likewise he cannot lower or raise the prices on goods which have been set according to the instructions from the Main Administration, nor can he forgive any debt to the Company without a decision from the Main Administration.

157. The Chief Administrator's responsibilities include the following:

A. He is to see that frontier outposts which are subject to attacks from savage tribes are adequately supplied with arms and garrisons and that measures are taken to guarantee the safety of the inhabitants.

B. He is to see that insofar as possible the coastal fortifications of the principal ports of the colonies are adequately supplied with weapons and are in a condition of defense.

C. He is to see that servitors in harbors and on ships are trained in firing guns and cannon so that if necessary they can substitute for a military garrison.

158. The Chief Administrator is to insist on military order and discipline and see that these are fully enforced.

159. He is to order that junior naval officers in Company

service take examinations on a regular basis, as is done in other ports of Russia. The results of these examinations, as well as service reports, are to be submitted to the Main Administration and through that body to the Inspection Department of the Naval Ministry. Such examinations are not required for senior naval officers in regard to their service in the colonies.

160. The Chief Administrator is strictly ordered to see that:

A. General governmental decrees on all matters pertaining to Russian subjects are carried out precisely; likewise conventions and treaties concluded with foreign powers.

B. Privileges and regulations set forth in this charter are not violated.

C. No one is oppressed, and each person enjoys the right of owning property and the right of personal safety.

D. All Company enterprises relating to the colonies, which are under his direct jurisdiction, are carried out for the benefit of the Company.

161. The Chief Administrator is especially responsible for the well-being of the colonies. He must diligently carry out the regulations set forth in articles 100, 101, 102 and 103, and he is to submit periodic reports to the Main Administration concerning needs and requirements he has found in carrying out the policies referred to in these articles.

162. The Chief Administrator has a special responsibility for ensuring:

A. That no one serving the Company is forcibly detained in Company settlements.

B. That such persons receive everything due them under the terms on which they were hired by the Company.

C. That such persons do not incur excessive debts.

D. That they receive such assistance as is stipulated in this Charter, and are well-treated.

E. That native inhabitants, creoles and independent neighboring peoples are treated appropriately.

F. That settled native peoples are not abused; on the contrary, that every effort is made to improve their living standards and that they receive food and clothing and assistance in case of need and privation; that they do not become overly desirous of extravagant goods which may be to their detriment or are beyond their means.

G. That they do not have secret or illegal relationships with foreign ships and powers.

163. The Chief Administrator is to provide, through his own conduct, an example of honesty and integrity beyond reproach. In all of his relations he is to maintain the dignity of his position. He is to enforce strict personal honor and conduct worthy of their situation in all the servitors in the colonies.

164. He is to try to improve the customs and habits of the [native] inhabitants and provide them the opportunity to spend their free time in decent and innocent amusements.

165. The Chief Administrator must fully carry out all instructions from the Main Administration, and see that all persons serving in the colonies carry out these instructions to the letter.

166. He is to exercise strict supervision to see that no one acquires for his own use through trade in goods, purchase, or as a gift, any furs or walrus tusks, or in general any colonial products to which the Company has exclusive rights.

167. The Chief Administrator does not personally hold the capital assets, but is responsible for supervising those who do. He must see to it that there is a universal commitment on the part of Company personnel under his jurisdiction to benefit and profit the Company through hunting and trade, and to ensure that the Company does not suffer loss or deprivation.

168. The Chief Administrator, as master of all Company enterprises in the colonies, is to exercise constant supervision to see that the following structures are maintained properly, with all due care and without undue expenses: churches, infirmaries, schools, barracks, warehouses, mills, and in general, all Company enterprises. He is to see that periodic inventories are made in the warehouses, and he is to verify the cash box inventories.

169. As senior naval officer, the Chief Administrator is responsible for seeing that all equipment used for Company navigation is in good condition. Toward that goal he must see that the buildings of the colonial maritime office are in proper order; that all related artisan workshops are in the best possible condition; that ship construction is carried out punctually and in accordance with the needs of the Company; that small boats and sailing vessels which are being readied are handled and maintained properly; that the use of shipbuilding materials and

supplies is constantly overseen for conservation and accountability, and avoidance of excessive expenditures; that materials are used which will not wear out prematurely; that when ships are at anchor in harbors the rigging and sails and other materials are taken down; that the ships are kept free of leaks; that ropes, cables and hawser are replaced with iron chain, as possible; that all persons who are employed are actually necessary for Company work in port; and that the harbor maritime administration is in complete and proper order, and its activity directed primarily to benefit the colonies.

170. In assigning vessels for voyages, the Chief Administrator is to make certain that these vessels are put to their best use, consonant with the skill of their commanding officers, so as to bring maximum benefit to the Company and recompense for the expenses for their maintenance.

171. Prior to the departure of a vessel from the harbor on a designated voyage, the Chief Administrator is to make a personal inspection of the roadstead to ascertain that the vessel is properly armed, is carrying a full cargo of goods, supplies and provisions, and that the commanding officers are well qualified and the ship is properly fitted out.

172. The Chief Administrator gives ships' officers all necessary instructions and insists they be carried out precisely. He pays special attention to colonial shipping, because the security of the colonies, their well-being, and the totality of Company wealth depends on the vessels being kept in good order; and as well, the success of commercial transactions and the lives of many people depend on this.

173. The Chief Administrator must balance the undertakings with the available means, and avoid excessive expenditures by appropriate regulations based on local circumstances.

174. The Chief Administrator is to see to it that the number of Russians, creoles and natives hired into Company service is no greater than necessary to perform Company work. He must distribute them wisely, and constantly try to hold down expenses and decrease the number of unnecessary personnel.

175. The Chief Administrator is responsible for seeing that the upbringing and education of children at Company expense is directed toward the genuine benefit of the young generation. To achieve this goal it is necessary to instill into these children honesty and obedience, and to arouse in them a sense of indus-

try and order. They must be taught useful crafts, the handling of baidarkas and the use of firearms and the bow and arrow. The care of the children must be based on local circumstances, so that subsequently they will not have to revert to their old traditional ways.

176. The Chief Administrator is to take care that extravagant ways of life are not allowed to flourish in the colonies, that is, that he must not permit expectations to exceed the possibility of their realization.

177. He is also to be concerned that supplies and goods be distributed to the servitors in the colonies as they become available and are necessary to sustain the real needs of the servitors; yet he must constantly see to it that the expenses of the servitors do not exceed their means of paying for them.

178. The Chief Administrator is personally to inspect the various parts of the colonies, the offices and departments, every year or as circumstances may permit. He is to review production and capital, and thoroughly investigate all aspects of colonial administration. He is to interview Aleuts, servitors, creoles, and in general, all the natives. He must act as a leader who is attentive and just to all segments of the population without exception.

179. The Chief Administrator is to see to it that there is a satisfactory account for all aspects of administration.

180. The Chief Administrator is to report to the Main Administration in detail about all of his rules, and about developments and conditions in the colonies, as well as about every aspect of his administration, in a clear manner.

181. The annual reports of the Chief Administrator are to contain the following information:

A. A full review of the civil condition of the natives and creoles on various islands and departments.

B. The condition of the infirmaries and the activities of the medical personnel. This information will then be transmitted from the Main Administration of the Company to the Medical Department of the Ministry of Internal Affairs.

C. Educational establishments.

D. Hunting in various departments; what varieties of animals are taken.

E. Economic benefits which have accrued to the Company.

F. Biannual requirements of materials, goods and supplies for the colonies which have been sent from Europe or from other parts of the world.

G. Shipping.

H. Work undertaken in naval shipyards; structures built in the departments.

I. Crews' supplies

J. Events and happenings.

K. Departmental instructions.

In addition, the Chief Administrator submits to the Main Administration reports from official papers and from instructions given.

When he surrenders his post to his replacement, the Chief Administrator must without delay present to the Main Administration a general review of the most important points regarding conditions in the colonies, and at the same time he must also submit his own thoughts concerning measures he feels would be useful in improving various parts of the administration.

182. The Chief Administrator will be called to account if he transcends the limits of his authority, or if he neglects the authority given him either through nonfeasance or by allowing serious abuses which may be detrimental to Company interests and to those of the government.

183. It will not be considered an usurpation of authority if in the face of unusual circumstances the Chief Administrator makes a decisive order and later justifies the fact that it was essential, and that under the circumstances at the time he could not permit an obviously detrimental situation to occur; he must, however, send that explanation to higher authorities for review.

184. Action will be brought [against the Chief Administrator] through the following:

A. Petitions submitted directly to His Imperial Majesty or to the Governing Senate.

B. Reports from local authorities who may have been forced to take or carry out illegal measures.

C. A review of court sentences for persons who prove their illegal actions stemmed from trying to carry out their instructions properly, or from unclear instructions.

D. Special inspections of the colonies.

E. Reviews of annual reports.

F. Personal misconduct.

185. The above will call for taking action [against the Chief Administrator] only if they are based on clear evidence, or are perceived to have caused any significant detriment to the Empire or to the Company, or if the Chief Administrator has been abusive or has besmirched his honor.

186. All reports stemming from responsibilities of the Chief Administrator are forwarded by the Main Administration of the Company for review by the Ministry of Finance, except for those concerning military personnel, which are forwarded directly to naval authorities.

. . . .

188. The Chief Administrator receives proposals from the Main Administration and submits his reports to the Main Administration. He sends his proposals to the offices under his jurisdiction, where they are to be carried out, and receives reports from those offices. The same procedure applies with regard to his relations with the Okhotsk office on matters which directly affect the colonies.

189. In his relations with foreign authorities the Chief Administrator acts in the capacity of a civil governor.

Reference: *PSZ*, Second Series, Vol. 19, No. 18,290, 626–631.

78

OCTOBER 11, 1844

FROM THE RENEWAL OF THE CHARTER OF THE RUSSIAN AMERICAN
COMPANY: THE RUSSIAN ORTHODOX CHURCH AND TO THE RUS-
SIAN AND NONRUSSIAN INHABITANTS OF THE RUSSIAN AMERICAN
COLONIES

Chapter VII. [The Russian Orthodox Church.] Section VI.
The Colonial Bishopric.

219. The administration of the colonial churches, religious personnel and church schools is entrusted to the Bishop of Kamchatka, the Kuril and Aleutian Islands.

220. In addition to their salaries, paid according to contract, priests may accept offerings voluntarily made by their parishioners for services performed. These offerings may be in cash or in certificates which can be exchanged for goods in colonial offices, but these absolutely cannot be exchanged for furs. This prohibition pertains to priests as well as to all other servitors in the colonies.

Chapter VIII. The Rights Of Persons Living In Places Granted To The Company.

Section I. Contractual servitors.

221. The contract for a person hired for service in the colonies includes mutual obligations in its legal foundation.

222. Company servitors who are from tax-paying categories are hired in part for service as garrison or frontier guards in the colonies. Thus the Company has the right to hire into colonial service state peasants who, during their stay in America will be exempted from military conscription in their gubernias where there is the system of drawing lots. However, only young persons who have already participated in this drawing of names and have remained free may be hired. In accordance with the conscript system, recruits are young men of 20 or 21 years of age. Men older than that are not subject to conscription, and consequently the Company may hire men of any age over 21 if their passports indicate they are not subject to the draft.

In gubernias where this conscription system has not yet been introduced, [the Company may hire] only from families not included in the first or second draft call. This fact must be clearly registered in their passports, which are issued to state peasants desiring to enter service in the colonies.

223. The Main Administration will issue certificates to sailors who have served in the colonies aboard Company ships and have taken part in at least five voyages lasting a minimum of six months; the certificate will identify them as experienced sailors with the right to join the present naval societies in Russia, and they will be exempt from paying taxes and from conscription.

224. These certificates will also specify whether the sailor has studied and is capable of handling the rudder and making soundings, or whether he has only the knowledge required of an ordinary seaman.

225. Such certificates are to be accepted throughout the entire Russian Empire on the same basis as those issued by the naval administration for the Black Sea.

226. All servitors in the colonies, without exception, are forbidden to obtain furs through purchase, exchange or as voluntary gifts.

Section II. Colonial citizens.

227. Russian subjects and others of free status who have the right to leave America, but have settled there of their own free will, on the basis of this charter as stated below, are part of a special category of colonial citizens.

228. Russian citizens and peasants who are in the American colonies, having by their own will been hired by the Company, who have married creoles or American natives, who may be old or infirm, who after their prolonged stay have adapted to the climate and way of life, or who have been so long absent from Russia they no longer have close relatives there, and who submit to the Company a written petition stating their desire to remain permanently in the colonies, should be settled along the Kenai coast of America, or wherever the Main Administration of the Company deems appropriate. However, [if they remain] within the Russian possessions, the Company must build suitable living quarters for them, furnish implements

necessary for hunting and farming, provide livestock, domestic fowl and grain for planting, give them sufficient provisions for one year, and insure that they will not suffer deprivation in the future.

229. Once the Company has notified the proper authorities, the names of these persons are to be removed from the roster of the previous categories to which they belonged in Russia.

230. However, they are to remain in the ranks in which they previously belonged and the Main Administration of the Company must pay their soul tax, based on the roster kept by the Chief Administrator of the colonies. The Company is not obliged to pay any other taxes or obligations previously levied against them.

231. The Main Administration of the Company, in its annual reports, must submit the names of these settlers, both townsmen and peasants, to the Ministry of Finance.

232. Children of these settlers are to be assigned to the category of creoles. They will be accepted into Company service upon their own request at a set wage.

233. The Company may purchase any surplus goods from these settlers at a mutually agreeable price, but must pay set prices for furs.

234. With the consent of the colonial administration, colonial citizens may enter Company service on contractual terms.

235. [The Company] is to take special care not to crowd the settled natives together, and it is to supervise them so the colonial citizens will support themselves through their own efforts, not by burdening the natives.

Section III. Creoles.

236. Persons born of the union of a European or Siberian father and an American native woman, or an American native father and some European or Siberian woman, are reckoned in the category of creoles, as will any future children [of theirs], and there is a special roster for them.

237. Creoles are Russian subjects. In that category they have the right of legal protection of the government everywhere, on an equal basis with all other subjects who are registered in the category of townsmen, unless, by virtue of their

service or special circumstances, they may have acquired additional rights granted to other classes.

238. As long as creoles remain in the colonies they are exempt from state taxes and obligations, until a new regulation concerning this matter is issued.

239. Colonial authorities are to exercise vigilant supervision and special care, both over the creoles themselves, and over their property.

240. Creoles who have entered the service of the Company and distinguished themselves through zeal and ability may, at the discretion of the authorities, enjoy privileges granted to Russian subjects of the townsmen category who enter Company service.

241. Creoles who study in institutions of higher learning in Russia at the expense of the Company and receive the rank of students or medical personnel or a military or civil rank, must remain and serve in the colonies for a period of ten years. They will receive appropriate wages and maintenance from the Company for their service. When this period has expired, they will have the right to leave the colonies if they wish, provided they are not indebted to the Company.

242. Creoles who receive training in trades in Russia at the expense of the Company are obliged to serve in the colonies for not less than ten years. Upon the expiration of this time they may leave the colonies and pursue their trade in other places, if they wish, and if they are not indebted to the Company.

243. Creoles who are trained at Company expense in the colonies are obligated to serve there at least fifteen years, beginning at the age of seventeen. At the end of that period they may choose their own way of life, and may even leave the colonies if they wish, and if they are not indebted to the Company.

244. Creoles who leave the colonies, however, forego the right to have the Company support them in Russia, and must provide for themselves through their own labor. The Company's sole obligation is to transport them from the colonies and provide them sea rations in the usual amount allotted to persons of similar status who leave colonial service.

245. Creoles who have chosen their way of life and wish to settle in the colonies are assigned to colonial citizenship and enjoy the rights outlined in a previous section.

246. Illegitimate creoles are to be supervised and trained at the expense of the Company, through the colonial administration.

Section IV. Settled natives.

247. The category of settled natives in the colonies includes the inhabitants of the Kuril and Aleutian islands, Kodiak Island and the islands near it, and the Alaska Peninsula; it also includes tribes who live along the coast of America, such as the Kenaits, Chugach and others.

248. Settled natives who profess the Christian faith are not identified with any special designation. Those who are heathens are referred to as settled nonbelievers, to distinguish them from the others.

249. The government considers these people on an equal basis with all other Russian subjects. As long as they live in the colonies they comprise a special category, unless their outstanding service or some circumstance causes them to be registered in another category.

250. As Russian subjects they are obligated to obey all government laws, and enjoy the protection of the same.

251. Since the government has not yet fully determined their precise status, it does not impose iasak, taxes or any other obligation on them. The Company is likewise prohibited from demanding such obligations from them, except for that of selling their furs only to the Company.

252. Settled natives are administered by their toions under the supervision of a starshina appointed by colonial authorities from among respected Company servitors.

253. The obligations of the toions and starshinas are to supervise the natives entrusted to them, resolve arguments and problems, and assist the natives in their needs.

254. The Chief Administrator bestows the title of toion and gives a written patent as testimony of this. He makes his selection on the basis of his own personal judgment from among those who are most distinguished by reason of their zeal and reliability.

255. Upon the recommendation of the Chief Administrator, toions are rewarded for outstanding fulfillment of duties and for their zeal, with caftans trimmed with gold braid, and with medals.

256. The position of toion is not hereditary. The succession and approval are the prerogative of the Chief Administrator. A toion who holds this position for fifteen years retains his title until he dies, even though a new toion has replaced him.

257. A toion is appointed for every settlement which is at a considerable distance from any other settlement; however, when settlements are close together, one toion may be appointed for several settlements, if it is deemed appropriate.

258. A toion may appoint a *nariadchik* [native aide] in each settlement, on the basis of his own judgment. The nariadchik serves as the *pomoshchnik* [assistant] to the toion.

259. Natives must obey all instructions from the appointed toions pertaining to communal well-being and organization. Toions have no authority over natives' own belongings, however.

260. In order to acquaint the natives with the advantages of communal life, and provide them the means of reaping benefits from this, the colonial authorities must locate the native settlements, as far as possible, in suitable places, and assign them sufficient land for their various needs.

261. The Company is to use persuasion and instruction, and set a good example, to institute the Christian style of married life everywhere. At the same time the Company is to encourage good work habits, neatness and prudent economy among families.

262. Starshinas and toions must set an example by keeping to the teachings of the Church and maintaining proper conduct and working toward improvement of standards of living.

263. A native may keep as his inviolable possession all property acquired through labor, purchase, exchange or inheritance. Anyone who attempts to appropriate such property or who causes injury will be prosecuted to the limits of the law.

264. Natives not in service to the Company, in their free time, may fish along the coast where they live to procure food for themselves and their families. However, they cannot do this in neighboring areas without special permission from the colonial administration. They may likewise hunt marine and land animals on the islands and places where they live, and everything thus acquired is their inviolable property. However, if they wish to sell any furs they acquire, they may sell only to the Company, at a price which the administration is to report

to the government within two years of the time these regulations are put into effect.

265. Natives are obligated to serve the Company by hunting furbearing animals. For that reason it is decreed that half of all male natives between the ages of 18 and 50 are required to serve the Company.

266. Consequently, every year at a time determined by the colonial administration, in accordance with No. 265 above, the toions will designate the required number. There is only one unalterable condition, which is that there will remain enough workers in each family to provide for the women, the children and the infirm. The colonial administration is absolutely required to enforce this rule.

267. Natives designated to serve the Company must be provided with suitable clothing, food and baidarkas by the colonial administration at the expense of the Company. In addition, they must be paid for the animals they catch at the price agreed upon, as per No. 264. Those designated for this service are not to be separated from their families for more than two years.

268. Natives who have served the Company for three years may, if they wish, be replaced.

269. If the colonial administration deems it necessary to give some sort of work to women, this is permissible, but only with mutual consent and at a stipulated rate of pay.

270. Natives who wish to enter Company service on contract have the right to do so.

271. Natives who do not profess the Christian faith are free to worship in accordance with their own traditions.

272. The rules of gentle behavior are to guide the Russian clergy in working with the natives; they are to use persuasion alone, without any compulsion whatsoever.

273. Colonial authorities are obligated to prevent any oppression of the natives under the pretext of converting them to the Christian faith.

274. Natives are not to be punished if they prove negligent in observing church ceremonies, through ignorance, after having accepted the Christian faith. Reprimand and persuasion are the only ways to deal with such cases.

275. It is prohibited either to sell or to give furs as pres-

ents, except to churches and charitable institutions, which may accept furs as donations at prices established in the colonies. They will accept the furs on behalf of the Company, which will pay the established prices for them.

276. The local toions and starshinas are to investigate and resolve arguments involving property which may arise among natives who are subject to Russia.

277. Local company officials, such as administrators of departments, islands, redoubts and so on, are to investigate and resolve such disagreements between Russians and creoles, between them and natives, and between natives and their toions. If one of the natives involved in a dispute makes a request, and if local circumstances permit, the investigation and resolution of the problem will be carried out by the toion of that settlement, or [from another settlement] of the tribe, who is asked to come to the native's settlement.

278. Anyone dissatisfied with the decision of the toion or Company official has the right to appeal to the Chief Administrator of the colony or his assistant, in person, at the time of their inspection of the various parts of the colonies, or else through local offices.

279. The Chief Administrator is to resolve all discords concerning property in the colonies in accordance with No. 149. However, if Russians, creoles and natives are dissatisfied with the decision of the Chief Administrator, they have the right to submit their complaints to the Governing Senate within six months of their departure from the colonies, in accordance with No. 13. The six-month period for submitting a complaint does not commence from the time they actually depart the colonies, but from the time the petitioners or their representatives arrive into the interior of the Empire, or at least into those parts of the Empire that have an organized judicial system.

Section V. Natives who are not completely dependent on colonial authorities, but who live in colonial possessions.

280. Natives who live within the boundaries of the Russian colonies but are not completely dependent are to enjoy the protection and defense of the colonial administration only if they request it, and if such request is deemed valid.

281. The colonial administration is not to use force to ex-

tend the Company possessions into interior parts of the country which are settled by natives who are independent of colonial authorities.

282. If the colonial administration finds it advantageous to establish factories, redoubts or odinochkas in certain places on the American mainland in order to provide security for its commercial operations, this is permissible, but only with the consent of the native inhabitants in those places. The Company must use all possible means to preserve the natives' good will, avoiding anything which could arouse suspicions that their independence might be violated.

283. The Company is prohibited from demanding from these people tribute, iasak, tax or any other assessment. Further, in times of peace with them the Company is not to take any person from them by force except hostages, whom they give in accordance with the prevailing custom. Such hostages must be cared for properly, and Company officials must take special care to see that they do not suffer any injury.

284. If some of these natives express the desire to move to places [belonging to] settled natives, the colonial administration may permit this, if this action will not endanger our colonies. New migrants are to be registered among the settled natives and enjoy the rights and privileges granted to that category.

285. Contacts between the colonial administration and the independent natives are limited to an exchange of European wares for furs or other native products, on the basis of mutually agreed terms.

286. Hard liquor and firearms are excluded from items of exchange for the reason that they may be used to the detriment of the inhabitants. At permitted entertainments, however, hard liquor maybe served in small amounts.

Reference: *PSZ*, Second Series, Vol. 19. No. 18,290, 633–638.

79

NOVEMBER 12, 1848

INSTRUCTIONS FROM COUNT NIKOLAI N. MURAVEV, GOVERNOR OF
EASTERN SIBERIA, TO NAVY CAPTAIN GENNADII I. NEVELSKOI, FOR
A SURVEY OF THE COAST OF SAKHALIN ISLAND AND THE AMUR
RIVER ESTUARY.

The Kuril Island archipelago, from the Kamchatka Peninsula to the island of Matsumai [Hokkaido], forms the east coast, in a manner of speaking, of the Sea of Okhotsk. The northern islands in that chain belong to Russia, and the southern islands, from Iturup down to and including Matsumai, belong to Japan. Northwest of Matsumai off the Asian mainland lies the large island Sakhalin, which is separated from Matsumai by La Pérouse Strait. To the west of the northern extremity of Sakhalin lies the newly discovered Segnekinsk Bay. Many famous seafarers have made descriptions of all these islands, but these are inadequate for a comprehensive survey of the entire southeastern coast of the Sea of Okhotsk, from Petropavlovsk Harbor to Okhotsk, especially now, when all the whaling in that part of the world is concentrated in the southern part of the Sea of Okhotsk.

Some whaling vessels have come to Petropavlovsk Harbor from the Sandwich Islands to trade and to take on fresh water; they sail out from there to hunt in the southern part of the Sea of Okhotsk at the end of May or early June. After they have spent the summer there and have taken on their cargo, they sail past Sakhalin and the Shantarskie Islands, spend some time near Okhotsk, and then return to Petropavlovsk in September. If God blesses your voyage aboard the transport entrusted to your command [*Baikal*], you will reach Petropavlovsk Harbor in the middle of May; with the zealous cooperation of local authorities you will sail out from there by the end of May, or by the first of June at the latest. You will then have three months, June, July, August and part of September, to survey the coast of the Sea of Okhotsk, since you are not required to be in Okhotsk until September 10. You must schedule your sailing in the Sea of Okhotsk so as to use your time to greatest advantage and effect.

Of the [various parts of the] coast of the Sea of Okhotsk, it is most important to make a detailed description of the following:

1. The northern part of Sakhalin Island, from the east and west sides;
2. The strait that separates Sakhalin from the mainland;
3. The estuary and mouth of the Amur River;
4. Segnekinsk Bay, discovered last year by the brig *Okhotsk* and named the Gulf of Grand Prince Konstantin.

In order to carry out this assignment I suggest that Your Excellency would be well advised to proceed directly from Petropavlovsk Harbor to the northern extremity of Sakhalin and from there to Cape Golovachev where you would select a suitable anchorage in that area and then commence the surveys, descriptions and measurements of:

A. The strait between capes Golovachev and Romberg;
B. Parts of the shoreline of the Amur estuary from Cape Romberg to the point where this river flows within its own banks;
C. The northern part of Sakhalin Island, in regard to population, soil and vegetation;
D. The southern strait from the mouth of the Amur to the Gulf of Tatary.

Of course it would be very useful to have some of the natives help Your Excellency with these descriptions, but in spite of all my desires to furnish you with such persons from our neighboring possessions, I doubt I will be able to do this, because your arrival in the strait should be kept a strict secret; consequently, the only thing I can do is suggest that you take two Aleuts from Bering Island who can be useful in every instance in describing the shores. Then, when you reach Cape Golovachev, invite some of the local coastal inhabitants who have a generally satisfactory understanding of this, and have good rapport with the Russians and are easily attracted by friendly treatment and gifts.

Independently of this, I will do everything possible to make contact with Your Excellency in July while the transport vessel temporarily entrusted to you is anchored in the Cape Golovachev area. For that reason it would be desirable that your transport vessel remain there all during July, unless some special circumstance arises, and that the description of the estuary and mouth of the [Amur] River be carried out by using rowboats.

It is generally thought here that Sakhalin Island obstructs exit from the Amur River, that the northern strait between capes Golovachev and Romberg is very narrow, and that during low tide the southern strait [is so shallow that it] does not exist at all. However, the fact is that so far no one is certain of this, or of who the inhabitants of the northern part of Sakhalin are.

Concerning Sakhalin Island our only certain knowledge is that the southern part belongs to and is populated by the Japanese. Our officials who were in Peking, however, maintain that after Captain [Vasilii M.] Golovnin was in Japan, the Chinese and the Japanese governments divided Sakhalin between them, the northern part going to China and the southern to Japan. I am giving you this information for your guidance, consideration and verification in carrying out your assignment. In this regard I consider it necessary to add that it is rumored here that perhaps the English have already been on Sakhalin. This is probably true, because the mouth of the Amur has always been important to them, and because the whale trade offers them a convenient pretext for concentrating in the southern part of the Sea of Okhotsk.

If you encounter any Europeans while you are anchored at the estuary, try to impress on them that our vessels sail there frequently to survey the coast, since we recognize that the northern part of Sakhalin and the left bank of the Amur belong to us.

When you describe the coastline of Sakhalin it is essential for us to know of a suitable place for a fortified harbor near Cape Golovachev which would control the entrance into the strait. Of course this will depend on the width and direction of the channel in the strait, and the distance between the two capes. For that reason you should make a detailed description. The southern strait deserves the same attention, if it is at all times navigable. It would also be useful to find a bay on the opposite eastern coast of Sakhalin so that if the strait and the Amur estuary freeze over, we would have in mind a winter shelter for ships on the other side of the island.

Once you have completed all these surveys, Your Excellency should depart for Segnekin Bay, where in 1847 the brig *Okhotsk* spent August 24 to September 1. This bay can only be significant when the mouth of the Amur is accessible to us. Also, it will of course be useful to know the size and navigability of the rivers which empty into Tugur Bay. However, in my opinion this information is secondary in importance; the primary thing is that by the end of 1849 I can obtain information from you about the northern part of Sakhalin, and descriptions of the strait, the Amur estuary and the mouth of that river.

If you do not receive any information from Okhotsk or Kamchatka while you are anchored in the Amur estuary, continue your surveys, in accordance with the instructions you received from the Chief of Naval Operations, as well as these, my instructions, without losing sight of the fact that it is most important in every way that I have the above information by the end of the year 1849.

Reference: Ivan Barsukov. *Graf Nikolai Nikolaevich Muravev-Amurskii.* Vol. 2, (Moscow: 1891), 36–39.

80

1848

A REPORT ON RUSSIAN AMERICAN COMPANY SHIPS FOR THE YEAR
1848

In the year 1848 the [Russian American] Company had eight seaworthy sailing vessels and two chartered freighters, *Sitka* and *Atka*. The colonial fleet was increased during that year by the addition of a three-masted vessel purchased in the Sandwich Islands; it is American-built, made of oak, and named the *Kniaz Menshikov*. These vessels made the following voyages:

Kniaz Menshikov, under the command of Lieutenant [Aleksandr I.] Rudakov, was dispatched on December 24, 1848 to the port of San Francisco in California and to the Sandwich Islands to collect the funds due from [John] Sutter [as payment for the purchase of Fort Ross from the Company]. The ship carried a full cargo of colonial and European goods for sale. The vessel had not yet returned to New Arkhangel by May 16, 1849, when the mail was sent out from the colonies.

The brig *Baikal*, under the command of the Russian skipper Garder, set out from New Arkhangel on April 1 bound for Petropavlovsk in Kamchatka, carrying a cargo of goods for sale. It returned on September 9. On its voyage the brig put in at the islands of Atka, Bering, Copper and Amchitka, making the annual delivery of supplies in all these places, and collecting the accumulated furs to take back to New Arkhangel. Under the same command the brig *Baikal* set out for San Francisco on October 16, 1848, and returned to New Arkhangel on January 17, 1849. The primary reason for this voyage was the necessity of entrusting the affairs of the Company in California to the commercial trading house of Starkey, Jane and Company, since the previous Company agent, Leidesdorf, had died.

Under the command of the Russian skipper [Martin] Klinkovstrem, the brig *Okhotsk* voyaged from August 9 to December 9, 1848, carrying supplies to Kodiak Island and from there, a cargo of cut lumber for sale to California. She carried a small cargo of supplies to New Arkhangel, and also the news of the discovery of gold in California.

The brig *Velikii Kniaz Konstantin*, under the command of the Russian skipper [Vasilii G.] Pavlov, sailed on May 22, 1848 to the Pribilof Islands, Unalaska and to the Mikhailovsk redoubt, to deliver the yearly supplies and to trade with the Chukchi in Michigmenskii Bay and Kodiak Island, by special request of the Chief Administrator [Mikhail Tebenkov]. That brig also carried the Bishop of Kamchatka who was to inspect part of his diocese. The brig returned to New Arkhangel on September 26 with cargo taken on at the places she had visited.

Between April 1 and October 7, 1848 the brig *Promysl* sailed to the Kuril Islands for the annual delivery of supplies and to pick up the furs designated for the port of Aian. From there on her return voyage to New Arkhangel she stopped at Attu Island to deliver the annual supplies.

The schooner *Tungus*, under the command of the Russian skipper [Aleksandr F.] Kashevarov, was dispatched on July 26, 1848 to carry supplies to the islands and redoubts of the Kodiak department. She returned to New Arkhangel with the summer catch of furs and with a cargo of bricks and other items. On October 19, commanded by the same skipper, she sailed with a supplementary cargo to the Kodiak department and spent the winter there, returning to New Arkhangel on April 7, 1849 with the winter catch of furs.

The steamer *Nikolai*, under the command of the Russian skipper Arkhimandritov, sailed into the bay to trade with the Kolosh, towed other vessels that came into port, and sailed back out to sea hauling lumber rafts and barges from the Ozersk redoubt mill and from nearby bays.

The keel for the steamer *Baranov* was laid in 1847 and the vessel was launched on July 5 of that year in the port of New Arkhangel. She was assigned to the same kind of harbor work as the steamer *Nikolai*; she has been fitted with engines and is at work.

In addition to building the steamer *Baikal*, on June 5, 1848 the keel was laid for the 35-ton schooner *Klinkit* [Tlingit] in New Arkhangel. She has a 46-foot keel, a 50-foot deck and a width of 15 feet. The schooner was launched December 30, 1848. On February 1, 1849, upon completion of fitting out, she was dispatched to California. This ship was built for coastal sailing by order of the former Russian American Company agent in California, Leidesdorf. After his death it was sold in San Francisco at a profit for the Company.

The brig *Promysl* was careened for replacement of her copper sheathing.

Seven vessels are no longer seaworthy. The galiot *Morekhod* has been used as a ferry for the steam tug; the ships *Aleksandr* and *Elena* and the schooner *Kvikhpak* were built from hulks; the sloop *Sitka* and the brigs *Polifem* and *Riurik* were beached and converted for use as storehouses. Two other new storehouses were built and then disassembled; one was shipped to California and the other to Kamchatka.

Reference: Rossiisko-Amerikanskaia Kompaniia. *Otchet za 1848 god.*

See: "Izvlechenie iz otcheta Rossiisko-Amerikanskoi Kompanii za 1848 god," in *Morskoi Sbornik*, Vol. 3 (St. Petersburg: 1850), 81–84.

81

1849–1850

THE VIEWS OF COUNT NIKOLAI N. MURAVEV REGARDING THE NE-
CESSITY FOR RUSSIA TO CONTROL THE AMUR RIVER

R ussia must occupy the mouth of the Amur River and that part of Sakhalin Island which lies opposite, as well as the left bank of the Amur River, for the following reasons.

I. Concern for the eastern frontier of the Empire.

Rumors have for quite some time circulated through Siberia concerning the intentions of the English to occupy the mouth of the Amur River and Sakhalin Island. God forbid they should become entrenched there before we do! In order to establish more thorough and complete control over trade with China, the English undoubtedly need to control both the mouth of the Amur and the navigation on that river. If the Amur were not the only river flowing from Siberia to the Pacific Ocean, we might not have any objection to their intentions, but navigation via the Amur is the only suitable route to the east. This is a century-old dream of Siberians of all classes; it may be instinctive, but it is no less well grounded.

Upon review of all circumstances known to me, I can state that whoever controls the mouth of the Amur will also control Siberia, at least as far as Baikal, and that control will be firm. It is enough to contol the mouth of this river and navigation on it for Siberia, which is increasing in population and flourishing in agriculture and industry, to remain an unalterable tributary and subject of the power which holds the key to it.

II. Strengthening and securing possession of the Kamchatka Peninsula.

Only when we have the left bank of the Amur and the navigation rights on it can we establish communication with Kamchatka, and thus be in a position to establish Russia's firm control over this peninsula. The reason is that the route via Iakutsk and Okhotsk or Aian offers no means of supplying Kamchatka with sufficient military capacity, nor to provide it with proper population, which in and of itself, under the protection of fortresses, would comprise the strength of this distant oblast and furnish local land and naval forces with their necessary provisions. With the establishment of steam navigation on the Amur, Kamchatka could be provisioned from Nerchinsk with people and all necessities in no more than two weeks. The Amur River flows from our frontiers to the island of Sakhalin for more than 2,000 versts, and according to all available information, is navigable for its entire length.

III. Support for our trade with China.

The decrease in the Kiakhta trade already indicates that the intentions of the English in China cannot be beneficial to us. During the first years after their war [Opium War, 1839–42], we did not realize this, because the Chinese, motivated by their enmity toward the English, preferred to turn to us as their reliable and gracious neighbors. But time and material benefits mitigate the outburst of animosity, and moderate a flame of friendship which does not represent substantial benefits. I believe that the only way to promote our trade with China is to change it from local to widespread, so that by sailing on the Amur we could supply the products of our manufacture to all the northeastern provinces of China, which are more distant from present activities of the English, and consequently, from their competition which is dangerous to our trade.

IV. Maintaining our influence in China.

The English war and peace in China have laid the foundation for the transformation of that populous empire under the influence of the English. But during the lifetime of the late Chinese Emperor, we still hoped he would personally announce that since he had been insulted by them, he could not be favorably disposed toward them and consequently would not allow the spread of English influence in his empire.

Now, with the ascension of his 18-year-old son, one can be certain that the English will hasten to turn this event to their advantage with their usual natural entrepreneurial spirit, speed and persistence, so as to gain control not only of trade, but also of China's politics. I cannot judge whether we can prevent this, when five of China's ports have been not only accessible to the English, but have actually almost become English cities.

I believe it would be prudent for us to have better security along the frontiers with China, to the extent of our domestic needs, so the English will not gain full control there, and thus we must control the Amur. I also think that we must capitalize on current developments in China so we can reveal our plans to them, based on the general benefits to both empires; to wit, that no one but Russia and China should control navigation on the Amur, and that the mouth of that river should be protected, and of course, not by the Chinese.

Reference: Ivan Barsukov. *Graf Nikolai Nikolaevich Muravev-Amurskii.* Vol. 2, (Moscow: 1891), 46–48.

82

A SECRET COMMUNICATION FROM COUNT NIKOLAI N. MURAVEV, GOVERNOR OF EASTERN SIBERIA, TO ADJUTANT GENERAL PRINCE MENSHIKOV, CHIEF OF NAVAL OPERATIONS, REGARDING MEANS OF ESTABLISHING RUSSIAN CONTROL OF THE AMUR RIVER

S ecret.
I have had the honor of receiving Your Highness' instructions of November 24, [1849], No. 586, regarding the commander and officers of the transport *Baikal*; and at the same time Captain Lieutenant [Gennadii] Nevelskoi has submitted to me a detailed report on how he carried out his special assignment in accordance with Your Highness' instructions and those I added following on the information and authorization you had given me.

Your Highness will want personally to examine the reports and maps Nevelskoi has made and submitted, and judge for yourself the importance of his discoveries. However, I consider it my sacred obligation to submit my own views of these findings, and proposals consequent upon them, for your own information and for the report to the Sovereign Emperor; as well as all the thoughts, correspondence and information I have gathered on these matters which have a direct bearing on the security and well-being of the regions which have been entrusted to my administration.

Historical research into the Far Eastern regions of Russia indicates that during the course of the seventeenth century Russian cossacks and promyshlenniks gained control of the coasts of the Sea of Okhotsk, of Kamchatka and the banks of the Amur River. Although we had no settlements at the mouth of the Amur, nonetheless the cossacks navigated it and entered into the Sea of Okhotsk. Kamchatka and the Sea of Okhotsk remain ours to the present time, but at the end of the seventeenth century we were driven out from the Amur by Manchus who came there in substantial numbers and entrenched themselves on the right bank of the river. These latecomers established their influence, even though rather weakly, on the left bank of the river as well, except for the mouth of the Amur and the island of Sakhalin near to it, where there live the Giliak people, who acknowledge no authority.

The renowned European seafarers, La Pérouse, Broughton, and Krusenstern, sailed from south to north in these waters, between Sakhalin Island and the mainland, but none penetrated completely through this strait. La Pérouse and Broughton in their descriptions stated that there is no passage from the south, and that between Sakhalin Island the the mainland there is a sandy isthmus which is covered by water only at high tide. This information has been placed on all European Mercator maps, as well as on the one Your Highness sent to me along with the correspondence of February 9, 1848, No. 7721.

Krusenstern left the existence of a strait from the north in doubt. He indicated that the depth between capes Golovachev and Romberg gradually decreased to three and a half sazhens. He did not carry out any investigations farther to the south.

The matter has remained in this state of knowledge to the present year. I was aware that in 1847 certain reconnaissances of the Amur estuary had been made from the north, but there was no concrete evidence about the outcome until this summer. It was only when I was in Kamchatka that I learned that second lieutenant Gavrilov, who has since died, had penetrated the Amur estuary from the north, but did not find an entry into the mouth of the river for ships, and did not extend his search to the south.

Nevelskoi has resolved all of these questions, and in addition has discovered near the mouth of the Amur, on the northern bank, a harbor site which he has named *Shchastie* [Good Fortune], where our ships sailing in the Sea of Okhotsk can enter, anchor safely, and from where they will have interior communication with that part of the Amur River where in my judgment we must establish ourselves, which is on the Konstantin Peninsula. But the most important of all his discoveries is that in the strait south of the estuary there is an unimpeded entry from the Strait of Tatary which makes it possible for ships even of the largest size to sail directly into the river. This discovery compels us to seize control of the mouth of the Amur River without delay, because at any time we may anticipate that it will be occupied by others approaching from the south.

I have reason to believe this southern strait is not unknown to foreigners: first, through information Nevelskoi obtained from the Giliaks in Uaspyn settlement; second, I heard from one of the whalers (whom we encountered near Sakhalin on August 22) that he intended to sail south between Sakhalin and the mainland; third, I had information in Aian that when one of the [Russian American] Company officials was on one of the southern Kuril islands in 1847 he saw a large steamer sailing from the Sea of Okhotsk into the Pacific Ocean; and fourth, when I was returning from Kamchatka on the transport *Irtysh*, on August 14 at 2:00 P.M. at the entry to the fourth strait from the ocean, I saw a large three-masted ship with frigate arms which had come from the Sea of Okhotsk. It was probably a naval vessel; we sighted it at about twelve miles distance just after a fog lifted; it was sailing with the wind from west to east. There was no way we could catch up with it, but we continued to tack in the strait. Finally, fifth, it is impossible not to suppose that of the 250 whaling vessels in the Sea of Okhotsk over a period of several months, some of them within the next few months will certainly reach the southern shores of the estuary of the strait, in the same way as those we encountered between the northern part of Sakhalin and the mainland.

If foreigners were to occupy the mouth of the Amur it would be so detrimental to the Empire that we would instantly have to resort to the use of force to expel the new intruders, and thus declare war against the power to which they belong, that is, America, France or England. And there is almost no doubt that this will come to pass.

I make bold to suggest that it would be more prudent to avoid this extreme by occupying the mouth of the Amur ourselves, and at least that part of Sakhalin Island which is opposite, which is inhabited by the Giliaks. In doing this we will be in a position to show even the Chinese the necessity and justice of this action by reason of first discovery; for although the Chinese may also be there, they came only after our cossacks did. Likewise the geographical position of the Kuril archipelago, which belongs to us to the present time [justifies this]; the last island to the south, Urup, is ours and is in the same latitude as the southern extremity of Sakhalin.

Of course by occupying the mouth of the Amur we would

be able to navigate freely on the river from the Nerchinsk region and occupy the left bank of the river all the way to the Giliak [settlements]. (The land inhabited by the Giliaks is similar in nature to that at the mouth of the Amur.) Even if there are now some obstacles in the way of achieving all these results which are necessary both for Siberia and for all of Russia, we can control the mouth of the river for some time even with those inconveniences of communication with which we control Kamchatka; and at last it will be acknowledged that it is possible to establish a natural frontier between us and China along the Amur River.

There is no doubt that prior occupation of the mouth of the Amur and the northern part of Sakhalin, without communication via the Amur with the Nerchinsk district, will require us to strengthen our naval forces in the Sea of Okhotsk and in the Pacific; however, these expenditures will be compensated hundredfold, not only in the future but in the present, if only we will exercise our rights in the Sea of Okhotsk relating to inland waters, which are not in the least counter to the Conventions of 1824 and 1825.

At the present time, with the growth of foreign whaling in this sea to the point that 250 vessels are sailing there to hunt whales, and every year take more than 100,000 tons of whales, it would be prudent to impose a just and reasonable tax of 10 percent for our use, so we would have a substantial revenue which would far exceed the cost of maintaining several cruisers to collect this tax. Moreover, these cruisers would protect and reinforce our possessions on Sakhalin and at the mouth of the Amur. Later, when the left bank of the Amur and navigation on the river are under our control, it will be quite natural that our fleet in the Sea of Okhotsk and in Avacha Bay should be greater than all the European fleets in the Pacific Ocean, inasmuch as we would have at our disposal all the enormous and rich resources of Eastern Siberia, if they could be transported by water to the Sea of Okhotsk. However, even the immediate vicinity of the mouth of the Amur, where the Giliaks live, has a large and excellent forest, even including oak trees; there are very likely metal ores there as well.

I suggest that during the summer of 1850 we send part of the Okhotsk Admiralty command to the harbor of Shchastie,

A view of the arsenal and lighthouse in New Arkhangel during the expedition of Captain "Fiery" Belcher, RN, with Baranov's headquarters surmounting all. (OHS OrHi neg. 82023).

with a small crew of some 60 men, and a year's supply of provisions and with construction equipment. From there they would proceed to the mouth of the Amur and build a *zimov'e* [winter hut] in a suitable location near the Konstantin Peninsula. The transport which would take them there could return to assist the others in the transfer of the Okhotsk port to Kamchatka, and the newly constructed vessel in Okhotsk could be dispatched to the Amur command for the winter. In 1851 they could be joined by those persons designated to be sent out from Irkutsk, in accordance with Imperial wishes. In the present year further orders will be forthcoming.

The command post at the mouth of the Amur will be evidence to foreigners of our possession. Our people will trade with the Giliaks of course, so they will benefit. For that reason the commanding officer should be issued goods and money in a special fund. In the future this outpost will cut lumber, and its commanding officer will carry on necessary observations such as the flood level of the Amur, the ice cover and when the ice breaks up; and he will also make measurements in the estuary and do his best to establish ever closer ties with these native people. In winter, through these Giliaks and the Tungus who come there, we will have communication with Aian across the Ud River; even now an official named Orlov is being sent to the land of the Giliaks by that route; I have mentioned this to Your Highness in my report.

At this time there will be almost no need for unbudgeted expenses. It will not be difficult to build a zimov'e where there is abundant forest land, and this will be an important step in preventing foreigners from occupying this region.

In one way or another Your Highness should undertake this matter. But, in any event, I have a particular need to most humbly request Your Highness to return Nevelskoi to my command. With all of his skills as an experienced naval officer, he will be absolutely indispensable to me all during the forthcoming reorganization in the Sea of Okhotsk. Of course this assignment will be no less difficult for him, and no less important for the government, than the service of naval officers in Okhotsk and Kamchatka. Therefore, I believe, I am fully justified to ask that at the time of his departure from St. Petersburg you grant him all the rights and prerogatives of rank and salary which were established for the previous commanding officer of the port of Okhotsk, and prior to his appointment as commanding officer of the Amur port, to give him the ration funds due to the commanding officer of a vessel which sails in foreign waters, taking into account his forthcoming frequent visits to places where costs are extraordinarily high.

During the assignments I will give him in the Sea of Okhotsk, he will become more and more familiar with the estuary, with Sakhalin and the mouth of the Amur River. When the government is pleased to establish firm control over these places, it will only remain to assign him the title of commanding officer of the local port.

I also need a practical and active naval engineer, especially since Lieutenant Molinari, who previously held that post in Okhotsk, was drowned this past autumn. I am taking the liberty of most humbly requesting this appointment, along with three commanders also to be placed under my authority. I will employ them as circumstances develop in areas of greater need.

In regard to my own views on all the matters outlined above, I will probably have an opportunity to present these in person to Your Highness at the end of this winter. However, if Your Highness is pleased to act favorably on my request, Nevelskoi should be instructed to return here at the end of March so he can travel to Okhotsk or Aian via the winter route. Upon his return from St. Petersburg he will meet with me and receive all the instructions I am empowered to give, in accordance with your orders.

As an addition to my report of September 28, No. 161, concerning the official, Orlov, I feel I must add that he will be quite indispensable to you in the appropriate military rank, that is, Officer of the Corps of Navigators. If Your Highness is pleased to grant him the raise I have requested, and to assign him to the Port of Okhotsk, I will employ him in the Giliak territory where the Company is presently sending him in mid-February.

Concerning the transfer of the port of Okhotsk, in consequence of the Imperial desires which Your Highness has communicated to me, I am presently issuing appropriate orders; but, in order to finalize this and to carry it out expeditiously, I have great need of Korsakov, whom I will send to Iakutsk and Okhotsk as soon as he returns, and of Nevelskoi, who will be sent there at the end of winter, if you are pleased to obtain approval for my assignment for him.

See: Ivan Barsukov. *Graf Nikolai Nikolaevich Muravev-Amurskii.* Vol 2, (Moscow: 1891), 48–54.

83

UNDATED

A CONFIDENTIAL REPORT FROM NIKOLAI N. MURAVEV, GOVERNOR
OF EASTERN SIBERIA, TO GENERAL-ADMIRAL GRAND PRINCE CON-
STANTINE, REGARDING FORTIFICATION OF KAMCHATKA, SAKHALIN
AND THE AMUR RIVER DELTA

In the present unstable condition of our relations with other
naval powers, we must attend to the security of our coasts
and ports in the Pacific Ocean and the Sea of Okhotsk.

Your Imperial Highness has already been pleased to adopt
important measures in that regard by dispatching naval vessels
into those areas, following the Imperial decision to increase the
46th naval squadron, and by dispatching a Cossack squadron
from the Transbaikal forces to the mouth of the Amur River.
Meanwhile the transport vessel *Dvina* should already have
made delivery this fall to the harbor of Petropavlovsk [Kam-
chatka] of the armaments necessary for the basic defense of the
fort. However, certain preliminary instructions and decisions
from high government authorities are necessary so that these
resources will be in place by the time they may be needed, and
will thus be deployed to best advantage.

In another direction, the imminent uprising in China [T'ai-
p'ing Rebellion, 1851–1864] demands particular attention.
Thanks to the foresight of the government, Eastern Siberia is
presently supplied with considerable military resources. In the
Transbaikal region there are some 16,000 infantry troops under
arms, and more than 5,000 cavalry. Of that number 13,000
infantry and cavalry and 20 pieces of artillery can easily and
freely be moved across the border, and if necessary, the number of troops can be increased to 16,000. But with these forces
we must defend our possessions from Kamchatka to Kharatsai,
along a land and sea frontier which extends for some 10,000
versts.

Your Highness may wish to know to what extent these
areas and expanses merit our attention and defense for the future of Russia. I only venture to state that no matter how im-

portant the developments are which are now taking place in the south and west along our European frontiers, and no matter how disturbing the prospect of war with Turkey, England and France may seem to us, Russia is so firmly united in spirit and so unconditionally devoted to her Sovereign that no danger from that direction can threaten her. Furthermore, Russia's internal strength and material resources are so sound and so vast, that the longer such a war might last, the more terrible would become the situation for our enemies, especially for England, even though the enemy could inflict some harm to our coastal cities in Europe.

However, the situation is entirely different in our Far East. Avacha Bay in Kamchatka, the Amur delta (the Sungari) and navigation on the Amur could be taken by force from Russia. Neighboring China, very populous, is powerless now because of ignorance, but can easily become dangerous for us under the influence and leadership of the English and the French. In such a case Siberia will cease to be Russian. In addition to Siberia's gold deposits, the expanse of land is important to us, because it can accommodate the excess of agricultural population from European Russia for an entire century to come. If we lose that vast space, we will never be able to compensate for it by any victory or conquest in Europe.

In order to protect Siberia, we must now preserve and strengthen Kamchatka, Sakhalin, the delta of the Amur River and navigation on the river itself, and establish firm influence with neighboring China. At present it is possible for us to achieve all of this by using the local resources of Eastern Siberia which have gradually been readied over the past five years. But it is essential to authorize and empower the Commander-in-Chief of Eastern Siberia to act within defined limits, depending on local circumstances, because in such a remote land and over such great distances, there will be too great a delay if he has to seek authority to act on each particular case. Most of all, there is an urgent need to issue preliminary instructions and to make decisions concerning the defense of the coasts and harbors against the English. Their rapid communication by sea with their various far-flung naval outposts gives them the ability to authorize their squadrons to attack us in the Pacific

Ocean once war is declared in Europe, whereas our usual route of communication across Siberia will bring that information to Kamchatka much later.

In accordance with all these considerations, I should like to recommend that Admiral [Efim V.] Putiatin's squadron, which is presently endangered by the English, immediately sail to the port newly discovered by Nevelskoi, which is free of ice by February. Upon arrival there, this squadron should come under the direct command of the Siberian commander who could be authorized to issue orders at an appropriate time to complete Putiatin's mission to Japan, if it has not yet been carried out. The steam schooner *Vostok* and her crew, presently part of the 46th Squadron, will be needed to communicate between the Siberian ports with the necessary speed.

As soon as the ice breaks up, the Commander-in-Chief of Eastern Siberia should open the shortest route of communication to the Amur River delta and deliver part of the reinforcements designated for the 46th Squadron. He should also dispatch both batteries of mountain artillery under his command, and two or three engineer officers from St. Petersburg, to help fortify the coastline and the ports in the Amur delta and in Kamchatka. Only in this manner and with these means can we prepare ourselves in good time to repel the English, who could appear there by the end of June or early July. Our squadron of three frigates and two corvettes, prudently assigned along our coastline and islands in the Sea of Okhotsk and along Kamchatka, will force the enemy to proceed very cautiously with any plans of attack, no matter how strong they may be.

Further, in order to establish the necessary swift communication between the Transbaikal region and the Amur delta, and from there with Kamchatka, and in order to supply these points with military personnel, provisions and other necessities, there should be steamship communication all summer long between the Amur delta and Petropavlovsk harbor, using the schooner *Vostok*; and between Nerchinsk and the Amur delta using the steamer *Argun* newly built on the Shilka River, and long boats as well.

It will be difficult for the English to land troops for several reasons: even by using all their resources they cannot bring

Early view of Petropavlovsk on Avacha Bay, Kamchatka. This port, along with Okhotsk, shared the same problems of remoteness and dietary imbalance as the Aleutian and Alaskan settlement. Private collection.

large numbers of landing forces into these remote regions; all during the war with China their landing forces and the crews of their steam and sail vessels numbered only 3,000 men; further, in Kamchatka and that region they have little knowledge of the land; and finally, the English will not suppose that it is necessary to employ huge forces against regions which in their judgment are unpopulated. For these reasons I believe that at first it will be sufficient for us to have 500 men in battle-ready condition at the port of Petropavlovsk, and another 500 along the banks of the Amur with four mountain artillery pieces, in case our ships could not fend off an attack at sea, thus enabling the enemy to land forces. However, if even in spite of these precautions we still had insufficient forces to repel an attack, and our land-based troops in Kamchatka had to retreat into the interior of the peninsula and to Bolsheretsk on the coast of the Sea of Okhotsk, and if those at the mouth of the Amur had to pull back to the settlement of Kizi and to Nikolaevsk outpost— even then, by using steamship communication, there would still be time that same summer to send down the Amur two battalions and several companies of mounted cossacks with appropriate artillery, who could expel the enemy from the Amur

495

and the Tatar Strait. Then the steam vessels could be used to transport sufficient forces across the Sea of Okhotsk to Bolsheretsk, without passing through the Pacific Ocean, to force the enemy from Petropavlovsk harbor.

It is essential, possible and justified for us to open navigation on the Amur under these circumstances. The present state of chaos in China provides us an ideal opportunity to do this, and our success and security for the last three years at the Amur delta (Sungari) are a positive guarantee of our future success. When we openly navigate on the Amur in strength, the Manchu authorities will undoubtedly make verbal protests to us, and possibly their Tribunal will send written protests to our Senate. But in both situations we can and should respond firmly, justifying the necessity of this navigation on the basis of our own benefit and defense, and also that of Manchuria. I am confident in predicting that the matter will end there.

Meanwhile, in the present situation the Chinese government has lost its authority and does not control half its empire. One may say that this has brought about the end of our trade in Kiakhta, and we have no assurance we will be able to assist in reestablishing that trade. Consequently, we should change the form of our relationship and inform the Tribunal that "it should refer to and establish contact with the Commander-in-Chief of Siberia, who is also the commanding officer of the armed forces there, and who has received from his government appropriate instructions concerning the matter."

This procedure will eliminate many dangerous disagreements which may arise under the present circumstances, and which can easily develop there as a result of the great distances and slow communication between those regions and St. Petersburg. Meanwhile it will indicate to the Chinese government that we are not deluded by its predicament, and are adopting our own appropriate measures. This form of relationship will be all the more just and reasonable, for we will probably soon be dealing not with the Chinese Empire, but with several separate provinces. It would be advantageous to appoint a special official from the Ministry of Foreign Affairs to be attached to the Commander-in-Chief of Eastern Siberia and to give him instructions in the form of basic guidelines for dealing with all manner of eventualities. In regard to precautionary measures concerning land forces along our frontiers with Mongolia, the following steps should be taken. By May 25 of next year two encampments of cossack forces should be assembled. One near Kiakhta should consist of the 12th or 13th Line Battalion with adequate artillery, and the lst, 5th and 6th mounted regiments of Transbaikal Cossacks. The second should be located between the settlement of Ologeia and the Vurukhoituevsk Fort, comprised of the lst and 2nd Cossack Infantry Brigades and three regiments of mounted cossacks with their entire light artillery.

It will not cause any major disruption in the economic lives of the cossacks to assemble the forces in these places, and will require quite small expenditures on the part of the Treasury. Furthermore, as a result of this demonstration and the timely negotiations on the part of the Commander-in-Chief of Eastern Siberia, we will undoubtedly succeed in all our proposals and demands which our government will find essential as a result of the current changes taking place in China.

The 14th and 15th Line Battalions will remain in their deployed positions along the Ingoda and Shilka rivers, from where they can easily be dispatched onto the Amur if necessary. The 3rd Cossack Infantry Brigade, deployed on the same rivers, will have summer assemblies in battalion units in their headquarters, and if necessary can also reinforce our men at the Amur delta.

During encampment, in case of movement across the frontier, our forces will be formed into the following detachments:

From six mounted cossack regiments, assemble five fully staffed	4,400	men
From 12 cossack infantry battalions, assemble six fully staffed	6,200	
From 4 regular army battalions, assemble two fully staffed	2,000	
Two batteries of artillery	400	
TOTAL	13,000	men

In order to fund all possible eventualities which might require expenditures over and above the anticipated budgets for the army and navy departments, the Commander-in-Chief of Eastern Siberia should be authorized to borrow from various sources of capital in Eastern Siberia, including philanthropic funds. These debts would be repaid by the government at a more convenient time after the end of a war in Europe, or from new sources of revenue to be developed in Eastern Siberia. Meanwhile, the budgeted funds for all departments should be placed under his direct authority, and he should have the right to alter the designated sums, with the understanding that these changes and other regulations would have to be submitted to the attention of higher authorities.

All of the above proposals offer the possibility of using local resources of Eastern Siberia, only adding ships presently in the Pacific Ocean and en route there; this will not only defend our long-established possessions there, but will also strengthen them and provide the necessary influence over neighboring lands. This will also demonstrate that it is now necessary to give the Commander-in-Chief of Eastern Siberia a vote of confidence from the Sovereign Emperor, and the power and authority corresponding to that confidence.

See: Ivan Barsukov. *Graf Nikolai Nikolaevich Muravev-Amurskii*. Vol. 2, (Moscow: 1891), 104–109.

84

JULY 22, 1854

THE RUSSO-AMERICAN CONVENTION CONCERNING THE RIGHTS OF
NEUTRALS AT SEA

The two High and Contracting Parties recognize as permanent and immutable the following principles, to wit:

1st. That free ships make free goods, that is to say, that the effects or goods belonging to subjects or citizens of a Power or State at war are free from capture and confiscation when found on board of neutral vessels, with the exception of articles contraband of war.

2nd. That the property of neutrals on board an enemy's vessel is not subject to confiscation, unless the same contraband be of war. They engage to apply these principles to the commerce and navigation of all such Powers and States as shall consent to adopt them on their part as permanent and immutable. . . .

Done at Washington the twenty-second day of July, the year of grace 1854.

W. L. March
Edouard Stoeckl

Reference: Mallory, William M., comp. *Treaties, Conventions, International Acts, Protocols and Agreements between the United States of America and Other Powers, 1776–1909*. Vol. 2 (Washington: 1910), 1519–1521.

---

*This is the first of four articles in the convention. We have chosen to leave out the introductory remarks and to print only the first article, which lays out the principles of the rights of neutrals at sea. The second and third articles deal with interpretation of the first article and the fourth explains how the convention will be approved. THE EDITORS.

85

INFORMATION ON THE ACTIVITY OF THE RUSSIAN AMERICAN COM-
PANY, ITS PERSONNEL AND CAPITAL GOODS

From the Report of the Russian American Company for the years 1854–1855 we present the following brief summaries. The entire property of the Company, both in Russia and in the colonies, amounted to 4,673,472 rubles 92 kopecks. Of this amount, 100,000 rubles were spent to organize the Russo-Finnish Whaling Company, and 511,161 rubles 39 kopecks for seagoing vessels: 332,516 rubles 51 kopecks in Russian ports, and 179,644 rubles 88 kopecks in colonial ports.

The following servitors were in the colonies: 1 Chief Administrator of the colonies; 4 naval staff officers; 4 senior officers; 2 Siberian line battalion senior officers; 2 civil officials; 1 mining engineer; 42 church personnel; 4 medical personnel; 2 medical assistants; 4 midwives; 12 ships' skippers and senior assistants from among the volunteer naval personnel; 4 junior assistants; 2 office administrators; 15 heads of district and command posts; 45 bookkeepers and prikashchiks; 4 master artisans, shipwrights and armourers; 68 government sailors; 99 lower ranking personnel from Siberian Line Battalion No. 14; 327 freely hired Russian servitors, artisans and workers; 230 natives; 31 freely hired women as helpers in the schools and infirmaries. [Total 903.]

The population of the colonies consisted of 5,100 males and 4,625 females, for a total of 9,725. Of this number there were the following: Russians—658 (597 male, 61 female); creoles—1,902 (935 male, 967 female); Aleuts—4,127 (2,081 male, 2,046 female); Kenaits—1,088 (513 male, 575 female); Chugach and others—1,863 (933 male, 930 female); and Kurils—87 (41 male, 46 female).

Twenty-one boys and nineteen girls were receiving an education in two schools in New Arkhangel. In addition, at Company expense, ten lads were being educated in St. Petersburg for their future service in the colonies.

[During this period] the New Arkhangel infirmary cared for 1,295 persons, 15 of whom died.

In 1854 Company ships completed the following voyages from New Arkhangel, for the most part prior to receiving news in the colonies about the outbreak of the [Crimean] war, and for communication between colonial departments where they did not anticipate the presence of enemy cruisers:

1) The ship *Kadiak*, under the command of the Russian skipper Pavlov, was sent out on January 8 to San Francisco with a cargo of lumber and salted fish; upon her return, she set out to take supplies to departments of the colonies, and returned to New Arkhangel on September 25.

2) The brig *Okhotsk*, under the command of the [Finnish-] Russian skipper Iuzelius, left New Arkhangel on April 8 with a cargo destined for the islands of Attu, Shumushu and Urup. She unloaded her cargo as directed, took aboard the furs that had been gathered and prepared there, and delivered the furs to Aian. From there she completed three voyages to the Amur region and returned to Aian on September 30 to spend the winter.

3) The brig *Shelikhov*, under the command of Lieutenant [Fedor K.] Verman was dispatched to Kodiak carrying workmen and lumber to build ice houses. After fulfilling this assignment, the brig sailed to the island of Unga with supplies, and upon her return to New Arkhangel on July 19, was immediately sent back to Kodiak with additional lumber. She also transported to the Chief Administrator of the colonies an assistant who was entrusted with supervising construction of ice houses and fish storage units on Kodiak. This brig returned to New Arkhangel on September 29.

4) The schooner *Tungus*, under the command of the Russian navigator [Aleksandr F.] Kashevarov, took supplies to the islands of Unga, Ukamok and Nushagak and wintered over in the Kodiak department.

5) The brig *Velikii Kniaz Konstantin*, under the command of the Russian skipper Arkhimandritov, sailed to Kamchatka with various goods and supplies for Petropavlovsk and for the Atkhinsk and Kuril departments; she returned to New Arkhangel on August 31.

6) An around-the-world vessel, *Kamchatka*, under the command of the skipper Ridell, reached New Arkhangel on October 2, having come from the port of Petropavlovsk. She was then dispatched with lumber to San Francisco, which she

reached safely on the night of December 1, having managed to avoid enemy [British and French] cruisers stationed along the coast of California, and an English frigate positioned at the entrance to San Francisco Bay. The *Kamchatka* eluded the latter through the skill of the Company agent in San Francisco, [Petr S.] Kostromitinov, who upon learning of the arrival of the ship immediately sent an American steamer to escort her under tow into the port. When they reached port the ship was completely safe, but since English vessels could have seized her on her return voyage, she was anchored in San Francisco until it was possible for her to return to the colonies safely.

7) The ship *Nikolai I*, under the command of the Russian skipper [Martin] Klinkovstrem, wintered near the Amur River settlements and returned to New Arkhangel on September 22. She carried lower ranking men of the Siberian line battalion who were assigned to duty in the colonies. Later she was sent to San Francisco with a cargo of colonial goods. She arrived there safely on January 1, 1855, but remained in San Francisco together with the *Kamchatka*, lest she be captured by enemy cruisers before she could reach the colonies.

8) The ship *Kniaz Menshikov*, which had taken part in the expedition of Adjutant General Count [Efim V.] Putiatin, returned safely to New Arkhangel on October 11, having brought from Aian various foodstuffs sent across Siberia for the colonies.

9) The around-the-world ship *Sitka* arrived in New Arkhangel from Hamburg on April 18, 1854, under the command of the Russian skipper Conrad. On May 16 she was dispatched to Aian with the year's catch of furs and other cargo for Aian, Kamchatka, and the Amur River region. After she had delivered the furs and other cargo to Aian, she continued her voyage. She approached Avacha Bay during the night of August 26–27, but the next morning was captured right at the entrance to the bay by an enemy squadron which had assembled there. Subsequently *Sitka* and her cargo were claimed as a legitimate prize-of-war, and were sold in France.

In 1855, because of the [Crimean] war, a large part of the Company vessels were idle. To supply colonial departments, and for other purposes, [the Company] used a neutral vessel, necessarily assisted by the brig *Shelikhov*, under the command of the Russian navigator Kashevarov, and the schooner *Tungus*, under the command of the hired navigator Kuritsyn, both of whom carried out their assignments successfully.

The brig *Okhotsk*, under the command of the skipper Iuzelius, sailed from the port of Aian to the mouth of the Amur with a cargo of various goods and supplies for local settlements. On July 16 she encountered an English steamer in the Amur estuary, which sent out five small armed sloops to capture *Okhotsk*. The brig's commanding officer, seeing no possibility of defending his ship or of escaping with it, ordered that a hole be cut in the underwater part of the brig. He ignited a fire near the powder storage area and transferred all of his crew onto small sloops and set out for shore. He was harried by pursuing gunfire from the enemy sloops, but Iuzelius and part of his crew in the sloop with him managed to reach shore; the rest of the crew on two other sloops were captured by the enemy, and the explosion and fire completely destroyed the brig.

In 1854 and 1855 the colonial fleet took possession of a 500-ton screw steamer built in New York, and acquired a 350-ton ship in San Francisco.

The following projects were undertaken in naval headquarters in New Arkhangel during this period:

1) They completed construction of a large lighter for a steam-driven lumber mill. The machinery was put into place and the mill made operational.

2) Two sloop sheds were built at the slip.

3) The brig *Promysl* was converted into a hulk; partitions and compartments were built into her.

4) Necessary repairs were made to Company vessels; two ships were built for the American-Russian Trading Company* and repairs were made to the whaling vessel *Aian*. In addition to these activities, masts and spars were made for all the ships which needed them.

Besides the ship *Sitka*, captured by the enemy, and the brig

---

* The American-Russian Trading Company was organized in San Francisco and headed by [Beverley] Sanders. Its purpose was to export ice, bituminous coal, lumber and fish from the Russian possessions to all countries bordering on the Pacific. On May 31, 1859, that company and the North West Ice Company in San Francisco concluded a contract. THE EDITORS.

Okhotsk, destroyed with its cargo by its captain, the Company also lost a small ironclad steamer which was destroyed by the enemy upon its second arrival at Petropavlovsk in the spring of 1855.

In compliance with the existing convention of neutrality between the Russian American Company and Hudson's Bay Company, the English Admiral Bruce, and the French, Fourichon, did not engage in any inimical activity during their 1855 visit to the port of New Arkhangel.

On March 10 and 11, 1855, a hostile uprising of natives took place in New Arkhangel. We lost 2 dead and 19 wounded. The Kolosh, on the other hand, lost between 60 and 80 men killed and wounded. As a sign of their renewed submission they surrendered eight hostages.

A very useful description was appended [to the Report] concerning the previously little known communication link between Aian and Iakutsk, along with a clear and very intelligible lithographed map of Eastern Siberia. The map shows trails from Iakutsk to Okhotsk, Aian and Ud ostrog, which existed prior to the discovery of a water route by way of the Amur River. These were the only three routes leading to the Sea of Okhotsk and to the Pacific Ocean. Now, thanks to this map, one can clearly see the advantages and disadvantages of these route.

See: "Otchet Rossiisko-Amerikanskoi Kompanii za 1854 i 1855 gody." In *Morskoi Sbornik*. Vol. 27 (Moscow: 1857), No. 1, 20–24.

86

1858–59

INFORMATION ON RUSSIAN AMERICAN COMPANY SHIPPING, COAL
MINING AND WHALING, FROM THE COMPANY'S 1858 REPORT

The total capital goods of the Russian American Company, both in Russia and in the colonies, amounted to 5,344,195.09 rubles (905,638.73 more than in 1857). Of that amount, 100,000 rubles (as in the previous year) represented assets of the Russian-Finnish Whaling Company, and 309,311.83 rubles (89,984.12 more than in 1857), the value of seagoing vessels.

The following servitors were in the colonies: 1 Chief Administrator, a Rear Admiral; 1 fleet staff officer; 3 senior officers; 1 fleet navigator, a senior officer; 4 Siberian line battalion senior officers; 2 civilian officials; 1 mining engineer; 2 mining foremen; 27 members of the clergy (17 less than in 1857); 6 medical officials; 4 medical assistants; 6 medical students; 2 midwives; 2 assistant mid-wives; 11 skippers and their senior assistants (hired navigators); 9 junior ship assistants (hired navigators and students of navigation); 6 master artisans, shipwrights and armourers; 2 scientists at the Sitka magnetic observatory; 9 office administrators and their assistants; 13 bookkeepers and their assistants; 34 prikashchiks; 18 administrators of isolated posts and commands; 23 clerks; 37 navy seamen; 166 lower ranks from Siberian line battalions; 467 hired servitors, artisans and workers (303 Russians and 164 natives); and 29 hired female workers in schools and infirmaries. From this it is apparent that in spite of the fact that the value of the seagoing vessels increased, the complement of servitors associated with navigation decreased from 1857 by 74 persons: 1 junior ship assistant; 1 artisan, shipwright and armourer; 32 sailors and 40 hired servitors, artisans and workers. From line battalions, there was one more officer and 21 fewer junior personnel.

The native population of the colonies consisted of 5,188 males and 4,804 females, a total of 9,992. Of that number 567 males and 45 females, a total of 612, were Russian. Creoles numbered 924 males and 986 females for a total of 1,910.

Aleuts and Kurils numbered 2,224 males and 2,227 females, a total of 4,451; foreigners, 2 males and 1 female, a total of 3; Kenaits, 540 males and 595 females, a total of 1,099; Kuskokvims and Aglegmiuts, 663 males and 669 females, a total of 1,332; Chugach and Mednovsk, 301 males and 281 females, a total of 585.

There were 14 pupils in a temporary school in New Arkhangel built for children of servitors. Two of these were sent aboard the around-the-world ship *Kamchatka* to gain further practical training in navigation. Instruction proceeded along the usual lines in the schools for children of workers, and orphaned children. As of May 1, 1858, 29 pupils were educated at Company expense in the school for boys; 9 were accepted during the year. Of these, 4 entered Company service upon reaching the proper age; 2 died; and as of May 1, 1859, the total number of pupils was 32. There were 25 pupils in the school for girls as of May 1, 1858, 3 of whom were accepted during the year. Of these pupils, 3 married workers, and so there were 25 pupils as of May 1, 1859.

On March 19, 1859 the Russian American Company received permission to establish a school for young boys in New Arkhangel; this is to be known as the Public School of the Russian American Colonies. Navigation and naval astronomy will be taught there also.

The newly established class of colonial citizens, who are settled in various departments of the colonies, numbered some 240 persons in 1858, including their family members. In the report concerning these citizens, they are described as "comprising a population who are moral and industrious" (of course from the desire for property). This category consists of Russian subjects, other persons of the free category who have the right to leave America, and hired townspeople and peasants who are in the Russian American colonies as hired persons, and who have married either creoles or American natives.

The question arises as to who are these "other people of the free category who have the right to leave America?" Are they Russians who have not incurred debts to the Company, or who have paid their debts? Or are they emancipated natives who are not mentioned in the information about citizens? Since the Report is read not only by shareholders of the Russian

American Company who should know the regulations of the Company, [but by others as well], and since many periodical publications reprint the Report or excerpts from it, it would be interesting to know whether natives are divided into free and non-free categories. Are American natives, Aleuts and especially creoles, colonial citizens? Or when they leave the previous lifestyle of their brothers in colonies of European powers, are they subdivided according to the color of their skin? If they are not actually bound to the land in the strictest sense of the term, are they not actually independent either? Or are they completely dependent on the colonial administration and deprived of some or many of their civil rights?

While we await the solution of this question, an explanation of which we will probably find in the history of the colonies which is in preparation [Tikhmenev], we will note here that in spite of the well-tried navigational skills of the creoles, they have not yet comprised the crew of a colonial circumnavigatory ship. There is no doubt that it would be very useful for them to display their skills to advantage, observe others, and cast their eyes on white society.

In 1858 Company ships undertook the following major voyages:

1) The ship *Tsaritsa*, 1,900 tons, purchased in Hamburg, sailed from Kronstadt with Company and government cargo, under the command of skipper Ridell on September 6, 1858. She left Hamburg on November 12 and encountered such heavy weather in the English Channel that she suffered considerable damage and was forced to put in at Plymouth for repairs. Passengers and cargo for the colonies were transferred to a foreign vessel, *Johann Kepler*, leased for that purpose in Plymouth. After repairs were made, *Tsaritsa* left Plymouth on May 26, 1859, and sailed directly to the Amur River to unload government cargo. On August 10 she passed through the [Korean] Strait and entered the China Sea.

2) The ship *Nikolai I* (commander Krogius), after delivering government cargo in the Amur region, reached Shanghai on October 3, 1858, where she took on a cargo of tea. She put out to sea again on December 13 and reached Kronstadt on April 26 [1859], having called at the Cape of Good Hope and Copenhagen.

3) The ship *Kamchatka* (commander Iuzelius), upon delivery of cargo in New Arkhangel which she had brought from Europe, was dispatched on July 19, 1858 to De Castries Bay to take on cargo for the colonies, which she delivered to the Amur. From there she returned to New Arkhangel on November 16. On November 27, carrying passengers and a cargo of furs, she put out to sea on a return voyage to Kronstadt, where she arrived on June 29, 1859, after stops in Honolulu, St. Catherine Island and Copenhagen.

4) The ship *Nakhimov* (commanded by Ensign of the Corps of Naval Navigators Benzeman) set out on June 11, 1858 for the port of Aian to deliver religious personnel and students from the New Arkhangel seminary, on the occasion of the transfer of the seminary to Iakutsk; she also carried other passengers. From Aian the ship sailed to De Castries Bay to take on grain which had been brought down the Amur for delivery to the colonies. Prior to setting out for the colonies the ship sailed to the harbor of St. Vladimir and to Hakodate [Hokkaido], and on December 8 returned to New Arkhangel. On February 5, 1859 she sailed with a cargo of ice to San Francisco and returned on March 18.

5) The ship *Kodiak* (commander Kadin) was dispatched on April 15, 1858 to Kodiak Island with lumber to complete the construction of ice sheds, and with supplies for the Kodiak department.

She took on a cargo of ice and delivered it to San Francisco, returning to New Arkhangel on July 8. On the 29th of that month (under the command of navigator Rozlund), she was again sent to Kodiak for ice, delivered it to California, and returned to Sitka on November 2.

On January 15, 1859 the ship again went from Sitka to California with a cargo of furs, and with salted fish and lumber to sell. She returned on March 12 and on the 24th again went to San Francisco with a cargo of ice. She returned to the colonies on May 31 carrying the newly appointed Chief Administrator of the colonies, Captain of the first rank [Hampus] Furuhjelm.

7) The ship *Shelikhov* (commander [Aleksandr F.] Kashevarov) delivered supplies to the islands of Atka, Attu, Bering and Copper, and took on furs for New Arkhangel. She carried out this assignment between April 9 and July 30, 1858. On March

29, 1859, *Shelikhov* was again sent to deliver supplies to the same islands as well as to the islands of Shumushu and Urup; she brought furs from these departments to Aian, reaching there July 17.

8) The steamer *Imperator Aleksandr II* (commander Arkhimandritov) set out on May 16, 1858 with supplies for the islands of Unalaska, St. Paul, St. George, and the Mikhailovsk and Kolmakovsk redoubts. From these places she carried furs back to New Arkhangel. On this occasion she sailed twice to English Bay to procure supplies of coal and on her return voyage she stopped twice at the harbor of Pavlovsk where she transferred supplies from there to English Bay for the coal mining expedition. She delivered passengers to New Arkhangel, as well as the annual catch from the Kodiak department. The steamer returned to New Arkhangel on August 28.

On March 29, 1859 the steamer sailed to Pavlovsk harbor and to English Bay, and returned to Sitka on April 23.

9) The steamer *Velikii Kniaz Konstantin* (commander Ofterdinger) was dispatched on May 8, 1858 to Aian with the annual colonial catch and the mail; she stopped at Shumushu and Urup to deliver supplies and pick up furs. From Aian the steamer sailed to Nikolaevsk to transfer goods and supplies to a Company vessel at De Castries Bay. These supplies had come down the Amur, but because of a delay en route, *Konstantin* sailed to Sakhalin Island to take on coal and then returned to De Castries Bay from where she returned to Nikolaevsk with news of the arrival at that bay of the ship *Kamchatka*.

With the assistance of the government barge *Iaponets*, the steamer transported the cargo which by then had reached the mouth of the Amur. On October 7 she sailed to Aian, and from there, on October 21, set out for Petropavlovsk harbor, reaching there on October 27. She remained there to make repairs and to spend the winter.

On May 12 the steamer set out for Sakhalin and Nikolaevsk, carrying passengers and the mail. From there, she set out on June 9 for Aian, carrying passengers. On June 10 she encountered the American ship *Melita* which had been shipwrecked. *Konstantin* picked up her passengers and crew, but had to remain there until June 13 because of storms in Nevelskii Bay; only then could she deliver the Americans to Nikolaevsk. She then returned to the damaged vessel, where the commander of the steamer salvaged everything possible and then took all the salvaged goods and *Melita*'s skipper to De Castries Bay.

10) The schooner *Tungus* (commander Kuritsyn) in the course of 1858 delivered supplies to the island of Unga, and then sailed all through the Kodiak department delivering supplies and picking up furs.

In this manner, in addition to successfully carrying out, aboard its own vessels, various assignments which involved great distances and sometimes a good deal of danger, the Company also had the honor of providing service to the government through the reliable transport of consular personnel and goods to Japan.

In 1858 there were 281 working days at the port of New Arkhangel, in the Admiralty Department and on Lesnoi Island. On each of these days an average of 334 men were involved in port activities.

In addition, a substantial amount of lumber was cut and prepared; part was sent to Kodiak for the construction of ice sheds and harbor facilities, and large shipments went to various colonial departments. Three steamers and six sailing vessels had capital and repair work. The ship *Shelikhov* was beached for careful inspection and repair of her underwater parts. Repairs were also made to harbor and oared vessels. In the sail shop new sails were made and old sails repaired. Various works were carried out as needed in other shops such as tools, joinery, blacksmith, metal, copper, turnery, tannery, rigging and caulking. Special workmen prepared ice, loaded and unloaded departing and arriving vessels. Construction of the lumber mill on Lesnoi Island was completed and the machinery was put into place.

In addition to information about procuring coal in English Bay, this Report gives an outline of the search and actual labor over the past four years to develop a coal mining industry in the colonies. In 1857, in the heart of the coal bed at English Bay some 600 feet from shore a shaft was built to extract coal and to pump out water. It was not until late in 1856 that a steam engine was emplaced to pump out the water in the shaft, and since it was impossible to use a hand pump to get rid of the water which appeared in the shaft at a depth of 17 feet, work had to be halted until the pump was installed. The necessary structures were completed in 1858, the pumping machinery was enclosed and the labor force increased. Consequently it became possible to proceed on the work of the shaft. By March 1, 1859 the depth of the shaft was 70 feet: 47 feet of sand and 23 feet of hard clay. Coal should be found at a depth of 160 feet. This estimate is based on the calculations of coal strata as seen from the coast.

To procure coal for our own use, small shafts were sunk at the very edge of the basin along the coast. Although this manner of mining is much more difficult, it nevertheless enabled provisioning of Company ships with coal and revealed important information about the formation of the coal strata. There are four shafts. The total length is 1,687 feet, of which 1,509 feet is in the coal itself, and 178 feet in nonproductive material. This temporary form of mining of coal yielded 4,200 tons, or about 25,000 puds. Almost the entire amount was used for steamships and other internal use, with only a small part, some 530 tons, sent to California for sale on an experimental basis.

Kodiak appears more suitable than any other place for procuring ice. In New Arkhangel ice is cut only eleven inches thick, and there are no more than ten days when this can be done. On Kodiak the temperature goes down to 20°, and therefore careful consideration is being given to establishing this operation there. The ice trade, in association with the American-Russian Trading Company, has not fulfilled expectations. That company suffered a substantial loss in the spring of 1858. Its vessel *Zenobia* was returning from New Arkhangel with a cargo of 836 tons of ice when it was wrecked near Cape Bonito. The crew and the colonial mail were saved, and the ship and its cargo were lost. The ship was not part of the general assets, and therefore the loss for the Russian American Company was limited to the ice itself.

As a result of this circumstance the American-Russian Trading Company hurriedly engaged the clipper *Vitula*, 1,177 tons, to sail to the colonies for ice. By June they loaded 1,200 tons aboard and set out from Sitka. In addition to this, two Company ships delivered 549 tons of ice to San Francisco. And aboard the newly chartered American-Russian Trading Company ship *Cartyne*, 1,000 tons of ice were sent from Kodiak. In all, except for the loss of the 836 tons of ice, 2,749 tons were shipped from the colonies to San Francisco, and of that amount only 1,167 tons were sold as of January 1.

This disappointing sale of ice in California, as well as a number of misunderstandings which arose as a result of the failure of the American-Russian Trading Company to fulfill certain parts of the contract, became the subject of special correspondence between both companies, as was stated in the Report for last year. Because of the possibility of causing serious repercussions for the Russian American Company, final negotiations about this matter have been delegated by the Main Administration to Captain of the first rank Furuhjelm, during his voyage via San Francisco to his assignment [in New Arkhangel]. The final resolution of these negotiations can be expected at the end of 1859. It is possible that the statistics on the amount of ice used annually by the citizens of San Francisco and its vicinity could explain the misunderstanding of the American-Russian Trading Company, and the dissatisfaction of the Russian American Company with the small sale of Russian ice, and the existence of a secret trade in ice by Americans outside the Russian American Company.

Ships of the Russian-Finnish Whaling Company, *Graf Berg* and *Turku*, sailed from the Sandwich Islands to the Sea of Okhotsk on March 31, 1858. When *Graf Berg* entered that sea on April 26, she encountered a Japanese ship in very serious condition. That vessel, after sailing from Simoda to one of the Japanese coastal harbors during a great storm, lost its mast and rudder, and in that condition was carried out to sea where it suffered disastrous events for the next three months. The crew of seventeen Japanese had not had a drop of fresh water for three weeks. They had quenched their thirst with the few fruits left in the cargo. Their total provisions consisted of just one sack of rice, of which the crew received only a handful each day. The commanding officer of *Graf Berg*, Enberg, lowered sloops into the water and took the crew of the wrecked ship aboard his vessel and continued his voyage. On May 1 *Graf Berg* anchored in the strait between the islands of Matsumai and Kunashiri, where Enberg put the Japanese ashore. The ship *Turku* also reached the Sea of Okhotsk on April 22, when the sea was not yet free of ice. For some time she did not sight any whales. *Graf Berg* was also there, and had the same experience, as did many other foreign whalers. They decided to break through the ice and sail to Tauisk Bay; both ships anchored there on June 2.

Hunting was not good in June, but in July they took six whales in Udsk Bay. However, by then the number of foreign vessels in that bay had increased to 130, so both [Russian] vessels decided to move on to Aian, and then continue to the north. Early in December *Turku* reached Honolulu. Its cargo consisted of 500 barrels of whale oil and about 6,000 pounds of whale whiskers, which were sent to be sold in Bremen. The skipper of the *Graf Berg* intended to remain in the Sea of Okhotsk until late in the season and then proceed to Kamchatka, in accordance with his orders. By October 1, 1858 he had 250 barrels of oil. He also reached the Sandwich Islands early in 1859, where he planned to rest and take on needed supplies.

See: "Otchet Rossiisko-Amerikanskoi Kompanii za 1858 god." In *Morskoi Sbornik*. Vol. 45 (Moscow: 1860), No. 2, 1–9.

87

MARCH 19, 1859

ESTABLISHMENT OF THE PUBLIC SCHOOL OF THE RUSSIAN AMERI-
CAN COLONIES IN NEW ARKHANGEL

The Sovereign Emperor, subsequent to a report from the Minister of Finance to the Siberian Committee concerning the establishment in New Arkhangel on Sitka Island of a Public Colonial School, and in accordance with the proposal of the Committee, issued the following decree on March 19, 1859:

1. The Russian American Company is hereby authorized to establish a school for boys in New Arkhangel; it is to be called the Public School of the Russian American Colonies.

2. Overall supervision and care of the school is to be entrusted to the Chief Administrator of the colonies, and direct supervision to an overseer, who will be one of the teachers, selected by the Chief Administrator.

3. The organization of this school is to be patterned after *uezd* [district] schools; the teachers will be considered in actual government service under the jurisdiction of the Ministry of Public Education. They will be granted the rank, uniform, pension and all rights and prerogatives of teachers in uezd schools in Siberia.

4. The curriculum and actual teaching of subjects are to be the same as in three-class uezd schools, namely:

   A. Catechism and church history
   B. Russian language
   C. Arithmetic, geometry and solid geometry
   D. Geography
   E. History of the Russian Empire and abridged world history
   F. Penmanship, sketching and drawing

For young people with a religious calling who are destined to enter the seminary, there will be supplementary studies of church singing, Slavonic language and a more detailed study of catechism, as is done in the uezd church schools. Students who will go directly into special Company service in the colonies should have additional instruction in bookkeeping; necessary aspects of mathematics, navigation and marine astronomy; German and English languages; and other commercial subjects needed for Company service for commercial navigation and business transactions.

NOTE: Young people with a religious calling who express a desire to learn language may also receive that instruction.

5. Graduates who successfully complete the entire course of studies and then enter Company service, upon completion of their six years of service on duties assigned by the Company, will be granted the rank of personal distinguished citizens.

6. The premises of the school, its upkeep, and the maintenance of the students, salaries of teachers and other expenses are to be charged to the Company, with the understanding that the amount of salary and pension will correspond to the salary scale of teachers in uezd schools in Siberia, and that authorized deductions from salaries for pensions will be held by the Treasury in a pension fund. This rule applies strictly to teachers of uezd school subjects such as catechism, Russian language, mathematics, geography and history.

7. To assist in teaching supplementary subjects for young people with a religious calling, who intend to enter a theological seminary, two supervisors are to be appointed, either from among local clergy or from the best students in Siberian seminaries, in consultation with the Bishop of Kamchatka and with local diocesan authorities. The salaries for these supervisors, who will be appointed by His Grace the Bishop of Kamchatka, are to come from the budget for the religious school, independent of the sum designated for the maintenance of the school in accordance with the decree of the Holy Synod approved by the Emperor on December 5, 1857.

8. The Main Administration of the Russian American Company is charged, in cooperation with the Ministry of Public Education, to appoint teachers and to adhere strictly to the rules governing their selection as set forth by the Ministry.

9. Individuals educated at Company expense in the Public Colonial School, upon completion of the curriculum, are obligated to enter Company service as recompense for their education, and to serve in the colonies for not less than ten years, in posts to be assigned to them by local authorities according to their qualifications. They will receive appropriate salaries

ХЛИШТИА́НАТЪ

ЛЮКУ́ДАХЧІ́ЧАДА ЛУ́ЛА́ГИГА,

а̂л̂ха́къ

ЛИКИ́ЛІ́ГУКЪ ТА̊И̊Г̑ИШКА́КЪ

ІІШТУ́ЛИ҇КЪ

чали́

ЛИКИ́ЛІ́ГУКЪ КА̊ТИХИ́ШІІША́КЪ.

Іл̑ьямъ Ты́жновамъ пи҇льля.

С. ПЕТЕРБУ́РГЪ.

Шинꙋ́дамъ Типꙋ́глаꙋни а̊ни.

1847.

Title page of a Russian Orthodox Christian Guide Book, compiled and translated into the Aleutian language by the missionary priest, Ilia Tyzhnov. Printed by the Synod Press in St. Petersburg in 1847. Following the example set by Veniaminov, Father Tyzhnov translated a number of religious books into the Aleutian language, and compiled a special primer for the use of the native people on Kodiak Island. Lada Mocarski. *Bibliography of Books on Alaska Published before 1868.*

and maintenance from the Company on the precise terms established in the Statute of the Company concerning the ten-year obligatory service. This rule applies to those born in the colonies who are educated there, or who have studied trades in Russia at Company expense.

Reference: *PSZ*, Second Series, Vol. 34, No. 34,258, 212–213.

88

MARCH 9, 1862

A DESCRIPTION OF HUNTING AND CONSERVATION IN THE RUSSIAN
AMERICAN COLONIES BY ALEKSANDR F. KASHEVAROV

Nearly everyone who has recently written about the Russian American colonies agrees that the present administrative structure of this distant possession of Russia in the New World needs radical reorganization. But at the same time it is quite clear that there may be the danger that valuable furbearing animals, the prime source of wealth of the country, would be exterminated if, as a result of giving citizenship and its full rights to the local inhabitants of Russian America, that is, Russians, Aleuts, creoles and other indigenous peoples, they were given free reign to hunt, and could consider hunting their lawful right.

Therefore, in order to balance necessary progress with conservation, some persons have suggested that for the conservation of marine animals in the Russian American possessions, the Russian American Company should be granted, for a definite but prolonged period of time, the right to hunt marine animals in those places where it has previously hunted; that is, where the Company has established economic practices, *zapusks* and the like, with the essential condition that they maintain and improve these places. Toward this end, "permit the Russian American Company to have permanent use of these places where it presently has settlements or various establishments." (Does this include fishing, coal mining, lakes, ice houses, good harbors, large rivers and their estuaries, i.e., *everything*!?)

A zapusk is a temporary halt or curtailment of hunting furbearing animals whose numbers are seriously depleted because of intense or prolonged hunting; the purpose is to allow the animal to increase in number.

The term *promyslovye zveri* refers to animals which only the Russian American Company has the right to hunt. These are divided into mainland, island, river and marine animals. Mainland animals have softer fur than the same kind of animal on the islands. Island animals such as the fox, polar fox and others, because they live on an island surrounded on all sides by the sea which never freezes over, can never leave the island. For that reason it is not difficult to ascertain when hunting should be closed down, and when traps may again be set to take these animals.

The fur seal and walrus are among island animals that can be hunted. By some secret law of nature which has never been explained, every year these fur seals come from the south to the Bering Sea and head for the Pribylov and Komandorskie Islands to breed. Long experience indicates the time to begin hunting, and at that time the fur seals are herded. They are driven from the shore into the interior of the island where these amphibious creatures become clumsy in the grass. Here they are killed by clubs (large wooden sticks held in the hand), almost at the discretion of the hunter, and in numbers permissible and necessary in accordance with the estimates.

At the conclusion of this slaughter the rest of the seals are again herded, but this time just back to the shore, where they are left in peace. In due time they leave their breeding grounds and swim southward, but no one knows where. Perhaps they spend the winter somewhere in the depths of a warm sea, in a manner similar to bears who hibernate in their lairs with no activity but sucking their paws.

Earlier I said that fur seals are killed almost by choice and in as large numbers as accord with the estimates. But this is done in order not to deplete the animals totally, and to give them the opportunity to reproduce. The estimate is based on long term observation of the fur seal's growth and reproduction. Some of the animals have been marked on the flipper or head by the intelligent and concerned administrator of the island of St. Paul, the creole Shaeshnikov, and by local Aleuts who have lived there for a long time. From their accounts Father Ioann Veniaminov (currently His Eminence, Innokentii, Archbishop of Kamchatka and other places) prepared an interesting table of the probability of increasing the fur seal population if the promyshlenniks in their annual hunt for that animal would limit themselves to taking the numbers given in his table; this would provide for a gradual increase from a minimum number over the course of a given period of time in the table until the animal has naturally replenished its own numbers. The brilliant success of the eminent author of this table justifies serious consideration [of his proposal].

That table, as I recall, is appended to his informative work, *Notes on the Unalaska Department*. I venture to say that by publishing this table it has been of genuine benefit to our country.

The situation regarding marine, river and mainland animals is an entirely different story! These animals have ample space to roam. The boundless uninhabited expanse and the severe winter give them the opportunity to multiply in peace. A native hunter comes on them by chance when he is in the mountains or tundra hunting reindeer or wolves, which are necessary for his life. Sable or marten are also essential to his life. But the most important creature for domestic economy in that inhospitable part of the world is the beaver. A substantial number are killed each year. They are the primary commodity in the fur trade, and for that reason the savages hunt them eagerly. It is possible that in time the number of beaver will diminish, but there is no need to think about conservation for them at the present time. They belong to the independent natives of the interior who live in that vast expanse and acknowledge no authority but custom and tradition which is handed down to them from their forebears.

I also believe it is impossible to take real conservation measures for sea otters. Possibly an objection may be raised to this simple statement. According to observations by Aleut promyshlenniks, the sea otter appears and spends the first part of the year only in areas where it can find abundant food and where it does not scent smoke, which it cannot abide. The feeding grounds are located in what are called sea otter banks near islands. These feeding grounds may be devoid of sea otters for a period of one, two or three years. Based on this, experienced sea hunters know in advance that there may be few or no animals in a particular place one year, but they can predict that the animal will come in large numbers to some other known place. They dispatch sea otter hunting parties to that place, and honor and glory are gained by taking as many of the animals as possible. But did the sea otters migrate from one place to another? The question is unresolved.

However, independent of the appearance of large numbers of sea otters in a new place, the success of the hunt depends largely if not entirely on good weather during the first part of the year. It happens that in the three-month period the hunters can make only three or four hunting trips at sea. In order to be successful, the sea must be calm so the men can follow the diving of the sea otter. This can be observed only with the aid of inflated bladders which come up to the surface of the sea [after the animal has been shot]. The shaft of the arrow separates from the head [after it hits the sea otter]; a long cord made from the intestines of large marine animals attaches the [inflated] bladder to the shaft, the cord wound around the middle of the shaft. When the sea otter comes up for air, the slack of the cord is taken in.

The cord unwinds, and the shaft floats some distance from the otter and impedes its progress, and at the same time forces the otter to remain on the surface of the water. Like a whale that needs air, the otter must come up for it, willingly or not. It becomes exhausted, surfaces near the baidarkas, and is then killed by one or more arrows. The slightest ripple on the sea obviously interferes with sighting the animal and thereby impedes the baidarka chase after the surfaced sea otter. The sea otter hunt in the Russian American colonies ends in early July because the animal leaves our shores and migrates, but no one knows where.

Under these circumstances, can one guarantee that foreign sailors will not accidentally discover the winter haunt of these free-moving precious furbearing animals? They spend winter in one place and summer somewhere else, and no one knows where they may appear. This is especially true at the present time when there is such an enormous amount of navigation in the northern part of the Great [Pacific] Ocean! Is it not possible that in some place seldom visited by ships in that ocean, someone may in time discover the previously unknown sea otter banks?

Sea lions and seals are also marine animals. How could a free Aleut citizen live if he did not have the right to hunt these creatures for himself? He needs lavtaks for the baidaras and baidarkas; he is a coastal dweller and hunter; his nature cannot be changed (and need not be), and he cannot exist adequately without the baidara and baidarka. He needs *kamleis* [outer garments], covers for baidarkas, boot tops made from [sea lion and seal] intestines and throats, and he needs the meat and fat of these sea creatures for food. And what about whales? walrus? and others?

Earlier I mentioned that I include the walrus among amphibious animals hunted and reserved for [the exclusive use of] the Russian American Company. This enormous and powerful animal is killed with deadly risk on the part of the Aleut promyshlenniks. This hunt for tusks is the most dangerous, most difficult, and the least rewarding for the promyshlenniks. The Aleuts carry their baidarkas and provisions from the southern coast of Alaska to the northern part; they leave provisions at Moller Bay, where the walrus breeding grounds are to be found on the west side. On the day set for the walrus hunt, they offer prayers to God, put on clean shirts, and in a group or unit spread out and encircle the walrus. They stand side by side facing the walrus and point their spears at it in order to take it head on. The walrus does not move until he is frightened. On the ground it moves only in a straight line. A large group of walrus will line up in rows. The most dangerous moment for the promyshlenniks is when they spear the first row; every single animal in that row must be killed. The second row of animals presents less danger. The walrus does not move sideways, as noted above. The animals in the second row clamber over the bodies of the walrus in the first row, and raise their heads, which makes it easier for the promyshlenniks to kill these giants than it was to kill those in the first row. The promyshlenniks thus kill the rest of the walrus from behind a barricade, as it were, without danger. But God forbid that the first row breaks through the line of the promyshlenniks! When that happens the rest of the rows of walrus instantly hurl themselves to the sea, and the promyshlenniks must seek safety in flight.

Immediately after the end of the slaughter the hunters begin to take the tusks from the dead animals. This is the goal of such difficult and dangerous work. By the fourth and fifth days the unbearable stench from the decomposition of hundreds of walrus carcasses forces the promyshlenniks to abandon the rookery, the scene of their exploit. They return to the southern coast of Alaska along the same route, but they have to haul 200 puds [of tusk ivory]. The bodies of the hundreds of walrus are left to be devoured by other animals.

I am completely convinced that it would be fruitless to attempt the conservation of marine animals except for the fur seal. And it would be strange to deprive the inhabitants of the coastal colonies of the right to the free use of the resources of their native sea, which God has given them for their own good! There is no need to fear that if local promyshlenniks are permitted to hunt marine animals freely the animals will be exterminated—Russian America simply does not have enough manpower to do that! Whenever and wherever it becomes necessary, temporary conservation of certain animals should be done, and this is a specialty of native hunters. Do we need government supervision to carry this out, using local inhabitants of the Russian American colonies, through legally instituted regulations for the development of their well-being and the prosperity of the country? [We cannot] compare private hunting with the terrible period of the past, carried on by unbridled foreign opportunists and crude intruders into our lands, with potential future hunting undertaken by local people, properly regulated. To suggest that the disastrous results of long ago will be repeated in the future is distressing.

Our future civilization must not be determined by memories of matters in days long since passed by. We yearn for the rights of property in our country. And when such gifts of the government are offered, why leave a loophole for someone to establish a monopoly? We are the same people as "all of our severe critics and judges." We see and understand what is white and what is black. For example, the Aleuts, "when the Company is no longer their nursemaid" will certainly not accept just a mere pittance as pay for the exhausting, deleterious work of prolonged paddling, the dangers of the sea otter hunt which must take place just during the time of year when it is best for them to prepare their own provisions for winter. And who but an Aleut can go out on the sea otter hunt? No one. Whalers in whaleboats? They love to smoke and eat well, they need fire, and thus make fire and smoke, which the Aleuts avoid throughout the entire time of the sea otter hunt. As I have said, the sea otter does not like smoke, if it smells smoke it instantly flees the area. Then where to look for it? And how many whalers would be needed? For this reason the Aleut has no rival, and he will very quickly come to realize this.

I could mention several other conflicts that might arise from the abrogation of the right of ownership, both private (cooperative and societal) and monopoly, when owners do not have governmental authority to influence the local populace for their own benefit, and thus are deprived of property rights in many ways, and of the benefit of the fruits of their own free productive labor. But it is time to conclude, and therefore I will end by saying "best for *all* or for *none*."

See: A. F. Kashevarov. "Chto takoe zapusk i promysel pushnykh zverei v Rossiisko-Amerikanskikh koloniiakh." in *Morskoi Sbornik*, Vol. 58 (St. Petersburg: 1862), 86–92.

89

APRIL 18, 1863

THE OPINION OF REAR ADMIRAL ARVID A. ETHOLEN, FORMER CHIEF
ADMINISTRATOR OF THE RUSSIAN AMERICAN COMPANY, CONCERN-
ING THE PROPOSED REORGANIZATION OF THE COLONIES

The means proposed by the Committee [on the Organization of the Russian American colonies] for the future re-
structuring of the colonies are completely at odds with the
purpose. The Committee has not expressed any reasons which
would prompt it to draw up plans so completely contrary to
reality, contradictory to the situation in the colonies, and detrimental to the future existence of the Company.

Furthermore, a view such as this can undermine the commercial enterprise which has labored for such a long time for
the well-being of the distant region, and for the benefit and
prestige of the Fatherland. The Company could little expect to
be subjected to such distrust, in view of all its aspirations to
serve the Imperial government through meticulous and generous fulfillment of all the difficult and costly assignments given
it, of which it is sufficient to recall the Amur expedition, and
the fact that the Company saved the garrison and the inhabitants of Kamchatka from terrible famine during the time of the
last [Crimean] war.

Observations from the Main Administration of the Company on the report of [Sergei A.] Kostlivtsov could have convinced the Committee that the various proposed changes in
colonial administration and in local lifestyle are in the first
place *premature*, and in the second place, would require *extensive expenditures* and financial resources, for which there is not
the slightest indication of appropriation. Is it possible at this
time to carry on free trade in the colonies, or to expect successful colonization of the American mainland in a country which
is totally desolate and inaccessible, which has a severe climate
and is unproductive, and where even at present the very small
population has great difficulty in procuring for itself the means
of existence?

In order to become intimately familiar with the land and
the region it is necessary not to have just a six-month visit to

Sitka and Kodiak, but an inspection of all the parts of the colonial possessions, especially in the northwestern part of the American mainland, which is very little known, even to the inhabitants of Sitka and Kodiak. If Kostlivtsov had set aside some time for this inspection, which is absolutely necessary for this purpose, then by using his good judgment and skills of observation in regard to those parts of the colonial administration which he personally observed, one can be certain he would not have made the above proposals.

I feel that I have more right to judge this because I am very familiar with all the places in our colonies where I spent 30 years of my life, first as commander of a ship, then as an assistant to the Chief Administrator, and finally for five years in the position of Chief Administrator. Since my return from there, for the past fifteen years I have taken part in the affairs of the Main Administration as a Director and member of the Executive Committee, a post which I still hold, although with the consent of the general shareholders at their meeting I am now on leave of absence in order to recover my health. My service in the Company has been honest and selfless and my efforts have been directed exclusively to carrying out honorably my responsibilities for the benefit both of the region and of the Company. All of this imposes on me the obligation to express my opinion, which such long years of service have shaped, with the hope that my view will be accepted as impartial.

In this belief, I base my ideas on substantial information and facts, and I say resolutely that if the Government approves the Committee's proposals in the form as they are now presented to the Main Administration of the Company, the entire region will be *completely lost* in the very near future, because the Company cannot exist under such conditions. It would have to terminate its activities immediately, and liquidate its assets and abandon the territory to its fate, territory which it has controlled and administered for almost 60 years now, and to which it has devoted so much labor, expenditure and sacrifice; territory which it has protected in times of peace and of war; territory where it has used every means to bring order and prosperity. In this regard no one can dispute the Company's beneficial service, and I make bold to say that such a beneficial enterprise deserves protection, not the destruction of its very existence and its interests.

I do not know what motives have forced the Committee to propose such drastic changes in the present structure of the colonial administration; in my judgment, there cannot be any reason for this. The inspectors who looked over the colonies at the request of the government [Pavel N. Golovin and Kostlivtsov]* very likely anticipated that they would find serious disorder in the colonies, as well as illegal activities and abuses on the part of local authorities. However, they had to report in clear conscience and justice that they found everything in proper order; the populace did not suffer from oppression; no one submitted valid complaints to them; and consequently they praised the Company with full approval for its activity in gaining due respect from foreigners,and in maintaining in their eyes the credit which they have everywhere. Would it seem that radical reorganization is needed there?

The only criticism cited is that the American Company enjoys a monopoly, to the detriment of other Russian subjects. I consider this opinion erroneous. This Company is not a *monopoly*; it is not even a tenant. Rather, it is a possessor of lands acquired at its own expense, settled through its own labors, and maintained with its own facilities. The Government limits its right of possession to twenty-year periods of privileges, and at the expiration of these periods can always cease granting extensions and take the colonies under its jurisdiction. This should only be done, however, with compensation to the Company for all its structures and enterprises there, as well as for materials, property, supplies and other things which the Company has acquired for local needs and requirements, and which would be of no use or profit to the Company once it ceased operations there.

It is likewise unfair to level the charge that the Aleuts are slaves to the Company. No one deprives them of their belongings; everything they acquire for themselves both at sea and on land belongs to them; but since they could not engage in hunting without the assistance of the Company, which furnishes them with everything, naturally they have the obligation to

---

*Golovin's official report: *The End of Russian America: Captain P. N. Golovin's Last Report, 1862*. Portland, 1979; his unofficial views: *Civil and Savage Encounters: the Worldly Travel Letters of an Imperial Russian Navy Officer, 1860–1861*. Portland, 1983. See Bibliography.

turn over their catch to the Company, which pays them at the established price, and often at an even higher price. One can rather call the Aleuts members of a family of which the American Company is the head. As head, or as solicitous guardian, the Company has obligations to them and constantly adheres to the rule that it must be responsible for the well-being and improvement of the lives of the natives, and responsible as well for supervising their moral and intellectual development, insofar as possible with the means at the Company's disposal. And on the other hand, by their nature the Aleuts are children, in the full sense of the word, without any thought for their future. They are extremely heedless, unconcerned and lazy. To grant every newcomer the right to settle among them and to entice them with goods or with strong drink, will mean to lead them unavoidably into complete ruin. The only thing they own is peltry, and thanks to the guardianship and orderly administration by the Company, furbearing animals have not yet been exterminated around the Aleutian Islands. When the animals are exterminated, and are gone, then indigence, famine and ruin will follow, since it is already too late for the Aleuts to revert to their primitive way of life.

It is appropriate here to draw certain comparisons between the colonies which have been under the jurisdiction of the Company for nearly 60 years, and the Kamchatka district, which has been under government administration for some 150 years, that is, under the same governance which the Committee proposes adopting for the colonies in the future.

At the time of its discovery the Kamchatka region had about 12,000 native Kamchadal inhabitants, plus the Koriaks and Chukchi. The wealth of the region in furbearing animals was not much inferior to that of the colonies [in Russian America]. The soil, at least in the southern part of Kamchatka, was infinitely better than that anywhere in the colonies. Not even taking into account the considerable sums of money which the Government has spent in that region, what is the situation there now?

The population numbers scarcely 2,000 to 3,000 people. Furbearing animals have disappeared except for a small number of sables which merchants acquire from the natives in exchange for vodka; and not infrequently officials do the same.

The superb Kamchatka fish, which is the best quality in the entire North Pacific, is still found there in abundance, but no one has tried to make it an item of trade. The Kamchadals have become accustomed to eating grain, which cannot be grown there because of the severe climate; yet there have been times when for several years in succession [the Government] did not bother to supply the region with this necessary foodstuff, although the port of Okhotsk, and later the substantial Amur fleet, were available.

It is not necessary to recall here the abuses which crept into Kamchatka, indeed some openly, under government administration, and even under the authority of judges, district police officers, attorneys and others. The Chukchi inhabit the northern part of the Kamchatka region; in their way of life and customs they are quite similar to the native inhabitants of North America and to the Aleuts; and to the very present day these people remain in their primitive state. Left to their own fate, no one concerns himself about them. The light of the Christian faith has not been able to penetrate to them; they have no churches or chapels; they neither know nor recognize any authority. An American whaler, James Reading, was shipwrecked on the Chukotsk coast in 1852 and he and 37 of his crew spent the entire winter among the Chukchi; Reading reported that [the natives] even learned the name of their own [Russian] sovereign from the Americans.

All these facts are indisputable. Kamchatka had and still has government administration. Trade is free and anyone can settle there, although until now there have been very few persons willing to do so. In short, Kamchatka has everything the Committee now proposes to introduce into the colonies, with one difference: in Kamchatka the government bears all the expense, and in the colonies the Company does. The Committee is recommending that the Company continue to provide the garrison, churches, clergy, the colonial school, other schools, infirmaries, provisions and housing for all servitors and workers, heat and light for their dwellings—all of this.

The Company will also have to continue to provide storehouses for provisions, and furnish supplies and fine quality goods, which are by no means inexpensive. And in spite of all these requirements the Committee still manages to suggest withdrawing many existing privileges for the Company such as the exclusive right to trade throughout the American mainland, through the entire expanse of territory from Cape Douglas to Lake Iliamna, and on to the northeast right up to the English frontier. The Company would also lose the right to exclusive trade in all the islands along that coast, including Sitka and its port of New Arkhangel and all of its buildings—and the Company spent nearly a million rubles on construction there. The Company is expected to give up all of this for the benefit of nonexistent settlers, who are to be generously rewarded with eternal possession of land and freedom to trade everywhere! Can the Company agree to such conditions?

According to the Committee's proposal, the Aleuts are to be permitted to settle and to roam wherever they wish, and to hunt individually for their own benefit, with no Company guardianship. But what will result from this? To permit the Aleuts to relocate without permission, and leave their settlements which it has taken twenty years of great effort to consolidate, would be to take a tremendous step backward.

Obviously the Committee did not understand this when it drew up its proposal, for it did not consider it necessary to consult on this matter with the Main Administration of the Company or with other highly regarded specialists. If the Committee had had the advantage of this information, it would have learned that prior to 1841 the Aleuts were free to settle on their islands wherever they wished. Quite apart from the danger [of hunting individually], which was the reason for hunting in groups, the Aleuts often vanished without a trace, and died before anyone could come to their rescue. There are several instances of this, when after a long search [rescuers] discovered entire families who had settled somewhere or other on distant headlands, all dead in their baraboras; every one of them poisoned from the foolish consumption of a dead whale or toxic shellfish. Such tragedies did not occur after the Aleuts, at my recommendation, gathered in permanent settlements under the supervision of their own toions. When the inspectors spent some time on Kodiak Island they had the opportunity to ascertain that the Aleuts were well satisfied with this arrangement.

How does the Committee propose to compensate the Company for all it will give up, for the expenses it must continue to underwrite, and for all its hard work and sacrifices? The Company will retain for twelve years the exclusive right to the furs in a *defined area*, but in the future the Company will not be able to lay claim to natural resources either above or below ground.

At this point let us introduce a brief summary of the revenues which the Company may expect under this proposed arrangement. Up to the present time the annual revenue from this designated territory has consisted of a total of 800–900 sea otters, 12,000–16,000 fur seals, some 1,600 blue foxes, 2,000 island red foxes, 300 island brown foxes, some 400 island cross foxes and several hundred otters. For all of these furs the Company can expect gross revenues of some 300,000 rubles in Russia. If one deducts the cost of acquiring these furs, freight and insurance to Europe, and the year or more that elapses between paying [the natives] for the furs and selling them, the Company would realize a profit of scarcely 200,000 rubles. And from this profit the Company would be expected to maintain its entire administrative structure in the colonies and in Russia, acquire and maintain a substantial fleet, buildings, shops and other structures, supply warehouses for provisions and goods, which are to be of good quality yet not expensive, and in addition to all of this the Company is to provide pensions for the aged and infirm servitors and for widows and orphans. One may well ask how much is to be left for the shareholders of the Company? Even more, how can the Company manage to carry out its primary responsibilities with such limited means?

I consider it unnecessary to respond separately to all the points of the Committee's proposals, since the Main Administration of the Company has probably already done this; therefore I will limit my remarks to just a few of the points.

In general it is apparent that the Committee expects special benefits to the Empire from colonizing the American mainland, but I can say with certainty that such colonization will not be successful. Who will sentence himself to settle in a totally barren, unproductive, bleak region, which abounds in nothing, not only for trade but even for daily existence, where the soil consists of tundra and marsh, and even in summer thaws to a depth of only a few inches?

There is very little hope of discovering gold fields which

might attract people there not only from Russia but from America and from Europe. Gold was first discovered in California, and then gradually farther north. Now fields have been discovered as far north as the Stikine River, whose estuary lies within our possessions. But the fields are in plains quite a distance east of the coastal mountains which form our frontier to Mt. St. Elias; the range extends no more than 30 Italian miles inland from the coast. In that intervening distance there is no gold. From Mt. St. Elias our frontier lies directly north to the Arctic Ocean, with the land west of that line belonging to Russia. This territory is very low, marshy, and intersected by many rivers. Generally speaking, we have not explored it for gold deposits. But even if we suppose that there are precious metals there, the deposits would have to be very rich to attract persons willing to take on the working of mines in view of the tremendous expenses involved in construction and supplying the region with all the necessary equipment and goods.

It is quite impossible to agree with the Committee's proposal that the government appoint a special *military governor* to administer the colonies and oversee the activities of the Company. This would accomplish nothing and would be damaging. If the government actually finds it necessary to supervise the colonies, in my judgment it would be sufficient to send a government agent there every five years or so; however, he should come from here [St. Petersburg], not from the Amur. With the present good communication with the colonies, this would not be difficult, nor would it involve any great expense. This agent could gather all the necessary information about the administration, inquire, receive claims and complaints, and without issuing any rules, report to higher authorities when he returns to St. Petersburg, relating all his findings and observations, and appending to his report the views and explanations of the Chief Administrator.

This kind of arrangement would not result in any detriment to the administration. Furthermore, the Chief Administrator of the colonies is as much a government official as the military governor would be, as proposed by the Committee. The Chief Administrator has previously been selected from among reliable staff officers of the Imperial Navy. The Emperor appoints him to this position. His obligations are to see that the Charter of the Company to administer the colonies, granted by the Emperor, is in no way violated, and that no one oppresses the natives. He must also preserve the colonies in totality, and prevent any clashes with foreign powers. In a word, in the person of the Chief Administrator are now concentrated all the responsibilities which the Committee proposes to assign to a military governor. For this reason I see no reason to deprive the Chief Administrator of governmental trust, especially considering the fact that ever since naval officers have served in that position there has not been a single instance of any of them using his authority and trust for maleficent purposes.

Furthermore the appointment of a special military governor and his staff and officials will result in new, substantial, and wholly useless expenses. If the title of Chief Administrator or Harbor Administrator does not sound right, rename the position Military Governor; but there must not be two authorities in the same place. In my opinion, as long as the [Russian] American Company exists, the Chief Administrator should have the entire administrative authority. One may have either Company administration or government administration, but nothing in between.

In conclusion, I would like to express my firm conviction that this region is still too unprepared for such reforms as the Committee proposes, and that the continued existence of the [Russian] American Company is absolutely essential for the purpose [of administration]. For this reason the government should not at the present time undertake this administration, nor assume such obligations, the fulfillment of which will involve the government in significant expense without any purpose or need.

See: [Arvid A. Etholen, in:] *Doklad komiteta ob ustroistve Russkikh Amerikanskikh kolonii*. Vol. 1 (St. Petersburg: 1863), 374–384.

90

1863

RECOMMENDATIONS FOR REORGANIZING THE RUSSIAN AMERICAN COLONIES, SUBMITTED BY THE OFFICIAL COMMITTEE

The Committee has taken note of the necessity of having cruisers [in the North Pacific Ocean], and the vital, primary role which their presence should exert in the matter of the reorganization and support of our American colonies; however, the Committee does not consider itself well enough informed for immediate discussion of the precise manner in which to carry out this assignment. This should depend completely on the opinions, the means and the perceptions of the Naval Ministry, which has special jurisdiction over our naval forces. In addition to the American colonies, Russia has other vital interests in the Pacific: we need to maintain ports and a fleet at the mouth of the Amur River, and along the eastern periphery of Siberia in general. A number of our naval vessels are already on permanent assignment to sail between Japan and China. Recently there has been a permanent Russian squadron of more than twelve vessels in those waters. We cannot provide support for our political influence in China and the Far East without these expeditions.

It appears that in conjunction with the cruisers which would be designated to protect our colonies, naval vessels should be dispatched there under the jurisdiction of a Military Governor, which could eventually be detached from the Pacific Ocean squadron and from the Amur flotilla; but it would be almost impossible not to have at least one naval steamer permanently assigned to New Arkhangel to be at the disposal of the Chief Administrator of the region.

In the Conclusion of the review, the Committee has felt obligated to give special attention to the governmental administration of affairs in our American colonies, which is centered in the Fatherland. Initially the former Commerce College had this responsibility; when it was abolished at the beginning of the present century, supervision first went to the Ministry of Internal Affairs, and since 1819 it has been assigned to the jurisdiction of the Ministry of Finance, Department of Manufacture and Internal Trade. This corresponds in some degree with the structure of the colonial administration, which is in every aspect a private commercial company with which the Government has tried to interfere as little as possible.

Actually, however, judging by the results, this form of organization should not be considered satisfactory. The Ministry of Finance does not have at its disposal the necessary means to supervise the colonies, and in particular it has no naval vessels. For this reason it could not maintain supervision over the local activities of the Company administration, as would have been proper for it to do. In these matters it could only rely on the reports of the Company itself, and for verification it had only information and evidence which came to it indirectly through reports of commanders of naval vessels, reports which were occasionally sent to the Naval Ministry. These reports were for the most part informal, and as such were not notable for thoroughness and adequate detail. Consequently, since governmental supervision is not positioned to provide proper local supervision, the policy [of St. Petersburg], willingly or not, has more and more come to favor the commercial interests of the Russian American Company, losing sight of the needs of the territory entrusted to the Company, and of the population there. Seemingly, its sole aim has been the prosperity of the Company, and it has not given adequate attention to the matter of whether there is some connection between this prosperity and the development and strengthening of our colonization in America, which of course has been the primary goal of the Imperial administration in this matter.

It would be neither opportune nor advisable to leave conditions as they are now for the future, even if we were to keep the present colonial administrative structure. This is completely impossible under the terms of the proposed reorganization.

The establishment of governmental authority in a distant land where one can only penetrate through prolonged sailing, and the founding of this authority mainly on naval power, obviously demands that it be subordinated in its administrative structure to a department which has the necessary ability and special means of handling relations with the colonies, and of supervising them and bringing them under appropriate governmental jurisdiction. The Naval Ministry is the only administrative governmental unit with the necessary means to do this.

The Ministry of Internal Affairs would have the same problem as the Ministry of Finance: how could it extend its authority over a territory with which there is not even any regular mail service, and where, even if this were organized, it takes at least seven or eight months to send a written message, and more than a year to receive a response? Furthermore, would it be wise to subordinate to civil authority an administration which by its very designation must consist primarily of naval officers, and act by means of naval cruisers? All of this leads the Committee to the conviction that the overall administration of the Russian American colonies, including the affairs pertaining to the Russian American Company, should in the future be removed from the Ministry of Finance and placed under the jurisdiction of the Naval Ministry, to whom, indirectly, must also be subordinated the Military Governor of the colonies, who, because of the requirements of the region, must be selected from among the naval ranks.

CONCLUSION

All of the above considerations lead the Committee to find that the structure of our American colonies is definitely in need of change. The Committee bases its judgment on reports submitted by the persons [S. A. Kostlivtsov and P. N. Golovin] who inspected the colonies in 1860 at the recommendation of the Ministry of Finance and the Naval Ministry; on oral reports to the Committee during its deliberations, made by members of the Main Administration of the Company; and on other information given to the Committee. The primary goals of the changes should be to rescue the region from the deterioration of hunting and trade; to improve the condition of the dependent natives and of the entire colonial population; and to provide greater protection for the colonies against hostile independent natives and lawless foreign whalers and contrabandists. But to carry out these reforms it is not necessary to have unconditional revocation of the privileges from the Russian American Company and from Company institutions in the region. It will suffice to limit the scope of its privileges and to grant privileges for a shorter period of time. The administration of the region could also be established for the same period, but with the proviso that a local supervisor, completely governmental, be appointed over it, with sufficient means to provide both internal and external security for the region. The colonial population should immediately have a local judicial system and means of enforcement.

The Committee considers it neither proper nor necessary to predict measures which may have to be adopted in the future, but it does feel bound to express an opinion concerning the need gradually to prepare the region for the introduction of an independent administration. Toward that end the Committee feels it is essential that the new charter of the Company contain specific terms on how to transfer to the government public institutions and works which the Company has established in the past or may establish in the future, if at the conclusion of the period of the Company's privileges and obligations the government should decide it best to relieve the Company of the same. With this in mind, the Committee proposes adopting the following basic rules for guidance.

I. REVISION OF THE CHARTER
OF THE RUSSIAN AMERICAN COMPANY

1) Beginning from January 1, 1874, i.e. the expiration of the current privileges, grant the Company for twelve years the exclusive right to hunt furbearing animals and carry on the fur trade on the Alaskan Peninsula, defining as its northern limits a line from Cape Douglas in the Kenai Peninsula to Upper Lake Iliamna; and on all islands off the southern coast of that peninsula: the Aleutian, Komandorskie, Kuril and those in the Bering Sea and along the entire west coast of the Bering Sea. Impose on the Company the obligation to carry on the hunt for furbearing animals in the designated areas with the observance of all precautionary measures necessary to prevent the reduction of the species. Revoke the Company's privilege of hunting and fur trading in the area northeast of the Alaska Peninsula, along the entire coast to the frontier of the possessions of Great Britain, also the islands along the entire coast, including Sitka and the entire Kolosh archipelago, and the mainland of the northern part of America, with the stipulation that the territory north and south of the Stikine River, pres-

ently leased to Hudson's Bay Company, remain in that use in accordance with the contract concluded with the Russian American Company, until June 1, 1865, or longer if the government should feel it useful to extend that lease.

2) Likewise revoke the Company's present exclusive privileges of fishing and whaling and the right to all resources above and below ground presently or in the future discovered. Grant the Company exclusive rights before all other Russian subjects to the use only of such mineral works and other enterprises and undertakings which the Company has already established at its own expense, or will do in the future.

3) Continue the Company's obligation, until January 1, 1874, of maintaining in the colonies a military garrison, churches, clergy, colonial institutions of learning, schools and infirmaries, as well as providing provisions for all its servitors, crews and workers. On the islands where the Company enjoys a monopoly in the hunt for furbearing animals and the fur trade, which islands are distant from ports open for free trade, the Company should build warehouses to provide the inhabitants with food and other necessities, of good quality, and insofar as possible at reasonable prices approved by the Chief Administrator of the region.

4) During the period [of the Charter], that is, until January 1, 1874, empower the administrators of Company offices and those in charge of odinochkas, and other persons in the colonies on Company service, to handle administrative duties in the region.

5) Grant the Company the privilege of dispatching its ships with goods and promyshlenniks to sail to all departments of the colonies, and also outside the colonies, for purposes of trade. However, impose on the Company the obligation to use those vessels, without special payment, to deliver to designated places persons dispatched by the colonial administration, and also to carry the mail.

6) Grant the Company the right to issue scrip for use in the colonies as small bills, with the provision however, that the Company establish an exchange facility in New Arkhangel where those holding scrip could convert it into hard currency or government notes.

7) Continue personal service privileges, as at present, for members of the Main Administration and officials in that of-

fice; other Russian subjects who serve the Company, but only those who fulfill their obligations in colonial administration, teaching, medical service, seafaring or technical work; and for the administrator of the Aian office and his assistant. Establish a special staff for this purpose.

8) Continue the Company's right to fly its flag aboard its ships, as approved by the Emperor on September 8, 1806. Servitors hired as skippers, navigators and apprentice seamen aboard Company ships are entitled to wear uniforms as stipulated in an Imperial decree of June 9, 1851. The Company may use the seal with the Imperial emblem when conducting business of the Main Administration, in its colonial offices in America, and in the port of Aian. It may also retain all special concessions which it presently enjoys in hiring persons in Russia and Siberia, in reference to the length of the validity of their passports and the matter of paying their taxes; however, it should lose its present right of exception from required billeting of military personnel. Finally, obligate the Company to take out a commercial certificate of the First Guild every year, and appropriate papers for all its offices, depots and warehouses in Russia and Siberia, except for the port of Aian.

9) In preparing a new charter for the Company based on the above, establish regulations concerning the participation of the Main Administration of the Company in administering the colonies, but eliminate the political aspect which is presently within the sphere of its activity.

10) In the new Charter, stipulate which of the social institutions and undertakings introduced by the Company should be transferred to the government, and under what conditions, if there is a need to make such transfer, and in case the privileges and obligations of the Company are revoked by the government when the period of the charter expires.

II. REGARDING THE CONDITION OF THE INHABITANTS, HUNTING AND TRADE IN THE COLONIES

11) Free the Aleuts and other dependent natives from obligatory work for the Russian American Company. Instead, authorize the Company to hire them for hunting and other work on a voluntary basis, at a set rate of pay either in cash or in kind. When Aleuts and other colonial inhabitants catch fur-

bearing animals through their own means, with Company permission but not on hire to the Company, in areas where the Company has exclusive hunting privileges and may grant natives the right to hunt, the furs thus taken should be sold only to the Company, at prices which the government establishes; however, these prices should in all cases be increased beyond the present level.

12) Do not prevent Aleuts and other islanders from settling in places they consider more advantageous for themselves. Give them the right to leave the places where they live, visit ports open for free trade, and acquire supplies and goods there, as they wish. Measures should be taken, however, to prevent these island people from illegally hunting furbearing animals in places set aside for the exclusive use of the Russian American Company in accordance with the terms of its Charter.

13) Limit to five years the term of obligatory service for creoles who have been educated at the expense of the Russian American Company either within or outside the colonies; however, do not prevent that term from being lengthened or shortened by mutual agreement.

14) Put an end to class difference which presently exists in the colonies, and establish, in addition to the natives, one class of people who have settled there permanently under the general classification of colonial settlers. Include in this class the present colonial citizens: both creoles, whose lifestyle has kept them from merging with the natives, and new settlers who come to the colonies. Organize local administration on communal lines so that natives elect their toions and settlers their elders.

15) In all parts of the colonial territory where Company enterprises have not been established, Russian people should have the right to settle, as also should foreigners who have accepted Russian sovereignty. The government should give all possible assistance to these settlements.

16) Give all permanent settlers and natives full and hereditary title to land which they occupy as their homes, their fields or workshops.

17) Until future review, do not tax colonial inhabitants. Do not impose direct taxes on natives or settlers; likewise do not extend to the colonies existing tax levies for the use of the official seal and for defense, or for licenses to trade and hunt.

18) Permit settlers who have decided to settle permanently in the colonies to hunt, in accordance with general rules which should be drawn up, in those places of Russian possession where the Russian American Company does not have exclusive rights.

19) Permit all colonial inhabitants and Russian subjects, without exception, to engage in all pursuits in the colonies except for the fur trade.

20) Allow Russian and foreign vessels to bring in, duty-free, all manner of supplies and goods except for hard liquor, arms and gunpowder, to the ports of New Arkhangel on Sitka Island and St. Paul on Kodiak Island, and eventually to other ports which may be designated. All colonial inhabitants without exception should have the right to resell imported goods at will. In this regard, repeal the present police regulation under which natives in the area around New Arkhangel can sell wild game and other items only to the Company office.

21) Impose taxes for the Treasury on hard liquor brought into the colonies. Permit only Russian vessels to bring in gunpowder and firearms; prohibit foreign vessels from importing these items. In regard to the sale of these items in the colonies, give the Chief Administrator of the colonies special authorization, based on local conditions, to control how these imported goods may be resold.

III. THE STRUCTURE OF THE COLONIAL ADMINISTRATION

22) Entrust to a Military Governor appointed by the Emperor the principal administration of the region and the supervision over Company administration with all rights and obligations pertaining to that position; however, he should be completely independent of the Russian American Company and not participate in its commercial and hunting activities. Establish a special office for him, solely for administrative purposes, with several staff members for special assignments.

23) In order to establish closer concern for the well-being of the natives, as well as to protect them against any oppression, the Government should appoint two officials for the Military Governor; they should be selected from among civil, military or naval officers and be in charge of natives.

24) Establish a Colonial Council under the chairmanship of

the Military Governor. The members should include the bishop, the two supervisors of natives, the colonial affairs administrator of the Russian American Company, the administrator of the New Arkhangel office and one other person, chosen by the Company who should be at the disposal of the Governor in case the government members should be absent or occupied with other matters.

25) Impose as an absolute obligation of the Military Governor that immediately upon his arrival at his designated post he give his closest attention to organizing a judicial system in the colonies, for both criminal and civil cases which may arise among the colonial population. He should submit his proposals to the government for approval.

Until final approval of special rules concerning this, empower the Colonial Council, as the highest local authority, to dispense justice and punishment in all administrative, police or disputed cases (involving property or contracts) when complaints are registered concerning the activity of local authorities, and also in cases which may somehow arise between the Company administration and private persons who have entered into obligations or agreements with the Company. This does not include criminal cases which are subject to the present rules in the colonies.

26) Give the Military Governor powers as broad as possible to preserve the security of peaceful colonial citizens against the Kolosh and other unsubjugated natives who live within the Russian possessions. He must commit the colonial administration to taking vital measures to prevent hostile activities and attacks by savages against colonial settlements. The military garrison maintained at the expense of the Russian American Company should be under the immediate command of the Military Governor.

27) On the instruction of the Naval Ministry, dispatch naval vessels to the colonies to maintain there a permanent cruising presence in local waters in order to prevent as well as to halt lawless behavior of foreign whalers and contrabandists. Put these vessels under the jurisdiction of the Military Governor and empower him, in agreement with the Russian American Company, to fit out cruisers and Company vessels for the same purpose.

28) Pay from the government Treasury account the maintenance of the Military governor, his office, supervisors of natives and the cruising expenses of naval vessels dispatched by the Naval Ministry.

29) The basic administration of the Russian American colonies, as well as of the Russian American Company, in accordance with the above rules, should be the responsibility of the Naval Ministry.

The Committee on the Reorganization of the Russian American colonies has submitted these views to the Minister of Finance for his review.

Signed: A. Butovskii; G. Nebolsin; I. Shestakov;
Iv. Bulychev; Ia. Ginkulov; Baron Iu. Korf;
Sergei Kostlivtsov, abstaining; A. Kriger; V. Rzhevskii;
N. Tizengauzen; Al. Shcherbinin; D.Neelov;
N. Ermakov.

See: [Sergei A. Kostlivtsov]. *Doklad komitetaob ustroistve Russkikh Amerikanskikh kolonii.* Vol.1 (St. Petersburg: 1863), 255–267.

91

MARCH 30, 1867

THE TREATY CEDING ALASKA TO THE UNITED STATES OF AMERICA

The United States of America and His Majesty the Emperor of All the Russias, being desirous of strengthening, if possible, the good understanding which exists between them, have, for that purpose, appointed as their Plenipotentiaries: the President of the United States, William H. Seward, Secretary of State; and His Majesty the Emperor of All the Russias, the Privy Councillor Edouard de Stoeckl, His Envoy Extraordinary and Minister Plenipotentiary to the United States.

And the said Plenipotentiaries, having exchanged their full powers, which were found to be in due form, have agreed upon and signed the following articles:

ARTICLE I.

His Majesty the Emperor of All the Russias agrees to cede to the United States by this convention, immediately upon the exchange of the ratifications thereof, all the territory and dominion now possessed by his said Majesty on the continent of America and in the adjacent islands, the same being contained within the geographical limits herein set forth, to wit: The eastern limit is the line of demarcation between the Russian and the British possessions in North America, as established by the convention between Russia and Great Britain, of February 16/28, 1825 and described in Articles III and IV of said convention, in the following terms:

"Commencing from the southernmost point of the island called Prince of Wales Island, which point lies in the parallel of 54 degrees 40 minutes latitude, and between the 131st and 133rd degree of west longitude (meridian of Greenwich), the said line shall ascend to the north along the channel called Portland Channel, as far as the point of the continent where it strikes the 56th degree of north latitude; from this last mentioned point, the line of demarcation shall follow the summit of the mountains situated parallel to the coast as far as the point of intersection of the 141st degree of west longitude (of the same meridian); and finally, from the said point of intersection, the said meridian line of the 141st degree, in its prolongation as far as the Frozen ocean.

"IV. With reference to the line of demarcation laid down in the preceding article, it is understood:

"1st. That the island called Prince of Wales Island shall belong wholly to Russia," (now, by this cession, to the United States).

"2nd. That whenever the summit of the mountains which extend in a direction parallel to the coast from the 56th degree of north latitude to the point of intersection of the 141st degree of west longitude shall prove to be at the distance of more than ten marine leagues from the ocean, the limit between the British possessions and the line of coast which is to belong to Russia as above mentioned (that is to say, the limit to the possessions ceded by this convention) shall be formed by a line parallel to the winding of the coast, and which shall never exceed the distance of ten marine leagues therefrom."

The western limit within which the territories and dominion conveyed are contained, passes through a point in Bering's Straits on the parallel of sixty-five degrees thirty minutes north latitude, at its intersection by the meridian which passes midway between the island of Ratmanoff, or Noonarbook, and proceeds thence in a course nearly southwest, through Bering Straits and Bering Sea, so as to pass midway between the northwest point of the island of St. Lawrence and the southeast point of Cape Chukotsk, to the meridian of one hundred and seventy-two west longitude; thence, from the intersection of that meridian, in a southwesterly direction, so as to pass midway between the island of Attu and the Copper Island of the Komandorskie couplet or group, in the degrees of west longitude, so as to include in the territory conveyed the whole of the Aleutian Islands east of that meridian.

ARTICLE II.

In the cession of territory and dominion made by the preceding article, are included the right of property in all public lots and squares, vacant lands, and all public buildings, forti-

545

The Russian American Company fort in New Arkhangel. *La Corvette Senavine.* (OHS neg. OrHi 82754)

fications, barracks, and other edifices which are not private individual property. It is, however, understood and agreed, that the churches which have been built in the ceded territory by the Russian government, shall remain the property of such members of the Greek Oriental [Russian Orthodox—eds.] Church resident in the territory, as may choose to worship therein. Any government archives, papers and documents relative to the territory and dominion aforesaid, which may now be existing there, will be left in the possession of the agent of the United States; but an authenticated copy of such of them as may be required, will be, at all times, given by the United States to the Russian government, or to such Russian officers or subjects as they may apply for.

ARTICLE III.

The inhabitants of the ceded territory, according to their choice, reserving their natural allegiance, may return to Russia within three years; but if they should prefer to remain in the ceded territory, they, with the exception of uncivilized native tribes, shall be admitted to the enjoyment of all the rights, advantages, and immunities of citizens of the United States, and shall be maintained and protected in the free enjoyment of their liberty, property, and religion. The uncivilized tribes will be subject to such laws and regulations as the United States may from time to time adopt in regard to aboriginal tribes of that country.

ARTICLE IV.

His Majesty, the Emperor of All the Russias shall appoint, with convenient dispatch, an agent or agents for the purpose of formally delivering to a similar agent or agents appointed on behalf of the United States, the territory, dominion, property, dependencies and appurtenances which are ceded as above, and for doing any other act which may be necessary in regard thereto. But the cession, with the right of immediate possession, is nevertheless to be deemed complete and absolute on the exchange of ratifications, without waiting for such formal delivery.

ARTICLE V.

Immediately after the exchange of the ratifications of this convention, any fortifications or military posts which may be in the ceded territory, shall be delivered to the agent of the United States, and any Russian troops which may be in the territory shall be withdrawn as soon as may be reasonably and conveniently practicable.

ARTICLE VI.

In consideration of the cession aforesaid, the United States agree to pay at the Treasury in Washington, within ten months after the exchange of the ratifications of this convention, to the diplomatic representative or other agent of His Majesty the Emperor of All the Russias, duly authorized to receive the same, seven million two hundred thousand dollars in gold. The cession of territory and dominion herein made is hereby declared to be free and unencumbered by any associated companies, whether corporate or incorporate, Russian or any other, or by any parties, except merely private individual property holders; and the cession hereby made, conveys all the rights, franchises and privileges now belonging to Russia in the said territory or dominion, and appurtenances thereto.

ARTICLE VII.

When this convention shall have been duly ratified by the President of the United States, by and with the advice and consent of the Senate, on the one part, and on the other by His Majesty the Emperor of All the Russias, the ratifications shall be exchanged at Washington within three months from the date hereof, or sooner, if possible. In faith whereof, the respective plenipotentiaries have signed this convention, and thereto affixed the seals of their arms.

Done at Washington, the thirtieth day of March in the year of our Lord one thousand eight hundred and sixty-seven.

Edouard de Stoeckl
William H. Seward

See: William M. Mallory, ed. *Treaties, Conventions, International Acts, Protocols and Agreements between the United States of America and Other Powers, 1776–1909*. Vol. 2 (Washington: 1910), 1521–24. Spelling slightly modified.

SELECTED
BIBLIOGRAPHY

Bibliographies

Allen, Robert V. "Alaska before 1866 in Soviet Literature." *Quarterly Journal of the Library of Congress*, Vol. 23, No. 3 (July, 1966), pp. 243–50.

Arctic Institute of North America and United States Department of Defense. *Arctic Bibliography*. 15 vols. Washington, D.C., 1953–71.

Basanoff, V. "Archives of the Russian Church in Alaska in the Library of Congress." *Pacific Historical Review*, Vol. 2, No. 1 (1933), pp. 72–84.

Dorosh, John T. "The Alaskan Russian Church Archives." *Quarterly Journal of Current Acquisitions of the Library of Congress*, Vol. 18, No. 4 (1961), pp. 193–203.

Falk, Marvin W. "Bibliography of Translated Alaska Materials." *Alaska History*, Vol. 1, No. 1 (1984), pp. 53–66.

Gibson, James R. "Russian Sources for the Ethnohistory of the Pacific Coast of North America in the Eighteenth and Nineteenth Centuries." *The Western Canadian Journal of Anthropology*, Vol. 6, No. 1 (1976), pp. 91–115.

Hussey, John A. *Notes Toward a Bibliography of Sources Relating to Fort Ross State Historic Park, California*. Sacramento, 1979.

Kerner, Robert J. "Russian Expansion to America: Its Bibliographical Foundations." *Papers of the Bibliographical Society of America*, Vol. 25 (1931), pp. 111–129.

Lada-Mocarski, Valerian. *Bibliography of Books on Alaska Published before 1868*. New Haven and London, 1969.

Pierce, Richard A. "Archival and Bibliographic Materials on Russian America outside the USSR." In S. Frederick Starr, ed., *Russia's American Colony*, Durham, 1987, pp. 353–365.

Polansky, Patricia. "Published Sources on Russian America." In S. Frederick Starr, ed., *Russia's American Colony*, Durham, 1987, pp. 319–352.

Ricks, Melvin. *Melvin Ricks' Alaska Bibliography: An Introductory Guide to*

Alaskan Historical Literature, edited by Stephen and Betty Haycox. Portland, 1977.

————. *Basic Bibliography of Alaskan Literature*. 4 vols. Juneau, 1961.

Sarafian, Winston. "Alaska Bibliography of History Sources." *Alaska Journal*, Vol. 6, No. 3 (1976), pp. 181–82; Vol. 6, No. 4, pp. 253–55; Vol. 7, No. 2 (1977), pp. 60–63.

Smith, Barbara. *Russian Orthodoxy in Alaska: a History, Inventory and Analysis of the Church Archives in Alaska, with an Annotated Bibliography*. Anchorage, 1980.

Tomashevskii, V. V. *Materialy k bibliografii Sibiri i Dalnego Vostoka, XV—pervaia polovina XIX veka* [Materials for a Bibliography of Siberia and the Far East, Fifteenth to the First Half of the Nineteenth Century]. Vladivostok, 1957.

VanStone, James W. *An Annotated Ethnohistorical Bibliography of the Nushagak River Region, Alaska*. Chicago, 1968.

Wickersham, James. *Bibliography of Alaskan Literature, 1724–1924*, Vol. 1. Cordova, 1927.

Sources

Alaska History Research Project. *Documents Relative to the History of Alaska*. College, Alaska, 1936–38.

Barker, Burt Brown, ed. *Letters of Dr. John McLoughlin Written at Fort Vancouver 1829–1832*. Portland, 1948.

Barsukov, Ivan. *Innokentii Mitropolit Moskovskii i Kolomenskii po ego sochineniiam, pismam i razskazam sovremennikov*. [Metropolitan Innokentii of Moscow and Koloma According to His Writings and Letters and the Accounts of Contemporaries]. Moscow, 1883.

Bashkina, N. N., et al., eds. *Rossiia i SShA: Stanovlenie otnoshenii 1765–1815*. Moscow, 1980. Simultaneously published in English: *The United States and Russia: The Beginning of Relations 1765–1815*. Washington, D.C., 1980.

Beechey, Frederick William. *Narrative of a Voyage to the Pacific and Bering's Strait . . . 1825, 26, 27, 28*. London, 1831.

Berkh, Vasilii. "Izvestie o mekhovoi torgovle, proizvodimoi Rossiianami pri ostrovakh Kurilskikh, Aleutskikh i severozapadnom beregu Ameriki" [Information on the Russian Fur Trade along the Kuril and Aleutian Islands and the Northwest Coast of America]. *Syn otechestva*, 1823, No. 88, pp. 243–64; No. 89, pp. 97–106;

————. "Nechto o Sandvicheskikh ostrovakh" [Something about the Sandwich Islands]. *Syn otechestva*, 1818, pp. 158–165.

————. *Opisanie neschastnogo korablekrusheniia fregata Rossiisko Amerikanskoi kompanii Nevy, posledovavshego bliz beregov Novo-Arkhangelskogo porta*. [A Description of the Unfortunate Wreck of the Russian American Company Frigate *Neva*, Bound for the Area Near the Shores of the Port of New Arkhangel]. St. Petersburg, 1817.

Bernhardi, Charlotte. *Memoir of the Celebrated Admiral John de Kruzenshtern.* Seattle, 1964 (reprint of 1856 edition).

Bilbasov, V. A., ed. *Arkhiv Grafov Mordvinovykh* [The Archive of the Mordvinov Counts]. St. Petersburg, 1902.

Black, James J. *Notes on the Russian-American Company's Trading Posts etc.* [San Francisco, 1867].

Blaschke, E. "Neskolko zamechanii o plavanii v baidarkakh i o Lisevskikh Aleutakh" [Some Observations About Voyaging in Baidarkas and About the Fox Island Aleuts]. *Morskoi sbornik,* 1848, No. 3, pp. 115–24; No. 4, 160–65.

―――. *Topographia Medica Portus Novi-Archangelscensis* [A Medical Description of the Port of New Arkhangel]. Petropoli, 1842.

Bolotov, Ivan I. (Ioasaf). "Kratkoe opisanie ob ostrove Kadiake" [A Brief Description of Kodiak Island]. *Drug prosveshcheniia,* October, 1805, pp. 89–106.

Campbell, Archibald. *A Voyage Round the World, from 1806–1812.* New York, 1819.

Chamisso, Adelbert von. *A Sojourn at San Francisco Bay 1816.* San Francisco, 1936.

Chernykh, Egor L. "O zemledelii v Verkhnei Kalifornii." *Zhurnal selskogo khoziaistva i ovtsevodstva,* 1841, No. 9, pp. 234–65. Translated by James R. Gibson: "Agriculture of Upper California. A Long Lost Account of Farming in California as Recorded by a Russian Observer at Fort Ross in 1841." *Pacific Historian,* Vol. 11 (1967) No.4, pp. 10–28.

―――. "Two New Chernykh Letters (1835–1836)." Translated by James R. Gibson. *Pacific Historian,* Vol. 12 (1968) No. 3, pp. 48–56; No. 4, pp. 54–60.

Choris, Louis. *Voyage Pittoresque autour du Monde . . .* [A Pictorial Voyage around the World]. Paris, 1820–22.

Cordes, Frederick C., "Letters of A. Rotchev, Last Commandant at Fort Ross and the Résumé of the Report of the Russian American Company for the Year 1850–51." *California Historical Quarterly,* June, 1960, pp. 97–115.

Corney, Peter. *Voyages in the Northern Pacific.* Honolulu, 1896.

Davis, William H. *Seventy-five Years in California.* San Francisco, 1929.

Davydov, Gavriil I. *Dvukratnoe puteshestvie v Ameriku morskikh ofitserov Khvostova i Davydova, pisannoe sim poslednim.* 2 vols. St. Petersburg, 1810–1812. Translated by Colin Bearne and edited by Richard A. Pierce: *Two Voyages to Russian America, 1802–1807.* Kingston, 1977.

Divin, V. A., K. E. Cherevko and G. N. Isaenko, eds. *Russkaia Tikhookeanskaia Epopeia* [The Russian Pacific Ocean Epic]. Khabarovsk, 1979.

Dmytryshyn, Basil, E. A. P. Crownhart-Vaughan and Thomas Vaughan, eds. *Russian Penetration of the North Pacific Ocean, 1700–1799: A Documentary Record.* Portland, 1988.

Pavlov, P. N. et al., eds. *K istorii Rossiisko-Americanskoi kompanii. Sbornik dokumentalnykh materialov.* Krasnoiarsk, 1957. Translated by Marina

Ramsey and edited by Richard A. Pierce: *Documents on the History of the Russian American Company*. Kingston, 1976.

Duflot de Mofras, Eugene. *Exploration du territoire de l'Oregon, des Californies et de la mer Vermeille, executée pendant les années 1840, 1841 et 1842*. Paris, 1844. Translated by Marguerite Eyer Wilbur: *Duflot de Mofras' Travels on the Pacific Coast*. Santa Ana, 1937.

Duhaut-Cilly, August Bernard de. "Duhaut-Cilly's Account of California in the Years 1827–1828." Translated by Charles Franklin Carter. *California Historical Quarterly*, Volume 8 (1929), pp. 131–66, 214–50, 306–36.

D'Wolf, Captain John. *A Voyage to the North Pacific and a Journey through Siberia*. Cambridge, Mass., 1861.

Eschscholtz, Johann Friedrich. *Zoologischer Atlas* [Zoological Atlas]. 5 vols. Berlin, 1829–1833.

Fisher, Raymond H. *Records of the Russian-American Company, 1802, 1817–1867*. Washington, D.C. 1971.

Gazunov, Andrei K. "Izvlechenie iz putevogo zhurnala pomoshchnika morekhodstva Andreia Glazunova" [Extract from the Travel Journal of the Assistant Navigator Andrei Glazunov]. *Zhurnal manufaktur i torgovli*, Vol. 1 (1836) No. 3, pp. 31–61. Translated (from an 1841 French translation) by James W. VanStone: "Russian Exploration in Interior Alaska. An Extract from the Journal (1833–1834) of Andrei Glazunov." *Pacific Northwest Quarterly*, Vol. 50 (1959), No. 2, pp. 37–47.

Golovin, Pavel N. "Iz Putevykh pisem P. N. Golovina." *Morskoi Sbornik*, Vol. 66 (1863) No. 5, pp. 101–182; No. 5, pp. 275–340. Translated by Basil Dmytryshyn and E. A. P. Crownhart-Vaughan, Introduction by Thomas Vaughan: *Civil and Savage Encounters: The Worldly Travel Letters of an Imperial Russian Navy Officer, 1860–1861*. Portland, 1983.

———. "Obzor russkikh kolonii v Severnoi Amerike, sostavlennyi kapitan-leitenantom Pavlom Nikolaevichem Golovinym (1861)." *Morskoi Sbornik*, Vol. 57 (1862), No. 1, Part 3, pp. 19–192. Translated with Introduction and Notes by Basil Dmytryshyn and E. A. P. Crownhart-Vaughan: *The End of Russian America: Captain P. N. Golovin's Last Report, 1862*. Portland, 1979.

Golovnin, Vasilii M. *Puteshestvie vokrug sveta, sovershennoi na voennom shliupe "Kamchatka" v 1817, 1818 i 1819 godakh kapitanom Golovninym*. Moscow, 1965. Translated with an Introduction and Notes by Ella Lurey Wiswell, Foreword by John H. Stephan: *Around the World on the Kamchatka, 1817 1819*. Honolulu, 1979.

———. *Puteshestvie na shliupe "Diana" iz Kronshtadta v Kamchatku* [A Voyage on the Sloop *Diana* from Kronstadt to Kamchatka]. Moscow, 1961.

Jameson, J. Franklin, ed. "Documents. Correspondence of Russian Ministers in Washington, 1818–1825." *American Historical Review*, 1913, Vol. 18, No. 2, pp. 309–346.

Kashevarov, Aleksandr F. "Chto takoe zapusk i promysel pushnykh zverei v Rossiisko-Amerikanskikh koloniiakh" [The meaning of "zapusk" and the Hunt for Furbearing Animals in the Russian American Colonies]. *Morskoi sbornik*, Vol. 58 (1862), No. 3, pp. 86–92.

———. "Zhurnal, vedennyi pri baidarnoi ekspeditsii . . . [Journal Kept on a Baidara Expedition]" *Zapiski Russkogo geograficheskogo obshchestva*, Vol. 8 (1879), pp. 275–361. Translated by David H. Kraus, edited with an Introduction by James W. VanStone. *Fieldiana: Anthropology* 1977, Vol. 69, pp. 1–104.

Khlebnikov, Kyrill T. "Statistika. Zapiski o Kalifornii, sostavlenniia K. Khlebnikovym [Statistics. Notes on California Prepared by K. Khlebnikov]. *"Syn otechestva i Severnyi arkhiv*, Vol. 2 (1829), No. 2, pp. 208–227, 276–288, 336–347, 400–410; No. 3, 25–35.

———. "Statisticheskie svedeniia o koloniiakh Rossiisko-Amerikanskoi kompanii" [Statistical Information on the Russian American Company Colonies]. *Kommercheskaia gazeta*, 1834, Nos. 80, 81, 87, 90, 93, 96, 98, 99. Translated by James R. Gibson: "Russian America in 1833. The Survey of Kirill Khlebnikov." *Pacific Northwest Quarterly*, Vol. 63 (1972), No. 1, pp. 1–13.

———. "Zhizneopisanie Aleksandra Andreevicha Baranova, Glavnogo pravitelia Rossiiskikh kolonii v Amerike." St. Petersburg, 1835. Translated by Colin Bearne and edited by Richard A. Pierce: *Baranov, Chief Manager of the Russian Colonies in America*. Kingston, 1973.

———. *Zapiski K. Khlebnikova o Amerike*. Supplement to *Morskoi sbornik*, 1861, No. 3. Translated, with Introduction and Notes by Basil Dmytryshyn and E. A. P. Crownhart-Vaughan: *Colonial Russian America: Kyrill T. Khlebnikov's Reports, 1817–1832*. Portland, 1976. Section on Novo Arkhangelsk reprinted, with Introduction and Notes by Svetlana G. Fedorova, under the general editorship of V. A. Aleksandrov: *Russkaia Amerika v "Zapiskakh" Kirila Khlebnikova: Novo Arkhangelsk* [Russian America in the Notes of Kyrill Khlebnikov: New Arhangel]. Moscow, 1985.

———. *Russkaia Amerika v neopublikovannykh zapiskakh K. T. Khlebnikova* [Russian America in the Unpublished Notes of K. T. Khlebnikov]. Leningrad, 1979. With Notes and Introduction by Roza G. Liapunova and Svetlana G. Fedorova.

Khromchenko, Vasilii S. "Zhurnal, vedennyi na brige *Golovnine* v 1822-m gode flota michmanom Khromchenko" [The Journal Kept on the Brig *Golovnin* by Midshipman Khromchenko]. *Severnyi arkhiv*, 1824, No. 11, pp. 263–276; No. 12, pp. 303–314; No. 13–14, pp. 38–64; No. 15, pp. 119–131; No. 16, pp. 177 186; No. 17, pp. 235–248; No. 18, pp. 297–312. Translated by David H. Kraus and edited by James W. VanStone: *Khromchenko's Coastal Explorations in Southwestern Alaska, 1822*. Chicago, 1973.

Kittlitz, Friedrich H. von. *Denkwürdigkeiten einer Reise nach dem russischen Amerika* . . . [Reminiscences of a Journey to Russian America . . .]. Gotha, 1858. *See* Lütke, below.

[Kostlivtsov, Sergei A.] *Doklad komiteta ob ustroistve Russkikh-Amerikanskikh kolonii* [Report of the Committee on the Organization of the Russian American Colonies]. 2 vols. St. Petersburg, 1863–64.

Kotzebue, Otto von. *Puteshestvie v Iuzhnyi okean i v Beringov proliv.* 3 vols. plus Atlas. St. Petersburg, 1821–23. Translated: *A Voyage of Discovery into the South Sea and Bering's Straits.* 3 vols. London, 1821.

————. *Puteshestvie vokrug sveta . . . v 1823, 24, 25, 26 godakh.* St. Petersburg, 1828. Translated: *A New Voyage Round the World, in the Years 1823, 24, 25, and 26.* 2 vols. London, 1830.

Krusenstern, Ivan F. *Atlas de l'Océan Pacifique . . .* [Atlas of the Pacific Ocean] 3 vols. St. Petersburg, 1827.

————. *Puteshestvie vokrug sveta v 1803, 4, 5 i 1806 godakh.* St. Petersburg, 1809. *Atlas,* 1813. Translated by Richard Belgrave Hoppner: *Voyage Round the World in the Years 1803, 1804, 1805, & 1806.* London, 1813.

————. *Wörter-Sammlungen aus den Sprachen einiger Völker des Östlichen Asiens und der Nordwest-Küste von Amerika . . .* [Selection of Words from Languages of Some Inhabitants of the East Coast of Asia and the Northwest Coast of America]. St. Petersburg, 1813.

Langsdorff, Georg Heinrich von. *Bemerkungen auf einer Reise um die Welt in den Jahren 1803 bis 1807.* 2 vols. Frankfurt am Main, 1812. Translated: *Voyages and Travels in Various Parts of the World.* 2 vols. London, 1814.

La Pérouse, Jean François Galaup, comte de. *Voyage de La Pérouse autour du monde . . .* Paris, (1797). Translated: *A Voyage Round the World.* London, 1798.

Lazarev, Andrei. *Plavanie vokrug sveta na shliupe "Ladoge" v 1822, 1823 i 1824 godakh* [A Voyage Around the World on the Sloop *Ladoga* in 1822, 1823, and 1824]. St. Petersburg, 1832.

————. *Zapiski o plavanii voennogo shliupa "Blagonamerennogo" v Beringov proliv i vokrug sveta dlia otkrytiia v 1819, 1820, 1821 i 1822 godakh* [Notes on the Voyage of the Naval Sloop *Blagonamerennyi* to Bering Strait and around the World for Discoveries in 1819, 1820, 1821 and 1822]. Moscow, 1950.

Lisianskii, Iurii F. *Puteshestvie vokrug sveta v 1803, 4, 5 i 1806 godakh* [Voyage Around the World in 1803, 4, 5, and 1806]. St. Petersburg, 1812.

Lütke, Fedor Petrovich, Count. *Puteshestvie vokrug sveta . . . na voennom shliupe "Seniavin" . . .* [A Voyage Around the World . . . Aboard the Naval Sloop *Seniavin . . .*] St. Petersburg, 1835. Atlas, St. Petersburg, 1832. Translated into French: *Voyage autour du monde.* Paris, 1835. Six chapters from the French translation, pertaining to Russian America and Siberia, have been translated into English by Renee Marshall. To these chapters are appended three chapters from the Kittlitz memoir (*see* above) (Gotha: 1858), translated by Joan Moessner. These are combined into one volume edited by Richard A. Pierce: *A Voyage Around the World 1826–1829.* Kingston, 1987.

Mallory, William M., comp. *Treaties, Conventions, International Acts, Protocols and Agreements between the United States and Other Powers, 1776–1909.* Washington, D.C., 1910.

Markov, Aleksandr I. *Russkie na Vostochnom okeane* [Russians on the Pacific Ocean]. Moscow, 1849.

Materialy dlia istorii russkikh zaselenii po beregam vostochnago okeana [Materials for a History of Russian Settlement on the Shores of the Eastern Ocean]. Printed as a supplement to *Morskoi sbornik*, 1861, III.

Merk, Frederick, ed. *Fur Trade and Empire: George Simpson's Journal*. Cambridge, Mass., 1931.

Minitski, Rear Admiral. "Opisanie Okhotskogo porta" [A Description of the Port of Okhotsk]. *Syn otechestva i Severnyi arkhiv*, 1829, pp. 136–53, 206–21.

Netsvetov, Iakov E. *The Journal of Iakov Netsvetov: The Atkha Years, 1828–1844*. Translated, with Introduction and supplementary material, by Lydia T. Black, from a manuscript in the Alaska Church Collection, Library of Congress. Kingston, 1980.

———. "The Travel Journal of Priest Iakov Netsvetov (the Yukon Parish) for 1849." Translated by Antoinette Shalkop from a manuscript in the Alaska Church Collection, Library of Congress. *Orthodox Alaska*, Vol. 6 (1975), pp. 31–39.

———. *The Journals of Iakov Netsvetov: The Yukon Years, 1845–1863*. Translated, with Introduction and supplementary material, by Lydia T. Black, edited by Richard A. Pierce. From a manuscript in the Archives of the Russian Orthodox Church in Alaska, St. Herman's Pastoral School, Kodiak. Kingston, 1984.

Pavlov, P. N., ed. *K istorii Rossiisko-Amerikanskoi kompanii: sbornik dokumentalnykh materialov* [Toward a History of the Russian American Company: A Collection of Documentary Materials]. Krasnoiarsk, 1957.

Roquefeuil, Camille de. *Journal d'un voyage autour du monde, pendant les années 1816, 1817, 1818 et 1819* [Journal of a Voyage Around the World During the Years . . .]. 2 vols. Paris, 1823.

Rotchev, Aleksandr G. "Novyi Eldorado v Kalifornii." *Otechestvennye zapiski*, Vol. 62 (1849), No. 2, pp. 216–224. Translated with an Introduction by Alexander Doll and Richard A. Pierce: "New Eldorado in California, by A. Rotchev, Last Commandant of Fort Ross." *Pacific Historian*, Vol. 14 (1970), No. 1, pp. 33–40.

———. "Vospominaniia russkogo puteshestvennika o Vest-Indii, Kalifornii i Ost-Indii" [Recollections of a Russian Traveler about the West Indies, California and the East Indies]. *Panteon*, No. 1 (1854) pp. 79–108; No. 2, pp. 93–114.

Rowand, Alexander. *Notes of a Journey in Russian America and Siberia, During the Years 1841 and 1842*. [Edinburgh?], n.d.

Russia. *Polnoe sobranie zakonov rossiiskoi imperii s 1649 goda* [Complete Collection of the Laws of the Russian Empire from 1649]. First and Second Series. St. Petersburg, 1850.

———. State Chancery. *Zapiska o Rossiisko-Amerikanskoi Kompanii* [A Memorandum on the Russian-American Company]. St. Petersburg, 1864.

Russian American Company. *Correspondence of the Governors. Communications*

Sent: 1818. Translated and with an Introduction, by Richard A. Pierce. Kingston, 1984.

Schafer, Joseph. "Letters of Sir George Simpson, 1841–1843." *American Historical Review*, October 1908, pp. 70–94.

Shemelin, Fedor. *Zhurnal pervogo puteshestviia Rossiian vokrug zemnogo shara* [The Journal of the First Russian Voyage Around the World]. St. Petersburg, 1916.

Shur, Leonid A. *K beregam Novogo Sveta: iz neopublikovannykh zapisok russkikh puteshestvennikov nachala XIX veka* [To the Shores of the New World: From the Unpublished Notes of Russian Travelers of the Early Nineteenth Century]. Moscow, 1971.

Simpson, Sir George. *Narrative of a Journey Round the World.* 2 vols. London, 1847.

[Sutter, John A.] "Inventaire des biens meubles et immeubles qui se trouvent au Port Bodego, a l'éstablissement de Ross et aux ranchos de la Compagnie Russe-Américaine [Inventory of Structures and Chattels Located at Port Bodega, the Ross Settlement, and the Russian-American Company Ranchos]." in: John A. Sutter: Correspondence and Papers, 1846–1870. Bancroft Library.

Tarakanov, Timofei Osipovich. *Krushenie Rossiisko-amerikanskoi kompanii sudna "Sviatoi Nikolai" pod nachalstvom shturmana Bulygina . . .* in V. M. Golovnin. *Sochineniia i perevody.* St. Petersburg, 1864, pp. 406–428. Translated by Alton S. Donnelly; edited and with an Introduction by Kenneth N. Owens: *The Wreck of the Sv. Nikolai: Two Narratives of the First Russian Expedition to the Oregon Country, 1818–1820.* Portland, 1985.

Tebenkov, Mikhail D., comp. *Atlas severozapadnykh beregov Ameriki. . . .* [n.p.], 1852. and *Gidrograficheskie zamechaniia k Atlasu . . .* [Hydrographic Notes to the Atlas . . .]. Both, translated and edited by Richard A. Pierce: *Atlas of the Northwest Coasts of America . . . with Hydrographic Notes.* Kingston, 1981.

United States Congress. House of Representatives. *Russian America.* 40th Congress, 2nd Session, Executive Document No. 177. Washington, D.C., 1868.

———. Senate. *Russian Administration of Alaska and the Status of the Alaskan Natives.* 81st Congress, 2nd Session, Senate Document No. 152. Washington, D.C., 1950.

United States. General Services Administration. National Archives. *Records of the Russian-American Company 1802–1867: Correspondence of Governors General.* Microfilm copies available: Mll: 65 reels. Washington, D.C., 1942.

United States. Library of Congress, Manuscript Division. *Archive of the Holy Synod.*

———. *Index to Baptisms, Marriages, and Deaths in the Archives of the Russian Orthodox Greek Catholic Church in Alaska.* 4 vols. Washington, D.C., 1964–73.

———. Yudin Collection.

U.S.S.R. Ministerstvo inostrannykh del. *Vneshnaia politika Rossii XIX i na-chala XX veka: Dokumenty.* Series I, II. [The Foreign Policy of Russia in the Nineteenth and Early Twentieth Centuries.] Moscow.

Vallejo, M. G. *Vallejo Documentos.* Bancroft Library. Berkeley.

Veniaminov, Ivan E. *Zapiski ob ostrovakh Unalashkinskogo otdela.* St. Petersburg, 1840. Translated by Lydia T. Black and Richard H. Geoghegan; edited with an Introduction by Richard A. Pierce: *Notes on the Islands of the Unalashka District.* Kingston, 1984.

———. *Sostoianie pravoslavnoi tserkvi v Rossiiskoi Amerike . . .* St. Petersburg, 1840. Translated by Robert Nichols and Robert Croskey: "The Condition of the Orthodox Church in Russian America: Innokentii Veniaminov's History of the Russian Church in Alaska." *Pacific Northwest Quarterly,* Vol. 63, No. 2, pp. 41–54.

Wrangel, Baron Frederick von. "Obitateli severozapadnykh beregov Ameriki" [Inhabitants of the Northwest Shores of America]. *Syn otechestva,* 1838, Vol. 7, pp. 51–82.

———. "O pushnykh tovarakh Severo-Amerikanskikh Rossiiskikh vladenii" [Concerning the Furs of the Russian North American Possessions]. *Teleskop,* 1835, pp. 496–518.

———. *Ocherk puti iz Sitkhi v S. Peterburg.* [A Sketch of a Journey from Sitka to St. Petersburg]. St. Petersburg, 1836.

———. "Putevia zapiski admirala barona F. P. Vrangelia" [The Travel Notes of Admiral Baron F. P. Wrangel]. *Istoricheskii vestnik,* 1884, pp. 162–80.

———. "Amerikantsy Verkhnei Kalifornii." *Teleskop,* 1835, ch. 26, otd. Nauka, pp. 441–456. Translated by James R. Gibson: "Russia in California, 1833. Report of Governor Wrangel." *Pacific Northwest Quarterly,* Vol. 60 (1969), No. 4, pp.205–215.

———. *Statistische und ethnographische Nachrichten über die Russischer Besitzungen an der Nordwestküste von Amerika.* St. Petersburg, 1839. Translated by Mary Sadouski; edited by Richard A. Pierce: *Russian America Statistical and Ethnographical Information . . .* Kingston, 1980.

——— and Baronin Elisabeth. "Briefe aus Sibirien und den russischen Niederlassungen in Amerika" [Letters from Siberia and the Russian Establishments in America]. *Dorpater Jahrbücher für Literatur, Statistik und Kunst, besonders Russlands,* 1833–34: I, 169–80, 263–66, 353–74; II, 179–86, 356–64.

Zagoskin, Lavrentii A. *Peshekhodnaia opis chasti russkikh vladenii v Amerike.* St. Petersburg, 1847 [1848]. Translated by Penelope Rainey, edited by Henry M. Michael: *Lieutenant Zagoskin's Travels in Russian America.* Toronto, 1967.

———. *Puteshestviia i issledovaniia leitenanta Lavrentiia Zagoskina v Russkoi Amerike v 1842–1844 gg.* [Travels and Explorations of Lieutenant Lavrentii Zagoskin in Russian America in the Years 1842–1844.] Moscow, 1956.

Zavalishin, Dmitrii. "Delo o kolonii Ross" [The Matter of the Ross Colony]. *Russkii vestnik*, 1836, pp. 36–65.

———. "Kaliforniia v 1824 godu." *Russkii vestnik*, 1865, pp. 322–68. Translated and annotated by James R. Gibson: "California in 1824." *Southern California Quarterly*, Vol. 55 (1973), No. 4, pp. 369–412.

———. "Krugosvetnoe plavanie fregata 'Kreiser' v 1822–1825 gg. pod komandoiu Mikhaila Petrovicha Lazareva" [The Circumnavigation of the Frigate *Kreiser* under the Command of Mikhail Petrovich Lazarev]. *Drevniaia i novaiai Rossiia*, 1877, No. 5, pp. 54–67; No. 6, pp. 115–125; No. 7, pp. 199–214; No. 10, pp. 143–158; No. 11, pp. 210–223.

———. *Rossiisko-Amerikanskaia Kompaniia* [The Russian American Company]. Moscow, 1865.

Monographic Literature

Adamov, A. G. *Po neizvedannym putiam: Russkie issledovateli na Aliaske i Kalifornii* [Along Unexplored Ways: Russian Explorers in Alaska and California]. Moscow, 1950.

———. *Pravda o russkikh otkrytiiakh v Amerike* [The Truth about Russian Discoveries in America]. Moscow, 1952.

Afonsky, Georgii (The Right Reverend Gregory, Bishop of Sitka and Alaska). *A History of the Orthodox Church in Alaska (1794–1917)*. Kodiak, 1977.

Alekseev, Aleksandr I. *Fedor Petrovich Litke*. Moscow, 1970.

———. *Ilia Gavrilovich Voznesenskii (1816–1871)*. Moscow, 1977.

———. *Osvoenie russkimi liudmi Dalnego Vostoka i Russkoi Ameriki do kontsa XIX veka* [The Assimilation by the Russian People of the Far East and of Russian America until the End of the Nineteenth Century]. Moscow, 1982.

———. *Russkie geograficheskie issledovaniia na Dalnem Vostoke i v Severnoi Amerike . . .* [Russian Geographical Explorations in the Far East and in North America]. Moscow, 1976

———. *Sudba Russkoi Ameriki* [The Fate of Russian America]. Magadan, 1975.

———. and V. A. Esakov and A. F. Plakhotnik. *Russkie okeanskie i morskie issledovaniia v XIV i nachale XX v.* [Russian Ocean and Sea Explorations from the Fourteenth to the Early Twentieth Century]. Moscow, 1969.

Andreev, A. I. *Russkie otkrytiia v Tikhom okeane i Severnoi Amerike v XVIII–XIX vekakh*. Moscow, 1948. Translated by Carl Ginsburg: *Russian Discoveries in the Pacific in the Eighteenth and Nineteenth Centuries*. Ann Arbor, 1952.

Bagrow, Leo S. *A History of Russian Cartography to 1800*. Wolfe Island, 1975.

Bancroft, Hubert H. *History of Alaska, 1730–1855*. San Francisco, 1886.

———. *History of California*. 7 vols. San Francisco, 1886–90.

Barratt, Glynn. *Russia in Pacific Waters, 1715–1825*. Vancouver, 1980.

———. *Russian Shadows on the British Northwest Coast of North America, 1810–1890*. Vancouver, 1983.

Barsukov, I. *Graf Nikolai Nikolaevich Muravev-Amurskii* [Count Nikolai Ni-kolaevich Muravev-Amurskii]. Moscow, 1891.

Berg, Lev S. *Ocherki po istorii russkikh geograficheskikh otkrytii* [Outlines of the History of Russian Geographical Discoveries]. Moscow, 1962.

Berkh, Vasilii N. *Khronologicheskaia istoriia otkrytiia Aleutskikh ostrovov ili pod-vigi Rossiiskogo kupechestva.* St. Petersburg, 1823. Translated by Dmitrii Krenov and edited by Richard A. Pierce: *A Chronological History of the Discovery of the Aleutian Islands.* Kingston, 1974.

————. *Opisanie neshchastnogo korablekrusheniia fregata Rossiisko Amerikanskoi kompanii "Nevy" . . .* [Description of the unfortunate shipwreck of the Russian-American Company frigate *Neva . . .*]. St. Petersburg, 1817.

Bolkhovitinov, Nikolai Nikolaevich. *Russko-amerikanskie otnosheniia, 1815–1832* [Russian-American Relations, 1815–1832]. Moscow, 1975.

————. *Russko-amerikanskie otnosheniia i prodazha Aliaski, 1834–1867* [Rus-sian-American Relations and the Sale of Alaska, 1834–1867]. Moscow, 1989.

————. *Stanovlenie russko-amerikanskikh otnoshenii, 1775–1815* Moscow, 1966. Translated by Elena Levin: *The Beginnings of Russian-American Re-lations*, 1775–1815. Cambridge and London, 1975.

————., ed. *Zarubezhnye issledovaniia po istorii russkoi Ameriki (konets XVIII-seredina XIX v.)* [Foreign Research on the History of Russian America (Late Eighteenth Century to Mid-nineteenth Century)]. Moscow, 1987.

Chevigny, Hector. *Lord of Alaska: The Story of Baranov and the Russian Adven-ture.* New York, 1942.

————. *Lost Empire: The Life and Adventures of Nikolai Petrovich Rezanov.* New York, 1937.

————. *Russian America: The Great Alaskan Venture, 1741–1867.* New York, 1965.

Cook, Warren L. *Floodtide of Empire: Spain and the Pacific Northwest, 1543–1819.* New Haven and London, 1973.

Dailey, Janet. *The Great Alone.* New York, 1986.

Dall, William H. *Alaska and Its Resources.* Boston, 1870.

Divin, V. A. *Povest o slavnom moreplavatele* [The Story of a Famous Sea-farer]. Moscow, 1976.

————. *Russkie moreplavaniia na Tikhom okeane v XVIII veke* [*Russian Seafaring on the Pacific Ocean in the Eighteenth Century*]. Moscow, 1971.

Dyson, George. *Baidarka.* Edmonds, 1986.

Efimov, A. V., ed. *Atlas geograficheskikh otkrytii v Sibiri i v severo-zapadnoi Amerike v XVII–XIX vv.* [Atlas of Geographic Discoveries in Siberia and in Northwest America, Seventeenth to Nineteenth Centuries]. Moscow, 1964.

Elliott, George. *Empire and Enterprise in the North Pacific, 1785–1825.* Un-published doctoral dissertation, University of Toronto, 1957.

Erdmann, H. *Alaska: Ein Beitrag zur Geschichte nordischer Kolonisation* [Alaska: A Treatise on the History of Northern Colonization]. Berlin, 1909.

Fainsberg, E. Ia. *Russko-iaponskie otnosheniia v 1697–1875 gg.* [Russo-Japanese Relations 1697–1875.] Moscow, 1960.

559

Farrar, Victor J. *The Annexation of Russian America*. Washington, 1937.

Farris, Glenn J. *Preliminary report of the 1981 Excavations of the Fort Ross Warehouse* (Unpublished manuscript for the California Department of Parks and Recreation), 1982.

Fedorova, Svetlana G. *Russkoe naselenie Aliaski i Kalifornii*. Moscow, 1971. Translated and edited by Richard A. Pierce and Alton S. Donnelly: *The Russian Population in Alaska and California, Late Eighteenth Century—1867*. Kingston, 1973.

Friis, Herman R., ed. *The Pacific Basin: A History of Its Geographical Exploration*. New York, 1967.

Gibson, James R. *Imperial Russia in Frontier America: The Changing Geography of Supply of Russian America, 1784–1867*. New York, 1976.

Gnucheva, Vera F. *Materialy dlia istorii ekspeditsii Akademii Nauk v XVIII i XIX vekakh. Khronologicheskie obzory i opisanie arkhivnykh materialov* [Materials for the History of Expeditions of the Academy of Sciences in the Eighteenth and Nineteenth Centuries. A Chronological Survey and Description of Archival Materials]. Moscow, 1940.

Golder, Frank A. *Russian Expansion on the Pacific 1641–1850* . . . New York, 1971 (reprint of 1914 edition).

Gsovski, V. *Russian Administration of Alaskan Natives*. Washington, D. C., 1950.

Harrison, John A. *The Founding of the Russian Empire in Asia and America*. Coral Gables, 1971.

Henry, John Frazier. *Early Maritime Artists of the Pacific Northwest Coast, 1741–1841*. Seattle and London, 1984.

Hernandez y Sanchez-Barba, M. *La Ultima Expancion en America* [The Last Expansion in America]. Madrid, 1957.

Hrdlicka, Ales. *The Aleutian and Commander Islands and Their Inhabitants*. Philadelphia, 1945.

———. *Anthropology of Kodiak Island*. Philadelphia, 1944.

Hunt, W.R. *Arctic Passage: The Turbulent History of the Lands and People of the Bering Sea, 1697–1975*. New York, 1975.

Jensen, Ronald. *The Alaska Purchase and Russian-American Relations*. Seattle and London, 1975.

Jochelson, W. *History, Ethnology and Anthropology of the Aleut*. Washington, D.C., 1933.

Kamenskii, Anatolii, Arkhimandrit. *Indiane Aliaski. Byt i religiia ikh*. Odessa, 1906. Translated, with an Introduction and Supplementary Material by Sergei A. Kan: *Tlingit Indians of Alaska*. Fairbanks, 1985.

Kavanov, P. I. *Amurskii vopros* [The Amur Question]. Blagoveshchensk, 1959.

Kushner, Howard. *Conflict on the Northwest Coast: American-Russian Rivalry in the Pacific Northwest, 1790–1867*. Westport and London, 1975.

Lebedev, D. M. and V. A. Esakov. *Russkie geograficheskie otkrytiia i issledovaniia* [Russian Geographic Discoveries and Explorations]. Moscow, 1971.

Lensen, George A. *The Russian Push Toward Japan: Russo-Japanese Relations, 1697–1875*. Princeton, 1959.

Liapunova, Roza G. *Etnografiia narodov tikhookeanskogo severa Ameriki: Russkie i sovetskie issledovaniia* [The Ethnography of the Peoples of the North Pacific Regions of America: Russian and Soviet Research]. Leningrad, 1979.

———. *Ocherki po etnografii Aleutov (konets XVIII-pervaia polovina XIX v.)* [Studies of the Ethnography of the Aleuts (Late Eighteenth to the First Half of the Nineteenth Century)] Leningrad, 1975.

Lower, J. Arthur. *Ocean of Destiny: A Concise History of the North Pacific, 1500–1978*. Vancouver, 1978.

Mahr, August C. *The Visit of the "Rurik" to San Francisco in 1816*. Palo Alto, 1932.

Majors, Harry. *Science and Exploration on the Northwest Coast of North America, 1542–1841*. Seattle, 1969.

Makarova, Raisa V. *Russkie na Tikhom okeane vo vtoroi polovine XVIII v.* Moscow, 1968. Translated and edited by Richard A. Pierce and Alton S. Donnelly: *Russians on the Pacific, 1743–99*. Kingston, 1975.

———. *Vneshnaia politika Rossii na Dalnom Vostoke : vtoraia polovina XVIIv.—60-e gody XIX v.* [Foreign Policy in the Far East: Second Half of the Eighteenth Century to the 1860's.] Moscow, 1974.

Markov, Aleksei I. *Vostochnaia Sibir, Aziia, Okhotsk, i russkie vladeniia v Amerike* [Eastern Siberia, Asia, Okhotsk and the Russian Possessions in America]. St. Petersburg, 1856.

Markov, Sergei N. *Letopis Aliaski* [A Chronicle of Alaska]. Moscow and Leningrad, 1948.

———. *Russkie na Aliaske* [The Russians in Alaska]. Moscow, 1946.

McCoy, Patrick. *Archaeological Research at Fort Elizabeth, Waimea, Kauai, Hawaiian Islands*. Honolulu, 1972.

McCracken, Harold. *Hunters of the Stormy Sea: The History of the Sea Otter Hunters of Alaska*. Garden City, 1957.

McFeat, Tom. *Indians of the North Pacific Coast*. Toronto, 1966.

Mehnert, Klaus. *The Russians in Hawaii, 1804–1817*. Honolulu, 1939.

Michener, James. *Alaska*. New York, 1988.

Miller, David H. *The Alaska Treaty*. Kingston, 1981.

Mitchell, Kathryn E. *Fort Ross: Russian Colony in California, 1811–1841*. M.A. Thesis. Portland State University, Portland, 1984.

Ogden, Adele. *The California Sea Otter Trade*. Berkeley, 1941.

Okun, Semen B. *Rossiisko-Amerikanskaia Kompaniia*. Moscow, 1939. Translated by Carl Ginsburg: *The Russian American Company*. Cambridge, 1951.

Orth, Donald J. *Dictionary of Alaska Place Names*. Washington, D.C., 1967.

Oulashin, Eric E. *Nicholas N. Muravev: Conqueror of the Black Dragon*. M.A. Thesis. Portland State University, Portland, 1971.

Pasetskii, V. M. *Ferdinand Petrovich Vrangel, 1796–1870*. Moscow, 1975.

———. *Ivan Fedorovich Kruzenshtern*. Moscow, 1974.

561

Pierce, Richard A. *Builders of Alaska: The Russian Governors, 1818–1867*. Kingston, 1986.

———. *Russia's Hawaiian Adventure, 1815–1817*. Berkeley and Los Angeles, 1965.

Pilder, H. *Die Russisch-Amerikanischer Handels-Kompanie bis 1825* [The Russian-American Trading Company Before 1825]. Berlin, 1914.

Poniatowski, Michel. *Histoire de la Russie de l'Amerique et de l'Alaska* [A History of Russian America and Alaska]. Paris, 1978.

Quested, R. K. I. *The Expansion of Russia in East Asia, 1857–1860*. Kuala Lampur and Singapore, 1968.

Ratner-Shternberg, S. A. *Otdel Severnoi-Ameriki: Putevoditel po muzeiu antropologii i etnografii AN SSSR* [The North American Department: A Guidebook to the Museum of Anthropology and Ethnography of the Academy of Sciences of the USSR]. Leningrad, 1929.

Ray, Dorothy J. *The Eskimos of Bering Strait, 1650–1898*. Seattle, 1975.

Rekliu, E. *Zhizn pervobytnykh narodov (eskimosy i aleuty-iniuty)* [The Life of Primitive Peoples (Eskimos and Aleut-Inuits]. Moscow, 1889.

Rich, Edwin E. *The Fur Trade and the Northwest to 1857*. Toronto, 1967.

———. *The History of the Hudson's Bay Company, 1670–1870*. London, 1958–59

Ricks, Melvin. *The Earliest History of Alaska*. Anchorage, 1970.

Riordan-Eva, Margot C.V. *The Cowlitz Corridor: The Passage through Time*. M.A. thesis, Portland State University, 1986.

Sarafian, Winston. *Russian-American Employee Policies and Practices, 1799–1867*. Los Angeles, 1970.

Sergeev, M. A. *Kurilskie ostrova* [The Kuril Islands]. Moscow,1947.

Shur, Leonid A. *K beregam Novogo Sveta* [To the Shores of the New World]. Moscow, 1971.

Siebert, Erna V. *North American Indian Art*. London and New York, 1969.

Shalkovskii, K. *Russkaia torgovlia v Tikhom okeane* [Russian Trade in the Pacific Ocean]. St. Petersburg, 1883.

Smith, Barbara. *Preliminary Survey of Documents in the Archive of the Russian Orthodox Church in Alaska*. Boulder, 1974.

———. *Russian Orthodoxy in Alaska*. Juneau, 1980.

Soler, Ana Maria Schop. *Un Siglo de Relaciones Diplomaticas y Comerciales entre España y Rusia, 1733–1833* [A Century of Diplomatic and Commercial Relations between Spain and Russia, 1733–1833].Madrid, 1984.

Spencer-Hancock, Diane. *Fort Ross: Indians-Russians-Americans*. Jenner, California, 1980.

Starr, S. Frederick, ed. *Russia's American Colony*. Durham, 1987.

Stephan, John J. *The Kuril Islands: Russo-Japanese Frontier in the Pacific*. Oxford, 1974.

———. *Sakhalin: A History*. Oxford, 1971.

Tarnovecky, Joseph. *The Purchase of Alaska: Backgrounds and Reactions*. Unpublished doctoral dissertation, McGill University, 1969.

Tikhmenev, Petr A. *Istoricheskoe obozrenie obrazovaniia Rossiisko Amerikanskoi kompanii i deistvii ee do nastoiashchego vremeni.* 2 vols. St. Petersburg, 1861, 1863. Text translated and edited by Richard A. Pierce and Alton S. Donnelly: *A History of the Russian-American Company.* Seattle and London, 1978. Selected documents translated by Dmitri Krenov and edited by Richard A. Pierce and Alton S. Donnelly: *A History of the Russian-American Company. Documents.* Kingston, 1979.

Tompkins, Stuart Ramsey. *Alaska: Promyshlennik and Sourdough.* Norman, 1945.

USSR. Academy of Sciences. *The Pacific: Russian Scientific Investigations.* Leningrad, 1926.

Valaam Monastery. *Ocherk iz istorii Amerikanskoi pravoslavnoi missii (Kadiakskoi missii 1794–1837 gg.)* [A Sketch from the History of the American Orthodox Ecclesiastical Mission (The Kodiak Mission, 1794–1837)]. 2 vols. St. Petersburg, 1894.

Vaughan, Thomas, ed. *The Western Shore: Oregon Country Essays Honoring the American Revolution.* Portland, 1976.

————, and Bill Holm. *Soft Gold; The Fur Trade and Cultural Exchange on the Northwest Coast of America.* Portland, 1982.

Vila Vilar, Enriqueta. *Los Rusos en America* [Russians in America]. Seville, 1966.

Vishnevskii, B. N. *Puteshestvennik Kirill Khlebnikov* [The Traveler Kyrill Khlebnikov]. Perm, 1957.

Vize, Vladimir Iu. *Russkie poliarnye morekhody iz promyshlennykh, torgovykh i sluzhilykh liudei XVII–XIX vv.* [Russian Polar Seafarers of the Seventeenth to Nineteenth Centuries: Promyshlenniks, Traders and Servitors]. Moscow and Leningrad, 1948.

Wagner, Philip Lawrence. *Russian Explorations in North America.* Unpublished M.A. Thesis. University of California, Berkeley, 1950.

Wheeler, Mary E. *The Origins and Formation of the Russian-American Company.* Chapel Hill, 1966.

Znamenskii, S. *V poiskakh Iaponii* [In Search of Japan]. Blagoveshchensk, 1929.

Zubkova, Z. *Aleutskie ostrova* [The Aleutian Islands]. Moscow, 1948.

Zubov, N. N. *Otechestvennie moreplavateli-issledovateli morei i okeanov* [The Fatherland's Navigator-Explorers of the Seas and Oceans]. Moscow, 1954.

Periodical Literature

Agranat, G. A. "Ob osvoennii Russkimi Aliaski" [Concerning the Assimilation of Alaska by the Russians]. *Letopis Severa,* Vol. 5 (1971).

Anon. "Obozrenie sostoianiia deistvii Rossiisko-Amerikanskoi Kompanii s 1797 po 1819 god" [A Review of the Condition of the Russian-American Company's Activities from 1797 to 1819], *Zhurnal manufaktur i torgovli,* 1835, pp. 12–124.

Arkadev, A. "Russkie na Tikhom okeane (obzor literatury)" [Russians on the Pacific Ocean (A Survey of the Literature)]. *Nauka i zhizn*, No. 3 (1949), pp. 41–45.

Bassin, Mark. "The Russian Geographical Society, the 'Amur Epoch,' and the Great Siberian Expedition, 1855–1863." *Annals of the Association of American Geographers*, Vol. 73 (1983), pp. 240–56.

Berkh, V. "Izvestie o mekhovoi torgovle, proizvodimoi Rossiianami pri ostrovakh Kurilskikh, Aleutskikh i severozapadnom beregu Ameriki" [Information Concerning the Fur Trade, Carried on by the Russians in the Kuril and Aleutian Islands and the Northwest Coast of America]. *Syn otechestva*, 1823, No. 88, pp. 243–64; No. 89, pp. 97–106.

Blomkvist, E. E. "Risunki I. G. Voznesenskogo (Ekspeditsiia 1839–1849 gg.)." *Sbornik Muzeia antropologii i etnografii*, Vol. 13, pp. 230–304. Translated by Basil Dmytryshyn and E. A. P. Crownhart-Vaughan "A Russian Scientific Expedition to California and Alaska, 1839–1849: The Drawings of I. G. Voznesenskii." *Oregon Historical Quarterly*, Vol. 73 (1972), No. 2, pp. 101–170.

Bolkhovitinov, Nikolai N. "Avantiura Doktora Sheffera na Gavaiiakh v 1815–1819 godakh". *Novaia i noveishaia istoriia*, No. 1 (1972), pp. 121–37. Translated by Igor V. Vorobyoff. "The Adventures of Dr. Schaffer in Hawaii, 1815–1891." *The Hawaiian Journal of History*, 7 (1973), pp. 55–78.

———. "Obshchestvennost SShA i ratifikatsiia dogovora 1867 g." [Public Opinion in the USA and the Ratification of the Treaty of 1867]. *Amerikanskii ezhegodnik*, 1987, pp. 157–174.

———. "Russia and the Declaration of the Non-Colonization Principle: New Archival Evidence." Translated by Basil Dmytryshyn, *Oregon Historical Quarterly*, Vol. 72 (1971), pp. 101–127.

———. "Russian America and International Relations." in S. Frederick Starr, ed., *Russia's American Colony*, Durham, 1987, pp. 251–270.

———. "Vopros o reorganizatsii Rossiisko-Amerikanskoi kompanii, 1860–1866." [The Question of the Reorganization of the Russian-American Company, 1860–1866.] Unpublished manuscript in Oregon Historical Society Manuscript Division.

———. "Zarubezhnye issledovaniia o russkoi Amerike" [Foreign Research on Russian America]. *SShA*, 1985, No. 4, pp. 87–95.

Carson, Gerald. "Mr. Seward's Icebox." *Timeline* (Ohio Historical Society), October-November 1987, pp. 34–49.

Cowdin, Elliot C. "The Northwest Fur Trade." *Hunt's Merchants' Magazine*, June 1846, 532–39.

Davidson, Donald C. "Relations of the Hudson's Bay Company with the Russian American Company on the Northwest Coast, 1829–1867." *British Columbia Historical Quarterly*, January 1941, pp. 33–51.

Dufour, Clarence John. "The Russian Withdrawal from California." *California Historical Quarterly*, Vol. 12 (1933), pp. 240–276.

Dumond-Fillon, Rémy. "Histoire de l'exploration scientifique du Pacifique par les Russes [A History of Russian Scientific Explorations in the Pacific]." *Cahiers d'histoire du Pacifique*, 1978, pp. 13–37.

Dzeniskevich, Galina I. "Kollektsiia A. F. Kashevarova v severo amerikan-skom otdele MAE" [The A. F. Kashevarov Collection in the North American Department of the Museum of Anthropology and Ethnography]. *Sbornik MAE*, Vol. 35 (1980), pp. 178–182.

Erman, Adolf. "Zufass-Bemerkungen uber Neu Californien" [Additional Remarks on New California]. *Annalen der Erd-, Volker- und Staatenkunde*, Series 2, June 1833, pp. 240–260.

Essig, E. 0. "The Russian Settlement at Ross." *California Historical Quarterly*, Vol. 12 (1933), pp. 191–216.

Farris, Glenn J. "Fathoming Fort Ross." *Historical Archaeology*, Vol. 17 (1983), No. 2, pp. 93–99.

Fedorova, Svetlana G. "Shturmany Ivany Vasilevy i ikh rol v izuchenii Aliaski (pervaia polovina XIX v.)" [The Navigators Ivan Vasilev and Their Role in the Study of Alaska (First Half of the Nineteenth Century)]. *Letopis Severa*, No. 9 (1979), pp. 167–210.

Fisher, Robin. "Indian Control of the Maritime Fur Trade and the Northwest Coast." In *Approaches to Native History*, edited by D. A. Muise. Ottawa, 1977. pp. 65–86.

Gentilcore, R. Louis. "Missions and Mission Lands of Alta California." *Annals of the Association of American Geographers*, March 1961, pp. 46–72.

Gerus, Oleh W. "The Russian Withdrawal from Alaska: The Decision to Sell." *Revista de Historia de America*, 1972–73, pp. 75–76.

Gibson, James R. "European Dependence upon American Natives: the Case of Russian America." *Ethnohistory*, Vol. 25 (1978), No. 4, pp. 359–85.

———. "Russia in California, 1833: Report of Governor Wrangel." *Pacific Northwest Quarterly*, October 1969, pp. 205–215.

———. "Russia on the Pacific: the Role of the Amur." *Canadian Geographer*, Vol. 12 (1968), pp. 15–27.

———. "Russian America in 1833: The Survey of Kirill Khlebnikov." *Pacific Northwest Quarterly*, January, 1972, pp. 1–13.

———. "Russian Dependence upon the Natives of Alaska." In S. Frederick Starr, ed. *Russia's American Colony*, Durham, 1987, pp. 77–104.

———. "Russian Expansion in Siberia and America." *Geographical Review*, Vol. 70 (1980), No. 2, pp. 127–136.

——— "A Russian Orthodox Priest in a Mexican Catholic Parish." *Pacific Historian*, Summer, 1971, pp. 57–66.

———. "Sables to Otters: Russia Enters the Pacific." *Alaska Review*, Vol. 3 (1968–69), pp. 203–217.

———. "Bostonians and Muscovites on the Northwest Coast, 1788 1841." In: Thomas Vaughan, ed., *The Western Shore: Oregon Country Essays Honoring the American Revolution*. Portland, 1976, pp. 81–120.

———. "The Sale of Russian America to the United States." *Acta Slavica Iaponica*, Vol. 1 (1983), pp. 15–37.

———. "Two New Chernykh Letters." *Pacific Historian*, Summer, 1968, pp. 48–56; Fall, 1968, pp. 55–60.

———. "Why the Russians Sold Alaska." *Wilson Quarterly*, Vol. 3 (1979), No. 3, pp. 179–188.

Golder, Frank A. "The Attitude of the Russian Government Toward Alaska." In H. Morse Stephens and Herbert E. Bolton, eds., *The Pacific Ocean in History*, New York, 1917, pp. 269–275.

———. "The Purchase of Alaska." *American Historical Review*, Vol. 25 (1920), No. 3, pp. 411–425.

Greene, C. S. "Fort Ross and the Russians." *Overland Monthly*, Vol. 22 (1893), No. 127.

Howay, F. W. "An Outline Sketch of the Maritime Fur Trade." *Annual Report of the Canadian Historical Association*, 1932, pp. 5–14.

Ivashintsov, N. "Russkiia krugosvetnia puteshestviia" [Russian Circumnavigations]. *Zapiski Gidrograficheskogo Departamenta*, 1849, pp. 1–116; 1850, pp. 1–190. Published in English: *Russian Round-the-World Voyages, 1803–1849*. Kingston, 1980.

Jackson, C. Ian. "The Stikine Territory Lease and Its Relevance to the Alaska Purchase." *Pacific Historical Review*, Vol. 36 (1967), pp. 289–306.

Komissarov, Boris N. "Dnevnik puteshestviia F. P. Litke na shliupe 'Kamchatka' v 1817–1819 gg." [The Journal of F. P. Lùtke's Voyage on the Sloop 'Kamchatka' in 1817–1819]. *Izvestiia Vsesoiuznogo geograficheskogo obshchestva*, Vol. 96 (1964), pp. 414–419.

Kozhin, P. M. "Etnograficheskie nabliudeniia I. G. Voznesenskogo v Kalifornii" [The Ethnographic Observations of I. G. Voznesenskii in California]. Trudy Instituta Etnografii, New Series, Vol. 7 (1977).

Kushner, Howard I. "'Hellships':Yankee Whaling along the Coasts of Russian America, 1835–1852." *New England Quarterly*, Vol. 45 (1972), pp. 81–95.

———. "The Significance of the Alaska Purchase to American Expansion." In: S. Frederick Starr, ed. *Russia's American Colony*, Durham, 1987. pp. 295–315.

Liapunova, Roza G. "Aleutskie baidarki" [Aleut Baidarkas]. *Sbornik MAE*, Vol. 21 (1963).

———. "Orudiia okhoty aleutov" [Hunting Weapons of the Aleuts]. *Sbornik MAE*, Vol. 21 (1963).

———. "Relations with Natives of Alaska." In: S. Frederick Starr, ed. *Russia's American Colony*, Durham, 1987. pp. 105–143.

Makarova, Raisa V. "Toward a History of the Liquidation of the Russian American Company." In: S. Frederick Starr, ed. *Russia's American Colony*, Durham, 1987, pp. 63–73.

Mamyshev, V., "Amerikanskie vladeniia Rossii" [Russia's American Possessions]. *Biblioteka dlia chteniia*, March-April 1855, pp. 205–292.

Mazour, Anatole G. "Russian-American Company: Private or Government Enterprise?" *Pacific Historical Review*, Vol. 13 (1944), No. 2, pp. 168–173.

Ogden, Adele. "Russian Sea Otter and Seal Hunting on the California Coast, 1803–1841." *California Historical Quarterly*, Vol. 12 (1933), pp. 217–239.

Okladnikova, Elena A. "Science and Education in Russian America." In: S. Frederick Starr, ed. *Russia's American Colony*, Durham, 1987, pp. 218–248.

Okun, Semen B. "Tsarskaia Rosiia i Gavaiskie ostrova" [Tsarist Russia and the Hawaiian Islands]. *Krasnyi arkhiv*, 1936, pp. 161–186.

Oleksa, Michael. "The Death of Hieromonk Juvenaly." *St. Vladimir's Theological Quarterly*, Vol. 30 (1986), No. 3, pp. 231–268.

Potekhin, V. "Selenie Ross" [The Ross Settlement]. *Zhurnal manufaktur i torgovli*, 1859, pp. 1–42.

Ray, Arthur J. "Fur Trade History as an Aspect of Native History." In: Ian A. L. Getty and Donald B. Smith, eds. *One Century Later*. Vancouver, 1978, pp. 7–18.

Senkevich, Anatole, Jr. "The Early Architecture and Settlements of Russian America." In: S. Frederick Starr, ed. *Russia's American Colony*. Durham, 1987, pp. 147–195.

Sgibnev, A. "Popytki russkikh k zavedeniiu torgovykh snoshenii s Iaponieiu v XVIII i nachale XIX stoletii" [Russian Attempts to Establish Trade Relations with Japan in the Eighteenth and Early Nineteenth Centuries]. *Morskoi sbornik*, Vol. 100 (1869), No. 1, pp. 37–72.

Shalkop, Antoinette. "The Russian Orthodox Church in Alaska." In: S. Frederick Starr, ed. *Russia's American Colony*. Durham, 1987, pp. 196–217.

Shashkov, S. S. "Rossiisko-Amerikanskaia Kompaniia" [The Russian American Company" In: *Sobranie sochinenii S. S. Shashkova*. St. Petersburg, 1898. Vol. 2, pp. 632–652.

Sherwood, Morgan B. "Science in Russian America, 1741–1865." *Pacific Northwest Quarterly*, Vol. 58 (1967), No. 1, pp. 33–39.

Shirokii, V. F. "Iz istorii khoziaistvennoi deiatelnosti Rossiisko—Amerikanskoi kompanii" [From the History of the Economic Activity of the Russian-American Company]. *Istoricheskie Zapiski*, Vol. 13 (1942), pp. 207–221.

Shur, Leonid A. "Dnevniki i zapiski russkikh puteshestvennikov kak istochnik po istorii i etnografii stran Tikhogo okeana (pervaia polovina XIX v.)" [Diaries and Notes of Russian Travelers as Sources for the History and Ethnography of the Countries of the Pacific Ocean (First Half of the Nineteenth Century)]. In *Avstraliia i Okeaniia: Istoriia i sovremennost*. Moscow, 1970.

———, and James R. Gibson. "Russian Travel Notes and Journals as Sources for the History of California, 1800–1850." *California Historical Quarterly*, Vol. 52 (1973), No. 1, pp. 37–63.

Siebert, Erna V. "Kollektsii pervoi poloviny XIX v. po severnym atapaskam" [The Collections from the First Half of the Nineteenth Century on the Northern Athabascans]. *Sbornik MAE*, Vol. 24 (1967), pp. 55–84.

Sokol, A. E. "Russian Expansion and Exploration in the Pacific." *American Slavic and East European Review*, Vol. 11 (1952), No. 2, pp. 85–106.

Stepanova, M. V. "Iz istorii etnograficheskogo izucheniia byvshikh russkikh vladeny v Amerike" [From the History of the Ethnographical Study of the Former Russian Possessions in America]. *Sovetskaia etnografiia*, Vol. 21 (1947).

Stephan, John J. "The Crimean War in the Far East." *Modern Asian Studies*, III 3 (1969), pp. 257–277.

Sturgis, William. "Examinations of the Russian Claims to the Pacific Northwest Coast of America." *North American Review*, Vol. 15 (1822), pp. 370–401.

Taylor, G. P. "Spanish-Russian Rivalry in the Pacific, 1769–1820." *Americas*, Vol. 25 (1958), pp. 109–127.

Tolstoy, M., Count. "Missionerskaia deiatelnost pokoinogo mitropolita Innokentiia" [The Missionary Activity of the Late Metropolitan Innokentii]. *Russkii arkhiv*, 1879, pp. 273–303.

Tumarkin, D.D. "Novie arkhivnye materialy o gavaitsakh" [New Archival Materials about the Hawaiians]. *Sovetskaia etnografiia*, Vol. 34 (1960), pp. 158–160.

Welch, R. E., Jr. "American Public Opinion and the Purchase of Alaska." *American Slavic and East European Review*, Vol. 17 (1958), pp. 481–494.

Wheeler, Mary E. "Empires in Conflict and Cooperation: The 'Bostonians' and the Russian-American Company." *Pacific Historical Review*, Vol. 40 (1971), No. 4, pp. 419–441.

———. "The Origins of the Russian-American Company." *Jahrbücher für Geschichte Osteuropas*, 1966, pp. 485–494.

Zubkova, Z. N. "Aleutskie ostrova (Fiziko-geograficheskii ocherk)" [The Aleutian Islands: A Physical-Geographical Study]. *Zapiski Vsesoiuznogo geograficheskogo obshchestva*, New Series, Vol. 4 (1948).

INDEX

Macao, 230, 231
McKenzie, Alexander, 178
Madeira, 96
Madrid, 133:
    Spanish government at, *see*
    Spain
Magee, Bernard, 161n
Magmiut people, 421
Maia River, 52, 61
Malakhov, —, 144
Malaspina Expedition, 377
Malegmiut people, xliii
Malimiut people, 421
Malin, Gavriil, 63
Malkinsk, 70
Manchu people, 485
Manchuria, 496
Manila, 133, 134, 206, 250, 327,
    389
Maps: Baranov (Sitka) Island, 76;
    Eastern Siberia-Western
    America, xcii–xciii; Kam-
    chatka and Japan, xciv; Kru-
    senstern voyage, 114–15; New
    Arkhangel (Sitka), endpapers;
    North Pacific Coast, xcv;
    North Pacific Ocean, 20–21;
    Pearl River and Canton, 185
March, W. L., 499
Maria (brigantine), 149: fur cargo,
    151
Mariia (ship), 48, 50
Mariia Magdalina (vessel), 99
Marikanka River, 55
Marquesas (Mendocino) Islands,
    65, 97
Martinez, Ignacio, 379
Mashin, Andrei V., 149
Matmai Island, 199
Matsumai Island, *see* Hokkaido
    Island
Maui, 186
Mauna Loa, 40
Meares, John, 45
Mednovsk (Atnakht) people, 143,
    406–408, 409, 410, 411, 416,

418, 420, 506: customs,
    407–408
Mednovsk trading post, 408
Meek, Thomas, 329
Melita (ship): wreck, 509–10
Mendocino Islands, *see* Marquesas
    Islands
Menshikov, —(Prince), 485
Mexican Revolution, lxvi
Mexico, 110, 120, 133, 138,
    214–15, 236–37, 392, 394,
    398:
    independence from Spain, lxvi,
    371, 376–78, 388–89, 401;
    Russian relations with,
    lxiv–lxv, 401–404, 441; Span-
    ish viceroy in, 205, 206,
    246–47, 251, 291, 386
Michigmenskii Bay, 480
Michurin, Dmitrii, 6
Michurin, Ivan Dmitriev, 6
Michurin, Nikolai, brother of Petr
    D., 6
Michurin, Nikolai, son of Petr D.,
    6
Michurin, Petr Dmitriev, 6
Michurin, Prokopii, 6
Middleton, Henry, 383
Mikhailovsk redoubt, xl, 419, 420,
    480, 509
Milbanke Sound, 161
Milchashna River, 334
Mirt Kadiak (ship), 165, 167, 241
Mitchell, Julian A., 442
Model (vessel), 144
Molinari, —(Lieutenant), 490
Moller Bay, 522
Molokai, 186
Molvo, Herman, 232, 241, 242
Monasterio, José Maria Ortiz,
    402–404
Mongolia, 497
Mongol people, lxi
Monroe, James, 383
Monterey, 116–19 *passim*, 126,
    128, 135, 153–57 *passim*, 190,

213, 237, 258, 263, 264, 274, 280, 331, 334, 376, 377–78, 381, 386, 387–88, 392

Monterey Bay, 260, 262, 273

Monterey Presidio, 121, 126, 260–62, 269, 271–72, 273, 282, 377, 386–88, 391

Montesquieu, Charles, Baron de, xxxii

Moorehead, Max L., lxxviii

Moorfield, — (shipwright), 147

Moravia, 139

Mordvinov, N. S., 31

Morekhod (galiot), 481

Moscow, xxxviii, 8, 9, 14, 32: guilds, 6; illustration 203

Mount Edgecumbe, 73

Mount St. Elias, xl, 532

Müller, G.F., lxxvi

Mulovskii, Grigorii I., xxxii

Mur (Moore), —(Midshipman on *Diana*), 199

Muravev, Matvei I., 474: Chief Administrator, Russian America, 322–25, 337, 378; report on Amur fortifications, 492–98; views on Russian control of Amur River, 482–84, 485–91

Museum of Anthropology and Ethnography, Leningrad, lx

Mylnikov, Dmitrii, 6

Mylnikov, Iakov, 6

Mylnikov, Mikhail, 6

Mylnikov, Nikolai Prokopev, xxx, 5, 6, 14

Mylnikov, Petr Prokopii, 7

Mylnikov Company, xxxiii

Nadezhda (vessel), lxii, 38, 65, 117, 145, 187, 261: map of route, 114–15

Nagasaki, lxiii, 38, 99: Atkinson painting, 200

Nakhimov (ship), 508

National Museum, Helsinki, lx

Near Islands, xl

Nebolsin, G., 543

Neelov, D., 543

Nektarii (ierodiakon), 62–64, 103

Nelba River, 56

Nelbar River, 56–59 *passim*

Nelson, Horatio, 29

Nerchinsk, 483, 488, 494: ammunitions factory, 22, 358, 454

Nesselrode, Karl V. (Charles Robert), 236, 246, 366–69, 383, 402–404: portrait, 403; reports to concerning Hawaiian Islands, 290–92, 299–302

Nesvetsov, Iakov, xlii

Neva (ship), lxii, 45, 65, 97, 117, 145, 153, 161, 166, 184, 186, 187, 191, 192, 193, 200: fur cargo, 193–94; Lisianskii journal, 72–90; map of route, 114–15

Nevelskii Bay, 509

Nevelskoi, Gennadii I., 475, 485, 486, 487, 490–91, 494

New Arkhangel, xxxv, xl, liii, lxiii, lxv, lxxv, 25, 30n, 44, 45, 112, 118, 130, 140, 142, 171, 197, 218, 229–32, 239, 241, 251, 305, 308, 322, 323, 324, 331, 335, 338, 370, 373, 375, 378, 386, 422, 441, 479, 480, 501–12 *passim*, 530, 538, 541, 542: established, 26, 224; fort, 143, 160, 331; Langsdorff painting, 157; naval unit, xxxv, lii, 534; schools, 500, 506, 514–17; shipbuilding, lviii, lxviii; Russian Orthodox church, xlii, lix; Tlingit (Kolosh) hostilities, 1, 72, 74–88, 105, 106, 160–61, 210–11, 224; views, 489, 546

New California, *see* California

New Helvetia, 441

New Mexico, 134